Time Out
Berlin

Penguin Books

PENGUIN BOOKS

Published by the Penguin Group
Penguin Books Ltd, 27 Wrights Lane, London W8 5TZ, England
Penguin Books USA Inc., 375 Hudson Street, New York, New York 10014, USA
Penguin Books Australia Ltd, Ringwood, Victoria, Australia
Penguin Books Canada Ltd, 10 Alcorn Avenue, Toronto, Ontario, Canada M4V 3B2
Penguin Books (NZ) Ltd, 182-190 Wairau Road, Auckland 10, New Zealand

Penguin Books Ltd, Registered Offices: Harmondsworth, Middlesex, England

First published 1993
Second edition 1995
Third edition 1998
Fourth edition 2000
10 9 8 7 6 5 4 3 2 1

Colour reprographics by Westside Digital Media, 9 Bridle Lane, London W1
and Precise Litho, 34-35 Great Sutton Street, London EC1
Printed and bound by Cayfosa-Quebecor, Ctra. de Caldes, Km 3 08 130 Sta, Perpètua de Mogoda,
Barcelona, Spain

Edited and designed by

Time Out Guides Limited
Universal House
251 Tottenham Court Road
London W1P 0AB
Tel + 44 (0)20 7813 3000
Fax + 44 (0)20 7813 6001
Email guides@timeout.com
www.timeout.com

Editorial

Editor Dave Rimmer
Deputy editor Peterjon Cresswell
Researcher John Fitzsimons
Indexer Cathy Heath

Editorial Director Peter Fiennes
Series Editor Caroline Taverne

Design

Art Director John Oakey
Art Editor Mandy Martin
Senior Designer Scott Moore
Designers Benjamin de Lotz, Lucy Grant
Picture Editor Kerri Miles
Deputy Picture Editor Olivia Duncan-Jones
Picture Admin Kit Burnet
Scanning & Imaging Chris Quinn

Advertising

Group Advertisement Director Lesley Gill
Sales Director Mark Phillips
International Sales Manager Mary L Rega
Advertisement Sales (Sydney) Samuel Childes Pty Ltd
Advertising Assistant Daniel Heaf

Administration

Publisher Tony Elliott
Managing Director Mike Hardwick
Financial Director Kevin Ellis
Marketing Director Gillian Auld
General Manager Nichola Coulthard
Production Manager Mark Lamond
Production Controller Samantha Furniss

Features in this guide were written and updated by:

Introduction Dave Rimmer. **History** Frederick Studemann. **Berlin Today** Natalie Gravenor, Dave Rimmer.
By Season Lisa Ellis. **Architecture** Francesca Rogier. **Sightseeing** Kevin Cote, Dave Rimmer, Ed Ward. **Museums**
John Fitzsimons, Dave Rimmer. **Art Galleries** Sophie Lovell. **Accommodation** Sophie Lovell. **Shopping & Services**
Julie Wedow. **Restaurants** J.J. Gordon, Dave Rimmer, Ed Ward. **Nightlife/Cafés** Harry Acton, Jonathan Gainer,
Natalie Gravenor, Martin Kaluza, April Lamm, Dave Rimmer, Paul Threlby, Ed Ward. **Love Parade** Mark Reeder,
Dave Rimmer. **Cabaret** Priscilla Be, Dave Rimmer. **Children** Kevin Cote. **Dance** Julie Wedow. **Film** Andrew Horn.
Gay & Lesbian Jens Friedrich. **Media** Kevin Cote. **Music: Classical & Opera** J.J. Gordon. **Music: Rock, Folk & Jazz**
Natalie Gravenor. **Sport & Fitness** Peterjon Cresswell, Natalie Gravenor, Connie Hanna. **Theatre** J.J. Gordon.
Day Trips Ed Ward. **Overnighters** Ed Ward. **Hamburg** Peterjon Cresswell. **Prague** Peterjon Cresswell, Will Tizzard.
Essential Information/Getting Around John Fitzsimons, Dave Rimmer, Fred Studemann. **Business** Kevin Cote.
Women Lisa Ellis. **Further Media** Chris Bohn, Biba Kopf, Dave Rimmer, Ed Ward.

The editor must thank and will remain forever indebted to:

Priscilla Be, Gosto Babka von Gostomski, Sophie Blacksell, Chris Bohn, Frank Charour, Chaos, Kevin Cote, Kevin
Ebbutt, Omar Elshami, Claus Erbskorn, John Fitzsimons, Dilek Gentner, Natalie Gravenor, Evelyn Hasshoff, Volker
Hauptvogel, Paul Hockenos, Edith Hoppe, Edison Lagos, Patrick Lonergan, Sophie Lovell, Mark Reeder, Pete
Robertson, Yasmin Röcker, Francesca Rogier, Thomas Wernecke, Trevor Wilson.

Maps by J.S. Graphics, 17 Beadles Lane, Old Oxted, Surrey RH8 9JG.

Photography by Hadley Kincade except: page 239 John Sibley/Action Images; page 240 (top) Sandra Behne/Sporting
Pictures Ltd; page 240 (bottom) Bongarts/Action Images; pages 4, 5, 6, 7, 8, 9, 10, 11, 12, 14, 15, 16, 17, 18, 19,
20, 21, 22, 23, 258, 259 and 260 AKG London; pages 252 (bottom) and 255 Toma Babovic/Black Star/Colorific!;
page 208 BFI Films; page 204 Dirk Bleicker; page 234 BMG Berlin Musik GmbH; page 99 David Brandt; page 209
The Ronald Grant Archive; pages 265 and 266 Sara Hannant; page 221 Megadyke Productions; page 227 David
Redfern; page 252 (top) Telegraph Colour Library; page 263 Trip/J Ellard; page 264 Trip/R Gibbs.

The following photographs were supplied by the featured establishments: 84, 114 and 198.

Contents

About the Guide

This is the fourth edition of the *Time Out Berlin Guide*, another of our wide-ranging series on the world's most vital cities. Our team of writers, resident experts in their fields, have been back on the town casing what's hot and what's not in Europe's newest capital – from the most extreme S&M salon to the least dynamic of downtown discos. Indeed, a whole new downtown – an uncritical mass of malls and multiplex cinemas – has sprung up since our last edition. Our writers pick it all apart: culturally, politically, architecturally, just as they delve deep into the ever-shifting alternative scene which has been drifting east from Mitte, to Prenzlauer Berg and on to Friedichshain.

Although any trip to Berlin will be enhanced with a copy of this *Guide*, it is not only a book for casual visitors and tourists. While listing the main sights and monuments, our team has also combed Berlin to provide the most complete picture of a city in flux, from the roof of the gleaming new Reichstag down to the dankest, darkest, dingiest dive. We aim to highlight not only the traditional must-sees, but also Berlin as the Berliners know it – a city that tourists seldom see.

Details, details, details

All information was checked and correct at the time of going to press, but please bear in mind that Berlin is still changing as its two halves are finally sewn back together. Little stays the same for long in this town. Clubs, restaurants, galleries and other venues wink in and out of existence.

Addresses & telephone numbers

In listing addresses we've included both the district name and the five-digit postcode. You don't need the district name when addressing a letter, but very few people are going to be able to direct you to 'Berlin 10783'. Telephone numbers in Berlin can be anything from four to eight digits long.

Prices

Prices, where listed, should be treated as guideline rather than gospel. Fluctuating exchange rates, inflation and the circumstances of Berlin's volatile economy can cause prices, especially in shops and restaurants, to change rapidly. Expect some fluctuation. But if prices vary wildly from those indicated here, please ask why. If there's no good

reason, go elsewhere – and then please let us know about it. We aim to give the most up-to-date advice, and always want to hear if you've been cheated, badly treated or given the runaround.

Credit cards

Compared the UK or USA, credit cards are still not widely used in Berlin. Larger shops will take them, and many of the more expensive restaurants, but you can basically forget about using them in clubs, galleries, bars, theatres, concert halls and cinemas. In Berlin, cash is king. We've used the following abbreviations for the major credit cards: AmEx – American Express; DC – Diner's Club; JCB – Japanese credit card; MC – Mastercard; V – Visa.

To boldly go

In chapters without listings, such as History or Architecture, names of places **highlighted in bold** are fully listed elsewhere in the book and can be found in the index.

Right to reply

It must be stressed that the information we offer in this *Guide* is impartial. No institution or enterprise has been included because they advertise in our publications. Rigorous impartiality and cosmopolitan criticism are the reasons why our guides are so successful and well-respected. But if you disagree with us, please, let us know. Your comments on places you have visited are always welcome – you'll find a reader's reply card in the back of this book.

There is an online version of this guide, as well as weekly events listings for over 30 international cities, at http://www.timeout.com

Introduction

People always have the same question, when they hear that you've been in Berlin. 'Oh, Berlin…Tell me, has it changed much?' I mean, what a question. Can any city have changed more in the last decade, short of those flattened by war in the Balkans or Transcaucasus? I usually end up tongue-tied, struggling to come up with some sensible one-liner.

Change is the nature of cities, of course. But to be in Berlin at the beginning of the 21st century is to experience this truth at its most complex and visceral. On any taxi ride through town, should the driver take a less familiar turn, you can abruptly find yourself in streets you thought you knew but now barely recognise, among unexpected new buildings, the laying of future foundations, whole city blocks going up. An entire new art quarter here. A new strip of nightclubs there. And in streets that once crackled with energy, sometimes now no life at all. At times this can all seem quite magical, a veritable fairyland of urban flux. This is Berlin at its restless best, living doggedly up to old clichés: becoming rather than being, regenerating itself from ruin.

But then there's a paradox, for to be in Berlin at the beginning of the 21st century is also to experience the dogged persistence of history. In any other city, could history be so, well… *present* in the conceiving of the future? In Berlin you can't lob a brick without hitting some thorny historical dilemma involving issues of guilt or memory, collective or individual responsibility. At every twist and turn of daily life, in every utterance of public debate, even embedded in the fabric of the newest new building – Foster's Reichstag, Libeskind's Jüdisches Museum – history is there. At every

level of culture, Berlin flexes between retro and modern, unable to make up its mind.

For yes, this is Berlin, the yin-yang city. And the more it changes, the more it damn well stays the same. Over a decade since the Wall was breached and it stubbornly remains two cities. Where once was no-man's-land, now there's a postmodern transition zone, a non-place of the future, neither east nor west. But old habits die hard in the boroughs, and Berlin is almost proud to be the 21st century schizoid town, perpetually united against itself.

And as the government moves in, and the developers map out some unnecessary new mall, and the bohemians decamp to the district next door, even the city's sense of time is changing. Daily life speeds up, a whole generation of party people has stopped dealing drugs and begun dealing with mornings, and the very fabric of the present is stretched into a new shape.

Past, present, future – one perspective can be had from the top of the Reichstag, now topped by Sir Norman Foster's high-tech dome – a piece of the future capping the ravaged symbol of Berlin's tempestuous 20th century.

From that surprisingly playful vantage, very much in the thick of it, with the representative buildings of the Berlin Republic all around, there rises up another vision of the future. As of the government's arrival, a whole new generation is now living in new apartment blocks, shopping in new malls, working in new offices… none of them connected to either east or west, a third city, slouching towards Berlin to be born.

Has Berlin changed much? 'Well, er, yeah… just a bit.'

Dave Rimmer

Money From Home In Minutes.

If you're stuck for cash on your travels, don't panic. Millions of people trust Western Union to transfer money in minutes to 176 countries and over 78,000 locations worldwide. Our record of safety and reliability is second to none. For more information, call Western Union: USA 1-800-325-6000, Canada 1-800-235-0000. Wherever you are, you're never far from home.

www.westernunion.com

WESTERN UNION | MONEY TRANSFER®

The fastest way to send money worldwide.

In Context

Key Events

1237 Cölln first mentioned in a church document.
1307 The towns of Berlin and Cölln officially united under the rule of the Ascanian family.
1319 Last of the Ascanians dies.
1359 Berlin joins the Hanseatic League.
1411 Friedrich of Hohernzollern is sent by the Holy Roman Emperor to bring peace to the region.
1447-48 The 'Berlin Indignation'. The population rebels and locks Friedrich II out of the city.

1535 Accession of Joachim I Nestor, the first protestant Elector. The Reformation arrives in Berlin.
1538 Work begins on the Stadtschloß.
1618-48 Berlin and Brandenburg are ravaged by the Thirty Years War – the population is halved.
1640-88 Reign of Friedrich Wilhelm, Grand Elector.
1662-68 Construction of the Oder-Spree canal.
1672 Jewish and Huguenot refugees arrive in Berlin.
1695 Work begins on Schloß Charlottenburg.
1701 Elector Friedrich III, son of the Grand Elector, has himself crowned Friedrich I, King of Prussia. Work begins on the German and French cathedrals at the Gendarmenmarkt.
1713-40 Reign of King Friedrich Wilhelm, who expands the army; Berlin becomes a garrison city.
1740-86 Reign of Frederick the Great – a time of military expansion and administrative reform.
1788-91 Construction of Brandenburg Gate.

1806 Napoleon marches into Berlin. Two years of French occupation. The Quadriga shipped to Paris.
1810 Wilhelm von Humboldt founds the university.
1813 Napoleon defeated at Grossbeeren and Leipzig.
1814 General Blücher brings the Quadriga back to Berlin and restores it on the Brandenburg Gate.

1837 Foundation of the Borsig Werke marks the beginning of Berlin's expansion into Continental Europe's largest industrial city.
1838 First railway line, from Berlin to Potsdam.
1840 Friedrich Wilhelm IV accedes to the throne. With a population of around 400,000, Berlin is the fourth largest city in Europe.
1848 The 'March Revolution' breaks out. Berlin briefly in the hands of the revolutionaries.
1861 Accession of King Wilhelm I.
1862 Appointment of Otto von Bismarck as Prime Minister of Prussia.
1871 Following victory in the Franco-Prussian war, King Wilhelm I is proclaimed German Emperor and Berlin becomes the Imperial capital.
1879 Electric lighting comes to Berlin, which also boasts the world's first electric railway. Three years later telephone services are introduced. The city emerges as Europe's most modern metropolis.
1888 Kaiser Wilhelm II comes to the throne.
1890 Kaiser Wilhelm II sacks Bismarck.

1894 Completion of the Reichstag.
1902 First underground line is opened.
1914-18 World War I.
1918 On 9 November, Kaiser Wilhelm abdicates, Philip Scheidemann proclaims Germany a republic and Karl Liebknecht declares Germany a socialist republic. Chaos ensues.
1919 Spartacist uprising suppressed.
1923 Hyperinflation – $1 is worth 4.2 billion marks.
1926 Joseph Goebbels comes to Berlin to take charge of the local Nazi party organisation.
1927 Berlin boasts more than 70 cabarets.
1933 Hitler takes power.

1936 The 11th Olympic Games are held in Berlin.
1938 Kristallnacht, 9 November. Jewish homes, businesses and synagogues in Berlin are stoned, looted and set ablaze.
1939 Outbreak of World War II, during which Berlin suffers appalling devastation.
1944 A group around Colonel Count von Stauffenberg attempts to assassinate Hitler.
1945 Germany signs unconditional surrender.

1948-49 The Berlin Blockade. The Soviets cut off all transport links to west Berlin. For 11 months the city is supplied by the Allied Airlift.
1949 Foundation of Federal Republic in May and of the German Democratic Republic on 7 October.
1953 17 June uprising in East Berlin is suppressed.
1961 The Wall goes up on 13 August.
1968 Student leader Rudi Dutschke is shot.
1971 Erich Honecker succeeds Walter Ulbricht as GDR head of state. The Quadrapartite Agreement formalises Berlin's divided status.
1980-81 'Hot Winter' of violent squatter protests.
1987 Berlin's 750th birthday.

1989 On 9 November, the Wall comes down.
1990 3 October, formal German Reunification.
1994 The last of the Allied military leave Berlin.
1999 The German government moves from Bonn and the 'Berlin Republic' is born.

History

Dragged from a medieval bog to trade, prosperity and Enlightenment, Berlin has entertained revolution, wars and evil empires, only to be divided and then rule again as Germany's sole capital.

Ascanian origins

Berlin's origins are neither remarkable nor auspicious. It emerged sometime in the 12th century from swamplands that pioneering German knights had wrested from the Slavs. The name Berlin is believed to be derived from the Slav word *birl*, meaning swamp.

Facing off across the Spree river, Berlin and its twin settlement Cölln (on what is now the Museumsinsel) were founded as trading posts halfway between the older fortress towns of Spandau and Köpenick. Today the borough of Mitte embraces Cölln and old Berlin, and Spandau and Köpenick are outlying suburbs. The town's existence was first recorded in 1237, when Cölln was mentioned in a church document.

The Ascanian family, who held the title of Margraves of Brandenburg, ruled over the twin towns and the surrounding region. Eager to encourage trade, they granted special rights to merchants with the result that Berlin and Cölln emerged as prosperous trading centres linking east and west Europe. In 1307 the two towns were officially united.

In the 13th century, construction began on the Marienkirche and Nikolaikirche churches, both of which still stand. The latter gave its name to the **Nikolaiviertel**.

Early years of prosperity came to an end in 1319 with the death of the last Ascanian ruler. This opened the way for robber barons from the outlying regions, eager to take control of Berlin. But despite political upheaval and the threat of invasion, Berlin's merchants did manage to continue business. In 1359 the city joined the Hanseatic League of free-trading European cities (more prominent members were Hamburg and London).

The Hohenzollerns arrive

But the threat of invasion remained. Towards the end of the 14th century two powerful families, the Dukes of Pomerania and the brutal von Quitzow brothers, began to vie for control of the city.

Salvation came with Friedrich of Hohenzollern, a nobleman from southern Germany sent by the Holy Roman Emperor in 1411 to bring peace to the region. Initially, Friedrich was well received. The bells of the Marienkirche were melted down to be made into weapons for the fight against the aggressors. (In a strange echo of history, the Marienkirche bells were again transformed into tools of war in 1917, in the reign of Kaiser Wilhelm II, the last of the Hohernzollerns to rule.)

Having defeated the von Quitzow brothers, Friedrich officially became Margrave. In 1416 he took the further title of Elector of Brandenburg, denoting his right to vote in the election of the Holy Roman Emperor – titular head of the German-speaking states.

With peace and stability came the loss of independent traditions as Friedrich consolidated power. In 1442 foundations were laid for Berlin Castle and a royal court was founded. Disputes rose between the patrician classes (representing trade) and the guilds (representing crafts).

Rising social friction culminated in the 'Berlin Indignation' of 1447-48 when the population rose up in rebellion. Friedrich's son (Friedrich II) and his courtiers were locked out of the city and the foundations of the castle were flooded. In months the uprising collapsed and the Hohenzollerns returned triumphant. While merchants were shouldered new restrictions, courtiers were exempted from communal jurisdiction. The city began to lose economic impetus. Berlin was transformed from an outlying trading post to a small-sized capital (in 1450 the population was 6,000).

Reformation & debauchery

The Reformation arrived in Berlin and Brandenburg under the reign of Joachim I Nestor (1535-71),

Friedrich II at the founding of Berlin Castle.

Berlin in 1652 – urban regeneration.

the first Elector to embrace Protestantism. Joachim strove to improve the cultural standing of Berlin by inviting artists, architects and theologians to work in the city. In 1538 Caspar Theyss and Konrad Krebbs, two master-builders from Saxony, began work on a Renaissance-style palace. The building took a hundred years to complete and evolved into the bombastic Stadtschloß which stood on the Spree island until the East German government demolished it in 1950.

Joachim's studious nature was not reflected in the behaviour of his subjects. In a foretaste of Berlin's later reputation for debauchery and decadence, self-indulgence characterised life in the late 16th-century city. Repeated attempts to clamp down on excessive drinking, gambling and loose morals had little effect. Visiting the city, Abbot Trittenheim remarked that 'the people are good, but rough and unpolished; they prefer stuffing themselves to good science'.

After stuffing itself with another 6,000 people, Berlin left the 16th century with a population of 12,000 – double that of a hundred years earlier.

WAR & RECONSTRUCTION

The outbreak of the Thirty Years War in 1618 dragged Berlin on to the wider political stage. Although initially unaffected by the conflict between Catholic forces loyal to the Holy Roman Empire and the Swedish-backed Protestant armies, Berlin was eventually caught up in the war which

Stadtschloß – Renaissance-style bombast.

was to leave the German-speaking states ravaged, divided and weakened for over two centuries.

In 1626 Imperial troops occupied Berlin and plundered the city. In the following years Berlin was repeatedly sacked and forced to pay special taxes to the occupying forces. Trade collapsed and its hinterland was laid waste. To top it all, there were four serious epidemics between 1626 and 1631 which claimed thousands of lives. By the time the war ended in 1648, Berlin had lost a third of its housing stock, the population had fallen to less than 6,000 and the municipal coffers were greatly depleted.

The Great Elector

Painstaking reconstruction was carried out under Friedrich Wilhelm, known as the Great Elector. He succeeded his father in 1640, but chose to see out the war in exile. Influenced by Dutch ideas on town planning and architecture (he was married to a Princess of Orange), Friedrich Wilhelm embarked on a policy that linked urban regeneration, economic expansion and solid defence.

New fortifications were built around the city and a garrison of 2,000 soldiers established as Friedrich expanded his 'Residenzstadt'. In the centre of town, the Lustgarten was laid out opposite the palace. Running west from the palace the first Lindenallee ('Avenue of Lime Trees' or Unter den Linden) was created.

To revive the economy, housing and property taxes were abolished in favour of a modern-style sales tax. With the money that was raised, three new towns – Friedrichswerder, Dorotheenstadt and Friedrichstadt – were built. (Together with Berlin and Cölln, today these make up the district of Mitte.) In the late 1660s a canal linked the Spree and Oder rivers, confirming Berlin's position as an east-west trading centre.

But Friedrich Wilhelm's most inspired policy was to encourage refugees to settle in the city. First to arrive were over 50 Jewish families from Vienna. In 1672 Huguenot settlers arrived from France. The influence of the new arrivals was pronounced, bringing new skills and industries to Berlin.

The growing cosmopolitan mix laid the foundations for a flowering of intellectual and artistic life. By the time the Grand Elector's son, Friedrich III, took the throne in 1688, one in five Berliners spoke French. This legacy can be seen in the many French words that still pepper Berlin dialect, such as *boulette* ('hamburger') and *étage* ('floor').

In 1695 work commenced on **Schloß Charlottenburg** to the west of Berlin. A year later the Academy of Arts was founded. And in 1700, intellectual life was further stimulated by the founding of the Academy of Sciences under Gottfried Leibniz. The construction of the German and French cathedrals at **Gendarmenmarkt** in 1701 gave Berlin one of its most beautiful squares.

Five years later the Zeughaus ('Armoury'), now housing the **Deutsches Historisches Museum** was completed on Unter den Linden .

In 1701 Elector Friedrich III took a step up the hierarchy of European nobility when he had himself crowned Prussian King Friedrich I (not to be confused with the earlier Elector). In little more than half a century, Berlin had progressed from a devastated town to a thriving commercial centre with a population of nearly 30,000.

The Prussians are coming

The common association of Prussia with militarism can broadly be traced back to the 18th century and the efforts of two men in particular: King Friedrich Wilhelm I and his son Friedrich II (also known as Frederick the Great). Although father and son hated each other and had very different sensibilities (Friedrich Wilhelm was boorish and mean, Friedrich II sensitive and philosophical), together they launched Prussia as a major military power and in the process gave Berlin the character of a garrison city.

King Friedrich Wilhelm (1713-40) made parsimony and militarism state policy – and almost succeeded in driving Berlin's economy into the ground. The only thing that grew was the army, which by 1740 numbered 80,000 troops. Many of these were deployed in Berlin and billeted in the houses of ordinary citizens.

With a king much more interested in keeping the books than reading them, intellectual life suffered. Friedrich had no use for art so he closed down the Academy of Arts; instead he collected soldiers, and swapped a rare collection of Oriental vases for one of the King of Saxony's regiments. The Tsar received a small gold ship in exchange for 150 Russian giants.

But the obsession with all things military did have some positive effects. The king needed competent soldiers, so he made school compulsory; the army needed doctors, so he set up medical institutes. Eventually Berlin's economy also picked up on the back of demand from the military. City administration was reformed. Skilled immigrants (this time mostly from Saxony) met the increased demand. The result was a population boom (from 60,000 in 1713 to 90,000 in 1740) and a growth in trade and manufacturing.

Frederick the Great

While his father was collecting soldiers, Frederick the Great deployed them in a series of wars with Austria and Russia (from 1740-42, 1744-45 and 1756-63, known as the Seven Years War) in a bid to win territory in Silesia in the east. Initially, the wars proved disastrous. The Austrians occupied the city in 1757, the Russians in 1760. However,

thanks to a mixture of good fortune and military genius, Frederick finally emerged victorious from the Seven Years War.

When not fighting, the king devoted his time to forging a modern state apparatus (he liked to call himself 'first servant of the state'; Berliners simply called him 'Old Fritz') and transforming Berlin and Potsdam. This was achieved partly through conviction – the king was friends with Voltaire and brought him to live at Potsdam, and Old Fritz saw himself very much as an aesthetically-minded figure of the Enlightenment – but it was also a political necessity. He needed to convince enemies and subjects that even in times of national crisis he was able to afford grand projects.

So Unter den Linden was transformed into a grand boulevard. At the palace end, the Forum Fredericianum, designed and constructed by the architect von Knobelsdorff, comprised the Opera House, St Hedwigskathedrale, Prince Heinrich Palace (now housing **Humboldt University**) and the State Library. Although it was never fully completed, the Forum remains one of Berlin's main attractions.

To the west of Berlin, the **Tiergarten** was landscaped and a new palace, Schloß Bellevue (now the Berlin residence of the German president), was built. Frederick also decided to replace a set of barracks at Gendarmenmarkt with a theatre, now called the **Konzerthaus**.

To encourage manufacturing and industry (particularly textiles), advantageous excise laws were introduced. Businesses such as the KPM (Königliche Porzellan-Manufaktur) porcelain works were nationalised and turned into prestigious and lucrative enterprises.

Legal and administrative reforms also characterised Frederick's reign. Religious freedom was enshrined in law; torture was abolished; and Berlin became a centre of the Enlightenment. Cultural and intellectual life blossomed around figures such as philosopher Moses Mendelssohn and poet Gottfried Lessing.

The Brandenburg Gate in 1790.

By the time Friedrich died in 1786, Berlin had a population of 150,000 and was the capital of one of Europe's grand powers.

ENLIGHTENMENT'S END

The death of Frederick the Great also marked the end of the Enlightenment in Prussia. His successor, Friedrich Wilhelm II, was more interested in spending money on architecture than wasting his time with political philosophy. Censorship was stepped up and the king's extravagance plunged the state into an economic and financial crisis. By 1788 over 14,000 peo-

Wilhelm von Humboldt.

ple in the city were dependent on state and church aid. The state apparatus began to crumble under the weight of incompetent and greedy administrators. When he died in 1797, Friedrich Wilhelm II left his son with huge debts.

However, the old king's expensive love of classicism left Berlin with its most famous monument: the **Brandenburg Gate**. It was built by Karl Gottfried Langhans in 1789, the year of the French Revolution, and modelled on the Propylaea in Athens. Two years later, Johann Schadow added the Quadriga, a sculpture of a bare-chested Victoria riding a chariot drawn by four horses. Originally one of 14 gates marking Berlin's boundaries, the Brandenburg Gate is now the geographical and symbolic centre of the city.

If the king did not care for intellect, then the emerging bourgeoisie did. Towards the turn of the century, Berlin became a centre of German Romanticism. Literary salons flourished, and remained a feature of Berlin's cultural life into the middle of the 19th century.

Despite censorship, Berlin still had a platform for liberal expression. The city's newspapers welcomed the French Revolution so enthusiastically that in the southern German states Jacobins were referred to as 'Berliners'.

The Napoleonic wars

In 1806 Berlin came face to face with the effects of revolution in France: following the defeat of the Prussian forces in the battles of Jena and Auerstadt on 14 October, Napoleon's army headed for Berlin. The king and queen fled to Königsberg and the garrison was removed from the city. On 27 October Napoleon and his army marched through the Brandenburg Gate. Once again Berlin was an occupied city.

Napoleon set about changing the political and administrative structure. He called together 2,000 prominent citizens and told them to elect a new administration called the Comité Administratif. This body oversaw the city's day-to-day adminis-

tration until the French troops left in 1808.

Napoleon decreed that property belonging to the state, the Hohenzollerns and many aristocratic families be expropriated. Priceless works of art were removed from palaces in Berlin and Potsdam and sent to France; even the Quadriga was taken from the Brandenburg Gate and shipped to Paris. The city also suffered financially. With nearly 30,000 French troops in the city, Berliners had no choice but to supply them with food and lodging. On top of this came crippling war reparations.

When the French left, a group of energetic, reform-minded aristocrats, grouped around Baron vom Stein, seized the opportunity to introduce a series of wide-ranging reforms in a bid to modernise the moribund Prussian state. One key aspect was the clear separation of state and civic responsibility, which gave Berlin independence to manage its own affairs. A new council was elected, based loosely on the Comité Administratif (though only property owners and the wealthy were entitled to vote). In 1810 the philosopher Wilhelm von Humboldt founded the university. All remaining restrictions on the city's Jewish population were removed.

Other reforms included the introduction of a new and simplified sales tax. A newly created 'trade police' was established to monitor trading standards. Generals Scharnhorst and Gneisenau completely overhauled the army.

Although the French occupied Berlin again in 1812 on their way home from the disastrous Russian campaign, this time they were met with stiff resistance. A year later the Prussian king finally joined the anti-Napoleon coalition and thousands of Berliners signed up to fight. When Napoleon tried to capture the city once more, he was defeated at nearby Grossbeeren. This, together with a subsequent defeat for the French in the

General Blücher brings back the Quadriga.

Battle of Leipzig, marked the end of Napoleonic rule in Germany.

In August 1814, General Blücher brought the Quadriga back to Berlin, and restored it to its place on the Brandenburg Gate. One symbolic addition was made to the statue: an Iron Cross and Prussian eagle were added to the staff in Victoria's hand.

Biedermeier & Borsig

The burst of reform initiated in 1810 was short-lived. Following the Congress of Vienna (1814-15), which established a new order for post-Napoleonic Europe, King Friedrich Wilhelm III reneged on promises of constitutional reform. Instead of a greater unity among the German states, a loose alliance came into being; dominated by Austria, the German Confederation was distinctly anti-liberal.

In Prussia itself, state power increased. Alongside the normal police, a secret service and vice squad were set up. The police president had the power to issue directives to the city council. Book and newspaper censorship increased. The authorities sacked Humboldt from the university he had set up.

With their hopes for lasting change frustrated, the bourgeoisie withdrew to their salons. It is one of the ironies of this time that although political opposition was quashed, a vibrant cultural movement flourished. Academics like Hegel and Ranke lectured at the university and enhanced Berlin's reputation as an intellectual centre. The period became known as Biedermeier after a fictional character embodying bourgeois taste, created by Swabian comic writer Ludwig Eichrodt.

Another legacy of this period is the range of neo-classical buildings designed by Karl Friedrich Schinkel, such as his Altes Museum and the Neue Wache (now the **Mahnmal**) on Unter den Linden. *See chapter* **Architecture**.

For the majority, however, the post-Napoleonic era was a period of frustrated hopes and bitter poverty. Industrialisation swelled the ranks of the working class. Between 1810 and 1840, the city's population doubled to around 400,000, making Berlin the fourth largest city in Europe. But most of the newcomers lived in conditions which would later lead to riot and revolution.

INDUSTRIAL REVOLUTION

Prussia was ideally equipped for the industrial age. By the 19th century it had grown dramatically and boasted one of the greatest abundances of raw materials in Europe.

It was the founding of the Borsig Werke on Chausseestraße in 1837 that established Berlin as the work-

Siemens – industrial ideal, technical genius.

shop of continental Europe. August Borsig was Berlin's first big industrialist. His factories turned out locomotives for the new railway network which had started with the opening of the Berlin to Potsdam line in 1838. Borsig also left his mark through the establishment of a suburb (Borsigwalde) that still carries his name.

The other great pioneering industrialist, Werner Siemens, set up his electrical engineering firm in a house by Anhalter Bahnhof. The first European to produce telegraph equipment, Siemens personified the German industrial ideal with his mix of technical genius and business savvy.

The Siemens company also left a permanent imprint on Berlin through the building of a new suburb (Siemensstadt) to house its workers. With the growth of companies like these, Berlin became continental Europe's largest industrial city.

1848 & all that

Friedrich Wilhelm IV's accession to the throne in 1840 raised hopes of an end to repression; and initially, he did appear to want real change. He declared an amnesty for political prisoners, relaxed censorship, sacked the hated justice minister and granted asylum to political refugees.

Political debate thrived in coffee houses and wine bars. The university was another focal point for discussion. In the late 1830s, Karl Marx spent a term there, just missing fellow alumnus Otto von Bismarck. In the early 1840s Friedrich Engels came to Berlin in order to do his military service.

August Borsig.

The thaw didn't last long. Friedrich Wilhelm IV shared his father's opposition to constitutional reform. Living and working conditions for the majority of Berliners worsened. Rapid industrialisation had also brought sweatshops, 17-hour days and child labour.

These poor conditions were compounded in 1844 by harvest failure

1848 – running street battles between revolutionaries and police.

which drove up prices for potatoes and wheat. Food riots broke out on Gendarmenmarkt when a crowd stormed the market stalls. It took the army three days to restore order.

Things came to a head in 1848, the year of revolutions. Berliners seized the moment. Political meetings were held in beer gardens and in the Tiergarten, and demands made for internal reform and a unification of German-speaking states. At the end of one demonstration in the Tiergarten, there was a running battle between police and demonstrators on Unter den Linden.

On 18 March, the king finally conceded to allowing a new parliament, and made vague promises about other reforms. Later that day, the crowd of 10,000 gathered to celebrate the victory were set upon by soldiers. Shots were fired and the revolution began. Barricades went up throughout central Berlin and demonstrators fought with police for 14 hours. Finally the king backed down (again). In exchange for the dismantling of barricades, the king ordered his troops out of Berlin. Days later, he took part in the funeral service for the 'March Dead' – the 183 revolutionaries who had been killed – and also promised more freedoms.

Berlin was now ostensibly in the hands of the revolutionaries. A Civil Guard patrolled the city, the king rode through the streets wearing the revolutionary colours (black, red and gold), seeming to embrace the causes of liberalism and nationalism. Prussia, he said, should 'merge into Germany'.

But the revolution proved short-lived. When pressed on unification, the king merely suggested that the other German states send representatives to the Prussian National Assembly. Needless to say, this offer was rebuffed.

Leading liberals instead convened a German National Assembly in Frankfurt in May 1848. At the same time, a new Prussian Assembly met in what is now the Konzerthaus on Gendarmenmarkt to debate a new constitution. Towards the end of 1848, reforming fervour took over Berlin.

THE BACKLASH

The onset of winter, however, brought a change of mood to the city. Using continuing street violence as the pretext, the king ordered the National Assembly to be moved to Brandenburg. In early November he brought troops back into the city and declared a state of siege. Press freedom was once again restricted. The Civil Guard and National Assembly were dissolved. On 5 December the king delivered his final blow to the liberals by unveiling a new constitution fashioned to his own particular tastes.

Throughout the winter of 1848-49 thousands of liberals were arrested or expelled. A new city constitution, drawn up in 1850, reduced the number of eligible voters to five per cent of the population, or around 21,000 people. Increased police powers meant that the position of police president was more important than that of mayor.

By 1857 the increasingly senile Friedrich Wilhelm had gone quite literally mad. His brother Wilhelm acted as regent until becoming king on Friedrich's death in 1861.

Once again, the people's hopes were raised: the new monarch began his reign by appointing liberals to the cabinet. The building of the **Rotes Rathaus** ('Red Town Hall') gave the city council a headquarters to match the size of the royal palace. Built between 1861 and 1869, the Rathaus was named for the colour of its bricks, and not (yet) the political persuasion of its members.

But by 1861, the king found himself in dispute with parliament over proposed army reforms. The king wanted to strengthen his direct control of the armed forces. Parliament wouldn't accept this, so the king went over its members' heads and appointed a new prime minister: Otto von Bismarck.

The Iron Chancellor

An arrogant genius who began his career as a diplomat, Bismarck was well able to deal with unruly parliamentarians. Using a constitutional loophole to rule against the majority, he quickly pushed through the army reforms. Extra-parliamentary opposition was dealt with in the usual manner: oppression and censorship. Dissension thus suppressed, Bismarck turned his mind to German unification.

Unlike the bourgeois revolutionaries of 1848 who desired a Germany united by popular will and endowed with political reforms, Bismarck strove to bring the states together under the authoritarian dominance of Prussia. His methods involved astute foreign policy and outright aggression.

Wars against Denmark (1864) and Austria (1866) brought post-Napoleonic order to an abrupt end. Prussia was no longer the smallest of the Great Powers but an aspiring initiator of geo-political change. Austria's defeat confirmed the primacy of Prussia among German-speaking states.

Victory on the battlefield boosted Bismarck's popularity across Prussia – but not in Berlin itself. He was defeated in his Berlin constituency in the 1867 election to the newly created North German League. This was a Prussian-dominated body linking the northern states and a stepping stone towards Germany's overall unification.

Bismarck's third war – against France in 1870 – revealed his scope for intrigue and opportunism. He exploited a dispute over the succession to the Spanish throne to provoke France into declaring war on Prussia. Citing the North German League and treaties signed with the southern

Otto von Bismarck.

German states, Bismarck brought together a united German army under Prussian leadership.

Following the defeat of the French army on 2 September, Bismarck moved quickly to turn a unified military campaign into the basis for a unified nation. The Prussian king would be German emperor: beneath him would be four kings, 18 grand-dukes and assorted princes from the German states, which would retain some regional powers. (This arrangement formed the basis for the modern federal system of regional *Länder*.)

On 18 January 1871, King Wilhelm was proclaimed German Kaiser ('Emperor') in the Hall of Mirrors in Versailles.

In just nine years, Bismarck had united Germany, forging an empire that dominated central Europe. The political, economic and social centre of this new creation was Berlin.

Imperial Berlin

The coming of empire threw Berlin into one of its greatest periods of expansion and change. The economic boom (helped by five billion gold francs extracted from France as war reparations) led to a wave of speculation. Farmers in Wilmersdorf and Schöneberg became millionaires overnight as they sold off their fields to developers.

During the decades following German unification, Berlin emerged as Europe's most modern metropolis. This period was later dubbed the Gründerzeit ('Foundation Years').

The Gründerzeit were marked by a move away from traditional Prussian values of thrift and modesty, towards the gaudy and bombastic. In Berlin, the change of mood manifested itself in numerous monuments and buildings. Of these the **Reichstag**, **Siegessäule** ('Victory Column'), the **Berliner Dom** and the **Kaiser-Wilhelm-Gedächtniskirche** are the most prominent.

Superficially, the Reichstag (designed by Paul Wallot and completed in 1894) represented a weighty commitment to parliamentary democracy, but in reality Germany was still in the grip of conservative, backward-looking forces. The authoritarian power of the Kaiser remained intact, as was demonstrated by the decision of Kaiser Wilhelm II to sack Bismarck in 1890 following disagreements over policy.

BERLIN BOOMS

When Bismarck began his premiership in 1861, his offices on Wilhemstraße overlooked potato fields. By the time he lost his job in 1890, they were in the centre of Europe's newest and most congested city. Economic boom and growing political and social importance attracted hundreds of thousands of new inhabitants to the city. At the time of unification in 1871, 820,000 people lived in Berlin; by 1890 the population had nearly doubled.

The growing numbers of the working class were shoved into hastily built *Mietskasernen* tenements (literally, 'rental barracks') which mushroomed across the city – particularly in Kreuzberg, Wedding and Prenzlauer Berg. Poorly ventilated and hopelessly overcrowded, the *Mietskasernen* (many of which still stand) are characterised by a series of interlinked courtyards. They became both a symbol of Berlin and a breeding ground for further social unrest.

The Social Democratic Party (SPD), founded in 1869, quickly became the voice for the city's have-nots. In the 1877 general election it won more than 40 per cent of the Berlin vote. Here was born the left-wing reputation of *Rotes Berlin* ('Red Berlin') which has followed the city to the present day.

In 1878 two assassination attempts on the Kaiser gave Bismarck an excuse to classify socialists as enemies of the state. He introduced restrictive laws to curb the 'red menace', and outlawed the SPD and two other progressive parties.

The ban existed until 1890 – the year of Bismarck's sacking – but did little to stem support for the SPD. In the general election held that year, the SPD dominated the vote in Berlin. And in 1912 it won more than 70 per cent of the Berlin vote to become the largest party in the Reichstag.

Kaiser Bill

Famed for his ridiculous moustache, Kaiser Wilhelm II came to the throne in 1880 and soon became the personification of the new Germany: bombastic, awkward and unpredictable. Like his grandmother Queen Victoria, he gave his name to an era. Wilhelm's epoch is associated with showy militarism and foreign policy bungles leading to a world war that cost the Kaiser his throne and Germany its stability.

The Wilhelmine years were also characterised by further explosive growth in Berlin (the population rose to two million by 1910 and by 1914 had doubled again) and a blossoming of the city's cultural and intellectual life. The Bode Museum was built in 1904 and in 1912 work began next door on the **Pergamon Museum**. In 1912 a new Opera House was unveiled in Charlottenburg (later to be destroyed by wartime bombing; the **Deutsche Oper** now stands on the same site). Expressionism took off in 1910 and the Kurfürstendamm became the location for many new art galleries. Although Paris still remained ahead of Berlin in the arts, the German city was fast catching up.

By the time of his abdication in 1918, Wilhelm's reign had also seen the emergence of Berlin as a centre of scientific and intellectual development. Six Berlin scientists (including Albert Einstein and Max Planck) were awarded Nobel Prizes.

In the years immediately preceding World War I, Berlin appeared to be loosening its stiff collar of pomposity. Tangoing became all the rage in new clubs around Friedrichstraße – though the Kaiser promptly banned officers in uniform from joining in the fun. Yet despite the progressive changes, growing militarism and international tension overshadowed the period.

Germany was not alone in its preparedness for war. By 1914 Europe was well and truly armed and almost waiting to tear itself apart. In June 1914 the assassination of Archduke Franz Ferdinand provided the excuse. On 1 August war was declared on Russia and the Kaiser appeared on a balcony of the royal palace to tell a jubilant crowd that from that moment onwards, he would not recognise any parties, only Germans. At the Reichstag the deputies, who had virtually unanimously voted in support of the war, agreed.

World War I & revolution

No one was prepared for the disaster of World War I. After Bismarck, the Germans had come to expect quick, sweeping victories. The armies on the Western Front settled into their trenches for a war of attrition that would cost over a million German lives. Meanwhile, the civilian population began to adapt to austerity and shortages. After the 1917 harvest failed, there were outbreaks of famine. Dog and cat meat started to appear on the menus in the capital's restaurants.

Karl Liebknecht declares a socialist republic.

The SPD's initial enthusiasm for war evaporated and in 1916 the party refused to pass the Berlin budget. A year later, members of the party's radical wing broke away to form the Spartacus League. Anti-war feeling was voiced in mass strikes in April 1917 and January 1918. These were brutally suppressed, but when the Imperial Marines in Kiel mutinied on 2 November 1918 the authorities were no longer able to stop the force of the anti-war movement.

The mutiny spread to Berlin where members of the Guards Regiment came out against the war. On 9 November the Kaiser was forced into abdication and subsequent exile. This date is weirdly layered with significance in German history; it's the anniversary of the establishment of the Weimar Republic (1918); Kristallnacht (1938); and the fall of the Wall (1989).

It was on this day that Philip Scheidemann, a leading SPD member of parliament and key proponent of republicanism, broke off his lunch in the second-floor restaurant of the Reichstag. He walked over to a window overlooking Königsplatz (now Platz der Republik) where a crowd had massed and declared to them: 'The old and the rotten have broken down. Long live the new! Long live the German Republic!'

At the other end of Unter den Linden, Karl Liebknecht, who together with Rosa Luxemburg headed the Spartacus League, declared Germany a socialist republic from a balcony of the occupied royal palace. (The balcony was the same one the Kaiser used when he spoke to Berliners on the eve of the war, and has been preserved as part of the Staatsratsgebäude ('State Council building') of the East German government.)

Liebknecht and the Spartacists wanted a Communist Germany similar to Soviet Russia; Scheidemann and the SPD wanted a parliamentary democracy. Between them stood those still loyal to the vanished monarchy. All were prepared to fight their respective corners. Barricades were erected in the city centre and street battles ensued.

It was in this climate of turmoil and violence that Germany's first attempt at republican democracy – the Weimar Republic – was born.

Terror & instability

The revolution in Berlin may have brought peace to the Western Front, where hostilities were ended on 11 November, but in Germany it unleashed a wave of political terror and instability. The new masters in Berlin, the SPD under the leadership of Friedrich Ebert, ordered renegade battalions of soldiers returning from the front (known as the Freikorps) to quash the Spartacists, who launched a concerted bid for power in January 1919.

Within days, the uprising had been bloodily suppressed and Liebknecht and Luxemburg went

into hiding. On 15 January Freikorps officers traced them to a house in Wilmersdorf and put them under arrest. They were then taken to a hotel near **Zoo Station** for interrogation. Between the hotel and Moabit Prison, the officers murdered both of them and dumped Luxemburg's body over the Liechtenstein Bridge into the Landwehr Canal. Today a plaque marks the spot.

Four days later, the national elections returned the SPD as the largest party: the Social Democrats' victory over the extreme left was complete. Berlin was deemed too dangerous for parliamentary business, so the government swiftly decamped to the quaint provincial town of Weimar from which the first German republic took its name.

Germany's new constitution ended up being full of good liberal intentions but riddled with technical flaws. And this left the country wide open to weak coalition government and quasi-dictatorial presidential rule.

Another crippling blow to the new republic was the Versailles Treaty, which set the terms of peace. Reparation payments (set to run until 1988) blew a hole in a fragile economy already weakened by war. Support for the right-wing nationalist lobby was fuelled by the loss of territories in both east and west. And restrictions placed on the German military led some right-wingers to claim that Germany's soldiers had been 'stabbed in the back' by Jews and left-wingers at home.

In March 1920, a right-wing coup was staged in Berlin under the leadership of Wolfgang Kapp, a civil servant from east Prussia. The recently returned government once again fled the city. For four days Berlin was besieged by roaming Freikorps. Some of them had taken to adorning their helmets with a new symbol: the *Hakenkreuz* or swastika.

Ultimately a general strike and the refusal of the army (the Reichswehr) to join Kapp brought an end to the putsch. But the political and economic chaos in the city remained. Political assassinations were commonplace. Food shortages lead to bouts of famine. Inflation started to escalate.

There were two main reasons for the precipitate devaluation of the Reichsmark. To pay for the war, the increasingly desperate imperial government had resorted simply to printing more money, a policy continued by the new republican rulers. The burden of reparations also lead to an outflow of foreign currency. In 1914 one dollar bought just over four Reichmarks; by 1922 it was worth over 7,000. And one hyperinflationary year later, a dollar was worth 4.2 billion marks. Workers needed suitcases to carry the near-worthless bundles of notes that made up their salaries. Wheelbarrows replaced wallets as almost overnight the savings of millions were wiped out.

In the same year, 1923, the French government sent troops into the Ruhr industrial region to take by force reparation goods which the German government said it could no longer afford to pay. The Communists planned an uprising in Berlin for October but lost their nerve.

In November a young ex-corporal called Adolf Hitler, who led the tiny National Socialist Party (NSDAP or Nazi Party), launched an attempted coup from a beer-hall in Munich. His programme called for armed resistance against the French, an end to the 'dictatorship of Versailles' and punishment for all those – especially the Jews – who had 'betrayed' Germany at the end of the war.

Hitler's first attempt at power came to nothing. Instead of marching on Berlin, he went to prison. Inflation was finally brought down with the introduction of a new currency (one new mark was worth one trillion old ones).

But the overall decline of moral and social values that had taken place in the five years since 1918 was not so easy to restore.

The Golden Twenties

Joseph Goebbels came to Berlin in 1926 to take charge of the local Nazi party organisation. On arriving, he observed: 'This city is a melting-pot of everything that is evil – prostitution, drinking houses, cinemas, Marxism, Jews, strippers, negroes dancing and all the off-shoots of modern art.'

The term 'evil' is better applied to Goebbels himself, but his description of 1920s Berlin was not far wrong. During that decade the city overtook Paris as continental Europe's arts and entertainment capital and in the process added its own decadent twist. 'We used to have a first-class army,' mused Klaus Mann, the author of *Mephisto*; 'now we have first-class perversions.'

By 1927 Berlin boasted more than 70 cabarets and nightclubs. At the Theater des Westens, near Zoo Station, cabaret artist Josephine Baker danced to a packed house. Baker also danced naked at parties thrown by playwright Karl Volmoeller in his

Die Dreigroschenoper premières in 1928.

flat on Pariser Platz. 'Berlin was mad! A triumph!' she later recalled.

While Brecht's *Dreigroschenoper* played at the Theater am Schiffbauerdamm, Berlin's Dadaists were gathered at the Romanisches Café on Tauentzienstraße (later destroyed by bombing – the **Europa-Center** now stands on the site). There was a proliferation of avant-garde magazines reflecting new ideas in art and literature.

But the flipside of all the frenetic enjoyment was an underbelly of raw poverty and glaring social tension reflected in the works of painters like George Grosz and Otto Dix. In the music halls, Brecht and Weill used a popular medium to ram home points about social injustices.

In architecture and design, the revolutionary ideas emanating from the Bauhaus school in Dessau (it briefly moved to Berlin in 1932 but was closed down by the Nazis a year later) were taking concrete form in building projects such as the **Shell House** building on the Landwehr canal, the Siemenstadt new town, and the model housing project Hufeisensiedlung ('Horse Shoe Estate') in Britz. Furniture, ceramics, sculptures and sketches, created in the Bauhaus workshop from 1919 until 1933, are kept in the **Bauhaus Archiv-Museum für Gestaltung**.

Street-fighting years

The stock market crash on Wall Street and the onset of global depression in 1929 ushered in the brutal end of the Weimar Republic.

The fractious coalition governments that had just managed to hold on to power in the brief years of prosperity in the late 1920s were no match for rocketing unemployment and a surge in support for extremist parties.

By the end of 1929 nearly one in four Berliners were out of work. The city's streets became a battleground for clashes between Nazis, Communists and social democrats. Increasingly the police relied on water cannons, armoured vehicles and guns to

Josephine Baker: 'Berlin was mad!'

quell street fighting across the city. One May Day demonstration left 30 dead and several hundred wounded. At Bülowplatz (now Rosa-Luxemburg-Platz) where the Communist Party, the KPD, had its headquarters, there were regular battles between Communists, the police and Nazi stormtroopers (the SA). In August 1931 two police officers were murdered on Bülowplatz. One of the men accused of the murders (and later found guilty, albeit by a Nazi court) was Erich Mielke, a young Communist, later to become the head of East Germany's secret police, the Stasi.

In 1932 the violence in Berlin reached crisis level. In just six weeks over the summer, 300 street battles left 70 people dead. In the general election in July, the Nazis took 40 per cent of the vote and became the largest party in the Reichstag. Hermann Göring, one of Hitler's earliest followers and a wounded veteran of the beer-hall putsch, was appointed Reichstag president.

The prize of government, however, still eluded the Nazis. At the elections held in November, the Nazis lost two million votes across Germany and 37,000 in Berlin, where the Communists emerged as the strongest party. (In 'Red' Wedding, over 60 per cent voted for the KPD.)

The election had been held against the backdrop of a strike by 20,000 transport employees who were protesting against planned wage cuts. The strike had been called by the Communists and the Nazis who vied with each other to capture the mass vote and bring the Weimar Republic to an end. Under orders from Moscow, the KPD shunned all co-operation with the SPD, ending any possibility of a broad left-wing front.

As Berlin headed into another winter of depression, almost every third person was out of work. A city survey recorded that almost half of Berlin's inhabitants were living four to a room and that a large proportion of the city's housing stock was unfit for human habitation. Berlin topped the European table of suicides.

The new government of General Kurt von Schleicher ruled by presidential decree. Schleicher had promised President von Hindenburg he could tame the Nazis into a coalition. When he failed, his rival Franz von Papen successfully overcame Hindenburg's innate dislike for Hitler and manoeuvred the Nazi leader into power. On 30 January 1933, Adolf Hitler was named Chancellor and moved from his headquarters in the Hotel Kaiserhof in Glinkastraße (it was central and his favourite band played there) to the Chancellery two streets away in Wilhelmstraße.

That evening, the SA staged a torchlight parade through the Brandenburg Gate and along to the Chancellery. Looking out from the window of his house next to the Gate, the artist Max Liebermann remarked to his dinner guests: 'I cannot eat as much as I'd like to puke.'

The Nazis take control

The government Hitler now led was a coalition of Nazis and German nationalists led by the media magnate Alfred Hugenberg. Together their votes fell just short of a parliamentary majority so another election was called for March. In the meantime, Hitler continued to rule by decree.

The last relatively free election of the Republic was also the most violent. Open persecution of Communists began. The Nazis banned meetings of the KPD, shut down Communist newspapers and broke up SPD election rallies.

On 27 February a fire broke out in the Reichstag. It was almost certainly started by the Nazis, who used it as an excuse to step up the persecution of opponents. Over 12,000 Communists were arrested. Spelling it out in a speech at the Sportspalast two days before the election, Goebbels said: 'It's not my job to practise justice, instead I have to destroy and exterminate – nothing else.'

The Nazis still didn't achieve an absolute majority (in Berlin they polled 34 per cent), but that no longer mattered. With the support of his allies in the coalition, Hitler pushed through an Enabling Law giving him dictatorial powers. By summer, Germany had been declared a one-party state.

Already ad hoc concentration camps – known as brown houses after the colour of the SA uniforms –

Gauleiter Goebbels speechifies in 1931.

had sprung up around the city. The SS established itself in Prinz Albrecht Palais where it was later joined by the secret police, the Gestapo. Just to the north of Berlin near Oranienburg, a concentration camp, **Sachsenhausen**, was set up.

Along the Kurfürstendamm squads of SA stormtroopers would go 'Jew baiting' and on 1 April 1933, the first boycott of Jewish shops began. A month later Goebbels, who became Minister for Propaganda, organised a book-burning, which took place in the courtyard at the university on Unter den Linden. Books by Jews or writers deemed degenerate or traitors were thrown on to a huge bonfire.

Berlin's unemployment problem was tackled through a series of public works programmes, growing militarisation, which drew new recruits to the army, and the 'encouragement' of women to leave the workplace.

Following the policy of *Gleichschaltung* (co-ordination), the Nazis began to bring all aspects of public life under their control. With a few exceptions, party membership became obligatory for doctors, lawyers, professors and journalists.

During the Night of the Long Knives in July 1934, Hitler settled some old scores with opponents within the SA and Nazi Party. At Lichterfelde barracks, officers of the SS shot and killed over 150 SA members. Hitler's predecessor as Chancellor, General von Schleicher, was shot together with his wife at their home in Wannsee.

After the death of President Hindenburg in August 1934, Hitler had himself named Führer ('Leader') and made the armed forces swear a personal oath of allegiance to him. Within less than two years, the Nazis had subjugated Germany.

Planning & persecution

A brief respite came with the Olympic Games in August 1936. In a bid to persuade foreign participants and spectators that all was well in the Reich, Goebbels ordered the removal of anti-Semitic slogans from shops. 'Undesirables' were also moved out of the city and the pavement display cases that held copies of the racist Nazi newspaper *Der Stürmer* ('The Stormtrooper') were dismantled.

The Games, mainly held at the newly-built **Olympiastadion** in Charlottenburg, were not such a success for the Nazis. Instead of blond, Aryan giants sweeping the field, Hitler had to watch the African-American Jesse Owens clock up medals and records. Whenever Owens won, Hitler fled the stadium so as not to have to shake hands with the real star of the Games.

The Games did work, however, as public relations. Foreign observers left glowing with reports about a strident and healthy nation. But had any of the foreign visitors stayed, they would have

The 1936 Olympics – a brief respite.

seen the reality of Hitler's policy of co-ordinating all facets of life in Berlin within the Nazi doctrine.

As part of a nationwide campaign to remove what the Nazis considered to be *Entartete Kunst* ('Degenerate Art') from German cultural life, works of modern art were collected and brought together in a touring exhibition designed to show the depth of depravity in contemporary ('Jewish-dominated') culture. But Nazi hopes that these 'degenerate' works would repulse the German people fell flat. When the exhibition arrived at Berlin's Zeughaus in early 1938, thousands queued for admission. The people loved the paintings.

After the exhibition, the paintings were sent to auction in Switzerland. Those that remained unsold were burnt in the fire station in Köpenicker Straße. More than 1,000 oil paintings and 4,000 watercolours were destroyed.

TOTALITARIAN TOWN-PLANNING

Shortly after taking power, Hitler ordered that the lime trees on Unter den Linden be chopped down to give Berlin's boulevard a cleaner, more sanitised form. This was just the first step in Nazi urban planning.

Hitler's plans for the redesign of Berlin reflected the hatred the Nazis felt for the city. Hitler entrusted young architect Albert Speer with the job of recreating Berlin as a metropolis to 'outtrump Paris and Vienna'. The heart of old Berlin was to be demolished and its small streets replaced by two highways stretching 37km (23 miles) from north to south and 50km (30 miles) from east to west. Each axis would be 90m (100 yards) wide. Crowning the northern axis would be a huge Volkshalle ('People's Hall') nearly 300m (328 yards) high with space for over 150,000 people. Speer and Hitler also had grand plans for a triumphal arch three times the size of the Arc de Triomphe and a Führer's Palace 150 times bigger than the one occupied by Bismarck. The new city was to be called Germania.

The onset of war meant that Speer only built a fraction of what was intended. Hitler's new Chancellery was constructed in under a year and finished in early 1939. It was demolished after the war. On the proposed east-west axis, a small section around the Siegessäule was widened for Hitler's 50th birthday in April 1939.

PERSECUTION

Of the half-a-million Jews living in Germany in 1933, over a third lived in Berlin. The Jewish community had played an important role in Berlin's development and its influence was especially prevalent in the financial, artistic and intellectual circles of the city.

The Nazis wiped out these centuries-old traditions in 12 years of persecution and murder. Arrests soon followed the initial boycotts and acts of intimidation. From 1933 to 1934, many of Berlin's Jews fled to exile abroad. Those who stayed were to be subjected to legislation (the Nuremberg Laws of 1935) that banned Jews from public office, forbade them to marry Aryan Germans and stripped them of citizenship. Jewish cemeteries were desecrated and the names of Jews chipped off war memorials.

Berlin business institutions that had been owned by Jews – such as the Ullstein newspaper group and the Tietz and Wertheim department stores on Alexanderplatz and Leipziger Straße – were 'Aryanised'. The Nazis either expropriated them from the owners or forced them to sell at ridiculously low prices.

On 9 November 1938, a wave of 'spontaneous' acts of vandalism and violence against Jews and their property began in response to the assassination of a German diplomat in Paris by a young Jewish emigré. Jewish businesses and houses across Berlin were stoned, looted and set ablaze. A total of 24 synagogues were set on fire. The Nazis rounded up 12,000 Jews and took them to Sachsenhausen concentration camp.

World War II

Since 1935, Berliners had been taking part in practice air-raid drills, but it was not until the Sudeten crisis of 1938 that the possibility of war became real. At that juncture Hitler was able to get his way and persuade France and Britain to let him take over the German-speaking areas of northern Czechoslovakia.

But a year later, his plans to repeat the exercise in Poland were met with resistance in London and Paris. Following Germany's invasion of Poland on 1 September 1939, Britain and France declared war on the Reich.

Despite the propaganda and spectacular early victories, most Berliners were horrified by the war. The first air raids came with the RAF bombing of Pankow and Lichtenberg in early 1940.

In 1941, following the German invasion of the Soviet Union, the 75,000 Jews remaining in Berlin were required to wear a yellow Star of David and the first large-scale and systematic deportations to concentration camps began. By the end of the war, only 5,000 Jews remained in Berlin.

Notorious assembly points for the deportations were Putlitzstraße in Wedding, Große Hamburger Straße and Rosenstraße in Mitte. On 20 January 1942, a meeting of the leaders of the various Nazi security organisations in the suburb of Wannsee agreed on a 'final solution' to the Jewish question. They joked and drank brandy as they sat around discussing mass murder.

The turning point in the war came with the surrender at Stalingrad on 31 January 1943. In a bid to grab some advantage from this crushing defeat, Goebbels held a rally in the Sportpalast where he announced that Germany had now moved into a state of 'total war'. By summer, women and children were being evacuated from Berlin and schools were shut down. By the end of 1943, over 700,000 people had fled Berlin.

The Battle of Berlin, which the RAF launched in November 1943, began to reduce much of the city centre to rubble. Between then and February 1944, more than 10,000 tonnes of bombs were dropped on the city. Nearly 5,000 people were killed and something like a quarter of a million were made homeless.

Roll-call at Sachsenhausen, 1940.

Red flag hoisted over the Reichstag, 1945.

THE JULY PLOT

On 20 July 1944, a group of officers, civil servants and former trades unionists launched a last-ditch attempt to assassinate Hitler and bring an end to the war. But Hitler survived the explosion of a bomb placed at his eastern command post in East Prussia by Colonel Count von Stauffenberg.

That evening Stauffenberg was killed by firing squad in the courtyard of army headquarters in Bendlerstraße, now Stauffenbergstraße. The other members of the plot were rounded up and put on trial at the People's Court near Kleistpark and subsequently executed at Plötzensee Prison.

In early January 1945, the Red Army launched a major offensive that carried it on to German soil. On 12 February, the heaviest bombing raid killed over 23,000 people in little more than an hour.

As the Red Army moved into Berlin's suburbs, Hitler celebrated his last birthday on 20 April in his bunker behind Wilhelmstraße. Three days later, Neukölln and Tempelhof fell. By 28 April, Alexanderplatz and Hallesches Tor were in the hands of the Red Army.

The next day Hitler called his last war conference. He then married his long-time companion Eva Braun and committed suicide with her the day after. As their bodies were being burnt by loyal SS officers, a few streets away a red flag was raised over the Reichstag. The city officially surrendered on 2 May. Germany's unconditional surrender was signed on 8 May at the Red Army command centre in Karlshorst.

Devastation & division

When Bertolt Brecht returned to Berlin in 1948 he encountered 'a pile of rubble next to Potsdam'. Nearly a quarter of all buildings in the city had been destroyed. The human cost of the war was equally startling – around 80,000 Berliners had been killed, not including the thousands of Jews who would not return from the concentration camps.

There was no gas or electricity and only the suburbs had running water. Public transport had all but completely broken down. In the first weeks following capitulation, Red Army soldiers went on a rampage of random killings and rapes. Thousands of men were rounded up and transported to labour camps in the Soviet Union. Food supplies were used up and later the harvest in the war-scarred land around the city failed. Come winter, the few remaining trees in the Tiergarten and other city parks were chopped down for firewood.

Clearing the rubble was to take years of dull, painstaking work. The *Trümmerfrauen* ('rubble women') cleared the streets and created mountains of brick and junk – such as the Teufelsberg, one of seven such hills which still exist today.

The Soviets stripped factories across the city as part of a programme to dismantle German industry and carry it back to the Soviet Union. As reparation, whole factories were moved to Russia.

Under the terms of the Yalta Agreement which divided Germany into four zones of Allied control, Berlin was also split into four sectors, with the Soviets in the east and the Americans, British and French in the west. A Kommandatura, made up of each army's commander and based in the building of the People's Court in Elßholzstraße, dealt with the administration of the city.

Initially the administration worked well in getting basics, like the transport network, back to some

Trümmerfrauen clear the streets of rubble.

The Reichstag, and the Reich, in ruins.

form of running order. But tensions between the Soviets and the western Allies began to rise as civilian government of city affairs returned. In the eastern sector, a merger of the Communist and Social Democratic parties (which had both been refounded in summer 1945) was pushed through to form the Socialist Unity Party (SED). In the western sector, however, the SPD continued as a separate party.

Events came to a head after elections for a new city government in 1946. The SED failed to get more than 20 per cent of the vote, while the SPD won nearly 50 per cent of all votes cast across the city. The Soviets vetoed the appointment to office of the SPD's mayoral candidate, Ernst Reuter, who was a committed anti-Communist.

THE BERLIN AIRLIFT

The situation worsened in spring 1948. In response to the decision by the Western Allies to merge their respective zones in western Germany into one administrative and financial entity and introduce a new currency, the Soviets walked out of the Kommandatura. In late June, all transport links to west Berlin were cut off and the blockade of the city by Soviet forces began. Three 'air-corridors' linking west Berlin with western Germany became life-lines as Allied aircraft transported thousands of tonnes of food, coal and industrial components to the beleaguered city.

Within Berlin, the future division of the city began to take permanent shape as city councillors from the west were drummed out of the town hall. They moved to Schöneberg Town Hall in the west. Fresh elections in the western sector returned Reuter as mayor. The **Freie Universität** was set up in response to Communist dominance of the Humboldt University in the east.

Having failed to starve west Berlin into submission, the Soviets called off the blockade after 11 months. The blockade also convinced the Western Allies that they should maintain a presence in Berlin and that their sectors of the city should be linked with the Federal Republic which had been founded in May 1949. The response from the East was the founding of the German Democratic Republic on 7 October. With the birth of the 'first Workers' and Peasants' State on German soil', the formal division of Germany into two states was complete.

The Cold War

During the Cold War, Berlin was the focal point for stand-offs between America and the Soviets. Far from having any control over its own affairs, the city was wholly at the mercy of geopolitical developments. Throughout the 1950s the 'Berlin Question' remained high on the international agenda.

Technically the city was still under Four-Power control, but since the Soviet departure from the Kommandatura and the setting up of the German Democratic Republic with its capital in East Berlin (a breach of the wartime agreement on the future of the city), this counted for little in practice.

In principle the Western Allies adhered to these agreements by retaining ultimate authority in West Berlin while allowing the city to be integrated as far as possible into the West German system. (There were notable exceptions such as the exemption of West Berliners from conscription and the barring of city MPs from voting in the West German parliament.)

Throughout the 1950s the two halves of Berlin began to develop separately as the political systems

US tanks rumble up to Checkpoint Charlie.

in East and West evolved. In the East, Communist leader Walter Ulbricht set about creating Moscow's most hard-line ally in eastern Europe. Work began on a Moscow-style boulevard – called Stalinallee – running east from Alexanderplatz. Industry was nationalised and subjected to rigid central planning. Opposition was kept in check by the newly formed Ministry for State Security: the Stasi.

West Berlin landed the role of 'Last Outpost of the Free World' and as such was developed into a showcase for capitalism. As well as the Marshall Plan, which paid for much of the reconstruction of West Germany, the Americans poured millions of dollars into West Berlin to maintain it as a counterpoint to Communism. The West German government, which at the time refused to recognise East Germany as a legitimate state, demonstrated its commitment to seeing Berlin reinstated as German capital by holding occasional parliamentary sessions in the city. The prominence accorded West Berlin was later reflected in the high profile of its politicians (Willy Brandt for example) who were received abroad by prime ministers and presidents – unusual for mere mayors.

Yet despite the emerging divisions, the two halves of the city continued to co-exist in some abnormal fashion. City planners on both sides of the sectoral boundaries initially drew up plans with the whole city in mind. The transport system crossed between East and West, with the underground network being controlled by the West and the S-Bahn by the East.

Movement between the sectors (despite 'border' checks) was relatively normal as Westerners went East to watch a Brecht play or buy cheap books. Easterners went West to work, shop or see the latest Hollywood films.

The secret services of both sides kept a high presence in the city, and there were frequent acts of sabotage on either side. Berlin became espionage capital of the world.

Reconstruction & refugees

As the effects of American money and the West German 'economic miracle' took hold, West Berlin began to recover. A municipal housing programme meant that by 1963 200,000 new flats had been built. Unemployment dropped from over 30 per cent in 1950 to virtually zero by 1961. The labour force also included about 50,000 East Berliners who commuted over the inter-sector borders.

In the East reconstruction was slower. Until the mid-1950s East Germany paid reparations to the Soviet Union. And to begin with there seemed to be more acts of wilful destruction than positive construction. The old palace, which had been only slightly damaged by bombing, was blown up in 1950 to make way for a parade ground which later evolved into a car park.

The Wall – sealing off West Berlin.

In 1952 the East Germans sealed off the border with West Germany. The only way out of the 'zone' was through West Berlin and the number of refugees from the East rose dramatically from 50,000 in 1950 to over 300,000 in 1953. Over the decade, one million refugees from the East came through West Berlin.

THE 1953 UPRISING

In June 1953, partly in response to the rapid loss of skilled manpower, the East German government announced a ten per cent increase in working 'norms' – the number of hours and volume of output that workers were required to fulfil each day. In protest, building workers on Stalinallee (now Karl-Marx-Allee) downed tools on 16 June and marched towards the government offices in the old Air Ministry on Leipziger Straße. The government refused to relent and by the next day strikes had broken out across the city. Communist Party offices were stormed and red flags torn from public buildings. By midday the government had lost control of the city and it was left to the Red Army to restore order. Soviet tanks rolled into the centre of East Berlin where they were met by stones thrown by demonstrators.

By nightfall the uprising was crushed. According to official figures 23 people died, though other estimates put the figure at over 200. There followed a wave of arrests across East Berlin with more than four thousand people detained. The majority went on to receive stiff prison sentences.

The 17 June uprising only furthered the wave of emigration. By the end of the 1950s it was almost possible to calculate the moment when East Germany would cease to function as an industrial state through the loss of skilled labour. Estimates put the loss to the East German economy through emigration at some DM100 billion. Ulbricht increased his demands on Moscow to take action.

In 1958, the Soviet leader Nikita Khrushchev tried to bully the Allies into relinquishing West Berlin with an ultimatum calling for an end to the military occupation of the city and a 'normalisation of the situation in the capital of the GDR', by which he meant Berlin as a whole. The ultimatum was rejected and the Allies made clear their commitment to West Berlin. Unwilling to provoke a world war but needing to prop up his ally, Khrushchev backed down and sanctioned Ulbricht's alternative plan for a solution to the Berlin question.

The Wall

During the early summer of 1961 rumours spread in town that Ulbricht intended to seal off West Berlin with some form of barrier or reinforced border. Emigration had reached a highpoint as 1,500 East Germans fled to the West each day and it became clear that events had reached a crisis point.

However, when in the early hours of 13 August units of the People's Police (assisted by 'Working Class Combat Groups') began to drag bales of barbed wire across Potsdamer Platz, Berlin and the world were caught by surprise.

In a finely planned and executed operation (overseen by Erich Honecker, then Politburo member in charge of security affairs), West Berlin was sealed off within 24 hours. As well as a fence of barbed wire, trenches were dug, the windows in houses lining or straddling the new border were bricked up, and tram and railway lines were interrupted: all this under the watchful eyes of armed guards. Anyone trying to flee West risked being shot, and in the 29 years the Wall stood, nearly 80 people died trying to escape. Justifying their actions, the East Germans later claimed they had erected an 'Anti-Fascist Protection Rampart' to prevent a world war.

Days later the construction of a brick wall began. When it was completed, the concrete part of the 160-km fortification ran to 112km; 37km of the Wall ran through the city centre. Previously innocuous streets like Bernauer Straße (where houses on one side were in the East, those on the other in the West) suddenly became the location for one of the world's most sophisticated and deadly border fortifications.

The initial stunned disbelief of Berliners turned into despair as it became clear that (as with the 17

John F. Kennedy: 'I am a doughnut!'

June uprising) the Western Allies could do little more than make a show of strength. President Kennedy dispatched American reinforcements to Berlin and for a few tense weeks, American and Soviet tanks squared off at **Checkpoint Charlie**.

Moral support from the Americans came with the visit of Vice-President Lyndon Johnson a week after the Wall was built. And two years later Kennedy himself arrived and spoke to a crowd of half-a-million people in front of the Schöneberg Town Hall. His speech linked the fate of West Berlin with that of the free world and ended with the now famous statement 'Ich bin ein Berliner!' (Literally, alas, 'I am a doughnut'.)

In the early years the Wall became the scene of many daring escape attempts (all documented in

Eastern escapee, shot and left to die, 1962.

the **Museum Haus Am Checkpoint Charlie**) as people abseiled off buildings, swam across the Spree river, waded through ancient sewers or simply tried to climb over the Wall.

But as the fortifications along the Wall were improved with mines, searchlights and guard dogs, and as the guards were given orders to shoot, escape became nearly impossible. By the time the Wall fell in November 1989 it had been 'updated' four times to incorporate every conceivable deterrent.

In 1971, the Four Powers met and signed the Quadrapartite Agreement which formally recognised the city's divided status. Border posts (such as the infamous Checkpoint Charlie) were introduced and designated to particular categories of visitors – one for foreigners, another for West Germans and so on.

Fun and games at the GDR's 30th birthday.

Tale of two cities

During the 1960s, with the Wall as infamous and ugly backdrop, the cityscape of modern Berlin (both East and West) began to take shape. On Tauentzienstraße in the West the Europa-Center was built and the bomb-damaged **Kaiser-Wilhelm-Gedächtniskirche** was given a partner – a new church made up of a glass-clad tower and squat bunker.

In the Tiergarten, Hans Scharoun laid out the Kulturforum as West Berlin's answer to the Museuminsel complex in the East. The first building to go up was Scharoun's **Philharmonie**, completed in 1963. Mies van der Rohe's **Neue Nationalgalerie** (which he had originally designed as a Bacardi factory in Havana) was finished in 1968.

In the suburbs work began on concrete minitowns, Gropiusstadt and Märkisches Viertel. Conceived as modern solutions to housing shortages, they would develop into alienating ghettos.

In the East, the **Alexanderplatz** was rebuilt along totalitarian lines and the **Fernsehturm** ('Television Tower') was finished. The historic core of Berlin was mostly cleared to make way for parks (such as the Marx-Engels Forum) or new office and housing developments. On the eastern outskirts of the city in Marzahn and Hohenschönhausen work began on mass-scale housing projects.

In 1965, the first sit-down was staged on the Kurfürstendamm by students protesting low grants and expensive accommodation. This was followed by political demonstrations as students took to the streets to protest against the state in general and the

Rudi Dutschke.

Vietnam war in particular. The first communes were set up in Kreuzberg, thereby sowing the seeds of a counter-culture which was to make that district famous.

In 1967 and 1968, the student protest movement came into increasingly violent confrontation with the police. One student, Benno Ohnesorg, was shot dead by police at a demonstration against the Shah of Iran, who visited the city in June 1967. A year later the students' leader, Rudi Dutschke, was shot by a right-winger. Demonstrations were held outside the offices of the newspaper group Springer, whose papers were blamed for inciting the shooting. It was out of this movement that the Red Army Faction (also known as the Baader-Meinhof gang) was to emerge. It was often to make headlines in the 1970s, not least through a series of kidnappings of high-profile city officials.

NORMALISING ABNORMALITY

The signing of the Quadrapartite Agreement confirmed West Berlin's abnormal status and ushered in an era of decline as the frisson of Cold War excitement and 1960s rebellion petered out. More than ever, West Berlin depended on huge subsidies from West Germany to keep it going.

Development schemes and tax-release programmes were introduced to encourage businesses to move to the city (to keep the population in the city, Berliners also paid less income tax), but still the economy and the population declined.

At the same time there was growth in the number of *Gastarbeiter* ('guest workers') who arrived from southern Europe and particularly Turkey, to take on menial jobs which most Germans shunned. Today there are over 120,000 Turks in the city, largely concentrated in Kreuzberg.

By the late 1970s, Berlin had was mired in the depths of decline. In the West the city government was discredited by an increasing number of scandals, mostly connected with property deals. In East Berlin, Erich Honecker's régime (he succeeded Ulbricht in 1971), which had begun in a mood of reform and change, became increasingly repressive. Some of East Germany's best writers and artists, who had previously been willing to support socialism, left the country. The Communists were glad to be rid of them. From its headquarters in Normannenstraße (a building which now incorporates the **Ministerium für Staatssicherheit** museum), the

Erich Honecker.

Stasi directed its policy of mass observation and increasingly succeeded in permeating every part of East German society. Between East and West there were squalid exchanges of political prisoners for hard currency.

The late 1970s and early 1980s saw the rise of the squatter movement (centred in Kreuzberg), which brought violent political protest back on to the streets. The problem was only diffused after the Senate caved in and gave squatters rent contracts.

In 1987 Berlin celebrated its 750th birthday twice, as East and West vied to outdo each other with exhibitions and festivities. In the East the Nikolaiviertel was restored in time for the celebrations and Honecker began a programme to do the same for the few remaining historical sites which had survived both wartime bombing and post-war planning. The statue of Frederick the Great riding his horse was returned to Unter den Linden.

The fall of the Wall

But restored monuments were not enough to stem the growing dissatisfaction of East Berliners. The development of perestroika in the Soviet Union had been ignored by Honecker, who stuck hard to his Stalinist instincts. Protest was increasingly vocal and only initially beaten back by the police.

By the spring of 1989, the East German state was no longer able to withstand the pressure of a population fed up with Communism. Throughout the summer, thousands fled the city and the country via Hungary, which had opened its borders to the West. Those who stayed began demonstrating for reforms.

By the time Honecker was hosting the celebrations in the Volkskammer ('People's Chamber') to mark the 40th anniversary of the GDR on 7 October 1989, crowds were demonstrating outside, chanting 'Gorby! Gorby!' to register their opposition. Honecker was ousted days later. His successor, Egon Krenz, could do little to stem the tide of opposition. In a desperate bid to defend through attack, he decided to grant the concession East Germans wanted most – freedom to travel. On 9 November 1989 the Berlin Wall was opened, just

over 29 years after it had been built. As thousands of East Berliners raced through to the sound of popping corks, the end of East Germany and the unification of Berlin and Germany had begun.

Reunifying Berlin

With the Wall down, Berlin was once again the centre-stage of history. Just as the division of the city defined the split of Europe, so the freedom to move again between east and west marked the dawn of the post-Cold War era.

Unsurprisingly such an auspicious moment went to Berlin's head and for more than a year the city was in a state of euphoria. Between November 1989 and October 1990 the city witnessed the collapse of Communism and the first free elections (March 1990) in the east for more than 50 years; economic unification with the swapping of the tinny Ostmark for the Deutschmark (July 1990); and the political merger of east into west with formal political unification on 3 October 1990. (It was also the year West Germany picked up its third World Cup trophy. The team may have come from the west, but in a year characterised by outbursts of popular celebration, easterners cheered too.)

But Unification also brought problems, especially for Berlin where the two halves had to be made into one whole. While western infrastructure in the form of roads, telephones and other amenities was in decent working order, in the east it was falling apart or non-existent. Challenges also came from the collapse of a command economy where jobs were provided regardless of cost or productivity.

The Wall cracks open, November 1989.

The Deutschmark put hard currency into the wallets of easterners, but it also exposed the true state of their economy. Within months thousands of companies cut jobs or closed down altogether.

The restructuring of eastern industry was placed with the Treuhandanstalt, a huge state agency which, for a while, was the world's largest industrial holding company. Housed in Goering's old air ministry on the corner of Leipziger Straße and Wilhelmstraße (now the Finance Ministry building), the Treuhand gave high-paid employment to thousands of western yuppies and put hundreds of thousands of easterners on the dole.

Understandably, easterners soon turned on the Treuhand, which was widely vilified as the main agent of a brutal takeover by the west. Few easterners, however, were prepared to go as far as some extremists – most probably members of the Red Army Fraktion (RAF), a left-wing terrorist group dating back to the 1960s – who in spring 1991 assassinated the head of the Treuhand, Detlev Karsten Rohwedder.

The killing of another state employee, Hanno Klein, drew attention to another dramatic change in Berlin brought about by Unification: a property boom. The biggest boost to the market ironically came from Bonn, the old federal capital, where in 1991 parliament voted to shift the seat of national government back to Berlin. The decision heralded a wave of speculative private investment and helped turn Berlin into one big building site.

Klein, who was responsible for drawing up a controversial master plan for the development of the new/old city centre where the Wall once stood and where the glossy new corporate developments of Potsdamer Platz now stand, sought to control the wilder demands of the construction community. Who killed him remains unknown.

Drifting to normality

The giddy excitement of the post-Unification years soon gave way to a period of disappointment. The sheer amount of construction work, the scrapping of federal subsidies and tax breaks to west Berlin, rising unemployment and a delay in the arrival of the government from Bonn all contributed to dampening spirits. In 1994 the last Russian, US, British and French troops left the city. With them went Berlin's unique Cold War status and also the added internationalism that came with occupation. After decades of being different, Berlin was on its way to becoming like any other big European capital. City politics were no longer dominated by the big issues of geopolitics but more by the details of how to cope with empty coffers and spending cuts.

The 1990s were characterised by the regeneration of the east. In the course of the decade the city's centre of gravity shifted towards Mitte. The government and commercial districts were revitalised. On their fringes, especially around Oranienburger Straße, the Hackische Höfe and into Prenzlauer Berg, a sprawl of trendy bars, restaurants, galleries and boutiques seemingly sprouted overnight in streets which under Communism had been grey and crumbling.

The fast-track gentrification in the east was matched by the decline of west Berlin. The proprietors of up-market boutiques and bars began to desert Charlottenburg and Schöneberg in favour of the east, or at least to open a branch there. Kreuzberg, once the inelegantly wasted symbol of a defiant west Berlin, degenerated to almost slum-like conditions while a new bohemia developed across the Spree in Friedrichshain.

Westerners did however benefit from the reopening of the Berlin hinterland. Tens of thousands took the opportunity to leave the city and move to greener suburbs and satellite towns in the state of Brandenburg. An attempt by the political leaders of Brandenburg and Berlin to merge the two was voted down in a 1996 referendum. Brandenburgers' resentment of the big city and antipathy for the east among some west Berliners conspired to kill the issue.

THE BERLIN REPUBLIC

Having spent the best part of the decade doing what it had so often done in the past – regenerating itself out of the wreckage left by history – Berlin exited the 20th century with a flourish. In spring 1999 the new Reichstag, remodelled by British architect Sir Norman Foster, was unveiled. By the end of the summer break the parliament, most of the government and the accompanying baggage of lobbyists and journalists had moved to the city.

From Chancellor Gerhard Schröder down, public figures and commentators sought to mark the transition as the beginning of 'the Berlin Republic'. In contrast to the decaying chaos of Weimar or the self-conscious timidity of Bonn, the Berlin Republic was regarded as standing for a Germany which was peaceful, democratic and self-confident enough to acknowledge, yet move on from, the horrors of the past.

Wall remnants at Niederkirchnerstraße.

Berlin Today

East is east and west is west and still the twain don't meet – beneath the glossy surface of 'new Berlin' lurk intractable social problems.

The federal government's move from Bonn and the opening of the new urban centre at Potsdamer Platz brought Berlin into the 21st century with the promise of democracy and prosperity. In preparation for this glittering future, the city prettied up showcase areas like Mitte and Tiergarten for Bonn newcomers, tourists, diplomats and businessmen, while more unsightly aspects such as homelessness, poverty and any expression of alternative culture and lifestyle (graffitti, squats) were relegated to the city's periphery or criminalised and eradicated. Potsdamer Platz as a Potemkin village concealing social unrest?

In any case, debissstadt (as the Daimler-Chrysler site is known) and the Sony Center have defied sceptics by attracting crowds of curious Berliners, Brandenburgers and tourists to the hypermodern buildings by Helmut Jahn (Sony Center), Hans Kollhoff (Klinker skyscraper), Renzo Piano (Stella Musical Theatre, debis IMAX cinema, debis head office building) and other star architects. The biggest draws, the multiplex cinemas and shopping mall, may be devoid of any specifically Berlin characteristics, whether east or west, but perhaps that's the appeal – challenging the city's lingering division not by crosstown dialogue or hybridisation, but by escaping from it altogether into a futuristic no-man's-land.

Sir Norman Foster's refit of the Reichstag is another architectural hit, but as the government rolls into town, social tension in the city is palpable. As of mid-1999, unemployment was running at over 15 per cent – the root of an existential anxiety often manifesting itself through racism and xenophobia. The last state-wide and municipal elections in Berlin saw the right-extremist Republikaner party move into the district assemblies of Pankow, Reinickendorf, Hohenschönhausen, Neukölln and Wedding, and some parts of town, especially in the east, can still be unsafe for anyone not adhering to the white/Aryan/hetero norm. Protest against the erection of the Memorial to the Murdered Jews of Europe – a design by Peter Eisenmann currently going up on the site south of Pariser Platz – saw 600 right extremists marching through the Brandenburg Gate in February 2000.

Another symptom of the divided city's growing pains is an increased general aggression level, with passers-by more apt to lash out for some perceived affront but less likely to to get involved when

Sign of the times at Checkpoint Charlie.

someone else is accosted on the street or in the S-Bahn. While the crime rate is still lower than that of New York City, whose zero-tolerance model captured the imagination of Berlin's law and order officials, and even lower than that of Frankfurt am Main, citizens feel more vulnerable to violence than ever before.

UP TO NO GOOD

In these difficult times, Berlin's youth is coming of age just as it is becoming a problem to a city increasingly depleted of the resources and ideas to help them to adulthood. Schools are being closed (ostensibly due to low student numbers resulting from rock-bottom birthrates) and after-school programmes discontinued, leaving youths to their own devices and sometimes up to no good – as evidenced by the emergence of occasionally violence-prone gangs. Club culture is a more benign channel for youthful energies, although it takes Deutschmarks out of pockets not necessarily refilled by employment. Youth unemployment is a major problem for the city, with adequate vocational training becoming a rarity. Those who opt for higher education encounter universities hoping to reduce Berlin's 130,000 students with stiff fees and a tightening of the academic screws. Yet for all the discussion of Draconian measures, Berlin still hasn't become the centre of academic excellence it would like to be.

But Berlin has most definitely become a centre of culture both high and low. The opening of the natural-light Gemäldegalerie at the Kulturforum near Potsdamer Platz and the hype surrounding the fashionable Mitte gallery scene, most recently the media hoopla accompanying the Berlin Biennale and 1999's Children of Berlin show in New York, have established Berlin in art circles as a major European force alongside London, Paris and Cologne. While gentrification and gentle ennui are beginning to creep into the nightlife of Mitte and Prenzlauer Berg, cutting-edge clubs and bars in Friedrichshain are setting the district up as the next boho borough. Berlin hasn't lost its edge, it's merely changing location.

Most cultural energy has been generated by private initiatives ranging from idealistic art-nerds to cash-conscious club-owners (the line between the two camps is increasingly blurred), but the city has also recognised culture as an economic factor. Not

'Those know-it-all Wessis!'

After the initial bedazzlement of the Ku'damm, consumer electronics and the Deutschmark, East Germans had to come to terms with the reality of the west. It didn't always live up to the land of milk and honey depicted on the western TV shows and adverts every East German – except those living in the 'valley of know-nothings' around Magdeburg and Dresden – could watch. Soon East Germans were confronted with a market economy mercilessly cruel to those unused to cutthroat competition. Upon the GDR joining the Federal Republic, the security of the cradle-to-grave social system dissolved. Ossis bemoaned a lack of solidarity from the government and in personal relationships, and seemingly in vain pleaded for compassion on behalf of a people whose previous way of life, for better or worse, had disappeared practically overnight.

The west, drunk on visions of having won the Cold War, came across as *Besserwessis* (a pun on *Besserwisser*, or know-it-all) or worse yet, ruthless vanquishers. On the one hand, west Berliners mourned the bygone days of splendid isolation and generous subsidies, blaming easterners for the new, less prosperous world order. On the other hand, western carpetbaggers greedily exploited the situation, buying up properties and businesses for a pittance and laying off workers in the name of profit margins. Ossis began feeling like second-class citizens in a no-win situation and turned an even more critical eye to Wessis, faulting a general callousness, shallowness, arrogance and lack of culture.

Tired of being designated a bunch of out-of-touch bumpkins, lazy bums and Stasi informants, Ossis began aggressively and spitefully to embrace any remnant of the old regime, be it consumer goods like Cabinet cigarettes or cultural icons such as the children's puppet show *Sandmännchen* or the rock band Puhdys (who actually had lost credibility towards the end of the GDR, but have suddenly got it back again). This desperate resistance against perceived Western annihilation of the Eastern identity even led to such controversial phenomena as the protective attitude towards former GDR politicians now on trial such as Erich Mielke or Egon Krenz. What right does the West have to judge these people, when the Ossis were the ones who had to put up with their parochial and paranoid stifling and exploitation of the GDR?

Small wonder then, that as Berlin enters the second decade since the fall of the Wall, 'mixed' relationships, that litmus test of integration, are still the exception rather than the rule. Those Wessis just don't understand....

'Those miserable Ossis!'

Ich will mein Mauer wieder!' – 'I want my Wall back!' T-shirts bearing this slogan were a common sight in West Berlin back when the initial euphoria over Reunification began to fade, and it's a lament still often muttered now. In their heart of hearts westerners know that the cushy old days of the cultural subsidy and tax breaks that kept West Berlin going when it was an isolated and economically unviable island are justifiably gone for good. But it's hard to shrug off annoyance at how much harder life has become since the Wall came tumbling down. Taxes are higher, so is unemployment. And even those West Berliners who uncomplainingly stumped up the extra 'solidarity tax' to help get their fellow Germans back on their feet in the early 1990s, can get irritated when some Ossi starts blaming them personally for every eastern misfortune. Hey, we didn't build the damn Wall! Learn to take some responsibility!

Na ja, it was tough on Ossis when their way of life vanished, but hell, they wanted those consumer durables. They voted for the CDU and CD-players in 1990. They ran to exchange their Ostmarks, one for one. Was the consequent collapse of eastern industry the West Berliners' fault?

And the West Berlin of old vanished just as completely, even if the effect was more subtle. From where the Wessi is sitting, it looks like a trade-off. In the last decade the East has been relatively enriched, but seemingly at the expense of the west in ways that echo all the way from the pay in the packet to the problems of finding a working phone box. Everything new and interesting seems to go up 'over there', western retail centres are in decline and fashionable life has pretty much totally decamped eastwards. Yet still they complain about Wessis. What do they want? Jam on it?

Many westerners would acknowledge that there were those among their number who were too quick to exploit the situation. Others would tell the Ossis: 'But we told you so!' Still others would see the problem not as themselves, but as west Germans, with whom they never felt much in common either. In the days of division West Berlin certainly wasn't part of the 'Hauptstadt der DDR', but it technically wasn't part of the Federal Republic either. It had its own unique status. Lonely but proud. Now west Berliners feel even lonelier than ever – still not part of West Germany, but also despised in the other half of their own city, where they often feel uncomfortable, and rarely proud at all.

Perhaps the arrival of all the bureaucrats and Bonners will give east and west Berliners common cause. But then again maybe not. Those Ossis just don't understand….

so much courting alternative culture, which thrives thanks to other resources, the city lends its support to mega-event art exhibitions, star-driven theatre performances and the annual Love Parade. (Imagine stern former Senator of the Interior Jörg Schönbohm, the man who cleansed Berlin of all squats, waving with a smile from a Love Parade float. It happened.)

THE (LACK OF) VISION THING

The city government (Senat) seems afflicted by a lack of vision. The grand coalition between the Christian Democratic Party (CDU) and Social Democratic Party (SPD) has been in power for the past decade. Ideological and personal infighting have precluded major policy strides, and the Senat's grand projects have been less imaginative than administrative: balancing the budget with spending cuts mostly in the social realm and privatising the gas and electricity utilities; streamlining local government by reducing the number of districts from 23 to 12. Another Senat-backed initiative, the state of Berlin's political fusion with surrounding Brandenburg, is back on the agenda despite a resounding 'no' in a 1995 referendum; some CDU advocates hope to see fusion on its way by 2004. And even erstwhile nay-sayers PDS (as the former communists are now known) have jumped on to this bandwagon, advocating the still more radical step of merging all eastern states except Thuringia.

To its credit, the Senat is attempting to make Berlin attractive for investors and new businesses. Property developers are seduced with subsidies and lenient zoning regulations in the hope of creating jobs, primarily in the service sector. Nevertheless, a lack of central coordination has fostered an explosion of shopping malls and multiplex cinemas which threaten to kill the mom-and-pop competition – and possibly each other if purchasing power continues to decline. Many new office buildings, especially around Friedrichstraße, have trouble finding tenants but are still lucrative tax write-offs. Affordable housing, on the other hand, is not made viable for landlords and developers, and the recent relaxation in the apartment market may soon be followed by another shortage, should the arrival of the government reverse cur-

Hot dogs and media hoopla – the tenth anniversary of the fall of the Wall.

rent depopulation tendencies. Coherent solutions to housing problems have yet to be articulated by the city government.

Other issues such as popular desire for more direct democracy and increasing social inequality, especially between east and west, are largely skirted – although governing mayor Eberhard Diepgen has somewhat surprisingly spoken out in favour of finally raising eastern wages and salaries to western levels since eastern costs of living have long approached those in the west. (At the time of writing, eastern wage levels average between 60-90 per cent of those in the west.)

The primary benefactor of this climate is the Party of Democratic Socialism (PDS), which grew out of East Germany's former ruling Socialist Unity Party (SED). The PDS presents itself as the mouthpiece for disillusioned and disenfranchised Ossis and is now gaining more votes in eastern districts (up to 40 per cent) than the CDU or SPD. Their recent national party programme reform accepting a socialised market economy may alienate their traditional constituency but could also lead to them encroaching upon the moribund Berlin SPD's turf on both sides of the city.

STILL A CITY OF TWO HALVES

The PDS success story shows that at the beginning of the second decade since Reunification, the two city halves haven't quite grown together. Homogenisation of everything from street signs to museum collections has been accomplished, and the architectural Berlin Wall may be a hazy memory save for a few surviving stretches turned into memorials or public art, but the proverbial *Mauer*

im Kopf ('Wall in the head') still stands tall. Ossi-Wessi interaction is still characterised by prejudices and misunderstandings on both sides. The east-west division and the social inequality it sometimes entails could turn this city into a minefield in years to come.

The federal government's move from quieter, safer Bonn to this potential minefield may prove the impetus needed to channel Berlin's corrosive division into an acceptance of diversity. The Bonners' imminent arrival may have precipitated the aforementioned 'clean-up' (squats all but eradicated in a clean sweep of police action instigated by former Senator of the Interior Schönbohm in 1998), experimentation with Orwellian surveillance systems in public places and the increased presence of private security forces. And Berliners fear that Bonn will have a generally provincialising influence on the city. But Bonners bring not only bad tidings and boredom. The government's proximity to the social issues festering in the city may make it more attuned to problems in the country at large, which was not always the case in cosy isolation on the banks of the Rhine. The influx of national and international organisations may finally give Berlin the business and media hub status it has long tried to hype into existence.

Yet even if Berlin's new role as capital of the republic now named for it doesn't provide the material basis, it may give the divided city the confidence and sense of purpose to face the challenges of the new century as one, and help Berlin to become comfortable as a multicultural metropolis of the future.

By Season

Berlin's streets enjoy sex, riots, gay parades and music for polar bears – all year round.

In Berlin there's always something going on – from dance, drug and sex parades to underground concerts, tattoo conventions, street riots and marathons. There are quieter periods like Christmas, but even then many clubs and cabarets make an effort to stage something extraordinary. That said, those spending the summer here will go away with a different impression from those who visit in winter. Berlin often seems deserted in winter as people retreat indoors to escape the freezing cold. In spring and summer, cafés, bars and life in general spill out into the street, making it easier to meet people and discover what's going on.

Information

Berlin – The Magazine (DM3.90 at tourist offices) has details in English and German on mainstream cultural events. Also look for listings in *tip* or *Zitty*.

Berlin-Tourismus-Marketing
Europa-Center, Budapester Straße, Charlottenburg, 10787 (01805 754 040). S3, S5, S7, S9/U2, U9 Zoologischer Garten. **Open** 8.30am-8.30pm Mon-Sat; 10am-6.30pm Sun. **Map D4**
Its website's not bad but the telephone situation is bonkers. The number above gets you to a call centre and costs an outrageous DM2.42 per minute when calling from within Berlin.
Branches: Tegel Airport; Brandenburg Gate.
Website: www.btm.de

Spring

Musik Biennale Berlin
Contact: *Berliner Festspiele, Budapester Straße 50, Tiergarten, 10787 (254 890).* **Dates** 2001 and every other year in March. **Admission** varies.
After Reunification, this former East German festival highlighting trends in contemporary music was spared extinction and put on the west Berlin life support system. Held every other year, the 12-day event invites international avant-garde composers and musicians to present music that is anything but harmonious. Held at the Philharmonie and other venues.
See chapter **Music: Classical & Opera**.

May Day Riots
Around Kottbusser Tor, Oranienstraße, Kreuzberg. **Date** 1 May.
The May Day Riot has been an annual fixture since 1987 when *Autonomen* engaged in violent clashes

Another Mexican picnic in the Tiergarten.

with police before going on to burn down their local supermarket. In the mid-1990s the action, along with the few remaining squatters, shifted from Kreuzberg to Prenzlauer Berg. Ironically, the increasing gentrification of the eastern borough led most of the rioters back to their old stomping ground in 1999. That year the police were also accused of extreme brutality after using water cannon and batons to disperse the crowd. These days, however, the riot is more of a social event than anything.

Theatertreffen Berlin
Contact: *Berliner Festspiele, Budapester Straße 50, Tiergarten, 10787 (254 890).* **Date** May.
Admission varies.
The best that German-speaking theatre has to offer. An independent jury picks ten of the most 'innovative, controversial and uncomfortable' new productions from theatres in Germany, Austria and Switzerland. The winners are awarded a trip to Berlin where they perform their piece during this fortnight-long meeting. There's also a Youth Theatre meeting at the end of May that is organised along the same principles.

German Open Berlin

Date third week of May. **Admission** DM25-160.
The world's fifth largest international women's tennis championship and a week-long get-together of Germany's rich and famous. Come match point, the focus switches to a gala ball and other glitzy social affairs. Mortals have a hard time getting tickets, especially for centre-court matches. For details *see chapter* **Sport & Fitness**.
Website: www.german-open.berlin.de

Deutsche Pokalendspiele

German Cup Final
*Olympiastadion, Charlottenburg, 14053 (300 633).
U2 Olympia-Stadion (Ost)/S5 Olympiastadion.*
Tickets & information *Deutscher Fußball-Bund, (Frankfurt) (069 678 80).* **Date** second weekend in June. **Admission** varies.
Berlin's dismal football scene was given a shot in the arm when the German FA awarded permanent hosting of the domestic cup final to the equally dismal Olympic Stadium in 1985. Every final has proved a great success since, 65,000 fans drinking and dancing in the aisles of a sold-out Olympic stadium. *See chapter* **Sport & Fitness**.

Karneval der Kulturen

Carnival of Cultures
Kreuzberg. **Information** (622 4232). **Date** Whit weekend in June.
Inspired by the Notting Hill Carnival and intended as a celebration of Berlin's ethnic and and cultural diversity, the procession involves dozens of floats, hundreds of musicians and thousands of spectators. Route changes every year, so phone for details.
Website: www.karneval-berlin.de

Summer

La Fête de la Musique

World Music Day
Date June 21. **Admission** free.
Since 1995 Berlin has been marking the start of summer with this one-day musical extravaganza. With stages set up in every district, la Fête de la Musique features hundreds of bands and DJs, playing everything from hip hop to *Schlager*.
Website: www.lafetedelamusique.com

Berlin Philharmonie at the Waldbühne

Waldbühne, Glockenturmstraße, Charlottenburg, 14053 (2308 8230). S5 Pichelsburg and shuttle buses. **Date** June. **Admission** varies.
The Philharmonic ends its season with a big concert at the atmospheric outdoor Waldbühne. The event marks the start of summer for 22,500 Berliners, who, once darkness falls, light up the venue with candles, lighters, matches and prohibited sparklers.

Schwullesbisches Straßenfest

Gay and Lesbian Street Party
Nollendorfplatz, Schöneberg. **Information** (216 8008). **Date** second or third week of June.
This sprawling two-day party is staged in the streets, bars and clubs around Nollendorfplatz in

Schöneberg. With hundreds of stalls and dozens of acts and DJs, it provides non-stop entertainment for straights and gays alike. It is designed as a primer for the **Christopher Street Day Parade**, usually a week later. *See chapter* **Gay & Lesbian**.

Christopher Street Day Parade

From Kurfürstendamm through Brandenburg Gate to Bebel Platz. Evening parties at different venues.
Date end of June.
Commemorating the 1969 riots at the Stonewall Bar in Christopher Steet, New York, which marked the beginning of modern gay liberation. The Saturday parade is a popular celebration of Berlin's lesbian and gay community and has developed into one of the most flamboyant summer tourist attractions. *See also chapter* **Gay & Lesbian**.

Love Parade

For details *see chapter* **Love Parade**.
In 1999, the Love Parade attracted over one million people who partied aboard and alongside floats sponsored by clubs from all over Europe. The ensuing raves and parties carry on for days. However the Parade also stokes up controversy and legal strife between organisers and environmentalists opposed to its route through the Tiergarten. At press time the route for 2000 was still under discussion.

Fuck Parade

Date first Sat in July. **Admission** free for parade.
Launched in 1997 as a 'counter-demonstration' to the Love Parade, the annual Fuck Parade is supposed to represent the non-commercial side of electronic dance music. With floats from dozens of techno, gabba and drum 'n' bass clubs from across Germany and Europe, it tends to attract 2-3,000 ravers. The route, out of earshot of the Love Parade, meanders through the backstreets of eastern Berlin.

Hanfparade

Alexanderplatz to Brandenburg Gate. **Information** (2472 0233). **Date** end of Aug.
Yep, another parade. Some German states relaxed laws on the use and possession of cannabis in 1998. However, 'Hemp Parade' organisers want nothing less than total legalisation. They're also hoping to promote the use of hemp as an eco-friendly raw material and pain killer. Previous processions have drawn as many as 50,000 people. Check local press for details of the route, which changes occasionally.

Internationales Bierfest

Strausberger Platz to Frankfurter Tor. U5 Frankfurter Tor. **Information** (508 6822). **Date** first weekend in Aug.
Showcases over one thousand beers from more than 60 countries. Stalls and marquees along east Berlin's Stalinist-style boulevard sell everything from Bavarian black beer to lager from Lapland.

Deutsch-Amerikanischer Volksfest

German-American Festival
Hüttenweg, Zehlendorf, 14195 (264 7480). U1 Oskar-Helene-Heim. **Date** late July-mid-Aug.
Admission varies.

Festival originally established by the US Forces, featuring lots of rides, gambling and stalls selling alcohol, German specialities and authentic American junk food. Tacky, but Berliners lap it up.

Heimatklänge
For details *see chapter* **Music: Rock, Folk & Jazz**. Berlin's biggest world music event. Through July and August the Tempodrom hosts acts from all corners of the globe. Expect anything from a chanting Mongolian shaman to Patagonian nose flautists.

Hofkonzerte
Dates every weekend July-Aug. **Admission** varies.
Held in the courtyard of the **Podewil** (*see chapter* **Music: Rock, Folk & Jazz**), this series of concerts brings together jazz and classical musicians from across Europe.

Tango Sommer
Date 8pm Thur, late June until mid-Aug.
Also outdoors at **Podewil**, 'Tango Summer' has proved tremendously popular since its 1996 launch. Attracting a mixed crowd, it's an opportunity to show off your footwork or soak up the music, played live by orchestras from Europe and Argentina.

Classic Open Air
Gendarmenmarkt, Mitte, 10117 (contact Media On-Line, 315 7540). U6 Französische Straße. **Date** July. **Admission** varies. **Map F3**
Organisers schedule big names such as José Carreras or Montserrat Caballe for the opening concert of this four-day festival set in one of the city's most beautiful squares. Many Berlin orchestras take part, plus soloists from all over Europe.

Internationale Funkaustellung
International Electronics Exhibition
Messe Berlin trade fair grounds, Messedamm 22, Charlottenburg, 14055 (3038 2274). U2 Kaiserdamm/S4 Witzleben. **Open** 10am-7pm daily. **Date** late Aug 2001 and every other year. **Admission** varies.
Nine-day trade fair in which market leaders present the latest in eclectic electrics, from audio, TV, video, camcorder and digital photography, to antennae, satellite reception stations and mobile communication. Visited by upwards of 400,000 people each year.

Berliner Festwochen
Contact: *Berliner Festspiele, Budapester Straße 50, Tiergarten, 10787 (254 890).* **Date** Sep. **Admission** varies.
The cultural summer closes with a month of themed events, concerts and performances. Classical music and international theatre are accompanied by exhibitions and readings, at various venues including the Philharmonie and Konzerthaus. *See chapter* **Music: Classical & Opera**.

Alberto Berliner Marathon
Contact: *Berlin Marathon, Alt-Moabit 92, Moabit, 10559 (302 5370).* **Date** last weekend in Sep. **Admission** DM70-120.
Berlin's biggest sporting event and the world's third largest marathon. Usually held on the last weekend

of September, the 2000 Berlin Marathon is being brought forward to 10 September to avoid clashing with the Olympics. Runners belt past most of Berlin's landmarks on their 42-km (26-mile) trek through seven districts. Some 30,000 take part, and if it's fine, they're cheered on by a million spectators. Admission depends on time and place of application. *See also chapter* **Sport & Fitness**.

Autumn

Urbane Aboriginale
Contact: *Freunde Guter Musik e.V, Erkelenzdamm 11-13, Kreuzberg, 10999 (615 2702).* **Date** autumn.
This festival of iconoclastic music and performance has been introducing experimental artists from different nations since 1985. Theatre, dance, music and performance groups and soloists spend about two weeks demonstrating that the global art underground is a very strange beast indeed. Past Urbane Aboriginale themes have included British ambient, Japanese avant-garde and music from the Polar regions. Most events are at **Podewil** and **Haus der Kulturen der Welt**. For listings *see chapter* **Music: Rock, Folk & Jazz**.

Art Forum
Messedamm 22, Charlottenburg, 14055 (303 80). U2 Kaiserdamm/S4 Witzleben. **Information** *European Galleries, Projektgesellschaft GmbH (8855 1643).* **Open** 10am-6pm daily. **Date** late Sept/early Oct.
Set up in 1996 as a networking opportunity for gallery owners and artists, this six-day fair of contemporary art attracts many of Europe's leading galleries plus thousands of lay enthusiasts from all over the continent. Non-trade visitors are advised to take a guide, preferably one familiar with the art scene who can chart a meaningful course through the dozens of hangar-type halls, each of which houses scores of exhibitions. *See chapter* **Art Galleries**.

JazzFest Berlin
For details *see chapter* **Music: Rock, Folk & Jazz**.
Jazz dominates the cultural scene for four days each autumn. The whole jazz spectrum is on offer, performed by a mixed bag of internationally renowned artists and the originators of local and German jazz projects. Going strong since 1964, the festival often is accompanied by sub-festivals highlighting specific categories of contemporary music, photo exhibitions and concerts at other venues.

Jüdische Kulturtage
Jewish Culture Days
Contact: *Jüdisches Gemeindehaus, Fasanenstraße 79-80, Charlottenburg, 10623 (880 280).* **Date** Nov. **Admission** varies.
Annual art and cultural festival over two to three weeks. Venues around town provide space for an extensive programme of theatre, music, film, readings, panel discussions, dance and workshops. Past themes have included 'Jewish Life in Eastern Europe' and 'Jewishness from California', and have brought to town the likes of Allen Ginsberg, Kathy Acker and Jeffrey Burns.

Christmas shopping by fairylight.

Winter

German Tattoo Convention

Columbiahalle, Columbiadamm 13-21, Tempelhof, 10965 (698 0908). U6 Platz der Luftbrücke. **Date** 4 days in Dec. **Admission** *day ticket* DM30. **Map F6**
Hundreds of long-haired, leather-wearing Lemmy lookalikes perform their art on any part of flesh you may choose to tattoo. There are food vendors and stands displaying jewellery to stick through holes in your nose, nipples, lip and clit. The largest gathering of its kind in the world.

Christmas Markets

Spandauer Altstadt, Marktplatz. U7 Altstadt Spandau. **Open** 9am-8pm Mon-Sat; 10am-7pm Sun; *Kaiser-Wilhelm-Gedächtniskirche, Breitscheidplatz. S3, S5, S7, S9/U2, U9 Zoologischer Garten.* **Open** 11am-9pm Sun-Thur; 11am-10pm Fri-Sat. **Dates** Nov-27 Dec. **Admission** free.
Yuletide markets shoot up in just about every district at the end of November. Visitors will inevitably run into the vast market around the centrally located **Kaiser-Wilhelm-Gedächtniskirche**, featuring a clutter of olde worlde, half-timbered stalls selling handicrafts and decorations as well as mulled wine, gingerbread and Christmas cake. It is also worth trekking out to the picturesque market in Spandau's old town on the western edge of the city.

Silvester

New Year's Eve
Thousands of Berliners climb the Teufelsberg at the northern tip of the Grunewald and the Kreuzberg in Viktoria Park to watch the firework spectacle that explodes over the city as church bells ring in the New Year. The Brandenburg Gate has also become a popular place to congregate since the Wall came down. The claustrophobic are advised to remain on the edge of the crowd as it can become overwhelming. Note that Berliners have few qualms launching rockets in all directions and flinging firecrackers at other people. Most clubs and bars are open all night, many keen to put on something out of the ordinary.

Lange Nacht der Museen

Information (2839 7444). **Date** last week in Jan and last week in Aug.
Every six months the civic museums throw an all-night party known as the Long Night of the Museums. As well as opening their collections until the small hours, they put on performances, concerts, readings and other unusual happenings. Visitors can shuttle between venues by boat, bus or tram.

Internationale Grüne Woche

Green Week
Messe Berlin trade fair grounds, Messedamm 22, Charlottenburg, 14055 (303 80). U2 Kaiserdamm/S4 Witzleben. **Open** 9am-6pm daily. **Date** Jan. **Admission** *day ticket* DM20.
Berlin's annual farm show is actually a ten-day orgy of food and drink from the far corners of Germany and the world. Hordes of Berliners and visitors flock to the exhibition halls to sample German gastronomic specialities and exotic foods. But bring your wallet – nothing is free.

Berlin International Film Festival

For details *see chapter* **Film**.
One of the world's major film festivals, the Berlinale features at least 300 movies each year by directors from around the globe. Injecting a shot of glamour in to the life of the city in the dead of winter, it is attended by the glitterati of the international film industry. As the city's centre of gravity moves eastward, so too does the Berlinale; February 2000 sees the festival switch its headquarters from west Berlin to Potsdamer Platz.

Transmediale

Date mid-Feb. **Admission** varies.
Running parallel to the Berlinale, the Transmediale at Podewil (*see chapter* **Music: Rock, Folk & Jazz**) is one of the largest events of its kind in the world. Bringing together artists from around the globe, it presents recent productions in video art, television, computer animation, the Internet and any other visual medium that might have been invented by the time you read this.

Architecture

After Schinkel and Sachlichkeit, destruction and division, can the birthplace of modern architecture meet its new urban challenge?

Mendelsohn's IG Metall building.

Their city might not be as old as Paris, but Berliners can boast of a long tradition of architectural experimentation. As a metropolis of the new culture of modernity – powered by the fast-paced, hardcore advance of big industry and finance that rapidly retreaded Prussian tradition after 1870 – it was only natural that Berlin would become the birthplace of modern architecture. During the 1910s and 1920s, it was the home of some of the century's greatest designers: Peter Behrens, Bruno Taut, Mies van der Rohe, Walter Gropius, Eric Mendelsohn and Hans Scharoun, to name just a few. But the path to modernism was launched on the heels of the Napoleonic occupation by Karl Friedrich Schinkel (1781-1841), who many still consider the city's greatest builder. In addition, fine specimens of nearly every style since the Baroque age can be found here, from neo-Renaissance to neo-Rationalism.

Though the Berlin we see today was really shaped by the rise of the modern era, nearly every political and economic transformation of the city before and since called a new set of architectural and planning principles into being. It was also nearly always a military post of one kind or another, not least during the Cold War. Not until the late 19th century could the city as a whole really begin to compete with grander European capitals, thanks to a construction boom, called the *Gründerzeit*, triggered by the rapid progress in industry and technology following the creation of the German Reich in 1871. From then on, the city quickly acquired a massive scale, while spreading out into the countryside, with wide streets and large blocks. These followed a rudimentary geometry set out by an 1862 plan by James Hobrecht and were filled in with five-storey *Mietskaserne* ('rental barracks') with minimal courtyards. Thankfully, the monotony – and the smoke and noise of nearby factories – was relieved by a handful of large public parks, while later apartment houses gradually became more humane and rather splendid. During the 1920s, this method of development was rejected in favour of Bauhaus-influenced slabs and towers, which were used to fill out the peripheral zones at the edge of the forests. The post-war years saw even more radical departures from the earlier tradition in all sectors of the city.

REMAKE, REMODEL

Today, as the cranes finally give way to a new layer of post-Wall architecture, the question becomes: how much of 'new Berlin' meets the cultural, technical, and urban design challenges posed by Reunification? On the whole, it is a mixture of contemporary design and historic emulation, some of it implementing new environmental strategies, much of it attempting to restore a sense of continuity to an urban fabric ruptured by division and heavy-handed reconstruction. Inevitably, many of the older architectural landmarks of today's Berlin are more important as markers of these cycles of history than as masterpieces. Many significant works were lost to the war, including Messel's Wertheim department store at Leipziger Platz and Mendelsohn's Columbushaus at Potsdamer Platz. The new buildings in these areas have been reworked with these losses in mind.

The spirit of historic revival has even taken in the city's most famous landmark, the Wall, which was dismantled with breathtaking speed within a year or two after 1989. It is now being commemorated in public art, from the **Dokumentationscentrum Berliner Mauer** at Bernauer Straße to Frank Thiel's portraits of the last Allied soldiers, suspended above former checkpoints in the city centre; other works are still being considered (any talk of reconstruction is premature). With so much new architecture by architects from all over the globe, however, the memory of the Wall is rapidly fading away.

Stadtmitte – a cored city

Berlin's long journey to world city status began in two tiny fishing and trading settlements on the Spree named Berlin and Cölln, originally Wendish/Slavic towns that were colonised by Germans around 1237. Among their oldest surviving buildings are the parish churches **Marienkirche** and Nikolaikirche. The latter was rebuilt in the **Nikolaiviertel** along with other landmarks, such as the 1571 pub Zum Nußbaum and the **Ephraim-Palais**, a Baroque corner building. Both are set among prefab town houses simulating Dutch gables, erected by the East Germans in time for the city's 750th anniversary in 1987 – a few decades after they had levelled nearly all of the surviving medieval fabric in the historic core.

Thanks also to the GDR's subtractive planning ideology, little survives of the massive Stadtschloß ('City Palace', 1538-1950) other than recently excavated foundations in front of the Palast der Republik, dating to the reign of Elector Joachim II. The Schloßbrücke crossing to Unter den Linden, adorned with figures by Christian Daniel Rauch, and the Neptunbrunnen ('Neptune Fountain', now relocated south of Marienkirche), modelled on Bernini's Roman fountains, were designed to embellish the palace.

In 1647, the Great Elector, Friedrich Wilhelm II (1640-1688) hired Dutch engineers to transform the route to the **Tiergarten**, the royal hunting forest, into the tree-lined boulevard of Unter den Linden. It led west toward **Schloß Charlottenburg**, built in 1695 as a summer retreat for Queen Sophie-Charlotte. Over the next century, the Elector's 'Residenzstadt' expanded to include Berlin-Cölln and the extension of Friedrichswerder to the southwest. Traces of the old stone **Stadtmauer** ('city wall') that enclosed them can still be seen in Waisenstraße in Mitte. Two further districts, Dorotheenstadt (begun 1673, named after the Great Elector's Dutch queen) and Friedrichstadt (begun 1688), expanded the street grid north and south of Unter den Linden. All were united under one civic administration in 1709.

Andreas Schlüter, the acclaimed architect who built new palace wings for Elector Friedrich Wilhelm III (1688-1713), crowned King Frederick I of Prussia in 1701), also built the alte Marstall

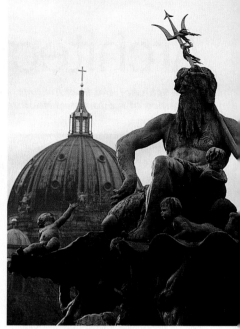

Neptunbrunnen – modelled on Bernini.

('Royal Stables', 1687) in Breite Straße. The bellicose ornamentation of the Zeughaus ('Royal Arsenal', 1695-1706, Nering and de Bodt; now **Deutsches Historisches Museum**) embodies the Prussian love of militarism. In the courtyard, Schlüter depicted the gruesome results of this love in 22 masks of dying warriors.

City life changed when William I, the Soldier King (1713-1740), imposed conscription and subjugated the town magistrate to the court and military élite. The economy now catered to an army comprising 20 per cent of the population (a fairly constant percentage until 1918). To spur growth in gridded Friedrichstadt – and to quarter his soldiers cheaply – the king forced people to build new houses, mostly done in a stripped-down classical style. He permitted one open square, Gendarmenmarkt, where twin churches were built in 1701, one of which now houses the **Hugenotten Museum**.

After the population reached 60,000 in 1710, a new customs wall enclosed four new districts – the Spandauer Viertel, Königstadt, Stralauer Vorstadt and Köpenicker Vorstadt; all now parts of Mitte. Built in 1737, the 14km border remained the city limits until 1860. Geometric squares later marked three of the 14 city gates in Friedrichstadt. At the square-shaped Pariser Platz, axial gateway to the Tiergarten, Langhans built the **Brandenburg Gate** in 1789, a triumphal arch later topped by Schadow's quadriga. The stately buildings around the square were levelled after the war, but are being reconstructed today, including the **Adlon Hotel** (Patzschke, Klotz, 1997), on an expanded version of its original site, and the twin buildings flanking the gate, Haus Sommer and Haus Liebermann (Kleihues, 1998). At the gate on the road to Potsdam, the Oktagon, which later evolved into the major commercial centre at Leipziger Platz, linked with Potsdamer Platz. The busy node at the circular Rondell (later Belle-Alliance-Platz, now Mehringplatz), was closed to through-traffic by a 1960s housing project. Still at its centre is the Friedensäule ('Peace Column', a lesser cousin to the **Siegessäule**), which is topped by Christian Daniel Rauch's statue of Victoria (1843).

Schinkel and his disciples

Even with the army, Berlin's population did not reach 100,000 until well into the reign of Frederick the Great (1740-1786), fan of Enlightenment ideas and absolutist politics. Military success inspired the French-speaking 'philosopher king' to embellish Berlin and Potsdam; many of the monuments along Unter den Linden stem from his vision of a 'Forum Fredericianum'. Though never completed, the unique ensemble of neo-classical, Baroque and rococo monuments includes the vine-covered **Humboldt University** (Knobelsdorff/Boumann, 1748-53, palace of Frederick's brother Prince Heinrich until 1810); the **Staatsoper** (Knobelsdorff, Langhans, 1741-3); the Prinzessinnenpalais (1733, now the **Operncafe**) and the Kronprinzenpalais (Unter den Linden 3; 1663, expanded 1732). Set back from the Linden on Bebelplatz are the alte Bibliothek, reminiscent of the curvy Vienna Hofburg (Unger, 1775-81, part of Humboldt University) and the pantheon-like St Hedwigs-Kathedrale, a gift to Berlin's Catholics (Legeay and Knobelsdorff, 1747-73).

Not long after the Napoleonic occupation, the prolific Schinkel became Berlin's most revered architect under Prince Friedrich-Wilhelm IV. Drawing on early classical and Italian precedents, his early stage-sets experimented with perspective, while his inspired urban visions served the cultural aspirations of an ascendant German state. His work includes the colonnaded **Altes Museum** (1828) regarded by most architects as his finest work, and the Neue Wache (Royal Guardhouse, 1818; now the **Mahnmal**) next to the Zeughaus, whose Roman solidity lent itself well to Tessenow's 1931 conversion into a memorial to the dead of World War I.

Other Schinkel masterpieces include the Schauspielhaus, a theatre to replace one lost to fire at Gendarmenmarkt (1817-21, now the **Konzerthaus**); the neo-gothic brick Friedrichwerdersche Kirche (1830, now the

Cubic – the Schinkel-Pavilion at Schloß Charlottenburg.

Schinkel-Museum); and the cubic Schinkel-Pavillon (1825) at Schloß Charlottenburg. Among his many collaborations with garden architect Peter Joseph Lenné is the picturesque ensemble of classical follies at Schloß Glienecke, overlooking the Havel near the Glieneckebrücke, which connects Berlin with Potsdam.

After Schinkel's death in 1841, his many disciples propagated his architectural lessons in brick and stone. Stüler most notably satisfied the king's desire to complement the Altes Museum with the Neues Museum (1841-59, Bodestraße 1-3, Mitte). Originally home of the Egyptian collection, it mixed new wrought-iron technology with classical architecture, terra cotta ceiling coffers and elaborate murals. By 1910, Museumsinsel comprised the neo-classical Alte Nationalgalerie (1864, also Stüler; Bodestraße, Mitte) with an open stairway framing an equestrian statue of the king; the triangular Bode Museum (1904, von Ihne; Am Kupfergraben/Monbijoubrücke); and the sombre grey **Pergamon Museum** (1906-9, Messel and Hoffmann). These are a stark contrast to the neo-Renaissance polychromy of the **Martin-Gropius-Bau** across town (1881, Gropius and Schmieden).

HISTORICISM AND ECLECTICISM

As the population boomed after 1865, doubling to 1.5 million by 1890, the city began swallowing up neighbouring towns and villages. Factory complexes and worker housing gradually moved to the outskirts. Many of the new market halls and railway stations used a vernacular brick style with iron trusses, such as Arminiusmarkt in Moabit (Blankenstein, 1892; Bremer Straße 9) and Franz Schwechten's Romanesque Anhalter Bahnhof (1876-80, now a ruin; Askanischer Platz). Brick was also used for civic buildings, like the neo-Gothic **Rotes Rathaus** (1861-69), while the orientalism of the gold-roofed **Neue Synagoge** on Oranienburger Straße (Knoblauch, Stüler, 1859-66) made use of colourful masonry and mosaics.

Restrained historicism gave way to wild eclecticism as the 19th century continued, in public buildings as well as apartment houses with plain interiors, dark courtyards and overcrowded flats behind decorative façades. Eclecticism was also rampant among lavish Gründerzeit villas in the fashionable suburbs to the south-west, especially Dahlem and Grunewald. There the modest yellow-brick vernacular of Brandenburg was rejected in favour of elaborately modelled plaster and stone.

The Kurfürstendamm, a tree-lined shopping boulevard built up in the 1880s, soon helped the 'new west' rival the finery of Leipziger Straße. Further out, in Nikolassee and Wannsee, private homes hit new heights of scale and splendour. Many were inspired by the English country house, such as Haus Freudenberg in Zehlendorf (1908, Muthesius; Potsdamer Chaussee 48).

The new metropolis

In anticipation of a new age of rationality and mechanisation, an attempt at greater stylistic clarity was made after 1900, in spite of the bombast of works such as the new **Berliner Dom** (Raschdorff, 1905) or the **Reichstag** (Wallot, 1894). The Wilhelmine era's paradoxical mix of reformism and conservatism yielded an architecture of *Sachlichkeit* ('objectivity') in commercial and public buildings. In some cases, like Kaufmann's **Hebbel-Theater** (1908), or the Hackesche Höfe (Berndt and Endell, 1906-07, Rosenthaler Straße 40-41, Mitte), Sachlichkeit meant a calmer form of art nouveau (or Jugendstil); elsewhere it was more sombre, with heavy, compact forms, vertical ribbing, and low-hanging mansard roofs. One of the most severe examples is the stripped-down classicism of Alfred Messel's Pergamon Museum; even Bruno Schmitz's food automat at Friedrichstraße 167 (1905), with its three central bays, is pretty dry.

The style goes well with Prussian bureacracy in the civic architecture of Ludwig Hoffmann, city architect from 1896-1924. Though he sometimes used other styles for his many schools, courthouses and city halls, his towered Stadthaus in Mitte (1919; Jüdenstraße) and the Rudolf-Virchow-Krankenhaus in Wedding (1906; Augustenburger Platz 1), then innovative for its pavilion system, epitomise Wilhelmine architecture.

In housing after 1900, Sachlichkeit led to early modernism to serve the masses of the metropolis, now totalling three million. Messel became architect to some of the first successful housing co-ops, designing with a country-house flair (Sickingenstraße 7-8, Moabit, 1895; and Stargarder Straße 30, Prenzlauer Berg, 1900). Paul Mebes launched his long career in housing, beginning with a double row of apartments with enclosed balconies (Fritschweg, Steglitz, 1907-08). He and others moved on to larger ensembles, forerunners of the Weimar-era housing estates. Schmitthenner explored a vernacular style with gabled brick terraces arranged like a medieval village in Staaken, built near Spandau for World War I munitions workers (1917). Taut and Tessenow substituted coloured stucco for ornament in the terraced housing of Gartenstadt Falkenberg in Altglienicke (1915), part of an unbuilt larger town plan.

Prior to the incorporation of metropolitan Berlin in 1920, many suburbs had been given full city charters and sported their own town halls, such the massive Rathaus Charlottenburg (1905; Otto-Suhr-Allee 100) and Rathaus Neukölln (1909; Karl-Marx-Straße 83-85). Neukölln's Reinhold Kiehl also built the Karl-Marx-Straße Passage (1910, now home of the **Neuköllner Oper**), and the Stadtbad Neukölln (1914; Ganghofer Straße 3-5), whose niches and mosaics evoke a Roman atmosphere.

Special care was also given to new suburban rail stations of the period, such as the S-Bahnhof Mexikoplatz in Zehlendorf, set on a lovely garden square with shops and restaurants (Hart and Lesser, 1905), and the U-Bahnhof Dahlem-Dorf, whose half-timbered style goes even further to capture a countrified look.

Radical Weimar reform

The work of many pioneers brought modern architecture to life in Berlin. One of the most important was Behrens, who reinterpreted the factory with a new monumental language in the building of the Turbinenhalle at Huttenstraße in Moabit (1909) and several other buildings for the AEG, for whom he also designed lamps and fittings. After 1918, the turbulent birth of the Weimar Republic offered a chance for a final aesthetic break with the Wilhelmine compromise.

A radical new architecture gave formal expression to long-awaited social and political reforms. The 'neues Bauen' began to exploit the new technologies of glass, steel and concrete, inspired by the early work of Tessenow and Behrens, Dutch modernism, cubism, Russian constructivism, civil engineering and even a bit of Japanese design.

Berlin architects could explore the new functionalism to their hearts' content, using clean lines and a machine aesthetic bare of ornament, thanks to the postwar housing demand and a new socialist administration that brought about the incorporation of the city in 1920 and put planner Martin Wagner at the helm after 1925. The city became the builder of a new form of social housing, and in spite of rampant inflation, several hundred thousand units were completed. The *Siedlung* ('housing estate') was developed within the framework of a 'building exhibition' of experimental prototypes – often collaborations among architects such as Luckhardt, Gropius, Häring, Salvisberg and the brothers Taut. Standardised sizes kept costs down and amenities like tenant gardens, schools, public transport and shopping areas were offered when at all possible.

Among the best known 1920s estates are Bruno Taut's Hufeisen-Siedlung (1927; Bruno-Taut-Ring, Britz), arranged in horseshoe shape around a communal garden, and Onkel-Toms-Hütte (Haring, Taut, 1928-29; Argentinische Allee, Zehlendorf), with Salvisberg's linear U-Bahn station at its heart. Most Siedlungen were housing only, such as the Ringsiedlung (Goebelstraße, Charlottenburg) or Siemensstadt (Scharoun and others, 1929-32). Traditional-looking 'counter-proposals' with pitched roofs were made by more conservative designers at Am Fischtal (Tessenow, Mebes, Emmerich, Schmitthenner et al, 1929, Zehlendorf).

Larger infrastructure projects and public works were also built by avant-garde architects under Wagner's direction. Among the more interesting are the rounded U-Bahn station at Krumme Lanke (Grenander, 1929), the totally rational Stadtbad Mitte (1930; Gartenstraße 5-6), the Messegelände (Pölzig, Wagner, 1928; Charlottenburg), the ceramic-tiled Haus des Rundfunks (Pölzig, 1930; Masurenallee 10, Charlottenburg), and twin office buildings on the southern corner of Alexanderplatz (Behrens, 1932).

Beginning with his expressionist Einsteinturm in Babelsberg, Erich Mendelsohn distilled his own brand of modernism, characterised by the rounded forms of the Universum Cinema (1928; now the **Schaubühne**) and the elegant corner solution of the IG Metall building (1930; Alte Jacobstraße 148, Kreuzberg). Before emigrating – as did so many other architects, Jewish and non-Jewish – Mendelsohn was able to build a few private homes, including his own at Am Rupenhorn 6 in Charlottenburg (1929).

Grand designs and demolition

In the effort to remake liberal Berlin in their image, the Nazis undertook a form of spatial re-education. This included banning modernist trademarks such as flat roofs and slender columns in favour of traditional architecture, and shutting down the Bauhaus school shortly after it was banished from Dessau. Modern architects fled Berlin as Hitler dreamt of refashioning it into the mega-capital 'Germania' designed by Albert Speer. The crowning glory was to be a grand axis lined with the

Reichsbank – downright scary.

embassies of newly subjugated countries with a railway station at its foot and a massive copper dome at its head, some 16 times the size of St Peter's in Rome. Work was halted by the war, but not before demolition was begun in parts of Tiergarten and Schöneberg.

Hitler and Speer's fantasy was that Germania would someday leave picturesque ruins à la ancient Rome. But ruins came sooner than expected. Up to 90 per cent of inner districts were destroyed by Allied bombing. Mountains of rubble cleared by women survivors rose at the city's edge, such as the Teufelsberg in the west and Friedrichshain in the east. In the reconstruction period, the ornate plaster decoration of many apartment buildings was never replaced; others never recovered from the three weeks of street combat prior to capitulation.

Fascism left an invisible legacy of a bunker and tunnel landscape, much of which was re-used as listening stations by the East Germans. The more visible fascist architecture is recognisable by its stripped-down, abstracted classicism, typically in travertine, and it has been used almost without interruption: in the west, **Tempelhof Airport** (Sagebiel, 1941) and the **Olympiastadion** (March, 1936); in the east, the marble-halled Reichsluftfahrtministerium (Sagebiel, 1936; Leipziger Straße 5-7, Mitte), served the GDR administration refurbished with socialist murals, while the downright scary Reichsbank (Wolff, 1938; Werderscher Markt, Mitte), a design personally chosen by Hitler, became home to the central committee of the Communist Party.

The two Berlins

The Wall, put up in a single night in 1961, introduced a new and more cruel reality which rapidly acquired a sense of permanence. The city's centre of gravity shifted as the Wall cut off the historic centre from the west, suspending the Brandenburg Gate and Potsdamer Platz in no-man's-land, while the outer edge followed the 1920 city limits.

Post-war architecture is a mixed bag, ranging from the crisp linear brass of 1950s storefronts to concrete 1970s mega-complexes. Early joint planning efforts led by Scharoun were scrapped, and radical interventions cleared out vast spaces. Among the architectural casualties in the East were Schinkel's Bauakademie and much of Fischerinsel, clearing a sequence of wide spaces from Marx-Engels-Platz to Alexanderplatz. In West Berlin, Anhalter Bahnhof was left to stand in ruins but Schloß Charlottenburg narrowly escaped demolition.

Though architects from East and West shared the same modernist education, their work became the tool of opposing ideologies, and housing was the first battlefield. The GDR adapted Russian social-

Mies van der Rohe's Neue Nationalgalerie.

ist realism to Prussian culture in projects built with great effort and amazing speed as a national undertaking. First and foremost was Stalinallee (1951-54; now Karl-Marx-Allee, Mitte/Friedrichshain). The Frankfurter Tor segment of its monumental axis was designed by Herman Henselmann, a Bauhaus modernist who briefly agreed to switch styles. In response, West Berlin called on leading International Style architects such as Gropius, Niemeyer, Aalto and Sert to build the Hansa-Viertel. A loose arrangement of inventive slabs and pavilions at the edge of the Tiergarten, it was part of the 1957 Interbau Exhibition for the 'city of tomorrow' (which included Le Corbusier's Unité d'Habitation in Charlottenburg). Oddly enough, today both the Hansa-Viertel and Karl-Marx-Allee are highly sought-after housing.

East and West stylistic differences diminished in the 1960s and 1970s, as new Siedlungen were built to even greater dimensions. The Gropiusstadt in Britz and Märkisches Viertel in Reinickendorf (1963-74) were mirrored in the East by equally massive (if shoddier) prefab housing estates in Marzahn and Hellersdorf.

To replace the cultural institutions then cut off from the West, Dahlem became the site of various museums and the new **Freie Universität**, with a daring rusted-steel exterior (Candilis Woods Schiedhelm, 1967-79). Scharoun conceived a

'Kulturforum' on the site cleared for Germania, designing two masterful prizes: the **Philharmonie** (1963) and the **Staatsbibliothek** (1976). Other additions were Mies' slick **Neue Nationalgalerie** (1968), and the Kunstbibliothek (1994; Matthäikirchplatz 6, Tiergarten). In its incomplete state, the Kulturforum has instigated years of debate.

The US presented Berlin with Hugh Stubbin's Kongreßhalle in the Tiergarten (1967, now the **Haus der Kulturen der Welt**), an entertainingly futuristic work, which rather embarrassingly required seven years of repair after its roof collapsed in 1980. East German architects brewed their own version of futuristic modernism in the enlarged, vacuous Alexanderplatz with its **Fernsehturm** (1969), the nearby Haus des Lehrers (Henselmann, 1961-64), and the enjoyable cinemas, **Kino International** (Kaiser, 1964) and Kosmos (Kaiser, 1960-62; Karl-Marx-Allee 131, Friedrichshain).

POSTMODERN PRESERVATION

Modernist urban renewal gradually gave way to historic preservation after 1970. In the West, largely in response to the squatting movement, the city launched a public-private enterprise, the Internationale Bauausstellung (IBA), to conduct a 'careful renewal' of the Mietskaserne and 'critical reconstruction' with infill projects to close up the gaps left in areas along the Wall. A few schools and recreation centres were also built, such as Langhof's cascaded **Stadtbad Kreuzberg** (1988). Within the huge catalogue of IBA architects are many brands of postmodernism, both local and foreign, from Ungers, Sawade and Behnisch, to Krier, Moore and Hertzberger; many had never built anywhere. It is a truly eclectic collection: the irreverent organicism of the prolific Ballers (Fraenkelufer, Kreuzberg, 1982-84) contrasts sharply with the neorationalist work of Eisenman (Kochstraße 62-63, Kreuzberg, 1988) and Rossi (Wilhelmstraße 36-38, Kreuzberg; 1988); a series of projects was also placed along Friedrichstraße. IBA thus became a proving-ground that created a new panorama of contemporary architectural theories about the city and its many layers of history.

In the East, urban renewal slowed to a halt when funds for the construction of new housing ran dry; and towards the end of 1970s, inner-city areas became economically attractive. Unlike the Nikolaiviertel, where the medieval core was replicated after total clearance, most East-bloc preservation focused on run-down 19th-century buildings on a few streets and squares in Prenzlauer Berg. Some infill buildings were also added on Friedrichstraße in manipulated grids and pastel colours, so that the postmodern theme set up by Abraham and other IBA architects on the street south of Checkpoint Charlie was taken over the Wall. But progress was slow, and in 1989, many sites still stood half-finished.

New critical reconstruction

The task of joining east and west was the challenge of the century, requiring new work of all kinds, from massive new infrastructure to daycare centres. But the first impulse of the city fathers (and former West Berliners) was to erase evidence of four decades of division, mainly by restoring as much of the pre-war past as possible. They thus created the notion of 'Berlinische Architektur' – a homogenised historicism imposing limits on height and materials in Friedrichstadt. Its pilot project was the Friedrichstadt Passagen, three blocks of urban shopping malls now housing **Galeries Lafayette** and **Quartier 206 Department Store** (Ungers, Cobb/Fried/Pei, Nouvel, 1993-5), which were followed by several other exercises in punched-window façades nearby. Pariser Platz features Frank Gehry's DG Bank (1998), the Akademie der Künste (Behnisch, 2000) and the French and British embassies (Wilford, 2000; Portzamparc).

A more modern interpretation of 'critical reconstruction' was attempted at the American Business Center (Philip Johnson, SOM, Lauber + Woehr, 1996-98; Friedrichstraße 200, Mitte) to fill in the open space left behind by Checkpoint Charlie. But it only half-succeeded; not all buildings could be financed. Hans Kollhoff's glitzy Internet-age concoction for a smaller Alexanderplatz (multiplying

Punched-window façade – Gehry's DG Bank.

Potsdamer Platz – stand-off between late modernism and neo-traditionalism.

the Rockefeller Center by twelve) does more to eradicate GDR memory; ten of his towers (out of 13 in the original plan) have been approved so far. Meanwhile, the fate of the bronze-tinted Palast der Republik (Graffunder, 1976; Schloßplatz, Mitte), the world's only parliament with a bowling alley, is contingent on its asbestos being removed and on a campaign to rebuild the Kaiser's Stadtschloß in its place. Interestingly, the new stone and glass Foreign Ministry (Mueller Reimann, 2000), built in front of the old Reichsbank on the Friedrichswerder, is oddly compatible with the Palast.

The largest commercial post-Wall project to be completed is the $4.8 billion makeover of Potsdamer Platz. This has been a true feat of engineering, from the use of scuba divers to pour foundations in water-filled sites to the special 'logistics centre' monitoring the removal of millions of tons of soil (and the delivery of enough truckloads of sand to have circled the globe several times), and the north-south tunnel for road and rail which passes under the project. As the new shopping mall, cinemas, hotel and office towers gradually become a fixture in Berlin life, the memory of its origins in a notorious pre-Unification land deal between the SPD and Daimler-Benz recedes. Larger than many downtowns, it is a denser and higher rendition of the thriving centre silenced by the war. An array of local and international stars (Piano, Rogers, Isozaki, Moneo) joined to create a 'European city' in architecture that paradoxically

could have been found just about anywhere, as if its motto was 'dare to be mediocre'. On an urban level, it has yet to meet its goal of suturing east and west. In fact it actually creates barriers on almost every edge, and even lacks internal gateways. These barriers include the water-filled moat at the tunnel entrance off the Landwehrkanal, awkwardly located building entrances and sculpture, and the way Scharoun's Staatsbibliothek next door is blocked off by its pushy new neighbours. At least Potsdamer Platz did achieve its principle goal: to bring a new commercial centre to Berlin, nothing more and nothing less.

SONY, SO FAR

The question of authenticity recurs in many of the new projects. Embedded somewhere within the triangular mega-block of Sony's 'urban entertainment centre' (Murphy, Jahn, 1996-2000) is one of the last real pieces of Wilhelmine Berlin: the grand old Kaisersaal Café from the Esplanade Hotel, which was moved 75m to fit into the new layered complex of eight buildings.

The focus of this media and film centre (with numerous shops, restaurants, cinemas, an IMAX theatre and a luxury hotel) is a large public 'forum', covered by a dynamic, permeable structure 12 storeys up. Made with an off-centre ringbeam supported by spokes and cables like an erratic bicycle wheel and draped with strips of translucent fabric, it allows natural light and provides a stage for media events. Framed with high-tech elements, and forming its own system of open spaces, the spatial logic of the complex is a direct challenge to the narrow streets and flattened public spaces of its neighbours in Potsdamer Platz. This translates in architecture to a stand-off between the late modernist aesthetic of Helmut Jahn's glazed, semi-circular 103-m office tower, and the neo-traditional throwback of the punched-windows and brick cladding of Hans Kollhoff's 88-m office tower (1996-2000) across Leipziger Straße. Together they form a gateway to Potsdamer Straße, where the old Potsdamer Tor once stood.

Still to follow will be a new Hertie department store on the Lenné Dreieck to the north of the Sony Center, and the completion of Leipziger Platz, dotted with assorted commercial buildings. The northern half of the octagonal square will accommodate a headquarters for the Deutsches Reisebüro and the Canadian Embassy. The Mosse Palais, built on the former site of publisher Rudolf Mosse's residence, has already been completed for the Berlin office of the American Jewish Committee (HDS & Gallagher, Boston, 1995-1997). The site of the former Wertheim department store (Alfred Messel, 1896; demolished 1958), under which passes the U2 U-Bahn line, will be broken up into smaller parcels for redevelopment. The red **Info-Box** will continue to stand on Leipziger Platz until 2005, when most of the construction in this area should be finished.

In short, there is already more than enough new work for visitors to take in, and a whole lot more to come. Only time will tell if the real estate market, which collapsed after the Bonn government delayed in making good on its 1990 decision to move here, has recovered enough to support all this new office and commercial space.

Also still to come is the Denkmal für die ermordeten Juden Europas ('Memorial to the Murdered European Jews') on the five-acre lot south of Pariser Platz. Quite what shape this will take has been mired in controversy for over a decade, but the city looks poised to go ahead with a design by Peter Eisenmann involving 1,500 rectangular concrete columns, each up to four metres high, forming a dense labyrinth of stelae. *See page 77* **Monumental controversy**.

ABSTRACTIONS OF FATE

Ironically, the two most important new architectural works of the post-Unification period were designed before 1989: Daniel Libeskind's Jüdisches Museum (Lindenstraße 14, Kreuzberg; *see page 84* **Reading between the lines**), and the **Reichstag** (orig. Wallot, 1884-1894) in the Spreebogen. Libeskind has created a masterful and well-built deconstructivist provocation, a silvery abstraction of fate guaranteed to confound its curators for some time to come – the interior will be closed to the public until 2001 while they compose an exhibition. Meanwhile, after its two-week wrap by Christo, the space where Hitler came to power

Nicholas Grimshaw's skeletal whale of a Stock Exchange.

Adlershof Science and Business Center – sign of modern metropolitanism.

was stripped, retrofitted, and brilliantly domed by Britain's Sir Norman Foster. With a double helix of ramps spiralling to the top, the light-filled dome is set on a generous roof terrace and has clean, elegant details: high-tech with class. It affords a new perspective of the city, gorgeous until late evening. *See page 71* **The dome of democracy**.

The Reichstag is neighbour to a second large-scale project, nearly complete: the Band des Bundes, designed by Axel Schultes, who built the Federal Chancellery. Together with the tightly packed maze of offices for the MPs, the Spreebogen ensemble joins east and west but walls off north and south and overwhelms the Reichstag (not easily done). It is built above the massive new tunnel for rail and road traffic, and linked to Moabit with an elegant new bridge by Santiago Calatrava. Adjacent to the Spreebogen are new buildings for political parties, press and media, such as the ARD studios (Ortner & Ortner, 1999); a group of buildings to house delegations from the German Länder (Ministeriengärten) will stretch down to Potsdamer Platz.

All this adds up to a new city within the city – which will complemented by the new railway station at Lehrter Bahnhof (von Gerkan Marg), flanked by even more office space. Since Berlin has never really had a central station, this is arguably as historically significant as the reconstruction of lost monuments. Built on the site of the original Lehrter Bahnhof, which was destroyed in World War II, the new station will function as a major junction for regional and inter-city rail routes as well as for the local U- and S-Bahn systems – north-south links will pass underground, while east-west routes sweep overhead. The glass upper hall will be covered with 3,500sq m of solar panels. Construction began in 1996 and should be completed by 2004.

More daring work may be found outside the old core, in Nicholas Grimshaw's skeletal whale of a Stock Exchange (1998; Ludwig-Erhard-Haus, Fasanenstraße 83-84), the silver disk of the **Velodrom** in Prenzlauer Berg (Claude Perrault, 1998), or among the scores of new embassies scattered from Mitte to the Tiergarten. Of the latter, one of the most innovative is the centre for Nordic delegations (Berger & Parkkinen, 1999; Rauchstraße 1, Tiergarten), a collection of irregularly shaped buildings within a medievalesque compound encircled by a blue wall. Further chances for good new architecture by younger architects lie in housing, infrastructure and parks on the periphery. Some is directly sponsored by the city, like the Adlershof Science and Business Center, and the 1999 Berlin building exhibition (to be completed in 2001) at Buchholz east and west, Karower Damm, and Buch V. Like the new Lehrter Bahnhof, this new ring of suburban development is the final confirmation that Berlin is on its way (back) to becoming a modern metropolis.

Sightseeing

Sightseeing

Between the scars of a troubled history and the foundations of a new future, Berlin has plenty of things to see – just don't expect many Baroque churches.

Construction time again.

A relatively young city and never a particularly beautiful one, Berlin is not a conventional sightseeing destination in the same way as, say, Paris or Rome. Few would come here just to look at churches. But this isn't to say that there's nothing to see. Berlin's turbulent history has left scars and reminders all over this huge town, while a new future on the global stage is only just beginning to take shape out of the many construction sites that currently dominate the centre – and have become a tourist attraction in themselves.

Most Berlin sights that could properly be described as unmissable – either because you really ought to see them or simply because you couldn't avoid them if you tried – are in and around the Mitte district. These include the **Brandenburg Gate**, the grand structures of Unter den Linden and Alexanderplatz, and the narrow streets of the Scheunenviertel, rich in Berlin's Jewish history.

But this is only a small segment of this enormous, sprawling city – carved up by rivers and canals, punctuated by pockets of green and fringed with lakes and forest. During its rapid growth in the latter part of the 19th century, it gobbled up a number of small communities and then, in the mid-20th century, became two cities with a wall between them. Today the Wall is down and the small towns exist only as names on the map, but there are still big differences between one part of town and another.

From beginnings as a small fortified enclave on an island in the Spree (now Museumsinsel), Berlin soon expanded into what is now the borough of Mitte. For many years, that's pretty much how it

stayed: the court preferred the pleasures of Potsdam or Königsberg, and Berlin remained little more than a trading town. But towards the end of the 17th century, Kaiser Friedrich Wilhelm took a town that had been devastated by war and disease and started shaping it into a modern metropolis – establishing a harbour, building **Schloß Charlottenburg**, and encouraging immigration, particularly of Jews and Huguenots.

Within a century, Berlin had been transformed into one of Europe's great cities: a military, commercial and cultural centre. This expansion was dwarfed by the enormous boom that started in 1871, when Berlin was named the capital of the newly unified German Reich. By the 1920s Berlin had become a world city, ranked with New York, London and its perennial rival, Paris. Greater Berlin was officially divided into 20 *Bezirke*, or boroughs. Latterly there have been 23 (the extra ones having been added to east Berlin) although from the beginning of 2001, most will merge into larger administrative units. *See page 53* **Bordering on the Bezirk**.

Hitler hated Berlin and directed Albert Speer to turn it into something more to his liking – the megalopolis of Germania, capital of the Thousand-Year Reich. World War II slowed down his plans, and only a few buildings (such as Tempelhof Airport or the **Olympiastadion**) and some grandiose street plans (the East-West Axis including the Großer Stern roundabout at the Siegessäule in the Tiergarten) were completed. *See page 67* **Remnants of the Reich**.

The Allies then bombed the city into submission, leaving a good 50 per cent of it completely uninhabitable. Massive rebuilding was necessary on both sides of the Cold War divide. As an island now stranded in the middle of East Germany, West Berlin had to come up with novel solutions, since there was nowhere for it to expand. This explains the amount of modern *Dachbau* ('roof-top') extensions of old buildings. East Berlin was under heavy pressure to serve as a showcase for the glories of communism, so what little money there was mostly went into architectural showpieces that were both cheap and overblown (such as Alexanderplatz). The rest either remained soot-encrusted and bullet-pocked, or else was flattened and flat-blocked.

This chapter concentrates first on the central boroughs. Beginning with the area around Potsdamer Platz, it then moves clockwise through Mitte, Prenzlauer Berg, Friedrichshain, Kreuzberg, Schöneberg, Charlottenburg and Tiergarten. There follows a brief section on other interesting neighbourhoods, divided into east and west, and then a look at places to go among the woods and waterways on the outskirts of town.

Bars, cafés, restaurants and other venues mentioned and highlighted **in bold** can be found listed elsewhere in the relevant chapters.

Around Potsdamer Platz

Though cranes still linger, and there are buildings yet to rise, much of Potsdamer Platz, intended as the city's new commercial centrepiece, is now completed. Since this once-bustling intersection was bombed flat and then wound up just on the East side of the Wall, it was a literal no-man's-land for many years. Now construction has transformed it into an area of corporate skyscrapers and seats of power, as well as the venue for the Berlinale Film Fest. For a quick, corporate-sponsored overview of plans for the finished project, head for the **Info-Box**, the big red structure on stilts that stands near the exits from the U-Bahn.

Among the skyscrapers which have now risen here are the corporate headquarters for Daimler-Chrysler's computer services division, Debis, and Sony's European operations. Their public spaces contain works of art by an international cast of artists, and the Sony building contains the Forum, conceived as an urban entertainment complex and including the **CineStar** multiplex and the interactive **Music Box** museum.

Some of the technological feats involved in the reconstruction of Potsdamer Platz are mind-boggling: one of the two buildings to survive the bombing and subsequent cleansing was the Kaisersaal Café from the old Grand Hotel Esplanade, a listed building. When the plans for the renovation were solidified, the café was found to be in a bad position, so the whole structure, weighing 1,300 tonnes, was moved 75m to its present position, where it has been integrated into the apartment complex on Bellevuestraße.

In anticipation of the increased human traffic through Potsdamer Platz, the Potsdamer Platz Arkaden were grafted on to the U-Bahn and S-Bahn stations, three storeys of what is essentially an American shopping mall (although employees there are forbidden to use that term). Despite the fact that nearly all of its chain-store tenants have outlets elsewhere in the city, it is filled with people during opening hours and seems to be popular with hicks from rural Brandenburg. Just outside the Arkaden, on Alte Potsdamer Straße, the other survivor of the bombing, Weinhaus Huth, is back selling wine at its old location. For more on the new Potsdamer Platz, what's been built and what's still to come, *see chapter* **Architecture**.

South along Stresemannstraße, of Anhalter Bahnhof, once the city's most important railway station, only a tiny piece of façade remains today,

Potsdamer Platz – don't even think of calling it a shopping mall.

Ivan's last stand – portrait of a Soviet soldier looms over Checkpoint Charlie.

preserved in its bombed state near the S-Bahn station that bears its name. Another ruin near the station is a modest section of the 18th-century city wall that was excavated and reconstructed in time for the city's 750th birthday celebrations. The **Grusel Kabinett**, a chamber of horrors, occupies an old air-raid shelter on the Schöneberger Straße side of the empty space where platforms and tracks once stood.

On Stresemannstraße, the Bauhaus-designed Europahaus was heavily bombed during World War II, but the lower storeys remain, and the Café Stresemann on the corner is a popular local neighbourhood hangout. Nearby, the **Martin-Gropius-Bau** hosts extravagant, well-curated shows. Next to it is a deserted patch of ground that once held the Prinz Albrecht Palais, which the Gestapo took over as its headquarters. In the basement, thousands of political prisoners were held and tortured to death, and the land was flattened after the war. In 1985, during an acrimonious debate over the design of a memorial to be placed on the land, a group of citizens cut the wire surrounding it and staged a symbolic 'excavation' of the site. To their surprise, they hit the Gestapo's basement, and immediately plans were made to reclaim the site. Today, the **Topographie des Terrors** exhibition there, with a ground-level photographic display of the site's history and railings overlooking the cells, is undergoing renovation and a library and document centre is due to open in late 2001. Along the northern boundary of the site stands one of the few remaining stretches of the Berlin Wall, its concrete pitted and threadbare after thousands

of souvenir-hunters in 1990 pecked away at it with hammers and chisels.

From here, it's a short walk down Kochstraße – once Berlin's Fleet Street and still home to both the Axel Springer publishing empire and to the left-wing daily, *die tageszeitung* – to Friedrichstraße, where the notorious Checkpoint Charlie once stood and where the **Haus am Checkpoint Charlie** museum documents the history of the Wall. Most of the space where the border post once stood has been claimed by new buildings, notably the Philip-Johnson-Haus, designed by the eminent American architect as a German-American business centre, although tenants have been slow to come – perhaps deterred by the strangely ugly spherical sculpture which stands outside. The actual site of the borderline itself is memorialised by Frank

Info-box – *the building site as tourist trap.*

Thiel's photographic portraits of an American and a Soviet soldier. A lone watchtower still stands just north of the former border but the small white building which served as the gateway between East and West is now in the **Allied Museum**; while what would have been a new control station had the Wall not fallen are now built into the apartment buildings at Friedrichstraße 207-208, right next to a Greek restaurant. **The British Bookshop**, a useful resource for Anglophones, stands round the corner on Mauerstraße, while the **Café Adler** on the corner with Zimmerstraße is a good refuelling stop.

Info-Box

Leipziger Platz 21, Mitte, 10117 (226 6240). S1, S2/U2 Potsdamer Platz. **Open** 9am-7pm Mon-Wed, Fri-Sun; 9am-9pm Thur. **Admission** free; *observation platform* DM2. **Map E4**
The huge construction site on Potsdamer Platz has been a major tourist attraction since its inception. To explain the vast changes being wrought in the area, a number of the players, including Daimler-Benz, Sony, Deutsche Bahn, and the Federal government, have installed exhibitions in this strikingly red structure floating over the mess. Many exhibitions are bilingual, many are interactive and computerised, and many of them may actually be working when you visit, at least partially. The view from the top helps you visualise what you've learned inside, and don't miss the replica of the world's first traffic light, which was installed at Potsdamer Platz, standing outside. The structure is scheduled to be moved elsewhere in the area after all the construction work on Potsdamer Platz is finished.

Mitte

When the Wall was up, the idea of this part of town calling itself Mitte – 'middle' – seemed faintly ludicrous. True, it was the place where the city was born on the sand islands in the Spree, and before World War II it had been the hub of the city. But it was by no means central to East Berlin, and, despite international-quality hotels and the International Business Centre at Friedrichstraße station, it didn't seem that important at all. In the reunited city, though, Mitte has regained its title as centre of the city in every way possible: culturally, scenically, administratively. With the historic old buildings scrubbed until they shine, an influx of capital promoting new construction, and a new energy from moneyed settlers, Mitte is very much back in the middle again.

Friedrichstraße

What the Kurfürstendamm pretended to be in post-war West Berlin, Friedrichstraße had been and may be again: Berlin's answer to the Champs-Élysées or Fifth Avenue. The street actually starts at Mehringplatz in Kreuzberg, site of the

Friedensäule, junior cousin to the **Siegessäule**, and ends at Orianienburger Tor in Mitte. The liveliest, glitziest stretch is that between Checkpoint Charlie and Friedrichstraße station. What's most evident is money; a huge amount has been poured into this part of the street, with office buildings and upmarket shopping malls, including the Friedrichstadt Passagen, into which **Galeries Lafayette** bravely moved early on. Also worth noting is **Dussmann Das Kulturkaufhaus**, a cultural department store which is seeking to take the place that both FNAC and Virgin's Megastore failed to capture in the west. Otherwise there are auto showrooms for Rolls Royce/Bentley/Volkswagen, Audi, and Mercedes-Benz, boutiques for Mont Blanc and Cartier, and everything from DKNY to Planet Hollywood in the Quartiers. *See chapters* **Shopping & Services** *and* **Architecture**.

Just to the east of this stretch lies Gendarmenmarkt, one of the high points of Frederick the Great's vision for the city. Here, the two cathedrals, the Französischer Dom (now the **Hugenotten Museum**) and the Deutscher Dom (home of the Questions of German History exhibit which was formerly in the Reichstag) frame the **Konzerthaus**. This was once a theatre (the Schauspielhaus) and now home to the Deutsches Symphonie-Orchester Berlin. *See chapter* **Music: Classical & Opera**.

Friedrichstraße station has been turned into one of Deutsche Bahn's shopping malls, the formerly grim building having been totally gutted in the process. The station interior was once notable mostly for its ability to confuse, since the checkpoint which once occupied it was the only East-West gateway for all categories of people (both East and West German plus foreigners), and necessitated a warren of passageways and interior spaces to maintain security. Looming over the nearby plaza is the Internationales Handelzentrum ('International Trade Centre') – the building from which East Germany conducted its trade in cheap consumer durables and coal, getting technology, raw materials and hard currency in return. The state held the monopoly in this trade, of course, and shortly after the government fell, most of the officials in this building were indicted for extortion. Its entire front has been demolished, and a new structure will soon stand in front of it. Following the train tracks to the east along Georgenstraße, you come upon the **Berliner Antik & Flohmarkt** – a succession of antique stores, bookshops, and cafés in the Bogen ('arches'), ending at Museumsinsel. The building just to the north of the train station is known as the **Tränenpalast** ('Palace of Tears'), since it was where departing visitors left their Eastern friends and relations who could not follow them back home through the border. Today, this former

Gendarmenmarkt – Frederick the Great's vision for the city.

checkpoint is a concert and cabaret venue, and a piece of the Wall can be seen in its beer garden.

North on Friedrichstraße, the **Metropol Theater** is a survivor of the bombing, a former venue for translated Broadway hits and home to the Distel Cabaret. Crossing the river on the wrought-iron Weidendammer Brücke, you turn left on Schiffbauerdamm towards the **Berliner Ensemble**, with its bronze statue of Brecht, who directed the company from 1948 to 1956, surrounded by quotations from his works. Behind it, on Schumannstraße, stands the **Deutsches Theater**, another of the city's important companies. Going back on to Friedrichstraße, you'll find the **Friedrichstadtpalast**, a large cabaret that was one of the entertainment hot-spots during the days of the GDR, since it took hard currency; it still pulls the crowds today, albeit mostly grannies from out of town. Billboards featuring the leggy chorines are inescapable in the area.

Museumsinsel & Unter den Linden

From before the Hohenzollern dynasty through the Weimar Republic, and from the Third Reich to the GDR, the entire history of Berlin can be found here. It's also the place where the city came into being, so the profusion of museums and historical sights is no accident. That said, if you decide not to go into the museums it can also be easily covered in one afternoon, since this concentration of history is easily walked around, starting at the **Brandenburg Gate**.

Berlin's famous gate was the scene of much partying after the Wall came down, having been stranded in no-man's-land for nearly 30 years. Once, only the monarch could drive through the central arch of the Gate; today, due to structural instability, it's closed to everyone. Immediately to the east of the Gate is Pariser Platz, which has been filled in with office buildings, so that the Gate no longer stands in isolation. Plans were drawn up in 1993 to present Pariser Platz as the 'Salon of Berlin', with new buildings on the same scale as the old ones, featuring conservative exteriors and contemporary interiors – *see page 64* **Won't You Come Into My Parlour?** Some of the old faces are back: the reconstructed Adlon Hotel is now at

Set books set out at Humboldt University.

its old address, and among the new buildings will be the French, British, and US Embassies, standing on the land they inhabited before World War II – although at press time, the US Embassy was being held up because of security concerns in the wake of the Nairobi bombing. The US government has asked Berlin to redesign its street plan to accommodate it, and for now, the city is baulking. To the south of the US Embassy site will be what is officially titled das Denkmal für die ermordeten Juden Europas – 'Memorial to the Murdered European Jews' – another project enmeshed in controversy over its location (it's not on any particular historical site), design (American sculptor Richard Serra parted ways with architect Peter Eisenman in 1998), and content (some feel that the memorial should honour all of the victims of the Holocaust, not just the Jewish ones). *See page 77* **Monumental controversy**.

Leading east from the Gate is Unter den Linden. Originally laid out to connect the town centre with the Tiergarten, Unter den Linden, which begins at the Brandenburg Gate, got its name from the *Linden* ('lime trees') that shaded its central walkway. Hitler, concerned that the trees obscured the view of his parades, had them felled, but they've been replanted. Between the Gate and the Spree, the side streets were laid out in a grid by the Great Elector Friedrich Wilhelm for his Friedrichstadt, which he hoped would provide the model for Berlin's continued growth.

The western end of Unter den Linden is all recent, having been badly bombed, and among the glories of Soviet-influenced architecture is the Russian and Ukrainian Embassy (formerly the Soviet Embassy). **Humboldt University** is now integrated into Berlin's university system, and its grand old façade has been restored, as have the two statues of the Humboldts, between which booksellers set up their tables in good weather. Across the street, Bebelplatz, the site of the huge Nazi book-burning (noted by Micha Ullmann's wonderful monument set into the Platz itself) is flanked by the **Deutsche Staatsoper**, whose cafés and restaurants are appropriately glitzy. A statue of Frederick the Great (taken down by the GDR, suddenly and mysteriously reappearing one night when the Party line on him changed) usually points toward the river at this spot, although recent restoration meant that Old Fritz was absent at the time of writing.

The island where Berlin started life is divided in half, with Werderstraße marking the line. The northern part with its collection of museums, is known as Museumsinsel, while the southern half (much enlarged by landfill), once a neighbourhood for the city's fishermen, Fischerinsel, is now a pleasant residential area with a couple of quiet hotels and some restaurants. Across a bridge is the **Märkisches Museum** (which houses an eclectic

Berlin's official bears.

exhibition of circus history), and Köllnischer Park, in which you can visit the official Berlin bears.

The museums on Museumsinsel are mostly more impressive seen from the outside than the inside. One exception is the **Pergamon-Museum**, a showcase for three huge and important bits of ancient architecture: the Great Altar of Pergamon (a Greek temple complex in what is now Turkey); the Blue Gate of Babylon, and the Market of Augustus from Caesarium. The Bode Museum had a strange assortment of displays, and is closed while they are rationalised; the Neues Museum is finally having its severe bomb damage repaired (although opening has not yet been scheduled, it won't be until after 2001); and Schinkel's **Altes Museum**, from 1830, has a small permanent collection and is currently hosting the works normally contained in the nearby Alte Nationalgalerie while that institution too is being refurbished. On Museumsinsel's eastern edge is the **Berliner Dom**, once again holding Sunday services after decades of communist opprobrium.

In between Museumsinsel and Fischerinsel, on Schloßplatz, stands the shell of the Palast der Republik. This asbestos-contaminated relic of the GDR has been closed to the public since 1990. Sadly all too obviously built in the mid-1970s as the main parliamentary chamber of the GDR, it also contained discos, bars and a bowling alley. The Palast der Republik replaced the remains of the war-ravaged Stadtschloß, residence of the Kaiser's – heavily bombed and in ruins until 1952, the GDR levelled it for both aesthetic and ideological reasons, leaving only the bit of the façade from which Karl Liebknecht proclaimed the German Republic in 1918. Arguments continue about whether to rebuild the Stadtschloß (the original plans are still on file), totally renovate the existing structure, or grace the site with some new structure. Further debate revolves around whether a new Stadtschloß would glorify Prussian military might, whether the existing Palast glorifies communism, or just what function a new structure would have (yet another shopping mall has been suggested). One way or another the communist

Altes Museum – Schinkel's finest.

Palast will eventually see a change. Just across the bridge is the Marx-Engels Forum, one of the few remaining monuments to the old boys – the huge statue of Karl and Fred begs you to take a seat on Karl's big lap.

Berliner Dom

Berlin Cathedral
Lustgarten, Mitte, 10178 (246 90). S3, S5, S7, S9 Hackescher Markt. **Open** 9am-7.30pm Mon-Sat; 11.30am-7.30pm Sun. **Admission** DM3; DM1.50 concs; *photo permission* DM3. **Map F3**
The dramatic Berliner Dom is now finally healed of its war wounds. Built around the turn of the century in Italian Renaissance style, it was destroyed during World War II and remained a ruin until 1973, when extensive restoration work began. It has always looked fine from the outside, but now that the internal work is complete, it is fully restored to its former glory. Crammed with Victorian detail, and containing dozens of statues of eminent German Protestants, it is now holding weekly services after several decades of existing in the face of GDR displeasure. Its lush 19th-century interior is hardly the perfect acoustic space for the frequent concerts which are held there, but it's worth a visit to see the crypt containing about 90 sarcophagi of the Hohenzollern dynasty.

Brandenburg Gate

Pariser Platz, Mitte, 10117. S1, S2 Unter den Linden. **Map E3**

Constructed in 1791 and designed by Langhans after the Propylaeus gateway into ancient Athens, the Gate was built as a triumphal arch celebrating the Prussian capital city. It was first called the Friedenstor ('Gate of Peace') and is the only remaining city gate left from Berlin's original 18. (Today a handful of U-Bahn stations are named after some of the other city gates, such as Hallesches Tor and Schlesisches Tor.)

The Quadriga statue, a four-horse chariot driven by Victory and designed by Schadow, sits on top of the gate. It has had a turbulent history. When Napoleon conquered the city in 1806 he took the statue home with him and held it hostage until his defeat in 1814. The Tor was later a favourite place for Nazi rallies. It was badly damaged during World War II, and during its renovation the GDR removed the Prussian Iron Cross. This was replaced after Reunification and repaired again after everyone had partied around it in 1990. The current Quadriga is a 1958 copy of Schadow's 18th-century original.

Deutches Historiches Museum (Zeughaus)

Unter den Linden 2, Mitte, 10115 (215 020). S3, S5, S7, S9, Hackescher Markt. **Open** 10am-6pm Mon-Tue, Thur-Sun. **Admission** free for most exhibits. **Map F3**
The Zeughaus is a former armoury with a deceptively peaceful pink façade which, after renovation, scheduled to be completed at the end of 2002, will once again house the Museum of German History.

Berliner Dom – *fully restored.*

The **Brandenburg Gate** – *Berlin's arch of triumph.*

Its exhibitions will no longer have the peculiar slant that made the place a favourite for Western tourists to visit in GDR times, but it does have frequent exhibitions on East-related themes. At Chrismas the gift shop has one of the finest selections of traditional German handcrafts in the city.

Friedrich-Werdersche-Kirche

Werderscher Markt, Mitte,10117 (208 1323). U2 Hausvogteiplatz. **Open** 10am-6pm Tue-Sun. **Admission** DM4; DM2 concs; free first Sun of the month. **Map F3**

Built according to a design by Schinkel during the 1820s, Friedrich-Werdersche Church currently houses the **Schinkel-Museum**, a collection of the artist/architect's sculptures. The neo-Gothic structure was, like almost everything else in the surrounding area, destroyed during World War II, but was successfully restored and re-opened in 1987. *See chapter* **Museums**.

Mahnmal

Unter den Linden 5, Mitte, 10115. S3, S5, S7, S9, Hackescher Markt. **Map F3**

The Mahnmal, constructed by Schinkel in 1821-24, was known as the Neue Wache when it served as a guardhouse for the royal residences in the area, and is today a memorial to the 'victims of war and tyranny', with an enlarged reproduction of a Käthe Kollwitz Pietà in its centre. The police presence is there in case someone takes exception (as some did at its re-dedication in 1993) to the inclusion of the Jews in that number.

The Scheunenviertel & Oranienburger Straße

If the area below the station is the new upmarket face of Mitte, the Scheunenviertel and Oranienburger Straße are the face of its moneyed bohemia – Berlin's main nightlife district and art quarter, littered with bars and galleries. Once so far out of town that the highly flammable hay barns (*Scheunen*) were built here, this was also historically the centre of Berlin's immigrant community, including many Jews from eastern Europe. During the 1990s it again began to attract Jewish immigrants, including both young Americans and Orthodox Jews from the former Soviet Union.

Immediately after the fall of the Wall, the Scheunenviertel became a magnet for squatters with access to the list of buildings supposedly wrecked by lazy urban developers, who had checked them off as gone in order to meet quotas – but had actually left them standing. With many other buildings in disrepair, rents were cheap, and the new residents soon learned how to take advantage of city subsidies for opening galleries and other cultural spaces. Result: the Scheunenviertel became Berlin's hot cultural centre.

The first of these art-squats was **Tacheles**. Built in 1907, the building originally housed the Friedrichstraße Passagen, an early attempt at a

Mahnmal – *shadows of tyranny.*

shopping mall, which in the 1930s was used by the SS. It had stood vacant for years and was falling apart when it was squatted by artists immediately following the fall of the Wall. It then became a rather arrogant arbiter of hip in the neighbourhood, offering studio space to artists, performance spaces for music, a cinema, and several bars and discos. In 1997, the city presented the squatters with an opportunity to buy it cheaply and was spurned, so now Tacheles is run by a new and friendlier management. The sculpture garden out back is nice when the weather's good, and frequently hosts tent shows in the summer.

Many visitors think the building on the corner of Tucholskystraße and Oranienburger Straße is the New Synagogue, but it's the Postführamt, once a postal building, albeit a very ornate one, currently hosting occasional art shows. Across Tucholskystraße at Oranienburger Straße 32 is an entrance to the new Heckmann Höfe (the other is on Auguststraße), a series of courtyards formerly belonging to an engineering firm, which have been delightfully restored to accommodate shops and restaurants. The free-standing building with the firm's coat of arms in the pavement in front of it was once the stables, as indicated by the sculpture of a horse's head, positioned as if peering out of the building.

A bit further down the block is the **New Synagogue**, with its gleaming golden Moorish-style dome. Turning into Große Hamburger Straße, you find yourself surrounded by Jewish

Bordering on the Bezirk

From the beginning of 2001, Berlin's administrative map will be redrawn – the number of districts or *Bezirke* will be reduced from 23 to 12. A reform of the Bezirk structure has been discussed since the mid-1990s, although wags say it has been up for grabs since 1920, when the original 20 districts comprising city boroughs and neighbouring villages constituted Greater Berlin. In 1998, the Berlin government decided upon 12 districts, each with around 300,000 inhabitants, with 20 districts merging with neighbouring boroughs. Only populous Neukölln, enormous Reinickendorf and the practically separate city of Spandau will each remain separate entities.

The financially beleaguered city government hopes to save up to DM2 million by reducing district overheads, and the business community is looking forward to a 'leaner, more efficient and customer-orientated' local administration. The general populace, however, is somewhat divided – opinion polls taken around the announcement of the Bezirk fusion showed that a middling percentage supported it. One popular sentiment seems to be: 'If it ain't broke, why fix it?' The administrative make-up of Berlin has survived Weimar turmoil, the Nazi régime and the division of the city, the only exception being the spinning off of Hellersdorf and Marzahn (from Lichtenberg) and Hohenschönhausen (from Weißensee) in the 1970s and 1980s to accommodate the new housing projects there.

Many suspect that the Bezirk fusion is nothing but a ploy to keep in check the formerly communist PDS , which has a greater following in the east than the governing Christian Democrats and Social Democrats and is making inroads into the west. Others moan that mostly eastern districts are affected. Financial experts predict that initially more money will be spent than saved in the process of joining the districts. Some merging boroughs feel too similar (social powderkegs Kreuzberg and Friedrichshain fear their combined district will become the city's poorhouse), others too different (fading boho cultural centre Schöneberg and conservative industrial Tempelhof are struggling to find common ground). Combining Mitte and Tiergarten, which both house federal government institutions, makes sense, but where does third partner Wedding fit in?

Besides fear of fewer local goverment services, the main issue is local identity. This is most saliently reflected in the discussion about names. Tiergarten, Mitte and Wedding have already decided upon 'Mitte', Köpenick and Treptow are considering the hyphenate option. Numbering the districts, as in Paris or Vienna, is a widely discussed but generally unpopular solution. Pankow, Prenzlauer Berg and Weißensee might take on the historical-geographical name Barnimhöhe. Hellersdorf and Marzahn will alas not be known as Hellerzahn – the district of bright teeth – but will possibly be named Wuhletal after the river that runs through them.

Aside from the name game, more traditional neighbourhoods or *Kieze* such as Moabit, Friedenau, Dahlem, Biesdorf or Schöneweide, which never enjoyed Bezirk status, will remain and perhaps even gain significance as Berliners reembrace 'regional' identities in the wake of more global reorganisation. Does any of this sound familiar?

Jewish deportees memorialised.

having miraculously survived two wars, they were restored from the old plans in the mid-1990s, and today house an upmarket collection of shops, galleries, theatres, cabarets, cafés, restaurants and cinemas. A few doors up Rosenthaler Straße is an alley alongside a cinema, in which a workshop for the blind was located during World War II. Its owner managed to stock it fully with 'blind' Jews, and helped them escape or avoid the camps. Across the street from the Hackesche Höfe, around the S-Bahn station, shines a welter of bars, restaurants and galleries. There are more fashionable bars and shops along Rosenthaler Straße and around the corner on Neue Schönhauser Straße.

Neue Synagoge
New Synagogue
Oranienburger Straße 28-30, Mitte, 10117 (2840 1316). S1, S2 Oranienburger Straße. **Open** 10am-6pm Mon-Thur, Sun; 10am-2pm Fri. **Admission** DM5; DM3 concs. **Tours** 2pm and 4pm Sun; 4pm Wed. **Admission** DM3; DM1.50 concs. **Map F3**
Built in 1857-66 as the Berlin Jewish community's showpiece, this was the synagogue attacked during Kristallnacht in 1938, but not too badly damaged – Allied bombs did that in 1945. The façade remained intact and the Moorish dome has been rebuilt and given a new gilding. Inside is an excellent exhibit about Jewish life in Berlin and a glassed-in area protecting the ruins of the sanctuary, a reminder for generations to come of what has been lost.

history. On the right, on the site of a former old people's home, there is a memorial to the thousands of Berlin Jews who were forced to congregate at this site before being shipped off to concentration camps. Following Jewish tradition, many visitors put a stone on the memorial in remembrance of those who died. Behind the memorial is a park which was once Berlin's oldest Jewish cemetery; the only gravestone left is that of the father of the German Jewish renaissance, Moses Mendelssohn, founder of the city's first Jewish school, next door at number 27. A few other stones can be seen piled in the park's south-east corner.

Across the street at number 15-16 is *The Missing House*, an artwork by Christian Boltanski, in which the walls left blank by a bombed-out house have the names and occupations of former residents inscribed on the site of each one's apartment. Sophienkirche, from which nearby Sophienstraße gets its name, sits behind wrought-iron fences a little further on, and is better looking from the outside than inside – although it is one of the few remaining Baroque churches in the city.

At the end of Oranienburger Straße, at the corner of Rosenthaler Straße, are the Hackesche Höfe, built in 1906-7 by some young Jewish idealists as just what they are today, a mixed-use complex with nine courtyards. The Hackesche Höfe never took off, despite their lovely Jugendstil design, but,

Neue Synagoge – *gleaming Moorish dome.*

Alexanderplatz's Fountain of the Friendship of Peoples.

Sophienstraße & Auguststraße

Sophienstraße is Mitte's jewel in the crown. This 18th-century street was restored in 1987 for the city's 750th anniversary, with craft people's ateliers that have replicas of old merchants' metal signs hanging outside them. The brick façade of the Handwerker Verein at number 18 is particularly impressive, and the interior has the excellent gallery **Asian Art Now**, as well as the Sophiensaele, a theatre space in what was once an old Jewish ballroom.

At 20-21 are the Sophie-Gips Höfe, which came into being when Erika and Rolf Hoffmann were denied permission to build a gallery in Dresden for their huge collection of contemporary art. Instead, they bought this complex, restored it, and installed the art here, along with their private residence, which includes an Olympic-sized swimming pool. Tours of the **Sammlung Hoffmann** are available – Saturdays, by appointment only, felt slippers de rigueur – but there are also text, earth and light works integrated into the structure, which can be seen until 10pm, as well as galleries, cafés and offices. Beyond is woodwind restorer **Johanna Petzold**'s wonderful shop of wood and straw handcrafts, the window of the book/stamp/postcard dealer, and, at night, the venerable Sophienclub, next to the Sophienstraße entrance to Hackesche Höfe.

Running from Oranienburger Straße to Rosenthaler Straße, Auguststraße is the very core of Berlin's eastern gallery district, with such important venues as **Eigen + Art** and **Kunst-Werk** among many others. This is now known as Mitte's 'Art Mile' and the street makes a good afternoon's stroll on any day of the week. Better still, many galleries on the Mile open their doors for a *Rundgang*, or 'walk around', generally on the first Saturday evening of each month. As you go from gallery to gallery, you could also possibly stop for refreshment at **Hackbarths** or **Ici**, or to watch a football kickaround on the pitch by Kleine Hamburger Straße.

Alexanderplatz & surrounds

Visitors who have read Alfred Döblin's *Berlin Alexanderplatz* or seen the multi-part television series by Faßbinder may arrive here and wonder what has happened. What happened was that in the early 1970s Erich Honecker decided that this historic square should reflect the glories of socialism, and tore it all down, replacing it with a masterpiece of commie kitsch: wide boulevards; monotonous white buildings filled with cafés and shops; and, of course, the impressive golf-ball-on-a-knitting-needle, the **Fernsehturm** ('Television Tower'), from whose observation deck and revolving restaurant you can soak in a fantastic view of the city on a clear day.

At ground level, capitalism's neon icons sit incongruously on Honecker's erections. A huge Panasonic television blares news and adverts at

Dominating Mitte's skyline – **Fernsehturm**.

The goofy World Time Clock.

busy shoppers; the goofy clock with the 1950s-style atom design on the top tells the time in (mostly) former socialist lands, water cascades from the Brunnen der Völkerfreundschaft ('Fountain of the Friendship of Peoples') and at the Markthalle you can sink beer or bite into a brand-name burger. There are plans to replace most of Alexanderplatz with a dozen or so skyscrapers, among which the Fernsehturm will likely remain standing.

Berliner Rathaus
Berlin Town Hall
Rathausstraße 10, Mitte, 10178 (902 60). S3, S5, S7, S9/U2, U5, U8 Alexanderplatz. **Open** 8am-6pm Mon-Fri. **Admission** free. **Map G3**
Berlin's town hall sits just off Alexanderplatz. This magnificent building was built of terracotta brick during the 1860s. The history of Berlin up to that point is illustrated in a series of 36 reliefs on the façade. During communist times, it served as East Berlin's town hall – which made its old nickname, Rotes Rathaus ('Red Town Hall'), after the colour of the façade, especially fitting. West Berlin's city government workers moved here from their town hall, Rathaus Schöneberg, in 1991. Guided tours are organised by appointment.

Fernsehturm
Television Tower
Alexanderplatz, Mitte, 10178 (242 3333). S3, S5, S7, S9/U2, U5, U8 Alexanderplatz. **Open** *Mar-Oct* 9am-1am daily; *Nov-Feb* 10am-midnight daily. **Admission** DM10; DM5 children 3-16; children under-3 free; last admission half an hour before closing. No disabled people admitted due to evacuation restrictions. **Map G3**
Built in the late 1960s at a time when relations between East and West Berlin were at their lowest ebb, the 365-metre tower – its ball-on-spike shape visible from all over the city – was intended as an assertion of communist dynamism and modernity. A shame then that such television towers were a West German invention. A shame, too, that they had to get Swedish engineers to build the thing. Communist authorities were also displeased to note a particular phenomenon: when the sun shines on the tower, reflections on the ball form the shape of a cross. Berliners dubbed this stigmata 'the Pope's revenge'. Nevertheless, the authorities were proud enough of the thing to make it one of the central symbols of East Germany's capital; its silhouette even used to form the 'i' in 'Berlin' on all GDR tourist information. No longer is it flaunted, but Berliners have grudgingly come to accept this modernist monstrosity. The Fernsehturm may be ugly, but it's a great way to orient yourself early on a visit to Berlin, as much of the city is visible from the top. Wend your way through the cheap tourist attractions in the lobby, take the elevator to the observation platform and you'll find a view of Berlin unbeatable by day or night – particularly looking westwards, where you can take in the whole of the Tiergarten and surrounding area. If heights make you hungry, take a twirl in the

revolving Telecafé restaurant, which offers an even better view plus a full menu of snacks and meals – including, for those who want something light, 'leg of lamp'.

Gedenkstätte Berliner Mauer

Wall Memorial
Bernauer Straße/Ackerstraße, Wedding, 13355 (464 1030). U8 Bernauer Straße. **Open** *documentation centre* 10am-5pm Wed-Sun. **Admission** free. **Map F2**
Immediately on Reunification, the city bought this stretch of the Wall to use as a memorial, and it was finally dedicated in 1998. Impeccably restored (graffiti disappears virtually overnight), it is also as sterile a monument as Berlin boasts, with a brass plaque decrying the communist 'reign of terror', which is regularly defaced. A documentation centre, featuring displays on the wall and a database of escapees, has recently opened across the street at Bernauer Straße 111, and from its roof you can view the Wall, and a 'Chapel of Reconciliation' – featuring the bells from a nearby church then trapped in no-man's-land – was under construction at press time. *See page 60* **The fall and decline of the Berlin Wall** *and chapter* **Museums**.

Marienkirche

Alexanderplatz, Mitte, 10178 (242 3600). S3, S5, S7, S9 Hackescher Markt. **Open** 10am-4pm Mon-Thur; noon-4pm Sat-Sun. **Admission** free. **Map G3**
Marienkirche, begun in 1270, is one of Berlin's few remaining medieval buildings. Just inside the door, a wonderful Berlinish Dance of Death fresco dating from 1485 is being painstakingly restored, and fans of organ music shouldn't miss a concert on the 18th-century Walther organ here, considered this famous builder's masterpiece. Marienkirche hit the headlines in 1989 when the new civil rights movement in East Berlin chose it for one of the first sit-ins in the city, since churches were one of the few places large numbers of people could congregate without needing state permission.

Nikolaiviertel

Mitte, 10178. S3, S5, S7, S9/U2, U5, U8 Alexanderplatz. **Map G3**
The oldest area in Berlin is centred around Nikolaikirche, dating from 1220, and was an awful GDR reconstruction job which contained an odd collection of artefacts that purported to tell the ancient history of Berlin. The 18th-century neighbourhood was severely damaged during the war, and the GDR's reconstruction, which involved bringing the few undamaged buildings from this period together into what is essentially a fake assemblage of history, is currently being re-reconstructed. There are a couple of historic residences, including the Ephraim-Palais, which once belonged to the court jeweller; Gottfried Lessing's house; restaurants; cafés (including a reconstruction of Zum Nußbaum, a contender for the oldest bar in Berlin); overpriced shops – and a definite old-time European feeling that's rare in Berlin these days.

Stadtmauer

City Wall
Littenstraße/Waisenstraße, Mitte, 10179. U2 Klosterstraße. **Map G3**
Long before the infamous Wall, Berlin had another one: the medieval city wall of the original 13th-century settlement. There's almost as much left of this wall as there is of the more recent one. Built along the wall is the old (and extremely popular) restaurant Zur Letzten Instanz, which takes its name from the neighbouring law court from which there was no further appeal. There has been a restaurant on this site since 1525, Napoleon among its customers. The building is one of four old houses that have been reconstructed.

Prenzlauer Berg

If the fall of the Wall has precipitated a renaissance in any neighbourhood in Berlin, it is surely Prenzlauer Berg. Long described as grey and depressing, an area of workers' houses unrelieved by any sites of historical or touristic interest, these days the east Berlin district has had its façades renovated, its streets cleaned, and its buildings newly inhabited by everyone from artists to yuppies. Galleries and cafés have sprung up, and hundred-year-old buildings have had central heating, bathrooms and telephones installed for the very first time.

Built around the turn of the century, Prenzlauer Berg seems to have had more visionary social planners than other neighbourhoods dating from the same period. It has wider streets and pavements, giving the area a distinctive, open look unique in Berlin. Although some buildings still await restoration, looking down a street that's been scrubbed and painted gives the impression of a 19th-century boulevard.

The hot centre of Prenz'lberg, as its inhabitants call it, is LSD, the section bounded by Lychener Straße to the east, Danziger Straße to the south and Schönhauser Allee to the west. Starting at the Senefelderplatz U-Bahn, up Schönhauser Allee to there's first a Jewish graveyard, Berlin's oldest and fairly gloomy even by local standards, due to its

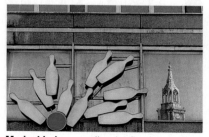

Marienkirche – *medieval reflection.*

closely-packed stones and canopy of trees. At Sredzkistraße stands an old brewery, the Kulturbraurei, that houses a huge furniture store, a grocery store, a huge restaurant/club/disco, called Soda, and a cinema.

The streets to the east of here are alive with other clubs, restaurants, and shops. One block of Husemannstraße was lovingly restored by the GDR for the city's 750th birthday and is today lined with boutiques, cafés like **November**, and restaurants like **Ostwind** and **Restauration 1900**. At number 12 the **Museum Berliner Arbeiterleben** is a reconstructed workers' apartment from around the same time that this neighbourhood was built.

Husemannstraße feeds into Kollwitzplatz, one of the prettiest spots in the area, a small park dedicated to the painter and social reformer Käthe Kollwitz, whose statue stands in the park. It was in the Café Westphal (now a Greek restaurant) here that the first meetings of East Berlin dissidents were held in the early 1980s, until they got too crowded and had to be moved to the nearby Gethsemane-Kirche. There are a few decent restaurants in this area, including **Gugelhof** and **Trattoria Lapeggi**.

It's well worth walking down Kollwitzstraße to take a look at the fluorescent cows installed in 1999 by a local artist, Sergei Alexander Dott, on the side

of number 18. From Kollwitzplatz, taking Knaackstraße brings you past a nicely restored synagogue to another pleasant square containing a small park with a water tower in it. Today there are apartments in the water tower, but the Nazis constructed a small prison in its basement, a fact noted by a memorial plaque. Again, this park is bounded by cafés such as **Pasternak** and **Anita Wronsky**, and is one of the centres of social life in Prenzlauer Berg.

Heading north on Prenzlauer Allee, you come to Ernst-Thälman-Park, named after the leader of the pre-1933 Communist Party in Germany. In its north-west corner stands the Zeiss Planetarium, a fantastic GDR interior space that once hymned Soviet cosmonauts and still runs programmes on what's up there in space. Considering the wide expanse of sky visible from most any street in Prenz'lberg, it seems a fitting symbol for the whole neighbourhood.

Another hot centre is the area around Kastanienallee, which has become a main commercial street with a decided Prenz'lberg flavour. The Volksbühne's Prater branch has a wonderful beer garden, and the **Bastard** club there is a major venue for hip hop.

Prenzlauer Berg has undergone rapid change, and has now reached the point where some of the original businesses are failing and being replaced by others. Like the more bohemian parts of Mitte, it hums with energy and creativity, much of it generated by the same artists, writers and musicians who lived here before the Wall came down – but, also as in Mitte, a certain yuppie sensibility is evident, particularly around Kollwitzplatz. It's a pleasant, somewhat edgy, place to walk around, sit in a café, or shop.

Friedrichshain

As first Mitte, then Prenzlauer Berg became gentrified, Berlin's restless bohemia needed new space, and this district was elected. It's a logical enough place, convenient to both Prenzlauer Berg and the incoming trains at Ostbahnhof, and it's the next step for an eastward-growing city. Although at the time of writing there were few galleries, the signs are there in the concentration of bars, restaurants, and natural-food stores on Simon-Dach-Straße and the parallel Gabriel-Max-Straße near Boxhagener Platz. You'll find one of the city's hipper musical venues, **Supamolly**, on Jessner Straße. North of Frankfurter Allee is another concentration of hangouts in the Rigaer Straße area. Friedrichshain, originally known as Stralau, was historically a largely industrial district, with Berlin's central wheat and rye mill and its first city hospital, and Osthaven, its eastern port. More than half of its buildings were destroyed by bombing in World War II.

U-Bahn over Schönhauser Allee.

Kollwitzstraße's, er....moo-ral.

The best way to get a feeling for both Friedrichshain and its place in the life of the GDR is to walk east from Alexanderplatz down Karl-Marx-Allee. The **Kino International** and the now-closed Café Moskau give hints, but at Lichtenberger Straße, with its twin cupolas, the street turns into socialist paradise, with row after row of Soviet-designed apartment buildings from the early 1950s, stretching as far as Proskauer Straße, giving you the distinct impression of being in Moscow. Keeping in mind the street's former name, Stalinallee, will just add to the feeling. These buildings are all listed, and are being restored, heroic statues of workers included. The theory was that each one should be a model of society, with apartments being let to all categories of workers, with artists and writers getting the top floors, odd for a supposedly egalitarian régime – and it was here that the workers' riots of 17 June 1953 started. An annual beer festival is held in August, a good time to visit, because the neighbourhood is out in force.

To the south, the area around Ostbahnhof features **Maria am Ostbahnhof**, one of Berlin's best-known clubs, and provides the current location for the **Tempodrom**, the tent which hosts the annual Heimatklänge festival of world music. (The Tempodrom will be moving to the Potsdamer Platz area sometime in 2001, if all goes according to plan.) It's also where you find the East Side

Gallery, a long stretch of former Wall along Mühlenstraße given to artists who decorated the original one. A bit shabby at the moment, it needs funds to restore the paintings; the city seems undecided as to whether to contribute. A number of other clubs are currently operating in the area – *see chapter* **Nightlife**. The industrial buildings here are in the process of undergoing transformation into shopping and business centres, and if you're interested in where the street got its name, the old mill is at number 8.

In Friedrichshain's north-west corner, abutting Prenzlauer Berg, is the Volkspark Friedrichshain, a huge park with assorted bits of socialist realist art, an open-air stage and an early 20th-century fountain of fairy tale characters among lush greenery. The graves of the fighters who fell in March 1848 in the battle for German unity are here. It's also a popular gay cruising zone.

Kreuzberg

Back in November 1994, one of the last Kreuzberg demonstrations attempted, rather pathetically, to prevent the opening of the Oberbaumbrücke. During the Cold War, this bridge across the Spree and into Friedrichshain was a border post and spy-exchange venue. Only pedestrians, most of them old-age pensioners from the East, could cross. Its renovation by Santiago Calatrava and its opening to the traffic that now surges across it, was effectively the fall of one of the last pieces of Wall. But it was also the fall of the Kreuzberg of old.

Around Oranienstraße

In the 1970s and 1980s, the eastern half of Kreuzberg north of the Landwehrkanal was off at the edge of inner West Berlin. Enclosed on two sides by the Wall, on a third by the canal, and mostly ignored by the rest of the city, its decaying tenements came to house Berlin's biggest, and most militant, squat community. The area was full of punky left-wing youth on a draft-dodging mission and Turks who came here because the rents

Landwehr Canal – dividing Kreuzberg.

The fall and decline of the Berlin Wall

In East German officialese it was known as the 'Anti-Fascist Protection Rampart'; in West Berlin it was simply Die Mauer; to the rest of the world it was the Berlin Wall. For 28 years it stood there, an historical reality made implacably concrete, snaking for 155km around the perimeter of West Berlin.

One of the most secure stretches of frontier in the world, star of stage, screen and radio and a handy backdrop for visiting politicians, it achieved the status of global symbol long before it was breached on 9 November 1989.

And now there is bugger all left of it.

The most central surviving stretch of Wall runs along Niederkirchnerstraße, just off Wilhelmstraße (S1, S2/U2 Potsdamer Platz), between the Luftfahrtsministerium and the **Topography of Terror** (*see chapter* **Museums**). It is a pock-marked piece, a block or two long, much of it chipped away by tourists with hammers. The remainder is now protected by a wire fence.

A longer stretch, now known as the East Side Gallery (*pictured*) and commemorating the Wall's traditional function as graffiti canvas, can be found along Mühlenstraße by the River Spree (S3, S5, S7, S9 Ostbahnhof). This is decked by mostly political work from various international artists and has been billed as the world's largest outdoor picture gallery. Its future is still in some doubt, as the paintings are faded fast and funds for restoration are short.

From the S-Bahn lines running across the Spree to the west of Friedrichstraße, you can see a length of Wall, graphically divided into 28 segments, each of them representing a year from 1961-1989.

For each year there is a body count of people killed trying to get over – over the years at least 80 people died. If you want to view this at ground level, it's at the corner of Reinhardtstraße and Schiffbauerdamm (S1, S2 Unter den Linden).

Another short stretch also stands in Bernauer Straße in Wedding, the main exhibit of the new **Dokumentationszentrum Berliner Mauer** attached to it. The Wall segment stands complete with a swathe of no-man's-land and various border defences.

There are also small hunks of Wall all over town. A few displaced slabs are still lying around on Potsdamer Platz. There is a piece at one of the Tauentzienstraße entrances to the Europa-Center. Various hotel lobbies also boast their very own chunks of Wall. Lo, how the mighty has fallen.

were cheap and people (mostly) left them alone. The air was filled with the smell of hashish, the sound of Turkish pop music and the clamour of political activity.

No area of west Berlin has changed quite so much since the Wall came down. This once isolated pocket found itself recast as desirable real estate in the centre of the unifying city. Gentrification threatened while Mitte and Prenzlauer Berg asserted themselves as the new centres of radical energy and underground nightlife. The entire alternative art scene uprooted and moved east into the Scheunenviertel and even the **May Day riots** – long an annual Kreuzberg tradition – began taking place in Prenzlauer Berg.

Oddly enough, gentrification never really took off in this end of Kreuzberg, but it did so in Prenzl'berg, and now the riots have moved back. Though Kreuzberg is no longer a magnet for young bohemia, enough of the anarchistic old

guard stayed behind to ensure that the area still has a distinct atmosphere. This half of Kreuzberg is still an earthy kind of place, full of cafés, bars and clubs, dotted with small cinemas, and is an important nexus for the city's gay community. It's just much, much quieter and a lot less radical than it used to be. A certain spark has gone. On some Tuesday nights, the once-teeming Oranienstraße might as well have tumbleweed blowing down the middle of the road.

One thing hasn't changed. It's still the capital of Turkish Berlin, the world's fifth-largest Turkish city. The area around Kottbusser Tor, with its kebab shops, Galatasaray supporters' club bars and Anatolian travel agents, is the heart of Turkish Berlin. The open-air **Türkischer Markt** stretches along the Maybachufer every Tuesday and Friday. Görlitzer Park, once an important train station, turns into one of the world's largest outdoor Turkish barbecues on fine weekends. The area is full of döner takeaways and Turkish grocery stores, while at night Turkish street gangs face off to defend their territories – mostly from other Turkish street gangs.

Oranienstraße is the area's main drag, still full of bars and clubs. Former punk venue **SO36** now hosts some of Berlin's most important gay one-nighters and **Roses**, the dyke/queer cruise bar, is along the road. Funky dance music still faintly rumbles from **Schnabelbar**. There are still more bars on this street than anyone could handle in one night out, and the area to the north and west of here is home to even more places – including **Café Anal**, **Markthalle** and **Abendmahl**. Fans of art deco in the service of commerce are urged to check out the gigantic warehouse on Pfuelstraße, which runs for a block towards the Spree.

South across Skalitzer Straße, Oranienstraße changes into Wiener Straße, running alongside the old Görlitzer Bahnhof, where bars and cafés such as **Madonna** and **Morena** welcome what's left of the old Kreuzberg crowd. A couple of blocks further south lies Paul-Linke-Ufer, the border with Neukölln, lined with canal-bank cafés that provide a favourite spot for weekend brunch.

The U1 line runs overhead through the neighbourhood along the middle of Skalitzer Straße. The onion-domed Schlesisches Tor U-Bahn station was once the end of the line. These days it continues one more stop across the Spree to Warschauer Brücke. You can also walk across into Friedrichshain and the post-industrial nightlife of Mühlenstraße. Heading east down Schlesische Straße leads you over the canal and into the borough of Treptow. The waterside **Club des Visionnaires** and the **Arena** concert venue are just along Puschkinallee, and Treptower Park with its **Soviet War Memorial,** lies beyond.

Around Bergmannstraße

The southern and western part of Kreuzberg, the one that actually has the 'cross hill' in Viktoriapark after which the borough is named, contains some of the most picturesque corners of west Berlin.

Viktoriapark is the natural way to enter the area. It has a cheery, fake waterfall cascading down the Kreuzberg, and paths wind their way to the summit, where Schinkel's 1821 monument commemorates victories in the Napoleonic Wars – most of the streets hereabouts are named after battles and generals of that era. From this commanding view over a mainly flat city, with the Schultheiss brewery at your back, the landmarks of both east and west spread out before you: Friedrichstraße dead ahead, the Europa-Center off to the left, construction around Potsdamer Platz in between the two, and the Fernsehturm over to the right. The view is better in winter, when the trees are bare, but the waterfall only runs in summer.

Back on ground level, walking along Kreuzbergstraße until it crosses Mehringdamm takes you on to Bergmannstraße, the main hub of neighbourhood activity. Bucking the general tendency of anything happening in Berlin to move eastwards, this street of cafés and junk shops, grocery stores and record shops by day does seem livelier than ever, although the area is relatively lacklustre at night (at a pinch it's worth trying **Galao** or the **Haifisch Bar**). It leads down to Marheineke-platz, site of one of Berlin's busiest market halls. Zossener Straße also bustles, and includes the **Freßco** café, **Space Hall** record shop (pick of the bunch, although there are several others in the area) and the **Grober Unfug** comic store, among its many businesses.

Bergmannstraße continues east to Südstern, past several large cemeteries, and eventually comes to the Hasenheide, the other of the neighbourhood's large parks, with another good view from atop the Rixdorfer Höhe.

If you've ever seen 'old Berlin' in a movie, chances are it was filmed in the streets just to the south of Bergmannstraße. Many buildings in this neighbourhood survived the wartime bombing and the area around Chamissoplatz has been immaculately restored. The cobbled streets are lined with houses still sporting their Prussian façades and illuminated by gaslight at night. This is one of the most beautiful parts of this largely unbeautiful city, and also contains **Ristorante am Chamissoplatz**, an excellent neighbourhood Italian joint, and two theatres noted for English-language work: **Theater Zerbrochene Fenster** and **Friends of Italian Opera**.

The edge of this area is dominated by the hulking presence of the Columbushaus, a red-brick monster that once had a Nazi prison in its basement and is currently used by the police for car registration. Beyond that, just across the border into the borough of the same name, stands the huge Tempelhof Airport. Once the central airport for the city, it was begun in the 1920s and later greatly expanded by the Nazis. The largest building in Berlin – and one of the largest in the world – its curving bulk looms with an authoritarian ominousness. (*See page 67* **Remnants of the Reich.**)

Tempelhof Airport was where main German national carrier Lufthansa Airlines started, but its place in the city's affections was cemented during the Berlin Airlift of 1948-49, when it served as the base for the 'raisin-bombers', which flew in and out at a rate of one a minute, bringing much needed supplies to the blockaded city and tossing sweets and raisins to kids who were waiting close by as the planes taxied in. The monument forking towards the sky on Platz der Luftbrücke nearby commemorates the pilots and navigators who flew these missions, as does a photo-realist painting stuck over in a corner of the terminal building.

Kreuzberg – centre of Turkish Berlin.

After commercial flights to Tempelhof were discontinued in the early 1970s, it became the centre of the US air operation in Berlin. Today it's once more a civil airport catering to small airlines running small planes on short-hop European routes.

This facility uses only a tiny fraction of the Tempelhof's enormous structure, other parts of which have been converted into entertainment venues, such as **Hangar II**, which occasionally houses a club of the same name, and the **La Vie en Rose** cabaret. Over on the other side of Columbiadamm are the **Columbiahalle** and **ColumbiaFritz** concert venues.

Schöneberg

Both geographically and in terms of atmosphere, Schöneberg lies between Kreuzberg and Charlottenburg. It's a diverse part of town, mostly built in the late 19th century and these days veering from 'alternative' to upmarket. Though largely devoid of conventional sights, it's rich in intriguing reminders of Berlin's recent history.

In English Schöneberg means 'beautiful hill' – oddly, because the borough's mostly as flat as a pancake. It does have an island, though: the triangular Schöneberger Insel, carved away from the rest of the city by the broad railway cuttings that carry S-Bahn lines 1 and 2, with an elevated stretch of line S45/46 providing the southern boundary. In the 1930s it was known as Rote Insel ('Red Island'), because, approached mostly over bridges and thus easy to defend, the area was one of the last to resist the Nazification of Berlin. Walking between the island and Kreuzberg's Viktoriapark, there's a fine view of central east Berlin from Monumentenbrücke. Around here can be found the pocket-sized **Scheinbar** cabaret and the agreeable **Café Aroma** Italian restaurant. On the north-west edge of the island is St Matthäus-Kirchhof, a large graveyard and last resting place of children's storytellers, the Brothers Grimm.

The Langenscheidtbrücke – named after the dictionary publishers whose offices stand on the western side – leads you towards the Kleistpark intersection. Here Schöneberg's main street is called Hauptstraße to the south and Potsdamer Straße to the north. Hauptstraße leads south-west in the direction of Potsdam. David Bowie and Iggy Pop once resided at number 152 – Bowie in a big, first-floor apartment at the front, Iggy in a more modest Hinterhof flat. The **Odeon** cinema, favourite haunt of Anglophone movie-goers, lies in this direction, but it's a good, long walk. Dominikuskirche nearby is one of Berlin's few Baroque churches.

North along Potsdamer Straße from Kleistpark U-Bahn is the entrance to Kleistpark itself – an 18th-century double colonnade which was moved here from near Alexanderplatz in 1910. The park was once Berlin's first botanical gardens. The mansion in it was formerly a law court (where the 1944 July bomb plotters were sentenced to death), and after the war it became the headquarters for the Allied Control Council. After the signing of the Ost-Verträge in 1972, which formalised the separate status of East and West Germany, the building stood virtually unused. What it did see were occasional Allied Council meetings, before which the Americans, British and French would observe a ritual pause, as if expecting the Soviet representative, who had last attended in 1948, to show up. In 1990, a Soviet finally did wander in and the Allies held a last meeting here to formalise their withdrawal from the city in 1994. This may be the place where the Cold War officially ended.

On the north-west corner of Potsdamer Straße's intersection with Pallasstraße stood the Sportpalast, site of many Nazi rallies and scene of Goebbels' 'Total War' speech of 1944. Leading west along Pallasstraße from here is a block of flats straddling the road and resting on the south side atop the huge hulk of a concrete Nazi air-raid shelter planners were unable to destroy. It, along with some of the used furniture shops on nearby Goebenstraße, featured in Wim Wenders' film *Wings of Desire*.

Nollendorfplatz to the north and west forms the central hub of Schöneberg's night-time activities. Outside Nollendorfplatz U-Bahn, the memorial to the homosexuals killed in concentration camps is a reminder of the immediate area's history – Christopher Isherwood chronicled Berlin from his rooming house at Nollendorfstraße 17, and currently Motzstraße is one of the hottest centres of Berlin's gay life. At number 5 can be found the **Mann-O-Meter** information centre and further along are bars, clubs and shops such as **Tom's Bar, Hafen** and **Scheune**. Gay Schöneberg continues around the corner and across Martin-Luther-Straße into Fuggerstraße, home of **Knaast, Connection, Prinzknecht** and other prime homosexual haunts.

South of Nollendorfplatz along Maaßenstraße, you come to Winterfeldtplatz, site of bustling Wednesday and Saturday morning produce markets, engendering a particularly lively café life. Winterfeldtstraße has many antiquarian bookshops and at night the area is full of bars and restaurants.

Down Goltzstraße cafés and bars mingle with rather pricey but nonetheless interesting shops. Across Grunewaldstraße the street turns into Akazienstraße and ends up back at Hauptstraße, but a left turn before this on Belziger Straße brings you eventually to Rathaus Schöneberg. At these steps John F Kennedy announced that he was a Berliner in 1963, and Berlin mayor Walter Momper welcomed East Berliners in 1989.

Perhaps the best way to get to know Schöneberg, though, is through its many lively restaurants, bars, and cafés – sipping a cappuccino at the **Café Berio**, tucking into a hearty plateful of Alsatian food at the **Storch**, downing a beer at the **Pinguin**. Talk to the locals. They won't mind – this is one of the most cosmopolitan areas of Berlin and most of them were once strangers here themselves.

Zoo area

Not as central as it once was, Bahnhof Zoo is still the arrival point for many Berlin visitors, and nearly everyone winds up here at some stage in their visit. It's the gateway to the centre of the former West Berlin, and, obviously, it's got the zoo, one of the world's largest.

Hymned by U2 and centrepiece of the film *Christiane F*, Bahnhof Zoo was once a spooky anomaly – slap in the middle of West Berlin but policed by the East, who controlled the inter-city rail system – and a seedy hangout for junkies and old soaks. Today it has a postmodernised interior full of glossy chain stores and self-service food outlets, and now the façades are also being spruced up. The original building was designed in 1882 by Ernst Dircksen; the modern glass sheds were added in 1934.

The surrounding area, with its mixture of sleaze and shopping, huge cinemas and bustling crowds (during the daytime, anyway) is the gateway to the

S-Bahn lines – defining the Schöneberger Insel.

Won't you come into my parlour?

If Potsdamer Platz represents an attempt to craft an urban space that will remain modern through the rest of this century, nearby Pariser Platz is a bizarre bid to recreate the essentials of a space that might have been relevant a hundred years ago.

The Brandenburg Gate is one of the city's original 18 – the one on the route to Brandenburg and at the end of Unter den Linden, the road leading into the power centre of Prussian Germany. Pariser Platz, lying just within the city boundary and site of the Gate, acquired a special significance: it was the city's *Empfangssaal* – reception room. The name commemorates the German occupation of Paris in 1814, and for a 135 years after that, foreign dignitaries would ceremoniously pass over it on their way from Lehrter Bahnhof to visit German tyrants and dictators downtown.

Sitting just inside East Berlin during the Cold War, for decades the only life visible on Pariser Platz was the occasional group of Russian soldiers posing for snapshots. It might have been ground zero of geopolitical tensions for decades, but Berlin's reception room had been rather unceremoniously re-zoned into a broom closet.

With the fall of the Wall, Pariser Platz quickly became filled with scores of vendors hawking Soviet militaria, Russian kitsch and assorted wall fragments, as city planners, investors and architects argued furiously over its future. The local government eventually prevailed in a scheme which seemed to be saying, 'Look, we'll let all hell break loose on Potsdamer Platz, but here, in front of the Brandenburg Gate, we want the kind of order and predictability that sum up what we think is the only acceptable version of our national heritage'.

Its original function as a reception room now irrelevant with the centre of power shifting to the new government quarter to the north, some inspired commentator described the new Pariser Platz as Berlin's *Gute Stube* – its front room or parlour, the kind that is kept in pristine condition but never gets used unless the vicar comes to call. In German the phrase has unfortunate, but fully intended, bourgeois undertones. As soon as it started circulating, the souvenir sellers were swept out of sight.

The application of private-space semantics to public-space planning is why Pariser Platz feels the way it does today. Whether you like it or not depends on how comfortable you feel in a stranger's finickity living-room.

The city placed strict codes on dimensions, regularity and materials to ensure structures differed little in tone from their pre-war predecessors. Flower beds and fountains were recreated (but oddly for a sitting-room, no benches) to restore linear discipline, and then the architects went to work, creating their own metaphor.

While outwardly conforming to the restrictions, inside, many buildings harbour flights of fancy prohibited at street level. Frank O Gehry's DG Bank contains a huge, biomorphic interior dome, like something out of *Alien*. The Dresdner Bank opposite is virtually hollow. And next door the French Embassy will feature a space-saving 'vertical garden' on the courtyard wall. It'll have benches all right. But not for sitting.

Kurfürstendamm, the main shopping street of west Berlin. The discos and bars along Joachimstaler Straße are best avoided – the opening of the **Beate Uhse Erotik-Museum** actually added a touch of class to the area – but the rest of this district is worth a wander.

The **Zoo Palast** cinema on Budapester Straße was once one of the central venues of the Berlinale Film Fest (now relocated to Potsdamer Platz), and still provides a touch of cinematic glitz. The **British Council** on Hardenbergstraße has a useful English-language library. Breitscheidplatz has the ruined **Kaiser-Wilhelm-Gedächtnis-kirche** rising in its midst and the **Europa-Center**, whose Mercedes star can be seen from much of the rest of the city, is a sort of monument to the West Berlin of the past. Its exterior looks best when neon-lit at night.

Tauentzienstraße is the westernmost piece of the *Generalzug*, a sequence of streets laid out by Peter Joseph Lenné to link the west end with Kreuzberg and points east. Constructed around 1860 they are all named after Prussian generals from the wars against Napoleon: Tauentzien; Kleist; Bülow; Yorck, and Gneisenau. The tubular steel sculpture in the central reservation east along Tauentzienstraße was commissioned for the city's 750th anniversary in 1987 and represents the then divided city in that the two halves twine around each other but never meet. The street runs along past **KaDeWe**, Berlin's most prestigious department store, to Wittenbergplatz. The 1911 neo-classical U-Bahn station by Alfred Grenander is a listed building and has been wonderfully restored with wooden kiosks and old ads on the walls. Outside stands a memorial to those who died in

Brothers Grimm – happily ever after.

concentration camps, looking eerily like a departure board in a train station.

A block further is the huge steel sculpture at an der Urania (no, we've never seen anybody skateboard it) with its grim monument to children killed in traffic by Berlin's drivers. This marks the end, or the beginning, of the western 'downtown'.

Europa-Center
Tauentzienstraße 9-12, Charlottenburg, 10789. S3, S5, S7, S9/U2, U9 Zoologischer Garten. **Map D4**
The Europa-Center, a 22-storey skyscraper attached to a shopping area and cultural centre, was built in 1965 and looks it. Intended as the anchor for the development of a new western downtown around Breitscheidplatz, it was the first of Berlin's genuinely tall buildings and was now the grande dame of the city's shopping malls. It houses a tourist information centre, around a hundred stores, restaurants,

the largest of Berlin's many Irish pubs, cinemas, a hotel (**Hotel Palace**) and Die Stachelschweine, a cabaret. It even contains the **Thermen**, a posh (and expensive) swimming pool and sauna facility. You can swim outside, even in winter. The strange sculpture in front was erected in 1983. It is officially called Weltenbrunnen ('Fountain of the Worlds'), but like almost everything else in Berlin, it has a nickname: *der Wasserklops* ('Water Meatball').

KaDeWe
Tauentzienstraße 21-24, Schöneberg, 10789 (212 10). U1, U2, U15 Wittenbergplatz. **Open** 9.30am-8pm Mon-Fri; 9am-4pm Sat. **Credit** AmEx, DC, MC, V. **Map D4**
Das Kaufhaus des Westens – 'Department Store of the West' – is the largest department store in continental Europe. Founded in 1907 by Adolf Jandorf, in 1926 acquired by Herman Tietz and later 'aryanised' and expropriated by the Nazis, it is the only one of Berlin's famous turn-of-the-century department stores to have survived the war intact. It was reconstructed in 1950 and extensively modernised in the 1990s. The most famous feature is the sixth-floor food hall, and rightly so. The array and variety of food is mind-boggling and there are numerous places to stop, eat and drink. *See also* chapter **Shopping & Services**.

Kaiser-Wilhelm-Gedächtniskirche
Kaiser-Wilhelm Memorial Church
Breitscheidplatz, Charlottenburg, 10789 (218 5023). S3, S5, S7, S9/U2, U9 Zoologischer Garten. **Open** 9am-7pm Mon-Sat; *old tower* 9am-4pm Mon-Sat; *guided tours* 1.15pm Wed-Fri. **Admission** free. **Map D4**

Rathaus Schöneberg – where Kennedy became a Berliner.

Europa-Center – *the grande dame of Berlin's malls. See page 65.*

One of Berlin's most well-known sights, and one at its most dramatic by night. The neo-Romanesque church was built at the end of the 19th century in honour of – you guessed it – Kaiser Wilhelm I. Much of the structure was destroyed during an Allied air raid in 1943. These days the church serves as a stark reminder of the damage done by the war, although some might argue that the bombing has improved what was originally a profoundly ugly structure. The ruin of the tower is flanked on either side by modern extensions – including tubes with stunning blue stained-glass windows that glow eerily at night – and which contain the sanctuary in use today by the congregation.

Zoologischer Garten

Hardenbergplatz 8, Tiergarten, 10787 (254 010). S3, S5, S7, S9/U2, U9 Zoologischer Garten. **Open** 9am-5pm daily. **Admission** *zoo* DM14; DM7 children; *aquarium* DM14; DM7 children; *combined admission* DM22.50; DM11.50 children. **Map D4**
Germany's oldest zoo was opened in 1841 to designs by Martin Lichtenstein and Peter Joseph Lenné. Various other architects designed the individual animal habitats, most of which were destroyed in the war. The site had previously been occupied by a pheasantry, founded in 1742 with the royal dinner table in mind. With 13,826 animals, the Zoologischer Garten is today one of the largest and most important zoos in the world, with more endangered species in its collection than any in Europe save Antwerp's. Given its age, it has some surprisingly modern exhibits. Try not to trip over the mouse deer running through the Vietnamese rain forest, which has no fence, and chance an encounter with a similarly

unencumbered rhinoceros, separated from you only by a trench. The zoo is huge, so if you're with the kids, zero in on some specific areas rather than try to see the whole thing at once. There are plenty of places to sit down and have a coffee, beer or *Bratwurst*, and in summer sometimes even an oom-pah band. The aquarium can be entered either from within the zoo or from its own entrance on Olof-Palme-Platz by the reconstructed Elephant Gate, and is a good option for a rainy day. It is also one of the world's most varied, comprising more than 500 species displayed in four sections: Oceanic; Freshwater; Crocodile Hall; and Insectarium. Its dark corridors and liquid ambience, with colourful tanks lit up and curious aquarian creatures moving behind thick refracting glass, are as absorbing as many an art exhibit.

Charlottenburg

Before the fall of the Wall, Charlottenburg *was* Berlin to most tourists. They stayed in hotels on and off the Kurfürstendamm, did their shopping there, and if they were museum-goers, went to the complex around **Schloß Charlottenburg**. There's much more Berlin to see now, but Charlottenburg, the city's west end again, is still worth a wander.

Around the Kurfürstendamm

West Berlin's tree-lined shopping boulevard is named after the Prussian Kurfürst ('Elector') – and for centuries it was nothing but a track leading

Remnants of the Reich

Hitler and his pet architect Albert Speer had grandiose plans for Berlin – or Germania, as it was to be renamed.

Once the rest of the world had been subjugated, the capital of the Thousand-Year Reich would be equipped with dinky features like a monstrous hall with a dome 16 times the size of St Peter's in Rome, a triumphal arch three times as tall as the one in Paris, a chancellery that would require visiting diplomats to take a chastening quarter-mile hike once inside the building, and a Führer's palace no less than 150 times the size of Bismarck's.

Well, war put a stop to all that and Allied bombs demolished much of what the Nazis actually did build. Some fine examples of fancy fascist architecture did, however, survive.

Fans of tyrannical town-planning might start with Flughafen Tempelhof (Tempelhofer Damm, U6 Platz der Luftbrücke). Originally opened in 1923, this airport was greatly expanded by the Nazis and had its place in Speer's plan for Germania. Not only the largest building in Berlin but one of the largest in the world, its 400m quarter-circle form is probably best appreciated from the air. At ground level it's impossible to take in all at once.

Somehow the Luftfahrtsministerium – the Nazi air ministry (corner of Leipziger Straße and Wilhelmstraße, S1, S2/U2 Potsdamer Platz) – survived wartime bombardment and went on to house various East German ministries until the Wall came down. Overbearing and bureaucratic, this is totalitarian architecture at its bleakest. The finance ministry is now moving in here as it arrives from Bonn.

The **Olympiastadion** in Neu-Westend, set for Leni Riefenstahl's ground-breaking documentary film *Olympische Spiele*, orchestrates height, space and enclosure in a way that is both chilling and thrilling. Built as a Nazi showpiece for the world on the occasion of the 1936 Olympic Games, this actually does what fascist architecture was intended to do: impress. It's not the most comfortable of stadiums to sit in, though, especially in winter. *See chapter* **Sport & Fitness**.

The one piece of Hitler's plans for Germania that did get built was Speer's East-West Axis, running from the Brandenburg Gate west through the city. The Siegessäule was moved in 1938 from the Reichstag to its present location, and four small guardhouses built at that time in Third Reich style survive today. The ornamen-

tal lamp posts (*pictured*) that still line Straße des 17. Juni, Bismarckstraße and Kaiserdamm were also part of the design for the East-West Axis.

Other remnants of the Third Reich include the ensemble of offices around Fehrbelliner Platz (U1, U7 Fehrbelliner Platz) which are now used by the city Senate; the Finanzamt at Bismarckstraße 48 (U2 Bismarckstraße), where the Nazi eagle now clutches the street number instead of a swastika; the Reichsbank building at Werderscher Markt in Mitte (U2 Hausvogteiplatz); and the ruins of the Gestapo HQ at the Topography of Terror.

There are also assorted blank, grey concrete Nazi flak towers around town, including one on Pallasstraße near the junction with Potsdamer Straße, one up at Humboldthain which has had a park landscaped around it, and one on Albrechtstraße in Mitte.

And at the corner of Loewenhardtdamm and General-Pape-Straße on the border of Tempelhof and Schöneberg stands a giant cylinder of concrete. This was to be the site of Hitler and Speer's outsized triumphal arch, and in 1941 the concrete was poured in to test whether the local sandy soil would bear the weight of its foundations. Now it stands alone and forgotten in an overgrown patch of weeds.

Kaiser-Wilhelm-Gedächtniskirche. *Page 65.*

from the Elector's residence to the royal hunting palace in the Grunewald. In 1881 Bismarck insisted it be built up into a 5.3m-wide street. To the south many villas were put up, and though few survive today, one surviving example is the ensemble now containing the **Käthe-Kollwitz-Museum**, the **Villa Griesbach** auction house and the Literaturhaus Berlin with its **Wintergarten am Literaturhaus** café on Fasanenstraße. The villas were soon replaced by upmarket tenement buildings with enormous apartments – sometimes upwards of ten rooms and as large as 500sq m. About half of the original buildings were destroyed in the war and replaced by functional office buildings, but there remain many bombastic old structures.

The ground-level Ku'damm soon developed into an elegant shopping boulevard. It remains so today with cinemas (mostly showing dubbed Hollywood fare), restaurants (from the venerable **Bovril** to assorted brand-name burger joints), and upmarket fashion shops – the Ku'damm (as locals call it) is a street dedicated to separating you from your Deutschmarks. The side streets to the south are a bit quieter, albeit even more upmarket, and Bleibtreustraße to the north has more shops and some of the most outrageous examples of 19th-century *Gründerzeit* architecture in Berlin.

The Ku'damm-Eck on the south-east corner of the intersection of Ku'damm and Joachimstaler Straße was formerly West Berlin's rather weak answer to Piccadilly Circus, with a giant video screen and neon ads. The old building was torn down in 1999 to make way for a new complex with a hotel, department store and gallery. Diagonally across from it at the Kranzler-Eck, a Helmut Jahn-designed ensemble is going up around the famous old Café Kranzler, with a 16-storey tower and pedestrian courtyards including a habitat for various exotic birds. Other notable new architecture in the area includes the Kant-Dreieck on the corner of Fasanenstraße and Kantstraße with its large metal 'sail'; and British high-tech architect Nicholas Grimshaw's Ludwig-Erhard-Haus for the Stock Exchange at Fasanenstraße 83-84.

Kantstraße more or less parallels the Ku'damm to the north, and has the grandiloquently eclectic **Theater des Westens** and more shops to look in. Since the opening of the **Stilwerk Design Center**, the stretch around Fasanenstraße and beyond Savignyplatz has become a centre for designer homeware stores. Leafy Savignyplatz has numerous foreign media offices, and more chic places, particularly the restaurants, cafés and shops on Grolmanstraße (**Florian**, **Café Savigny**) and in the Savignypassage (**XII Apostoli**, **Aedes**, **Bücherbogen**). Knesebeckstraße is a street for bookshops, including many antiquarian dealers on the northern stretch and the excellent **Marga Schoeller Bücherstube**.

Charlottengrad

The sound of throaty Russian vowels on Charlottenburg's streets is almost as common as Turkish tones in Kreuzberg. A highly visible community of Russian émigrés, ranging from migrant workers to mobile-toting nouveaux riches, contributes to the flair of this western district.

From 1919 to 1923, Berlin was haven to Russian émigrés of all stripes – monarchists fleeing the October Revolution, but also Mensheviks and anarchists, as well as artists and intellectuals attracted to Dadaism's new centre. Artists such as Marc Chagall, El Lissitzky, Naum Gabo and Vassily Kandinsky, writers Ilya Ehrenburg, Marina Zvetaeva, Maxim Gorky, Andrei Bely, Nina Berberova, Victor Sklovsky and Vladimir Nabokov, actor Ivan Mosjukin and film producer Josef Yermolev, all sojourned in the city, profiting from and contributing to the experimental edge of 1920s Berlin.

There are estimated to have been over 300,000 Russian émigrés in Berlin at this time, and the lion's share settled in Charlottenburg, so earning the district the nickname of

*Aquarium at the **Zoologischer Garten** – don't try this in the Crocodile House. Page 66.*

'Charlottengrad'. Here was the most significant Russian exile community in Europe, surpassing even the one in Paris. Schools, restaurants, grocers', churches, libraries, art galleries, newspapers and journals, not only catered to the emigrant community but also enriched the city's cosmopolitan tapestry. The Blauer Vogel cabaret gained renown beyond expat circles, and the Bauhaus wouldn't have been the same without the influence of Kandinsky and El Lissitzky.

Yet the expats seem to have received less than they gave – few Russian writers, for example, refer to their host city in works from this time – Nabokov's *The Gift* (actually set in the 1930s after Charlottengrad's heyday) being the one notable exception. Many shared El Lissitzky's sentiment that Berlin was merely a 'transit station', and by the mid-1920s, the creative exiles had either returned home to an intermittently stabilised Soviet Union or moved on to Paris and the US. Only Nabokov held out until 1937, before leaving for France and later the country that would inspire his signature work *Lolita*. The rise of the Nazis and ensuing hostile relations between Germany and the Soviet Union, Non-Aggression-Pact aside, severed Berlin's Russian connection.

East Berlin, capital of the 'socialist brother country', was populated by diplomats, KGB agents and other Soviet functionaries throughout the life of the GDR. The dissolution of the Soviet Union in 1991 then saw renewed immigration from Russia. Jews and Russians with German ancestry were allowed to settle, and post-Wall boomtown Berlin attracted cultural movers and shakers as well as merchants in legal and not-so-legal commerce. While nowhere near the high-water mark of the 1920s, more than 23,000 Russians and other nationals of former European CIS states constitute the city's fourth largest non-German community after Turks, ex-Yugoslavs and Poles. Once again, more Russians live in Charlottenburg than in any other district.

While most landmarks of Charlottengrad were destroyed in World War II, the district still harbours many focal points of the Russian community: Saria, selling home-made pyel'meni (Russian ravioli); Knigi Russkiye, purveying Russian books and assorted artefacts at Kantstraße 82; the culinary institutions of the fancy Samovar restaurant (Luisenplatz 3); the more bohemian Café Hegel (Savignyplatz 2), plus an irregular Russian *Stammtisch* (regulars' table) at **Florian** (*see chapter* **Restaurants**). With Berlin as a turnstile between east and west, Russians will continue to gravitate towards the Charlottengrad outpost.

Concerts & conferences

The futuristic International Conference Centre (ICC) at the top of Neue Kantstraße was built in the 1970s and is used for pop concerts, political rallies and alike. Next door, the even larger Messe- und Ausstellungsgelände ('Trade Fair and Exhibition Area'), bits of which date back to the late 1920s, plays host to trade fairs ranging from electronics to food to aerospace (the annual **Grüne Woche** and **Funkaustellung** are popular); from the top of the **Funkturm**, you can get a panoramic view of western Berlin. Hans Poelzig's nearby Haus des Rundfunks (Masurenallee 9-14) is an expressive example of monumental modernism in brick.

A little further out of the centre, Hitler's impressive **Olympiastadion** is the home turf for the revived **Hertha BSC** football club and other sports and concert events. (*See page 67* **Remnants of the Reich**) Its swimming pool is popular in summer. The Maifeld, once the parade-ground for the British Army, is now open to the public again, for rock concerts and other large gatherings, and the **Waldbühne** beyond is Berlin's most popular outdoor concert and cinema venue in the summertime.

Funkturm

Radio Tower
Messedamm, 14055 (3038 1905). U2 Theodor-Heuss-Platz. **Open** 11am-9pm Mon; 10am-11pm Tue-Sun. **Admission** DM6; DM3 concs. **Map A4**
The 138 metre-high Funkturm was built in 1926 and looks not unlike a smaller version of the Eiffel Tower. The Observation Deck stands at 126m. Vertigo sufferers should seek solace in the restaurant, which is only 55m from the ground.

Olympiastadion

Olympic Stadium
Olympischer Platz 3, Charlottenburg, 14053 (3006 3430). U2 Olympia-Stadion (Ost)/S5 Olympiastadion. **Open** 8am-8pm daily, except event days. **Admission** DM2; DM1 concs.
Designed by Werner March and opened in 1936 for the Olympic Games – an attempt at aryan propaganda that was gloriously sunk by Jesse Owens, much to Hitler's chagrin. The 76,000-seat stadium has been recently equipped with new plastic bucket seats, but is still mostly uncovered. It may be an impressive piece of architecture, but it still is an uncomfortable place – until it gets an overhaul for the 2006 World Cup. Home of Hertha BSC, it also hosts the German Cup Final, plus other sporting events and rock concerts.

Around Schloß Charlottenburg

Impressive though a lot of the buildings on the long street variously named Bismarckstraße or Kaiserdamm are, the building that brought Charlottenburg into being is still the ruler here. Coming into view as you walk up Schloßstraße, Queen Sophie Charlotte's summer palace – **Schloß Charlottenburg** – was intended to be Berlin's answer to Versailles. Today, the Schloß is most interesting as a park – the guided tours are conducted in German only, and the museums on the grounds proper are mostly of interest to specialists – but they easily transport the visitor back to the 18th century. The museums across the street are another matter, and worth visiting, especially: the **Ägyptisches Museum**, the **Bröhan Museum** and the **Museum für Vor- und Frühgeschichte**.

International Conference Centre – mid-1970s rallying point.

The dome of democracy

Described by Kaiser Wilhelm II as the 'Imperial Monkey House', scene of unseemly Weimar squabblings, left as a burnt-out ruin during the Third Reich, regarded by the Red Army as its main prize, and stranded for forlorn decades beside the Wall which divided the *Deutsches Volk* whose representatives it was intended to house, the Reichstag has never had an exactly happy history. Classically the place has satisfied neither democrats nor autocrats. It was controversial from the very beginning, as architect Paul Wallot struggled to find a style that would symbolise German national identity at a time – 1884-94, shortly after Unification – when no such style (or identity) existed.

Shortly after Reunification, the 1995 Christo wrap was meant to draw a somewhat ironic line under all that, and five million visitors enjoyed the building's familiar contours parcelled up in aluminium-coated fabric. For Christo, the 20-year struggle to gain approval was as important as the project itself, his intention explicitly to stimulate 'a discussion about the significance of the building and its place in Berlin, in Germany, and in history'.

Sir Norman Foster, whose brilliant refitting of the building was unveiled to the general public in April 1999, has sim-

ilarly conceived his architectural approach as a 'dialogue between old and new'. Graffiti scrawled by Russian soldiers in 1945, for example, has been left in view and there has been no attempt to clean up or even deny the building's turbulent history.

His crowning achievement is the new cupola. No dome appeared on his original competition-winning plans, but the German government insisted upon one. Foster in turn insisted that unlike the structure's original dome (damaged in the war and demolished in the 1950s), the new one should be a public space, open to visitors, and this he has achieved.

A trip up to the top of the Reichstag dome is one of the most worthwhile experiences the 'new Berlin' has to offer. It's free, there's rarely more than a 15-minute wait, and a lift whisks you to the roof in seconds. From there, a double-helix of ramps lead up to the top, affording fine views of the new capital that is taking shape all around. The only comparable experience is

ascending the Fernsehturm, but that's so much taller than anything which surrounds it the visitor feels totally divorced from the city below. In the Reichstag cupola you feel very much in the thick of things – emphasising the building's new connection to the city and the society in which it functions.

The dome has other uses too. Open at the top, it serves as an air-extraction system, eliminating the need for air conditioning. At its centre is a funnel of mirrors angled so as to shed light on the workings of democracy below, providing exactly the kind of scattered light that news crews need to film their reports. They also have an almost funhouse effect: strolling the spiral walkways, the visitor can see his head in this mirror, his legs in that one. Foster has managed to create a space that is open, playful and defiantly democratic. It's difficult not to see this as an excellent omen for the infant Berlin Republic: a house of representatives that is now truly representative in character.

Schloß Charlottenburg – Berlin's answer to Versailles.

The streets just south of Bismarckstraße, particularly those named after philosophers (Leibniz, Goethe) have a lot of interesting small shops selling antiques, books, and the fashions that well-to-do residents sport around Charlottenburg's cafés and restaurants.

Gedenkstätte Plötzensee

Plötzensee Memorial

Hüttigpfad, Charlottenburg, 13627 (344 3226). Bus 123. **Open** *Mar-Sept* 8am-6pm daily; *Oct, Feb* 8.30am-5.30pm daily; *Nov, Jan* 9.30am-4.30 pm daily; *Dec* 9.30am-4pm daily. **Admission** free.

The Nazis executed 2,500 political prisoners here. In a single night in 1943, 186 people were hanged in groups of eight. In 1952 it was declared a memorial to the victims of fascism. There is little to see today, apart from the execution area with its meat hooks upon which victims were hung, and a small room with an exhibition of death warrants and pictures of some of the leading members of the resistance. Booklets in English are available from the information office. The stone urn near the entrance is filled with earth from Nazi concentration camps. Today the rest of the prison is a juvenile corrective centre.

Tiergarten

Originally a hunting reserve for the local princes, the park which has given this district its name is one of the most pleasant in Europe. It was opened to the public at the same time as the Brandenburg Gate was dedicated – and they're still flocking to the place today. On a sunny day, the Tiergarten plays host to thousands of nature-lovers, joggers, kids, football players, gay cruisers and any number of Turkish barbecues. It's so lovely that you may be tempted to pitch a tent, but don't – that would be *streng verboten*. Around the park's outskirts, there are lots of hints of the past, such as the stretch of Tiergartenstraße which contains pre-war Embassy Row, currently being rebuilt. Just beyond this is the Kulturforum, housing the **Neue Nationalgalerie**, the **Gemäldegalerie**, the **Staatsbibliothek**, and the **Philharmonie**, home to the Berlin Philharmonic Orchestra and famous for offering near-perfect acoustics and near-perfect vision from all of its 2,200 seats. (There's also the **Musikinstrumenten Museum** tucked away in a corner of the Philharmonie complex.) Also in this area is the **Bauhaus Archiv-Museum für Gestaltung**, documenting the work and history of the famous design school.

Even the street which cuts through the park as its main thoroughfare, Straße des 17. Juni, has a Cold War reference, its name serving as a grim reminder of the East Berlin workers' strike of 1953. The street itself, with its enormous roundabout, the Großer Stern, is one piece of Hitler's plan for Germania (*see also page 67* **Remnants of the Reich** *and chapter* **Architecture**). The **Siegessäule** ('Victory Column') at the Großer Stern was moved there from in front of the Reichstag, where Hitler complained that it spoiled his view. To the east, Straße des 17. Juni runs past the **Sowjetisches Ehrenmal** ('Soviet War Memorial') and into the Brandenburg Gate (on the other side it becomes Unter den Linden), with a couple of small monuments in the central reservation proclaiming freedom for those living behind the Berlin Wall.

The **Haus der Kulturen der Welt** (former-ly the Kongreßhalle), is an impressive piece of modern architecture whose reflecting pool con-tains a Henry Moore sculpture. The Haus was designed by Hugh Stubbins, its nearby carillon by Bangert, Jansen, Scholz and Schultes. A gift from the Americans, known to the locals as the 'preg-nant oyster', it opened in 1957, and collapsed in 1980 – an event that gave the name to one of Berlin's best-known bands, Einstürzende Neubauten. Today, it houses changing exhibits of world culture and hosts musical ensembles and cinema screenings from far-off lands.

Beyond all this rises the immense Spreebogen government complex – the 'Band des Bundes' – the most notable building of which is the Axel Schultes' Bundeskanzleramt, the Federal Chancellery. The entire complex, built over a ser-pentine twist in the River Spree (*Bogen* meaning 'bend'), crosses the river twice, although it is built in a straight line.

Schloß Bellevue, a minor palace from 1785, just off the Großer Stern, now houses the German pres-ident when he's in town, the flag flying from its roof the signal that he's in. His 150 employees are found just next door in a new oval office building, discreetly shielded from the street. East across Lutherbrücke, a mammoth 718-apartment resi-dence for federal workers, already nicknamed 'The Snake', has arisen on a large plot of land which for-merly held bonded warehouses. From the bridge, you can also see the mirrored towers housing the Ministry of the Interior.

To the west of Schloß Bellevue is the Englischer Garten, which came about because King Ludwig I of Bavaria decided that the fact that there weren't constant revolutions in England was due to the plentiful open green spaces in the cities. The idea caught on, and these gardens became such an inte-gral part of German life that Lenin once com-mented that revolution in Germany was impossible because it would require people to step on the grass.

Just beyond the Schloß at the Großer Stern, there is a monumental statue of Bismarck set back from the road, flanked by statues of Prussian gen-erals Moltke and Roon, reminders of the past which, judging from the constantly reappearing graffiti, seem to have a few people worried. Following the circle around from here halfway, you can walk through a piece of the Tiergarten down Hofjägerallee to Tiergartenstraße, along which rises Berlin's past and future diplomatic quarter. Part of Albert Speer's plan for Germania, the original embassy buildings were designed by German architects as a means of proving German superiority. Damaged by bombing, they were largely abandoned, and Tiergartenstraße became an eerie walk past decaying grandeur. But with the grounds still the properties of the respective gov-ernments, when the move from Bonn came, they were reconstructed or in the case of the complex which houses the Nordic countries' embassies, for instance, new buildings were constructed from scratch. Today, many of Berlin's embassies can again be found here.

The Philharmonie – near-perfect acoustics, near-perfect vision.

A little further behind Schloß Bellevue, bounded by Bachstraße, Altonaer Straße, and the Tiergarten, is the Hansaviertel, a post-war housing project whose buildings were designed by a *Who's Who* of architects. Perhaps of most interest to specialists, it draws busloads of architecture students from around the world, who see something other than a group of fairly sterile modern buildings. *See chapter* **Architecture**.

Gedenkstätte Deutscher Widerstand

Memorial of the German Resistance
Stauffenbergstraße 13-14, Tiergarten, 10785 (265 40). U1 Kurfürstenstraße. **Open** 9am-6pm Mon-Fri; 9am-1pm Sat-Sun. **Admission** free. **Map E4**
An exhibition chronicling the German resistance to National Socialism is housed here. The building is part of a complex known as the Bendlerblock, which was owned by the German military from its construction in 1911 until 1945. At the back is a memorial to the conspirators killed during their attempt to assassinate Hitler at this site on 20 July 1944.

Reichstag

Platz der Republik, Tiergarten, 10557 (2272 2152). S1, S2 Unter den Linden. **Open** *dome* 8am-midnight daily, *last entry* 10pm. **Map E3**
The Reichstag, hugely imposing, with its grand lawn stretching towards the Tiergarten now in tatters, is currently behind a huge building site. Designed by Frankfurt architect Paul Wallot, in Italian High Renaissance style, the Reichstag was completed in 1894 to house the government of Bismarck's united Germany. It was burned on 17 February 1933 – an event the Nazis may or may not have done themselves but which they blamed on the Dutchman Marius van der Lubbe and certainly used as an excuse to clamp down on communists and suspend basic freedoms. Today, after a memorable wrapping by Christo which turned the front lawn into Berlin's major party venue, it has been renovated and once again sports a dome, designed by Sir Norman Foster – and is again the house of the German parliament. *See page 71* **The dome of democracy.**

Shell House

corner of Reichpietschufer and Stauffenbergstraße, Tiergarten, 10785. U1 Kurfürstenstraße. **Map E4**
Designed by Emil Fahrenkamp in 1932, Shell House, these days offices for the BEWAG electricity company, is a curvaceous architectural masterpiece. It survived the war, but it's not standing up to the march of time too well, and the undulating façade, after which it is named, is currently being restored.

Siegessäule

Straße des 17. Juni, Tiergarten, 10785 (391 2961). S3, S5, S7, S9 Bellevue. **Open** 1-5.30pm Mon; 9am-6pm Tue-Sat. **Admission** DM1.50. **Map D3**
The Tiergarten's biggest monument is the Siegessäule, built between 1871 and 1873 to commemorate the Prussian campaigns against Denmark (1864), Austria (1866) and France (1870-71). On top of the column is an eight-metre (26-foot) gilded Goddess of Victory by sculptor Friedrich Drake; captured French cannons and cannonballs, sawn in half and gilded, provide the decoration of the column proper. Fans of Wim Wenders' *Wings of Desire* can climb the 285-step spiral staircase to the viewing platform to the top for a fine view.

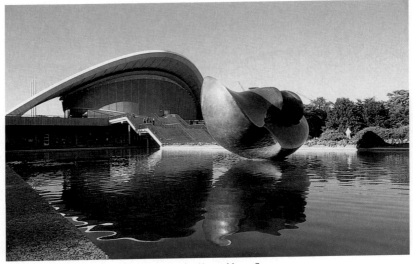

Haus der Kulturen der Welt – any more for Henry Moore?

Sowjetisches Ehrenmal im Tiergarten

Soviet War Memorial

Straße des 17. Juni, Tiergarten, 10557. S1, S2 Unter den Linden. **Map E3**

The impressive Soviet War Memorial, once the only piece of Soviet property in West Berlin, stands on the north side of the street just across Entlastungsstraße and was built during 1945-1946 from the same marble that came from the ruins of Hitler's Reich Chancellery. Once, this monument posed quite a political problem: built in the British Zone, it was surrounded by a British military enclosure, which was in turn guarded by the Berlin police, and all to protect the monument and the two Soviet soldiers who stood 24-hour guard there. Today, you can walk right up to the memorial and read its Russian inscriptions when it's not undergoing renovation. The two tanks flanking it are alleged to have been the first two Soviet ones into Berlin, but this is probably legend.

Tiergarten

Tiergarten, 10785. S3, S5, S7, S9 Tiergarten. **Map E3/D4**

Hunting grounds of the Prussian electors since the 16th century, the Tiergarten was turned into a park in the 18th century. During the war, bombs damaged much of it, and in the desperate winter of 1945-6 almost all the trees that were left were cut down for firewood. The park was left as a depressing collection of wrecked monuments and sorry-looking shrubbery interspersed with vegetable plots. Rehabilitation began in 1949 with the symbolic planting of a young lime tree by then mayor Ernst Reuter. Some of the trees were donated by Queen Elizabeth II. A stone on the Großer Weg, the large path in the park, is inscribed with names of the German towns that contributed trees. Today the bucolic Tiergarten is one of the largest city parks in Europe. You can take a stroll across lovely Löwenbrücke ('Lion Bridge'), a major gay cruising area at night, marked by four huge iron lions – or just get lost roaming through the 167-hectare (412-acre) park.

Other hoods

Because Berlin's underlying soil is sandy, until recently large buildings could not be built here, which means that the city sprawls on for miles– but the U-Bahn and S-Bahn system can take you to lesser-known neighbourhoods in minutes. Here are some suggestions for further exploration.

West Berlin

To the north, the city eventually gives itself up to block after block of industrial works and housing for the people employed there, and while the Moabit section of Tiergarten has some charm, particularly along the river, it's hard to summon up any reasonable kind of enthusiasm for areas like Wedding and Reinickendorf.

South-west Berlin was the American Sector, and sections like Steglitz, Dahlem and Zehlendorf contain some of the city's wealthier residences. Besides the museum complex (*see chapter* **Museums**), Dahlem is the home of the **Freie Universität**, some of whose departments occupy former villas seized by the Nazis from their Jewish owners. In Zehlendorf, Mexikoplatz is a beautifully-preserved plaza with one of the city's best-known left-wing book stores in its S-Bahn station. Elsewhere in Zehlendorf, the Onkel-Toms-Hütte development is a historically important collection of workers' houses designed in the 1920s and 1930s by architects like Bruno Taut, Hugo Häring, and Otto Rudolf Solvisberg. It is painted in colours only available from one firm in Germany, and today is lived in by workers in professions that are a far cry from the ones the original inhabitants toiled at. Take the U-Bahn to Onkel-Toms-Hütte and walk down Onkel-Tom-Straße towards the woods. (*See also chapter* **Architecture**.)

Perhaps the best way to ogle the mansions in Steglitz and Dahlem is by car or bicycle, wandering down the streets wondering at the mélange of architectural styles and trying to guess which Steglitz mansion is the one Helmut Kohl bought in anticipation of moving here in 1999. Perhaps one with a For Sale sign on it.

Another southern district, Neukölln, was a pocket south-east of Kreuzberg until the Wall came down, and now is the most direct neighbour of Schönefeld Airport. Karl-Marx-Straße here is a major shopping district, and the Rixdorf section around Richardplatz is charming because of the many old buildings that remain there. Further south, at Britz-Süd, the Bruno-Taut-Ring, a horseshoe-shaped housing estate, is a fine example of Bauhaus architecture. *See chapter* **Architecture**.

One other tourist attraction in a seldom-visited neighbourhood should be mentioned: in a tiny cemetery just off the Südwestkorso in Friedenau, south-west of Schöneberg, lies Marlene Dietrich's grave. Like most graveyards here, this one has a card with the location of some of the more prominent residents by its gateway, giving their names and occupations, so she's easy to find.

South of Charlottenburg and west of Schöneberg lies Wilmersdorf. This is a mostly boring district of smart apartments that has a bit of night-time sparkle and street life in the area around Ludwigkirchplatz.

Botanischer Garten

Botanical Garden

Königin-Luise-Straße 6-8, Zehlendorf, 14195 (830 060). S1 Botanischer Garten/S1, U9 Rathaus Steglitz. **Open** 9am-dusk daily. **Admission** DM4; DM2 concs.

The Botanical Garden was landscaped at the beginning of the 20th century on a 42-hectare (104-acre) plot of land. Today it is home to approximately

Sowjetisches Ehrenmal – *stone reliefs depict Stalin's triumph.*

18,000 species of plants, and includes 16 greenhouses and a museum with special displays on herbs and dioramas of flowers. *See chapter* **Museums**.

East Berlin

Much of this side of town is generally thought of as a wasteland of decaying communist apartment blocks with few redeeming features, but there's still a lot of the flavour of old Berlin in the east.

Not all of the neighbourhoods here are attractive: especially if you're not white, it's best to avoid Marzahn's grim housing projects after dark, although its Biesdorf district is quite nice and has a small park with a castle in it. Another park worth a visit is Treptower Park, with its immense **Sowjetisches Ehrenmahl** ('Soviet War Memorial'), the **Insel** nightclub on an island in the Spree, and pleasant picnic areas. From here, several excursion boats leave in the summer for trips along the Spree, and there are other boats with restaurants on them. The park continues to the south, where it becomes the Plänterwald and houses a big amusement park.

Sowjetisches Ehrenmahl

Soviet War Memorial
Treptow, 12435, S6, S8, S9, S10 Treptower Park.
Treptower Park is home to a huge, sobering monument to the Soviet soldiers who died in the war against Hitler, as well as a mass grave for 5,000 of them. As you walk down the tree-lined avenue you arrive at a statue of Mother Russia, weeping for her dead children. Fascinating if heavy-handed white stone reliefs, set up almost as stations of the cross and bearing quotations from Stalin, depict the story of how the Soviets triumphed over fascism. On top of the tomb at the far end of the park is an enormous statue of a valiant, square-jawed Soviet soldier, clasping a child in one arm and trampling a swastika underfoot.

Outskirts

The late New York songwriter David Ackles once wrote a song called 'Subway to the Country', about how he wished he could jump on the underground and get out of the metropolis to where the land was green. Berlin is where he should have been, not least at station termini like Königs Wusterhausen and Strausberg Nord – particularly if he had taken a bicycle and had been willing to pedal for half an hour or so. Even a handful of the stations to be found closer to town, particularly on the eastern side, could have offered him the pleasant surroundings of two-family houses with backyards filled with fruit trees.

Grunewald

The largest of Berlin's many forests also happens to be its most visited. On a fine Sunday afternoon, its lanes and paths are as packed as the Kurfürstendamm, but with walkers, runners, cyclists, horse riders and dog walkers. This is because it's so easily accessible by S-Bahn. There are several restaurants next to Grunewald station, and on the other side of the motorway at Schmetterlingsplatz, open during the season, April to October. Follow Schildhornweg (past Sandgraben, from which high-quality Berlin sand was dug for building and to supply its glass industry) to Teufelssee, a tiny lake which is packed with bathers in summer.

Nearby Teufelsberg is a product of war-time devastation. A railway was laid from Wittenbergplatz, along the Kurfürstendamm, to carry rubble from the city centre for depositing in a great pile at the terminus here. There are great views from the summit, on which sits a now-disused American electronic listening post.

To the south, there are kiosks for sausages, beer, drinks and ice creams at Großer Stern on Hüttenweg (also an exit from the motorway) in the summertime. It's a busy pit stop for hundreds of cyclists pelting up and down the paths, Kronprinzessinweg and Königsweg, which parallel the road.

At Grunewaldsee, the **Jagdschloß** ('Hunting Lodge') is a good example of hundreds of such buildings which once maintained the country life of the landed gentry, the Prussian Junkers. There you can find bathing by the lake in the summer-

time, including a well-signposted nudist section. The Grunewaldsee is also a favourite promenade for chic dogs and their owners, who refresh themselves in the deer-horn-bedecked Forsthaus Paulsborn.

A further kilometre east through this pleasant forest, you'll find Chalet Suisse, an over-the-top Swiss-themed restaurant popular with families because of its extensive playground and petting zoo. Another ten-minute walk takes you to the **Allied Museum**. Also nearby, the **Brücke Museum** houses many of the surviving works by

Monumental controversy

Of all the debates about history, architecture and the shape of Berlin's post-Wall cityscape, few have lumbered on so long or conjured up so much controversy as the argument about the memorial to Holocaust victims – the Denkmal für die ermordeten Juden Europas – proposed for the 20,000sq m site south of Pariser Platz. Since the mid-1990s, every deadline for any kind of decision has led to yet more indecision, mired in political disagreements about the nature of historical memory and responsibility, both individual and collective.

The idea of some kind of central memorial has been around since the late 1980s, but the fall of the Wall opened up the possibility. The winning design in a competition held in 1995 was by Berlin artist Christine Jackob-Marks. It proposed a huge, slanted concrete tablet – about the size of two football fields – bearing the names of all 4.2 million identified Holocaust victims. This was promptly rejected by then-Chancellor Kohl, distressed at its very immensity. But it also found disfavour with left-wing opponents of traditional '19th century-style' monuments that seek to draw a line under history, rather than invite the public to think about and engage with it. Many of the same people didn't actually want any central memorial at all, and especially not at a site with no particular historical links to the Holocaust. Why not just preserve the concentration camps? Or memorialise the perpetrators rather than the victims? And wasn't it in any case a lamentable cliché to try and match the enormity of the crime with the enormousness of the memorial?

Four finalists emerged from a second competition held in 1998: Jochen Gurz (39 light masts), Gesine Weinmiller (18 scattered walls), Daniel Libeskind (5 'solidified voids' orientated towards the Wannsee villa where Final Solution logistics were hammered out) and Peter

Eisenmann and Richard Serra (4,000 concrete columns of varying heights). It was the last that was finally accepted, though in the meantime Eisenmann and Serra parted ways and Libeskind stopped talking to either as he saw their field of columns as plagiarising his own garden of columns at the Jüdisches Museum in Kreuzberg (*see page 84* **Reading between the lines**).

Meanwhile, arguments broke out between atrocity victims. Roma representatives argued that the extermination of their own people must not be separated from that of the Jews, each side invoking the Third Reich's own racial categories in the ugly debate that ensued. The Roma were then promised their own memorial, though there were disagreements about whether it should be nearby or at the suburban location of a former Gypsy prison camp. Roma leaders, in turn, refused to share their memorial with homosexuals or communists who, they argued, had not been victimised on racial grounds. Was Berlin to become a landscape of segregated victims' memorials?

Georg Konrad, the head of the Akademie der Künste, condemned the winning proposals as kitsch, proposing instead a garden for children to play in, as at many Jewish museums. James T Young, one of the competition jurors, responded: 'The only thing worse than making the monument now would be to reverse course and deliberately choose not to make it.' Let the people decide if they like it, he suggested, or let them stay home and make it 'a victim of their not-so-benign neglect'.

The ground-breaking ceremony for Eisenmann's design (now scaled down to a mere 1,500 columns) was held in February 2000. A sizeable contingent turned up to protest. It seems the controversy itself has become the true Holocaust memorial.

the influential Brücke group (including Kirchner, Heckel and Schmidt-Rottluff), known for their impressionistic views of Berlin.

Krumme Lanke and Schlachtensee are pleasant urban lakes along the south-eastern edge of the Grunewald, perfect for picnicking, swimming or rowing – and each with its own eponymous station, U1 for Krumme Lanke, S1 for Schlachtensee.

Half way up Havelchaussee, the Grunewald-turm, a tower built in 1897 in memory of Wilhelm I, has an observation platform 105m (115 yards) above the lake with views as far as Spandau and Potsdam. There is a restaurant at the base, the Ausflugsrestaurant am Grunewaldturm, and another on the other side of the road, Waldhaus Wildspezialitäten, both with garden terraces. A short walk along Havelufer brings you to the ferry to Lindwerder Island, which also has a restaurant, Lindwerder Insel Restaurant.

Jagdschloß Grunewald

Grunewaldsee, Zehlendorf, 14193 (813 3597). S7 Grunewald. **Open** 10am-5pm Tue-Sun. **Admission** DM2.50; DM1 concs.

Built by Elector Joachim II von Brandenburg in 1542, who described it as 'zum grünen Wald' ('in the green wood'), thus coining the name of the forest in which it stands. Considerably altered by Graf Rochus zu Lynar and Frederick the Great (1770), much of the Renaissance façade was pulled down and thrown into a nearby pit. Later excavations unearthed it and recently the building has been restored to its original 16th-century appearance.

Wannsee

Boats and beaches in summer, castles and forests all through the year, are the highlights of the 'Berlin Riviera'. **Strandbad Wannsee** is the largest inland beach in Europe. Between May and September it is the most popular resort in Berlin, with service buildings housing showers, toilets, cafés, shops and kiosks. There are boats and ped-aloes and hooded, two-person wicker sunchairs for hire (enquire about all these at the entrance), a children's playground and separate sections for nud-ists and the severely disabled.

The waters of the Havel are extensive and in summer are warm enough to make swimming comfortable; there is a strong current, so do not stray beyond the floating markers. The rest of the open water is in constant use by ferries, sailing boats, speedboats and water-skiers.

Beyond the Strandbad lie the Wannseeterrassen, a couple of rustic lanes on the slopes of the hill, at the bottom of which private boats and yachts are moored. There is a good view from the restaurant Wannseeterrasse, but less remarkable food. A small bridge takes you across to Schwanenwerder, once the exclusive private island retreat of Goebbels and now home to the international think-tank, the Aspen Institute.

The town of Wannsee to the south is clustered around the bay of the Großer Wannsee and is dom-inated by the long stretch of promenade, Am Großen Wannsee, which is scattered with hotels and fish restaurants. Also here is the **Gedenkstätte Haus der Wannsee-Konferenz**. At this house, in January 1942, a meeting of prominent Nazis chaired by Reinhard Heydrich laid out plans for the extermination of the Jewish race – the Final Solution. The house, an elegant Grunderzeit mansion, is now a museum. *See chapter* **Museums**.

A short distance from S-Bahn Wannsee along Bismarckstraße is a little garden where the German dramatist, Heinrich von Kleist, shot him-self in 1811; the beautiful view of the Kleiner Wannsee was the last thing he wanted to see. On the other side of the railway tracks is Düppler Forst, a little-explored forest including a nature reserve at Großes Fenn at the south-western end. Travelling on the S-Bahn to Mexikoplatz and then the 629 bus to Krummes Fenn brings you to **Museumsdorf Düppel**.

Gedenkstätte Haus der Wannsee-Konferenz

Am Großen Wannsee 56-58, Zehlendorf, 14109 (8050 0125). S1, S7 Wannsee, then bus 114. **Open** 10am-6pm Tue-Fri; 2-6pm Sat-Sun. **Admission** free.

A lovely house with a grim history, and the first Holocaust museum in Berlin.

Museumsdorf Düppel

Clauertstraße 11, Zehlendorf, 14163 (802 6671). Bus 115, 211. **Open** *May-Sept* 3-7pm Thur; 10am-5pm Sun & hols. **Admission** DM3; DM1.50 concs.

A working reconstruction of a medieval Brandenburg village, and a great place to take the kids. *See chapter* **Children**.

Strandbad Wannsee

Wannseebadweg, Nikolassee, 14219 (803 5440). S1, S7 Nikolassee. **Open** 7am-8pm daily. **Admission** DM5; DM3 concs.

Pfaueninsel

This 98-hectare (242-acre) non-smoking island in the Havel River is part of the Potsdam complex (though within Berlin's borders) and is reached by the shortest private ferry ride in the city.

The island was inhabited in prehistoric times, but wasn't mentioned in archives until 1683. Two years later the Grand Elector presented it to Johann Kunckel von Löwenstein, a chemist who experimented with alchemy and instead of gold produced 'ruby glass', examples of which are on view in the castle. But it was only at the start of the Romantic Era that the island's windswept charms began to attract more serious interest. In 1793, Friedrich Wilhelm II purchased it and built a Schloß for his mistress but died in 1797 before they had a chance to move in.

Open waters of the Wannsee – great for sailors, dodgy for swimmers.

Its first residents were the happily married couple, Friedrich Wilhelm III and Queen Luise, who spent much of their time together on the island, even setting up a working farm there.

The island was later added to and adorned. A huge royal menagerie was developed, with enclosed and free-roaming animals (most of which were moved to the new Tiergarten Zoo in 1842). Only peacocks, pheasants, parrots, goats and sheep remain. Surviving buildings include the Jakobsbrunnen ('Jacob's Fountain'), a copy of a Roman temple; the Kavalierhaus ('Cavalier's House'), built in 1803 from an original design by Schinkel; and the Swiss cottage, also based on a Schinkel plan. All are linked to each other by winding, informal paths laid out in the English manner by Peter Joseph Lenné. A walk around the island, with its extreme quiet, its monumental trees and rough meadows, and its views of the waters of the Havel and the mainland beyond, provides one of the most complete sensations of escape from urban living to be had within the borders of Berlin.

Back on the mainland, a short walk south along the bank of the Havel, is the Blockhaus Nikolskoe, a recreation of a huge wooden chalet, built in 1819 by Friedrich Wilhelm II for his daughter Charlotte, and named after her husband, the future Tsar Nicholas of Russia. There is a magnificent view of the Havel from the terrace, where you can also enjoy an excellent choice of mid-price Berlin cuisine, or just coffee and cakes in the afternoon. The nearby Church of St Peter and St Paul dates from 1834-37 and has an attractive interior.

Blockhaus Nikolskoe

Nikolskoer Weg, Wannsee, 14109 (805 2914). S1, S7 Wannsee, then bus 216. **Open** *May-Oct* 10am-10pm Mon-Wed, Fri; 9am-10pm Sat-Sun; *Nov-Apr* 10am-10pm Mon-Wed, Fri; 10am-8pm Sat-Sun.

Pfaueninsel

Peacock Island
In der Havel, Zehlendorf, 14109 (805 3042). Bus 216 or 316 to hourly ferry at Nikolskoer Weg. **Open** 8am-6pm daily.

Schloß Pfaueninsel on the island is open April-October, with hourly guided tours between 10am and 5pm (4pm in October).

Glienicke

The centre of this park, now a conference centre, and its outbuildings, is Schloß Glienicke. Although closed to the public, its surrounding park invites a walk along the Havel. At Moorlake, there's a restaurant in a Bavarian-style 1842 hunting lodge – the Historisches Wirtshaus Moorlake – which is good for game dishes or afternoon coffee and cakes. Close by the park, where the main road comes down from Wannsee, the suspension bridge over the Havel (1909) was named Brücke der Einheit ('Bridge of Unity') because it joined Potsdam with Berlin. The name continued to be used even when, after the building of the Wall, it was painted different shades of olive green on the east and west sides and used only by Allied soldiers and for top-level prisoner and spy exchanges – Anatoly Scharansky was one of the last in 1986.

Glienicke's Brücke der Einheit – joining Potsdam and Berlin.

Schlößer & Park Glienicke
Glienicke Park and Palaces
Königstraße, Zehlendorf, 14109 (805 3041). Bus 116. Palace is closed to public.

A hunting lodge designed by Schinkel for Prinz Carl von Preußen, who quickly became notorious for his ban on all women visitors. On at least one occasion, Prinz Carl's wife was turned away at the gate by armed guards. The Prinz adorned the walls of the gardens with ancient relics collected on his holidays around the Mediterranean, and decided to simulate a walk from the Alps to Rome in the densely wooded park, laid out by Pückler in 1824-50. The summerhouses, fountains and follies are all based on original Italian models, and the woods and fields surrounding them make an ideal place for a Sunday picnic, since this park is little visited.

Spandau

Berlin's western neighbour and eternal rival, Spandau was home to Rudolf Hess, the city's last Nazi chieftain, until 1987 and is a little Baroque town which seems to contradict everything about the city of which it is now, reluctantly, a part. Spandauers still talk about 'going into Berlin' when they head off to the rest of the city. Berliners, for their part, basically consider Spandau as part of west Germany, though travelling there is easy on the U7, alighting at either Zitadelle or Altstadt Spandau, depending on which sights you want to visit. Spandau's original town charter lies in the **Stadtgeschichtlichesmuseum** (which in turn lies in the **Zitadelle**) and dates from 1232, a fact which Spandauers have relied on ever since to assert their legitimacy before Cölln and Berlin to be the historical heart of the capital.

The old town centre of Spandau is mostly pedestrianised, with two- and three-storey 18th-century town houses interspersed with burger joints and department stores. One of the prettiest examples is the former Gasthof zum Stern in Carl-Schurz-Straße; older still are the houses in Kinkel- (until 1933, Juden-) and Ritterstraße; but perhaps the best preserved district is across Am Juliusturm in the area bounded by Hoher Steinweg, Kolk and Behnitz. Steinweg contains a fragment of the old town wall from the first half of the 14th century; Kolk has the Catholic garrison church (Alte Marienkirche, 1848); and in Behnitz, at number 5, stands the Heinemannsche Haus, perhaps the finest late Baroque town house in Berlin. And at Reformationsplatz, the brick nave of Nikolaikirche dates from 1410-1450, the west tower having been added in 1468, and with further additions by Schinkel. All these landmarks, of course, had to be thoroughly restored after the last war.

One of the most pleasant times to visit the town is in the run-up to Christmas, when the market square houses a life-size Nativity scene with real sheep. The café and bakery on Reformationsplatz are excellent.

Rudolf Hess, Hitler's deputy, was imprisoned in the Allied jail after the Nuremberg trials, where he remained (alone after 1966) until his suicide on 17 August 1987, hanging from a piece of lamp flex at the age of 93. Once he'd gone, the 19th-century brick building at Wilhelmstraße 21-24 was demolished to make way for a supermarket for the British forces – who have since left the city. Hess' story has attracted controversy for decades but, until the official documents are released by the British government, there's still little evidence to contradict the official version: that Hess parachuted into Scotland in May 1941 on a secret special mission to negotiate an end to the war with Britain. On hearing this news, Churchill remained unimpressed: 'Hess or no Hess, I'm going off to the cinema to see the Marx Brothers'.

Stadtgeschichtlichesmuseum Spandau
Spandau Museum of Local History
*Am Juliusturm, Spandau, 13599 (339 1264). U7
Zitadelle.* **Open** 9am-5pm Tue-Fri; 10am-5pm Sat-Sun. **Admission** DM1.50; DM 1 concs. Combined
with Juliusturm/Palas ticket.
Located in the Palas, which has stones in its cellar
dating back to 1200. The base of the south front contains Jewish tombstones from 1244-1347, when
Spandau was the only place guaranteeing safety for
Jewish graves, but these can only be seen on the
twice-daily guided tour.

Zitadelle (Juliusturm, Palas)
*Am Juliusturm, Spandau, 13599 (339 11). U7
Zitadelle.* **Open** 9am-5pm Tue-Sun. **Admission**
DM1.50; DM1 concs. **Tours** noon, 3pm, daily; DM5;
DM3 concs.
The oldest building here (and the oldest secular
building in Berlin) is the Juliusturm, probably dating back to an Ascanian (*see chapter* **History**) water
fortress from about 1160. The present tower, with
154 steps and walls measuring up to 3.6m thick, was
home until 1919 to the 120-million Goldmark reparations, stored in 1,200 boxes, which the French paid
to Germany in 1874 after the Franco-Prussian War.
In German financial circles, state reserves are still
referred to as *Juliusturm.* The bulk of the Zitadelle
was designed in 1560-94, in the style of an Italian
fort. Its purpose was to dominate the confluence of
the Spree and Havel rivers. Since then it has been
used as everything from garrison to prison to laboratory. Today, most of the huge 300m by 300m site
is under restoration and archaeological excavation
– and not accessible to the public, except for its
museums, galleries and ateliers.

Friedrichshagen & the Müggelsee
The village of Friedrichshagen was annexed by
the GDR to bring the number of neighbourhoods
in East Berlin into parity with West Berlin, yet it
has retained a lot of its independent character. The
main street, Bölschestraße, leading down from the
S-Bahn station, is lined with steep-roofed
Brandenburg houses, and ends at the shores of the
large lake called the Müggelsee. Worth a visit on
any nice day, Friedrichshagen is particularly
enjoyable when the Berliner Burgerbräu brewery,
family-owned since 1869, throws open its gates for
its annual celebration in the summertime. The
town lines Bölschestraße with booths selling all
manner of goods, the brewery lays on musical
entertainment, and people sit on the shores with
cold beer and look out onto the lake. Boat tours are
available, and the restaurant Braustubl, next to the
brewery, serves particularly good Berlin cuisine.

Köpenick
The name Köpenick is derived from the Slavonic
copanic, meaning place on a river. The old town
stands at the confluence of the Spree and Dahme,
and having escaped bombing, decay and develop-

ment by the GDR, still maintains much of its 18th-century character.
Köpenick's imposing Rathaus ('Town Hall') is a
good example of late Victorian Wilhelmenisch
civic architecture. It was here, in 1906, two years
after the building's completion, that Wilhelm
Voigt, an unemployed cobbler who'd spent half his
life in jail, disguised himself as an army captain
and ordered a detachment of soldiers to accompany him into the Treasury, where they confiscated
the town coffers. He instantly entered popular folklore as the Hauptmann von Köpenick ('Captain of
Köpenick'), and was pardoned by the Kaiser
because he had shown how obedient Prussian soldiers were.
His theft is re-enacted every year during the
Köpenicker summer festival in late June, when a
parade of locals in period costume marches to the
Town Hall steps. There they are presented with a
box containing a list entitled Mach-Mit-Wettbewerb (the 'Get Involved Competition') – the
winners of the annual competition for the best
charitable or social work in the community.
Köpenick, of all the areas of east Berlin, was and
still is the most sought after, with handsome and
increasingly affluent shops, cafés and restaurants
clustered around the old centre. With its old buildings and extensive riverfront, it's a fine place for
a Sunday afternoon wander.
On Schloßinsel stands Köpenick's Schloß, with
its medieval drawbridge, Renaissance gateway
and Baroque chapel. Occasional open-air concerts
are held here in the summer months, and the late-medieval and classical-style **Kunstgewerbe-museum** ('Museum of Applied Art') houses a
collection of porcelain, glass, gold and splendid
Berlin iron. It was also here in the Weapons Room
in 1730 that Friedrich Wilhelm I ordered the trial
for desertion of his son, the future Frederick the
Great, who had attempted to flee to England with
his close personal friend, Lieutenant von Katte.
The couple were betrayed by a third man involved
in the escape attempt. The court martial sentenced
them both to two years' imprisonment, but the
king then altered the verdict, forcing his son to
watch von Katte's decapitation from his cell.
A few minutes' walk from the castle is the old
town centre. It stands on the site of a fishing community founded by Slavonic Wendish settlers a
thousand years ago, and fishing weirs are still set
in the river today. The pokey little streets, lined
with narrow, cramped houses, are currently being
restored and taken over by the new east Berlin
Schickeria, or trendies. There's now a good choice
of art galleries and antique dealers.

Schloß and Kunstgewerbemuseum
*Schloßinsel, Köpenick, 13507 (657 2651). S3
Köpenick, then tram 60, 61, 62 Schloßplatz.* **Open**
9am-5pm Tue-Sun. **Admission** DM4; DM2 concs;
free Sun.

Museums

Although many are closed for renovation, Berlin's museums can still offer dildos, hemp, Egyptology, clowns and a virtual orchestra.

If you came to Berlin just to visit its many museums, you've arrived at the wrong time. Continued renovation and reorganisation mean that around ten major museums are closed until sometime after the year 2001. This doesn't mean there's nothing to see – far from it – but it does, for example, make a trip to the Dahlem complex in south-west Berlin more daunting given that instead of the usual five museums, you'll currently find only two.

Despite temporary closures, many museums are still clustered around Museumsinsel in Mitte (**Altes Museum**, **Pergamon**), around Schloß Charlottenburg (**Ägyptisches Museum**, **Bröhan-Museum**, **Museum für Vor- und Frühgeschichte** and **Schloß Charlottenburg** itself) and in Dahlem (**Museum für Europäische Kulturen**, **Museum für Völkerkunde** and **Brücke-Museum**).

English guided tours of most state museums can be arranged in advance. For those in Dahlem and Charlottenburg, contact the Besucherdienst at Dahlem (830 1466, open 8am-noon Mon-Fri). For tours of the Pergamon, phone 209 050, 8am-4pm. In both cases give at least 14 days' notice. Tours for up to 25 people, costing around DM80 plus admission, last about an hour. As a general rule, only the larger museums are likely to have either booklets or information sheets in English. Where there are none, we have indicated it in the review.

Archaeology & ancient history

Ägyptisches Museum
Egyptian Museum
Schloßstraße 70, Charlottenburg, 14059 (3209 1261).
U2 Sophie-Charlotte-Platz/U7 Richard-Wagner-Platz.
Open 10am-6pm Mon-Fri; 11am-6pm Sat-Sun.
Admission *combined ticket* DM8; DM4 concs; *single ticket* DM4; DM2 concs; free Sun. **Map B3**
Just across the street from Schloß Charlottenburg and one of the most popular museums in Berlin,

Prime commie kitsch on display at the former **Ministerium für Staatssicherheit**. *Page 89.*

mainly because of the bust of Egyptian Queen Nefertiti. This piece of art, crafted in 1350 BC, was buried for more than 3,000 years until German archaeologists dug it up in the early 1900s. Nefertiti has her own room on the second floor. Also notable are a mummy and sarcophagi, a papyrus collection and the Kalabasha Gate. No English booklets are available, but there is a DM14 catalogue in German.

Pergamon Museum

Am Kupfergraben, Mitte, 10178 (209 050). S3, S5, S7, S9 Hackescher Markt. **Open** 9am-5pm Tue-Sun. **Admission** DM4; DM2 concs; free first Sun of the month. **Map F3**

Dedicated to ancient spaces and equipped with the gates, altars and gathering places of antiquity, the Pergamon is the next best thing to being there. The vast Hellenistic Pergamon Altar (from which the museum takes its name) dates from 180-160 BC. It is made of white marble and carved with figures of the gods. The Market Gate of Miletus, a two-storey Roman gate erected in AD 120, once provided access to a market and was large enough to contain a few shops of its own. In an adjoining room, the Babylonian Processional Street leads to The Gate of Ishtar, a striking cerulean and ochre tiled structure dating from the reign of King Nebuchadnezzar (605-562 BC). Built 1909-1930, the Pergamon is a relative newcomer to Museumsinsel but is one of the world's most important archaeological museums.

Museum für Vor- und Frühgeschichte

Primeval and Early History Museum
Spandauer Damm 20, Charlottenburg, 14059 (3267 4811). U2 Sophie-Charlotte-Platz/U7 Richard-Wagner-Platz. **Open** 10am-6pm Tue-Fri; 11am-6pm Sat-Sun. **Admission** DM4; DM2 concs; free Sun. **Map B3**

The evolution of Homo Sapiens from 1,000,000 BC to the Bronze Age (for which they've recently opened a new room) is the subject of this museum next to the west wing of the palace. Keep an eye out for the 6th-century BC grave of a girl buried with a gold coin in her mouth. Beats Christmas pudding. Information is available in English.

Art & architecture

Altes Museum

Lustgarten, Mitte, 10178 (209 050). S3, S5, S7, S9 Hackescher Markt. **Open** 10am-6pm Tue-Thur, Sun; 10am-8pm Fri-Sat. **Admission** DM4; DM2 concs; free first Sun of the month. **Map F3**

Opened as the Royal Museum in 1830, this original-ly housed all the art treasures on Museumsinsel. It was designed by Schinkel and is considered one of his finest buildings, with a particularly magnificent entrance rotunda. Currently hosting the major works of the nearby Alte Nationalgalerie which, like so many Berlin museums, is undergoing renovation.

Bauhaus Archiv-Museum für Gestaltung

Bauhaus Archive Museum of Design
Klingelhöferstraße 13-14, Tiergarten, 10785 (254 0020). Bus 100, 187, 341. **Open** 10am-5pm Mon, Wed-Sun. **Admission** DM5; DM2.50 concs. **Map D4**

Walter Gropius, founder of the Bauhaus school, designed this modern white building, just across the canal from the **Grand Hotel Esplanade** (*see chapter* **Accommodation**). The museum presents fur-niture, ceramics, metal objects, prints, sculptures, photographs and sketches created in the Bauhaus workshop from 1919 until 1933. Designs and mod-els by Gropius and Mies van der Rohe and paintings and drawings by Paul Klee, Georg Muche, Oskar Schlemmer and Kandinsky are also on show. For architecture experts and novices, there's a comput-erised introduction in German and English which provides a useful context to the museum. There's a cafeteria, plus a library with Bauhaus documents (open 9am-1pm Mon-Fri), and a book on the exhibit (available in English) costs DM22.

Bröhan-Museum

Schloßstraße 1a, Charlottenburg, 14059 (321 4029). U2 Sophie-Charlotte-Platz/U7 Richard-Wagner-Platz. **Open** 10am-6pm Tue-Sun. **Admission** DM6; DM3 concs. **Map B3**

Opposite the **Ägyptisches Museum** and a wel-come break from tourist traps, this quiet, private museum contains three levels of art nouveau and art deco pieces that businessman Karl Bröhan began collecting in the 1960s. The wide array of paintings, furniture, porcelain, silver and sculptures dates from 1890 to 1939. Hans Baluschek's paintings of social life in the 1920s and 1930s, and Willy Jaeckel's series of portraits of women, are the pick of the bunch.

Brücke-Museum

Bussardsteig 9, Zehlendorf, 14195 (831 2029). U1 Oskar-Helene-Heim, then bus 115. **Open** 11am-5pm Mon, Wed-Sun. **Admission** DM7; DM3 concs.

Some distance from the other Dahlem museums, an exhibit dedicated to the work of Die Brücke ('The Bridge'), a movement of artists established in Dresden in 1905 and credited with introducing expressionism to Germany. On display are oils, watercolours, drawings and sculptures by the main members of the movement: Schmidt-Rottluff; Heckel; Kirchner; Mueller, and Pechstein. Although a little out of the way, the Brücke is definitely worth seeing: a connoisseur's museum, small but satisfy-ing and coherently arranged, full of fascinatingly colourful work. Wander through the fancy neigh-bourhood of Dahlem to the edge of the Grunewald.

Ephraim-Palais

Poststraße 16, Mitte, 10178 (2400 2121). S3, S5, S7, S9/U2, U5, U8 Alexanderplatz. **Open** 10am-6pm Tue-Sun. **Admission** DM5; DM2.50 concs; free Wed. **Map G3**

In reconstructed Nikolaiviertel, this is part of the Foundation of City Museums. It was built in the 15th century, remodelled in late Baroque style in the 18th century, demolished by the communists, and then rebuilt by them 12m from its original location for the 750th anniversary of Berlin in 1987. Today it is home to temporary art exhibitions. Its soft, chande-lier lighting, parquet floors and spiral staircase add a refined touch to exhibited works without over-whelming them. Recent exhibitions have included

Reading between the lines

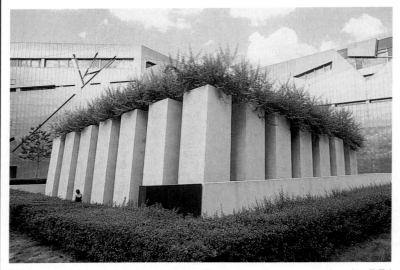

Is there any other museum in the world that could say so much while still standing so empty? The Jüdisches Museum is unlikely to house an exhibit any time before the end of 2001, and for now the curators are still conceptualising and collecting eventual contents that will document Jewish history and culture in the German lands from the ninth century to the present. In the meantime, Daniel Libeskind's landmark work of deconstructivist architecture, striking the map of 'new Berlin' like a silvery bolt of lightning, and in the process illuminating the pallour of most other new building in the city, is exhibit enough in itself.

Libeskind's working title for the project was 'Between the Lines'. The extraordinary ground-plan is in part based on an exploded Star of David, in part on lines drawn between the site and former addresses of great figures in Berlin Jewish cultural history – Heinrich von Kleist, Heinrich Heine, Mies van der Rohe, Arnold Schönberg, Walter Benjamin. It's a structure that makes its own laws yet points in all directions towards the city and its history. One even enters through history – through the baroque Kollegienhaus next door, formerly the Berlin Museum of which this was orginally intended as an annex, and once home to Berlin's Supreme Court, where German romantic writer E.T.A Hoffmann served as a judge.

Stairs lead to an underground labyrinth where the geometry is startlingly independent from that of the above-ground building, contrasting rather than conforming. One passage leads up to the exhibition halls, two others intersect en route respectively to the chillingly bleak tower memorialising the Holocaust, and outside to the E.T.A. Hoffmann Garden – the 'garden of exile and emigration' – a grid of 49 columns, tilted to disorientate. Elsewhere in the grounds, a playground (part of the original planning stipulation) is named after Walter Benjamin, whose *One-Way Street* is (along with Schönberg's *Moses und Aron*) one of the building's chief inspirations. Throughout the building, diagonals and parallels carve out surprising spaces, while windows slash through the structure and its zinc cladding like the knife-wounds of history.

And then there are the 'voids', cutting through the convoluted layout in an absolutely straight line – negative spaces that can be viewed or crossed but not entered, standing for the emptiness left behind by the destruction of German Jewish culture. A present absence, resonant throughout a building where every angle, every space, serves a symbolic, almost literary pur-

the paintings of Theo von Brockhausen and the photographs of Marianne Breslauer. Your ticket is valid for nearby **Nikolaikirche** (*see below*).

Gemäldegalerie

Picture Gallery
Matthäikirchplatz 8, Tiergarten, 10785 (266 2951). S1, S2/U2 Potsdamer Platz. **Open** 10am-6pm Tue-Sun. **Admission** DM5; DM3 concs. **Map E4**
Has an astonishing number of works by most of art history's big boys, including Rubens, Dürer, Breughel, Holbein, Raphael, Gainsborough, El Greco, Canaletto and Caravaggio. Room after room of paintings await exploration. There are works by German, Dutch and Italian artists from the 13th-17th centuries; French and English paintings from the 18th century; Dutch, French and Flemish works from the 17th century; Italian Baroque and rococo; and many Spanish works. Devotees of Rembrandt won't be disappointed by the 20 or so of his canvases displayed here, which constitute one of the world's largest collections of his works. Also on display is a version of Botticelli's *Venus Rising* (the complete painting is in Florence) and Correggio's brilliant *Leda With The Swan*. Look also for Lucas Cranach's *Fountain of Youth* (1546), depicting old, haggard women entering a pool and emerging from the other side young and beautiful again.

Georg-Kolbe-Museum

Sensburger Allee 25, Charlottenburg, 14055 (304 2144). Bus x34, x49, 149. **Open** 10am-5pm Tue-Sun. **Admission** DM5; DM3 concs.
Georg Kolbe's former studio in a quiet corner of Charlottenburg has been transformed into a showcase for his work. The Berlin sculptor, regarded as Germany's best in the 1920s, mainly focused on naturalistic human figures. The museum features examples of his earlier, graceful pieces, as well as his later sombre and larger-than-life works created in accordance with the ideals of the Nazi régime. One of his most famous pieces, *Figure for Fountain*, is outside in the sculpture garden.

Hamburger Bahnhof, Museum für Gegenwart Berlin

Hamburg Station, Museum of Contemporary Berlin
Invalidenstraße 50-51, Mitte, 10557 (397 8340). S3, S5, S7, S9 Lehrter Stadtbahnhof. **Open** 10am-6pm Tue-Thur, Sun; 10am-8pm Fri-Sat. **Admission** DM12; DM6 concs. **Map E3**
Opened with much fanfare in 1997 and housed in a huge and expensive refurbishment of a former railway station, the exterior features a stunning fluorescent light installation by Dan Flavin, which is worth whizzing by at night to observe. There are various temporary exhibits and retrospectives while the permanent exhibition within comes principally from the bequested Marx Collection. This includes wings for works by Andy Warhol and Joseph Beuys along with works by Bruce Nauman, Amseln Kiefer and many others – lots of macho metal and grey art from the 1980s. Some relief is on the first floor – the sculptures of Rosemarie Trockel and charming pre-pop Warhol drawings from the 1950s. The museum

pose. Between the lines is, after all, where something should be read.

Nothing could be further from Potsdamer Platz, where former no-man's-land has been replaced by the postmodern void of an anyplace mall. It's not even necessary to understand Libeskind's intent to feel the drama and emotion of the structure he has created. According to Tom Freudenheim, the museum's Deputy Director, a huge percentage of visitors wonder why they don't just leave the place empty. His challenge is to compose an exhibit that will do justice not just to Jewish history, but also to this wonderful building. Until that exhibit is complete, for now we recommend you take the tour of Libeskind's virgin void.

Jüdisches Museum

Jewish Museum
Lindenstraße 14, Kreuzberg, 10969 (2839 7444). U1, U6 Hallesches Tor. Guided tours in English 1.30pm, 3pm, daily; in German hourly 11am-4pm Mon-Wed, Fri; 11am-7pm Thur; half-hourly 11am-4pm Sat-Sun. **Admission** DM8.
Map F4
Guided tours of the empty building are scheduled to continue through 2000. The museum will close sometime in 2001 while the exhibit is installed, and reopen again that year.

has one of the best art bookshops in Berlin and an *Aktionraum* hosting various events such as performances and symposia, plus a video archive of all Joseph Beuys' performances that were taped.

Käthe-Kollwitz-Museum

Fasanenstraße 24, Wilmersdorf, 10719 (882 5210). U15 Uhlandstraße. **Open** 11am-6pm Wed-Sun. **Admission** DM6; DM3 concs.

Käthe Kollwitz's powerful work embraces the full spectrum of life, from the joy of motherhood to the pain of death. Charcoal sketches and sculptures by this Berlin artist (1867-1945) are housed in a beautiful four-storey villa on one of Berlin's most elegant streets. Guided tours on request.

Martin-Gropius-Bau

Stresemannstraße 110, Kreuzberg, 10963 (254 860). S1, S2 Anhalter Bahnhof. **Open** 10am-8pm Tue-Sun. **Admission** DM12; DM7 concs. **Map F4**

Cosying up to where the Wall once ran (you can still see a short and pitted stretch of it running along the south side of nearby Niederkirchnerstraße), the Martin-Gropius-Bau is named after its architect, uncle of the more famous Walter. Built in 1881, it was recently renovated and serves as a venue for large-scale art exhibitions and major touring shows, for which it is ideal. Recent exhibitions have included Art from Germany 1960-2000 (from the collection of Hans Grothe) and drawings by Leonardo da Vinci and Joseph Beuys. No permanent exhibition.

Neue Nationalgalerie

Potsdamer Straße 50, Tiergarten, 10785 (266 2662). S1, S2/U2 Potsdamer Platz. **Open** 10am-6pm Tue-Thur, Sun; 10am-8pm Fri-Sat. **Admission** DM4; DM2 concs. **Map E4**

The modern building, designed in the 1960s by Mies van der Rohe, houses German and international paintings from the 20th century. It's strong on German expressionists and surrealists such as Max Beckmann, Otto Mueller, Ernst Ludwig Kirchner, Paul Klee and Max Ernst. The Neue Sachlichkeit is also well represented by George Grosz and Otto Dix. Many major non-German 20th-century artists are also featured, Picasso, de Chirico, Léger, Munch, Wols and Dali among them. However, the pleasure of the gallery is in discovering lesser-known artists like Ludwig Meidner, whose post-World War I apocalyptic landscapes exert the great, garish power of the most action-packed *Marvel* comic centrefold.

Note: Its 19th-century exhibits are now part of the Alte Nationalgalerie's collection; this has in turn been moved for the time being to the **Altes Museum** (*see above*).

Schinkel-Museum

Werderscher Markt (in Friedrich-Werdersche-Kirche), Mitte, 10117 (208 1323). U6 Französische Straße. **Open** 10am-6pm Tue-Sun. **Admission** DM4; DM2 concs. **Map F3**

The brick church, designed by Karl Friedrich Schinkel, was completed in 1830. Its war wounds were repaired in the 1980s and it reopened in 1987 as a homage to its architect. Inside are statues by Schinkel, Schadow and others, rubbing shoulders in the soft light from the stained glass windows. Pictures of Schinkel's works that didn't survive the war (like the Prinz-Albert-Schloß) are also displayed.

Schloß Charlottenburg

Luisenplatz and Spandauer Damm, Charlottenburg, 14059 (320 911). U2 Sophie-Charlotte-Platz/U7 Richard-Wagner-Platz. **Open** *Apr-Oct* 9am-5pm Tue-Fri; 10am-5pm Sat-Sun. **Admission** *combination ticket* DM15; DM8 concs; *single ticket* DM1-4; DM1-2 concs; free Sun. **Map B3**

Queen Sophie-Charlotte was the impetus behind this sprawling palace and garden – hubbie Friedrich III (later King Friedrich I) built it in 1695 as a modest summer home for his Queen. Later kings also summered here, tinkering with and adding to the buildings. Unless you have a whole day, it's best to tackle only a part of the Schloß. The central and oldest section houses the bedrooms of its original residents, Sophie-Charlotte and her husband. The apartments can only be seen on guided tours in German; English group tours must be arranged weeks in advance.

Highlights of the newer west wing are the living quarters of Frederick the Great, including his collection of 18th-century paintings. The Romantic Gallery downstairs includes the beautifully bleak work of Caspar David Friedrich, alongside the paintings of Schinkel and a number of lesser German romantics. The Schinkel Pavilion, named after its designer, used to be a summer house. Built in 1825, it contains sculpture, drawings, furniture, porcelain and more paintings by the indefatigable Schinkel.

The Belvedere, a tea house designed in 1788 by Langhans, architect of the Brandenburg Gate, contains three floors of fine porcelain from the 18th and 19th centuries, including pieces by KPM Berlin, porcelain-makers to the Kaiser. The Mausoleum houses the tombs of Queen Louise, Friedrich Wilhelm III, Kaiser Wilhelm I and Kaiserin Augusta.

Botany

Botanisches Museum

Botanical Museum

Königin-Luise-Straße 6-8, Zehlendorf, 14195 (830 060). U1 Dahlem-Dorf/S1 Botanischer Garten. **Open** *Oct-Feb* 9am-5pm Tue-Sun; *Mar, Sept* 9am-6pm Tue-Sun; *Apr, Aug* 9am-7pm Tue-Sun; *May, July* 9am-8pm Tue-Sat; *June* 9am-9pm Tue-Sat. **Admission** DM8; DM4 concs.

Within the Free University's Botanical Gardens (*see chapter* **Sightseeing**), this museum is meant to show behind the scenes of the plant kingdom. There are fossils and dioramas showing plant life through the ages, examples of mushrooms, sponges, leaves, seeds and woods in vitrines, as well as the different types and uses of commodities such as rice, tobacco, hemp and cotton. There is no information in English, and the museum looks like it was finished around the time the Wall went up and has never been redecorated since, but it's free with a ticket for the gardens. The cross-section of the California redwood, as well as the herbs stolen from ancient Egyptian and Roman graves, are both worth seeing.

Märkisches Museum – *clowns abound.*

Cabaret & circuses

Märkisches Museum
Am Köllnischen Park 5, Mitte, 10179 (308 660). U2 Märkisches Museum. **Open** 10am-6pm Tue-Sun. **Admission** DM3; DM1 concs. **Map G4**
All kinds of circus and variety show paraphernalia are displayed at the Märkisches Museum: old clown costumes, handbills, posters and brief histories of circuses and the artists who performed in them. In the back, and perhaps the most interesting exhibit, is a selection of programmes and newspaper articles from the scandalous variety shows and cabaret acts that made Berlin notorious in the 1920s. The highlight is the stuffed body of a famous circus lion that gave up the ghost in 1987. The rest of the museum is a bit stuffy and static, but diehard circus-lovers shouldn't be disappointed. In the park outside is the bearpit housing the Berlin bears, the city's official symbol – albeit a rather forlorn one.

Commodities

Hanf Museum
Hemp Museum
Mühlendamm 5, Mitte, 10178 (242 4827). U2 Klosterstraße. **Open** 10am-8pm Tue-Fri; noon-8pm Sat-Sun. **Admission** DM5. **Map G3**
The world's largest hemp museum has the aim of teaching the visitor about the uses of hemp throughout history, as well as touching on the controversy

surrounding the herb today. There are a few booklets to leaf through in English, as well as books in the shop such as *Growing Marijuana in Cool Climates* and *Industrial Hemp*, about hemp-based products. The exhibit starts with the history of hemp growing and interesting displays of the plant's many traditional uses in textiles and industry – from ropes and sails to wigs and beauty cream. There is then a section on its medicinal properties, including a 1900 advert touting hashish as 'the ideal cure for calluses and warts'. Another section is devoted to hemp's cultural meaning, including a display of hookahs and pipes, and explanations of the plant's uses around the world. (In Vietnam it's used as a spice, while the Turks have used it as a drug since ancient times.) Finally, there is a section on the current controversy surrounding its legalisation. The café (doubling as a video and reading room) has cakes made with and without hemp. Everything, though, is sadly THC-free.

Zucker Museum
Sugar Museum
Amrumer Straße 32, Wedding, 13353 (3142 7574). U9 Amrumer Straße. **Open** 9am-4.30pm Mon-Thur; 11am-6pm Sat. **Admission** DM4.50; DM2 concs. **Map D1**
Any museum devoted to the chemistry, history and political importance of sugar would have problems thrilling the punters. But the Zucker does have a very unusual collection of sugar paraphernalia. Most interesting is a slide show on the slave trade, on which the sugar industry was so dependent. Something to ponder over a coffee.

Ethnology

Museum für Völkerkunde
Ethnological Museum
Lansstraße 8, Zehlendorf, 14195 (830 1438). U1 Dahlem-Dorf. **Open** 10am-6pm Tue-Fri; 11am-6pm Sat-Sun. **Admission** DM4; DM2 concs.
The Ethnological Museum is much too big to be covered in one visit. Eight regional departments cover two floors: Oceanian; American; African; East Asian; South Asian; West Asian and European, as well as Music Ethnology. There is also an educational department which includes a junior museum and museum for the blind. No need to bother with all the collection, though, as some sections are pretty tedious (the early American exhibits, for instance, can easily be bypassed). But the South Sea (Südsee) collection should not be missed, nor should the beaded artefacts from Cameroon: the beaded throne is quite amazing (although it looks less than comfy). The displays themselves are a joy – no doubt the curators had a lot of fun putting them together. The most interesting collection contains New Guinean masks and effigies suspended from the ceiling in well-lit cabinets; a large assortment of boats and canoes; a number of curious façades; even a fully intact men's clubhouse. The figure of a woman, suspended over the doorway with her legs wide open, just goes to show that boys have always been boys.

Museum für Europäische Kulturen

Museum of European Cultures
Im Winkel 6-8, Zehlendorf, 14195 (8390 1287). U1 Dahlem-Dorf. **Open** 10am-6pm Tue-Fri; 11am-6pm Sat-Sun. **Admission** DM4; DM2 concs.
Traditional clothes, jewellery, furniture, cooking utensils and toys of the people of Europe, from the Rhine to Silesia, are collected here. Exhibits are artfully arranged and informative. Particularly worth seeing is the traditional clothing, much of which was still worn regularly up to the first half of the 20th century. The displays of weaving and spinning machines are also admirable. The museum is near but not a part of the immense Dahlem complex (of which the **Museum für Völkerkunde** is currently the only open component). Follow the sign at Dahlem-Dorf U-Bahn station.

History

See also **Schloß Charlottenburg** *under* **Arts & architecture**.

Allied Museum

Outpost, Clayallee 135, Zehlendorf, 14195 (818 1990). U1 Oskar-Helene-Heim. **Open** 10am-6pm Mon-Tue, Thur-Sun; 10am-8pm Wed. **Admission** free.
The Allied forces arrived as conquerors, kept West Berlin alive during the 1948 Airlift and left many Berliners with tears in their eyes when they finally went home again in 1994. Housed in what used to be a cinema for US Forces personnel (audiences used to stand for the Stars and Stripes), the exhibition is mostly about the period of the Blockade and the Airlift, documented with photos, tanks, jeeps, planes, weapons, uniforms, cookbooks and music. Outside you can find the building that was once the stop-and-search centrepiece of Checkpoint Charlie.

Anti-Kriegsmuseum

Anti-War Museum
Brüsseler Straße 21, Wedding, 13353 (4549 0110). U9 Amrumer Straße. **Open** 4-8pm daily.
Admission free. **Map D1**
The original was founded in 1925 by Ernst Friedrich, author of the book *War Against War*. It was destroyed in 1933 by the Nazis, and Friedrich fled to Brussels. There he had another museum from 1936-1940, at which point German troops once again showed up and trashed the place. In 1982 a group of teachers including Tommy Spree, grandson of Friedrich, reestablished the museum in West Berlin. It now hosts changing exhibitions (for example on the work of Gandhi, or persecution of Kurds in Turkey), as well as a permanent display including some grim World War I photos and artefacts from the original museum, children's war toys, information on German colonialism in Africa, pieces of anti-Semitic material from the Nazi era. World War II memorabilia includes a medal of honour awarded to German mothers who bore lots of children, and a 1940s air-raid shelter in the cellar. In addition, there is a 15-minute video in German on Friedrich and his

work. Information on the museum and copies of *War Against War* are available in English, but the exhibitions themselves are only in German. Call ahead to arrange a tour in English with British director Tommy Spree.

Museum Berliner Arbeiterleben

Museum of Berlin Working-Class Life
Husemannstraße 12, Prenzlauer Berg, 10435 (442 2514). U2 Eberswalder Straße. **Open** 10am-3pm Mon-Thur. **Admission** free. **Map G2**
Reconstruction of a Berlin worker's flat as it would have been around 1900. It's an interesting way to tell the story of everyday life in Berlin, with all kinds of articles on display, ranging from a stove-heated curling iron to a weirdly shaped baby carriage. The front room is set aside for changing exhibitions.

Deutsch-Russisches Museum Berlin-Karlshorst

Berlin-Karlshorst German-Russian Museum
Zwieseler Straße 4/corner Rheinsteinstraße, Karlshorst, 10318 (5015 0841). S3 Karlshorst. **Open** 10am-6pm Tue-Sun. **Admission** free.
Built between 1936-38, this place was used until 1945 as a German officers' club. After the Soviets took Berlin, it was commandeered as a headquarters for the military administration and it was here, during the night of 8-9 May 1945, that German commanders signed the final and unconditional surrender of the Nazi army, thus ending the war in Europe. It was also here, five years later, that Soviet General Chuikov authorised the first communist government in the GDR. The building now houses a museum which looks at the German-Soviet relationship over 70 years. Divided into 16 small rooms including the Allied flag-adorned conference room in which the Nazis surrendered, it takes us through two world wars and one cold one, assorted pacts, victories and capitulations, and varying degrees of hatred and camaraderie. The permanent exhibit includes lots of photos, memorabilia, documents, campaign maps, video footage and propaganda posters. Buy a guide in English for DM4; the exhibits are explained in German and Russian. Interesting enough to warrant a couple of hours.

Dokumentationszentrum Berliner Mauer

Berlin Wall Documentation Centre
Bernauer Straße 111, Wedding, 13355 (464 1030). U8 Bernauer Straße. **Open** 10am-5pm Wed-Sun. **Admission** free. **Map F2**
Like communism never happened, it's hard to find much evidence of the Wall these days. But you can still see a short stretch of it, plus the accompanying swathe of no-man's-land and various border defences, here at this memorial, which stands on the district boundary line separating Mitte and Wedding. The attached Documentation Centre presents a complete history of the Wall, with hundreds of photos and documents plus slide shows and videos. Die Kapelle der Versönung ('Chapel of Reconciliation'), built on the site of a former church destroyed by the East Germans, stands as a memorial to those killed attempting to escape.

Museum Haus am Checkpoint Charlie

Friedrichstraße 44, Kreuzberg, 10969 (253 7250).
U6 Kochstraße. **Open** 9am-10pm daily. **Admission**
DM8; DM5 concs. **Map F3**
An essential trip for anyone interested in the Wall
and the Cold War. The museum opened not long
after the GDR erected the Berlin Wall in 1961 with
the purpose of documenting the grisly events that
were taking place. The exhibition charts the history of the Wall, and gives details of the ingenious and
hair-raising ways people escaped from the GDR –
as well as exhibiting some of the contraptions that
were used, such as suitcases and a weird car with a
propeller. There's also a display about non-violent
revolutions – including information about Mahatma
Gandhi, Lech Wałesa and, of course, the peaceful
1989 upheaval in East Germany.

Gedenkstätte Haus der Wannsee-Konferenz

Wannsee Conference Memorial House
Am Großen Wannsee 56-58, Zehlendorf, 14109 (805
0010). S1, S7 Wannsee, then bus 114. **Open** 10am-
6pm Mon-Fri; 2-6pm Sat-Sun. **Admission** free.
On 20 January 1942, a grim collection of prominent
Nazis – Heydrich and Eichmann among them –
gathered here on the Wannsee to draw up plans for
the Final Solution, making jokes and sipping brandy
as they sorted out the practicalities of genocide.
Today, this infamous villa has been converted into
a place of remembrance, with a standing photo exhibition about the conference and its consequences.
Call in advance if you want to join an English-language tour, otherwise all information is in German.

Grusel Kabinett

Chamber of Horrors
Schöneberger Straße 23a, Kreuzberg, 10963 (2655
5546). S1, S2 Anhalter Bahnhof. **Open** 10am-7pm
Mon-Tue, Thur, Sun; 10am-9pm Fri; noon-8pm Sat.
Admission DM12; DM8 concs. **Map E4**
The 'Berlin Creepy Show', as they call it, is housed
in the city's only visitable World War II air-raid shelter. Built in 1943, the five-level bunker was part of
an underground network connecting various other
bunkers and stations throughout Berlin, and today
houses both the Grusel Kabinett and an exhibit on
the dark and chilly bunker itself. The latter includes
a few personal effects found here after the War, various bunker plans and a video documentary in
German only. The actual structure is the most interesting thing. The 'horrors' begin at ground level with
an exhibit on medieval medicine (mechanical figures
amputate a leg to the sound of canned screaming).
Elsewhere there's a patented coffin designed to call
attention to your predicament should you happen to
be buried alive. Upstairs is scarier: a shadowy,
musty labyrinth with a simulated cemetery, strange
cloaked figures, lots of spooky sounds and a few surprises. Kids love it, but not those under ten.

Hugenotten Museum

Gendarmenmarkt, Mitte, 10117 (229 1760). U6
Französische Straße. **Open** noon-5pm Tue-Sat; 11am-
5pm Sun. **Admission** DM3; DM2 concs. **Map F3**

An exhibition on the history of the French
Protestants in France and Berlin-Brandenburg is
displayed in the Französischer Dom, still the congregation's main church. The museum chronicles
the religious persecution Calvinists suffered (note
the bust of Calvin on the outside of the church) and
their subsequent immigration to Berlin after 1685,
at the behest of the Hohenzollerns. The development
of the Huguenot community is also detailed with
paintings, documents and artefacts. One part of the
museum is devoted to the church's history, particularly the effects of World War II – it was bombed
during a Sunday service in 1944 and remained a ruin
until the mid-1980s. Other exports from France can
be found in the wine restaurant upstairs.

Luftwaffe Museum

Air Force Museum
Ritterfelddamm, Gatow, 14089 (3687 2601). U7
Rathaus Spandau, then bus 135 to Gutsstraße. **Open**
10am-5pm Tue-Sun. **Admission** free.
On the western fringes of the city at one of the air-
bases integral to the Berlin Airlift (and a 25-minute
walk from the nearest bus stop), this is a 'museum
in progress'. An old hangar houses much of the
exhibit, which includes information on the history
of the Luftwaffe as well as fighter and surveillance
planes from the beginning of the century through to
1970s NATO equipment. There's a World War I tri-
plane, a restored Handley Page Hastings (as used in
the Airlift) and an Antonov An-2 from the GDR Air
Force. Outside are more recent aircraft, including
modern fighter planes and helicopters.

Ministerium für Staatssicherheit Forschungs- und Gedenkstätte Normannenstraße

Stasi Museum
Ruschestraße 59, Lichtenberg, 10365 (553 6854).
U5 Magdalenenstraße. **Open** 11am-6pm Tue-Fri; 2-
6pm Sat-Sun. **Admission** DM5; DM3 concs.
These days you almost need evidence that communism ever happened. This museum, housed in part
of what used to be the gruesome headquarters of the
Ministerium für Staatssicherheit (the *Stasi* – the East
German equivalent of the KGB), offers some proof.
You can look round the old offices of secret police
chief Erich Mielke – his old uniform still hangs in
his wardrobe – and view displays of bugging
devices and spy cameras concealed in books, plant
pots and Trabant car doors. There's also a lot of
communist kitsch: tasteless furniture, tacky medals,
banners and busts of Marx and Lenin. The documentation is in Germany only.

Nikolaikirche

Nikolaikirchplatz, Mitte, 10178 (240 020). U2
Klosterstraße. **Open** 10am-5.30pm Tue-Sun.
Admission DM5; DM2.50 concs. **Map G3**
Inside Berlin's oldest congregational church, from
which the Nikolaiviertel takes its name, is an interesting historical collection chronicling Berlin's development from its founding (c1230) until 1648. Old
tiles, tapestries, stone and wood carvings – even old
weapons and punishment devices – are on display.

The Story of Berlin – *Nazi book-burning in 3D sound and vision.*

The collection includes photographs of the extensive wartime damage, plus examples of how the stones melted together in the heat of bombardment. Reconstruction was completed in 1987, in time to celebrate Berlin's 750th anniversary. Your ticket is also valid for the nearby **Ephraim-Palais** (*see above*).

Museum für Post und Kommunikation

Museum of Post and Communication
Leipziger Straße 15, Mitte, 10117 (202 940). U2 Mohrenstraße. **Map F4**
At press time this was about to reopen, having relocated from west Berlin premises. The old post museum had several short videos, exhibits and displays for kids to push, pull and turn, and traced the Prussian/German postal system from the late 19th century to the present.

Stiftung Topographie des Terrors

Niederkirchnerstraße 8, Mitte, 10117 (2548 6703). S1, S2/U2 Potsdamer Platz. **Open** 10am-6pm Tue-Sun. **Admission** free. **Map F4**
The Topography of Terror is a piece of waste ground where once stood the Prinz Albrecht Palais, headquarters of the Gestapo. It was from here that the Holocaust was directed, and where the Germanisation of the east was dreamt up. You can walk around – small markers explain what was where – before examining the fascinating exhibit documenting the history of Nazi state terror. This is housed in some former basement cells of the Gestapo complex. The catalogue (DM13 and available in English) is excellent. A surviving segment of the Berlin Wall runs along the northern boundary of the site and a library and document centre is due to open in late 2001.

The Story of Berlin

Kurfürstendamm 207-208, Charlottenburg, 10719 (01805 992 010). U15 Uhlandstraße. **Open** 10am-8pm daily. **Admission** DM18; DM14 concs. **Map C4**
If you're interested in the city's history, The Story of Berlin should not be missed. Some 7,000sq m are filled with superbly designed rooms and multimedia exhibits created by renowned authors, designers and film and stage specialists telling Berlin's story from its founding in 1237 to the present day. Equipped with an activated head-set, visitors are taken from a futuristic room through a series of 20 historically themed ones, recalling with sound and narration various stages in the city's history: from Frederick the Great's world of war to the Golden Twenties; from the Nazi era to daily life in East Berlin – all in excellent 3D sound in German or English. Underneath all this is a massive nuclear shelter. Built by the Allies in the 1970s, this low-ceilinged, oppressive bunker is still a fully functional shelter and can hold up to 3,500 people. Guided tours are given several times a day.

Museum der Verbotenen Kunst

Museum of Prohibited Art
Schlesichen Busch, Puschkinallee, Treptow, 12435 (204 2049). U1 Schlesisches Tor. **Open** *Apr-Nov* noon-6pm Sat-Sun. **Admission** DM1.
This former Cold War watchtower, which stands right on the border between Treptow and Kreuzberg, is now home to a modest but interesting exhibition on the history of the Wall. Photos and documentation illustrate its construction, operation and security measures. There's also a gallery of art with Wall themes.

Natural history

Naturkundemuseum

Invalidenstraße 43, Mitte, 10115 (209 38591). U6 Zinnowitzer Straße. **Open** 9.30am-5pm Tue-Sun. **Admission** DM5; DM2.50 concs. **Map E3**

This Natural History Museum is one of the world's largest and best organised. Also one of the oldest: the core of the collection dates from 1716. A tall skeleton of a brachiosaurus greets you in the dinosaur-filled first room, each exhibit thought to be at least 150 million years old. The archaeopteryx is perhaps the most perfectly preserved example yet unearthed. Another room has an vast display of fossils, from trilobites to lobsters, while other highlights include the skeleton of a giant armadillo. The animal collection, assembled in the 1920s, is almost like a zoo – except that these critters are stuffed. The huge mineral collection is a wonder: row upon row of rocks, set up just as they were when the building first opened in 1889. Don't miss the meteor chunks in the back. Part of the Humboldt University, the museum has over 60 million exhibits in total.

Music

Music Box

Sony Center, Kemperplatz 1, Tiergarten, 10785 (5513 7137). S1, S2/U2 Potsdamer Platz. **Open** 10am-10pm daily. **Admission** DM20; DM12 children. **Map E4**

Museum der Verbotenen Kunst.

Unveiled as part of the Sony Center complex in January 2000, and clearly intended to showcase Sony technology, this interactive exhibit is supposed to 'take visitors on a journey through the world of music'. The visitor can go on a 'Beatles Yellow Submarine Adventure', conduct a virtual Berlin Philharmonic, play with exotic new digital instruments and scrutinise a 'Musical Map' of the world. At press time we had only seen a press release, so are unable to judge just how exciting all this actually is in (virtual) reality. *See also chapter* **Children**.

Musikinstrumenten-Museum

Tiergartenstraße 1, Tiergarten, 10785 (254 810). Bus 142, 148. **Open** 9am-5pm Tue-Fri; 10am-5pm Sat-Sun. **Admission** DM4; DM2 concs; free under-12s; free Sun. **Map E4**

Over 2,200 string, keyboard, wind and percussion instruments dating back to the 1500s are crammed into this small museum next to the **Philharmonie**. Among them are assorted rococo musical clocks, for which 18th-century princes commissioned jingles from Mozart, Haydn and Beethoven. The place comes alive during tours, when guides play such obsolete instruments as the Kammerflugel. Concerts on the first Saturday of the month.

Sexuality

Beate-Uhse Erotik-Museum

Joachimstaler Straße 4, Charlottenburg, 10623 (886 0666). S3, S5, S7, S9/U2, U9 Zoologischer Garten. **Open** 9am-midnight daily. **Admission** DM10; DM8 concs. **Map C4**

The three floors of this collection (above a flagship Beate-Uhse retail outlet offering the usual videos and sex toys) contain varied oriental prints, some stupid showroom-dummy tableaux, and glass cases containing such delights as early Japanese dildos, Andean penis flutes, Javanese erotic dagger hilts, 17th-century chastity belts, a giant coconut that looks like an arse and a vase used in the film *Caligula*. A small exhibit on pioneering sex researcher Magnus Hirschfeld sadly comprises nothing more than a few boards of dry documentary material, worthily considering the history of his Institut für Sexualwissenschaft, which was opened in Berlin in 1919 and eventually closed down by the Nazis. The only other things with any connection to Berlin are an inadequate item on Heinrich Zille and a corner documenting the career of Frau Uhse herself, who went from being a Luftwaffe pilot and postwar potato-picker to annual sex-aid sales of DM100 million. Oddly respectable, given its subject.

Schwules Museum

Gay Museum

Mehringdamm 61, Kreuzberg, 10961 (693 1172). U6, U7 Mehringdamm. **Open** 2-6pm Mon-Wed, Fri-Sun; 2-9pm Thur; *tours* 5pm Sat. **Admission** DM7; DM4 concs. **Map F5**

This museum, opened in 1985, is the first and still the only one in the world dedicated to the research and public exhibition of homosexual life in all of its

Schwules Museum – *the first and only of its kind. See page 91.*

forms. The museum, its library and archives are staffed by volunteers and function thanks to private donations, including bequests (such as the archive of GDR sex scientist Rudolf Klimmer). On the ground floor is the actual museum, which (in rather limited space) houses temporary exhibitions that include photography, video, installations, sketches, sculpture, and so forth. More impressive are the library and archives on the third floor. Here can be found around 8,000 books (around 500 in English), 3,000 international periodicals, collections of photos, posters, plus TV, film and audio footage, all available for lending. Information about the whole place is available in English and many other languages.

Theatre

Brecht-Weigel-Gedenkstätte

Chausseestraße 125, Mitte, 10115 (282 9916). U6 Zinnowitzer Straße/Oranienburger Tor. **Open** 5-7pm Tue-Fri; 5-6.30pm Thur; 9.30am-noon Sat. **Admission** DM6; DM3 concs. **Map F2**
Brecht's home, from 1948 until his death in 1953, has been preserved exactly as he left it. Tours of the house last about half an hour and give interesting insights into the life and reading habits of the playwright. The window at which he worked overlooked the grave of Hegel in the Dorotheenstädtische und Friedrichs-Werdersche Friedhof, which is where Brecht, too, is buried (*see chapter* **Sightseeing**). His wife, actress Helene Weigel, continued living here until she died in 1971. The Brecht archives are kept upstairs. Tours take place every half-hour – phone in advance for one in English. The Kellerrestaurant near the exit serves 'select wines and fine beers and Viennese cooking in the style of Helene Weigel', in case you want to extend your Brecht-Weigel experience. *See chapter* **Restaurants**.

Technology

Computer und Videospiele Museum

Rungestraße 20, Mitte, 10179 (279 3315). U8 Heinrich-Heine-Straße. **Open** noon-6pm Sun. **Admission** DM6; DM3 concs. **Map G4**
A 1953 chess computer, Eliza, Pong, Pac Man, and nearly everything from the dawn of digital to the present day, to be viewed and played on the original machines. Kids love it, but any buff can enjoy the exhibits. The main curiosity is the GDR computer games played on clanky Robotron machines. *Website: www.computerspielemuseum.de*

Deutsches Technikmuseum Berlin

German Museum of Technology
Trebbiner Straße 9, Kreuzberg, 10963 (254 840). U1, U7 Möckernbrücke. **Open** 9am-5.30pm Tue-Fri; 10am-6pm Sat-Sun. **Admission** DM5; DM2 concs. **Map E5**
Opened in 1983 in the former goods depot of the once thriving Anhalter Bahnhof, a quirky collection of industrial objects. The rail exhibits have pride of place, with the station sheds providing an ideal setting for locomotives and rolling stock from 1835 to the present. On view are also exhibitions on the industrial revolution; street, rail, water and air traffic; computer technology and printing technology. Oddities, such as vacuum cleaners from the 1920s and a large collection of sextants, make this a fun spot for implement enthusiasts. Behind the main complex is an open-air section with two functioning windmills and a smithy. The Spectrum annex, in an old railway administrative building, houses 200 interactive devices and experiments. A further new wing to house an exhibit on ship, air and space travel is under construction. While this is going on, passers-by cannot fail to notice the hulk of half a plane sticking out towards Tempelhofer Ufer – it's an Allied DC3 from the Berlin Airlift.

Art Galleries

As Mitte turns professional, Berlin art remains balanced between the transient and the traditional.

The Berlin art scene is a strange animal. First there are the established west Berlin private galleries with big name artists that radiate an affluent and tasteful calm, then there are the big museums and galleries full of classical treasures and modern titans that span the city. And then there is Mitte, a mad, wild, scaffolding-clad hubbub hovering in the balance between yuppie wonderland and underground frisson. It is quite clear which way the scales are tipping, but for the moment Mitte is still in the strange transience that makes it so exciting. And meanwhile politicians, property developers, young commercial gallerists and a diverse assortment of artists are all contributing to a scene characterised by a variety of different and often conflicting visions. Among the dwindling war ruins, massive building sites and pastel concrete renovations, contemporary art in Berlin is enjoying renewed energy and international attention.

The 1990s were characterised by the clubs and bars that sprang up in the former East Berlin and became the hippest sites for underground or alternative art actions. Whether broadcasting on the net, exhibiting sardonic urban video or collaborating with DJs, the goal for artists was to do it weird, do it with others and, best of all, do it in a damp, squatted bunker.

The clubs and bars and experimental galleries got crowded, got popular, got press and started to get closed down as developers moved in. It wasn't long, however, before it dawned on investors that this scene was a potentially valuable asset. Which in turn created a shift in attention for the artists in their never-ending need for cash to finance their work. As local government funding receded in the arts, the money started to come from the builders, the bankers and the Bonners.

There has been a subtle and tangible shift to the art scene as the key to longer-term survival lies increasingly not in staying one step ahead of the authorities, but in professionalisation. Galleries large and small have had to wise up, get smart, sort out their marketing agenda or bite the dust. Some of the wackiest, most alternative -looking venues have had a media profile strategy that would make a Saatchi man blush.

The grubby, badly lit, crumbling cellars that were housing the work of the grubby, badly-dressed new avant garde in the mid- to late 1990s are now replastered, repainted, restyled and low

Deutsche Guggenheim. *See page 94.*

voltaged. The artists now have central heating and running water and their work is losing its rougher edges. Even **aktionsgalerie**, once last bastion of the grubby anarchic underground at Hackescher Markt, has bowed to the new broom.

Generally speaking (there are some important exceptions) work by historical figures of German art is still found in the older galleries in and around Charlottenburg, but gallery-goers who've been to Berlin before – even recently – won't recognise the rest of the scene. Mitte is now where international contemporary and cutting-edge work is found, and in the area around Hackescher Markt and Auguststraße there are galleries everywhere you turn. Many alternative and temporary exhibitions have moved further out to Friedrichshain and Treptow, where there are still some empty old buildings to be found.

An easy way to orient yourself in the Mitte scene is to attend a Rundgang ('walk around'). On a

Rundgang evening the Mitte galleries all open at the same time, allowing visitors to stroll from one to another. They tend to be on the evening of the first Saturday in each month. You will need to check listings (*see below*) for dates. There are two major events in the Berlin art calendar: **Art Forum Berlin** and the **Berlin Biennale**. The former, an international art fair, takes place late October at the Messehallen unter dem Funkturm (for details contact European Galleries, Projektgesellschaft GmbH, 8855 1643). *See chapter* **By Season**.

Listings & information

Most galleries provide free copies of the *Mitte Gallery Guide* and/or *Berliner Galerien* (which covers all Berlin). Both have maps; neither list all galleries. Also look out for other written material in galleries, cafés and bars, as invitations to forthcoming exhibitions are often there for the taking.

Buying a copy of the *Berlin Artery* from a gallery for DM3.50 is a far better bet. Published every two months, it contains comprehensive gallery listings with maps to pinpoint their locations, reviews in both English and German, and a calendar of openings and special events, including the Mitte Rundgang.

Public galleries & collections

See also chapter **Museums** *for* **Bauhaus Archiv-Museum für Gestaltung, Bröhan Museum, Brücke Museum, Gemäldegalerie, Georg-Kolbe-Museum, Hamburger Bahnhof, Käthe-Kollwitz-Museum, Martin-Gropius-Bau,** *and* **Neue Nationalgalerie.**

Akademie der Künste

Hanseatenweg 10, Tiergarten, 10557 (390 760). U9 Hansaplatz/S3, S5, S7, S9 Bellevue. **Open** Mon;10am-7pm Tue-Sun. **Admission** DM6; DM4 concs; Wed free. **Map D3**
Founded by the Prussian Prince Friedrich III in 1696, the Akademie der Künste is one of the oldest cultural institutions in Berlin. By 1938, however, the Nazis had forced virtually all of its prominent members into exile. Re-established in 1954, in a new building from architect Werner Duttmann, to serve as 'a community of exceptional artists' from the world over, its multi-faceted programme now offers a great variety of events ranging from free jazz concerts and poetry readings to performances and film screenings as well as art exhibitions.
Café. Group discounts. Wheelchair access.

DAAD Galerie

Kurfürstenstraße 58, Tiergarten, 10785 (261 3640). U1, U2, U4 Nollendorfplatz/U1, U2 Wittenbergplatz. **Open** 12.30-7pm daily. **Admission** free. **Map D4**
Above the Café Einstein, this is gallery for the German Academic Exchange Service (DAAD) that initiated an 'Artists-in-Residence' programme in West

Berlin in 1965. The list of DAAD-sponsored artists reads like a 'Who's Who' of the international art world. John Armleder, Daniel Buren, Edward Kienholz, Mario Merz and Nam June Paik have all partaken. More recent recipients of this grant include Andrea Zittel, Steven Pippin and Johan Grimonprez.

Deutsche Guggenheim Berlin

Unter den Linden 13-15, Mitte, 10017 (202 0930). U6 Französische Straße. **Open** 11am-8pm daily. **Admission** DM8; DM5 concs; free Mon. **Map F3**
In partnership with the Deutsche Bank (and housed in one of their buildings) this is perhaps the least impressive European branch of the Guggenheim museums. Big bucks, big ads, big boring. Huge, safe, famous name, glossy corporate art that you can take your granny to and buy a catalogue afterwards.
Website: www.deutsche-guggenheim-berlin.de

Haus am Lützowplatz

Lützowplatz 9, Tiergarten, 10785 (261 3805). U1, U2, U4 Nollendorfplatz. **Open** 11am-6pm Tue-Sun. **Admission** free. **Map D4**
One of the first non-commercial, private galleries to re-open in West Berlin after World War II. It shows mostly figurative work from Berlin neo-realists such as Elvira Bach plus paintings, sculpture and photography from Hungary, Bulgaria, Russia and Poland. Run under the iron hand of curator Karin Pott, the gallery has a reputation of some standing. The Studiogalerie at the back is given over to young curators and artists annually to produce their own programme of events and shows.
Wheelchair access from parking lot in the back of the house.

Haus am Waldsee

Argentinische Allee 30, Zehlendorf, 14163 (8091 2234). U1 Krumme Lanke. **Open** noon-8pm Tue-Sun. **Admission** DM6; DM4 concs.
Founded in 1946 by the local arts council, in a villa in the wealthy suburb of Zehlendorf. During the first two decades after World War II the Haus mounted a series of pioneering exhibitions which presented the work of artists who had been banned by the Nazis and, as a result, were almost unknown in Germany at the time: Käthe Kollwitz (in 1946); Hermann Blumenthal (in 1947); Karl Schmidt-Rottluff (in 1948) and Max Ernst (in 1951). But even as late as 1980, with its show *Heftige Malerei* ('Violent Painting'), the gallery broke new ground for those neo-Expressionist Junge Wilde painters who – just three years later – were to be the main attraction of the international Zeitgeist show at the Martin-Gropius-Bau. But that's history. These days you should check what's on before making the trip to the suburbs.

Haus der Kulturen der Welt

Kongreßhalle, John-Foster-Dulles-Allee 10, Tiergarten, 10557 (397 870). 100, 248 bus. **Open** 10am-7pm Tue-Sun. **Admission** DM6; DM4 concs. **Map E3**
A unique institution and an important part of Berlin's cultural life. Funded by the Federal government and the Berlin Senate, the 'House of World Cultures' was set up in January 1989 to promote

The man who made Mitte?

If one name came to be held synonymous with the 1990s art boom in Berlin Mitte, it would most likely be that of Klaus Biesenbach – gallerist, curator and marketing supremo. Other names might be tossed into the ring. That of Friedrich Loock, for example, whose Galerie Wohnmaschine was the first art outpost in Auguststraße. Or that of Eigen + Art's Gerd Harry 'Judy' Lybke. Or administrator/facilitator Jutta Weitz. But one suspects that Biesenbach will always scoop the pool, and his is certainly the name currently most muttered (as often as not darkly) at Mitte's artier parties.

Former medical student Biesenbach arrived in Berlin from Munich in the winter of 1989-90 at the age of 23. Within two years he and others had taken over a former margarine factory in Auguststraße to use as a centre for contemporary art projects and began inviting curators and artists from other international art hot spots. He orchestrated the 37 Rooms exhibition in empty spaces all over Auguststraße and initiated its status as Berlin's now internationally renowned 'Art Mile'.

By his late twenties Biesenbach had projects running with artists of significant standing such as Katharina Sieverding, Bruce Nauman and Joseph Kosuth. The crumbling rooms of the factory, now named **Kunst-Werke**, or KW, were host to many exhibitions and served as studios and performance spaces for a number of artists.

The professionalisation of what appeared on the surface to be an anarchic, underground scene was swift, assured and subtle. Biesenbach took control of the organisation and maintained the cutting-edge profile while securing private, local government and lottery investment in building restoration. The elegant new Kunst-Werke complex reopened its first phase in 1998 and a further new exhibition hall completed in 1999.

Biesenbach, in the meantime, had been consolidating his reputation by curating 'hybrid work space' at the Documenta X in Kassel and in New York's P.S. 1, by working in Japan and London and by being on the jury of the 1997 Venice Biennale. In 1998 he hosted, along with curators Hans-

Klaus, but no cigar.

Ulrich Obrist and Nancy Spector, the first Berlin-Biennale. The show highlighted Berlin's status as a major centre for young contemporary art with Biesenbach leading the charge.

With his lupine eyes, sharp suits and bottle-blond hair Biesenbach, a deft self-publicist, is evidently not a man content to work quietly behind the scenes. He is at pains to emphasise that artists produce work together with the KW. It is not an institution that holds with 'the 19th-century idea that art is made and then preserved'. Rather the KW 'produces lots of art with artists'. On the surface this approach appears to be a claim of some arrogance but the sort of work KW artists are concerned with – drawing together contemporary lifestyle, political, club and nightlife influences – often has less to do with 'individual works of art' than with the complexity of stage productions where the 'house' takes credit for its visionary approach and its choice of director.

That is not to say that a number of KW's featured artists are not becoming stars in their own right. Critical attention and public attendance at the shows are high and this means reaching an international audience and market. Top billing, however, always goes to the Kunst-Werke itself. And, of course, to Klaus Biesenbach.

Biesenbach sees the KW as fulfilling a similar role to that of P.S. 1 in New York or London's ICA: a venue for cutting-edge contemporary art that facilitates production, presentation and discussion under one roof. This he has most certainly achieved, but there is more. When you are involved in the moulding of a cultural infrastructure from zero then the knock-on effects can be extraordinary. The Auguststraße area is unrecognisable from the decayed back streets of ten years ago. Biesenbach may have his detractors, the achievements of KW may not be his alone, but there is no doubt that his dynamism and personality have played a significant role in the creation of an international image for a district of Berlin, with all its cultural, economic and political repercussions. He is one of the shapers of the new capital.

artists from developing countries, mounting spectacular large-scale exhibitions such as contemporary Indian art, Bedouin culture in North Africa and the avant-garde in China. The programme also features film festivals, readings, lectures, panel discussions, concerts and dance performances. Hugh A Stubbins' oyster-like Kongreßhalle was erected in 1957-58 as America's contribution to Berlin's first international building exhibition. When the original structure collapsed in 1980, the building was rebuilt almost from the ground up.

Bookshop. Restaurant. Wheelchair access; toilets for the disabled.

Hochschule der Künste

Hardenbergstraße 33, Charlottenburg, 10623 (318 50). U2 Ernst-Reuter-Platz/S3, S5, S7, S9/U2, U9 Zoologischer Garten. **Open** 6am-midnight Mon-Sat. **Admission** free. **Map C4**

Enter the main lobby and you'll find a colourful diversity of student displays ranging from traditional painting to video installations and computer graphics. Most of the Junge Wilde painters are in some way connected with the HdK – either as teachers (Karl-Horst Hödicke, Georg Baselitz) or as former students (Salomé, Helmut Middendorf, Rainer Fetting). The school has annual open days and also hosts symposia and other events.

Wheelchair access.

Kunst-Werke

Auguststraße 69, Mitte, 10117 (281 7325). U6 Oranienburger Tor. **Open** noon-6pm Tue-Sun. **Admission** DM5; DM3 concs. **Map F3**

Originally a pioneering but modest undertaking, Kunst-Werke is now the funding-fattened HQ of artistic director Klaus Biesenbach (see page 95 **The man who made Mitte?**) and the most high-profile venue in Berlin for young and emerging contemporary art. It has been fully refurbished with a 'café pavilion' by Dan Graham and a new exhibition hall from architect Hans Düttmann. Two tubular slides snake down the outside of the building and serve as fire escapes – great diversion for the young and young-at-heart if all that art gets too intense. Featured artists include: Marina Abramović; Gary Hill; Carsten Höller and Sol Le Witt. From September 2000 it co-hosts the Berlin Biennale.

Café.

Künstlerhaus Bethanien

Mariannenplatz 2, Kreuzberg, 10997 (616 9030). U1, U8 Kottbusser Tor/U1 Görlitzer Bahnhof. **Open** 2-7pm Tue-Sun. **Admission** free. **Map G4**

Located in a huge 19th-century complex of former hospital buildings, this Berlin institution was originally squatted in the 1970s and back then hosted alternative art and theatre. These days it offers studio residencies to foreign artists; USA, Europe, Russia and Japan are often represented (Bruce McLean was one of numerous artists-in-residence to work here) and both Sweden and Australia have permanent studio programmes. There are three main galleries almost permanently running exhibitions by the resident artists (who often sit their own

shows too), along with talks, screenings and symposia. In the same building on the ground floor is the Kunstamt Kreuzberg – Kreuzberg's local government art office – which often mounts large thematic exhibitions of contemporary art.

Wheelchair access (ask the doorman for key to elevator).

NBK

Neuer Berliner Kunstverein
Chausseestraße 128-129, Mitte, 10115 (280 7020/2). U6 Oranienburger Tor. **Open** noon-6pm Tue, Thur-Fri; noon-7pm Wed; noon-4pm Sat. **Admission** free. **Map F2**

In a new building that could just as easily have housed an insurance office, this is a well-funded society that hosts mainly curated group exhibitions by contemporary artists chosen from proposals submitted to a jury of the NBK's members. Choices and results are somewhat variable.

Website: www.nbk.org

NGBK

Neue Gesellschaft für bildende Kunst
Oranienstraße 25, Kreuzberg, 10999 (615 3031). U1, U8 Kottbusser Tor. **Open** noon-6.30pm daily. **Admission** free. **Map G4**

An offshoot of the late 1960s student movement, the NGBK has for more than 20 years produced a highly diversified and ambitious programme featuring photography, ethnic art, Berlin art and documentary shows. Exhibitions are consistent and to a high standard. Enter via the ground floor bookshop or the courtyard to the left of the bookshop.

Bookshop. Wheelchair access.
Website: www.snafu.de/ngbk

Sammlung Berggruen

Westlicher Stülerbau, Schloßstraße 1, Charlottenburg, 14059 (3269 5811). U2 Sophie-Charlotte-Platz. **Open** noon-6pm Tue-Fri; 11am-4pm Sat. **Admission** DM8; DM4 concs. **Map B3**

A satisfying and important collection compiled by Berggruen, an early dealer of Picasso's in Paris, offering a superb overview of Picasso's work. Also on display are works of his contemporaries such as Braque, Klee and Giacometti. The collection is on loan to Berlin and is housed in relatively intimate rooms in a building opposite the **Schloß Charlottenburg** (*see chapter* **Museums**).

Sammlung Hoffman

Sophienstraße 21, Mitte, 10178 (2849 9121). U8 Weimeisterstraße. **Open** by appointment only 11am-4pm Sat. **Admission** DM10. **No credit cards. Map F3**

This is Erika and Rolf Hoffmann's private collection of international contemporary art, including a charming floor installation work by Swiss video artist Pippilotti Rist and work by Douglas Gordon, Felix Gonzalez-Torres and AR Penck. The Hoffmans offer guided tours through their chic apartment every Saturday by appointment only – felt slippers supplied. For some, this kind of ritzy development signals the beginning of the end of what was good about Mitte; for others it means the exact opposite. Both camps are exaggerating.

Commercial galleries
Charlottenburg & the west

The Charlottenburg galleries are mostly within short walking distance of one another and are nestled between the district's designer stores and restaurants. These days they rarely receive much attention from the press and at the Berlin Art Forum most are most conspicuous by their absence. They do, however, remain reliable in their fields of interest, particularly for canvases by German artists of the pre-1990s generation – something you'd rarely find in Mitte. As elsewhere in Berlin, none of the following galleries take credit cards.

Galerie Anselm Dreher
Pfalzburger Straße 80, Wilmersdorf, 10719 (883 5249). U1 Hohenzollernplatz. **Open** 2-6.30pm Tue-Fri; 11am-2pm Sat. **Map C5**
Anselm Dreher's unique gallery has been around for more than 30 years now, uncompromisingly promoting the concrete, minimal and conceptual tendencies in contemporary art. He was the first in Berlin – and for quite some time the only one – to show the work of Carl André, Joseph Kosuth, Jochen Gerz and Ange Leccia.
Wheelchair access.

Galerie Barbara Weiss
Potsdamer Straße 93, Tiergarten, 10785 (262 4284). U1 Kurfürstenstraße. **Open** noon-6pm Tue-Fri; 11am-4pm Sat. **Map E4**
A beautiful conceptual art-oriented gallery in a gracious old apartment down the road from the Neue Nationalgalerie. Gallerist Barbara Weiss represents, among others, Maria Eichorn, Roaul de Keyser, John Miller and Janet Cardiff.

Galerie Eva Poll
Lützowplatz 7, Tiergarten, 10785 (261 7091). U1, U2, U4 Nollendorfplatz. **Open** 10am-1pm Mon; 11am-6.30pm Tue-Fri; 11am-3pm Sat. **Map D4**
When Eva Poll established her gallery in 1968, it was with the intention of supporting a local group of young 'critical' realists who had emerged in the mid-1960s. She currently represents Harald Duwe, GL Gabriel, Maxim Kantor, Ralf Kerbach, Volker Stelzmann, Hans Schieb and Sabine Grzimek.
Branch: Kunststiftung Poll, Gipsstraße 3, Mitte, 10178 (2649 6250).
Wheelchair access.
Website: www.artnet.com/epoll.html

Fine Art Rafael Vostell
Knesebeckstraße 30, Charlottenburg, 10623 (885 2280). S3, S5, S7, S9 Charlottenburg. **Open** 11am-7pm Mon-Fri; 11am-4pm Sat. **Map C4**
An upmarket gallery representing established artists like Francis Bacon, Nam June Paik and Yoko Ono, along with younger Berlin types such as Axel Lischke, Dead Chickens and MK Kähne.
Website: www.vostell.de

Galerie Franck + Schulte
Mommsenstraße 56, Charlottenburg, 10629 (3240 0440). U7 Adenauerplatz/S3, S5, S7, S9 Savignyplatz. **Open** 11am-6pm Mon-Fri; 11am-3pm Sat. **Map C4**
Eric Franck came from Geneva and Thomas Schulte from New York to challenge the Berlin market with

Galerie Franck + Schulte – *from blue-chip art to funky Swiss video.*

fresh ideas in 1991. Now it's one of Berlin's main blue-chip, upmarket galleries. The work of famous Americans dominates. Recent exhibitions have included artists such as Chuck Close and Gordon Matta-Clark, but funky Swiss video artist Pippilotti Rist has also exhibited. The gallery represents Rebecca Horn, Sol Le Witt, Katharina Sieverding, Tony Oursler and Robert Mapplethorpe.

Galerie Georg Nothelfer

Uhlandstraße 184, Charlottenburg, 10623 (881 4405). U15 Uhlandstraße. **Open** noon-6.30pm Mon-Fri; 10am-4pm Sat. **Map C4**
Nothelfer, a longtime doyen of the Berlin art world, concentrates on German Informel, Tachism and Lyrical Abstraction as well as gestural, scriptural and narrative painting by more established artists from Europe such as Pierre Alechinsky, Arnulf Rainer, Antoni Tàpies and Cy Twombly.

Galerie Springer & Winkler

Fasanenstraße 13, Charlottenburg, 10623 (315 7220). S3, S5, S7, S9/U2, U9 Zoologischer Garten. **Open** 10am-1pm, 2.30pm-7pm Tue-Fri; 11am-3pm Sat. **Map C4**
Until the end of 1997 this was the gallery of Rudolf Springer, one of the grand old men of Berlin's art world, who opened his first gallery as early as 1948. Now his son and partner run it, having moved up together from their gallery in Frankfurt-am-Main to take over. Among the greats Springer has presented are Alexander Calder, Joan Miró, André Masson, Max Ernst and Henri Laurens. But he's also had a continuous passion for German post-war artists (Wols, Ernst Wilhelm Nay, AR Penck, Jörg Immendorf and Markus Lüpertz).

Raab Galerie

Potsdamer Straße 58, Tiergarten, 10785 (261 9217/18). U1 Kurfürstenstraße/129, 148, 248, 348 bus. **Open** 10am-7pm Mon-Fri; 10am-4pm Sat. **Map E4**
Ingrid Raab's established gallery is known for the expressive and figurative painting that Berlin was once identified with. Exhibited artists include Markus Lüpertz, Elvira Bach, Luciano Castelli, Adolph Gottlieb, Rainer Fetting and Daniel Spoerri.
Wheelchair access.

Galerie Volker Diehl

Ladenbergstraße 16, Charlottenburg, 10629 (881 8280). U15 Uhlandstraße/S3, S5,S7, S9 Savignyplatz. **Open** 2-6.30pm Tue-Fri; 11am-2pm Sat. **Map C4**
Mainly contemporary German, Italian and American painters of the post-war generation, but you may also find minimal sculpture by Donald Judd and work by younger locals. Volker Diehl, a prominent figure in the Berlin art world, is one of the main organisers of the Berlin Art Forum.
Wheelchair access.

Mitte

The Scheunenviertel district of Mitte is the undoubted heart of Berlin's contemporary art scene, with the Auguststraße 'art mile' as its main street. We have listed below the principal galleries as of early 2000, but these spaces come and go and there are many others in this neighbourhood – mostly within walking distance of one another along these old and, for Berlin, uncharacteristically narrow streets.

aktionsgalerie

Auguststraße 20, Mitte, 10178 (2859 9654). U8 Weinmeisterstraße. **Open** 2-7pm Tue-Sat. **Map F2**
Originally at Große Präsidentenstraße 10, at press time this gallery was relocating to the new premises listed here while their old building was being renovated. Telephone for further details. Founder Hans Nowak is a great supporter of young experimental art in Mitte. He set up the annual festival Und ab die Post which takes place in the derelict former Postfuhramt at Oranienburger Straße 19-21 (on the corner with Tucholskystraße) each May – a non-commercial three-week exhibition, dance, video, film, club, theatre and concert whirl which gives a good overview of what's happening in underground trends. Again, call the gallery or check listings for further information as venue and dates are liable to change at short notice.

Arndt & Partner

Auguststraße 35, Mitte, 10119 (280 8123). U8 Rosenthaler Platz. **Open** noon-6pm Tue-Sat. **Map F2**
Established in 1994 by Matthias Arndt to show international contemporary art. Exhibited artists include Via Lewandowsky, Peter Friedl (a conceptual artist responsible for the 'KINO' sign at Documenta X) and young locals Johannes Kahrs and Susan Turcot.
Website: www.arndt-partner.de

Asian Fine Arts

1st Hof, Sophienstraße 18, Mitte, 10178 (2839 1387). U8 Weinmeisterstraße. **Open** noon-7pm Tue-Sat. **Map F3**
Founded by Jaana Prüss and Alexander Ochs with the aim of correcting west-centric bias in the contemporary arts scene. Showing artists from China, Hong Kong, Korea, Japan, Vietnam, India and Indonesia, they have, since 1997, opened up a rich source of often breathtaking (and not at all ethnic) new Asian art. Of particular note are Fang Lijun, Chiharu Shiota and Yuan Shun. The gallery participated in the 2000 Venice Biennale, and exhibitions in MoMA and P.S. 1, New York, Kunstmuseum, Bonn and the Museum of Contemporary Art, Tokyo.
Website: www.asianfinearts.de

Galerie Barbara Thumm

Dircksenstraße 41, Mitte, 10178 (2839 0347). S3, S5, S7, S9 Hackescher Markt. **Open** 1-4pm Tue-Fri; 1-5pm Sat. **Map G3**
Opened in 1997 with an international programme focusing on British and Berlin-based artists. The gallery has moved for the second time but is now in excellent new rooms that complement the high standard of the works shown. Artists represented include Fiona Banner, Bigert + Bergström, (e.) Twin Gabriel, Julian Opie and Bridget Smith.

Galerie Barbara Thumm – *British and Berlin-based artists such as Julian Opie.*

Galerie Berlin
Kunsthof, Oranienburgerstraße 27, Mitte, 10117 (251 4420). S1, S2 Oranienburger Straße/U6 Oranienburger Tor. **Open** 1-7pm Tue-Fri; 1-6pm Sat. **Map F3**

Formerly the international branch of the GDR's official art trade and since November 1990 a thriving private venture. The owners concentrate on expressive painting from eastern Germany including work by artists such as Bernhard Heisig and Werner Liebmann. They also have works from early 20th-century German Expressionism and Impressionism (Max Beckmann, Käthe Kollwitz, Max Liebermann). In 1999 it moved to these new premises among the designer cafés and shops in the recently refurbished Kunsthof.

Galerie Bodo Niemann
Hof VI, Hackesche Höfe, Rosenthaler Straße 40-41, Mitte, 10178 (2839 1928). U8 Rosenthaler Platz. **Open** 1-6pm Tue-Sat. **Map F3**

Best known for its exhibitions of photography and figurative and abstract art from the 1920s, mostly by German artists such as Hannah Höch, Emil Orlik, Kurt Scheele or photographer August Sander. The gallery moved here from Charlottenburg towards the end of 1997.
Wheelchair access with assistance.

Contemporary Fine Arts
Sophienstraße 21, Mitte, 10178 (283 6580). U8 Weinmeisterstraße. **Open** 10am-6pm Mon-Sat. **Map F3**

One of Berlin's more upmarket galleries, established by the partnership of Bruno Brunnet and Nicole Hackert. It's in Sophien-Gips Höfe, the same building as the Hoffman Sammlung (*see above*). This is where to see expensive British imports such as Damien Hirst, Sara Lucas and Angus Fairhurst, and big canvas boys such as Daniel Richter and Olav Christopher Jenssen.

Galerie EIGEN + ART
Auguststraße 26, Mitte, 10117 (280 6605). S1, S2 Oranienburger Straße/U6 Oranienburger Tor. **Open** 2-7pm Tue-Fri; 11am-5pm Sat. **Map F2**

The success of the Auguststraße phenomenon can be contributed in a large part to charismatic gallerist Gerd Harry 'Judy' Lybke. Originally from Leipzig, he ran an independent gallery there for many years and still does. Shortly after the collapse of the Wall, he started his second venture in Auguststraße. Since then he's tirelessly promoted artists from the former East Germany and emerging international artists. A tribute to his effectiveness was the inclusion of five of them in Documenta X. Among those exhibited here are Dresden painter Neo Rauch, 1997 Turner prize nominee Christine Borland and Carsten and Olaf Nicolai.
Wheelchair access with assistance.
Website: www.eigen-art.com

Galerie Gebauer
Torstraße 220, Mitte, 10115 (280 8110). U6 Oranienburger Tor. **Open** noon-6pm Tue-Sat. **Map F3**

Once together with Barbara Thumm, Ulrich Gebauer has now gone his separate way, although the two stables of artists remain pretty comparable. The work of Fred Thomaselli, Jan van Imschoot, Thomas Schütte, Luc Tymans is represented here. The gallery itself is a little difficult to find – it's on the first floor in a former apartment.

Galerie Hilgemann

*Linienstraße 213, Mitte, 10119 (2838 4388). U6
Oranienburger Tor.* **Open** 2-7pm Tue-Fri; 1-5pm Sat.
Map F3
The name Hilgemann is more often associated with the
imploding metal sculptures of his father Everdt but
son Kai runs a gallery with an interesting, varied and
ambitious collection of work from international artists.
Worthy of mention are the huge 'Russian pop art'
works from painter duo Dubosarsky and Vinogradov.
Website: www.galerie-kai-hilgemann.de

Klosterfelde

*Linienstraße 160, Mitte, 10115 (283 5305). U6
Oranienburger Tor.* **Open** 11am-6pm Tue-Sat. **Map
F2**
Martin Klosterfelde's narrow ground-floor gallery
was formerly a vaulted passageway to a courtyard
typical of old Berlin. The gallery opened in 1996 on
the heels of the closure of a number of larger squats
in the same street, in microcosm reflecting the general state of affairs in Mitte. His programme to date
has been a mix of contemporary Germans, such as
painter Nader with his large-scale philosophical oil
tableaux, and established artists such as Vito
Acconci and Dan Peterman.

Kuckei Kuckei

*Linienstraße 158, Mitte, 10115 (883 4354). U6
Oranienburger Tor.* **Open** 11am-6pm Tue-Fri; 11am-
5pm Sat. **Map F3**
Once a gallery called Vierte Etage in Wilmersdorf
founded by Ben and Hannes Kuckei, it's been open
in Mitte under this name since summer 1998. It deals
solely with 'young art from the 1990s'. The location
is one of the more tastefully renovated courtyards
in Linienstraße directly behind the Kunst-Werke.
Artists include Ingmar Alge, Hlynur Hallsson,
Michael Laube and Gerhard Winkler.

Kunstruimte Berlin

*1st Hof, Sophienstraße 18, Mitte, 10178 (2859
9070). U8 Weinmeisterstraße.* **Open** 2-6pm Thur-Sat.
Map F3
Tiny but elegant space in the picturesque historical
Hof of the Sophiensaele Theatre. This Dutch-run
gallery shows mainly installation work, often, but
not always, from young Dutch artists. Also project-
based Internet work.

Galerie Leo Coppi

*Hof III, Hackesche Höfe, Rosenthaler Straße 40-41,
10178 (283 5331). U8 Weinmeisterstraße.* **Open** 1-
6.30pm Tue-Fri; noon-6pm Sat. **Map F3**
Doris Leo and Helle Coppi opened this gallery in
1991 to promote a number of painters and graphic
artists, most of whom live and work in east Berlin
and Dresden, but it all seems terribly old-fashioned.

Galerie Max Hetzler

*Zimmerstraße 89, Mitte, 10117 (229 2437). U6
Kochstraße.* **Open** 11am-6pm Tue-Sat. **Map F4**
Another new upmarket gallery (recently relocated
from Cologne and closer to Checkpoint Charlie than
Auguststraße) with a proclivity towards architec-
tural discourse. Established figures such as Günther

Another Dutch installation at **Kunstruimte.**

Förg, Robert Gober, On Kawara, Jeff Koons, Terry
Winters and Christopher Wool are represented here.
Branch: Schillerstraße 94, Charlottenburg, 10625
(315 2261).

Mehdi Chouakri Berlin

*Gipsstraße 11, Mitte, 10119 (2839 1153). U8
Weinmeisterstraße.* **Open** 11am-6pm Tue-Sat. **Map
F3**
Opened in October 1996 by Mehdi Chouakri (formerly
of Paris) and a slick you-can-eat-off-the-floor type of
space, this gallery has a pan-European/North-
American programme. Exhibitions are heavy on conceptual photography and hip-looking furniture-as-art
by the likes of Sylvie Fleury with her fashionable vac-
uumable fluffy stuff. Also represented are John M
Armleder, Claude Closky and local Monica Bonvicini.

museumsakademie

*3rd Hof, 2nd Floor, Rosenthaler Straße 39, Mitte,
10178 (3087 2580). S3, S5, S7, S9 Hackescher
Markt.* **Open** 2-7pm Tue-Sat. **Map F3**
Once you have made your way through the yard and
up the back stairs of this crumbling building you
are greeted by a surprisingly large and airy space
housing one of Berlin's most interesting private galleries. Featured artists from as far afield as Cuba,
Dublin, Israel and North Yorkshire include Heidi
Stern, Lorcan O'Byrne, Daniel Ben-Hur and Emma
Rushton. British gallerist Helen Adkins also runs a
course offering professional training and qualifica-
tion for would-be curators.

Galerie neugerriemschneider
Linienstraße 155, Mitte, 10115 (3087 2810). U6 Oranienburger Tor. **Open** 11am-6pm Tue-Sat. **Map F2**
Another *arriviste* from Charlottenburg, exhibiting the latest and hippest from the USA, Europe and more recently even some local talent. Among the artists represented here are artists Franz Ackermann, Sharon Lockhart, Tobias Rehberger and Rirkrit Tiravanija.

Galerie Paula Böttcher
Kleine Hamburger Straße 15, Mitte, 10117 (281 1236). U8 Weinmeisterstraße. **Open** 2-7pm Mon-Fri; 1-6pm Sat. **Map F3**
Opened by 25-year-old Paula Böttcher in June 1997, the gallery is working with young local and international artists. One of her first shows was entitled How To Make A Good Group Show If You've Only Got One Room. Thirteen artists answered using models of the gallery.

Projektraum Berlin
Auguststraße 35, Mitte, 10119 (2839 1862). S1, S2 Oranienburger Straße. **Open** 2-6pm Thur-Fri; 1-6pm Sat. **Map F2**
Andreas Binder and Mathias Kampl are the directors of this small gallery dedicated to the display of primarily conceptual installation art. Recent exhibitions have included Fred Sandback, Matt Mullican and Sabine Groß.

Radio Berlin
Veteranenstraße 22, Mitte, 10119 (0173 407 7666), U8 Rosenthaler Platz. **Open** 4-10pm Thur-Sat. **Map F2**
A refreshing break from all the marketing that passes itself off as art. Here you can visit, get chatting, enjoy the art and buy a piece to take home, if you fancy, at prices that even a student budget might allow. And it's not just any old junk. Jim Avignon, DAG, Lisa Brown, Dump Art Ginelli and Ulli Lust are all contributors and are some of the best representatives of the post-pop, comic, club, underground, whatever-you-want-to-call-it art in town. Few artistic pretensions but colour and quality in abundance.

Galerie Schipper und Krome
Auguststraße 91, Mitte, 10117 (2839 0139). S1, S2 Oranienburger Straße. **Open** 11am-6pm Tue-Sat. **Map F3**
An arrival from Cologne in 1997, this is the place to see work by the kind of artists currently featured in the important art magazines. Among others, Vanessa Beecroft, Matti Braun, Angela Bulloch, Liam Gillick and Raymond Pettibon are all represented.

Volker und Freunde
Oranienburger Straße 2, Mitte, 10117 (2809 6115). S1, S2 Oranienburger Straße. **Open** 1-7pm Tue-Fri; 11am-7pm Sat. **Map F3**
How do small, independent galleries ever survive long enough to support and represent their artists adequately? This gallery's solution is to provide a leasing and rental service to companies needing art in their work spaces and thus encourage business to become more involved in helping support exhibitions and projects. Artists include Stefan Pfeifer, Manfred Fuchs and Juliet Mars-Toussaint. *Website: www.voelcker.de*

Galerie Wohnmaschine
Tucholskystraße 35, Mitte, 10117, (3087 2015). S1, S2 Oranienburger Straße. **Open** 2-7pm Tue-Fri; noon-5pm Sat. **Map F3**
The owner of this important experimental gallery, Friedrich Loock, was born on Auguststraße and can quite literally claim to have been there from the beginning. He set up the gallery in his flat in Auguststraße in 1988 and gave it the German name for Le Courbusier's *machine à habiter*: living with art and in art. It moved across the street in 1998 into the rooms of his old local butcher's shop.

Zwinger Galerie
Gipsstraße 3, Hinterhof, Mitte, 10119 (2859 8907). U8 Weinmeisterstraße. **Open** 2-7pm Tue-Fri; 11am-5pm Sat; 11.30am-5pm Sun. **Map F3**
A long-established and reputable commercial gallery that in 1997 moved with the crowd from Kreuzberg to an atmospheric courtyard space near Hackesche Höfe. Gallerist Werner Müller didn't want to miss out on the international visitors that the Mitte galleries now attract. Artists represented include Bettina Allamoda and Tobias Hauser.

Radio Berlin – *a refreshing break.*

Shopping & Sleeping

Accommodation

It's boom time for Berlin's hotel industry, but businessman or backpacker, it's best to book ahead.

In 1999 Berlin became Germany's most visited city, with 3.4 million visitors and eight million overnight stays. The hotel industry continues to boom and at press time it's expected that the year 2000 will see a further 60 new hotels with 19,000 beds. This means more variety, more choice and more central accommodation for the visitor at prices that remain lower than in many other major European cities. But don't be lulled into a false sense of security. A new hotel needn't mean a good hotel and good hotels have a tendency to be full. Try and book well ahead, especially at times when there are major holidays, conventions or festivals. Many hotels now have websites which are worth checking for information about facilities and special deals, such as cheaper weekend rates.

Hotels are mostly concentrated in Mitte in the east and around the Zoo and Savignyplatz in the west. The selection of cheaper options in the east has dramatically improved in recent years with various new pensions and backpacker hostels. New places are opening all the time, especially around Oranienburger Straße and in Prenzlauer Berg and Friedrichshain. Do check the up-to-date lists available from **Berlin Tourismus Marketing** (*below*) or look at their website which has hotel listings in English and budget hostels listed under *Preiswert Schlafen*. While location is important, it's worth remembering that the Berlin public transport system is excellent. Unless you really are out in the sticks, you're rarely more than a 30 minutes from anywhere you may want to be.

For a longer stay, your best bet (besides word of mouth) is either a *Mitwohnagentur* (*see page 122* **Flat-share agencies**) or the classifieds in *Zweite Hand*, tip, *Zitty* and *Berliner Morgenpost*. You can also look on the noticeboards in the city's various colleges for student accommodation, or pin up your own notice. Prices vary wildly, but if you look for something *auf Zeit* (for a limited period) you can get a good deal. Expect to pay DM600-800 per month for a two-room flat in the more central parts of Kreuzberg, Prenzlauer Berg and Schöneberg. Mitte is more difficult; you would probably expect to pay more, although you might get lucky.

The listings below aim to give a rounded idea of what to expect from each establishment. Remember that many add breakfast to your bill, prices as quoted. If the price of breakfast is not listed, then it is inclusive with the cost of the room.

Most hotels offer breakfast as a buffet which can be as simple as coffee and rolls with cheese and salami, or the full works complete with smoked meats and salmon, muesli with fresh fruit and yoghurt and a glass of sparkling wine.

Our price categories work as follows: a De Luxe hotel is one where a double room costs DM350 or more; an Expensive hotel is DM220 or more; Moderate is DM125 or more; the rest are Budget.

Information

Berlin Tourismus Marketing

Europa-Center, Budapester Straße, Charlottenburg, 10787 (reservations 250 025/information 0190 754 040/information when calling from outside Germany +49 1805 754 040/fax 2500 2424/information @btm.de). S3, S5, S7, S9/U2, U9 Zoologischer Garten. **Open** 8am-10pm Mon-Sat; 9am-9pm Sun. **Map D4**

This privatised tourist information service can sort out hotel reservations and provides a free and fairly up-to-date hotel booklet (but note that the hotels listed have paid to be included). It also has a photocopied list of youth hostels and camping sites that costs DM1, and another of private apartments and holiday homes for DM2. The website is reasonably comprehensive but bug-ridden, difficult to navigate, not updated often enough and contains no phone numbers – you have to book through the service. Calling the info number costs an outrageous DM2.42 per minute (and you'll usually spend about DM10 listening to menu options and tunes from *Cabaret* just waiting for a human operator). Normal rates apply when calling from abroad. The reservations number is free, however.

Branches: Brandenburg Gate, Tegel Airport. *Website: www.berlin.de*

De Luxe

Adlon Hotel Kempinski Berlin

Unter den Linden 77, Mitte, 10117 (226 10/fax 2261 2222/Adlon@Kempinski.com). S1, S2 Unter den Linden. **Rates** *single DM440-590; double DM510-660; suite from DM590; breakfast buffet DM48.* **Credit** AmEx, DC, JCB, MC, V. **Map F3**

The original Adlon, world-renowned for its luxurious interiors and discreet atmosphere, opened in 1907 but burned down shortly after World War II. The new Adlon, rebuilt by the Kempinski group on the original site, opened in 1997 and aims to pick up

Bristol Hotel Kempinski Berlin – *perhaps Berlin's most famous hotel.*

where its predecessor left off, ostentatiously listing previous guests such as Albert Einstein, Theodore Roosevelt and Marlene Dietrich as though they only checked out last week. Right by the Brandenburg Gate and handy for Berlin's diplomatic quarter, it immediately became a first-stop choice for heads of state and the like, but, if you are not a Kennedy or McCartney, expect to be peering up nostrils here – the staff are very frosty. There are 337 rooms including 81 suites, six rooms for allergy sufferers, two for travellers with disabilities and two bulletproof presidential suites. There are also marble and black granite bathrooms, hairdressers, 12 boutiques and wardrobes with hanging rails that light up.

Hotel services *Boutiques. Business and press centre. Conference and banqueting salons. Fitness spa. Garage. Restaurants (3) and lobby-bar. Swimming pool.* **Room services** *Air conditioning. CD. Fax. ISDN. PC outlet. Telephones(2). TV. Website: www.hotel-adlon.de*

Berlin Hilton

Mohrenstraße 30, Mitte, 10117 (202 30/fax 2023 4269/ berlin-hilton@compuserve.com). U2, U6 Stadtmitte. **Rates** *single DM340-550; double DM380-590; suites DM480-1,500; breakfast DM35.* **Credit** AmEx, DC, JCB, MC, V. **Map F4**

Well-placed on the Gendarmenmarkt, the Hilton offers top-quality rooms and services in a pleasant atmosphere. The plant-filled lobby is huge and airy, with a slightly tacky waterfall and a restaurant in the middle. It suffers rather from a style clash since half the hotel has been renovated in a newer, more opulent style and the rest seems to have been left as it was. The standard rooms are cream, apricot and wood. The 'executive floor' has more expensive rooms. For that you get separate check-in facilities, a desk with modem connection, an exclusive clubroom, breakfast, an alarm clock, an ironing board and a free international newspaper in the morning.

Hotel services *Bicycle rental. Bowling alley. Disco. Fitness centre. Laundry service. Lift. Massage. Non-smoking rooms (14). Parking. Restaurants and bars (9). Sauna. Solarium. Squash court. Swimming pool. Whirlpool.* **Room services** *Bathrobe. Hairdryer. Minibar. Radio. Telephone. TV.*

Bristol Hotel Kempinski Berlin

Kurfürstendamm 27, Charlottenburg, 10719 (884 340/fax 883 6075). U9, U15 Kurfürstendamm. **Rates** *single DM375-525; double DM435-585; suite DM680-2,300; breakfast buffet DM36.* **Credit** AmEx, DC, JCB, MC, V. **Map C4**

Perhaps Berlin's most famous hotel, if not its best, the Kempinski exudes a faded charm. But even though the rooms are plush, you never really feel you're living in the lap of luxury, as you certainly should for this price. The Bristol Bar on the ground floor, with its fat leather sofas and lots of old, dark wood, has a long cocktail list and snooty waiters. Naff restaurant and grill bar.

Hotel services *Bar. Conference services. Cosmetic salon. Laundry service. Lift. Massage. Restaurants (3). Sauna. Solarium. Swimming pool.* **Room services** *Air conditioning. Minibar. Pay TV. Telephone. TV.*

Four Seasons Hotel

Charlottenstraße 49, Mitte, 10117 (203 38/fax 2033 6166). S1, S2, S3, S5, S7, S9/U6 Friedrichstraße. **Rates** *single DM390; double DM460-560; suite DM590; breakfast DM40.* **Credit** AmEx, DC, JCB, MC,V. **Map F3**

Grand Hotel Esplanade – *grand, spacious and beautifully decorated.*

This is what five-star luxury is all about: marble bathrooms; huge soft towels and dressing gowns; big beds with pure wool blankets, and a highly trained and elegant staff who know what you need before you do. The décor is English country-house style: wood panelling; loads of marble; open fireplaces; oil paintings of flowers and Scottish landscapes, and heirloom porcelain vases. The whole effect is one of having been invited up to the country estate for the weekend. Hard to believe it only opened in 1996. A discreet establishment.
Hotel services *Bar. Conference rooms. Disabled facilities. Fitness Club. Non-smoking rooms. Overnight laundry service. Parking. Restaurant. Safe. Sightseeing trips. Ticket reservations. 24-hour business services.* **Room services** *Air conditioning. Cable TV. Fax. Hairdryer. Minibar. PC-modem connection. Radio. Telephone.*
Website: www.fourseasons.com

Grand Hotel Esplanade

Lützowufer 15, Tiergarten, 10785 (254 780/fax 265 1171/info@esplanade.de). U1, U2, U4 Nollendorfplatz. **Rates** *single* DM380-500; *double* DM430-550; *suite* DM750-2,600; *breakfast* DM35. **Credit** AmEx, DC, JCB, MC, V. **Map D4**
One of Berlin's better luxury hotels, by the Landwehr Canal and the Tiergarten. The entrance is grand, with a huge, gushing wall of water across from the door and hundreds of lights glittering above your head. The lobby is spacious and beautifully decorated, with art adorning some of the walls on the ground floor. The well-tended rooms are sparkling white and an added benefit is being within stumbling-back-to-bed distance of Harry's New York Bar on the ground floor.

Hotel services *Bar. Conference facilities. Laundry service. Lift. Non-smoking rooms (30). Parking. Restaurant. Sauna. Swimming pool. Wheelchair access.* **Room services** *Air conditioning. Minibar. Pay TV. Radio. Telephone.*
Website: www.esplanade.de

Grand Hyatt

Marlene-Dietrich-Platz 2, Tiergarten, 10785 (2553 1234/fax 2553 1235). S1, S2/U2 Potsdamer Platz. **Rates** *single* DM320-500; *double* DM360-540; *suite* DM570-3,500; *breakfast buffet* DM35. **Credit** AmEx, DC, MC, V. **Map E4**
Part of the new Potsdamer Platz complex, the Grand Hyatt may have been designed under the watchful eye of Renzo Piano but still manages to look rather like a branch of Habitat. It's so 1990s – perhaps it's the sushi bar that does it. However, the Hyatt is what Potsdamer Platz is all about and, as such, it is interesting to be there and contemplate that the whole thing is standing on what was a patch of waste ground less than a decade ago. The lobby is all matt black and wood-panelled slick surfaces with discreet and minimal art touches – a welcome break from the usual five-star country mansion/marble look. The rooms are fairly spacious with not a floral print in sight, the Internet access/TV is a nice touch and the rooftop fitness centre has a splendid pool with views across the city as you swim.
Hotel services *Bar. Bistro. Conference rooms. Disabled facilities (2 rooms). Fitness Club. Parking. Restaurant. Safe. Solarium. Sushi bar. Swimming pool. Whirlpool.* **Room services** *Air conditioning. Hairdryer. Internet TV. Minibar. Nintendo. PC-modem connection. Radio. Telephone. Voicemail.*
Website: www.berlin.hyatt.com

Grand Hyatt – *so new, so 1990s. See p107.*

Hotel Intercontinental

Budapester Straße 2, Tiergarten, 10787 (260 20/fax 2602 2600/berlin@interconti.com). S3, S5, S7, S9/U2, U9 Zoologischer Garten. **Rates** *single* DM365-495; *double* DM415-545; *suite* DM575-3,500; *breakfast* DM35. **Credit** AmEx, DC, JCB, MC, V. **Map D4**

If you're on a generous expense account, this is the place to stay. Extraordinarily plush and spacious, the Intercontinental exudes a sense of luxury. The rooms are large, tastefully decorated and blessed with elegant bathrooms. The lobby is enormous; its soft leather chairs are the ideal place to read the paper or wait for your next appointment. One of the restaurants has a Michelin star.

Hotel services *Bar. Conference facilities. Laundry service. Lift. Parking. Restaurants (2). Sauna. Swimming pool.* **Room services** *Air conditioning. Minibar. Modem connection. Radio. Safe. Telephone. Trouser press. TV. Voicemail.*
Website: www.interconti.com

Maritim pro Arte Hotel Berlin

Friedrichstraße 151, Mitte, 10117 (203 35/fax 2033 4209/reservierung.bpa@maritim.de). S1, S2, S3, S5, S7, S9/U6 Friedrichstraße. **Rates** *single* DM247-469; *double* DM298-528; *suites and apartments* DM530-3,600; *breakfast buffet* DM32. **Credit** AmEx, DC, JCB, MC, V. **Map F3**

This gleaming new edifice calls itself a 'designer hotel' and is certainly one of the more stylish luxury hotels Berlin has to offer. Adorned with huge paintings and designer furniture, the foyer, three restaurants and bar are chic and luxurious. The 403 rooms, apartments and suites all are equipped with fax and PC connections, air conditioning and marble bathrooms. The staff are polite and helpful, particularly when you're dressed to match the surroundings – and meanwhile the Brandenburg Gate, Unter den Linden, the swanky boutiques of Friedrichstraße, and the bars and galleries of the Scheunenviertel are all close at hand.

Hotel services *Bar. Boutiques. Conference facilities (2 halls, 9 rooms). Gym. Parking. Restaurants (3). Sauna. Solarium. Swimming pool.* **Room services** *Fax & modem. Minibar. Pay TV. Safe. Telephone.*

Hotel Palace

Budapester Straße 38, Charlottenburg, 10787 (250 20/fax 262 6577/hotel@palace.de). S3, S5, S7, S9/U2, U9 Zoologischer Garten. **Rates** *single* DM375-540; *double* DM410-590; *suite* DM650-3,500; *breakfast buffet* DM35. **Credit** AmEx, DC, MC, V. **Map D4**

A Best Western hotel in the middle of the Europa-Center. The rooms are luxurious, reasonably spacious and complete with all the amenities. One nice extra is free access to the lavish sauna facilities of the Thermen am Europa Center.

Hotel services *Bar. Conference facilities. Laundry service. Lift. Parking. Restaurant.* **Room services** *Minibar. Radio. Telephone. TV.*
Website: www.palace.de

The Westin Grand

Friedrichstraße 158-164, Mitte, 10117 (202 70/fax 2027 3362/info@westin-grand.com). U6 Französische Straße. **Rates** *single* DM395-520; *double* DM 445-570; *suite* DM750-3,500; *breakfast buffet* DM35. **Credit** AmEx, DC, JCB, V. **Map F3**

Just around the corner from Unter den Linden, providing five-star luxury in a top location. Gratifyingly elegant, despite its prefabricated East German construction, the hotel manages to live up to its name rather well. Its recently renovated 35 suites are individually furnished with period décor according to whoever they are named after (try the Schinkel or Lessing suites), and its 358 rooms exude traditional taste, design and comfort. There's a hotel garden with a sun patio and atrium as well as bars, two restaurants and a non-smoking floor. Best of all is the bombastic staircase and foyer.

Hotel services *Aroma therapy. Bar. Coiffeur. Conference facilities. Laundry service. Lift. Massage. Restaurant. Safe. Sauna. Shops and boutiques. Solarium. Swimming pool. Whirlpools.* **Room services** *Air conditioning. Cable TV. Fax, desks and printer for business use. Internet TV. Minibar. Modem. Nintendo. Pay-TV. Radio. Safe. Telephone. Voicemail.*
Website: www.westin-grand.com

Expensive

Hotel-Restaurant Albrechtshof

Albrechtstraße 8, Mitte, 10117 (308 860/fax 308 86100/albrechtshof-hotel@t-online.de). S1, S2, S3, S5, S7, S9/U6 Friedrichstraße. **Rates** *single* DM180-350; *double* DM220-410; *suite* DM350-550. **Credit** AmEx, DC, MC, V. **Map F3**

The only hotel in this *Guide* with its own chapel – it's a member of the Verband Christlicher Hotels (Christian Hotels' Association), although it doesn't make a song and dance about it. There is a pleasant Hof garden for breakfast in the summer and a restaurant specialising in local dishes. The staff are kind and the hotel is situated in a quiet, village-like area remarkably close to Friedrichstraße station and several theatres. Décor is universal Posh-Hotel Style.
Hotel services *Chapel. Conference rooms. Parking. Restaurants. Rooms with handicapped facilities (3). Safe. Ticket reservations.* **Room services** *Fax. Minibar. PC-modem connection. Radio. Shower/bath. Telephone. TV. WC.*
Website: www.hotel-albrechtshof.de

Hotel Alexander

Pariser Straße 37, Wilmersdorf, 10707 (8867 5260/ fax 881 6094). U7 Adenauerplatz. **Rates** *single* DM175-215; *double* DM195-260. **Credit** DC, MC, V. **Map C5**
On a lively street south of the Ku'damm, this self-styled 'art hotel' has rooms with ultra-modern furnishings. The doubles are spacious, the singles are small but cosy. If you don't like the grey marbled wallpaper and metal trimmings of the opulent-looking 'café-bistro', the surrounding area is packed with bars and restaurants. The staff speak English.
Hotel services *Bar. Fax facilities. Restaurant.* **Room services** *Cable TV. Minibar. Radio. Room service. Safe. Telephone.*

Alexander Plaza Berlin

Rosenstraße 1, Mitte, 10178 (240 010/fax 2400 1777/info@alexanderplaza.com). S3, S5, S7, S9 Hackescher Markt. **Rates** *single* DM235-365; *double* DM255-385; *suite* DM550; *breakfast buffet* DM25. **Credit** AmEx, DC, MC, V. **Map G3**
A four-star hotel that outdoes a few of Berlin's five-star giants. Well situated between Alexanderplatz, Museumsinsel and Hackescher Markt, this handsome, renovated building houses a delightful modern establishment. Despite the proximity of a dozen building sites and the frisky Mitte nightlife district, the hotel stands in an oasis of quiet near the river. The staff are charming and overall décor is tasteful. There are 90 rooms, 30 for non-smokers and three for disabled travellers. Each room has modem facilities and there is also a fitness centre. The hotel has left the Mercure group of which it was originally a member and prices have increased significantly.
Hotel services *Fitness centre. Function rooms (4). Garage. Hairdressers. Non-smoking rooms (15). Restaurant. Safe. Sauna. Solarium.* **Room services** *Hairdryer. Minibar. Pay TV. Shower. Telephone. TV. WC.*
Website: www.alexanderplaza.com

Art'otel Ermelerhaus Berlin

Wallstraße 70-73, Mitte, 10179 (240 620/fax 2406 2222/berlin@artotel.de). U2 Märkisches Museum. **Rates** *single* from DM235; *double* from DM275; *suite/apartment* from DM290. **Credit** AmEx, DC, JCB, MC, V. **Map G4**
On the banks of the Spree, a delightful fusion of old and new. The building houses both immaculately restored rococo dining rooms and an ultra-modern residential section designed by architects Nalbach & Nalbach. The entire hotel is dedicated to the work of artist Georg Baselitz and all the rooms and corridors contain originals of his work as well as others by AR Penck and Andy Warhol. Besides the art, every detail

Art'otel Ermelerhaus – *Warhol works, scenic views and Philippe Starck bathrooms, too.*

of the décor has been meticulously attended to, from Philippe Starck bathrooms to Marcel Breuer chairs in the conference rooms. Service is friendly, views from the top suites across Mitte are stunning, and the food in both restaurants is imaginatively traditional. In summer a barge moored by the towpath in front of the hotel becomes a terrace with picturesque views. Buffet breakfast included.

Hotel services *Babysitting. Bar. Business office with computer, fax and modem.Conference facilities. Foyer Internet terminal. Garage. Laundry service. Restaurant.Theatre tickets.* **Room services** *Desk. Hairdryer. Internet access. Pay TV. Radio. Telephone. TV.*
Website: www.artotel.de

Berlin Plaza Hotel

Knesebeckstraße 62, Charlottenburg, 10719 (884 130/fax 8841 3754/info@plazahotel.de). U15 Uhlandstraße. **Rates** *single* DM179; *double* DM229; *extra bed* DM50. **Credit** AmEx, DC, JCB MC, V.
Map C4
Be prepared to be dazzled by the Berlin Plaza's mirror and brass foyer, which mixes well with several pink sofas and pieces of modern art from local galleries. The hotel has seven floors, one of them non-smoking. Its 131 rooms are tastefully decorated in pink, maroon and white, but are rather small and plain. All double rooms and some singles have both shower and bath. You can mix your own muesli at the breakfast buffet – the food is freshly made and bread is baked on the premises. German specialities are served in the restaurant and bar. Be aware that you are paying for its off-Ku'damm location.
Hotel services *Bar. Conference facilities. Laundry service. Lift. Parking (DM20 a day). Restaurant.* **Room services** *Hairdryer. Minibar. Radio. Safe. Telephone. TV.*
Website: www.plazahotel.de

Hotel Berliner Hof

Tauentzienstraße 8, Schöneberg, 10789 (254 950/fax 262 3065). U1, U2, U12, U15 Wittenbergplatz. **Rates** *single* DM134-195; *double* DM164-240; *extra bed* DM60. **Credit** AmEx, DC, MC, V. **Map D4**
If you want the west end, you won't get much more central than this: the Europa-Center is next door and the Ku'damm round the corner. The Berliner Hof's rooms face the courtyard rather than the street and are quiet, spacious and pleasantly decorated.
Hotel services *Lift. Parking (DM16).* **Room services** *Minibar. Radio. Telephone. TV.*

Boardinghouse Mitte

Mulackstraße 1, Mitte, 10119 (2838 8488/fax 2838 8489) U8 Weinmeisterstraße. **Rates** *single apartment* DM155-240; *double apartment* DM210-270; *extra person* DM60. **Credit** AmEx, MC, V. **Map G3**
Apartment hotel in the Scheunenviertel. It's not cheap, especially as extras can add up, but room prices get lower the longer you stay. The apartments are small and kitted out in modern German designer style. There are dozens of good cafés and restaurants on the doorstep and Hackescher Markt is just a stroll away.

Hotel services *Garage (DM15). Ironing board & iron rental (DM15). Laundry Service (DM25 per load).* **Room services** *Kitchen. Stereo.TV. Video.*

Concept Hotel

Grolmanstraße 41-43, Charlottenburg, 10623 (884 260/fax 8842 6500/info@concept-hotel.com). S3, S5, S7, S9 Savignyplatz. **Rates** *single* DM220-280; *double* DM280-350; *suite* DM350-500. **Credit** AmEx, DC, MC, V. **Map C4**
Formerly the Curator Hotel, this has been significantly refurbished and is generally pretty smart. There are conference facilities, a big roof terrace for sunbathing, restaurant and a boring bar. The hotel is quiet and situated in the best smart shopping area with a good restaurant selection nearby. Hard to see what the 'concept' is, though.
Hotel services *Bar. Conference facilities. Parking. Sauna. Solarium.* **Room services** *Minibar. Radio. Rooms equipped for disabled guests (2). Safe. Telephone. TV.*
Website: www.concept-hotel.com

Forum Hotel

Alexanderplatz, Mitte, 10178 (2389 4333/fax 2389 4305/forumBerlin@interconti.com). S3, S5, S7, S9/ U2, U5, U8 Alexanderplatz. **Rates** *single* DM207-319; *double* DM227-393; *suite* DM237-263; *breakfast* DM24. **Credit** AmEx, DC, MC, V. **Map G3**
It's hard to be very enthusiastic about any of the 1006 rooms here. They are expensive, grey, cramped and so full of fans, minibars and trouser presses there's scarcely room to swing a suitcase. But oh the view! From a corner room somewhere above the 16th floor facing the Fernsehturm and Karl-Marx-Allee at sunset, it is really quite something. On the other hand you could eat in the Panorama restaurant or play in the casino at the top (open 7pm-1am Fri, Sat) and save the bother and expense of actually having to stay here. Usually full of Chinese tour groups.
Hotel services *Bar. Casino. Conference facilities. Disabled facilities. Fitness centre. Laundry. Non-smoking floors. Parking. Restaurant (2). Sauna. Solarium.* **Room services** *Minibar. Telephone. TV.*

Hotel Hackescher Markt

Große Präsidentenstraße 8, Mitte, 10178 (280 030/fax 2800 3111/Hohama@aol.com). S3, S5, S7, S9 Hackescher Markt. **Rates** *single* DM210-310; *double* DM280-380; *suite* DM340-440. **Credit** AmEx, DC, MC, V. **Map F3**
Elegant new hotel in a nicely renovated old town house that solves the noise problem at Hackescher Markt by having most rooms facing the tranquil green courtyard. Some have balconies, most have baths and the suites are roomy and comfortable. Staff speak good English and are smiling and helpful.
Hotel services *Covered parking (DM20). Non-smoking floor. Restaurant.* **Room services** *Hairdryer. Minibar. Safe. TV.*
Website: www.hackescher-markt.de

Opposite: **Forum Hotel** – *take your pick from any of these 1006 rooms.*

Hecker's Hotel

*Grolmanstraße 35, Charlottenburg, 10623 (889
00/fax 889 0260/info@heckers-hotel.com). U15
Uhlandstraße.* **Rates** *single*
DM310-370; children under-12 free; *breakfast* DM25.
Credit AmEx, DC, JCB, MC, V. **Map C4**
Unremarkable on the outside, quite pleasant inside.
Although there's not much of a lobby, the
bar/restaurant off the entrance is a fine place to sit
and wait. Rooms are a good size and comfortable,
with lots of nice little touches – pencil sharpeners,
for example, and fresh fruit. Bathrooms are small,
but clean and well lit. The walk-in closets are easily the best in Berlin. Quiet and comfortable. There
is a roof terrace in summer. Some rooms have a fax
connection, a safe and/or a kitchenette.
Hotel services *Bar (until 10pm). Conference
facilities (up to 200 people). Parking.* **Room
services** *Minibar. Non-smoking rooms (2 floors).
Radio. Telephone. TV.*
Website: www.heckers-hotel.com

Holiday Inn Garden Court

*Bleibtreustraße 25, Charlottenburg, 10707 (881
4076/fax 880 93939/berlinhigc@aol.com). S3, S5,
S7, S9 Savignyplatz.* **Rates** *single* DM245-375;
double DM245-400; *suite* DM310-410; under-12s
free. **Credit** AmEx, DC, JCB, MC, V. **Map C4**
Quiet, charming hotel just off the Ku'damm. The 73
rooms and suites, though cramped, are tastefully
decorated while the bathrooms, also a bit tight, are
bright and clean. The glass-enclosed breakfast room
on the fifth floor offers a stunning view. The lobby
bar stays open around the clock and there are tables
and comfy chairs in the light, elegant lobby.
Hotel services *Bar. Conference facilities. Laundry
service. Lift. Parking.* **Room services** *Minibar.
Radio. Room service. Telephone. TV.*

Hotel Luisenhof

*Köpenicker Straße 92, Mitte, 10179 (241 5906/fax
279 2983/info@luisenhof.de). U8 Heinrich-Heine-
Straße.* **Rates** *single* DM199-290; *double* DM235-390;
suite DM350-450. **Credit** AmEx, DC, JCB, V. **Map
G4**
The beautiful building housing the Luisenhof dates
from the late 19th century and was the headquarters
and stables of a Berlin coaching company. When the
communists held sway, it was home to the party
training centre of the SED. In the middle of old
Berlin, close to the major cultural sights and the
city's business district, it was reopened after renovation in early 1992 and tastefully restored in original town-house style.
Hotel services *Conference facilities. Fax. Laundry
service. Lift. Photocopying. Restaurants (2).* **Room
services** *Fax connection. Minibar. Radio. Safe.
Telephone. TV.*
Website: www.luisenhof.de

Sorat Art'otel Berlin

*Joachimstaler Straße 29, Charlottenburg, 10719
(884 470/ fax 8844 7700/art-otel@SORAT-
Hotels.com). U9, U15 Kurfürstendamm.* **Rates**
single DM225-375; *double* DM265-435. **Credit** AmEx.
DC, JCB, MC, V. **Map C4**

Just off the Ku'damm in the heart of the west end,
this hotel's theme is the work of artist Wolf Vostell
– his collages and prints adorn the walls. The rooms
are modern, tasteful and big with great bathrooms.
Ask to see a couple of rooms, as they range from
good to great with little apparent relation to the
price. The *Eckzimmern* ('corner rooms') are the best.
The breakfast room is a joy with a sumptuous buf-
fet and it opens out into the garden in summer.
Hotel services *Bar (24 hours). Conference facilities.
Disabled facilities. Non-smoking rooms (2 floors).
Parking. Restaurant.* **Room services** *Cable TV.
Fax/modem connection. Minibar. Radio. Telephone.*
Website: www.SORAT-Hotels.com

Moderate

Alpenland Hotel

*Carmerstraße 8, Charlottenburg, 10623 (312
3970/fax 313 8444). S3, S5, S7, S9 Savignyplatz.*
Rates *single* DM75-130; *double* DM110-190; *extra bed*
DM55. **Credit** MC, V. **Map C4**
A no-frills, friendly hotel. The rooms are fresh and
clean, as well as reasonably spacious. The large,
pristine bathrooms are especially fine, although not
every room has its own – communal toilets are on
every floor. Breakfast is taken in the restaurant
downstairs, which also has a pleasant bar.
Hotel services *Bar. Restaurant.* **Room services**
Safe. Telephone. TV.

Hotel am Scheunenviertel

*Oranienburger Straße 38, Mitte, 10117 (282
2125/2830 8310/fax 282 1115). S1, S2
Oranienburger Straße.* **Rates** *single* DM130; *double*
DM150. **Credit** AmEx, DC, MC, V. **Map F3**
One of the best-value, best-located little hotels in
town. In the historical heart and old Jewish Quarter
of Berlin, Museumsinsel, Friedrichstraße and
Hackesche Höfe are all nearby. By night the area is
alive with cafés, bars, clubs, restaurants and prostitutes. Rooms are clean and comfortable, but a little
dark, each with WC and good strong shower. The
ample buffet breakfast is included in the price and
the staff are friendly and helpful. Rooms at the front
can be noisy. A good base from which to explore
Berlin, but book ahead – there are only 18 rooms.
Room services *Telephone. TV.*

Best value – **Hotel am Scheunenviertel.**

A view with a room

There are a lot of so-called 'art hotels' in Berlin. Hanging a few pictures on the walls or sticking a statue or two in the foyer helps give a cultivated impression and attracts the punters which is, after all, the name of the game. But at **Künstlerheim Luise** the art is not in the rooms so much as the rooms themselves are art. Over 30 artists were each given a budget and a free hand to create their own unique rooms within the hotel and the result, unveiled summer 1999, is a wonderland of colours, styles, ingenuity and delightful surprises.

Take your pick from the grandly proportioned suites and rooms on the Bel Étage. Room 107 houses *Mammel's Traum* from artist David Mammel, in which a huge French-style bed three times life-size fills the room and makes you feel tiny and child-like. Or there's the Professoren Suite in 105 from Oliver Jordan, dark and manly with desk and comfortable chairs to finish writing your latest seminal work. Thomas Baumgärtel's regal and witty Königsuite is completely gold with silk-screened bananas everywhere, even on the toilet seat. Unless you are a teetotaller it might be wise to give Elvira Bach's room 101 a miss: thick vertical black-and-white stripes and bright expressive paintings of women in stockings and stilettos add up to a distinctly queasy effect.

Upstairs the rooms become smaller and simpler but by no means lesser treasures. The Money Room in 316 from JJ Anniroc is tiny and basic with a single bed and little else but the floor is covered with bank notes and as you lie on the bed and look through the window which has a screen print as a blind you have a perfect view of the Reichstag – even better than from the Adlon. Jessika Miekely's room 318 is covered in blue butterflies and Chez Rose in 317 there are painted roses everywhere. The phosphorescent room 308 is perfect for insomniacs, its walls decked with glow-in-the-dark letter puzzles from artist Stefan Brée.

On the first and third floor are two fully equipped communal kitchens. The one on the third floor is decked out like an old station waiting room with a jukebox playing James Bond theme tunes and a fantastic view across the Spree to the new government cityscape. A small breakfast is included in the room price but if you want something more substantial the new restaurant Sion am Reichstag downstairs, open from 8am to 1am, will cater to your needs.

Owners Torsten Modrow (yes, he is related to the last GDR Prime Minister), Mike Buller and former gallerist Christian Brée have created a hotel with a real difference. They intend to redo the rooms every two years with new artists so guests can expect an ever-changing live-in art experience and all at budget prices. More power to their elbows.

Künstlerheim Luise

Luisenstraße 19, Mitte, 10117 (284 480/fax 280 6942/info@kuenstlerheim-luise.de). U6 Oranienburger Tor. **Rates** *single* DM75-135; *double* DM110-190; *suite* DM240. **Hotel services** *Art shop. Bar. Restaurant/brasserie.* **Room services** *Telephone. Website: www.kuenstlerheim-luise.de*

Hotel Bogotá

*Schlüterstraße 45, Charlottenburg, 10707 (881
5001/fax 883 5887/hotel.bogota@t-online.de). S3,
S5, S7, S9 Savignyplatz.* **Rates** *single DM78-130;
double DM125-190; extra bed DM50.* **Credit** AmEx,
DC, MC, V. **Map C4**
More functional than fancy, a 125-bedroom, two-star
hotel with good service and very good prices. It's
slightly to the south of Ku'damm and frequented by
backpackers, businessmen and tourists. This is
made possible by the range of rooms and prices
available. About half of the double rooms have
showers and toilets and most of them, though plain-
ly furnished, are comfortable. If there are four of you
on a small budget, you can take a double room and
pay an extra DM50 per person (including breakfast)
for the two extra beds.
Hotel services *Lift. TV room.* **Room services**
Telephone. TV.
Website: www.hotelbogota.de

Hotel California

*Kurfürstendamm 35, Charlottenburg, 10719 (880
120/fax 8801 2111/reserv@hotel-california.de). U15
Uhlandstraße.* **Rates** *single DM165-245; double*
DM195-295; extra bed DM70; breakfast buffet DM18.
Credit AmEx, DC, JCB, MC, V. **Map C4**
Smack in the middle of some of Berlin's best shops
and right next to a new McDonalds. The unimpos-
ing lobby sports a small fountain and a large piece
of the Berlin Wall, as well as some deep sofas to sink
into after a hard day's sightseeing. The rooms are
basic and comfortable. The lift stops only on every
half-floor, so there are still 12 stairs to climb to your
room. Bicycle rental in summer.
Hotel services *Bar. Conference facilities. Lift.
Sauna. Solarium (DM5 for ten minutes). TV room.*
Room services *Hairdryer. Minibar. Radio. Safe.
Telephone. TV.*
Website: www.hotel-california.de

Hotel Pension Castell

*Wielandstraße 24, Charlottenburg, 10707 (882
7181/fax 881 5548/messe@hotel-castell.de). U7
Adenauerplatz/U15 Uhlandstraße.* **Rates** *single*
DM125-170; *double* DM150-190. **Credit** AmEx, MC,
V. **Map C4**
Tucked away just off the Ku'damm and near many
designer shops, this 22-room pension has friendly
staff and good-sized rooms. All have a shower and
TV but some haven't their own WC.
Hotel services *Lift.* **Room services** *Telephone.
TV.*
Website: www.hotel-castell.de

Hotel Charlot am Kurfürstendamm

*Giesebrechtstraße 17, Charlottenburg, 10629 (323
4051/fax 327 96 66/hotelcharlot@bln.net). U7
Adenauerplatz/S3, S5, S6, S7, S9 Charlottenburg.*
Rates *single DM90-145; double* DM120-230. **Credit**
AmEx, MC, V. **Map B4**
There aren't many better hotels in this price range.
It's in a beautiful residential area full of chic shops
and great cafés; the historical Jugendstil building
has been well restored; it has friendly management;
and the 42 bedrooms are spotlessly clean. Not all

Hotel California – *deep sofas, few Eagles.*

have showers and toilets, but the communal ones are
quite clean. Despite the name, it's actually about five
minutes away from the Kurfürstendamm.
Hotel services *Bar. Lift. Parking. TV room.* **Room
services** *Telephone. TV.*
Website: www.hotel-charlot.bln.net

Hotel-Pension Elba

*Bleibtreustraße 26, Charlottenburg, 10707 (881
7504/fax 8804 5955/882 3246/hotelelba@aol.com).
S3, S5, S7, S9 Savignyplatz.* **Rates** *single DM95-138;
double DM158-175.* **Credit** AmEx, MC, V. **Map C4**
Closer to a hotel than a pension in atmosphere and
size, which is reflected in the prices. But it's known
for the friendliness of its staff and is housed in a
splendid, and splendidly located, town house. Its 16
rooms range from the cramped to the capacious, but
all are well equipped with showers and toilets, and
are decorated in plain white and wood.
Hotel services *Lift.* **Room services** *Hairdryer.
Minibar. Telephone. TV.*
Website: www.members.aol.com/hotelelba

Hotel-Pension Funk

*Fasanenstraße 69, Charlottenburg, 10719 (882
7193/fax 883 3329). U15 Uhlandstraße.* **Rates**
single DM65-130; double DM100-190. **Credit** AmEx,
MC, V. **Map C5**
In the former apartment of Danish silent movie star
Asta Nielsen. The proprietor does his best to maintain the ambience of a pre-war flat, and the rooms
are furnished with pieces from the 1920s and 1930s.

The effect is cosy, and the 14 rooms are comfortable and large, even if not all have their own showers. For an extra DM45 per person (including breakfast) you can fit up to another three people into a double room. Two of the doubles have their own bathrooms. **Hotel services** *Lift.* **Room services** *Telephone.*

Pension-Gästezimmer Gudrun

Bleibtreustraße 17, Charlottenburg, 10623 (881 6462/fax 883 7476). S3, S5, S7, S9 Savignyplatz. **Rates** *single* DM105; *double* DM135-145. **No credit cards. Map C4**
Only four rooms (just two with WC) but they are huge and comfy with old-fashioned furniture and have a shower and TV. For a small group travelling together or a family they are really good value. **Room services** *TV.*

Hotel Jurine

Schwedter Straße 15, Mitte, 10119 (443 2990/fax 4432 9999/mail@hotel-jurine.de). U2 Senefelderplatz. **Rates** *single* DM150-190; *double* DM190-240; *breakfast* DM19. **Credit** AmEx, DC, V. **Map G2**
This freshly renovated building housing a three-star hotel, at the foot of Prenzlauer Berg, is within walking distance of the cafés and restaurants around Kollwitzplatz and has good transport connections into town. The rooms are bright and airy and the hotel has a friendly, family atmosphere but has yet to develop much character as it really is brand-new throughout. Also possible to board for longer stays. **Hotel services** *Bar. Conference room. Garage Gardens with terrace.* **Room services** *Fax. ISDN telephone. Pay TV. Radio. Room with disabled facilities (1). Satellite TV. Shower/bath. WC. Website: www.hotel-jurine.de*

Hotel-Pension Kastanienhof

Kastanienallee 65, Mitte, 10119 (443 050/fax 4430 5111). U8 Rosenthaler Platz/U2 Senefelderplatz. **Rates** *single* DM130; *double* DM180; *2-room apartment* DM210. **Credit** MC, V. **Map G2**
If you can handle the pastel peach and pink décor, rooms here are generously proportioned and well equipped. Staff are friendly and there are two breakfast rooms (one non-smoking) and a bar. Well situated for exploring Prenzlauer Berg and Mitte, lying on the border between the two districts. **Hotel services** *Bar. Lift. Parking (DM10 per day). Ticket booking.* **Room services** *Clock radio. Hairdryer. Minibar. Safe. Satellite TV. Shower. Telephone. WC.*

Pension Kettler

Bleibtreustraße 19, Charlottenburg, 10623 (883 4949/fax 882 4228). S3, S5, S7, S9 Savignyplatz/U15 Uhlandstraße. **Rates** *single* DM145; *double* DM155-180. **No credit cards. Map C4**
The six quiet and light bedrooms in this grand old building overlook an impressive courtyard. Most of the double rooms and some of the single rooms (rather small for the price) have showers. Double rooms can be booked as singles. All have showers, save one, and the toilets are in the corridor. **Room services** *Shower. Telephone.*

Hotel Märkischer Hof

Linienstraße 133, Mitte, 10115 (282 7155/fax 282 4331). U6 Oranienburger Tor. **Rates** *single* DM95-150; *double* DM140-198; *triple* DM210. **Credit** V. **Map F3**
A family-run hotel that's well placed by the junction of Friedrichstraße and Oranienburger Straße. You'll be within walking distance of some of Berlin's main attractions – the Berliner Ensemble, the Metropol Theater and the Staatsoper – and some of the city's most beautiful districts. The hotel is quiet and intimate, with friendly staff, comfortable though drab rooms and a pension atmosphere. **Hotel services** *Parking.* **Room services** *Minibar. Radio. Telephone. TV.*

Propeller Island City Lodge

Albrecht-Achilles-Straße 58, Wilmersdorf, 10709 (891 9016/fax 892 8721). U7 Adenauerplatz. **Rates** DM145-350; breakfast DM10. **No credit cards. Map B5**
This wonderful place, the most original hotel in Berlin, has been so successful since we listed it in our last edition it has now expanded around the corner. Still in the original building are the 'Symbol Room', squared off with 300 wacky graphics like a scene from a computer game; the 'Blaueszimmer', with mirrors hanging like sails in a monochrome blue environment; the Burgzimmer, where you sleep on top of a castle in a kind of Toontown-type fantasy; and the minimal 'Orangenes Zimmer' which is, well, orange. There is now also the choice of a further 27 rooms ranging from a totally mirrored room with crooked walls and infinite reflections to a four-person dormitory wrapped in wrapping paper. The 'Therapie Zimmer' is pure white with changing coloured lighting and in another you can sleep in a coffin. All are the product of the fertile mind of the artist and musician Lars Stroschen, and come complete with a stereo playing ambient sounds especially created for each room. Every stick of furniture has been custom-built and designed. A real labour of love and totally far out. Check website for pictures, booking and further information. **Hotel services** *Acupuncture. Alternative relaxation treatments. Holistic medicine.* **Room services** *Bathroom. ISDN telephone. Stereo. TV. Website: www.propeller-island.net4.com*

Pension Silvia

Knesebeckstraße 29, Charlottenburg, 10623 (881 2129/fax 885 0435). S3, S5, S7, S9 Savignyplatz. **Rates** *single* DM55-90; *double* DM90-100; *extra persons* DM50; *breakfast* DM9.50. **No credit cards. Map C4**
This pension has been in business for more than a hundred years and its present owner, Silvia, is an abrasive Saxon with a story or two to tell visitors about the hotel trade. The 15 rooms range in price from the cheap to the moderate, but they are all large, white and airy and have modern bathrooms. The location is convenient and don't be put off by the shabby dining room. You can get a decent breakfast for a little more in many of the nearby cafés. **Hotel services** *TV room.*

Artist Hotel-Pension Die Loge – *reduced rates for artists, perfect for small groups.*

Taunus Hotel

Monbijouplatz 1, Mitte, 10178 (283 5254/fax 283 5255). S3, S5, S7, S9 Hackescher Markt. **Rates** *single* DM150; *double* DM180. **Credit** AmEx, DC, MC, V. **Map F3**

Small hotel in a newly renovated building tucked away behind Hackescher Markt S-Bahn station. The interior is plain but clean and the location is excellent – close to Museumsinsel and an ideal base for exploring Mitte nightlife. A little too near the tram terminus with the windows open but you are in the city centre and there is a decent Italian restaurant on the corner opposite.

Hotel services *Bar. Parking (DM20).* **Room services** *Shower. Telephone. TV. WC.*

Hotel Unter den Linden

Unter den Linden 14, Mitte, 10117 (238 110/fax 2381 1100). S1, S2, S3, S5, S7, S9/U6 Friedrichstraße. **Rates** *single* DM109-150; *double* DM159-210. **Credit** AmEx, DC, MC, V. **Map F3**

The best thing about the sprawling, dated lobby of this 1960s hotel is the Le Corbusier-style chrome and black leather chairs. Images of old spy films come to mind with the extraordinary clash of décor. The staff are friendly but slow, and the food is nothing special – but who eats in their hotel with all Berlin to choose from? The corridors are stuffy, the rooms and bathrooms cramped but clean. However, there is a café terrace on Unter den Linden, and if you want to walk out of the door on to Berlin's most famous boulevard without paying Adlon prices, then this is an option.

Hotel services *Bar. Bistro. Conference facilities. Laundry service. Lift.* **Room services** *Minibar. Radio. Telephone. TV.*

Pension Viola Nova

Kantstraße 146, Charlottenburg, 10623 (313 1457/fax 312 3314/viola_nova@t-online.de). S3, S5, S7, S9 Savignyplatz. **Rates** *single* DM90-130; *double* DM120-160; *breakfast buffet* DM9.50. **No credit cards. Map C4**

In a popular tourist area, close to Ku'damm and Savignyplatz nightlife, the Viola Nova is one of many similar pensions in the district. Like the others, this is an old, converted Berlin house, and notable for its friendly owners, its pleasant breakfast room and its value for money.

Room services *Telephone. TV.*
Website: www.violanova.de

Hotel-Pension Waizennegger

Mommsenstraße 6, Charlottenburg, 10629 (883 1709/fax 881 4528/hotel.pension@t-online.de). S3, S5, S7, S9 Savignyplatz. **Rates** *single* DM80-100; *double* DM110-180. **No credit cards. Map C4**

In a delightful residential area, slightly off the beaten track, but still close enough to Savignyplatz to be convenient. The owners have made a real effort to make this a home away from home: six cosy rooms, filled with overstuffed furniture, all with a shower and two with a toilet.

Hotel services *Lift.* **Room services** *Shower. TV.*

City Hotel Westerland

Knesebeckstraße 10, Charlottenburg, 10623 (312 1004/fax 313 6489). S3, S5, S7, S9 Savignyplatz. **Rates** *single* DM120-160; *double* DM140-190; *suite* from DM180. **Credit** V. **Map C4**

A very pleasant hotel. The elegant wooden reception desk is stunning, and the breakfast room and bedrooms keep up the standard. Rooms come with either bath or shower and are very comfortable – if there were ever anything good on German TV, it would almost be worth foregoing the sights to luxuriate in some of their armchairs.

Hotel services *Lift. Parking.* **Room services** *Bath or shower. Room service. Telephone. TV.*

Budget

Pension Acksel Haus

Belforter Straße 21, Prenzlauer Berg, 10405 (4433 7633/fax 441 6116). U2 Senefelderplatz. **Rates** *single* DM85-100; *double* DM99-130. **No credit cards. Map G2**

A lovely place in a picturesque area, with great prices. There are seven apartments with a bedroom, sitting room, bathroom and kitchenette. Each has lovely old wooden floorboards, white walls and antique furniture with a Mediterranean feel. Most apartments have two beds, one of them can house four or five people. There is a pretty back garden for the summer. Walk round to Kollwitzplatz a block away for sumptuous café breakfasts. Highly recommended but be sure to book ahead.

Artist Hotel-Pension Die Loge

Friedrichstraße 115, Mitte, 10117 (280 7513/dieloge@t-online.de). U6 Oranienburger Tor. **Rates** *single* DM70-90; *double* DM100-140; *apartment for four* DM220; *breakfast* DM5-10. **No credit cards. Map F3**

It's not quiet here but you are very much in the thick of things as far as nightlife is concerned. This small, friendly, young pension has special reduced rates for artists and musicians (DM60) and is perfect for small groups travelling together. WC and showers are in the corridor. There is a cosy foyer with comfy sofas and rooms have decorative friezes painted by the owners. A second more upmarket hotel, Riverside, is close to completion nearby. Call here for details.

Room services *Telephone, TV.*
Website: www.artist-hotels.de

Pension Finck

Güntzelstraße 54, Wilmersdorf, 10717 (861 2940/fax 861 8158). U9 Güntzelstraße. **Rates** *single* DM50-80; *double* DM90-100. **No credit cards. Map C5**

On the third floor of a residential building, and directly above another pension. It's a homely jumble, with lots of knick-knacks hanging on the walls of the lobby and breakfast room. The 14 good-sized rooms are decorated in the same eclectic fashion as the rest of the place, and eight have a shower. The toilets are in the hallway. Friendly owner and slap next to an U-Bahn station.

Hotel services *Lift.*

Honigmond Pension

Borsigstraße 28, Mitte, 10115 (284 4550/fax 2844 5511/honigmond@t-online.de). U6 Oranienburger Tor. **Rates** *single* DM69; *double* DM99-129; *triple* DM149; *quad* DM199. **No credit cards. Map F2**

Simply and pleasantly decorated with white walls, and stripped wooden doorframes and floorboards.

A really good place for a family on a budget. No breakfast but there are plenty of places in the neighbourhood, for example the Honigmond restaurant downstairs, which does weekend breakfasts from 9am (*see chapter* **Restaurants**). Walking distance from the Scheunenviertel. Recommended.

Hotel services *Bar. Restaurant.* **Room services** *Telephone, TV.*

Hotel-Pension Imperator

Meinekestraße 5, Charlottenburg, 10719 (881 4181/fax 885 1919). U9, U15 Kurfürstendamm. **Rates** *single* DM80-120; *double* DM150-190; *breakfast* DM12-20. **No credit cards. Map C4**

One of the best places to stay in Berlin. The building is a huge town house and the Imperator occupies the second floor. Its 11 bedrooms are vast and stylishly furnished with a mixture of antique and modern. All but two have modern showers. The breakfast and TV rooms are gorgeous and the proprietor's taste in paintings is not bad. In the kitchen is one wall plastered with photos of the jazz musicians and artists who have stayed here, Cecil Taylor and John Cage among them.

Hotel services *Conference facilities. Laundry service. Lift. TV room.* **Room services** *Room service.*

Pension Kreuzberg

Großbeerenstraße 64, Kreuzberg, 10963 (251 1362/fax 251 0638). U6, U7 Mehringdamm. **Rates** *single* DM75; *double* DM98; *extra persons* DM43. **No credit cards. Map F5**

Small, friendly pension in a typical old Berlin building – but not for the unfit as there are four steep flights of stairs to the reception. Communal bathroom on each floor, some rooms with washbasins. Good location.

mitArt Pension

Friedrichstraße 127, Mitte, 10117 (2839 0430/fax 2839 0432/mitart@t-online.de). U6 Oranienburger Tor. **Rates** *single* DM90-150; *double* DM130-180. **No credit cards. Map F3**

Opposite Tacheles, this surprisingly peaceful and elegant pension is also a gallery. The friendly owner originally let out three rooms to visiting artists and then expanded to nine. The grand proportions of the breakfast room, which serves a healthy *Naturkost* repast, are typical 19th-century Berlin town house. The best room is the *Mädchenkammer* – a set of wooden steps up to a platform and simple white unadorned walls where the maid used to sleep. A good spot if you are in Berlin to look at art – Auguststraße is around the corner and the owner can give good insider tips. Recommended, and not to be confused with the Artist Hotel-Pension Die Loge up the road (*see above*).

Room services *Telephone.*

Hotel-Pension München

Güntzelstraße 62, Wilmersdorf, 10717 (857 9120/fax 853 2744). U9 Güntzelstraße. **Rates** *single* DM75-105; *double* DM130; *breakfast* DM10. **Credit** AmEx, MC, V. **Map C5**

Even though the lift looks suspiciously antiquated, it's better to brave its cage than hike up the stairs to the third floor of this residential building. Owned by artists, this pension features lots of natural wood,

'Russian visa, Miss, or perhaps an opera ticket?' – **Circus – The Hostel**.

modern art, and eight bright, cheerful rooms decorated in red, white and bright floral hues with modern furniture. All double rooms have a shower and WC. A welcome change from the average Berlin pension, not least because of its friendly owner.
Hotel services *Garage. Lift.* **Room services** *Telephone. TV.*

Studentenhotel Hubertusalle

Delbrückstraße 24, Grunewald, 14193 (891 9718/fax 892 8698). S7 Grunewald. **Open** *Mar-Oct office* 7am-2pm Mon-Fri. **Rates** *single* DM45-80; *double* DM70-110; *triple* DM90-126. **No credit cards. Map A6**
The Studentenhotel is right by Hubertus Lake and a good place to stay in summer. The building is an ugly 1980s construction, the 60 rooms are plain and functional and with bathrooms on the corridor. Cafeteria meals until 10pm. Often packed, so book in advance. A ten-minute ride to the city centre.
Hotel services *TV room.*

Youth & backpacker hostels

Official youth hostels in Berlin (there are three) are crammed most of the year so do book ahead. If you book more than two weeks in advance use the central reservations office on 262 3024. You must be a member of the YHA to stay in these and they all have single-sex dormitories. For your YHA membership card, if you don't already have one, you need to go to the **Mitgliederservice des DJH Berlin-Brandenburg** (*see below*).

A better bet may be one of the newer hostels in nicer surroundings, who waive membership requirements and often give good advice for the budget traveller. More are opening all the time and most will pass you on to a competitor if full. Of the hostels listed, breakfast is included and none take credit cards.

Mitgliederservice des DJH Berlin-Brandenburg

Tempelhofer Ufer 32, Kreuzberg, 10963 (264 9520/fax 262 0437/djh-berlin-brandenburg@jugendherberge.de). U1, U7 Möckernbrücke/U1, U2 Gleisdreieck. **Open** 9am-4pm Mon, Wed, Fri; 9am-6pm Tue, Thur. **Map E5**
The office can supply YHA membership cards. Bring your passport and a passport-sized photo. *Websites: www.djh.de; www.jugendherberge.de*

Youth hostels

Jugendgästehaus am Wannsee

Badeweg 1, Zehlendorf, 14129 (803 2034/5). S1, S7 Nikolassee. **Rates** *under-27s* DM34; *over-27s* DM42. Book as early as possible. All rooms have four beds.

Jugendgästehaus am Zoo

Hardenbergstraße 9a, Charlottenburg, 10623 (312 9410/fax 401 5283). S3, S5, S7, S9/U2, U9 Zoologischer Garten. **Rates** from DM35. **Map C4**
Not an official YHA hostel, so no membership required, and not a bad place. Some single rooms, plus doubles and four- to eight-bed dorms. No long-term reservations, but you can call one or two days in advance. Open 24 hours.

Jugendgästehaus Berlin
Kluckstraße 3, Schöneberg, 10785 (261 1097/8 or 257 99 808). U1 Kurfürstenstraße. **Rates** *under-27s* DM24-34; *over-27s* DM32-42. **Map E4**
Phone for reservations at least two weeks in advance. Four- to eight-bed dorms.

Jugendherberge Ernst Reuter
Hermsdorfer Damm 48-50, Wedding, 13467 (404 1610). U6 Alt-Tegel, then bus 125. **Rates** *under-27s* DM28; *over-27s* DM35.
Four- to six-bed dorms.

Backpacker hostels

Circus – The Hostel
Rosa Luxemburg Straße 39-41, Mitte, 10118 (2839 1433/fax 2839 1484/circus@mind.de). U2 Rosa-Luxemburg-Platz. **Rates** *dormitory* DM25-40; *single* DM50; *compulsory bedlinen* DM4. **No credit cards. Map G3**
New and well-located hostel with clean and bright rooms, open 24 hours and with single-sex accommodation if required. The owners are young travellers themselves and have worked hard to offer good value for money, striving to help both with your stay and your onward journey – everything from arranging Russian visas to opera tickets and booking your next place of stay. Guests can also go on free tours of little-known corners of Berlin. Often full so be sure to book. Highly recommended.
Hostel services *Bar. Bike hire. Breakfast service. Fast-track visas to eastern Europe. Internet café. Laundromat. Restaurant. Storage, locker room and safe. Tickets for football, travel and shows. Tours.*
Website: www.circus-berlin.de

The Clubhouse Hostel
Kalkscheunestraße 2, Mitte, 10117 (2809 7979/fax 2809 7977/mailto@clubhouse-berlin.de). S1, S2 Oranienburger Straße. **Rates** *dormitory* DM25-40; *single* DM50; *compulsory bedlinen* DM4; *breakfast buffet* DM7. **No credit cards. Map F3**
Housed in a central and historic but newly renovated building and culture centre, the **Kalkscheune** (*see chapters* **Cabaret** *and* **Nightlife**) this is just behind the famous Tacheles. The staff are friendly and English-speaking. The rooms smell a bit of socks but that's budget travelling for you. This is offset by an attractive communal room. Oh, and a free welcome beer on arrival.
Hostel services *Bike hire. Internet service. Luggage room and safe. No curfew or lockout. Pay phone. Ticket service.*
Website: www.clubhouse-berlin.de

Frederik's
Straße der Pariser Kommune 35, Friedrichshain, 10243 (2966 9450/fax 2966 9452/hostel@frederiks.de). S3, S5, S7, S9 Ostbahnhof/U5 Weberwiese. **Rates** *dormitory* DM25-35; *single* DM49; *compulsory bedlinen* DM4; *breakfast* DM6. **No credit cards. Map H3**
In a renovated Jewish girls' secondary school dating from 1903. The building and surrounding area is packed with history and dramatic east-European

architecture. Well connected for public transport as Ostbahnhof is only a short walk away. Prices vary according to whether the room has a washbasin.
Hostel services *Bike hire. Internet service. No curfew or lockout. Parking. Self-catering facilities. Shuttle service. Ticket service. Tours by bus, bike or skates.*
Website: www.frederiks.de

Lette'm Sleep Hostel
Lettestraße 7, Mitte, 10437 (4473 3623/fax 4473 3625/info@backpackers.de). U2 Eberswalder Straße. **Rates** *dormitory* DM26-35; *double with cooking facilities* DM45; *compulsory bedlinen* DM4. **No credit cards. Map G1**
A small hostel, run by Australians with a poor line in puns, on a ground floor and in the middle of Prenzlauer Berg's café, club and bar scene. No breakfast provided but you can either cook your own in the communal kitchen or splash out on the meal that Berlin does best in one of many nearby establishments. Excellent facilities for disabled travellers.
Hostel services *Cooking facilities. Disabled facilities. Free city map and information. Internet service. No curfew or lockout. Payphone. Snacks and beverages. Ticket service. TV.*
www.backpackers.de

Mitte's Backpacker Hostel
Chausseestraße 102, Mitte, 10115 (2839 0965/fax 2839 0935/info@backpacker.de). U6 Zinnowitzer Straße. **Rates** *dormitory* DM25-38; *single* DM50; *compulsory bedlinen* DM5; *breakfast* from DM5. **No credit cards. Map F2**
Open since 1994, this is the oldest backpacker hostel in Mitte. The rooms are all individually decorated by past guests with an artistic flair and have been named accordingly. The 'map room' is mildly amusing with light fittings in the shape of Berlin's two telecom towers. There is a video room with English-language films and a kitchen for self-catering which means the hostel tends to smell of frying food but this all just adds to the homey, student-digs atmosphere. The staff are multilingual, friendly and helpful.
Hostel services *Bike hire. Cooking facilities. Email service. Free city map and information. No curfew or lockout. Tours. Vegemite.*
Website: www.backpacker.de

Odyssee Globetrotter Hostel
Grünberger Straße 23, Friedrichshain, 10243 (2900 0081/Odyssee@hostel-berlin.de). U5 Frankfurter Tor. **Rates** *dormitory* DM24-36; *buffet breakfast* DM5. **No credit cards.**
Not far from Frederik's hostel, the Odyssee Globetrotter too is just off Karl-Marx-Allee and in the reasonably priced arty-studenty area of town with a good selection of alternative clubs and bars nearby. Rooms are brightly decorated, which livens up the standard pine furniture. The communal space is a good size for meeting and drinking and the bar is open until dawn.
Hostel services *Bar. Bike hire. Free lockers. Luggage room and safe. No curfew or lockout. Table football and assorted games.*
Website: www.hostel-berlin.de

Hotel Transit

Hagelberger Straße 53-54, Kreuzberg, 10965 (789 0470/fax 7890 4777). U6, U7 Mehringdamm. **Rates** *dormitory* DM33-47; *single* DM90. **Credit** AmEx, MC, V. **Map F5**

A converted factory houses this unexpectedly bright, airy hotel with 49 rooms. It's nicely located in one of the most beautiful parts of Kreuzberg, handy for Viktoria Park, a host of cafés and restaurants. The rooms are basic but clean and the DM33 dormitory bed is good value but you can't book, so you have to take pot luck with what's available. All rooms have showers and the friendly staff speak English, but overall not as user-friendly as the newer backpacker hostels. Reception open 24 hours.

Hostel services *Bar (24 hours). Internet access. Laundry service. Lift. TV.* **Room services** *Safe. Website: www.hotel-transit.de*

Camping

If you want to explore the camp sites of surrounding Brandenburg, ask for a camping map from **Berlin Tourismus Marketing** (*above*). Below we list those within the Berlin city limits. They are all quite far out of town, so check timetables for last buses if you want to enjoy some nightlife while in town. Prices don't vary much between sites: for tents, expect to pay around DM7.50 per night; for caravans DM13 plus DM10 per person and DM5 for children.

Landesverband des DCC (Deutscher Camping Club)

Geisbergstraße 11, Schöneberg, 10777 (218 6071/72). U4 Viktoria-Luise-Platz. **Open** 10.30am-6pm Mon; 8am-4pm Wed; 8am-1pm Fri. **Map D5**

Can provide information about all camping sites in Berlin and elsewhere in Germany.

DCC am Krossinsee

Wernsdorfer Straße 38, Köpenick, 12527 (675 8687/ fax 3680 8492). S8 Grünau, then tram 68 to Schmöckwitz, bus 733 to site.

Situated within quiet woodlands. Rooms in holiday homes and bungalows, restaurant also available. Open all year round. Caravans welcome.

Services *Boat, windsurf and bike hire. Disabled facilities.*

DCC Gatow

Kladower Damm 207-213, Spandau, 14039 (365 4340/ fax 3680 8492). Bus x34 from S3, S5, S7, S9/U2, U9 Zoologischen Garten.

Quiet with good sanitary facilities. Caravans and mobile homes welcome. Open all year round.

Services *Disabled facilities.*

DCC Kladow

Krampnitzer Weg 111-117, Kladow, 14089 (365 2797). Bus x34 to Alt-Kladow from S3, S5, S7, S9/U2, U9 Zoologischer Garten, then bus 234 to Selbitzer Straße.

Follow the DCC signs from Selbitzer Straße, about five minutes' walk. Caravans welcome, or you can

hire one from the site. Open all year round. Kladow's plus is that you can also take the ferry from Wannsee for the price of a normal city transport ticket.

Services *Children's playground. Food shop. Handicapped toilet. Open-air swimming and bathing. Restaurant. Shower. Sportsground.*

DCC Kohlhasenbrück

Neue Kreisstraße 36, Wannsee, 14109 (805 1737). S1, S7 Wannsee, then bus 118 to Neue Kreisstraße.

In a nature reserve area and open 1 March to 31 October. Within easy reach of Potsdam.

Services *Children's playground. Laundry facilities. Showers.*

Flat-share agencies

The *Mitwohnagenturen* ('flat-share agencies') listed below will find you anything from a rented flat for two or three years to a short-let room in a shared house. These are much easier to find in summer, when Berlin is less crowded – at other times of the year it may be more difficult. Most flat-share agencies accept bookings in advance, so the best advice is to book ahead.

If you're staying for a couple of weeks and manage to find something through a Mitwohnagentur, you will probably pay DM40-80 a night. For longer stays, the agencies charge commission at different rates – don't forget to check what this will cost you. Private rooms can also be booked through **Berlin Tourismus Marketing** (*above*).

Agentur Streicher

Immanuelkirchstraße 8, Prenzlauer Berg, 10405 (441 6622/fax 441 6623/info@housingagencies-berlin.com). U2 Senefelderplatz/tram 1 Knaackstraße. **Open** 11am-2pm Mon-Fri; 3-6pm Sat. **Map G2** *Website: www.housingagencies-berlin.com*

fine + mine Internationale Mitwohnagentur

Neue Schönhauser Straße 20, Mitte, 10178 (235 5120/fax 2355 1212/office@fineandmine.de). S3, S5, S7, S9 Hackescher Markt/U8 Weinmeisterstraße. **Open** 10am-6pm Mon-Fri. **Map G3** *Website: www.fineandmine.de*

Freiraum

Wiener Straße 14, Kreuzberg, 10999 (618 2008/fax 618 2006/info@freiraum-berlin.com). U1 Görlitzer Bahnhof. **Open** 10am-7pm Mon-Fri; 10am-2pm Sat. **Map G5** *Website: www.freiraum-berlin.com*

HomeCompany

Joachimstalerstraße 17, Charlottenburg, 10719 (194 45/fax 8826 6940/homecompany-berlin@t-online.de). U9, U15 Kurfürstendamm. **Open** 9am-6pm Mon-Fri; 11am-2pm Sat-Sun. **Map C4** *Website: www.homecompany.de*

Mitwohnzentrale Mehringdamm

Mehringdamm 66, Kreuzberg, 10961 (786 6002/fax 785 0614). U6, U7 Mehringdamm. **Open** 9am-6pm Mon-Fri. **Map F5**

Shopping & Services

Multi-million dollar malls and dapper designer districts shine in Berlin's retail revival – but not the dull department stores.

Few would come to Berlin with a shopping spree at the top of their must-do list. During the 40 years when one half of the city was an island and the other a cash-strapped communist capital, its grand pre-war department stores and boutique-lined boulevards mostly disappeared. With them went Berlin's reputation as a trend-setting, thriving centre of commerce. Retail in the West was characterised by merchandise drab in both selection and presentation, and in the East there was little worth buying at all. But Berlin's elevation to a capital city has changed all that. So rearrange the priorities on that list of things to do. No other city offers as much (affordable) space to the visions of young entrepreneurs as it does to the wares of big-name international companies.

Both jockey for customers unaccustomed to travelling across town to shop in a neighbourhood other than their own. Breathing life into multi-million dollar projects such as the malls of Potsdamer Platz or the Friedrichstadt Passagen has been a slow process. But gradually Berliners are waking up to the joys of retail therapy. There are days when Friedrichstraße, with its sophisticated international names such as Donna Karan, Gucci, Galeries Lafayette and Etro looks as busy as Fifth Avenue (though they must do a fraction of the turnover). A kilometre further north, an influential designer enclave has taken root by the bars, cafés and galleries of the revived Scheunenviertel.

The shopping heartland of the west around the Kurfürstendamm has responded to the shifting emphasis to the east – and subsequent waning custom – by undergoing a much-needed facelift. That has attracted more major players from abroad: the west end now boasts Europe's first Niketown and Germany's largest Benetton, as well as design houses from Prada to Hermès. In all parts of the city, Berlin's young, energetic population continues to feed a profusion of excellent second-hand shops and flea markets, music stores, bookshops and fashion outlets. Browse and you'll discover the dynamism of the city's retail revival.

Opening hours

Though it's mostly only the larger and more central ones that stay open late, shops can sell goods until 8.30pm on weekdays, and 4pm on Saturdays. Most big stores normally open their doors between 8.30am and 9am, newsagents and bakeries as early as 6am; smaller or independent shops tend to open around 10am or later.

In the days before Berlin's opening hours were liberalised, the only late day was the *Lange Donnerstag* ('long Thursday'). Force of habit makes many still shop late on Thursdays, leading to queues at downtown checkouts.

Galeries Lafayette – *French dressing, p143.*

Antiques

Collectors and browsers with an interest in the 18th and 19th centuries will find many of the better dealers clustered on Keithstraße and Goltzstraße in Schöneberg. The streets surrounding Fasanenplatz in Wilmersdorf are worth exploring, as is Suarezstraße in Charlottenburg.

In the east, streets such as Kollwitzstraße and Husemannstraße in Prenzlauer Berg are home to small, unpretentious *Antiquariaten* selling inexpensive books, household equipment and assorted communist memorabilia.

Most shops don't accept credit cards and you can negotiate a much better price for cash. *See also below* **Souvenirs** *and* **Flea Markets**.

Deco Arts
Motzstraße 6, Schöneberg, 10777 (215 8672). U1, U2, U4 Nollendorfplatz. **Open** 2-6pm Tue-Fri; 11am-3pm Sat. **No credit cards. Map D5**
Shell-shaped 1930s sofas and other art deco furniture at fair prices, as well as the odd piece by Marcel Breuer and Carl Jacobs, and treasures from the 1950s and 1960s. If an American bar is too big to take home, pick up a stylish tea set, vase or ashtray.

Fingers
Nollendorfstraße 35, Schöneberg, 10777 (215 3441). U1, U2, U4 Nollendorfplatz. **Open** 2.30-6.30pm Tue-Fri; 11am-2.30pm Sat. **No credit cards. Map D5**
Splendid finds from the 1940s, 1950s and 1960s, including lipstick-shaped cigarette lighters, vintage toasters, weird lighting and eccentric glassware.

Historische Bauelemente
Bärenklauer Weg 2, Marwitz, 16727 (03304 502 242). Berliner Ring Nord, exit Schwante and follow signs to Henningsdorf and Marwitz. **Open** 10am-6pm Mon-Sat. **No credit cards.**
In the early 1990s building boom, Olaf Elias began combing the region for construction sites throwing away old doors, window frames, wrought-iron garden fences, tiles and other old building materials. His collection now occupies 20,000sq m in a former pig farm 30 minutes from the city. It includes stunning Jugendstil bathtubs, 1920s sinks, angel sculptures and decorative but practical artefacts from various decades of Berlin-Brandenburg history. You'll need a car to get here, but it's a real treat.

Jukeland
Crellestraße 14, Schöneberg, 10827 (782 3335). U7 Kleistpark. **Open** 2-6pm Tue-Fri; 11am-2pm Sat. **No credit cards. Map E5**
Jukeland has everything you need to turn your home into an American diner: neon signs, Cadillac couches, diner-style tables and, of course, jukeboxes. Also a plentiful supply of signs from the 1940s and 1950s.

Lehmanns Colonialwaren
Grolmanstraße 46, Charlottenburg, 10623 (883 3942). S3, S5, S7, S9 Savignyplatz. **Open** 2-6.30pm Mon-Fri; 11am-2pm Sat. **No credit cards. Map C4**

Turn-of-the-century luggage, clothing and furniture deck out this small shop like a cluttered Victorian parlour. The eccentric stock runs to a colonial theme, so don't be surprised to come across a set of snakeskin luggage or a guide to hunting big game.

Timmerman's Indian Supply
Berliner Straße 88, Potsdam, 14467 (0331 292 076). S1, S7 Wannsee, then bus 116 to Glienicker Brücke. **Open** 9am-6pm Mon-Fri; 11am-6pm Sat, Sun. **No credit cards.**
This beautifully restored 1930s gas station alone is worth the trek. Inside are big toys for big kids, including vintage Indian motorcycles.

Ubu
Bleibtreustraße 55, Charlottenburg, 10623 (313 5115). S3, S5, S7, S9 Savignyplatz. **Open** 3pm-6.30pm Mon-Fri; 11am-2pm Sat. **No credit cards. Map C4**
Fine collection of vintage travel books and goods, with early Baedekers, travel cases and model ships.

Wolfgang Haas
Suarezstraße 3, Charlottenburg, 14057 (321 4570). U2 Sophie-Charlotte-Platz/204 bus. **Open** 3-7pm Tue-Fri; 11am-3pm Sat. **No credit cards. Map B4**
Period, lacquered-timber furniture, glassware, ceramics and other small antiques dating from 1800 to 1960. There are classic tables, chairs and cabinets, as well as art nouveau pieces. The selection of German crystal from the 19th and 20th centuries is particularly good; the paintings are all post-1945.

Auctions & appraisals

Leo Spik
Kurfürstendamm 66, Wilmersdorf, 10707 (883 6170). U7 Adenauerplatz. **Open** 10am-1pm Mon-Fri; 2.30-6pm Sat. **No credit cards. Map B5**
The only auction house that survived the war was founded in 1919 and specialises in art and antiques from the Renaissance period to classical modern pieces. Four annual auctions put paintings, jewellery, furniture and carpets under the hammer. The stress is on German art, but foreign goodies are also on offer. No in-house appraisals.

Villa Griesebach
Fasanenstraße 25, Charlottenburg, 10719 (882 6811). U15 Uhlandstraße. **Open** 10am-6.30pm Mon-Fri; 10am-2pm Sat. **No credit cards. Map C4**
One of the world's largest auction houses, Villa Griesebach specialises in Impressionist and Expressionist art, most of it German. Auctions are held in May and November. Free appraisals for paintings and sculptures that could be considered for a Griesebach auction.

Beauty salons

Aveda
Kurfürstendamm 29, Charlottenburg, 10719 (8855 2757). U9, U15 Kurfürstendamm. **Open** 10am-8pm Mon-Fri; 10am-4pm Sat. **Credit** AmEx, DC, V. **Map C4**

Aveda – *all lined up for a Comforting Eye Treatment.*

Berlin business people are extending their lunch breaks to treat themselves to a Comforting Eye Treatment (20 minutes, DM30) or a Himalayan Rejuvenation Treatment (two hours, DM250). At the back of this cosmetics shop, the hair and beauty salon offers hair-styling and cutting, aromatherapy massage, manicure, facials and body treatments, using products based on natural flower essences.
Branch: Quartier 206, Friedrichstraße 71, Mitte, 10117 (204 9504)

Hautfit Bio Kosmetik

Goltzstraße 18, Schöneberg, 10781 (216 5259). U7 Eisenacher Straße. **Open** 10am-6.30pm Mon-Fri; 10am-2pm Sat. **Credit** MC, V. **Map D5**
This salon uses only plant-based products including the brand widely considered to be the purest of the pure, from the German anthroposophical company Dr Hauschka. Products used vary according to skin type: an introduction facial costs DM65, as does the algae-based Sea Treatment; a flower essence facial DM95; and the two-hour Dr Hauschka treatment including facial, foot bath and hand massage is DM95-140. Products are for sale in the shop, a fin-de-siècle butcher's tiled in Jugendstil ceramics.

Marie France

Fasanenstraße 42, Charlottenburg, 10719 (881 6555). U15 Uhlandstraße. **Open** 9am-6pm Tue-Wed, Fri; 9am-8pm Thur; 9am-2pm Sat. **No credit cards.** **Map C4**
The cosmeticians speak English with a French accent and use luxurious French products at this clean, pleasant salon, which has been glamming up Berliners for more than 30 years. Hot-wax depilation is a speciality (DM46 for a half-leg), and they also offer a range of relaxing and beautifying treatments.

Cosmetics

Belladonna

Bergmannstraße 101, Kreuzberg, 10961 (694 3731). U7 Gneisenaustraße. **Open** 10am-7pm Mon-Fri; 10am-4pm Sat. **Credit** AmEx, MC, V. **Map F5**
Natural and flower-essence products from German firms Logona, Lavera, Dr Hauschka, Weleda and others, plus the entire range of Primavera essential oils and lamps to burn them in. The shop also stocks brushes, make-up and baby clothes.

DK Cosmetics

Kurfürstendamm 56, Charlottenburg 10707 (3279 0123). U15 Uhlandstraße. **Open** 10am-7pm Mon-Wed; 10am-8pm Thur-Fri; 10am-6pm Sat. **Credit** AmEx, DC, MC, V. **Map C4**
Lotions and potions for pampered globetrotters from cult beauty companies such as Kiehl's, Remde, Eve Lom and Bloom, make-up by Nars and Hard Candy, haircare from Bumble & Bumble and jewelled accessories from slides to tiaras. Diptyque scented candles and Sarah Schwartz's shaped or text-bedecked soaps make for more fun in the bath.

Shiseido Beauty Gallery

Bleibtreustraße 32, Charlottenburg, 10707 (8867 9840). U15 Uhlandstraße. **Open** 10am-7pm Mon-Fri; 10am-4pm Sat. **No credit cards. Map C4**
You can't actually buy anything here, but you'll need an appointment anyway. For 45 minutes, you can try out Shiseido's entire product range with no pressure to purchase. Friendly staff conduct a computer skin analysis, then advise on the right skincare régime and make-up application – all for free! The SBG is unique, boosting Shiseido's Berlin sales in the number of Ku'damm stores stocking the brand nearby.

World of Beauty

Augsburger Straße 37, Schöneberg, 10789 (885 4892). U1 Augsburger Straße. **Open** 9am-7pm Mon-Fri; 9am-4pm Sat. **No credit cards. Map D4**
Afro-American cosmetics plus real and fake hair pieces and extensions in many colours and styles.

Hair salons

Berlin hair stylists' technical skills tend to out-match their judgment or taste. And the state of the average Berlin barnet might convince you never to trust your crowning glory to the locals. That said, the city does boast a few stylists and colourists that can do a pretty fair job, as well as some international salons that can cut it with the best of them.

Hanley's Hair Company

*Hackesche Höfe, Rosenthaler Straße 40-41, Mitte, 10178 (281 3179). U8 Weinmeisterstraße/S3, S5, S7, S9 Hackescher Mark*t. **Open** 9am-8pm Mon-Fri; 10am-4pm Sat. **No credit cards. Map F3**
Friendly, trendy salon run by Thomas Schweizer and Deborah Hanley. Full range of styling and treat-ments, offering a wash, cut and head massage for DM54 (men) or D74 (women).

Locke & Glaze

Kastanienallee 3, Mitte, 10119 (448 2620). U2 Eberswalder Straße. **Open** 9.30am-7pm Mon-Fri; 9.30am-8pm Thur. **No credit cards. Map G2**
Great colour jobs and cuts by stylists who are not allowed to ask what you would like before offer-ing their own suggestions. The results fall some-where between what you thought you wanted and what they think would suit you, and most clients come out happy. Follow-up trims are cheaper. Dodgy decor.
Branch: Boxhagener Straße 53, Friedrichshain, 10245 (294 9778)

Udo Walz

Kempinski-Plaza, Uhlandstraße 181-183, Charlottenburg, 10623 (882 7457). U15 Uhlandstraße. **Open** 9am-6pm Mon; 9am-7pm Tue-Fri; 9am-3pm Sat. **Credit** AmEx, MC, V. **Map C4**
Udo is the darling of the Berlin hair brigade, and likes to have his picture taken with Claudia Schiffer. Whether he actually cuts her hair is a different mat-ter. The stylists are well-trained and friendly (wash, cut and dry, DM110).
Branch: Hohenzollerndamm 93, Wilmersdorf, 14199 (826 6108)

Vidal Sassoon

Schlüterstraße 38-39, Charlottenburg, 10629 (884 5000). S3, S5, S7, S9 Savignyplatz. **Open** 9.45am-6.15pm Tue, Thur; 9am-6.15pm Wed; 9am-7pm Fri; 8.30am-3pm Sat. **No credit cards. Map C4**
International safe bet. A cut from a top stylist will cost you DM105, and from the 'German Creative Director' DM150. 'Cut' includes massage, wash, hair treatment, conditioning and styling. Modelling cuts DM25-45. Full colouring and treat-ments on offer.

Udo Walz *– but alas no Claudia Schiffer.*

Opticians

Brille 54

Friedrichstraße 71, Mitte, 10117 (2094 6060). U6 Französische Straße. **Open** 10am-8pm Mon-Fri; 10am-4pm Sat. **Credit** AmEx, DC, MC, V. **Map F4**
A small but functionally sleek space in Quartier 206 designed by hot young Berlin architects Plajer & Franz. In stock are Helmut Lang, Armani, Gucci, Oliver Peoples, Paul Smith and Japan's Takumi Oval. Also handmade, platinum-coated frames by German designer Lunor, and aluminium, screwless frames with coloured shades from IC Berlin, popu-lar industrial design graduates.
Branch: Kurfürstendamm 54, Charlottenburg, 10107 (882 6696)

Brilliant

Schlüterstraße 53, Charlottenburg, 10629 (324 1991). S3, S5, S7, S9 Savignyplatz. **Open** 10am-7pm Mon-Wed; 10am-8pm Thur, Fri; 10am-4pm Sat. **Credit** AmEx, DC, MC, V. **Map C4**
Sip tea or espresso in the chic sitting room while try-ing out frames by Vivienne Westwood, CK, Yamamoto, Boss, Gaultier, D & G, Mikli, Persol, Starck Eyes and German institution Zeiss.

Fielmann

Passage, Alexanderplatz, Mitte, 10178 (242 4507). S3, S5, S7, S9/ U2, U5, U8 Alexanderplatz. **Open** 9am-8pm Mon-Fri; 9am-4pm Sat. **Credit** AmEx, DC, MC, V. **Map G3**
Germany's biggest chain of opticians. Large selec-tion of frames and competitive prices. Eye-tests in-house. Branches all over town.

Dussman Das Kulturkaufhaus – *spacious.*

Tanning studios

If you fancy bathing your bod in UV, you're in luck – there are bronzing parlours all over Berlin. Try the *Gelbe Seiten* under *Bräunungsstudios.*

City-Sun

First floor, Tauentzienstraße 16 (entrance in Marburger Straße), Charlottenburg, 10789 (218 8037). U1, U2, U15 Wittenbergplatz. **Open** 10am-10pm daily. **Credit** V. **Map D4**

Eight minutes in a super-intensive frying coffin costs DM6. Also an vast range of massage, nail and make-up services, with permanent lip, eyelid and eyebrow make-up.

Tattoos & piercing

Blut & Eisen

Alte Schönhauser Straße 6, Mitte, 10119 (283 1982). U8 Weinmeisterstraße/U2 Rosa-Luxemburg-Platz. **Open** 1-7pm Tue-Wed, Fri-Sat; 1-9pm Thur. **No credit cards. Map G3**

Book a good three weeks in advance for a bit of body piercing or tattooing courtesy of 'Blood & Iron'. The three, self-taught staff are walking advertisements for their own artistry. Their work is accomplished and original but not cheap – they won't touch you for less than DM150, and on average customers leave DM300-500 the lighter. No under-14s admitted.

Germany is still blessed with a lively independent bookshop scene, though chain stores are spreading. If the EU succeeds in scrapping the price maintenance system, then the dominance of the chains will undoubtedly increase.

Another Country

Riemannstraße 7, Kreuzberg, 10961 (6940 1150). U7 Gneisenaustraße. **Open** 11am-8pm Mon-Fri; 11am-5pm Sat. **No credit cards. Map F5**

Spacious premises housing an ambitious bookshop and private library stocked with more than 10,000 English-language titles – around half of them science fiction – from the collection of British owner Alan Raphaeline. A small membership fee allows you to use the reading room downstairs and help yourself to tea and coffee, or borrow books for varying fees. Return them to recoup a deposit, or else hang on to the book. Also stocks antiques.

Buchhandlung Herschel

Anklamer Straße 38, Mitte, 10115 (440 7599). U8 Bernauer Straße. **Open** 10am-7pm Mon-Fri; 10am-2pm Sat. **No credit cards. Map F2**

Located in the **Weiberwirtschaft** (*see chapter* **Women**), this is a small and personal shop that doesn't stock a huge range but Frau Herschel goes to great lengths to track down any German book you're looking for. Interesting new German writers give readings in the gallery once or twice a month.

The British Bookshop

Mauerstraße 83-84, Mitte, 10117 (238 4680). U2, U6 Stadtmitte. **Open** 10am-7pm Mon-Fri; 10am-4pm Sat. **Credit** AmEx, MC, V. **Map F4**

With a large stock of contemporary and classic fiction in English, the British Bookshop also boasts comprehensive teaching, travel and children's sections. Good selection of newspapers and magazines.

Bücherbogen

Savignyplatz Bogen 593, Charlottenburg, 10623 (3186 9511). S3, S5, S7, S9 Savignyplatz. **Open** 10am-8pm Mon-Fri; 10am-4pm Sat. **Credit** MC, V. **Map C4**

Great art-book shop and prime browsing spot. This branch has painting, sculpture and some architecture; the one at S-Bahnbogen 585 film; and the Kochstraße branch architecture.

Branches: S-Bahnbogen 585, Charlottenburg, 10623 (312 1932); Kochstraße 19, Kreuzberg, 10969 (251 1345)

Dussman Das Kulturkaufhaus

Friedrichstraße 90, Mitte, 10117 (202 50). S1, S2, S3, S5, S7, S9/U6 Friedrichstraße. **Open** 10am-10pm Mon-Sat. **Credit** AmEx, MC, V. **Map F3**

A spacious three-floor store mixing books with CDs, videos with magazines, also with internet terminals, an interactive video-viewing room and DVD shop.

Grober Unfug

Zossener Straße 32-33, Kreuzberg, 10961 (6940 1491). U7 Gneisenaustraße. **Open** 11am-7pm Mon-Fri; 11am-4pm Sat. **Credit** AmEx, MC, V. **Map F5**

Stockists of comics in all languages, including annuals and comic art from *Viz* to French arty stuff. The new Mitte branch includes a comic gallery.
Branch: Weinmeisterstraße 9b, Mitte, 10178 (281 7331)

Hugendubel
Tauentzienstraße 13, Charlottenberg, 10789 (214 060). U1, U2, U15 Wittenbergplatz. **Open** 9.30am-8pm Mon-Fri; 9am-4pm Sat. **No credit cards. Map D4**
After Kiepert, Berlin's second largest bookshop. Its four floors house more than 140,000 books, including a big English-language section.
Branch: Friedrichstraße 83, Mitte, 10117 (2063 5100)

Kiepert
Hardenbergstraße 4-5, Charlottenburg, 10623 (311 880). U2 Ernst-Reuter-Platz. **Open** 9am-8pm Mon-Fri; 9am-4pm Sat. **Credit** AmEx, MC, V. **Map C4**
Berlin's biggest bookshop. Wide selection of fiction and non-fiction, guides, maps and a decent selection of foreign-language books. Can arrange postal delivery at DM7 for a standard-sized hardback. Other branches have less English-language material.
Branches: Friedrichstraße 63, Mitte, 10117 (201 7130); Georgenstraße 2, Mitte, 10117 (203 9960)

Kohlhaas & Company
Fasanenstraße 23, Wilmersdorf, 10719 (882 5044). U15 Uhlandstraße. **Open** 10am-8pm Mon-Fri; 10am-4pm Sat. **Credit** MC, V. **Map C4**
Elegantly housed beneath the Literaturhaus, this small, well-run bookshop aims towards the highbrow. German literature predominates. Service is friendly and helpful.

Marga Schoeller Bücherstube
Knesebeckstraße 33, Charlottenburg, 10623 (881 1112/1122). S3, S5, S7, S9 Savignyplatz. **Open** 9.30am-7pm Mon-Wed; 9.30am-8pm Thur-Fri; 9.30am-4pm Sat. **Credit** MC, V. **Map C4**

Rated by *Bookseller* as Europe's fourth best independent literary bookshop, this excellent establishment, founded in 1930, also gets a resounding thumbs-up from us. It includes a self-contained English-language section which, though not the largest selection in town, is certainly the most interesting, with more English titles scattered throughout various specialist sections. Staff are sweet, helpful, know their stock and will track down anything that's not on their shelves.

Antiquarian & second-hand books

If you're particularly interested in second-hand books, take a walk down Knesebeckstraße in Charlottenburg, Winterfeldtstraße in Schöneberg, or Kollwitzstraße and Husemannstraße in Prenzlauer Berg. Most places can provide you with a leaflet listing all the *Antiquariaten* in Berlin.

Antiquariat Senzel
Knesebeckstraße 13-14, Charlottenburg, 10623 (312 5887). U2 Ernst-Reuter-Platz. **Open** noon-6.30pm Mon-Fri; 11am-2pm Sat. **No credit cards. Map C4**
Most of the books are in German, though odd English and French volumes can be found. Also some beautifully leather-bound tomes and old maps.

Dwal
Schlüterstraße 17, Charlottenburg, 10625 (313 3030). S3, S5, S7, S9 Savignyplatz. **Open** noon-6.30pm Mon-Fri; 11am-2pm Sat. **No credit cards. Map C4**
Large store with everything from recent best-sellers to rare first editions. Good selection of foreign titles.

Fair Exchange
Dieffenbachstraße 58, Kreuzberg, 10967 (694 4675). U8 Schönleinstraße. **Open** 11am-6.30pm Mon-Fri; 10am-4pm Sat. **No credit cards. Map G5**
Large selection of second-hand English-language books, with an emphasis on literature.

Shirley at **Marga Schoeller Bücherstube** *– sweet, helpful, knows her stock.*

Schönhauser – *classics of doubtful taste.*

Children's clothes & toys

Wooden toys are a German speciality and though pricey, are often original enough to warrant the expense. Puppets from the Dresdener puppet factory and Erzgebirge's tiny wooden figures are particularly distinctive. Stuffed toys are another traditional offering: Steiff and its competitor Sigikid offer beautifully made cuddly animals that are full of character and highly collectable. Steiff claims to have invented the teddy bear a century ago, and you can pick up a Steiff or Sigikid teddy, or one of the hundreds of their other cuddly pets for DM130-400. A really huge or exotic beast could set you back thousands. *See also chapter* **Children**.

Emma & Co
Niebuhrstraße 1, Charlottenburg 10629 (882 7373). S3, S5, S7, S9 Savignyplatz. **Open** 11am-6.30pm Mon-Fri; 11am-7.30pm Thur-Fri; 11am-4pm Sat. **Credit** AmEx, MC, V. **Map C4**
Melanie Wöltje's charming shop within **Bramigk & Breer** (*below*) offers well-made but not exorbitant children's wear, bedding, toys and gift items like name books and terry-cloth teddies.

Heidi's Spielzeugladen
Kantstraße 61, Charlottenburg, 10627 (323 7556). U7 Wilmersdorfer Straße. **Open** 9.30am-6.30pm Mon-Fri; 9.30am-4pm Sat. **Credit** V. **Map B4**

Wooden toys, including cookery utensils and child-sized kitchens, are the attraction here. Also a good selection of books, puppets and wall-hangings.

H&M Kids
Kurfürstendamm 234, Charlottenburg, 10719 (884 8760). U9, U15 Kurfürstendamm. **Open** 10am-8pm Mon-Fri; 9am-4pm Sat. **Credit** AmEx, DC, MC, V. **Map C4**
The place for cute, cheap clothes for kids up to 14.

Michas Bahnhof
Nürnberger Straße 24a, Schöneberg, 10789 (218 6611). U1 Augsburger Straße. **Open** 10am-6.30pm Mon-Fri; 10am-4pm Sat. **Credit** AmEx, DC, V. **Map D4**
Small shop packed with model trains both old and new, and everything that goes with them.

Spielen
Hufelandstraße 18, Prenzlauer Berg, 10407 (208 4298). S3, S5, S7, S9/U2, U5, U8 Alexanderplatz then bus 100, 257. **Open** 9.30am-7pm Mon-Fri; 10am-3pm Sat. **Credit** AmEx, DC, MC, V. **Map H2**
Mostly handmade wooden toys by small German manufacturers and other dated playthings. Highlights are dolls' houses and furnishings (tiny mangles and microscopic groceries), handmade puppets, mechanical tin toys and glockenspiels.

Tam Tam
Lietzenburger Straße 92, Charlottenburg, 10719 (882 1454). U15 Uhlandstraße. **Open** 10am-6.30pm Mon-Fri; 10am-4pm Sat. **Credit** MC. **Map C4**
A bright, charming shop filled with stuffed animals and wooden toys, including building blocks, trains, trucks, dolls' houses, plus child-sized wooden stoves.

v. Kloeden
Wielandstraße 24, Charlottenburg, 10707 (8871 2512). U15 Uhlandstraße. **Open** 9am-7pm Mon-Fri; 10am-4pm Sat. **Credit** AmEx, MC, V. **Map C4**
Oldest and friendliest toy store in town, run by a brother-and-sister team who make it their policy to help you find the perfect present. The wide selection includes children's books in English, toys and reading material from the Montessori and Steiner schools, building blocks by German aeronaut Otto Lilienthal, handmade Käthe Kruse dolls, Erzgebirge wooden figures, and all kinds of modern-day fare.

Design & household goods

Berlin's lack of good design shops was a market gap developers could smell miles away. The answer was **Stilwerk** (*below*), a project that has attracted retailers to transform this stretch of Kantstraße into an oasis for home improvers. Small shops offering ethnic fare are also new arrivals.

Bella Casa
Bergmannstraße 101, Kreuzberg, 10961 (694 0784). U7 Eisenacherstraße. **Open** 11am-7pm Mon-Fri; 10am-4pm Sat. **Credit** MC, V. **Map F5**
Inexpensive Oriental lamps, rugs, pillows, bed throws and ceramics from North Africa and Egypt.

Bramigk & Breer

*Niebuhrstraße 1, Charlottenburg 10629 (882 7373).
S3, S5, S7, S9 Savignyplatz.* **Open** 11am-6.30pm
Mon-Fri; 11am-7.30pm Thu-Fri; 11am-4pm Sat.
Credit AmEx, MC, V. **Map C4**
Strikes a balance between Mediterranean and
Brandenburg country style with stripped-down fur-
niture, warm lighting and irresistable ornaments. A
fine selection of natural linens, hand-blown coloured
drinking glasses, and realistic silk flowers.

dadriade

*Rosenthaler Straße 40-41, Mitte, 10178 (2852
8720). U8 Weinmeisterstraße/S3, S5, S7, S9
Hackescher Markt.* **Open** 10am-8pm Mon-Fri; 10am-
4pm Sat. **Credit** AmEx, MC, V. **Map F3**
The pioneering presence of this glossy flagship store
was instrumental in establishing Mitte as a hip place
to shop. A Mecca for disciples of (mostly Italian)
high style, it is filled with breathtaking tableware,
cunningly functional kitchens and steel-and-glass
furnishings – much of it by Philippe Starck.

Galerie Weinand

*Oranienplatz 5, Kreuzberg, 10999 (614 2545). Bus
129.* **Open** only by appointment. **No credit cards.**
Map G4
Herbert Jakob Weinand is Berlin's star interior
designer and his shop stocks objects made by himself and an international group of designers.

IKEA

*Am Rondell 8, Waltersdorf, 15732 (0337 62660).
Autobahn 113 to Grunau.* **Open** 9.30am-8pm Mon-
Fri; 8.30am-4pm Sat. **No credit cards.**
All you could want in the way of Scandinavian
value-for-money design. Delivery to a Berlin address
costs 10% of the purchase price, to a DM150 limit.

M&M

*Ludwigkirchstrasse 11a, Wilmersdorf, 10719 (883
2151). U1, U9 Spichernstraße.* **Open** 11am-7pm Mon-
Fri; 10am-4pm Sat. **Credit** AmEx, MC, V. **Map C5**
Walk into the Far East. High-quality Indonesian furniture and festive silk umbrellas, plus more unusual decorative finds from Afghanistan and Pakistan.

Ruby

*Oranienburger Straße 32, Mitte, 10117 (2838
6030). S1, S2 Oranienburger Straße.* **Open** 11am-
8pm Mon-Fri; 11am-6pm Sat. **Credit** AmEx, MC, V.
Map F3
Flying the minimalist banner, this small shop in the
beautifully restored courtyard of the Heckmann
Höfe offers furniture by Spencer Fung, bowls and
Linares lamps as well as rugs, fabrics, candles and
an alluring selection of ceramics in earth tones.

Schönhauser

*Neue Schönhauser Straße 18, Mitte, 10178 (281
1704). U8 Weinmeisterstraße.* **Open** noon-8pm Mon-
Fri; 11am-4pm Sat. **No credit cards. Map G3**
All you need to deck out your front room like the
flightdeck of the Starship Enterprise, like bright
plastic swivel chairs, GDR lighting fixtures, bubble
TVs and other design classics of doubtful taste.

Stilwerk

*Kantstraße 17, Charlottenburg, 10623 (315 150).
S3, S5, S7, S9 Savignyplatz.* **Open** 10am-8pm Mon-
Fri; 10am-4pm Sat. **Map C4**
The Stilwerk concept of bringing together interior
design retailers under one stylish roof breathed
new life into Hamburg's fish-market district. The
makers of Stilwerk Berlin, which opened in
November 1999, designed the centre as if Berlin's
image as a capital city depended on them. Here 48
shops around an atrium span the five floors of this
impressive, new 20,000sq-m building, offering
some of the best in international designer furniture
and related homeware and high-tech design products. The project has attracted big international
names like B&B Italia and The Conran Shop,
encouraged established local retailers like the
excellent Lichthaus Mösch lighting store to open a
second branch, and persuaded enough shop owners of similar ilk to develop the area into a haven
for home improvement. The Design and Craft
Platform on the fourth floor is a forum of Berlin talent who have shops elsewhere in town. There's also
design exhibitions and child-care facilities.

Glass & ceramics

Bürgel-Haus

*Friedrichstraße 154, Mitte, 10117 (204 4519). U6
Französische Straße.* **Open** 9am-8pm Mon-Sat.
Credit AmEx, MC, V. **Map F3**
This distinctive blue-and-cream pottery from the
state of Thüringen makes an inexpensive present
for lovers of cosy kitchenware.

Galerie Workshop

*Fasanenstraße 11, Charlottenburg, 10623 (312
2567). S3, S5, S7, S9/U2, U9 Zoologischer Garten.*
Open 10am-6.30pm Mon-Fri; 10am-4pm Sat. **Credit**
MC, V. **Map C4**
Modern works in glass, ceramic and porcelain, representing some of Europe's leading artists. Some of
the stuff is downright tacky, but other pieces are
breathtaking – such as the kaleidoscope-coloured
vases by France's Robert Pierini.

Keramikladen

*Rykestraße 49, Prenzlauer Berg, 10405 (441 9109).
U2 Senefelderplatz.* **Open** 1-6.30pm Tue-Fri; 11am-
4pm Sat. **No credit cards. Map G2**
Bright, inexpensive, humorous household ceramics
from this collective of five east German potters.

KPM

*Wegelystraße 1, Tiergarten, 10623 (3900 9215). S3,
S5, S7, S9 Tiergarten.* **Open** 9.30am-8pm Mon-Fri;
9am-4pm Sat. **Credit** AmEx, DC, MC, V. **Map D4**
Frederick the Great liked porcelain so much he
bought the company: Königliche Porzellan
Manafaktur. Eat from a king's plate, inexpensively
too if you pick up some seconds at this factory shop.
The full-priced version is at the Kempinski branch.
Branches: Kempinski Hotel, Kurfürstendamm 27,
Charlottenburg, 10719 (884 340); Unter den Linden
35, Mitte, 10117 (2064 1529)

Fashion

A quick glance at the average man in the Straße should tell you that Berlin is a long way from the cutting edge of style. But this sorry state of affairs is changing and the past years have seen some interesting developments in retail fashion.

One of the most productive places to hunt for stylish, affordable clothing has sprung up in the Scheunenviertel. The renovated Hackesche Höfe, the Heckmann Höfe and the surrounding streets are now home to many of Berlin's designers, their shops and ateliers. The merchandise on offer may sometimes seem limited, but the advantage of having workshops as part of the store is that styles can be run up quickly in your size and preferred fabric. Many of these shops are on short, cheap rental contracts, so it's best to call and check they're still there before setting out.

Designers of a more hefty calibre have moved into the retail developments on Friedrichstraße, where new shopfronts are slowly filling with high-profile, international labels.

But despite all this excitement in the east, there is still no avoiding the Ku'damm and its affluent offshoots. Here department stores and clothing giants (Gap, Esprit, Benetton, Eddie Bauer) jostle for space with high-end fashion boutiques. Most of the designer merchandise is stuff you'd be able to buy in any major city, but cross-town competition for business makes for some lively end-of-season sales (*Schlußverkauf*) and there is usually a lot of merchandise left over. With a favourable exchange rate, you can pick up bargains. The most sophisticated Berlin gets is Fasanenstraße, where you will find the likes of Gucci, Chanel, Tiffany and Bvlgari. Much of the money spent here is Russian, and literal wads of cash change hands.

The following shops are by no means a comprehensive survey of all that Berlin has to offer, but they aim for a flavour of the more dynamic elements of the city's fledgling fashion culture.

Antonie Setzer

Bleibtreustraße 19, Charlottenburg, 10623 (883 1350). S3, S5, S7, S9 Savignyplatz. **Open** 10am-7pm Mon-Wed; 10am-8pm Thu-Fri; 10am-4pm Sat. **Credit** AmEx, DC, JCB, MC, V. **Map C4**
Fashion for women with an intelligent selection of styles from Capucine, D&G, Miu Miu, Streness and the unusual designs of Italian label Gembalies.

Blue Moon

Wilmersdorfer Straße 80, Charlottenburg, 10629 (323 7088). U7 Adenauerplatz. **Open** noon-8pm Mon-Fri; 11am-4pm Sat. **Credit** AmEx, MC, V. **Map B4**
A clothing suppliers favoured by casual clubbers for over 20 years, with high-fashion shoes, including Dr Martens, and some of the tallest platforms in town. **Branches**: Uhlandstraße 33, Wilmersdorf, 10719 (881 4157); Zossener Straße 20, Kreuzberg, 12061 (6981 6544)

Bramigk Design

Savigny Passage, Bogen 598, Charlottenburg, 10623 (313 5125). S3, S5, S7, S9 Savignyplatz. **Open** 11am-6.30pm Mon-Fri; 11am-4pm Sat. **Credit** AmEx, MC, V. **Map C4**
Nicola Bramigk specialises in quietly distinctive womenswear in luxurious Italian fabrics (also for sale by the metre). Her simple, flattering styles can be made up in the fabric and size of your choice.

Brummer

Tauentzienstraße 17, Charlottenburg, 10789 (211 1027). U1, U2, U15 Wittenbergplatz. **Open** 10am-7pm Mon-Fri; 10.30am-4pm Sat. **Credit** AmEx, MC, V. **Map D4**
This 1930s department store was totally revamped to cater to the Anglomania of its owner, and now stocks traditional English clothing and accessories: impeccable suiting by Hackett, Mulberry leather goods and Penhaligon's fragrances and toiletries.

Chiton

Goltzstraße 12, Schöneberg, 10781 (216 6013). U7 Eisenacher Straße. **Open** noon-6.30pm Mon-Fri; 11am-2pm Sat. **Credit** AmEx, MC, V. **Map D5**
Young husband-and-wife team Robert and Friederike Jorzig are the winning ticket for beautiful bridal and evening gowns. Worked in high-quality fabrics, their striking cuts – from the very simple to designs recalling early Hollywood sophistication – attract many customers from Britain and the US. They also put out summer and winter collections in their signature reductionist style. Allow at least two or three weeks for gowns and men's suits – dresses can be done in three days.

Claudia Skoda

Linienstraße 154, Mitte, 10115 (280 7211). U6 Oranienburger Tor. **Open** 11am-7pm Mon-Fri. **Credit** AmEx, DC, MC, V. **Map F3**
Berlin's most established womenswear designer chose to launch her ready-to-wear collection, après skoda, through her new shop (and studio) in Mitte. Using high-tech yarns and innovative knitting techniques, the range bears her signature combination of stretch fabrics and graceful drape effects. Skoda's more costly couture line is available at her Marc Newson-designed Ku'damm branch. **Branch**: Skoda Attendance, Kurfürstendamm 50, 10707 (885 1009)

Eisdieler

Kastanienallee 12, Prenzlauer Berg, 10435 (285 7351). U2 Eberswalder Straße. **Open** noon-7pm Mon-Fri; noon-6pm Sat. **Credit** MC, V. **Map F3**
Five young designers pooled their resources to transform this former ice shop and each manages a label under the Eisdieler banner – clubwear, second-hand gear, casualwear and street style. Till Fuhrmann jewellery in silver and wood is particularly distinctive, and it's his spiky ironwork adorning the façade.

Essenbeck

Auguststraße 72, Mitte, 10117 (2838 8725). U8 Weinmeister Straße. **Open** noon-8pm Mon-Fri; noon-6pm Sat. **Credit** MC, V. **Map F3**

Jil Sander – *sleek silhouettes, fine fabrics and Spartan cuts.*

Seeking to introduce new names to Germany, owners Sabine Hartung and Dirk Schulte scout around London and bring back the likes of Shirley Fox and Dexter Wong. They also order men's and women's collections in styles ranging from functional to futuristic from places such as Iceland's SVO label.

Façon

Gipsstraße 5, Mitte, 10119 (2839 0966). U8 Weinmeisterstraße. **Open** 1-8pm Tue-Sun. **Credit** AmEx, MC, V. **Map F3**

After 14 years in the Paris fashion industry, Jan Murmann visited Berlin and was inspired by the creative energy buzzing in Mitte. Amid all the art galleries, he opened up his 'clothing gallery', a multi-functional space presenting mostly French labels unknown to Germany. By day, the collections for both sexes by Isabel Marant, Hannoh and Daniel Jasiak are on sale. At night, the clothes turn into an installation, with selected pieces moving up and down the space and into the window on a carousel.

Flex/Melting Point

Neue Schönhauser Straße 2, Mitte, 10178 (283 4836/44). U8 Weinmeisterstraße. **Open** 1-8pm Mon; 11am-8pm Tue-Fri; 10am-4pm Sat. **No credit cards. Map G3**

Clubwear store and dance record shop in one – this is one of the buzziest stores on the street, especially in the evening when Mitte's young, bad and beautiful pick out an outfit from German rave labels, including Sabotage and Thatchers.

Groopie Deluxe

Goltzstraße 39, Schöneberg, 10781 (217 2038). U7 Eisenacher Straße. **Open** 11am-7pm Mon-Fri; 11am-4pm Sat. **Credit** AmEx, JCB, MC, V. **Map D5**

Trendy, sexy gear to party in – lots of bright, skimpy numbers, fake fur, and accessories. On her travels the stewardess owner fills her suitcase with whatever suits her fancy, from Chinese dragonlady dresses to laidback SoHo chic for boys.

Harvey's

Kurfürstendamm 186, Charlottenburg, 10707 (883 3803). U15 Uhlandstraße. **Open** 10.30am-8pm Mon-Fri; 10am-4pm Sat. **Credit** AmEx, MC, V. **Map C4**

Frieder Böhnisch has held the fort of cutting-edge men's labels for 20 years. Now he stocks clothes and shoes by the Japanese – Yohji Yamamoto and Comme des Garçons – and the Belgians, Bikkembergs and Martin Margiela. His enthusiasm for the designers he sells may persuade you to splurge, but there are no hard feelings if you don't.

Hautnah

Uhlandstraße 170, Charlottenburg, 10719 (882 3434). U15 Uhlandstraße. **Open** noon-8pm Mon-Fri; 10am-4pm Sat. **Credit** AmEx, MC, V. **Map C4**

Cult fetish gear for those into latex, leather and stilettos, plus a proud range of 'English' PVC macs.

Hut Up

Oranienburger Straße 32, Mitte, 10117 (2838 6105). S1, S2 Oranienburger Straße. **Open** 11am-6pm Tue-Sat. **Credit** AmEx, MC, V. **Map F3**

Christine Birkle's imaginative felt designs come in bold colours for a wide variety of uses. Her wares are handcrafted in one piece shaped from raw wool using traditional methods. The clothes combine felt with silk or gauze, and there's a witty range of accessories for the body or home including hats, slippers, vases, hot-water bottles, mobile phone cases, wine coolers and egg cosies shaped like dunce hats.

Jil Sander

Kurfürstendamm 185, Charlottenburg, 10707 (886 7020). U9, U15 Kurfürstendamm. **Open** 10am-7pm Mon-Fri; 10am-4pm Sat. **Credit** AmEx, DC, JCB, MC, V. **Map C4**

This smart, understated store is a perfect foil for the doyenne of German minimalism. Sander's secret is her sleek silhouettes, fine fabrics and Spartan cuts, and this combination has won her an global audience who unflinchingly pay her top-dollar prices.

Lisa D

Hackesche Höfe, Rosenthaler Straße 40-41, Mitte, 10178 (282 9061). U8 Weinmeisterstraße/S3, S5, S7, S9 Hackescher Markt. **Open** noon-6.30pm Mon-Sat. **Credit** AmEx, DC, JCB, MC, V. **Map F3**

Long, flowing womenswear in subdued shades from this avant-garde designer. Austrian-born Lisa D is a well-known face on the Berlin fashion scene and was one of the first tenants to move into the renovated Hackesche Höfe.

Mientus Studio 2002

Schlüterstraße 26, Charlottenburg, 10707 (323 9077). U15 Uhlandstraße. **Open** 10am-8pm Mon-Fri; 10am-4pm Sat. **Credit** AmEx, DC, MC, V. **Map C4**

Clean cuts for sharp men from a range of collections including Dsquared, Neil Barrett, Helmut Lang, Miu Miu, Andrew Mackenzie and German rave labels. **Branch:** Wilmersdorfer Straße 73, Charlottenburg, 10629 (323 9077)

Molotow

Gneisenaustraße 112, Kreuzberg, 10965 (693 0818). U7 Gneisenaustraße. **Open** 2-8pm Mon-Fri; noon-4pm Sat. **Credit** AmEx, DC, MC, V. **Map F5**

Showcasing local talent, Molotow sells a selection of fashion and millinery from Berlin designers. The clothes are fresh and eye-catching, ranging from futuristic creations to classical sharp tailoring.

Nix

Oranienburger Straße 32, Mitte, 10117 (281 8044). U6 Oranienburger Tor. **Open** 11am-7pm Mon-Fri; noon-6pm Sat. **Credit** MC, V. **Map F3**

Designers Barbara Gebhardt and Angela Herb's atelier and store sells their New Individual X-tras (or Nix) label for men, women and children. This urban collection is unusual in cut, not extravagantly priced and has a dash of humour.

Patrick Hellman

Fasanenstraße 26, Charlottenburg, 10719 (882 4201).U15 Uhlandstraße. **Open** 10am-7pm Mon-Fri; 10am-8pm Thur; 10am-4pm Sat. **Credit** AmEx, DC, MC, V. **Map C5**

Prolific Berlin retailer with five stores to his name, specialising in international chic for men and women. A bespoke tailoring service offers men the choice of the Hellman design range in a variety of luxurious fabrics, including some by Italian textile maestro Ermenegildo Zegna.

Okida Sales

Friedrichstraße 203, Mitte, 10117 (2045 3590). U2, U6 Stadtmitte. **Open** 10am-8pm Mon-Fri; 10am-4pm Sat. **Credit** AmEx, JCB, MC, V. **Map F4**

Clothes, shoes and accessories for men, women and children 'inspired', shall we say, by international designers. The quality of imitation Stephan Kelian shoes, Todd's totes and Calvin Klein-esque suits is high, and though some of the shoes are ghastly, there are real finds to be made.

Planet

Schlüterstraße 35, Charlottenburg, 10629 (885 2717). U15 Uhlandstraße. **Open** 11am-6.30pm Mon-Wed; 11am-8pm Thu-Fri; 11am-4pm Sat. **Credit** AmEx, MC, V. **Map C4**

Calling themselves Wera Wonder and Mik Moon, the owners have been supplying Berlin's club scene with appropriately hip gear since 1985. Their DJ friends pump out deafening music to put you in club mode, and the rails and shelves are full of sparkling spandex shirts, fluffy vests and dance durable footwear.

RespectMen

Neue Schönhauser Straße 14, Mitte, 10178 (283 5010). U8 Weinmeisterstraße. **Open** noon-8pm Mon-Fri; 11am-4pm Sat. **Credit** AmEx, MC, V. **Map G3**

When seen on the rail, Dirk Seidel and Karin Warburg's menswear seems to be traditionally tailored, yet when worn it shows off its contemporary, body-conscious cut. Suits, trousers, jackets and coats can be made to order from the many fabrics on offer. The inventive cut may not appeal to fashion conservatives, but this is some of the most interesting menswear you'll find in Berlin. Stupid name, though.

RespectMen – *traditional but contemporary.*

Schenck

Gipsstraße 9, Mitte, 10119 (2839 0785). U8 Weinmeisterstraße. **Open** noon-8pm Mon-Fri; noon-4pm Sat. **Credit** AmEx, DC, MC, V. **Map F3**

Walk into Stephanie Schenck's small boutique and you'll probably hear her at her state-of-the-art knitting machines in the basement. Schenck studied textile design before fine-tuning her skills in the studio of **Claudia Skoda** (*above*). Her own designs combine fresh colours with innovative yarns into attractive, original pieces.

Schwarze Mode

Grunewaldstraße 91, Schöneberg, 10823 (784 5922). U7 Kleistpark. **Open** noon-7pm Mon-Fri; 10am-4pm Sat. **Credit** AmEx, DC, MC, V. **Map E5**

Leatherette, rubber and vinyl are among the particular delicacies stocked here for *Gummi* (rubber) enthusiasts. As well as the fetish fashions, erotic and S&M literature in German and English, comics, videos, CDs and magazines are on offer next door in Schwarze Medien.

Tenderloin

Alte Schönhauser Straße 30, Mitte, 10119 (4201 5785). U8 Weinmeisterstraße. **Open** noon-8pm Mon-Fri; noon-4pm Sat. **Credit** MC, V. **Map G3**

Once a purely second-hand store – there are still flares and flower prints left over from its retro period – it's the mix of 1960s and 1970s GDR furniture, luminous wigs in rainbow colours and new clothes

Schwarze Mode – *fetish fashions, S&M lit.*

that make this shop worth a visit. Berlin label Stoffrausch draws on the hip-hop and techno scene and each unisex handmade item is an original, so you can rest assured you won't be caught clubbing in the same clobber as some beautiful stranger.

To Die For

Neue Schönhauser Straße 10, Mitte, 10178 (2838 6834). U8 Weinmeisterstraße. **Open** noon-8pm Mon-Fri; noon-6pm Sat. **Credit** AmEx, MC, V. **Map G3**

Opened with the aim of providing a platform for Berlin labels, this shop offers fashion every bit as dynamic as the city itself. Check out the Viva Maria range of 'forbidden lingerie' – religious-themed underwear by Berlin designer Simone Franze. **Branch**: Akazienstraße 24, Schöneberg, 10823 (787 5004)

T&G

Rosenthaler Straße 34-35, Mitte, 10178 (2859 9343). U8 Weinmeisterstraße/S3, S5, S7, S9 Hackescher Markt. **Open** 10am-7pm Mon-Wed; 10am-8pm Thur-Fri; 10am-4pm Sat. **Credit** MC, V. **Map F3**

Kai Angladegies is not the first to fuse fashion and fine art, but T&G is a bold and stylish attempt. The interior is camply decked out in rococo splendour, with candelabras and muslin-draped changing cubicles, and the selection of clothing is equally impressive. Menswear is especially strong, with names such as Kenzo, Jeremy Scott and Givenchy. The gallery is accessed via a beautiful 1860 wrought-iron staircase and features exhibitions of fine art, design and haute couture including Balenciaga.

Yoshiharu Ito

Sophienstraße 7, Hackesche Höfe, Mitte, 10178 (2859 9170). U8 Weinmeisterstraße. **Open** noon-8pm Mon-Sat. **Credit** AmEx, DC, MC, V. **Map F3**

Tokyo-born Ito came to Berlin to study classical music and sold kimonos at the flea market to get by. But he had lots of ideas and in 1989 founded Studio Ito, a dynamic label which shot to national fame. Unpaid orders bankrupted the small company, and Ito went to work in theatre. Now he's back with purist collections in the tradition of Asian designers like Yamamoto but with strong European influences. His clothes are practical, with great attention to detail like perfectly worked pockets and unusual seams. Ito mixes a futuristic style with classic wool or laquered cotton for fun and wearable clothes.

Sports gear

360°

Pariser Straße 23-24, Wilmersdorf, 10707 (883 8596). U7 Adenauerplatz. **Open** 11am-7.30pm Mon-Fri; 10am-4pm Sat. **No credit cards. Map C5**

Designer sportswear and sundry accessories from Quicksilver, Stüssy, Sky & High and Vans, plus rollerblades, snowboards and windsurfing gear.

Karstadt Sport

Quartier 205, Friedrichstraße 67, Mitte, 10117 (2094 5000). U2, U6 Stadtmitte. **Open** 10am-8pm Mon-Fri; 9.30am-4pm Sat. **Credit** AmEx, DC, MC, V. **Map F3**

The purist **Yoshiharu Ito** *– fun, wearable and futuristic.*

Three-level megastore with a wide selection of gear by both name brands and cheaper alternatives. Also US sportswear and equipment, German football paraphernalia and children's clothes. Includes skating area, Alpine ski simulator, Internet terminals and sports restaurant.
Branch: Joachimstaler Straße 5-6, Charlottenburg, 10623 (8802 4153)

Niketown

Tauentzienstraße 7b-7c, Schöneberg, 10789 (250 70). U1, U2, U15 Wittenbergplatz. **Open** 10am-8pm Mon-Fri; 10am-4pm Sat. **Credit** AmEx, DC, MC, V. **Map D4**
Brand retail outlet in state-of-the art glass and neon design. Training gear – jerseys, sweatpants, even sunglasses and watches – embossed with the Nike trademark if you like to show off while working out.

Second-hand clothes & shoes

Berlin has a huge market in cheaper clothing, with flea markets, junk shops and second-hand stores offering unique and colourful bargains. The best hunting grounds are around Mehringdamm in Kreuzberg and Prinzenallee in Wedding.

Calypso – High Heels For Ever

Münzstraße 16, Mitte, 10178 (281 6165). U8 Weinmeisterstraße. **Open** noon-7pm Mon-Fri; noon-4pm Sat. **No credit cards. Map G3**
Hundreds of gravity-defying stilettos, wedges and platforms in the vivid shades and exotic shapes of the 1960s and 1970s, almost all in fine condition.

Also a selection of stilettoed, thigh-high fetish boots, some in men's sizes. Prices range from DM40-80, but expect to pay up to DM250 for truly kinky boots.

Checkpoint

Mehringdamm 57, Kreuzberg, 10961 (694 4344). U6, U7 Mehringdamm. **Open** 10am-6.30pm Mon-Fri; 10am-4pm Sat. **No credit cards. Map F5**
Huge selection of 1970s gear: Lurex skinny-knit jumpers, printed bellbottoms (DM39), leather coats and jackets (DM125-200), and even wedding dresses (DM200) from the heyday of *Charlie's Angels*.
Branch: Monroe, Kollwitzstraße 102, Prenzlauer Berg, 10435 (440 8448)

Colours

1st courtyard, Bergmannstraße 102, Kreuzberg, 10961 (694 3348). U7 Gneisenaustraße. **Open** 11am-7pm Mon-Wed; 11am-8pm Thur-Fri; 10am-4pm Sat. **No credit cards. Map F5**
Row upon row of jeans, leather jackets and dresses, including party stunners and some fetching Bavarian dirndls. The odd gem from the 1950s and 1960s is thrown in too. Prices vary from DM5-200 depending on condition and vintage.

Garage

Ahornstraße 2, Schöneberg, 10787 (211 2760). U1, U2, U4 Nollendorfplatz. **Open** 11am-7pm Mon-Wed; 11am-8pm Thur-Fri; 10am-4pm Sat. **No credit cards. Map D4**
One of Berlin's cheapest second-hand shops with clothing priced at DM25 per kilo. Surprisingly well organised, given the barracks-like nature of the place. Good for cheap, last-minute party outfits.

Humana

*Karl-Liebknecht-Straße 30, Mitte, 10178 (242 3000).
S3, S5, S7, S9/U2, U5, U8 Alexanderplatz.* **Open**
10am-6.30pm Mon-Wed, Fri; 10am-8pm Thur; 10am-
4pm Sat. **No credit cards. Map G3**
Huge Humana charity megastores are sprouting all
over the city, selling acres of cheap second-hand
clothing, household textiles, fur and leather. This is
the biggest and most central. They usually have a
'trend' section of more fashionable, original numbers
and this is worth hunting through for bargains.

Macy's

*Mommsenstraße 2, Charlottenburg, 10629 (881
1363). S3, S5, S7, S9 Savignyplatz.* **Open** 10am-7pm
Mon-Wed; 10am-8pm Thur-Fri; 10am-4pm Sat.
Credit AmEx, DC, MC, V. **Map C4**
Nearly new designer wear for women from the likes
of Jil Sander and Gaultier, including shoes and handbags, at super prices.

Made in Berlin

*Potsdamer Straße 106, Tiergarten, 10785 (262
2431). U1 Kurfürstenstraße.* **Open** 11am-7pm Mon-
Wed; 11am-8pm Thur-Fri; 10am-4pm Sat. **No credit
cards. Map E4**
Sister store of **Garage** (*above*), where the 'better
stuff' supposedly goes. It's still pretty cheap with
dresses and jackets in the DM40-60 range.

Sgt. Peppers

*Kastanienallee 91-92, Prenzlauer Berg, 10435 (448
1121). U2 Eberswalder Straße.* **Open** 11am-7pm
Mon-Fri; 11am-3pm Sat. **Credit** DC, MC, V. **Map G2**
Bright gear from the 1960s and 1970s, arranged by
size, which is helpful. Men's suits go for around
DM50, party dresses for DM40.

Sterling Gold

*Oranienburger Straße 32, Mitte, 10117 (2809
6500). S1, S2 Oranienburger Straße.* **Open** noon-
8pm Mon-Fri; noon-6pm Sat. **Credit** MC, V. **Map F3**
Michael Boenke couldn't believe his luck when he
was offered a warehouse full of 'prom' dresses during a trip to America. He immediately shipped them
straight to Berlin and has done so well with them
he's opened this second shop – decorated in
Cinderella style – in Mitte's Heckmann Höfe. These
wonderful ball- and cocktail gowns, from the 1950s-
1980s, are in terrific condition and attract the attention of fashion aficionados from places as far afield
as Hamburg, Cologne and Düsseldorf. Cocktail
dresses in every conceivable shade and fabric range
in price from DM100-150, but expect to pay anything
up to DM500 for one of Boenk's classic vintage silk
ballgowns or elegant wedding dresses.

Waahnsinn

*Neue Promenade 3, Hackescher Markt, Mitte, 10178
(282 0029). S3, S5, S7, S9 Hackescher Markt.* **Open**
noon-8pm Mon-Sat. **Credit** MC, V. **Map F3**
Unashamedly tacky clothes and jewellery from the
1960s and 1970s, chosen to outrage the eye and complement the plastic egg chairs and lava lamps also
on sale. Not the cheapest second-hand clobber, but
in good nick and on a strong party-girl theme.

Trippen – *idiosyncratic foot fashions.*

Shoes & leather goods

Bleibgrün

*Bleibtreustraße 29, Charlottenburg, 10707 (882
1689). S3, S5, S7, S9 Savignyplatz.* **Open** 10.30am-
6.30pm Mon-Fri; 10am-4pm Sat. **Credit** AmEx, DC,
MC, V. **Map C4**
Berlin's best designer shoe shop, with a nifty selection from the likes of Lagerfeld, Maud Frizon and
Jan Jansen. Bleibgrün has opened a swanky boutique next door at number 30 which has an equally
discriminating choice of cutting-edge womenswear.

Bree

*Kurfürstendamm 44, Charlottenburg, 10719 (883
7462). U15 Uhlandstraße.* **Open** 10am-7pm Mon-Fri;
10am-4pm Sat. **Credit** AmEx, JCB, MC, V. **Map C4**
German leather goods company whose practical,
durable and easy-to-organise handbags, briefcases,
rucksacks and suitcases are sported by many a
German professional.

Budapester Schuhe

*Kurfürstendamm 199, Charlottenburg, 10719 (881
1707). U15 Uhlandstraße.* **Open** 10am-7pm Mon-
Wed; 10am-8pm Thur-Fri; 10am-4pm Sat. **Credit**
AmEx, DC, JCB, MC, V. **Map C4**
Impressive selection of conservative Italian footwear
for men from the likes of Prada, Dolce & Gabbana
and Ferragamo plus handmade classics from
Austrian Ludwig Reiter. Average price is DM400-
500 per pair, or you can wait for sales when prices
are slashed by around 50%. The Bleibtreustraße
branch nearby is the best women's shoe shop in
town, with the above brands plus Sergio Rossi, JP
Tod's, Miu Miu, Mia Jahn.
Branches: Bleibtreustraße 24, Charlottenburg,
10707 (881 7001); Friedrichstraße 81, Mitte, 10117
(2038 8110)

Penthesileia

*Tucholskystraße 31, Mitte, 10117 (282 1152). U6
Oranienburger Tor.* **Open** 10am-7pm Mon-Fri;
10am-4pm Sat. **Credit** MC, V. **Map F3**
Named after an Amazon queen, this is showroom,
shop and workspace for Sylvia Müller and Anke
Runge, who design and make their highly individual range of handbags and rucksacks here. Shapes
are novel and organic – sunflowers, cones, shells and
hearts – and crafted from calfskin and nubuck.

Scarpe Milano

Bleibtreustraße 25, Charlottenburg, 10707 (8855 4175). U15 Uhlandstraße. **Open** 10am-7pm Mon-Wed; 10am-8pm Thu-Fri; 10am-4pm Sat. **Credit** MC, V. **Map C4**

Last season or surplus Italian designer shoes for men and women at cut prices.

Trippen

Hackesche Höfe, Rosenthaler Straße 40-41, Mitte, (2839 1337). U8 Weinmeisterstraße/S3, S5, S7, S9 Hackescher Markt. **Open** noon-7pm Mon-Fri; 10am-4pm Sat. **Credit** V. **Map F3**

Not the most reassuring name for a shoe shop, but home to an idiosyncratic selection of foot fashion designed by Angela Spieth and Michael Oehler. Oddly shaped wooden-soled platforms, heels that shoot out at right angles and 'horned' toes are just a few of the surprises here.

Shoemakers

See also **Repairs**.

Breitenbach

Bergmannstraße 30, Kreuzberg, 10961 (692 3570). U7 Gneisenaustraße. **Open** 8am-1pm, 2-6.30pm Mon-Fri; 10am-2pm Sat. **Credit** AmEx, MC, V. **Map F5**

Gentlemen's shoe- and bootmaker, who also provides first-class repairs for men's and women's footwear. A made-to-measure pair of leather shoes costs upwards of DM600.

Accessories

Fiona Bennett

Große Hamburger Straße 25, Mitte, 10115 (2809 6330). S3, S5, S7, S9 Hackescher Markt. **Open** noon-6pm Tue-Fri; noon-4pm Sat. **Credit** AmEx, DC, MC, V. **Map F3**

Fiona's hats are works of art. Redefining traditional shapes, her imagination leaves trends by the wayside to create horned headdresses, feathered fedoras, hats reminiscent of insects or sea urchins, and delicate hairpieces made of a single feather shaped into a curl or shimmering sequins spilling over into a filigree fountain. For all their theatrics, the hats always display their maker's sense for beauty and the interior is a crown jewel of compact design.

Fishbelly

Sophienstraße 7a, Mitte, 10178 (2804 5180). U8 Weinmeisterstraße. **Open** noon-8pm Mon-Fri; noon-4pm Sat. **Credit** AmEx, DC, MC, V. **Map F3**

Often compared to London's Agent Provocateur, this tiny Hackesche Höfe shop is licensed to thrill with extravagant under- and bathing garments by Dolce & Gabbana Intimo, Undressed and Moschino.

Kaufhaus Schrill

Bleibtreustraße 46, Charlottenburg, 10623 (882 4048). S3, S5, S7, S9 Savignyplatz. **Open** 11am-7pm Mon-Fri; 11am-4pm Sat. **Credit** AmEx, MC, V. **Map C4**

Feather boas, sequins, tiaras, pearls, rhinestones, shocking colours, frills and loud, fruity patterns.

Les Dessous

Fasanenstraße 42, Wilmersdorf, 10719 (883 3632). U1, U9 Spichernstraße. **Open** 11am-7pm Mon-Fri; 10am-3pm Sat. **Credit** AmEx, DC, MC, V. **Map C5**

A beautiful shop featuring luxurious lingerie, silk dressing gowns and striking swimwear by Capucine, Eres, Dior, La Perla, and Andres Sarda. **Branch:** Schlüterstraße 36, Charlottenburg, 10629 (881 3660)

Rio

Bleibtreustraße 52, Charlottenburg, 10623 (313 3152). S3, S5, S7, S9 Savignyplatz. **Open** 11am-6.30pm Mon-Wed; 11am-7pm Thur; 11am-6.30pm Fri; 10am-4pm Sat. **No credit cards. Map C4**

Eye-catching costume jewellery, with a stunning array of earrings from Vivienne Westwood, Armani, and Herv van der Straeten. Plus Rio's own range of luminescent frosted-glass necklaces, bracelets and earrings designed by shop owner Barbara Kranz.

Roeckl

Kurfürstendamm 216, Charlottenburg, 10719 (881 5379). U9, U15 Kurfürstendamm. **Open** 10am-8pm Mon-Fri; 10am-4pm Sat. **Credit** AmEx, DC, MC, V. **Map C4**

Gloves in all colours and materials, plus scarves, pashminas and shawls by international designers.

Tagebau

Rosenthaler Straße 19, Mitte, 10119 (2839 0890). U8 Weinmeisterstraße/S3, S5, S7, S9 Hackescher Markt. **Open** 11am-8pm Mon-Fri; 11am-6pm Sat. **Credit** MC. **Map F3**

Fiona Bennett – *hats reminiscent of insects and sea urchins.*

Rio – *eye-catching jewellery. See page 139.*

The six young designers who share this airy, spacious store-cum-workshop specialise in jewellery, fashion, millinery and furniture. Their work also shares a collective sculptural quality which, when it is combined with the Tagebau's generous space and subtle spot-lighting, gives the whole establishment the impression of a gallery.

Handmade jewellery

Feinschmeide

Windscheidstraße 24, Charlottenburg, 10627 (323 4048). U2 Sophie-Charlotte-Platz. **Open** 11am-6pm Tue-Fri; and by appointment. **No credit cards.** **Map B4**

Inventive, hand-crafted metalwork brooches, earrings and necklaces. Also on display are steel candleholders, chairs and sculptures.

Fritz & Fillman

Dresdener Straße 20, Kreuzberg, 10999 (615 1700). U1, U8 Kottbusser Tor. **Open** 11am-6pm Tue-Fri; 11am-2pm Sat. **Credit** V. **Map G4**

Highly original designs from these two native Berliners, plus work from goldsmiths all over Germany. A dazzling range of rings attracts many brides and grooms-to-be, with prices ranging from hundreds to thousands of marks. Fritz & Fillman also take on work to commission and offer courses in jewellery-making.

Branch: Fasanenstraße 47, Wilmersdorf, 10719 (881 5797)

Treykorn

Passage, Savignyplatz 13, Charlottenburg, 10623 (312 4275). S3, S5, S7, S9 Savignyplatz. **Open** 11am-7pm Tue-Fri; 11am-4pm Sat. **Credit** AmEx, DC, MC, V. **Map C4**

This smart gallery specialises in metal- and stone-worked jewellery, with styles ranging from the ultra-modern to contemporary classics. Stock changes every five weeks and Treykorn also hosts three major international jewellery design shows a year.

Costume & formal-wear hire

Graichen

Klosterstraße 32, Spandau, 13581 (331 3587). U7 Rathaus Spandau. **Open** 10am-6pm Mon-Fri; 10am-1pm Sat. **Credit** MC.

Tuxedos for men, short and long eveningwear for women. Bridal gowns, too. Rental for black tie runs from DM120-200; womenswear from DM100-300.

Theaterkunst

Eisenzahnstraße 43-44, Wilmersdorf, 10709 (864 7270). U1, U7 Fehrbelliner Platz. **Open** 8am-4.30pm Mon-Thur; 8am-3.30pm Fri. **No credit cards.** **Map B5**

Three warehouses crammed floor to ceiling with period costumes to kit out any historical fantasy. The choice is immense so allow time to browse and be fitted and go back later to collect. Founded in 1908, the impressive collection was destroyed during the last war and re-established in 1951. Staff know their stuff and give good advice, and there's a free alterations service. Elaborate rococo outfits cost up to DM900 to hire; costumes from more recent times cost around DM250.

Spitze

Weimarer Straße 19, Charlottenburg, 10625 (313 1068). U7 Wilmersdorfer Straße. **Open** 2-6.30pm Mon-Fri; 11am-2pm Sat. **Credit** MC, V. **Map C4**

A goldmine for clothes and accessories from 1860 to 1960, raided by Donna Karan whenever she's in town. Spitze will rent out some of its nuggets for a third of the sale price. Evening gloves, handbags, shoes and other accessories also available.

Dry-cleaning & alterations

Good laundry and dry-cleaning services are in short supply, and almost non-existent in the east, so to have a garment cleaned it's worth a trip west. Many fashion designers offer an alterations or made-to-measure service as part of the cost, or for a small charge. To get a zip fixed or rip mended, alterations shops (many of them Turkish) will usually provide a next-day service. Consult the *Gelbe Seiten* under *Änderungsschneidereien*.

Kim Jang Woon

Pestalozzistraße 69, Charlottenburg, 10627 (327 5151). U7 Wilmersdorfer Straße. **Open** 10am-6pm Mon-Fri; 10am-1pm Sat. **No credit cards.** **Map B4**

Quick turnaround for all manner of alterations. Trouser-shortening or taking-in from DM16.

Are Berliners being served?

Imagine for a moment. You're in a major capital city. You ring up the leading department store for some information. You're put on hold. For seven minutes. And the asinine, please-don't-hang-up music they are piping into your ear is sung to a tune from *Cabaret*: 'Willkommen, bienvenue, welcome/In KaDeWe au KaDeWe to KaDeWe'. Over and over again. Naturally, you'd hang up.

It's hard to have patience with Berlin's department stores. **KaDeWe** (*see page 143*) is the largest department store in continental Europe and a top tourist attraction. But apart from the magnificent food hall, it simply doesn't match up to its reputation as one of the world's best retailers. Yes, it carries name brands in all departments, the service is friendly enough and a DM400-million renovation has improved the layout. But like its hold-the-line tune, the presentation is outdated, the decor tacky, and much of the merchandise merely average.

The city's department stores had their heyday in the early 20th century. Wertheim on Leipziger Straße (1896-1913) and Tietz on Alexanderplatz (1904-11) were commercial wonders of their day. Wertheim, by Alfred Messel, stunned visitors with its glass-roofed atrium, 10,000 lightbulbs and 83 elevators. Today, nothing is left of it save the old subterranean safe-deposit-box room, now part of the Tresor nightclub (*see chapter* **Nightlife**). KaDeWe was founded in 1907 in what was then a peripheral residential area – the first big commercial development in the New West. Today the Kaufhaus des Westens belongs to the **Karstadt** group, a high-street chain which has also swallowed up Hertie (as Hermann Tietz's name was 'Aryanised' in the 1930s) and **Wertheim**. Together they rule in the west. Meanwhile the Kaufhof group bought the old East-German Centrum stores and dominate the eastern market. Its Alexanderplatz branch façade is so 1970s it's almost hip. **Kaufhof** is structured on the shop-in-shop principal and expat London girls go there to stock up on Oasis. Apart from clothing, all these stores offer everything you might need in decent quality and at reasonable prices, including stationery, kitchenware, electronic equipment, luggage and gourmet food departments.

But for a more up-to-the-minute department-store shopping experience, head over to the new developments around Friedrichstraße. The Jean Nouvel glass block which houses **Galeries Lafayette** (*see page 143*) offers state-of-the-art architecture and a refreshing shopping experience. All the merchandise is French, and though the selection of accessories, cosmetics and clothing is good (highlight is the Agnès B boutique), here too the best feature is the food floor in the basement, where you'll feel transported to Paris among fresh cheeses, chocolates, wines, breads and condiments.

One block down is another architectural new kid, IM Pei's Friedrichstadt Passagen centrepiece. The **Quartier 206 Department Store** (*pictured*) is entered at its corners and takes up the entire first floor. Reminiscent of New York's Takashimaya and designed by that city's Calvin Tsao, it is the developer's wife's pet project, fusing her predilection for eastern and western aesthetics to offer the most lusted-after designer labels, statement jewellery, interior trends, cult cosmetics, connoisseur cigars and fresh flowers from foreign fields.

The Friedrichstraße newcomers testify to the changing face of Berlin retail. And with a dose of Berlin *Schadenfreude* we can now say to the others: 'Please hold on, somebody will be with you in a moment'.

Karstadt

Wilmersdorfer Straße 118, Charlottenburg, 10627 (311 050). U7 Wilmersdorfer Straße. **Open** 9.30am-8pm Mon-Fri; 9am-4pm Sat. **Credit** AmEx, DC, MC, V. **Map B4**

Kaufhof

Alexanderplatz 9, Mitte, 10178 (2474 3265). S3, S5, S7, S9/U2, U5, U8 Alexanderplatz. **Open** 9am-8pm Mon-Fri; 9am-4pm Sat. **Credit** AmEx, DC, MC, V. **Map G3**

Quartier 206 Department Store

Friedrichstraße 71, Mitte, 10117 (2094 6800). S1, S2, S3, S5,S7, S9/U6 Friedrichstraße. **Open** 10am-8pm Mon-Fri; 10am-4pm Sat. **Credit** AmEx, DC, MC, V. **Map F3**

Wertheim

Kurfürstendamm 231, Charlottenburg, 10719 (880 030). U9, U15 Kurfürstendamm. **Open** 10am-8pm Mon-Fri; 9am-4pm Sat. **Credit** AmEx, DC, MC, V. **Map C4**

Spitze – *vintage accessories. See page 140.*

Kleenothek

Schönhauser Allee 186, Prenzlauer Berg, 10119 (449 5833). U2 Rosa-Luxemburg-Platz. **Open** 7.30am-7.30pm Mon-Fri; 9am-1.30pm Sat. **No credit cards. Map G2**
Reliable dry cleaners which will also take in laundry for service (machine) washing.

Michael Klemm

Wörtherstraße 31, Prenzlauer Berg, 10405 (442 4549). U2 Senefelderplatz. **Open** 10am-6pm Mon-Fri. **No credit cards. Map G2**
Friendly tailor for all types of alterations. Will also run up garments on request. Skirts taken in for DM14; jeans patched for DM15.

Nantes

Uhlandstraße 20-25, Charlottenburg, 10623 (883 5746). U15 Uhlandstraße. **Open** 8am-6pm Mon-Fri; 9am-noon Sat. **No credit cards. Map C4**
Recommended by designer shops, Nantes charges slightly more than most for dry cleaning (DM15 for a man's jacket; DM35 for a ballgown), but takes up to four days. It's worth the wait for valuable items.

Trendy

Möllendorffstraße 74, Lichtenberg, 13067 (9599 73033). S4, S8, S10/U5 Frankfurter Allee. **Open** noon-6pm Mon-Fri. **No credit cards.**
Sonja Geier spent seven years working for a major retailer altering the likes of Armani, Galliano and Gucci. Her sewing is impeccable and she will pick up and deliver to your home or hotel.

Flea markets

There's many a treat in store at Berlin's flea markets, especially for music lovers, collectors of old books, fans of art deco and those with a fetish for old GDR knick-knacks. It's worth checking out *Zitty* and *tip* for the most up-to-date listings.

Berliner Antik & Flohmarkt

Bahnhof Friedrichstraße, S-Bahnbogen 190-203, Mitte, 10117 (208 2645). S1, S2, S3, S5, S7, S9/U6 Friedrichstraße. **Open** 11am-6pm Mon, Wed-Sun. **Map F3**
More than 60 dealers have taken up residence in the renovated arches under the S-Bahn tracks, selling furniture, jewellery, paintings and interesting vintage clothing, some of it from the 1920s and 1930s.

Kunst und Nostalgie Markt

Museumsinsel, by Zeughaus, Mitte, 10178 (03341 309 411). S1, S2, S3, S5, S7, S9/U6 Friedrichstraße. **Open** 11am-5pm Sat-Sun. **Map F3**
One of the few places you can still find true GDR relics, with anything from old signs advertising coal briquets to framed pictures of Honecker. Also a section devoted to modern arts and crafts.

Straße des 17. Juni

Straße des 17. Juni, Charlottenburg, 10787 (2255 0096). U2 Ernst-Reuter-Platz/S3, S5, S7, S9 Tiergarten. **Open** 8am-5pm Sat-Sun. **Map C4**
Early 20th-century objects of a high quality with prices to match, alongside a jumble of vintage and alternative clothing, second-hand records, CDs and books. Arts and crafts further along the street. Best flea market in town, albeit an insanely cramped one.

Zille-Hof

Fasanenstraße 14, Charlottenburg, 10623 (313 4333). U15 Uhlandstraße. **Open** 8am-5.30pm Mon-Fri; 8am-1pm Sat. **Map C4**
Almost next door to the Kempinski Hotel, a neat and tidy junk market where you can track down everything from an antique hatpin to a chest of drawers. You'll find the better bric-à-brac indoors, while the real bargains lurk in the courtyard outside.

Flowers

Blumen 31

Bleibtreustraße 31, Charlottenburg, 10707 (8847 4604). U15 Uhlandstraße. **Open** 9am-8pm Mon-Fri; 9am-6pm Sat. **Credit** AmEx, DC, MC, V. **Map C4**
Specialising in roses from Ecuador, creatively combined into bulging bouquets with little more than an array of greens. Roses start at DM4 a piece, but are long-lasting, and you can pick up a one-rose nosegay for as little as DM8. Delivery from DM10.

Blumenwiese

Dorotheenstraße 151, Mitte, 10117 (2016 5067). S1, S2, S3, S5, S7, S9/U6 Friedrichstraße. **Open** 9am-6pm Mon-Fri; 9am-4pm Sat. **No credit cards. Map F3**

Tastefully exotic arrangements are something of a rarity in east Berlin, but Blumenwiese pulls off the most extraordinary floral tributes with panache and numbers the Adlon Hotel among its many corporate clients. Delivery free within Mitte, and throughout Berlin for a few marks more. A Fleurop shop.

Fleurop

(713 710). **Open** 7.30am-6.30pm Mon-Fri; 8am-2pm Sat. **Credit** AmEx, DC, MC, V.

Call to have flowers delivered anywhere in the western world. Bouquets start at DM25, but hard-up Romeos can have a single flower delivered to their sweetheart's door for only DM20. Within Germany, your flowers can arrive within an hour, sent via any one of 7,000 shops nationwide.

Food

There's little joy shopping in Berlin supermarkets. They are small and cramped, encourage check-out queues, keep idiosyncratic opening hours and never take credit cards. The alternative are specialist shops, from ethno to gourmet, which range from expensive Italian delis to cheap Asian minimarkets. The organic food market is booming, the variety of produce sold in *Biolåden* is huge and subject to strict controls.

Aquí España

Kantstraße 34, Charlottenburg, 10625 (312 3315). U7 Wilmersdorfer Straße. **Open** 9am-8pm Mon-Fri; 9am-6pm Sat. **No credit cards**. **Map B4**
Neighbourhood store stocking Spanish wines and groceries, plus ingredients for Mexican and Latin-American dishes, including a full array of dried chillies, flour and corn tortillas and Central-American seafood in the freezer.

Bier Company

Körtestraße 10, Kreuzberg, 10967 (693 2720). U7 Südstern. **Open** 3-8pm Mon-Thur; noon-9pm Fri; 10am-6pm Sat. **No credit cards**. **Map G5**
Micro-brewery that sells its own stout, British and Belgian ale and a host of other superb brews. Most notable is Turn, which instead of being hopped with hops, is 'hemped' with hemp. Also sells home-brewing kits and offers brewing courses.

Brotgarten

Seelingstraße 30, Charlottenburg, 14059 (322 8880). U2 Sophie-Charlotte-Platz. **Open** 7.30am-6.30pm Mon-Fri; 7.30am-1.30pm Sat; 9am-noon Sun. **No credit cards**. **Map B4**
Health food store notable for its mixes of muesli, dried fruits and nuts, and its delicious wholesome breads, made with a variety of nuts and seeds. Natural-product sweets are also available.

English Food Shop

Fechnerstraße 21, Wilmersdorf, 10717 (861 0607). U7 Blissestraße. **Open** noon-6pm Mon-Fri. **No credit cards**. **Map C5**
Widest selection in Berlin of foodstuffs the Brits miss, ranging from English mustards to mar-malades, from jelly to prawn-cocktail crisps and from Marmite to PG Tips.
Branch: Seeburger Straße 3, Spandau, 13581 (332 9420)

Galeries Lafayette

Französische Straße 23, Mitte, 10117 (209 480). U2, U6 Stadtmitte. **Open** 9.30am-8pm Mon-Fri; 9am-4pm Sat. **Credit** AmEx, DC, JCB, MC, V. **Map F3**
Prices are reasonably high in the French-oriented basement food hall of this flash department store. Nevertheless the delicatessen counter offers high-quality cuts, and the staff are often happy to help out with gastronomic suggestions. It also features a wide selection of French cheese and wines. *See page 141* **Is Berlin being served?**

KaDeWe

Tauentzienstraße 21-24, Schöneberg, 10789 (212 10). U1, U2, U15 Wittenbergplatz. **Open** 9.30am-8pm Mon-Fri; 9am-4pm Sat. **Credit** AmEx, DC, MC, V. **Map D4**
Most famous for its lavish food hall which takes up the whole of the sixth floor and features foodstuffs from around the globe. Seafood and *Wurst*-lovers will think they've died and gone to heaven. The delicatessen is famous for its specialities, the gourmet bars offer everything from oysters to smoked sausage, and special orders for more *outré* items can be made by phone (213 2455). Some may take a few days to be fulfilled, same-day delivery is possible until 4pm in Berlin and Potsdam, with a DM10 charge for orders less than DM200. Allow two or three days for delivery of large drinks orders.
See page 141 **Is Berlin being served?**

Kolbo

Auguststraße 77-78, Mitte, 10117 (no phone). U6 Oranienburger Tor. **Open** 11am-1.45pm, 2.15-7pm, Tue-Thur, Sun; 9am-2pm Fri. **Credit** AmEx, MC, V. **Map F3**
Small friendly store and bakery in Berlin's old Jewish quarter selling kosher foodstuffs and wines, plus a selection of books (including kosher cookbooks) and ritual objects.

Königsberger Marzipan

Pestalozzistraße 54a, Charlottenburg, 10627 (323 8254). S3, S5, S7, S9 Charlottenburg. **Open** 11am-6pm Mon-Wed; 2-6pm Tue, Thur-Fri; 11am-2pm Sat. **No credit cards**. **Map B4**
Irmgard Wald and her late husband moved from Kaliningrad to Berlin after the war and began again in the confectionery trade. With her smiling American-born granddaughter, Frau Wald still produces fresh, soft, melt-in-your-mouth marzipan. Small boxes of assorted sweets make great gifts.

Leysieffer

Kurfürstendamm 218, Charlottenburg, 10719 (885 7480). U15 Uhlandstraße. **Open** 10am-8pm Mon-Sat. **Credit** AmEx, DC, MC, V. **Map C4**
Beautifully packaged confitures, teas and handmade chocolates from this German fine food company make perfect high-calorie gifts. Café upstairs and bakery attached.

Clothes to the edge

It may not have anything comparable to St Martin's, but with six fashion schools Berlin churns out its fair share of aspiring designers. In recent years its graduates have been going boldly where no one in the years of division could: to fashion's final frontier, where critical acclaim meets commercial success.

It is nothing short of sensational that the Berlin label Thatchers has been chosen as a client by the prestigious French fashion agency Girault-Totem. With its synthesis of street and clubwear, Thatchers has its finger on the pulse of the city's thriving underground – a beat which is grabbing the attention of trend scouts the world over.

Much has changed since 1989. While you'll still see the barrage of bad taste that once gave Berlin its bad rep as the worst-dressed city in Europe, locals are finding the multitude of fashion retailers that have moved in to town, from cheap chic to high-end luxury labels. In a city characterised by its individuality, not everyone is happy to buy into globalised Gucci or Gap.

With the growing public interest in local designers has come increased support from city government. It now recognises fashion as an asset and subsidises start-up businesses as well as studios where designers share equipment. The standard of garments on offer has made a quantum leap in both style and quality. Shoddy workmanship is no longer accepted either by shop owners or their increasingly discerning clientèle, and many labels meet their expecta-tions. For men, Firma, Coration, **RespectMen** and Ralf Handschuh are respected for their subtle urban utility styles and contemporary cuts. Women's fashions by Ute Henschel, Nardini, Christine Birkle's **Hut Up** and Jane Garber's Kostümhaus have made their mark with imaginative use of fabrics and good tailoring.

Mitte's Hackesche Höfe are home to bright local stars and have attracted others to the area. That's helped establish the Scheunenviertel as the city's answer to the Sohos of London and New York. Vivienne Westwood calls her students at the Hochschule der Künste the best in the world. A lecturer there since 1991, she spends a long weekend drilling them in how the tricks, techniques and silhouettes of historical costumes can be reinterpreted for modern attire.

Having names in town like Westwood or the HdK's other famous designer professor, Wolfgang Joop, naturally lends hope that the city will establish its name in the fashion stakes. But it'll never be a fashion capital. It doesn't want to be. Berlin is happy to go its own way. And in fashion, that can only be a good thing.
Coration is available at **To Die For***; Ralf Handschuh at* **Essenbeck** *and T&G; Firma at* **Quartier 206***; Thatchers at* **Groopie Deluxe** *and* **To Die For***; Ute Henschel at* **Molotow***. Nardini is at Schlüterstraße 70 in Charlottenburg (131 1464) and Kostümhaus is in the Hackesche Höfe on Mitte's Rosenthaler Straße (282 7018). Vivienne Westwood's students present shows each May. Information on 318 50.*

Hackesche Höfe – home of bright, local fashion stars.

Lindenberg

Morsestraße 2, Charlottenburg, 10587 (3908 1523).
U9 Turmstraße. **Open** 8am-7pm Mon-Fri; 8am-2pm
Sat. **No credit cards. Map D3**
Wholesaler where the city's pro and amateur chefs
stock up on live lobster, fresh seafood, New Zealand
lamb, local ducks, out-of-season fruit and veg,
assorted French cheeses, and wines and spirits.
Anyone can walk in but most things are sold only
in industrial quantities. Advance orders taken.

LPG

Mehringdamm 51, Kreuzberg, 10961 (694 7725).
U6, U7 Mehringdamm. **Open** 10am-7.30pm Mon-Fri;
10am-4pm Sat. **No credit cards. Map F5**
If you're staying a while and are an organic shop-
per, co-ops are great alternatives to expensive
Bioläden. For a DM100 deposit and a monthly fee of
about DM25, you can save up to 30% on food, wine,
juice, cosmetics and household detergents.

Macchina/Caff

*Alte Schönhauser Straße 26, Mitte, 10009 (2838
4414). U8 Weinmeisterstraße.* **Open** noon-6pm Mon-
Fri; 11am-4pm Sat. **Credit** AmEx, MC, V. **Map G3**
Treat your caffeine addiction with a fix from the
selection of quality Italian coffee such as Illy and
Manresi, and pick up a state-of-the-art espresso
machine. Also a wide selection of simple aluminium
espresso cans, and a DM59 solar-powered milk
frother patented by Berlin company SoLait.

Vinh-Loi

*Ansbacher Straße 16, Schöneberg, 10787 (235
0900). U1, U2, U15 Wittenbergplatz.* **Open** 9am-7pm
Mon-Fri; 9am-4pm Sat. **No credit cards. Map D5**
Asian groceries including Thai fruit, veg and herbs
fresh from the airport on Mondays and Thursdays.
Plus woks, rice steamers and Chinese crockery.

Weichardt-Brot

Mehlitzstraße 7, Wilmersdorf, 10715 (873 8099).
U7, U9 Berliner Straße. **Open** 8am-6.30pm Mon-Fri;
8am-1pm Sat. **No credit cards. Map C5**
The very best bakery in town, Weichardt-Brot grew
out of a Berlin collective from the 1960s. Stone-
ground organic flour and natural leavens make this
a Mecca for bread-lovers.

Street markets

Berlin's many *Wochenmärkte* offer an alternative
to stores, and usually sell better, cheaper fresh produce. There's probably one at the end of your road.

Farmers' Market

*Wittenbergplatz, Schöneberg, 10787. U1, U2, U15
Wittenbergplatz.* **Open** 9am-6pm Thur. **Map D4**
Predominantly organic produce, including 'bio'
cheese, bread, fresh pasta and meat stands, plus fruit
and vegetables from farms in the region. You'll also
come across inedible items such as wooden brushes
and sheepskins.

Kollwitzplatz

*Kollwitzplatz, Prenzlauer Berg, 10435. U2
Senefelderplatz.* **Open** noon-7pm Thur. **Map G2**

Whisky & Cigars – *Scotch 'n' smoke, p145.*

Open-air food markets are still rare in the east. This
one is a small and unassuming organic market,
much more lively in summer than in winter.

Türkischer Markt

*Maybachufer, Neukölln, 12045. U1, U8 Kottbusser
Tor.* **Open** noon-6.30pm Tue, Fri. **Map G5**
A noisy, crowded market just across the canal from
Kreuzberg, catering for the needs of the neighbour-
hood's Turkish community. Good buys, great tastes.

Winterfeldt Markt

*Winterfeldtplatz, Schöneberg, 10781. U1, U2, U4
Nollendorfplatz.* **Open** 8am-2pm Wed, Sat. **Map D5**
Saturday's multicultural experience. Everybody
shows up to buy their vegetables, cheese, whole-
grain breads, *Wurst*, meats, flowers, clothes, pet supplies and toys; or simply to meet over a coffee, beer
or falafel at one of the many cafés off the square.

Wine & spirits

Getränke Hoffmann

Kleiststraße 23-26, Schöneberg, 10787 (2147 3096).
U1, U2, U15 Wittenbergplatz. Open 9am-8pm Mon-
Fri; 8am-4pm Sat. **No credit cards. Map D4**
Branches offer a wide range of everyday booze at
everyday prices. Call 753 9606 to make orders for
delivery anywhere in town or check the *Gelbe Seiten.*
Branch: Schönfließer Straße 19, Prenzlauer Berg,
10438 (444 0682)

Klemke Wein & Spirituosenhandel

*Mommsenstraße 9, Charlottenburg, 10629 (8855
1260). S3, S5, S7, S9 Savignyplatz.* **Open** 9am-7pm
Mon-Fri; 9am-2.30pm Sat. **No credit cards. Map C4**

Respected specialists in French and Italian wines from the tiniest vineyard to the grandest chateau. Also *digestifs* and whiskies. Free delivery in Berlin.

Vendemmia

Akazienstraße 20, Schöneberg, 10823 (784 2728). U7 Eisenacher Straße. **Open** 10am-6.30pm Mon-Fri; 10am-2pm Sat. **No credit cards. Map D5**
Bulk importers of first-class Italian wines which are decanted into bottles bearing photocopied labels. Not the most impressive bottle you can take to a party, but it's good stuff and very cheap. Several other good wine and spirits shops on this street, plus an Italian deli with a good wine selection.

Whisky & Cigars

Sophienstraße 23, Mitte, 10178 (282 0376). S3, S5, S7, S9 Hackescher Markt. **Open** noon-7pm Tue-Sat. **No credit cards. Map F3**
Two friends sharing a love of single malts are behind this shop, which stocks 150 whiskies, and cigars from Cuba, Jamaica and Honduras. Top of the range is a bottle of Milroys Imperial at DM160 or a DM80 Havana Montecristo.

Food delivery & catering

It is still almost impossible to get anything better than an industrial pizza or cheap Chinese takeaway. Few restaurants will deliver past 11pm. Look in the *Gelbe Seiten*, or keep an eye out for flyers.

Liberty Pizza

(445 0412). **Open** orders taken 11.30am-9.30pm daily. **No credit cards.**
Delivery service started by a homesick group of Brooklyn Italians to fill the gap in the market for thick-crusted American-style pizza. Serves Mitte, Prenzlauer Berg, Wedding and Weissensee.

Rogacki

Wilmersdorfer Straße 145, Charlottenburg, 10585 (341 4091). U7 Wilmersdorfer Straße. **Open** 9am-7pm Mon-Fri; 8am-3pm Sat. **No credit cards. Map B4**
Established in 1928, Berlin's fish institution provides smoked eel, salads, sandwiches, *Wurst* and meat dishes. Party service, delivery charge DM10-35.

Photography

Foto Klinke

Friedrichstraße 207-208, Kreuzberg, 10969 (2529 5530), U6 Kochstraße. **Open** 9am-7pm Mon-Fri; 9am-2pm Sat. **Credit** MC, V. **Map F4**
The large processing department can turn around films in an hour; passport photos (four for DM12.95) arrive in ten minutes. Also a large range of cameras and photo equipment. Branches all over town.
Branches: Schönhauser Allee 105, Prenzlauer Berg, 10439 (444 1380); Potsdamer Straße 141, Schöneberg, 10783 (216 3876)

PPS

Rosenthaler Straße 28-31, Mitte, 10178 (2852 8400). U8 Weinmeisterstraße. **Open** 8am-9pm Mon-Fri; 2-

6pm Sat-Sun. **Credit** AmEx, DC, MC, V. **Map F3**
Professional colour lab offering two-hour developing, digital service, scanning, black-and-white hand-developed enlargements, large format print and other services. Also sells cameras, rents out sophisticated equipment and sends off repairs.

Wüstefeld

Grolmanstraße 36, Charlottenburg, 10623 (883 7593) U15 Uhlandstraße/S3, S5, S7, S9 Savignyplatz. **Open** 9.30am-7pm Mon-Fri; 10am-4pm Sat. **Credit** MC, V. **Map C4**
In exchange for a glance at your passport or ID card and a credit-card deposit, you can rent Nikon, Canon, Hasselblad and Leica cameras and photo equipment here. Also professional processing service.

Records, tapes, CDs

See also **Flex/Melting Point** *under* **Fashion** *and* **Dussman Das Kulturkaufhaus** *under* **Books.** At *www.platten.net* there is a complete online guide to every record shop in Berlin, from Turkish music shops to second-hand stores, calling at all points in between.

Canzone

Savigny Passage, Bogen 583, 10623 (313 1578). S3, S5, S7, S9 Savignyplatz. **Open** 10.30am-7pm Mon-Thur; 10.30am-8pm Fri; 10.30am-4pm Sat. **Credit** V. **Map C4**
Stocks hard-to-find CDs in a Latin, tango, African or Brazilian vein. Belly-dancing videos also on offer.

D-Fens

Greifswalder Straße 224, Prenzlauer Berg, 10405 (4434 2250). U2 Rosa-Luxemburg-Platz. **Open** noon-7pm Mon-Fri; noon-3pm Sat. **No credit cards. Map G3**
Small DJ shop in a revamped garage, specialising in house, trance, electro, techno and disco. Home base of Berlin labels Formaldahyde and BCC. Owner Ralf Ballschuh, a DJ himself, is happy to turn up the volume on any track you wish. Hard to find so follow the signs for the Knaack Klub. See *chapters* **Music: Rock, Folk & Jazz** *and* **Nightlife.**

DNS

Alte Schönhauser Straße 39-40, Mitte, 10178 (247 9835). U8 Weinmeisterstraße. **Open** 11am-8pm Mon-Fri; 11am-4pm Sat. **Credit** AmEx, DC, MC, V. **Map G3**
Old vinyl, including some rare finds, as well as the latest pressings in the world of techno.

Gelbe Musik

Schaperstraße 11, Wilmersdorf, 10719 (211 3962). U1 Augsburger Straße. **Open** 1-6pm Tue-Fri; 11am-2pm Sat. **Credit** MC, V. **Map C5**
Arguably Europe's number one outlet for avant-garde music, with racks filled with minimalist, electronic, world, industrial and extreme noise. Rare vinyl and import CDs, music press and sound objects make absorbing browsing, and the store is a hang-out for the international and the odd.

D-fens – *the best form of sonic attack.*

Berlin's leading address for independent and underground rock, with lots of British, US and Australian imports, a huge vinyl section, and staff who know and love their music.

Space Hall

Zossenerstraße 33, Kreuzberg, 10961 (694 7664).
U7 Gneisenaustraße. **Open** 11am-7pm Mon-Wed; 11am-8pm Thur-Fri; 10am-4pm Sat. **No credit cards. Map F5**
Spacious shop offering a broad range of new and second-hand CDs at decent prices and with a huge techno/house vinyl room at the back. Two other good record shops on this street and more round the corner on Bergmannstraße.

WOM

Augsburger Straße 36-42, Schöneberg, 10789 (885 7240). *U1 Augsburger Straße.* **Open** 10am-8pm Mon-Fri; 9am-4pm Sat. **Credit** AmEx, MC, V.
Map D4
The World Of Music chain offers a no-frills approach to music retailing, and its wide selection of CDs includes a good selection of jazz recordings.
Branch: Hertie, Wilmersdorfer Straße 118, Charlottenburg, 10585 (315 9170)

Repairs

Bicycle repairs

FNC

Mommsenstraße 35, Charlottenburg, 10629 (323 3503). *U7 Adenauerplatz.* **Open** 9am-6pm Mon-Wed; 9am-7pm Thur, Fri; 9am-2pm Sat. **No credit cards. Map B4**
Best bike store in town. It specialises in trekking and racing bikes, but staff will repair any old rattler.

Computer repairs

Pabst Computer

Bundesallee 137, Friedenau, 12161 (859 5200). *S4/U9 Bundesplatz.* **Open** 10am-8pm Mon-Fri; 10.30am-2pm Sat. **Credit** AmEx, MC, V. **Map C6**
Mac dealer with its own repair workshop.
Website: www.pabst.de

J·E

Poststraße 12, Mitte, 10178 (2472 1741). *U2 Klosterstraße.* **Open** 10am-8pm Mon-Fri; 10am-4pm Sat. **No credit cards. Map G3**
PCs repaired, software sold and classes given.
Website: www.je-computer.de

Luggage repairs

Kofferhaus Meinecke

Meinekestraße 25, Wilmersdorf, 10719 (882 2262). *U9, U15 Kurfürstendamm.* **Open** 10am-7pm Mon-Fri; 10am-4pm Sat. **Credit** AmEx, MC, V. **Map C4**
Specialists in Samsonite, Delsey, Airline, Traveller, Rimova and Picard. The staff will be pleased to repair your suitcases within three working days and deliver new ones within the Berlin city limits.

Hans Riedl Musikalienhandel

Uhlandstraße 38, Wilmersdorf, 10719 (882 7395). *U15 Uhlandstraße.* **Open** 8am-6.30pm Mon-Fri; 9am-2pm Sat. **Credit** MC, V. **Map F4**
Probably the best address for classical music in Berlin, this huge, slightly old-fashioned shop stocks a wide selection of CDs and sheet music, as well as string and brass instruments. Staff are knowledgeable and the shop is patronised by music professionals as well as Berlin's classical music-lovers.
Branch: Konzerthaus, Gendarmenmarkt, Mitte, 10117 (204 1136)

Hardwax

2nd courtyard, 3rd floor, Paul-Lincke-Ufer 44a, Kreuzberg, 10999 (6113 0111). *U8 Schönleinstraße.* **Open** noon-8pm Mon-Fri; 10am-4pm Sat. **No credit cards. Map G5**
One of the best places in Europe to buy techno records. Also a small selection of CDs, including the excellent minimalist releases on their own Chain Reaction label. The mail-order service includes an auction of rarities where you bid by phone, mail, fax or e-mail and the record gets shipped COD to the highest bidder the next day.

Mr Dead & Mrs Free

Bülowstraße 5, Schöneberg, 10783 (215 1449). *U1, U2, U4 Nollendorfplatz.* **Open** 11am-7pm Mon-Wed; 11am-8pm Thur-Fri; 11am-4pm Sat. **No credit cards. Map D5**

Witt
*Hauptstraße 9, Schöneberg, 10827 (781 4937). U7
Kleistpark.* **Open** 9am-6pm Mon-Fri; 9am-2pm Sat.
Credit AmEx, DC, MC, V. **Map E5**
Probably Berlin's most extensive assortment of suitcase spare parts, including patches. Luggage repairs
can be completed in a day, and if damage has happened during a flight and you have written airline
confirmation of this, the repairs will be billed to the
airline. Evening delivery possible.

Shoe repairs
See also **Shoemakers**, Breitenbach (*above*).

Picobello
*KaDeWe, Tauentzienstraße 21, Schöneberg, 10789
(2121 2349). U1, U2, U15 Wittenbergplatz.* **Open**
9.30am-8pm Mon-Fri; 9am-4pm Sat. **Credit** AmEx,
DC, MC, V. **Map D4**
Staff will heel and sole shoes while you wait, and
also engrave and cut keys. There are branches all
over Berlin, often to be found in department stores.

Souvenirs

As Berlin becomes ever more 'westernised', it's getting hard to find relics from its communist past.
You'll find the odd stand selling commie kitsch
such as Party badges, Russian hats or Soviet
binoculars plus bits of graffitied plaster, said to be
from the Wall, at Checkpoint Charlie and
Potsdamer Platz. The **Museum Haus am
Checkpoint Charlie** (*see chapter* **Museums**)
sells items such as key rings, lighters and mouse
pads with a 'You Are Leaving The American
Sector' theme. The **Kunst und Nostalgie** and
Straße des 17. Juni flea markets (*above*) have
stalls devoted to artefacts from the old East.

Berlin Story
*Unter den Linden 40, Mitte, 10117 (2016 6139). S1,
S2 Unter den Linden.* **Open** 10am-8pm daily. **Credit**
AmEx, DC, MC, V. **Map F3**
You won't find a better source of Berlin-related books
(in both German and English), with subjects ranging
from the history of the Hohenzollerns and the GDR
to Prussian architecture and Norman Foster's domed
Reichstag. A huge selection of historical city maps,
posters, videos, CDs, and souvenirs such as toy
Trabbies (DM9.90), mounted wall chunks (DM300),
and various von Schadow sculptural plaster replicas.

Berliner Zinnfiguren Kabinet
*Knesebeckstraße 88, Charlottenburg, 10623 (313
0802). S3, S5, S7, S9 Savignyplatz.* **Open** 10am-6pm
Mon-Thur; 10am-8pm Fri; 10am-3pm Sat. **Credit**
AmEx, MC, V. **Map C4**
Armies of tin soldiers line up alongside farm ani-
mals and historical characters, all handworked in tin
and painted with incredible attention to detail. Take
home an entire battalion of Prussian Grenadiers for
DM300. Also a fascinating collection of books on
Prussian military history.

J&M Fässler
*Europa-Center, Charlottenburg, 10787 (342 7166).
S3, S5, S7, S9/U2, U9 Zoologischer Garten.* **Open**
10am-6.30pm Mon-Fri; 10am-6pm Sat. **Credit** AmEx,
DC, MC, V. **Map D4**
Nasty German ornaments, from Hummel cuckoo
clocks to Bavarian beer mugs and musical boxes.

Johanna Petzoldt
*Sophienstraße 9, Mitte, 10178 (282 6754). S3, S5,
S7, S9 Hackescher Markt.* **Open** 10am-6pm Mon-Sat.
Credit AmEx, JCB, MC, V. **Map F3**
Tiny, charming shop filled with traditional hand-
made wooden figurines, musical boxes and candle-
mobiles by Erzebirge. Quirky figures depict rural
German life, Christmas figures and military types.
Appropriate and appealing souvenirs, prices range
up to DM400 for a musical box.

Stationery & art supplies

Perhaps it is the national predilection for bureau-
cracy, but Germans love stationery – particularly
anything with a whiff of office efficiency about it.
Notebooks and files are taken very seriously and
designed to last. The quality on offer is high.

Ferdinand Braune
*Grunewaldstraße 87, Schöneberg, 10825 (7870
3773). U7 Kleistpark.* **Open** 10am-6.30pm Mon-Fri;
10am-2pm Sat. **Credit** MC, V. **Map E5**
Berlin's painters flock here for Herr Braune's hand-
blended oil paints, acrylics, sketchbooks and the
finest canvas stretches. Delivery service available.

Grüne Papeterie
*Oranienstraße 196, Kreuzberg, 10999 (618 5355).
U1, U8 Kottbusser Tor.* **Open** 9.30am-7.30pm Mon-
Fri; 10am-4pm Sat. **No credit cards. Map G4**
Eco-friendly stationery, wrapping paper, wooden
fountain pens as well as small gifts and toys.

J Müller
*Neue Schönhauser Straße 16, Mitte, 10178 (283
2532). U8 Weinmeisterstraße.* **Open** 8am-6pm Mon-
Fri. **No credit cards. Map G3**
Family-run business selling fine stationery and rub-
ber stamps. Also prints signs and business cards.

Papeterie
*Uhlandstraße 28, Charlottenburg, 10719 (881
6363). U15 Uhlandstraße.* **Open** 9.30am-7pm Mon-
Wed; 9.30am-8pm Thur-Fri; 9.30am-4pm Sat. **Credit**
AmEx, DC, MC, V. **Map C4**
Upmarket stockists of nicely made notebooks, agen-
das, diaries, albums and organisers, plus Mont Blanc
pens and Count Faber-Castell gilded pencil sets.

Propolis
*Oranienstraße 19a, Kreuzberg 10999 (615 2464).
U1, U8 Kottbusser Tor.* **Open** 10am-6pm Mon-Fri.
No credit cards. Map G4
Specialising in pigments, with over 300 to choose
from, plus recipes and ingredients for wall finishes.
Also available are oil, water and acrylic paints,
resins, gold and silver leaf, brushes and canvases.

On the Town

Restaurants

Don't just prepare for the Wurst – dining options in cosmopolitan Berlin are decent, diverse and designed for all tastes and budgets.

First, the bad news. No one comes to Berlin to eat. It's simply not a world gastronomic capital like Rome, New York or Bangkok. There is, for example, no restaurant which serves as gourmet short-hand for the city the way the Tour d'Argent does for Paris or Galatoire's for New Orleans. Plus, it's in Germany, a land whose cuisine conjures images of heavy, pork-laden, fat-saturated, salty, under-seasoned, starchy... well, you get the picture.

But of course, when in Berlin you have to eat, and the good news is that even though the city may lack an international reputation for good eating, there are scores of excellent restaurants here. Given the funds and the inclination, you could spend months hitting a different place each day and wander away happy. True, there are a lot of places which serve non-German cuisine warped to please the conservative local palate, but they are no longer the only choice. Even vegetarians are having an easier time these days, as younger Germans become more health-conscious and innovative chefs raise the standards of vegetarian cooking to new heights.

One big advantage Berlin has had for some time is the presence of the Turkish minority, whose numerous fruit-and-vegetable stands are found throughout the city, laden with fresh produce gathered in the pre-dawn hours at the huge Westhafen wholesale market. Another bright side is Germans' relentless *Wanderlust*, which has brought them into close contact with the food of their favourite holiday destinations. Italian, in particular, is well-served in Berlin, as are Japanese, Thai, Greek and Indian food along with various eastern European cuisines. Now, if we could just get the locals to travel to China more often – Chinese food in Berlin is a grim proposition indeed.

And, for those who don't mind a touch of the pig, there is traditional Berlin food, which can be tasty indeed even though no one's ever going to call it health food: Königsberger Klöpse (veal and pork meatballs in a cream sauce dotted with capers), variations on the roast pork theme, *Thüringer Bratwurst, Currywurst* and *Bouletten* for main course, and Kaiserschmarren (pancakes sliced up and mixed with liqueur-enhanced whipped cream) for dessert.

There is also no dearth of young cooks who, inspired by French nouvelle cuisine, have invented *neue deutsche Küche*, its German half-cousin.

This is not, perhaps, as wonderful (or as meagre in its portions) as its inspiration, but, since there's a goodly touch of Italian in it, is very much worthy of your attention.

Breakfast in Berlin is usually served in cafés, and usually until well into the afternoon in many places: they understand their clientèle's lifestyle well. It can be a cup of *Milchkaffee* with a croissant or a heavier meal of cheese and cold-cuts with a soft-boiled egg, or even a *Bauernfrühstuck*, that inimitable German variation on the omelette. The very brave can attempt the weekend ritual of *Frühschoppen*, in which breakfast is accompanied by a shot of *Korn*, the local attempt at whisky, or a bottle of *Sekt*, sparkling white wine.

Unlike the rest of Germany, Berliners often save their main meal for the end of the day, so that a light lunch is easily enough found. If all you want is a sandwich, these are often available in bakeries as *belegte Brötchen*, served on fresh-baked rolls. Or stop by an *Imbiß* for a sausage or *Döner Kebap*. On the higher end of the economic scale, lunch in one of Berlin's better restaurants – those which open for lunch – can be a good way of getting an idea of the place's cooking at a reasonable price.

In the evenings, particularly at weekends, restaurants can be packed, so ingrained is the dining-out experience in Berliners' lifestyle. A reservation may not be essential, but it doesn't hurt to make one anyway to avoid disappointment and the possibility of a subsequent search for another place to eat. This is particularly so in the east, where decent dining options are still relatively thin on the ground and the better restaurants often over-subscribed.

German restaurants still dominate in Berlin and these we have organised by price-range – Expensive (an average of DM45 and up), Moderate (DM25-44) and Inexpensive (under DM25). These are followed by restaurants organised according to cuisine rather than cost, reflecting the cosmopolitanism of Berlin's gastronomic culture. Then we pay homage to the Imbiß. This word can denote a takeaway-only joint, or a place with stand-up tables, or a self-service sit-down eaterie. Whatever the precise format, Imbiße come in a variety of cuisines and offer a way of stretching your budget – in some you can order a fine, filling dinner for a fraction of the price you'd fork out in a normal restaurant.

The average prices listed are intended to reflect the cost of a starter and main course, but take these as guideline rather than gospel – in most restaurants it's easy to spend much more or a lot less, and the addition of wine or a pre-dinner cocktail will kick the bill up considerably. One welcome sign is that some of the top-drawer places have taken a cue from their French counterparts and opened bistros, where smaller or different dishes from the same kitchen can be enjoyed for lower prices.

In restaurants, a service charge of 17 per cent is usually added to the bill, but unless service has been awful (not impossible in Berlin, alas), diners usually round up the bill or, in the classier joints, add ten per cent. Tips are handed to the server (or you tell them how much to take) and never left on the table, which is considered insulting by some. Be warned: when handing over the cash, only say *danke* if you want the waiter to keep the change.

German

Expensive

Adlon

Hotel Adlon, Unter den Linden 77, Mitte, 10117 (22 610). S1, S2 Unter den Linden. **Open** 6-11pm daily. **Average** DM80. **Credit** AmEx, DC, V. **Map F3**

Try master chef Karlheinz Hauser's orgasmic lemon grass soup as a starter and be equally astonished by his lobster *en gêlée*. He's also caused a sensation among gastronomes with his duck served in

two courses – an astonishing feat of culinary skill. The airy, bright dining area with great views over Unter den Linden and the Brandenburg Gate may be geographically the city's best. A gourmet restaurant named Lorenz (after the hotel's original founder, Lorenz Adlon), to be helmed by Maestro Hauser, is due to open on the first floor in 2000.

Alt-Luxemburg

Windscheidstrase 31, Charlottenburg, 10627 (323 8730) U2 Sophie-Charlotte-Platz. **Open** 7pm-midnight Mon-Sat. **Average** DM70. **Credit** AmEx, DC, MC, V. **Map B4**

We're happy to report that Karl Wannemacher, who combines classic French flavours with Asian influences in a wonderfully romantic dining room, is back on form with such wonders as horseradish terrine with smoked eel and monkfish in a succulent saffron sauce informed with tomato. But this truly pretty little restaurant's wine list could do with a few more moderately priced bottles.

Altes Zollhaus

Carl-Herz-Ufer 30, Kreuzberg, 10961 (692 3300). U1 Prinzenstraße. **Open** 6-11.30pm Tue-Sat; *kitchen closes* 11pm. **Menu** DM80-100. **Credit** AmEx, DC, JCB, MC, V. **Map G5**

This former customs house on the Landwehrkanal does a brilliant job of modernising German cuisine, using only the freshest, locally grown ingredients, many of them organically raised. The superb wine-list and attentive service in pleasant surroundings – plus the healthy-sized portions – make this establishment a value-for-money splurge, if that's not something of a contradiction.

Altes Zollhaus – *modernising German cuisine in an old customs house.*

Bamberger Reiter

Regensburger Straße 7, Schöneberg, 10777 (218 4282/bistro 213 6733). U4 Viktoria-Luise-Platz. **Open** 6pm-1am daily; *kitchen closes* 12.30am. **Average** DM75. **Credit** AmEx, DC, V; *bistro* **no credit cards. Map D5**
This romantic and subdued, country-elegant restaurant is now run by former head chef Franz Raneburger's daughter, Doris, but there's been no noticeable drop in quality. Enjoy tender monkfish or flounder, succulent Bresse pigeon or the foie gras served with plums in balsamic vinegar and a sprinkling of delicate beans. The cellar does a fine turn in Austrian wines, the cheeseboard is impeccable and the service fresh and youthful. The bistro next-door serves Alsatian cuisine at considerably lower prices.

Blue Goût

2nd Hinterhof, Anklamer Straße 38, Mitte, 10115 (448 5840). U8 Rosenthaler Platz. **Open** 7pm-1am daily; *kitchen closes* 11.30pm. **Average** DM40. **Menu** *three courses* DM60. **Credit** AmEx, MC, V. **Map F2**
This spacious, airy room remains one of the city's hidden gems. Serving top-notch fresh ingredients including organic meat and with a wide variety of vegetarian dishes on the daily menu, it flirts with Asia while reinventing its French, Italian and German roots. Excellent wine list, decent prices and the garden out back is lovely in summertime – the only drawback is occasionally high-handed waiing staff. At some point in 2000, the restaurant is due to move to Chausseestraße 8, a short walk from U6 Oranienburger Tor.

Borchardt

Französische Straße 47, Mitte, 10117 (2038 7110). U6 Französische Straße. **Open** 11.30am-1am daily; *kitchen closes* midnight. **Average** DM50. **Credit** AmEx, MC, V. **Map F3**
In the late 19th century Friedrich Wilhelm Borchardt opened a restaurant of this name right next door at number 48. It became the place for politicians and society folk but was destroyed by bombing in World War II. Since 1991 the name has belonged to Roland Mary and Marina Richter, who have reconstructed a highly fashionable, Maxim's-inspired bistro serving highly respectable French food. Still one of the few places in the area with character. So why not snorkel down a dozen oysters and tuck into a fillet of pike-perch or beef after an evening at the Komische Oper, the Staatsoper or the Konzerthaus?

Bovril

Kurfürstendamm 184, Charlottenburg, 10707 (881 8461). U7 Adenauerplatz. **Open** 10am-2am Mon-Sat. **Average** DM60. **Credit** MC, V. **Map B5**
A bright Ku'damm bistro popular among business, intellectual and artist types – it's long been a FilmFest favourite – for its selection of light, German-French meals, exquisitely prepared. The menu changes daily but the soups are always superb. It's almost impossible to get a table for the set DM28 lunch, particularly on Saturdays, when it turns into one of Berlin's favourite after-shopping venues.

StäV – *Rheinland by the Spree. Page 156.*

Café Einstein

Kurfürstenstraße 58, Tiergarten, 10785 (261 5096). U1, U2, U4, U12 Nollendorfplatz. **Open** 10am-2am daily. **Average** DM45. **Credit** AmEx, DC, JCB, V. **Map D4**
The Tiergarten branch of Cafe Einstein is a decades-old institution: a bustling pseudo-Viennese coffeehouse serving anything from a superb cup of coffee with a slice of sinfully delicious *Apfelstrudel* to a full meal of fine Austrian cooking. A second, less characterful branch opened on Unter den Linden in 1996. **Branch:** Unter den Linden 42, Mitte, 10117 (204 3632)

First Floor

Hotel Palace, Budapester Straße 38, Charlottenburg, 10787 (2502 1020). S3, S5, S7, S9/U2, U9 Zoologischer Garten. **Open** noon-3pm, 6pm-midnight, Mon-Fri; 6pm-midnight Sat. **Average** DM70. **Menu** DM78-190. **Credit** AmEx, DC, MC, V. **Map D4**
Some say head chef Rolf Schmidt is one of Berlin's top toques. He proffers, for example, Bresse pigeon served with chanterelles and a ragout of potatoes, venison richly stuffed with foie gras, or loup de mer and Breton lobster served with saffron and tomato confit. Three menus at different price ranges are proposed daily. The frozen Grand Marnier soufflé is as honourable as the unobtrusive service. Don't let the fact that this is a hotel dining-room in the architectural blot of the Europa-Center put you off – it's one of Berlin's top tables.

Florian

Grolmanstraße 52, Charlottenburg, 10623 (313 9184). S3, S5, S7, S9 Savignyplatz. **Open** 6pm-3am daily; *kitchen closes* 1am. **Average** DM50. **No credit cards. Map C4**

A light, white restaurant in the attractive area around Savignyplatz. A sprinkling of celebrities can often be spotted among the members of the film, media and art scene who cluster around the bar sipping sparkling wine, before sitting down to order from a small menu of nouvelle European dishes. It's also a favoured haunt of Charlottenburg's Russian community. Nice ambience but somewhat overpriced and useless for vegetarians.

Grand Slam

Gottfried-von-Cramm-Weg 47-55, Grunewald, 14193 (825 3819). S7 Grunewald. **Open** 6.30-11pm Tue-Sat. **Average** DM80. **Credit** DC, V.

One of Berlin's worst-named restaurants (it's part of a sports club) is helmed by Jürgen Fehrenbach, who has proven his ability with such delights as lasagna with morels and parmesan, scallops with leek risotto and chocolate soufflé with passion fruit. Dig-deep wine list, impeccable service. Great for power dining.

Guy

Jägerstraße 59-60, Mitte, 10117, (942 600). U6 Französische Straße. **Open** noon-3pm, 6pm-1am, daily. **Average** DM50. **Credit** AmEx, DC, MC, V. **Map F4**

Guy's burgundy velvet and dark wood interior (shades of Gaultier's designs for Greenaway's *The Cook, The Thief, His Wife and Her Lover*) is so theatrical that it just might distract your attention from the stunningly banal food in what, as we go to press, is Berlin's hottest restaurant – viz the watery 'wild mushroom risotto' without the slightest hint of porcini, the undercooked catfish on tough pasta or the niggardly cheese platter. Incompetent service; and a hugely popular downstairs bar. Named after Franco-German proprietor Hartmut Guy.

Hackescher Hof

Rosenthaler Straße 40-41, Mitte, 10178 (283 5293). S3, S5, S7, S9 Hackescher Markt. **Open** 7am-1am Mon-Thur, Sun; 7am-2am Fri-Sat. **Average** DM35. **Credit** AmEx, MC, V. **Map F3**

It's huge, it's loud, it's almost always full, and the overpriced food will never win any prizes for originality. So why on earth is the Hackescher Hof so popular? Location, for one, and long opening hours, for another. If you manage to get a window table, it's not a bad place for watching the crowds over a cup of coffee or a beer.

Lutter & Wegner

Charlottenstraße 56, Mitte, 10117 (2029 5410). U6 Französischer Straße. **Open** noon-2am daily; *kitchen closes* midnight. **Average**: DM45; *bistro* DM25. **Credit** AmEx, MC, V. **Map F4**

This place has it all: history, as one of Berlin's earliest wine merchants, when its champagne became known locally as Sekt, a word now applied to all sparkling white wine; atmosphere, its airy, elegant rooms embellished with plenty of fresh flowers; great German-French cuisine; and excellent service. The wine list is justifiably legendary, and if the tariff looks high, just head for the bistro, where the same list holds sway along with perfect salads, cheese and ham plates and excellent desserts, as well as a more informal atmosphere.

Henne – *there ain't nobody here but us chickens. See page 157.*

Shootout at the gourmet corral

For years, the KaDeWe's food floor, with its overwhelming selection of edibles and cosy pavilions featuring everything from fresh oysters to pasta, has been a Berlin landmark for food fans. Who, after all, could even challenge it? Recently, an answer came: the French. When Galeries Lafayette opened on Friedrichstraße, word quickly got out that the only part worth bothering with was its basement food department. But, lacking the square metres, could the Galeries seriously compete with the KaDeWe? A recent spot-check would indicate the answer to be both yes and no.

First, Gal Laf is completely French in its orientation. This means in turn that its fish and oyster bar, its steak/frites bar, its baked-potato bar and its sandwiches (for which there's always a massive queue – allow yourself a good 15 minutes) lack any non-Francophone touch. On the

other hand, KaDeWe does offer sushi and (not-so-fantastic) Chinese food, as well as boasting a very good pasta pavilion.

KaDeWe's little pavilions are discreet, so there's no crossover with other areas; in Gal Laf, the sections bleed into each other, so that diners at a table can have selections from three different areas and still sit together. KaDeWe's pavilions are a bit dark, while Gal Laf is brightly lit. On the other hand, KaDeWe's bars have high stools, while Gal Laf puts diners below the level of the shoppers thronging the floor.

As for the groceries, KaDeWe wins in the bakery department, but of its sheer quantity, much can be found in any well-stocked Berlin supermarket. The winner? KaDeWe is still the *ne plus ultra*, but Gal Laf is homier and more intimate and let's face it, Berlin could do with a few more places like these.

Maxwell

Bergstraße 22, Mitte, 10115 (280 7121). U8 Rosenthaler Platz. **Open** 6pm-1am daily; *kitchen closes* 11.30pm. **Average** DM70. **Menus** *three courses* DM70; *four courses* DM85. **Credit** AmEx, DC, MC, V. **Map F2**

Housed in a beautifully reconstructed old brewery, set at the back of a courtyard, Maxwell is certainly worth a look to take a look at, and Uwe Popall's toothsome modern cooking is very popular with Berlin's smart set. The service can be terribly slow, the portions served are small, but nobody seems to mind when they're surrounded by so many artworks from Damien Hirst, a friend of the owner.

Paris Moskau

Alt-Moabit 141, Tiergarten, 10557 (394 2081). S3, S5, S7, S9 Lehrter Stadtbahnhof. **Open** 6-11.30pm daily. **Average** DM65. **Menu** DM80-110. **No credit cards**. **Map E3**

Once a railway workers' canteen right by the tracks which connected Paris and Moscow, this well-established place always has at least one fish dish, and often poultry and venison with Russian-French influences. It's fine fare but all save the most dedicated nouvelle cuisine fans will blanche at the portion sizes. It used to be a beautiful backwater location, but right now it's so near the Lehrter Stadtbahnhof building site that you can hear the construction work while you're eating.

Seasons

Four Seasons Hotel, Charlottenstraße 49, Mitte, 10117 (2033 6363). U2, U6 Stadtmitte. **Open** 6.30am-2.30pm, 6pm-1am, daily; *kitchen closes* 11.30pm. **Menus** *three courses* DM81; *three courses* DM94. **Credit** AmEx, DC, MC, V. **Map F4**

This restaurant offers great value for money and fine seasonal cooking. The room exudes relaxed grandeur, with large tables spaced so far apart that they allow for considerable discretion. To the dinner menus add DM13 for the admirable cheese platter and try the tortellini with mange-tout, rocket and cream cheese in a pine nut sauce and sublime *pot au feu* of lobster and sea bass with pepper crostini.

Rockendorf's Restaurant

Passauer Straße 5-7, Schöneberg, 10789. U1, U2 Wittenbergplatz. **Open** noon-1am daily; *kitchen closes* 10pm. **Credit** AmEx, DC, MC, V. **Map D4**

No sooner did *Gault-Millau* vote Siegfried Rockendorf Berlin's greatest chef than he announced that he was shutting up shop at his old haunt in the northern suburbs (lack of customers due to its isolated position) and reopening on 1 May 2000 at this address, near KaDeWe. The name remains the same, as will, presumably, his magnificent Franco-German cuisine – Rockendorf is a dynamo in the kitchen. And if he still charges a jaw-dropping DM23 for a bottle of mineral water, you can always seat yourself in his new neighbouring bistro, which will apparently offer refined versions of Berlin-Brandenburg cuisine at slightly less ruinous prices.

Vau

Jägerstraße 54-55, Mitte, 10117 (202 9730). U6 Französische Straße. **Open** noon-2.30pm, 7pm-midnight, daily. **Average** DM85. **Credit** AmEx, DC, MC, V. **Map F4**

Innovative, formal, well-designed and catering to a wealthy clientèle, Vau's reputation is due to chef Kolja Kleeberg. Try his lobster with pasta and fried rocket in lemon vinaigrette with pignoli or the duck breast cooked rare with Brussels sprouts. The wine

list is ruinously expensive and needs mid-range rein-
forcement but don't overlook the Neuburger
Beerenauslese 1995, or an equally sweet-complex
Banyuls by the glass, to go with your wine tart with
Gewurztraminer ice cream – or the superlative
cheeses. Terrific bar downstairs. Booking essential.

Moderate

Café Restaurant Jolesch

*Muskauer Straße 1, Kreuzberg, 10997 (612 3581).
U1, U12 Schlesisches Tor.* **Open** 10am-1am daily;
kitchen closes 11.30pm. **Average** DM30. **No credit
cards. Map H4**
Deservedly popular spot serving brilliant interpretations of Austrian cuisine: the goulash is thick
with hot paprika and caraway, and the Tafelspitz
is tender. There are also always at least a couple of
inventive vegetarian entrées on the daily menu, and
the soups, too, can be ingenious. Dinner reservations suggested.

Diekmann

*Meinekestraße 7, Charlottenburg, 10719 (883 3321).
U9, U15 Kurfürstendamm.* **Open** noon-1am Mon-
Sat; 6pm-1am hols. **Average** DM40. **Menu** DM55.
Credit MC, V. **Map C4**
Just off the Ku'damm, this is a former grocer's shop
remodelled into a comely restaurant. It's a big,
relaxing space in which the owners have kept most
of the old shop fittings and even a few odd products adorning the ornate shelves. Although these
have clearly been chosen for their packaging, you
can also buy some of the stuff. The menu, which
changes daily, comprises hearty portions of fine
German cuisine. The wine list is long, the music
classical and the service friendly and multilingual.

Ganymed

*Schiffbauerdamm 5, Mitte, 10117 (2859 9046). S1,
S2, S3, S5, S7, S9/U6 Friedrichstraße.* **Open** noon-
3pm, 5pm-1am, Mon-Fri; noon-1am Sat; 10am-1am
Sun. **Average** DM35. **Credit** AmEx, DC, MC, V.
Map F3
Wine is the star at this renovated holdover from the
GDR, the anchor of Mitte's new Restaurant Row.
Nothing wrong with the food, either; it's simply not
too innovative. Nor need it be, serving as a foil for
the small, but exquisitely chosen list of wines, with
an emphasis on German medal-winners.

Gugelhof

*Knaackstraße 37, Prenzlauer Berg, 10435 (442
9229). U2 Senefelderplatz.* **Open** 10am-1am daily.
Average DM40. **Menus** DM47, DM55. **Credit**
AmEx, MC, V. **Map G2**
On a corner of Kollwitzplatz, a busy establishment
that packs them in with south German and Alsatian
cuisine. It has a long and complicated meat-heavy
menu with a couple of fish and vegetarian options.
Specialities include fondue and an excellent raclette
– smoked cheese grilled on a tabletop contraption
then dished out over baked potatoes and served with
pickled onions. Biggest drawback is the lack of
elbow room – there really are too many tables for
the space – but the bar is generously proportioned
and staffed by some of the best in Berlin. Frequented
by local artists and actors during the week, it fills
with tourists and west Berliners at weekends.

Heinrich

*Sophie-Charlotten-Straße 88, Charlottenburg, 14059
(321 6517). U2 Sophie-Charlotte-Platz.* **Open** 4pm-
midnight daily. **Average** DM35. **Credit** AmEx, MC,
V. **Map B4**

Honigmond – *for a quiet neighbourhood beef stew. See page 157.*

Named after satirist and illustrator Heinrich Zille, who used to live at this address, this is the only place in Berlin where you'll find horse ragout on the same menu as buckwheat pancakes. A wide spread of vegetarian options rubs shoulders with traditional German standbys, and original wooden fittings are interspersed with Zille's photos of the area at the turn of the century. Service is courteous and unhurried, the wine list is long, the cheese soup and dandelion salads are particularly good.

Kellerrestaurant im Brecht Haus

Chausseestraße 125, Mitte, 10115 (282 3843). U6 Oranienburger Tor. **Open** *noon-1am Mon-Fri, Sun; 6pm-1am Sat.* **Average** *DM35.* **Credit** *AmEx, MC.* **Map F3**
Bertold Brecht got that sleek, well-fed look from the cooking his wife, Helene Weigel, learned in Vienna and Bohemia, and this atmospheric place, crammed with model stage sets and other Brecht memorabilia, serves up a number of her specialities, including Fleischlabberln (spicy meat patties) and a mighty Weiner Schnitzel. In summer, the garden more than doubles the capacity, but arriving after a reading at the literature forum next door can make you wish you'd reserved.

Marjellchen

Mommsenstraße 9, Charlottenburg, 10629 (883 2676). S3, S5, S7, S9 Savignyplatz. **Open** *5pm-1am Mon-Sat.* **Average** *DM45.* **Credit** *DC, JCB, MC, V.* **Map C4**
There aren't many places like this anymore, serving specialities from East Prussia, Pomerania and Silesia in an atmosphere of old-fashioned *Gemütlichkeit.* There's a beautiful bar, service is great and the larger-than-life owner likes to recite poetry and sings sometimes, too.

Offenbach-Stuben

Stubbenkammerstraße 8, Prenzlauer Berg, 10437 (445 8502). S4, S8, S10 Prenzlauer Allee. **Open** *6pm-2am daily; kitchen closes 11.30pm.* **Average** *DM35.* **Credit** *AmEx, DC, MC, V.*
An eccentric survivor from the old East Berlin, this was one of the few private restaurants operating back then, and certainly one of the best. Nothing fancy in the kitchen, just classic German cuisine prepared with top-notch ingredients and the sure skill that comes from long practice. The walls are covered with memorabilia relating to the French composer from which it takes its name, and the waiters can be very odd indeed, although they won't cancan.

stäV

Schiffbauerdamm 9, Mitte, 10117 (285 98725). S1, S2, S3, S5, S7, S9/U6 Friedrichstraße. **Open** *11am-1am daily.* **Average** *DM25.* **Credit** *MC, V.* **Map F3**
A *ständige Vertretung* ('permanent agency' – the term West Germany used for their non-embassy in the East) of the Rheinland in Berlin, stäV makes good money from homesick Bonners. Both Berliners and Rheinlanders-in-exile can dine on Himmel und Ääde ('heaven and earth' – blood sausage with mashed potatoes and apples), raisiny Rheinisch Sauerbraten, and drink Cologne's sneakily powerful

Markthalle *– Golden Teapot Award.*

beer, Kölsch, while puzzling over the political in-jokes on the wall. Good list of wines from the Rheinland, as might be expected.

Storch

Wartburgstraße 54, Schöneberg, 10823 (784 2059). U7 Eisenacher Straße. **Open** *6pm-1am daily; kitchen closes 11.30pm.* **Average** *DM38.* **No credit cards.* **Map D5**
It's hard to recommend Storch too highly. The Alsatian food – one soup starter, a sausage and sauerkraut platter, plus varying meat and fish dishes from the place where German and French cuisines rub shoulders – is finely prepared and generously proportioned. House speciality is tarte flambée: a crispy pastry base cooked in a special oven and topped with either a combination of cheese, onion and bacon or – as a dessert – with apple, cinnamon and flaming calvados. The cosmopolitan front-of-house staff are one of the best and nicest crews in Berlin. Long wooden tables are shared by different parties and the atmosphere nearly always buzzes. Not the place for a quiet chat and occasionally you get stuck next to someone you don't like, but the only real drawback here is that there's rarely very much for vegetarians – but ask the English-speaking proprietor what he can rustle up (and mention that we told you to do so) and he'll always produce something more than edible. Booking essential and no reservations accepted for after 8pm. Twice winner of the *Time Out Berlin Guide* Golden Sausage for generosity of spirit and all-round attention to detail.

Inexpensive

Café Hardenberg

Hardenbergstraße 10, Charlottenburg, 10623 (312 2644). U2 Ernst-Reuter-Platz. **Open** *9am-1am daily; kitchen closes midnight.* **Average** *DM15.* **No credit cards.* **Map C4**
Across from the Technical University, this café is usually packed with students drinking coffee. Simple, decent plates of spaghetti, omelettes, salads and sandwiches are sold at reasonable prices. It's also a good place for cheap vegetarian food.

Großbeerenkeller

Großbeerenstraße 90, Kreuzberg, 10963 (251 3064).
U1, U7, U12 Möckernbrücke. **Open** 4pm-2am Mon-
Fri; 6pm-2am Sat. **Average** DM22. **No credit
cards. Map F5**
Going strong since 1862, this cellar Kneipe is a real
institution. Berliners from all walks of life come for
the substantial Hoppel-Poppel breakfast and home-
made meat and potato dishes.

Henne

Leuschnerdamm 25, Kreuzberg, 10999 (614 7730).
U1, U8 Kottbusser Tor. **Open** 7pm-1am Wed-Sun;
kitchen closes midnight. **Average** DM15. **No credit
cards. Map G4**
Only one thing on the menu here: half a roast chick-
en. What sets Henne apart from other Imbiße with
chickens rotating in their windows is that its birds
are organically raised, milk-roasted and, in short, the
Platonic ideal of roast chicken. The only other deci-
sions are whether to have cabbage or potato salad
(we'd say cabbage) and which beer to wash it down
with (try Bavarian Mönchshof). Check the letter from
JFK over the bar, regretting missing dinner here.

Honigmond

Borsigstraße 28, Mitte, 10115 (2854 4550). U6
Zinnowitzer Straße. **Open** noon-2am Mon-Fri; 9am-
2am Sat-Sun. **Average** DM25. **No credit cards.
Map F2**
This quiet, neighbourhood place serves up traditional Königsberger Klöpse and beef stew alongside
a bi-weekly menu of innovative dishes using strictly fresh local ingredients in surroundings designed
to evoke a 1920s nostalgia without overdoing it.
Excellent small wine list, lunch dishes, and remarkable home-made bread. Small hotel upstairs, too.

Marché

*Kurfürstendamm 14, Charlottenburg, 10719 (882
7578). U9, U15 Kurfürstendamm.* **Open** 8am-
midnight daily. **Average** DM20. **Credit** AmEx, V.
Map C4
Healthy and freshly prepared food is what you'll find
here, not ambience. This Swiss-owned chain offers
vegetables, meats and desserts at various stands,
buffet-fashion. Mood livens in summer when tables
are set out on the pavement.

Markthalle

*Pücklerstraße 34, Kreuzberg, 10977 (617 5502). U1,
U12 Görlitzer Bahnhof.* **Open** 8am-2am Mon-Thur,
Sun; 8am-4am Fri-Sat; *kitchen closes* midnight.
Average DM24. **No credit cards. Map H4**
This unpretentious restaurant and bar, with chunky
tables and wood-panelled walls, has become a
Kreuzberg institution. They serve breakfasts until
5pm, salads from noon, and in the evening a selec-
tion of filling and reasonably priced meals, though
the kitchen is nothing to write home about.
Afterwards pop down into the basement club Privat
or over the road for a drink in the Der Goldene Hahn
(*see chapter* **Nightlife**). Good selection of grappa.
The loveable weekend bar-staff bag the *Time Out
Berlin Guide* Golden Teapot for most enjoyably
camp crew in town.

Tiergarten Quelle

*Stadtbahnbogen 482, Bachstraße, near Haydnstraße,
Tiergarten, 10555 (392 7615). S3, S5, S7, S9
Tiergarten.* **Open** 11am-midnight Mon-Fri; 11am-
1am Sat-Sun; *kitchen closes* 5pm. **Average** DM20.
No credit cards. Map D3
TU students jam this funky bar for huge servings
of the food Grandma used to make: potatoes with
quark and linseed oil; pork medallions with tomatoes and melted cheese with Käsespätzle; mixed grill
with sauerkraut; Maultaschen on spinach, and to
wash it down, stone litre mugs of foaming
Schultheiss beer. The Kaiserschmarren at DM9.50
is a meal in itself. Go when school's out of session or
you'll never get a table.

The world on your plate

African

Café Asmarino

Grunewaldstraße 82, Schöneberg, 10823 (782 7282).
U7 Eisenacher Straße. **Open** 5pm-1am Tue-Sun.
Average DM20. **No credit cards. Map D5**
Quiet, friendly establishment offering Eritrean specialities mostly hingeing on *ingera*, a millet pancake
either rolled and stuffed or used to mop up sauces,
with beef, chicken and vegetable accompaniments.
More interesting than excellent, but a genuine
change from more common cuisines.

Americas

Andy's Diner & Bar

*Potsdamer Straße 1, Mitte, 10785 (2300 4990). S1,
S2/U2 Potsdamer Platz.* **Open** 9am-3am daily;
kitchen closes 2am. **Average** DM25. **Credit** AmEx,
MC, V. **Map E4**
Avert your eyes from the decor and the sports TVs,
avoid the hamburgers and milkshakes (which are
presented as 'health food'), and dig into a pretty good
steak, or come for breakfast and enjoy authentic
American-style pancakes and eggs. Film Festival-
goers, in particular, will find this place convenient.

Hard Rock Café

Meinekestraße 21, Charlottenburg, 10719 (884 620).
U9, U15 Kurfürstendamm. **Open** noon-2am daily;
kitchen closes midnight. **Average** DM35. **Credit** AmEx,
JCB, MC, V. **Map C4**
It is with deep regret that we announce that Berlin's
best hamburger is to be found in this loud, pricey
chain – but it's true. It may cost DM14.50, but it's a
winner. Other main courses are forgettable, but onion
rings and chicken wings also score for authenticity
and the desserts are a study in American overkill.

Jimmy's Diner

Pariser Straße 41, Wilmersdorf, 10707 (882 3141).
U1 Hohenzollernplatz. **Open** 11am-2am Mon-Thur,
Sun; 11am-4am Fri-Sat. **Average** DM15. **No credit
cards. Map C5**
The grand old man of Berlin American restaurants,
Jimmy's has inspired a raft of inferior copies with
its scrupulously authentic decor, decent (albeit

Trattoria Lappeggi – *hamming it up, p161.*

frozen) hamburgers and big portions. Despite the fluorescent lighting, it's a mecca for late-night meals and gets pretty loud at times.

Joy

Sredzkistraße 30, Prenzlauer Berg, 10435 (442 2578). U2 Eberswalder Straße. **Open** 4pm-2am daily. **Average** DM20. **No credit cards. Map G2**

A typical 'American' restaurant for Berlin: half the menu is faux-Mexican, the hamburger patties are the same frozen ones that everyone else uses, and the ubiquitous college-kid cocktails. What is good about Joy, however, are the blackboard specials, the fried catfish and, each November, an authentic Thanksgiving dinner.

Las Cucarachas

Oranienburger Straße 38, Mitte, 10115 (282 2044). S1, S2 Oranienburger Straße. **Average** DM20. **Credit** AmEx, MC, V. **Map F3**

Chileans in the kitchen mean an odd take on Mexican food at times, and between the blaring salsa and the margarita-fuelled customers, the noise level can be unbearable, but Las Cucs (named after Villa's revolutionaries, not any kitchen denizens) is a popular hangout for tourists and expats. The Lone Star branch emphasises tacos, including fine tacos al pastor, and is altogether more relaxing. Watch out for the crap mariachis, though.

Branch: Lone Star Taqueria, Bergmannstraße 11, Kreuzberg, 10691 (692 7182).

Café Nola

Dortmunder Straße 9, Tiergarten, 10555 (399 6969). U9 Turmstraße. **Open** 9.30am-1am daily; *kitchen closes* 11.30pm. **Average** DM22. **Credit** AmEx, MC. **Map D3**

Two Swiss chefs bravely attempt Californian cuisine in this uncharacteristically picturesque corner of Moabit, and, more often than not, succeed. A light hand on the sauces with fruit and chillies providing some of the flavour, an emphasis on fish and vegetarian entrées, as well as a well-chosen wine list with some unusual Chilean and South African bottles add up to a refreshingly un-Berlinisch dining experience.

¡Viva México!

Chausseestraße 36, Mitte, 10115 (280 7865). U6 Zinnowitzer Straße. **Open** noon-11pm Mon-Fri; 2pm-midnight Sat; 5pm-midnight Sun. **Average** DM15. **No credit cards. Map E2**

A true find: a Mexican woman and her family preparing authentic interior Mexican food in Berlin. Home-made refried beans and at least four salsas (three of which are good and spicy) to put on your tacos, burritos and tortas, plus a decent range of dinner items. This place would be good in Mexico, let alone Germany, and they do catering, as well. A bit out of the way, but worth the trip.

Chinese

Ostwind

Husemannstraße 13, Prenzlauer Berg, 10435 (441 5951). U2 Senefelderplatz. **Open** 6pm-1am Mon-Sat; 10am-1am Sun. **Average** DM25. **No credit cards. Map G2**

Good Chinese food is rare in Berlin, so Ostwind's stabs at authenticity are welcome. True, some of it is pretty bland, but such light dishes as dan-dan noodles sauced with spicy meat and bean-sauce, or steamed dumplings with pork and vegetables, make a great lunch. Main courses are, by Chinese tradition, keyed to the seasons and change four times a year. It's not all great, but choose carefully and you'll be rewarded with superb country cooking of a sort rarely found in Chinese restaurants anywhere.

French

Bistro Chez Maurice

Bötzowstraße 39, Prenzlauer Berg, 10407 (4280 4723). S4, S8, S10 Greifswalder Straße/bus 257. **Open** noon-midnight daily. **Average** DM25. **Credit** MC, V.

French food is hard enough to come by in Berlin, let alone solid working-class fare like this. The low prices are deceptive, due to a supplement system for many of the items on offer, but you won't regret the extra expenditure. Service is sometimes manic and there aren't any grands crus on the wine-list, but the portions are good, the preparation excellent, and if you like what you had, you can come back to the delicatessen next door and buy the ingredients.

Paris Bar

Kantstraße 152, Charlottenburg, 10623, (313 8052).
S1, S5, S7, S9 Savignyplatz. **Open** noon-2am daily;
kitchen closes 1am. **Average** DM50. **Credit** AmEx.
Map C4
Berlin's most eclectic dining-room. It has always
been next to impossible to get a table here during
the Berlin Film Festival, and the stars and wannabes
may still be flocking here from the Sony Center as
there is nowhere to eat in and around Potsdamer
Platz. But honestly, DM90 for a dozen oysters is just
outrageous – as is the contumely of the arrogant
waiters. Much of the art on the walls has been
swapped by the daubers for a free feed. Excellent
spot for lunch.

Ty Breizh

Kantstraße 75, Charlottenburg, 10627 (323 9932).
U7 Wilmersdorfer Straße. **Open** 5pm-1am Mon-Fri;
6pm-2am Sat; *kitchen closes* 11pm. **Average** DM35.
No credit cards. Map B4

A mad place. The 'Breton House' specialises in two
geographically opposed French cuisines: Breton and
Savoyarde. This slight schizophrenia is reflected in
le patron's physique; he has half a moustache on his
lip, tends to burst into song, opens his oysters with
a drill, plays games and performs tricks for the
guests and hand-paints every bill personally. Good,
if slightly overpriced – and indisputably unique.

Greek

Skales

Rosenthaler Straße 12, Mitte, 10119 (283 3006). U8
Weinmeisterstraße. **Open** 5pm-1am Mon-Thur, Sun;
5pm-3am Fri-Sat. **Average** DM35. **Credit** AmEx,
DC, MC, V. **Map F3**
To look at this huge, high-ceilinged room, you'd
never guess that it was once a storage space for uniforms and other paraphernalia of the Freie Deutsche
Jugend, the GDR's youth organisation. It's gone
through a severe ideological change, too: the often

One good idea

Basing a restaurant around one ingredient
sounds like either a gimmick or a not-very-rev-
olutionary idea, depending on how you look at
it. After all, doesn't a seafood restaurant specialise in fish? A steakhouse in steak? Aren't
most German restaurants erected on a foundation of pork?

But narrowing down the focus can provide a
creative cooking team with a challenge, and
recently Berlin has seen some single-ingredient
places open which, their gimmicky potential
notwithstanding, can provide not just food, but
food for thought.

The one which has grabbed all the press
recently is **Knofel**, the all-garlic restaurant. Its
name is a slangy version of *Knoblauch* (garlic)
and chef Mario Brand is certainly a fan of the
pungent bulb. Here, everything from appetizer
to dessert is redolent of garlic, although it's not
all as successful as it could be because of
Germans' innate mistrust of ethnic foods. What
Brand has mostly done is to adapt various
German dishes by lacing them with his preferred seasoning, with greater or lesser success.
Garlic soups, of course, are a long-standing
Mediterranean tradition, as is the famous
Provençal chicken with 40 cloves of garlic, and
these work very well, as does a garlicked variation on the traditional Bratkartoffeln. The
Hackbraten, basically a meatloaf, is also excel-
lent, but the so-called Banditen-Spieß, garlic-
marinated beef cubes on a skewer with slices of
bell pepper and raw garlic cloves, is not. Nor is

the garlic ice-cream, basically vanilla ice cream
with raw garlic spun into it, nor the garlic
Schnapps, both versions of which were rank
with the raw taste. Still, if you're intent on foil-
ing vampires and choose wisely, you can get a
good meal here.

Closer to the locals' hearts is the potato, first
grown in Germany at Schloß Monbijou, which
stood where you'll now find Monbijou Park on
Oranienburger Straße. There are at least two all-
potato restaurants in town, the best of which is
Kartoffelkeller, in a cellar on Albrechtstraße
near Friedrichstraße station. Potato soups, salads, casseroles, pancakes and, yes, dessert and
Schnapps (the latter unsurprising, since cheap
vodka has been made from potatoes since time
immemorial) are the stars here, and the German
devotion to the humble tuber is reflected in a
packed house night after night. Nothing particularly revolutionary here, but, rather, a hymn to
the many uses this country, and particularly this
region, has wrung out of the Kartoffel.

Knofel

Wichertstraße 33a/Dunckerstraße 2, Prenzlauer
Berg, 10439 (447 6717). S4, S8, S10
Schönhauser Allee. **Open** 6pm-1am Mon-Thur;
2pm-1am Fri; 1pm-1am Sat-Sun. **Average** DM25.
Credit AmEx, MC, V. **Map G1**

Kartoffelkeller

Albrechtstraße 14b, Mitte, 10117 (282 8548). S1,
S2, S3, S5, S7, S9/U6 Friedrichstraße. **Open**
11am-1am daily. **Average** DM20. **Credit** AmEx,
MC, V. **Map F3**

Sale e Tabacchi – *minimalist design, impeccable trattoria cooking. See page 164.*

snooty service matches the often snooty customers, but at least the Greek food is well prepared and worth the tariff, and it's an alternative to the many Italian eateries in this neighbourhood.

Indian

Chandra Kumari
Gneisenaustraße 4, Kreuzberg, 10961 (694 3056). U6, U7 Mehringdamm. **Open** noon-1am daily. **Average** DM20. **No credit cards**. **Map F5**
Authentic Sri Lankan food at this and its Prenzlauer Berg branch, including fiery curries, many involving exotic vegetables like jackfruit, others with organic Neuland meat. Try the hoppers (a cross between pasta and crêpes) instead of rice if you're there on a day when they're offered, and cool down afterwards with an avocado milkshake. There's usually a wait, but it's worth it.
Branch: Suriya Kanthi, Knaackstraße 4, Prenzlauer Berg, 10405 (442 5101).

India Haus
Feurigstraße 38/corner Dominicusstraße, Schöneberg, 10827 (781 2546). U4 Rathaus Schöneberg. **Open** 5pm-midnight Mon-Fri; noon-1am Sat-Sun. **Average** DM28. **Credit** AmEx, DC, V. **Map D6**
Though more and more places are opening, Berlin is not a great town for Indian food and most places seem to have the same menu. India Haus is a cut above. Just off Schöneberg's Hauptstraße and near the Odeon cinema, it offers a long menu with wide choices for vegetarians. The almond soup is excellent and the malay kofta delicious, but avoid the chicken tikka – the bird comes dry and the sauce is too hot. There's a cheaper Imbiß attached.

Kashmir Palace
Marburger Straße 14, Charlottenburg, 10789 (214 2840). U1 Augsburger Straße. **Open** 5pm-midnight Mon, Sun; noon-3pm, 6pm-midnight, Tue-Fri; noon-midnight Sat. **Average** DM35. **Credit** AmEx, DC, JCB, V. **Map D4**

This upmarket curry house is a life saver if you're in bad need of an authentic Mughlai or tandoori dish. The portions are small, the setting is formal and the clientèle can include anyone from Indian businesspeople to travel story-swapping trekkers of the subcontinent just back from their latest expedition. No one eats with their fingers, though.

Surya
Grolmanstraße 22, Charlottenburg, 10623 (312 9123). S3, S5, S7, S9 Savignyplatz. **Open** noon-1am daily. **Average** DM25. **No credit cards**. **Map E5**
A fairly standard range of Indian food, done particularly well, has turned this place into an institution as well as one of the more affordable options on this ritzy street. With a bit of encouragement the chef will up the spice levels, as the service is top-drawer.

Italian

Café Aroma
Hochkirchstraße 8, Schöneberg, 10829 (782 5821). S1, S2/U7 Yorckstraße. **Open** 6pm-1am Mon-Fri; noon-midnight Sat-Sun. **Average** DM35. **Menu** DM30. **No credit cards**. **Map E5**
A temple of Tuscanophilia, Café Aroma has informal language classes on Sunday mornings, a wide selection of Italian magazines to read and some of the best northern Italian food in Berlin, with a wine list and wide variety of wines by the glass to match it. Appetisers and pastas are so good you may never stray over to the main dishes, but if you do, all the meat is organic. Reservations advised.

Cantamaggio
Alte Schönhauser Straße 4, Mitte, 10119 (283 1895). U2 Rosa-Luxemburg-Platz. **Open** 7pm-1am daily. **Average** DM40. **Credit** AmEx, DC, MC, V. **Map G3**
One of the longest-lasting 'new' restaurants in Mitte; and, since it's out of the hot centres of activity, this must be down to the superbly made food. That said, it's had its share of disappointingly uninspired

moments of late, which, to be fair, may have been as much to do with the time of year we visited as a failure of creativity in the kitchen. Tables are also uncomfortably close to each other, but on a good night everyone's too absorbed with their food to pay attention to what you're saying.

Ristorante Chamisso

Willibald-Alexis-Straße 25, Kreuzberg, 10965 (691 5642). U6 Platz der Luftbrücke. **Open** 6pm-1am daily. **Average** DM35. **Credit** DC, MC, V. **Map F5**
Excellent and charming Italian neighbourhood joint by picturesque Chamissoplatz – a wonderfully quiet and leafy spot to sit outside in summer – offering daily menus of fresh pastas, inventive salads and other authentic Italian dishes.

Enoteca Il Calice

Giesebrechtstraße 19, Charlottenburg, 10629 (324 2308). U7 Adenauerplatz. **Open** 6am-1am daily; *kitchen closes* midnight. **Average** DM50. **Credit** AmEx, V. **Map B5**
One for the wine enthusiast – a relaxed place serving mostly Italian food conceived to complement its 40-page list of bottles. Many of the wines are listed with full and rather fruity descriptions; there's also a selection of rather complicated offers, including menus of seasonal specialities (DM69) with recommended bottles, and staff will organise a Weinkarusell with four wines, all of one grape or region, for your own private tasting (DM340 for six people). Carpaccio is a speciality and six fin-de-Claire oysters will set you back DM24. Staff are friendly and will help you through it all.

Gorgonzola Club

Dresdener Straße 121, Kreuzberg, 10999 (615 6473). U1, U8, U12 Kottbusser Tor. **Open** 6pm-midnight Mon-Thur, Sun; 6pm-2am Fri-Sat.
Average DM35. **No credit cards. Map G4**
Popular place with a very simple Italian menu. In front you'll find a bar area with tables where you can also eat. An appealing main dining space leads you through to a rather gloomy back room which is probably best avoided. The authentic pizzas run between DM11-19. Spaghetti, tagliatelli, gnocchi or ravioli are served with a choice of basic sauces including, of course, gorgonzola. The salad selection is excellent. It's handy before or after an English-language movie at the Babylon cinema (*see chapter* **Film**) down the road, or before sinking a few drinks at the Würgeengel (*see chapter* **Nightlife**).

Trattoria da Enzo

Großbeerenstraße 60, Kreuzberg, 10965 (785 8372). U6, U7 Mehringdamm. **Open** 6pm-1am daily; *kitchen closes* midnight. **Average** DM30. **No credit cards. Map F5**
A bustling little place that serves up authentic pizzas and recommended pasta dishes as well as commendable meat, chicken and a decent antipasti selection. You can wash it all down with a philanthropically priced Salentino.

Trattoria Lappeggi

Kollwitzstraße 56, Prenzlauer Berg, 10405 (442 6347). U2 Senefelderplatz. **Open** 10am-2am daily; *kitchen closes* 11pm. **Average** DM50. **Credit** AmEx, MC, V. **Map G2**

Schwarzenraben – *chicest of Berlin's Italian joints. See page 164.*

What's on the menu

The traditional Berlin menu revolves around a holy trinity of pork, cabbage, and potatoes. Locals say the signature dish is Eisbein, an incredibly fatty hunk of pork, but this may be a ploy to frighten non-Berliners. Although many restaurants have English translations on their menus, not all are terribly accurate: we still remember the Chinese place with the sign in its window declaring 'We have Crap!' Best, then, to absorb a little vocabulary before venturing out.

Useful phrases

I'd like to reserve a table for... people. **Ich möchte eine Tisch für... Personen reservieren.**
Are these places free? **Sind diese Plätze frei?**
The menu, please. **Die Speisekarte, bitte.**
I am a vegetarian. **Ich bin Vegetarier.**
I am a diabetic. **Ich bin Diabetiker.**
We'd/I'd like to order. **Wir möchten/Ich möchte bestellen.**
We'd/I'd like to pay. **Bezahlen, bitte.**

Basics

Frühstück breakfast
Mittagessen lunch
Abendessen dinner
Imbiß snack
Vorspeise appetiser
Hauptgericht main course
Nachspeise dessert
Besteck cutlery
Brot/Brötchen bread/rolls
Butter butter
Ei/Eier egg/eggs
Spiegeleier fried eggs
Rühreier scrambled eggs
Gemüse vegetables
Käse cheese
Fleisch meat
Fisch fish
Obst or **Fruchte** fruit
Nudeln/Teigwaren noodles/pasta
Soße sauce
Salz salt
Pfeffer pepper
gekocht boiled
gebraten fried/roasted
paniert breaded/battered
nach...Art in the style of...

Soups (Suppen)

Bohnensuppe bean soup
Brühe broth
Erbsensuppe pea soup
Hühnersuppe chicken soup
klare Brühe mit Leberknödeln clear broth with liver dumplings
Kraftbrühe clear meat broth
Linsensuppe lentil soup

Meat, poultry and game (Fleisch, Geflügel und Wild)

Ente duck
Gans goose
Hackfleisch ground meat/mince
Hirsch venison
Huhn/Hühnerfleisch chicken
Hähnchen chicken (when served in one piece)
Kaninchen rabbit
Hase hare
Kohlrouladen cabbage-rolls stuffed with pork
Kotelett chop
Lamm lamb
Leber liver
Nieren kidneys
Puter turkey
Rindfleisch beef
Sauerbraten marinated roast beef
Schinken ham
Schnitzel thinly pounded piece of meat, usually breaded and sautéed
Schweinebraten roast pork
Schweinefleisch pork
Speck bacon
Truthahn turkey
Wachtel quail
Wurst sausage

Fish (Fisch)

Aal eel
Forelle trout
Garnelen prawns
Hummer lobster
Kabeljau cod
Karpfen carp
Krabbe crab or shrimp
Lachs salmon
Makrele mackerel
Matjes/Hering raw herring
Miesmuscheln mussels
Schellfisch haddock
Scholle plaice
Seezunge sole
Tintenfisch squid
Thunfisch tuna
Venusmuscheln clams
Zander pike-perch

Herbs and spices (Kräuter und Gewürze)

Basilikum basil
Kümmel caraway
Kürbiskerne pumpkin-seeds
Mohn poppy-seed
Nelken cloves
Origanum oregano
Petersilie parsley
Sonnenblumekerne sunflower seeds
Thymian thyme
Zimt cinnamon

Vegetables (Gemüse)

Blumenkohl cauliflower
Bohnen beans
Bratkartoffeln fried potatoes
Brechbohnen green beans
Champignons/Pilze mushrooms
Erbsen green peas
Erdnüsse peanuts
Feldsalat lamb's lettuce
grün Zwiebel spring onion
Gurke cucumber
Kartoffel potato
Knoblauch garlic
Knödel dumpling
Kohl cabbage
Kürbis pumpkin
Linsen lentils
Möhren carrots
Paprika peppers
Pommes chips
Rosenkohl Brussels sprouts
Rösti Swiss grated roast potatoes
rote Bete beetroot
Rotkohl red cabbage
Salat lettuce
Salzkartoffeln boiled potatoes
Sauerkraut shredded white cabbage
Schwarzwurzel comfrey root
Spargel asparagus
Steinpilze boletus mushrooms
Tomaten tomatoes
Zwiebeln onions

Fruit (Obst)

Ananas pineapple
Apfel apple
Apfelsine orange (increasingly rare)
Birne pear
Erdbeeren strawberries
Granatapfel pomegranate
Heidelbeeren blueberries
Himbeeren raspberries
Kirsch cherry
Limette lime
Stachelbeeren gooseberries
Zitrone lemon

Drinks (Getränke)

Bier beer
dunkles Bier dark beer
Glühwein mulled wine
helles Bier lager, light beer
Kaffee coffee
Mineralwasser mineral water
Orangensaft orange juice
Saft juice
Sprudelwasser sparkling mineral water
Tafelwasser still water
Tee tea
Wein wine

Big, lively and fashionable place, with windows that overlook Kollwitzplatz, serving up a variety of well-prepared and beautifully presented Italian regional dishes to a mixed clientèle of every age and from every scene. The pasta is particularly good. The crew are all Italian and mostly seem to be friends, which adds to the atmosphere although you suspect they're hamming it up a bit. Between noon and 5pm, there's a salad and pasta menu (DM15) and a soup, pasta and dessert menu (DM19). Chairs and tables set outside in summertime.

Trattoria á Muntagnola

Fuggerstraße 27, Schöneberg, 10777 (211 6642). U4 Viktoria-Luise-Platz. **Open** 4pm-1am daily; *kitchen closes* midnight. **Average** DM35. **Credit** AmEx, MC, V. **Map D5**
Berlin's first family – literally – of southern Italian food. Muntagnola is the flagship, Contadino its eastern branch, and La Rustica a new pizzeria. All feature huge portions with an authenticity rare in Berlin, waiters who speak heavily-accented German, home-baked sourdough bread, rustic china and a superbly chosen wine list. The two larger places require reservations because they're jammed nightly with diners enjoying perfectly cooked pastas and secondi. Meanwhile, at La Rustica, the pizzas may be twice as expensive as at other pizzerias but they're twice as good. La Rustica also serves a couple of non-pizza selections from the blackboard and is one of Mitte's best lunch bargains. All are seriously addictive.
Branches: Al Contadino Sotto Le Stelle, Auguststraße 34, Mitte, 10119 (281 9023); La Rustica, Kleine Präsidentenstraße 4, Mitte, 10178 (218 9179).

Trattoria Paparazzi

Husemannstraße 35, Prenzlauer Berg, 10435 (440 7333). U2 Senefelderplatz. **Open** 6pm-midnight daily; *kitchen closes* 11pm. **Average** DM30. **No credit cards. Map G2**
Hiding behind a truly stupid name and a fairly ordinary façade is one of Berlin's best Italian restaurants, with the awards to prove it. Cornerstone dishes are malfatti, pasta rolls seasoned with sage, and strangolapretti, 'priest stranglers', of pasta, cheese and spinach with tiny slivers of ham – but pay attention to daily specials. The southern Italian waiters can be a bit spaced out, but they get the job done. Excellent house wines, but few others; reservations a must.

Petite Europe

Langenscheidtstraße 1, Schöneberg, 10827 (781 2964). U7 Kleistpark. **Open** 5pm-1am daily. **Average** DM30. **No credit cards. Map E5**
Rough-and-ready neighbourhood Italian joint serving decent and well-priced food. It's acceptable rather than exceptional fare but vegetarians get a wide choice, and all diners get a free bruschetta before and a free grappa after the meal. Avoid any salad except the rucola variations. Staff work their arses off and however crowded this bustling place gets (expect a short wait mid-evening), the prompt service rarely falters. Occasional Phil Collins in the background earns the only black mark.

Mäcky Messer – *innovative sushi.*

Sale e Tabacchi
Kochstraße 18, Kreuzberg, 10969 (252 1155). U6 Kochstraße. **Open** 9am-2am daily; *kitchen closes* midnight. **Average** DM40. **Credit** MC, V. **Map F4**
Attractions here are minimalist design and impeccable trattoria cooking. Artichokes alla romana, linguini with fresh clams and mussels, rucola and parmesan salad and decent wines at fair prices keep the place packed – especially with architects. Portions, however, tend to be quite small. The front of the house serves as a café, where you can sip a fine espresso while watching the Kochstraße scene.

Schwarzenraben
Neue Schönhauser Straße 13, Mitte, 10178 (2839 1698). U8 Weinmeisterstraße. **Open** 11am-2am daily; *kitchen closes* midnight. **Average** DM40. **Credit** AmEx, V. **Map G3**
Some contend that so many of Berlin's young film and theatre stars eat here because they're non-paying shills to draw other punters to owner Rudolf H Girolo's most chic of Berlin's Italo-Mediterranean joints. Savour, if you can, overpriced, banal Italian food (and wildly overpriced wine) surrounded by pseudo film stars. Service with a snarl. Hugely popular, hugely overrated, although the downstairs club sometimes features interesting DJs and live acts.

XII Apostoli
Savigny Passage, Bleibtreustraße 49, Charlottenburg, 10623 (312 1433). S3, S5, S7, S9 Savignyplatz. **Open** 24 hours daily. **Average** DM40. **No credit cards.** **Map C4**
It's overcrowded, it's cramped, it's pricey, the service varies from rushed to rude, the music is trad jazz doodling irritatingly at the very edge of perception – but the pizzas are excellent and, more to the point, it's open 24 hours. Excellent selection of breakfast pastries. The same goes in all respects for the Mitte branch.
Branch: S-Bahnbogen 177-180, Georgenstraße, Mitte, 10117 (201 0222).

Japanese

Mäcky Messer
Mulackstraße 29, Mitte, 10119 (283 4942). U8 Weinmeisterstraße. **Open** 6pm-midnight Tue-Sun. **Average** DM35. **No credit cards.** **Map G3**
A German sushi chef wouldn't inspire consumer confidence in most, but the craftsman who runs this tiny place is a master of traditional and innovative sushi dishes – no surprise, therefore, that he's from Hamburg, where they know fish. Add to that the Oriental-influenced soups and usually a fusion dish or two as a daily special, and you've got one of Berlin's best meals at the price. Extra points for the sharks carved from radishes.

Sabu
Damaschketraße 31, Wilmersdorf, 10711 (327 4488). U7 Adenauerplatz. **Open** noon-1am Mon-Fri; 6pm-1am Sat. **Average** DM45. **Menu** DM80. **Credit** MC, V. **Map B5**
Probably the best Japanese restaurant in Berlin. A smart, white place with a calm atmosphere serving traditional dishes given an individual slant. The tempura is heavenly, the noodle soups are the stuff of legend, and the sushi is so good that this is the restaurant of choice for sushi chefs from other Japanese places. It's on a quiet street and there's a tiny veranda with a table for two that's wonderful on summer nights – if you can get it.

Sachiko Sushi
Grolmanstraße 47, Charlottenburg, 10623 (313 2282). S3, S5, S7, S9 Savignyplatz. **Open** noon-midnight Mon-Sat; 4pm-midnight Sun. **Average** DM20. **Credit** AmEx, MC, V. **Map C4**
Not just Berlin's best sushi bar, but its first kaiten sushi ('revolving sushi') joint. The scrummy morsels come round on little boats that circumnavigate a chrome and black stone bar. Inevitably packed with upmarket Charlottenburg 30- and 40-somethings.

Udagawa
Feuerbachstraße 24, Steglitz, 12163 (792 2373) S1 Feuerbachstraße. **Open** 6pm-1am daily; *kitchen closes* 11pm. **Average** DM50. **Credit** AmEx, MC, V.
This small, somewhat out-of-the-way eaterie has it all, from fresh sushi, sashimi and tempura down to humbler noodle dishes. Worth the detour, but lacking in intimacy due to its lack of space.

Middle Eastern

Café Oren

*Oranienburger Straße 28, Mitte, 10117 (282 8228).
S1, S2 Oranienburger Straße.* **Open** 10am-1am
daily; *kitchen closes* midnight. **Average** DM27.
Credit AmEx, V. **Map F3**

A Jewish (not kosher) restaurant right next to the
Neue Synagoge and offering standard fish and vegetarian dishes with Middle Eastern specialities.
The garlic cream soup is thick and tasty, the salad
fresh and crispy, and the soya cutlet breaded with
sesame, in a light curry sauce served with fried
banana and rice, is absolutely heavenly. There's an
excellent vegetarian borscht and the Orient
Express platter, a large selection of meze, is very
good value indeed. As bustly as Oranienburger
Straße outside, it's best to book. Summer tables in
the courtyard. Breakfast too.

Mesa

*Paretzer Straße 5, Wilmersdorf, 10713 (822 5364).
U1 Heidelberger Platz.* **Open** 4pm-midnight daily.
Average DM38. **Credit** V. **Map C6**

Out of the way but worth the effort. This classy
Lebanese restaurant serves up neat variations on
the usual staples. There are lots of lamb and chick-
en dishes, couscous, and plenty for vegetarians –
try the vegetable *rosti* that comes with three dip-
ping sauces and the spicy lentil soup. It's a classy
kind of place, elegant and with a relaxed atmosphere. Egyptian cigarettes are on sale and free
Lebanese chiclets arrive with the bill.

Pacific rim

Angkor Wat

*Seelingstraße 36, Charlottenburg. 14059 (325 5994).
U2 Sophie-Charlotte-Platz.* **Open** 6-11.30pm Mon-
Thur, Sun; noon-11.30pm Fri-Sat. **Average** DM25.
No credit cards. **Map B3**

Extraordinarily friendly service and exotic decor
make this a good spot for dinner. Spicy Cambodian
food – think twice before asking for extra hot. Try
the cold ricepaper rolls stuffed with shrimp, or the
beef with Asian aubergine and coconut sauce.

Fournier

*Gipsstraße 3, Mitte, 10119 (283 86622). U8
Weinmeisterstraße.* **Open** noon-1am daily.
Average DM40. **Credit** AmEx, MC, V. **Map F3**

Berlin's art scene sighed in relief when Fournier reopened in late 1999, since this had been one of its
top hangouts. Redecorated from its previous stark-
ness, it still features Pacific Rim cuisine at its finest,
with the rice served in appealingly cheesy plastic
Thai buckets. Vegetarians are well taken care of,
fish-lovers too, and the soups are good enough to
support a little soup bar in the basement, which is
open late on weekends. Asian food, so why the
French name? A tribute to the owner's grandmother, who inspired him to become a chef.

Shima

*Schwäbische Straße 5, Schöneberg, 10781 (211
1990). U7 Eisenacher Straße.* **Open** 6pm-2am daily;
kitchen closes midnight. **Average** DM40. **Credit**
MC, V. **Map D5**

Shima – *cosmopolitan Asian fusion on a quiet Schöneberg corner.*

An innovative 'Asian fusion' menu originally conceived by the Canadian 'food designer' Gordon W (now at **Wasserwelt**, *see below*) has been drawing diners to this quiet Schöneberg corner since Shima first opened in 1999. Gado gado, dim sum and satay mingle on a menu that also offers chapatis (the Indian bread served with a cosmopolitan variety of accompaniments), various noodle dishes and outstanding soups. There's a neat cocktail lounge area to complement a dining space that spills on to pavement tables in summer. Service is cool and efficient, though sometimes the kitchen can take its time.

Wasserwelt
Altonaer Straße 20, Tiergarten, 10557 (3990 6933). U7 Hansaplatz. **Open** 11am-3am daily. **Average** DM35. **No credit cards**. **Map D3**
The folks who gave us the Zoulou Bar and Mr. Hu's (*see chapter* **Nightlife**) have now taken the full leap to restauranthood, and have wisely chosen Indian-trained Canadian chef Gordon W to supervise a wide-ranging fusion menu featuring hearty American breakfasts, moderately-priced lunches, and a maddeningly large choice for vegetarians. Other attractions include the bar, with its freshly-pressed juices, including low- and no-alcohol cocktails, and the beer-garden, studded with illuminated world globes, which has its own wok and tandoori cooks in summertime. Decor's a bit odd, but you probably won't notice because the food's so good. *Website: www.restaurant-wasserwelt.de*

Woolloomooloo
Röntgenstraße 7, Charlottenburg, 10587 (3470 2777). U7 Richard-Wagner-Platz. **Open** 5pm-1am daily. **Average** DM30. **No credit cards**. **Map C3**
The name is Aboriginal for 'where the waters cross' – it's close by where two canals intersect the river Spree – and this is an Australian restaurant serving kangaroo or ostrich steak, stir-fried crocodile and other delights from Down Under with a lot of Thai and Japanese influences on the preparation. An interior of exposed brickwork, good and cheery service. Surprisingly few actual Aussies in evidence, but there's a long and authoritative list of Australian wines.

Portuguese

Casa Portuguesa
Helmholtzstraße 15, Tiergarten, 10587 (393 5506). U9 Turmstraße. **Open** 5pm-1am Mon-Sat; noon-1am Sun. **Average** DM40. **Credit** MC, V. **Map D3**
Do what the regulars do – despite a commendable *bacalhau* (salt cod – 24 hours' notice required) ignore the menu and order a fresh salad, an honest vinho verde and whatever fish is chalked up on the board to experience the best grilled fish in Berlin.

Russian

Pasternak
Knaackstraße 22-24, Prenzlauer Berg, 10405 (441 3399). U2 Senefelderplatz. **Open** 10am-2am daily. **Average** DM27. **No credit cards**. **Map G2**

Monsieur Vuong *– a true oasis. Page 168.*

Book at least a day in advance if you want to dine in this small bar and Russian restaurant on Prenzl'berg's most chic corner: it's usually crammed to the gunnels, which can be irritating as people constantly brush past you looking for places. Try for a table in the small back room. The staff also let buskers in to play, so avoid if you don't want to hear ancient Neil Young songs strangled to death. But the atmosphere is friendly and the food fine and filling. Kick off with the borscht or the ample fish plate, then broach the pel'meni or vareniki – Russian ravioli filled with either meat or potatoes – or the hearty beef Stroganoff.

Thai

Kien-du
Kaiser-Friedrich-Straße 89, Charlottenburg, 10585 (341 1447). U2 Sophie-Charlotte-Platz. **Open** 5pm-1am daily. **Average** DM30. **No credit cards**. **Map B4**
It still doesn't look much – lots of Buddhas and other south-east Asian paraphernalia – but Kien-du serves some of Berlin's best Thai curries. There's a huge selection of them too, and though the selection for vegetarians is small, it's very good indeed. Try the beef, potatoes and peanuts in hot yellow sauce or the curried pineapple, bamboo and peppers – then take the edge off with a Singha beer. They're extremely flexible here, and happy to prepare things to your specifications.

Mahachai

Schlüterstraße 60, Charlottenburg, 10629 (313 0879). S3, S5, S7, S9 Savignyplatz. **Open** 5pm-1am Mon-Fri; noon-1am Sat-Sun. **Average** DM30. **No credit cards. Map C4**
This little jewel of a Thai eaterie is slap next to the S-Bahn tracks, but retains a serenity inside that belies the location. The food is superb, with most of the usual choices but fresher-than-usual ingredients, and service is equally sterling.

Mao Thai

Wörther Straße 30, Prenzlauer Berg, 10405 (441 9261). U2 Eberswalder Straße. **Open** noon-11pm daily. **Average** DM30. **Credit** AmEx, DC, MC, V.
Gorgeous interior, always packed, Mao Thai is perhaps not the most authentic Thai restaurant in town, but it's definitely one of the most popular. So much so that it's spun off two others: Kamala Siam is in a cellar on Oranienburger Straße, which makes it very convenient, particularly for lunch (although sometimes getting the waiting staff to remember where you've been stashed can be tough); and Tuans Hütte, hidden away by the railroad tracks near Alexanderplatz. Back in Wörther Straße, the chicken served in a coconut is the signature dish, but everything is of a high quality, so look around. And if it's Mao Thai you're headed for, reserve!
Branches: Kamala Siam, Oranienburger Straße 69, Mitte, 10117 (283 2797). Tuans Hütte, Dircksenstraße 40, Mitte, 10178 (283 6948)

Turkish

Hitit

Corner Danckelmannstraße/Knobelsdorffstraße, Charlottenburg, 14059 (322 4557). U2 Sophie-Charlotte-Platz. **Open** noon-1am daily. **Average** DM50. **Credit** V. **Map B4**
Completely different from most of the other Turkish restaurants in the city, Hitit serves excellent Anatolian/Turkish food in an elegant setting, complete with Hittite wall-reliefs, stylish high-backed chairs and pale walls. You can choose from more than 150 dishes listed, with plenty of options for vegetarians. The service is extremely friendly and the atmosphere is calm and soothing, embellished by the small waterfall running down the wall at the front of the restaurant.

Istanbul

Knesebeckstraße 77, Charlottenburg, 10623 (883 2777). S3, S5, S7, S9 Savignyplatz. **Open** noon-midnight daily. **Average** DM45. **Credit** AmEx, DC, JCB, MC, V. **Map C4**
The oldest Turkish restaurant in Berlin serves well-cooked meals at steepish prices. The menu is extensive, offering a wide selection of starters, meat and fish dishes: vegetarians can opt for a selection of hot and cold meze. From the street you can't see inside: open the door and you could almost be in Constantinople. The interior is dark and lavishly decorated with all manner of Islamic and Turkish paraphernalia. At the weekends belly dancers perform in the room at the back.

Merhaba

Hasenheide 39, Kreuzberg, 10967 (692 1713). U7 Südstern. **Open** noon-midnight daily. **Average** DM40. **Credit** AmEx, V. **Map G5**
A Turkish hotspot heavy on authentic wines and traditional food. Ignore the main courses and share a selection of spicy appetisers instead. Effusive service but uninspiring decor of mirrors and chrome.

Vegetarian

Abendmahl

Muskauer Straße 9, Kreuzberg, 10997 (612 5170). U1 Görlitzer Bahnhof. **Open** 6pm-1am daily; *kitchen closes* 11pm. **Average** DM45. **No credit cards. Map H4**
The name means 'Last Supper' and the warm decor is enlivened with a little Catholic kitsch. The menu changes regularly and all dishes bear wacky names such as News From The Moon, Murder Ahoi and (always on the menu) Flammendes Inferno (Thai fish curry). What you get is inventive and wonderfully presented fish and vegetarian dishes followed by spectacular desserts. It's a short menu but the soups are unsurpassable and their seitan dishes alone are worth the trek out to deepest Kreuzberg. Service is charming, efficient and laid-back. An ideal place to linger in good company. Book at weekends.

Hakuin

Martin-Luther-Straße 1, Schöneberg, 10777 (218 2027). U1, U2, U15 Wittenbergplatz. **Open** 5pm-midnight Tue-Sat; noon-11 pm Sun. **Average** DM50. **No credit cards. Map D5**
Excellent but expensive Buddhist vegetarian food. In the beautiful main room people eat quietly amid a jungle of plants and a large fish pool with a gentle fountain. Fruit curries are often served on bamboo serving-plates, in tune with the decor.

Imbiß & fast food

All over Berlin you will see the sign Imbiß – a catch-all term embracing just about anywhere you get food but not table service, from stand-up street corner Currywurst or Döner Kebap stalls, to self-service snack bars offering all manner of exotic cuisine. The quality varies wildly, but some excellent, cheap food can be found in these places. Here is a selection of some of the more interesting ones.

Fish & Chips

Yorckstraße 15, Kreuzberg, 10963 (0173 801 3855). U6, U7 Mehringdamm. **Open** noon-1am daily. **Map E5**
Alarmingly authentic British chippy, serving battered fish and real chips with salt and vinegar or a variety of sauces, plus mushy peas, a selection of British ales and strong English tea. It's just DM6.50 for a huge and excellent plateful, there's a small seating area and a variety of magazines about fishing and diving to read while they fry up your fresh fish. Heaven for long-term expats or British travellers weary of *Wurst* and Wiener Schnitzel.

Fleischerei Bachhuber's bei Witty's

*Wittenbergplatz, Charlottenburg, 10789 (no phone).
U1, U2, U15 Wittenbergplatz.* **Open** 11am-1am
daily. **Map D5**

Berlin's best Currywurst? We won't touch that question, but consider that this friendly place serves only
Neuland organic meat, has stunning French fries
with a variety of sauces, and always has a queue
even though service is quick and it's directly across
the street from the KaDeWe and its food halls. You
do the maths.

Habibi

*Goltzstraße 24, Schöneberg, 01781 (215 3332). U1,
U2, U4, U12 Nollendorfplatz.* **Open** 11am-3am Mon-
Fri, Sun; 11am-5am Sat. **Map D5**

Freshly made Middle Eastern specialities including
falafel, kubbe, tabouleh and various combination
plates. Wash it down with freshly squeezed orange
or carrot juice, and finish up with a complimentary
tea and one of the wonderful pastries. The premises are light, bright and well-run. Everything is excellently presented and served with a flourish. The
Winterfeldtplatz branch can get very full; the others
stay open only until 2am.
Branches: Akazienstraße 9, Schöneberg, 10823 (787
4428); Körtestraße 35, Kreuzberg, 10967 (692 2401).

Konnopke's Imbiß

*Under U-Bahn tracks, corner Danziger
Straße/Schönhauser Allee, Prenzlauer Berg, 10435
(no phone). U2 Eberswalder Straße.* **Open** 5am-7pm
Mon-Sat. **Map G1**

The quintessential Berlin Imbiß, going strong under
family management since 1930, Konnopke's makes
its own *Wurst* and serves a variety of sandwiches,
including several vegetarian offerings, which people eat in a kind of Biergarten under the tracks.

Ku'damm 195

*Kurfürstendamm 195, Wilmersdorf, 10707 (no
phone). S3, S5, S7, S9 Savignyplatz.* **Open** noon-2am
daily. **Map C4**

Berlin's best-known German Imbiß, and one that's
not frequented by tourists. Buy Russian shashlik
kebab and Currywurst fresh from the grill.

Kulinarische Delikatessen

*Oppelner Straße 4, Kreuzberg, 10997 (618 6758).
U1, U12 Schlesisches Tor.* **Open** 8am-2am daily.
Map H5

Why do Berliners eat such bad Turkish food?
Probably because they know deep in their hearts
that some day they'll come upon a place like this,
where the same old leaden selections are transmuted into gold. The Döner's not bad, but it's the vegetarian offerings that make it really special: try an
aubergine-falafel combo kebab, a zucchini kebab or
even one of the salads.

Marcann's

*Invalidenstraße 112, Mitte, 10115 (2832 8388). U6
Zinnowitzer Straße.* **Open** 7am-6pm Mon-Fri;
10am-4pm Sat; 10am-1pm Sun. **Map E2**

Marc, Ann and the crew came to Berlin from France
to work in Galerie Lafayette's bakery and then quit

to open their own place. Hitting this corner just as a
bunch of offices opened nearby, they serve packed
lunchtime crowds with panini, home-baked
baguettes, and also offer a fine selection of French
pastries, soft drinks and even a few bottles of wine.
Fillings include home-made pâtés, various French
cheeses and tuna Niçois.

Misuyen Asia-Bistro

*Torstraße 22, Mitte, 10119 (247 7269). U2 Rosa-
Luxemburg-Platz.* **Open** 11am-9pm Mon-Sat. **Map
G2**

Sometimes, if you look behind the surface of one of
Berlin's many Asian Imbiße, you'll find something
unexpected. In Misuyen's case, it's Laotian food,
albeit mixed with the usual greatest hits: some Thai,
some Indonesian, some fake Chinese. Lighter and
with more fresh vegetables than the usual Asian
fare, the Laotian dishes can also be made without
MSG if you say the three magic words: '*Ohne
Glutamat, bitte*'.

Monsieur Vuong

*Gipsstraße 3, Mitte, 10119 (308 72643
/datv@usa.net). U8 Weinmeisterstraße.* **Open** noon-
midnight Mon-Fri; 2pm-1am Sat. **Map F3**

Doing the gallery thing in Mitte and hungry for the
clean, refreshing tastes of south-east Asia? Don't
have the time or money for **Fournier**? Well, next
door, the eponymous Vietnamese chap who runs
this attractive little place will serve soup, noodle
dishes and that turbo Vietnamese espresso with help
from his extended family. Charming service, and the
garden out back is a true oasis in the summer.

Pagoda

*Bergmannstraße 88, Kreuzberg, 10961 (691 2640).
U7 Gneisenaustraße.* **Open** noon-midnight daily.
Map F5

This essential Imbiß is as good as some of the more
costly Thai joints in town. Dozens of menu selections, the proper amount of chillis already in the dish
making a dip into the hot-sauce jar only minimally
necessary, and fast, friendly service.

Safran

*Knaackstraße 14, Prenzlauer Berg, 10405 (no
phone). U2 Senefelderplatz.* **Open** 11am-1am Mon-
Fri, Sun; 11am-3am Sat. **Map G2**

'The best falafel in east Berlin,' the counterman says,
and he's right, but it doesn't stop there: shredded
chicken-breast with herbs, almonds and pine-nuts
(available as a plate or pitta-stuffer), stewed okra
with aromatic rice, fish soup and many other daily
specials. Inexpensive, open late, and right in the middle of the Wasserturm area.

Spätzle

*S-Bahnbogen 390, Lüneberger Straße, Tiergarten,
10557 (no phone). S3, S5, S7, S9 Bellevue.* **Open**
9am-8pm Mon-Sat; 11am-8pm Sun. **Map D3**

A lovely little place serving the pastas of Swabia,
including Spätzle (with Bratwurst, lentils or meatballs), Kasespätzle (with cheese), *Maultaschen* (like
giant ravioli) and Schupfnudelen (a cross between
pasta and chips), accompanied by a dark Berg beer.

Nightlife

No closing times, a savage drinking culture, cocktails for any budget, scenes to suit every sexual proclivity, stylistic bent or musical mutation. You want nightlife? Welcome to Berlin.

Tresor/Globus – *pioneering party in no-man's-land location. See page 174.*

Rumour has it that when the mayor sent a statistician out to count the number of bars and nightclubs in Berlin, he never returned. First time surveyors of Berliner nightlife may find themselves alternately mystified and daunted by the variety, intensity, stamina and tolerance that characterises nightlife in this shadowy city.

Berlin has always had a reputation for the extreme. Until the end of the 1980s, the walled city attracted radicals with its military service-exemption and subsidised dissidence. Geopolitical circumstances also made it hard to get out of town at weekends, so drinking and nightclubbing became the central form of leisure. After the Wall fell many scenes moved east, converting abandoned warehouses and industrial buildings into techno and house clubs that opened for days at a time. As the Love Parade grew and the underground scene spilled out on to the streets and into the mainstream, at times it seemed like the whole city was a club that wouldn't close. Liberal licensing laws

still do not specify any closing hours and evenings out follow the classic continental time-frame, with restaurants serving until 11pm or midnight and clubs peaking between 2am and 4am.

Scenes vary according to neighbourhood, style, sexual persuasion and degree of sanity. And like club and bar cultures in most big cities, Berlin's nightlife can be seen as a confluence of both locally expressed global developments in music and fashion and nocturnal distortions of the frictions and trends of daily life. Much of the variety of Berlin after dark is due to the fact that it's a city of independent bar and club owners – there is a happy absence of door security with wireless headsets, standardised drink menus and the other signs of the corporatised clubbing experience now drearily ubiquitous in the UK.

While a comprehensive survey of Berlin clubland would require a whole book, musically oriented stylistic indicators can give rough impressions of particular Berlin scenes. Techno, house, trance, drum 'n' bass, hip hop, kitchy electronica, African, R&B/soul, blaxploitation, biker, neo-rockabilly, headbanger, gothic, neo-grunge, industrial, neo-wave, post punk, lounge-core and Latin scenes all make their presence felt in regular and non-recurring venues around Berlin.

Clubs and bars appear and disappear like pimples on the city's changing face. The listings here were as current as we could get them at the time of going to press (February 2000), but who knows what will have happened in a year's time. Particularly for clubs, we recommend you cross-check against local listings. To this end, clubbers and party-goers of all persuasions will be happy to find Berlin has a very developed information infrastructure. Pamphlets and party flyers can be found on bartops and in postcard and newspaper racks in cafés across the city. The pocket-sized weekly freebie *Flyer* is very in-the-know, and anyone without a local guide should make it their bible. *Uncle Sally's* and *[030]* also carry nightlife listings, information and adverts for the larger parties. The clubradio website (*www.klubradio.de*) features streams from performances at **Maria am Ostbahnhof**, **Ostgut** and **Tresor**, and bars and clubs are generally quite present on the web.

The distinction between bars and nightclubs is often blurred, with many bars offering DJs and dancefloors and nightly changes of theme and atmosphere. And recurring parties without home venues may be thrown in several places over the course of a season (*see page 181* **Declassifying carousing**). We've organised our listings by area partly because the different areas have different characters of nightlife, but also because any system of categorisation squelches particularities of scene and venue. Still, basic trends in Berliner nightlife can be summarised as follows.

THE BEAT GOES ON

Techno and house are alive and throbbing. House parties at the **Kalkscheune** and techno, house and trance nights at **Tresor** and **Matrix** have a surprising endurance, and can, at times, be reminiscent of the post-historical electro utopianism that plagued central-eastern Berlin in the early 1990s. **Tresor** has a longstanding connection to Detroit, importing DJs such as George Morel, Juan Atkins and Derrick May on a semi-regular basis. Frankfurt grandmaster Sven Väth still also packs the house several times a year. Decidedly East Berlin techno reverberations can be experienced at Prenzlauer Berg's **Icon**, albeit mixed with delicate touches of hip hop and rare groove. The closure of 90ü and WMF while this book was in preparation have left something of a void for the happy house crowd, but as this is a substantial nightlife demographic, either or both may soon reopen in new locations, or new clubs will sprout to take their places.

In recently opened Friedrichshain clubs such as **Ostgut**, **Stellwerk** or Maria am Ostbahnhof (*see chapter* **Music: Rock, Folk & Jazz**) local and experimental bands and erudite DJs play emerging electronica, neo-punk, various electro-rock hybrids and anything that party organisers think will appeal to the neighbourhood's semi-radical appetite for provocation. Interiors in Mühlenstraße's 'clubbing mile' (between Ostbahnhof and the Oberbaumbrücke) are generally lacerated, ex-industrial structures that evoke the rougher edges of authentic clubbing. The Volksbühne's **Roter Salon** often houses slightly pretentious performances and evenings for cultural-studies savants. **Cookies** preserves the playfully retro approach to warehouse decoration that began in the early 1990s, with an attitude that manages to be housey, unpretentious and current all at the same time.

Newer clubs appearing in Mitte such as **Kurvenstar**, **Oxymoron** and **Lore.Berlin** are more concerned with design and profile than actual atmosphere. The result of predictions about the future of clublife in a city taking its new role as capital seriously, they stand without shaking. Neglecting the dogged eccentricities and stylistic traditions of Berlin's turbulent nightlife history, they look to other cities for clues as to how to attract money and position in the 'European Capital'. This often results in over-designed interiors, graceless vacillations between worn styles, and altogether too many crap cocktails.

Mitte

Mitte is everything it wants to be and more – just ask anyone who lives there. In the centre of unified Berlin there's no shortage of confidence or ostentation but commercial utility and wanting it badly have brought more cultural representation than real life to the district.

Squatters in Oranienburger Straße were the first to open cafés and initiate culture programmes after the Wall fell. As a thank you, the city evicted most of them, often quite violently, and treated the eternal leisure mill that is the Oranienburger Straße-Rosenthaler Straße nexus as if it were a tabula rasa for their own cultural designs. Planners were so meticulous in their licensing agreements that in quiet moments acute visitors will hear the Oranienburger Straße whispering stipulations for calming pastel walls and requisite ratios of Italian lamps per square metre of dining space.

That said, many of the cafés and bars look good and do fulfil their mandates of providing contemporary, in-the-know environments. In summer, Oranienburger Straße proper is about 60 per cent tourists. Things calm down and become more tasteful as you move up Auguststraße. The corner of Auguststraße and Tucholskystraße is a bustling area in the evenings.

Summer nights in Oranienburger Straße – wanting it badly.

Like Potsdamer Platz, Hackescher Markt promises everything and draws a lot of tourists. The restored buildings across from the S-Bahn are indeed impressive, but their renovation coincided with the disappearance of the neighbourhood's most intense nightspots. Oxymoron manages to pack crowds of cosmopolitan aspirants on weekends, as do various other identikit bars in the area.

Friedrichstraße is the Champs-Élysées without a pulse, and should be avoided by anybody looking for a good time out.

Acud

Veteranenstraße 21, Mitte, 10119 (4435 9497). U8 Rosenthaler Platz/bus N8. **Open** from 10pm daily. **Map F2**

This bedrock of cultural life in Mitte, comprising a theatre, alternative cinema, café and exhibitions along with a subterranean club, was at press time struggling to gather funds to buy the house from the newly found original owners who were expropriated by the Nazis. The club may not be the most trendy, but it's a magnet for reggae, drum 'n' bass and hip hop enthusiasts who want to get into the music and not just parade their wardrobe.

Bar Lounge 808

Oranienburger Straße 42-43, Mitte, 10117 (2804 6727) U6 Oranienburger Tor. **Open** 10am-3am daily. **Credit** AmEx, DC, MC, V. **Map F3**

New venture by former 90° and Café Moscow impresario Bob Young who, like most people now setting up shop in this part of Mitte, seems to be betting on

a lot of money flowing into the area and being spent on cocktails. Triangular front bar with gold columns and windows on to the corner with Auguststraße; roomy back lounge with large aquarium, heavy drapes, chill-out sounds and lots of places to sit and chat. Still too new at press time to tell how it was going to work, but a well-dressed, expensive sort of place and looking to attract the same kind of crowd.

Bergwerk

Bergstraße 68, Mitte, 10115 (280 8876). U8 Rosenthaler Platz/bus N8. **Open** from 5pm Mon-Fri; from noon Sat; from 10am Sun. **Map F2**

Dependable basement club populated by people eager to avoid trendy clubs and expensive beer. Despite the many DJs named in listings, there is in fact only one guy who changes his repertoire depending on the night. Just the sort of idiosyncrasy that makes a place worthwhile for a night of slumming and slamming to the Beastie Boys, whose various incarnations seem to be the starting points for all the various club nights here.

Broker's Bierbörse

Schiffbauerdamm 8, Mitte, 10117 (3087 2293). S1, S2, S3, S5, S7, S9/U6 Friedrichstraße. **Open** 8am-3am daily. **Map F3**

Mad little place where 'market forces' dictate beer prices, which rise and fall throughout the evening. One minute there's a run on Jever, the next everyone gets bullish about Beck's. Tends to get going after the nine-to-fivers come out to play, and can get so full in mid-evening that there are queues outside. Breakfasts, snacks and sausages served.

Delicious Doughnuts

Rosenthaler Straße 9, Mitte, 10119 (2809 9274).
U8 Weinmeisterstraße. **Open** from 10pm.
Admission varies. **Map F3**

The legendary Mitte rare groove and acid jazz club no longer sells doughnuts at the bar, so far has it wandered from the old, smokin' turntable daze of the early 1990s. Several changes of ownership and a slicker-than-thou renovation – black leather booths and everything else lounge red – have cost it some regulars, but it appears to be making a comeback. The cocktail menu is extensive, the staff cool and it is still a DJ-orientated venue. At the time of going to press the scheduling was as follows: open club night on Thursday; 'Kinky Euro Club' on Friday; 'Real Scratchin' Grooves' on Saturday. Look out for DJs Copasetic or Martin Rank (choice groove and the occasional rockabilly provocation).

Gipson

Gipsstraße 12, Mitte, 10119 (3087 2520). U8
Weinmeisterstraße. **Open** 7pm-3am Mon-Sat. **Map F3**

Formerly a bar based around arty video installations, but new owners from west Berlin have refocused on cocktails and fine spirits and hiked the prices to the skies. As such, an interesting barometer of the way this neighbourhood is heading, but otherwise eminently avoidable.

Greenwich

Gipsstraße 5, Mitte, 10119 (no phone). U8
Weinmeisterstraße. **Open** 6pm-6am daily. **Map F3**

Named after the Millennium, co-owned by Cookie, and just about Berlin's most happening bar as the century turned. Beautifully designed with space age curves and glowing aquaria, and packed to the gills with well-heeled young scenesters – at weekends, uncomfortably so. Long ground-floor bar is complemented by mezzanine lounge.

Hafenbar

Chausseestraße 20, Mitte, 10115 (282 8593). U6
Zinnowitzer Straße. **Open** from 9pm Fri; from 10pm Sat. **Admission** DM10-15. **Map F2**

Somewhat past its 1990s prime, when it was the home to lounge lizards Le Hammond Inferno. Hafenbar still serves up easy listening, 1970s disco and *Schlager*, but other places have since encroached on its turf. Still, a good place for mindless fun off the rather too well beaten path of Oranienburger Straße.

Im Eimer

Rosenthaler Straße 68, Mitte, 10117 (282 2074). U8
Rosenthaler Platz/bus N8. **Open** from 11pm Fri-Sat.
Admission DM8. **Map F3**

This still-crumbling monument of the original 1989 alternative invasion of Mitte is still true to its punk/squatter roots – even though the music played here these days is mostly digital hardcore. The house's labyrinth of psychedelically tatty cave-like spaces is the venue for readings and performances to complement the general mayhem – 'Holger Lang reads Pipi Langstrumpf' an example of one recent offering. Worth a visit, if only to experience a fast-disappearing world.

Jubenal

Tucholskystraße 34, Mitte, 10117 (2833 7377). U6
Oranienburger Tor. **Open** from 8pm daily. **Map F3**

Kurvenstar – *fashion victims' failed escape route from provincial pasts.*

Consciously cool lounge (with occasionally snooty doorman) for scrubbed hipsters featuring lava lamps, sexy bartenders (who mix well) and a small stage for jazz-related performances. Unfortunately, much of the music performed here would better be described as 'sound'. No problem, though, as Jubenal regulars quaff about four drinks a set.

Kurvenstar

Kleine Präsidentenstraße 3, Mitte, 10178 (2859 9710). S3, S5, S7, S9 Hackescher Markt. **Open** from 8pm Tue-Sun. **Map F3**
A meeting-point for second-rate DJs and fashion victims trying to escape from provincial pasts, this would-be-slick lounge with dancefloor exemplifies the neurotic side of the new Mitte's will to flower.

Lime Club

Dircksenstraße 105, 10178, Mitte (2472 1397). S3, S5, S7, S9/U2, U5, U8 Alexanderplatz. **Open** from 10pm Wed-Sat. **Admission** DM10. **Map G3**
Noteworthy for their Friday and Saturday-nighters, when Goths crawl out from under their rocks and congregate here in droves. Dress in black to feel at home. Also house, techno and hip hop events.

Lore.Berlin

Neue Schönhauser Straße 20, Mitte, 10178 (2804 5134). S3, S5, S7, S9 Hackescher Markt. **Open** 5pm-3am daily. **Map G3**
Possibly the most unpleasant new bar in the whole of Mitte, this is worth a look just for the morbid thrill of seeing what the combined forces of too much money and too little imagination may do for the city in the future. It's underground, there's a lame theme involving coal wheelbarrows, there are well-tanned, unintelligent bar staff, lots of balding young men in ties at the very long bar, and some beautifully dressed young women. Apparently they pay DJs to play things like 'vocal house' on Saturdays, but it's hard to find anyone who'll verify this, and the weekend queues are unconscionable.

Lumumba

Steinstraße 12, Mitte, 10119 (2838 5465). U8 Weinmeisterstraße. **Open** from 8pm Tue-Sun. **Map G3**
Laidback bar with dancefloor where a mixed crowd of African and German academic types shimmy to zouk, highlife, salsa, merengue, reggae and other African and Afro-Caribbean grooves, with the occasional hip hop track thrown in. Come early in the evening for a crash course in salsa dancing.

Mitte Bar

Oranienburger Straße 46, Mitte, 10117 (283 3837). U6 Oranienburger Tor. **Open** from noon daily. **Map F3**
During the day locals involved with nightlife or students with a few hours' break will congregate for coffee or the first beer of the day. Later it fills with people just finished gawking at the tourist sights of Oranienburger Straße. Still, at night the music is sometimes adventurous, the decor dark, and a back room is frequently occupied by a wide spectrum of DJs playing everything from trip hop to 1960s sleaze.

Obst & Gemüse

Oranienburger Straße 48, Mitte, 10117 (no phone). U6 Oranienburger Tor. **Open** from noon. **Map F3**
Next door to the Mitte Bar (above) this former greengrocers ('Obst & Gemüse' means 'fruit & veg') has large windows through which you can watch the wildlife on Oranienburger Straße. Nothing much else special about it, though, and it's usually too crowded for comfort. A place to meet and move on.

Odessa

Steinstraße 16, Mitte, 10119 (no phone). U8 Weinmeisterstraße. **Open** 7pm-2am daily. **Map G3**
Beautiful minimalist bar that's unusually quiet for this part of town. Wooden tables in the small back room are complemented by a bar out front, behind which can usually be found the well-travelled proprietor from Lichtenstein. No music, nor room for many guests, and only a small but carefully chosen selection of drinks, but this is a welcome antidote to too much fake cool on nearby Rosenthaler Straße.

Oscar Wilde

Friedrichstraße 112a, Mitte, 10117 (282 8166). U6 Oranienburger Tor. **Open** 4pm-2am Mon-Thur; 1pm-3am Fri; 11am-3pm Sat; 11am-2am Sun. **Map F3**
Typical Irish pub, offering the obligatory ingredients of Guinness, fry-up breakfasts, and a big video screen in the back for watching Premier League matches on Sky. Live music at weekends.

Oxymoron

Hof 1, Hackesche Höfe, Rosenthaler Straße 40-41, Mitte, 10178 (2839 1886). S3, S5, S7, S9 Hackescher Markt. **Open** *restaurant* from 11am daily; *club* from 11pm daily. **Map F3**
A salon-à-club with elegantly recessed booths in the heart of Hackescher Markt leisure mall, Oxymoron is a book begging to be judged by its expensive cover charges (DM15-20). In the restaurant/café, tourists and ad execs vie with couples from Charlottenburg for the attention of demi-mondettes modelling waitress aprons. The club (in the rear) is small but efficient, catering to guests who would be very hip in Munich. DJs play anything from house to acid jazz to package-tour dance.

Roberta

Zionskirchstraße 7, Mitte, 10119 (4405 5580). U8 Bernauer Straße. **Open** from 6pm daily. **Map F2**
All the elements seem to be here – high ceilings, apricot walls, civilised drink prices and turntables playing house, bigbeat, easy listening, funk, soul and other musics dear to the pleasantly mixed straight and gay crowd's heart. And yet there's something hip-bar-by-numbers about the place. Something's gotta give before Roberta replaces the older, DJ-less, but infinitely more enjoyable Kapelle (*see chapter* **Cafés**) across Zionskirchplatz in barcrawlers' affections. DJs most nights.

Roter Salon

Linienstraße 227, Mitte, 10119 (247 7694). U2 Rosa-Luxemburg-Platz. **Open** varies. **Map G3**
While this part of town may no longer be red, the Roter Salon's lights and seats still proudly are, and

the velvet, mirrors and chandelier elegance seem perfect for cultured conversation and tango-dancing. Tango is on Wednesdays and on the other days of the week, you'd be at a loss to find a more eclectic mix anywhere else in the city: on Monday drum 'n' bass; Tuesday salsa; Fridays and Saturdays club nights running the gamut from Britpop to Northern Soul, indie rock to Blaxploitation funk.

Sage-Club

Köpenicker Straße 78, Mitte, 10179 (no phone). U8 Heinrich-Heine-Straße. **Open** from 10pm Thur-Sun. **Admission** DM10-25. **Map G4**

Upmarket and self-consciously fashionable club with an emphasis on house. There's a bit of a see-and-be-seen kind of vibe, coupled with a lot of looking down noses, so dress to feel your best. 'Funky Friday' and Sunday's Niteclub 2000 featuring funk and old school or garage and techno respectively are the least intimidating evenings, and rock nights on Thursday have a different atmosphere altogether.

Schokoladen

Ackerstraße 169-170 Mitte, 10115 (282 6527). U8 Rosenthaler Platz. **Open** from 8pm daily. **Map F2**

This eastern scene stalwart, located in the former ZAR chocolate factory, is still going strong and never fails to amaze with its adventurous mixing of theatre, poetry and music off the beaten track, both live and from turntables. Attracts a knowing, but not terminally hip, student and intellectual-artsy crowd with humane drink prices and a playful, yet down-to-earth atmosphere.

Tresor/Globus

Leipziger Straße 126a, Mitte, 10117 (609 3702). S1, S2/U2 Potsdamer Platz/bus N52, 84. **Open** from 11pm Wed-Sun. **Admission** DM15. **Map E4**

Pioneering no-man's-land club partly in the subterranean safe-deposit box room of the otherwise vanished pre-war Wertheim department store, partly in the old Globus bank building on the surface. This was the place in techno's good old days, and the legend just about manages to linger. Still good for catching Juan Atkins, Derrick May, Blake Baxter and other Detroit greats when they pass through town, but Sven Väth is the only DJ who packs the place these days. The summer Trancegarden out back, with tables and fairy lights among the shrubbery, is the club's finest feature, complementing two internal dancefloors and a bar. But often there's no longer much happening and it's unlikely to survive much longer in its current form. There's talk of constructing a 'techno tower' on the site, full of shops and studios.
Website: www.tresor-berlin.de

Kalkscheune

Johannisstraße 2, 10117, Mitte (2839 0065). S1, S2, S3, S5, S7, S9/U6 Friedrichstraße. **Open** varies. **Admission** DM12-20. **Map F3**

The 'chalk stable' is great just in the summer when the courtyard bar is open, but in winter everyone has to cram into one big, smoky, poorly-lit, low-ceilinged room where, if you don't want to dance (or can't find the space), you also can't talk over the

It's a Latin thing

German album chart-topper, the *Buena Vista Social Club* soundtrack, has got even the most unhip secretary taking salsa lessons and strutting her stuff at clubs playing Afro-Cuban and Afro-Brazilian music. So-called 'Latin' music, a term lumping together these disparate styles along with bossa nova, tropicalia, merengue, tango and more, is the latest manifestation of German passion for all things *südländisch*. This likewise somewhat indiscriminate term encompasses anything from *Wirtschaftswunder* fantasies of holidays in Capri to the whole Ibero-Latin American cultural complex.

But Berlin's 'Latin' scene has a long history. There's a small but significant community of Latin American who settled in the city and brought their musical heritage with them. Once centred around the legendary Salsa in Charlottenburg, the scene has also fostered the **Havanna Club**, **La Máquina** and El Barrio (Potsdamer Straße 84, Tiergarten).

These places are popular with the Cuban and South American communities as well as with Germans. Most places offer dancing instruction in salsa or merengue for the uninitiated. The submissive and subjugating moves of tango are also popular, with regular evenings at the **Roter Salon** (*pictured*) plus less Teutonically repressed Mondays at Checkpoint (Leipziger Straße 55, Mitte), Tuesdays at **Kalkscheune**, Wednesdays at La Charanga (Brüsseler Straße 3, Wedding), Thursdays at Mambo (Danckelmannstraße 20, Charlottenburg), Fridays at Encuentro (Hagelberger Straße 53-53, Kreuzberg) and Sundays at **Chamäleon Varieté** (*see chapter* **Cabaret**).

Even after 'Latin' music has receded into the memory as yet another faded flavour of the month, the rhythms of Central and South America will still pulsate from Berlin clubs. The **Canzone** record shop (*see chapter* **Shopping & Services**) and the SFB4 Multikulti radio station are other good points of departure for this journey into *sueño*.

Havanna Club

Hauptstraße 30, Schöneberg, 10827 (784 8565). U7 Eisenacher Straße. **Open** from 10pm Fri, Sat; *dance instruction* 9pm. **Map D6**

La Máquina

Lietzenburger Straße 86, Charlottenburg, 10719 (0172 304 3921). U9, U15 Kurfürstendamm. **Open** from 9pm Thur-Sun; *dance instruction* 9-11pm Thur, Sun. **Map C4**

music. Nice wooden bar at one end, though. There's no real defined scene here, but a variety of events and parties ranging from cabaret to house music, so check local listings for what's on.

Sophienclub

Sophienstraße 6, Mitte, 10178 (282 4552). U8 Weinmeisterstraße. **Open** from 10pm daily. **Admission** varies. **Map F3**
One of a handful of youth-oriented clubs that existed in East Berlin prior to Reunification, Sophien went from jazz roots to accessible acid jazz and funk. Its legendary status in the east made it a favourite destination for west Berliners and visiting celebs after the Wall fell, but the club resolutely ignored musical trends and still does, attracting people looking to party and not terribly concerned about the music.

Zucca

Am Zwirngraben 11-12, Mitte, 10178 (2472 1212). S3, S5, S7, S9 Hackescher Markt. **Open** 10pm-3am daily. **Map F3**
Considering that its location in the S-Bahn arch at Hackescher Markt screams 'tourist trap', the elegant Zucca is a surprisingly pleasant place to start an evening. Chandeliers and dark wood panelling give the place a ballroom air, while the prices and crowd aren't overly upmarket. DJs supply the suitably subdued soundtrack.

Prenzlauer Berg

A centre of pre-war Jewish life and the one genuinely bohemian district in communist East Berlin, Prenzlauer Berg has always taken its cultural status very seriously. Most of its fin-de-siècle buildings have been studiously renovated, and green yuppies have opened dozens of health-food shops. Kollwitzplatz is a delightful green square surrounded by scores of cafés and bars where young professionals court one another over gourmet food and cocktails.

In Rykestraße, the local literati and green strategists discuss perennial political issues. The cafés near Helmholtzplatz are a bit further downmarket and somewhat more spontaneous than those in the vicinity of Kollwitzplatz and the Wasserturm, staying lively from 7-8pm until 2-3am. The Prater Biergarten in nearby Kastanienallee is a pleasant place for a Hefeweizen on warm summer evenings, and a fine starting point for interminable drinking tours down Kastanienallee and Oderberger Straße.

Akba

Sredkistraße 64, Prenzlauer Berg, 10405 (441 1463). U2 Eberswalder Straße. **Open** from 7pm daily. **Map G2**
In front is a quiet, terribly smoky café that can host an eclectic crowd, especially late at night. Through the back is the Akba Lounge, a mini-club devoted to a broad selection of music – featuring everything from cheesy 1960s *Schlager* to hip hop.

Aroma

Kastanienallee 40, Prenzlauer Berg, 10435 (no phone). U2 Eberswalder Straße. **Open** from 9pm Fri. **Map G2**
A shoebox bar for a shoestring budget, where an old couch and loopy plastic chairs encroach upon the mini-dance space. Run by an art student, this tiny storefront isn't hard to find – just hard to squeeze in. Always open on Fridays, and randomly open on other days. Ask the bartender for details of that week's parties.

Casino

Prenzlauer Allee/corner of Saarbrücker Straße, Prenzlauer Berg, 10405 (no phone). S3, S5, S7, S9/U2, U5, U8 Alexanderplatz. **Open** from 10pm Fri-Sat. **Map G2**
Trashy, unfrilly and vaguely industrial atmosphere in this comfortably makeshift club housed in another part of the same former bread factory as **Cookies** (*below*). There's a young crowd numbering maybe 1,500 in here on a good night, crowding on to a large dancefloor fired by trance and techno (watch out for kids doing a strange robotic dance called the Lufthacker) or retreating into the small downtempo bar. At its best in summer when the action spills into the wonderful courtyard.

Cookies

Prenzlauer Allee/corner of Saarbrücker Straße, Prenzlauer Berg, 10405 (no phone). S3, S5, S7, S9/U2, U5, U8 Alexanderplatz. **Open** from 11pm Tue, Thur. **Map G2**
While the daze of happy house and electro-sleaze illicitly pulsing through dark bunkers and post-bombardments warehouses may be over, Tuesdays at Cookies preserves some of the cocktails and coal-heated ambience of the early 1990s. Then, Wessi decadents brought clubland to the corroding corridors of east Berlin, wrapping themselves in vintage velvet and urbane oblivion. Now, though they may serve websites by day, their Wednesday mornings are clouded from that seventh gin fizz and the girl they spilled it on. Cookie, surprisingly easy-going for a Berlin legend, can usually be seen shaking cocktails behind one of the indoor-outdoor club's three bars.

H2O

Kastanienallee 16, Prenzlauer Berg, 10435 (no phone). U2 Eberswalder Straße. **Open** from 10pm daily. **Map G2**
The abstract patterns on the wall evoke graffitti without actually using spray pieces, echoing this place's general vibe of paying respect to hip hop while also embracing other forms of dance music. DJs are at the turntables on weekends and on occasional weekday nights, and you may catch young local MC hopefuls rapping live so well that you end up mistaking it for the record of some big-name German hip hop crew.

Haus Bar

Rykestraße 54, Prenzlauer Berg, 10405 (4404 7606). U2 Senefelderplatz/tram 1. **Open** 7pm-5am daily. **Map G2**

All bright red and gold with a glorious cherub-filled sky on the ceiling, this small pocket of fabulousness seats about 15 people at a push. Much more fun than the wanky cafés with Russian literary names around the corner, and particularly inviting at three or four in the morning.

Icon

Cantianstraße 15, Prenzlauer Berg, 10437 (no phone). U2 Eberswalder Straße. **Open** from 10pm Thur-Sun. **Map G1**
A tricky-to-locate entrance in the courtyard just north of the junction with Milastraße leads to an interesting space cascading down several levels into a long stone cellar. It's a well ventilated little labyrinth, with an intense dancefloor space, imaginative lighting, good sound and a separate bar insulated enough for conversation to remain possible. Sometimes techno events, sometimes drum 'n' bass. At its best when the core crowd of young locals is augmented by a wider audience for some special event, but a cool place on any night.

Knaack

Greifswalder Straße 224, Prenzlauer Berg, 10405 (442 7060). S4, S8, S10 Greifswalder Straße/tram 2, 3, 4. **Open** 8pm-4am Wed-Sat. **Map H2.**
Multi-level club that hangs on from eastern beginnings by attracting a very young audience with a changing programme of hard, aggressive music in

the basement, and generic party music upstairs. The concert hall books a steady stream of interesting international acts. *See also chapter* **Music: Rock, Folk & Jazz.**

Lampion

Knaackstraße 54, Prenzlauer Berg, 10435 (442 6026). U2 Eberswalder Straße. **Open** 4pm-3am daily. **Map G2**
Small and quiet bar with a distinguished bohemian pedigree and dozens of umbrellas hanging from the ceiling. Occasional puppet shows in the small theatre at the back. Locals predominate. Tourists tolerated if they're respectful.

Nemo

Oderberger Straße 46, Prenzlauer Berg, 10435 (no phone). U2 Eberswalder Straße. **Open** 6pm-3am Mon-Sat; 11am-3am Sun. **Map G2**
When the Wall came down, the owner of this former grocer's emigrated to Costa Rica, and it is his dreams of a warmer clime that inspired the cartoonish beach and cactus murals and the straw matting on the ceiling. A variety of cheap meals and snacks are served until late along with Mexican and Bavarian beers, there's an all-you-can-eat buffet on Sunday for DM12, and lots of games machines. If it's too crowded you'll have no problem finding other cheap eats and drinks on a street now hosting a dozen other bars and restaurants.

The *Geheimtip* for furtive fun

The answer to the question, 'Where should we meet for a drink tonight?' is not always easy. But having a calendar handy will help. Is it the second Thursday of the month? The third Sunday of a month without an 'r' in it? Or a day that is a multiple of the number six? Once you have the date settled, you can turn your attention to further complications. Are you prepared, for example, to navigate yourself through a rubbish-filled lot, after ducking underneath a rusty chain loosely holding together the locked doors of a dilapidated gate?

Glamourous it is not, but deliciously secretive it is. A *Geheimtip* (literally 'secret tip') is a happening place that only you and a select few (hundred) know about. Usually by the time the hoi polloi hears about this secret hideout, the place is long gone. But unlike the 'in' places of London or New York, you don't have to be on a list, or drop a wad of cash to get in. No, you just need to have heard about it and know how to get there. And these mostly illegal Geheimtips give the cold shoulder to the money-with-an-attitude-set.

The unscenic scene is what nocturnal Berliners thrive on, sometimes rather morbidly.

Only the dead could dance at one recent spot. A former morgue, Kunst und Technik is the name you won't find in neon lights or advertised in *Flyer* – and if it does turn up in listings, then it's no longer a Geheimtip. The name exists only in the heads of those who know – and some of them call it the Six Bar, for this is the place only open on dates that are multiples of six. More like an extended private party, the DJs and cheap drinks – not fancy lighting or pretty decor – are the real attraction to this hideout somewhere on the banks of the Spree.

Other Geheimtips have sprung up in a white-tiled former butcher's shop, in the back offices of a former supermarket and other post-industrial locations. Rough and ready, these Geheimtips celebrate the architectural wounds of war, the collapse of the GDR economy, Berlin's capacity for continual reinvention and the need of various scenes to find spaces not easily penetrable by tourists and out-of-towners.

If you do manage to track one of them down, you'll find that they're friendly enough places. It's just that even to hear about them, first you have to get involved.

Wohnzimmer – *suspiciously bar-like.*

Pfefferbank
Schönhauser Allee 176, Mitte, 10119 (4404 9669).
U2 Senefelderplatz. **Open** from 9pm Mon-Wed; from
11pm Thur-Sat. **Map G2**
Smallish but vibrant club with music that tends
towards the funky, housey end of the spectrum.
Escobar 2000 provides bouncy reggae and ragga at
the start of the week.

Wohnzimmer
*Lettestraße 6, Prenzlauer Berg, 10437 (445 5458). U2
Eberswalder Straße.* **Open** 10am-4am daily. **Map G1**
Days are rather slow at this shabbily elegant café.
Visitors who make it past the poignantly drunken,
would-be anarchists sunning in Helmholtzplatz will
find, behind the door to this 'living room', a suspiciously bar-like structure made from an inspired
ensemble of kitchen cabinets. Threadworn divans
and artsy bargirls make this the perfect place to discuss Dostoevsky with career students over a tepid
borscht. Evening light from candelabra reflects on
gold-sprayed walls as students and maudlin poets
chase brandies with Hefeweizen and bodily fluids.

Friedrichshain

In the downmarket eclecticism of its bars and
cafés, Friedrichshain today is much like the Mitte
or Prenzlauer Berg of the early 1990s. But working-class, underdeveloped and not very central, the
neighbourhood has neither Prenzlauer Berg's

bohemian history nor Mitte's architectural flair.
Mühlenstraße is a litany of crumbling industrial
architecture – mecca, in other words, for aspiring
club owners with limited budgets – while the area
around Simon-Dach-Straße is full of fun bars,
cheap cafés and ethnic restaurants.
    Cheap rents have attracted students, and Rigaer
Straße and Mainzer Straße were hubs of the squatter scene. Apart from proles, neo-fascists, part-time
prostitutes   and   disgruntled   pensioners,
Friedrichshain is still home to radicals of many
stripes and swaggers. Many of these people are
unhappy these days, as modernisation has meant
rising rents and crumbling social institutions.
Locals may sneer at you if you wear flashy designer clothes or attempt to pay with credit cards.
    Apart from venues listed here, **Maria am
Ostbahnhof** (*see chapter* **Music: Rock, Folk &
Jazz**) also host various club nights.

Astro Bar
*Simon-Dach-Straße 40, Friedrichshain, 10245 (no
phone). U5 Frankfurter Tor.* **Open** from 9pm. **No
credit cards**.
At the Grünberger Straße end of the Simon-Dach-
Straße strip, this is a charming dusk-till-dawn venue
to see the locals at their favourite pastime: drinking
and listening to funny music. The control panel in
the back room could have come from a *Thunderbirds*
set, and the DJs play anything from Slim Galliard to
Atari Teenage Riot.

Barfly
*Boxhagener Straße 108, Friedrichshain, 10245 (2949
2072). U5 Samariterstraße.* **Open** from 5pm daily.
The name recalls Bukowski but this isn't the seedy
hole you might expect. In fact, by Friedrichshain
standards Barfly is a pretty elegant little place
behind frosted glass windows, aiming to usher a bit
of a cocktail culture into the neighbourhood. While
in other bars around here you can meet the scene,
this is where you meet the well-dressed crowd.

Dachkammer
*Simon-Dach-Straße 39, Friedrichshain, 10245 (296
1673). U5 Samariterstraße.* **Open** *restaurant* from
1pm daily; *cocktail bar* 7pm-1am daily.
There's a pub/restaurant on the ground floor, but
the interesting part is the upper-level cocktail bar. If
you buy a beer downstairs they won't let you take
it upstairs, just to keep the atmosphere relaxed and
loungey. Sounds odd, but you'll appreciate it as soon
as you stretch out on one of the sofas. Youngish,
casual crowd.

Dezibel
*Scharnweberstraße 54, Friedrichshain, 10247 (2900
3939). U5 Samariterstraße.* **Open** from 4pm daily.
Co-owned by a South African and positioned away
from the circus that is Simon-Dach-Straße, this is a

Astro Bar – *Friedrichshain locals at play in
their controlled habitat.*

Tagung – not bitter or sad.

pleasantly unspectacular pub that's become a hang-out for local Anglophones. Irish beer, indie rock, occasional movies in the back room plus DJs, open-mike nights and performances by drunk singer-songwriters. Sunday is 'family day', which means they're open from noon and smoking is *verboten*.

Ex

Rigaer Straße 25, Friedrichshain, 10247 (422 3545). U5 Samariterstraße. **Open** from 5.30pm daily.
The pioneer purveyor of cocktails in the Rigaer Straße area and still one of the best. Maybe its secret is stripping things down to basics: bare walls and spartan tables make it look like a simple pub rather than a fancy cocktail bar. And in spite of the variety of drinks on offer, everyone just chooses the two or three frighteningly cheap daily specials.

Matrix

Warschauer Straße 18, Friedrichshain, 10243 (2949 1047). S3, S5, S6, S7, S9/U1, U12 Warschauer Straße. **Open** from midnight Fri-Sat. **Admission** DM15. **Map H4**
A real hole, under the U-Bahn arches and notable for its absurd computerised drinks system, stringent door policy and what is possibly the best sound system in Berlin. The music's mostly house, techno and wet & hard, but the atmosphere depends very much on the DJ and the event.

Non-Tox

Mühlenstraße 12, Friedrichshain, 10243 (2966 7206). S3, S5, S6, S7, S9/U1, U12 Warschauer Straße. **Open** varies. **Map H4**
Grungy club in the cellar of an abandoned commercial building on Mühlenstraße, Friedrichshain's new clubbing mile. Diverse musical programme encompasses everything from hardcore techno to punk. Not suitable for headbangers, as you might knock the noggin on pipes hanging from the ceiling.

Ostgut

Mühlenstraße 26-30 (access from Rummelsburger Platz), Friedrichshain, 10243 (2900 0597). S3, S5, S7, S9 Ostbahnhof. **Open** from 11pm Fri-Sat. **Admission** DM20.
Warehouse-type venue hosting occasional big events with internationally renowned DJs such as Westbam or George Morel – pulsating and not too pretentious. The vibe is more commercial than relaxed and friendly, however, but Ostgut is worth a visit if you can fight your way through the crowds and survive the stifling atmosphere.

Stellwerk

Danneckerstraße 1, Friedrichshain, 10245 (291 1229). S3, S5, S6, S7, S9/U1, U12 Warschauer Straße. **Open** from 11pm Fri-Sat. **Admission** DM10-20.
In an old steelworks at the end of a muddy track stuck somewhere between Warschauer Straße and Ostkreuz, this is one of the harder, grungier and, on a good night, most hectic clubs in Berlin. If you like over-the-top sounds in a dark, seedy atmosphere, then this is the place – from hardcore, techno and hardtrance to Gothic industrial metal favoured by a predominantly male crowd all dressed in black. *Website: www.Stellwerk-Berlin.de*

Supamolly

Jessnerstraße 41, Friedrichshain, 10247 (2900 7294). S4, S8, S10/U5 Frankfurter Allee. **Open** from 3pm-late daily. **Admission** varies.
Having started life in the early 1990s as a semi-legal bolt-hole fronting a lively squat, Supamolly is a miracle of survival. It's still murky, candle-lit and Mandela-muralled, still very cheap, and still filled with all types and ages of a fuck-the-system persuasion – from dreadlocked commune-dwellers to ageing punks and tidy young eastern activists. In the best Berlin tradition, rebellion goes with an ethos of real tolerance – people are too focused on problems like fighting far-right groups to take much account of surface differences – but that said, leave the Armani coat at home. The bar's back door still gives on to the former squat, now venue for a laudably unfiltered stream of performances, from folk drumming to digital light shows.

Tagung

Wühlischstraße 29, Friedrichshain, 10245 (292 8756). U5 Samariterstraße. **Open** from 7pm daily.
Small bar decked out in GDR memorabilia and still serving things like Club Cola, the old Eastern brand. The patrons are 20- and 30-somethings and not bitter or sad the way you might expect. Instead, the

place seems to provide good laughs and drunken nights for all. The Cube Club downstairs is likewise 'ostalgically' decorated and offers mainstream dance music and occasional one-off events.

Weinsalon

Schreinerstraße 59, Friedrichshain, 10247 (4201 9408). U5 Samariterstraße. **Open** from 7pm daily.
This is the result when squatters get comfy. The armchairs and sofas are just dodgy enough to make you feel at home, and in the back room you can lean on an old coal oven as you watch the usual suspects play pool. As the name suggests, a good selection of wines by the glass, plus a cheese plate to go with it. If here is too crowded, there are several other bars in formally squatted houses on this street or on Rigaer Straße.

Kreuzberg

West Berlin's former art and anarchy quarter is nowadays very quiet compared to the madness and mayhem of old – the artists have moved to Mitte, the anarchists to Friedrichshain. But enough ageing scenesters and alternative types have hung on to ensure that the atmosphere hasn't completely evaporated.

The Bergmannstraße neighbourhood, though lively and enjoyable by day, is these days pretty somnolent after dark, with **Haifisch** and **Galao** providing the only really decent late-night options, though there are plenty of fading bars along Bergmannstraße, and more still on Gneisenaustraße and around Südstern.

The area around Oranienstraße and Wiener Straße offers a much better range of opportunities for partying and drinking, and remains one of the city's gay hubs. Even though it's not much more than a shadow of its former chaotic self, it's still possible to have fun in these parts.

Anker-Klause

Kottbusser Brücke/corner Maybachufer, Neukölln, 10967 (693 5649). U8 Schönleinstraße. **Open** from 10am Tue-Sun; from 4pm Mon. **Map G5**
Although looking over Kreuzberg's Landwehr canal, the only thing nautical about this 'anchor retreat' is the midriff-tattooed, punk-meets-portside swank of

Declassifying carousing

The nebulous border between bars and clubs can be disorienting for those who like to classify their carousing. Like nightclubs, bars often open late (8-11pm) and don't close until early morning (anywhere from 3-9am). They often have dancefloors with DJs and charge covers on weekends – **Schnabelbar** or **Mitte Bar**, for example – offering essentially nightclub environments. They may also be combinations: Kreuzberg's bi-gay **Bierhimmel** (*see chapter* **Gay & Lesbian**) features a kind of subdued lounge reachable through doors at the convivial bar's rear, and Prenzlauer Berg's petite **Akba** has a hip hop/drum 'n' bass nightclub nestled behind its rear stairway. Clubs may conversely contain bars, ranging from traditionally bar-like spaces to the proverbial chill-out room (**Cookies**, **Tresor** and Maria am Ostbahnhof – *see chapter* **Music: Rock, Folk & Jazz** – all feature separate dancing and relaxing rooms). Whether or not bars become clublike depends on the DJs listed, the night of the week and the particular crowd.

The emergence of Lounge has further consummated this blurring of club/bar distinctions. While the Teutonic temperament hardly allows for lizard-like behaviour, Germans are nonetheless aping this new design-behavioural hybrid which seems to have emerged from the Internet. The fab-coloured sunglasses and shiny-collared excesses of late-house fashion in recent times have been de-amplified for less kinetic interactions. For a cultural experience, go to **Jubenal**, or the **Bar Lounge 808** lounge to observe local attempts to lay back and talk shite. Friedrichshain's **Dachkammer** and **Astro Bar** are funny, easy places to hang with local artists and eccentric students.

And then there's the nebulous border between clubs and parties. A professional group of party-throwers (modular teams of DJs, doormen and promoters/organisers) may stage events at several different bars and clubs in the same season, linked together by theme or title rather than mere location. Similar to the profile-conscious posses and tribes in early 1990s English techno and house scenes (DIY, Spiral Tribe), these later party varieties can be quite intense and/or luxurious, and are often more interesting than simple club nights.

The Comet group's Playboy's Paradise parties are glamorous, bubbly and powdery affairs, extravagant when they come off – and tacky and over-posey when they don't. NO UFOS have been packing clubs and warehouses for several years with their upbeat – and upmarket – techno and house parties, and Sons of Shaft stage masterful Blaxploitation events. New groups and new themes appear all the time so check *Flyer* or [030] for announcements.

Madonna – *reflecting on different ways to burn a car or squat a building.*

the barstaff. A slammin' jukebox (rock, sleaze, beat) a weathery terrace and the best sandwich melts in Berlin offer ample excuse to dock here from afternoon until whenever they decide to close. Convivial during the week, packed at weekends.

Galao
Nostitzstraße 12, Kreuzberg, 10961 (no phone). U6, U7 Mehringdamm. **Open** from 8pm Thur-Sun. **Map F5**
Beautifully designed (a fortuitous pairing of 1970s sci-fi furnishings and the ubiquitious apricot walls) and perfectly laid out, with the front bar and cosy dancefloor connected by a lounge, the Galao is a gorgeous package in search of some worthwhile content – the trip hop/Latin/rare groove policy is unadventurous and misses by half. The owners are aware of the problem, though, and are rethinking the musical concept. We can't help but root for this welcome addition to a nice area otherwise pretty much bereft of noteworthy nightlife.

Der Goldene Hahn
Pücklerstraße 20, Kreuzberg, 10997 (618 8098). U1, U12 Görlitzer Bahnhof. **Open** 7pm-3am daily. **Map H4**
A small bar with unpretentious brick walls, old wooden pharmacist's fittings and lots of stuffed chickens, 'The Golden Cock' is relaxed and smart, and the barstaff DJ their own choice of vintage vinyl on a bartop turntable. Menu of light meals. Good spot for an intimate rendezvous.

Haifisch
Arndtstraße 25, Kreuzberg, 10965 (691 1352). U6, U7 Mehringdamm. **Open** 8pm-3am Tue-Thur, Sun; 8pm-5pm Fri-Sat. **Map F5**
Well-run and friendly bar where the staff are expert cocktail-shakers, the music's always hip and taste-

ful in a laid-back trancey groove kind of way, and the back room, equipped with a sushi bar, is a good place to chill out at the end of an evening. Certainly the most happening place in the Bergmannstraße neighbourhood and with some kind of crowd any night of the week.

Konrad Tönz
Falckensteinstraße 30, Kreuzberg, 10997 (612 3252). U1, U12 Schlesisches Tor. **Open** from 8pm daily. **Map H5**
Named after a 1970s true crime show policeman, Konrad Tönz carries the TV detective theme to its logical extreme: beige geometrically patterned wallpaper and DJs spinning easy-listening and beat faves on mono turntables. Not much room for dancing and you probably wouldn't want to anyway, lest you be sneered at by the stubbornly cool crowd. DJs from 9pm at weekends.

Madonna
Wiener Straße 22, Kreuzberg, 10999 (611 6943). U1, U12 Görlitzer Bahnhof. **Open** 11am-3am daily. **Map H5**
With over a hundred whiskies and frescoes detailing a lascivious pageant of falling angels and clerical inebriation, this bar and café offers a friendly vantage on the debauched, counterculture erudition of Kreuzberg 30-somethings who don't care if or where the government resides. Particularly interesting as neutral ground for subcultures which, until Berlin's modernisation frenzy gave them common cause, had differing opinions on the proper way to burn a car, squat a building or play a guitar.

Privat
Pücklerstraße 34, Kreuzberg, 10997 (617 5502). U1, U12 Görlitzer Bahnhof. **Open** from 10pm Fri-Sat. **Admission** DM10. **Map H4**

This long, low space in the basement of the Markthalle (*see chapter* **Restaurants**) hosts a variety of events from ambient performances and occasional live acts to retro parties and dance music of all stripes. Occasionally worth a look, though it's hard to predict what you'll find. Enter through the restaurant above, and retreat back to the bar there when downstairs doesn't cut it.

Schnabelbar

Oranienstraße 31, Kreuzberg, 10999 (615 8534). U1, U8, U12 Kottbusser Tor. **Open** from 10pm daily. **Map G4**
Once an essential stop on any Oranienstraße crawl and still open all night, this place is recognisable by the metal beak (*Schnabel*) which pokes out over the door. Inside there's a long bar and a tiny dancefloor, over which DJs can be found spinning funk, reggae and rare groove. Long past its best, though.

SO36

Oranienstraße 190, Kreuzberg, 10999 (6140 1306). U1, U8, U12 Kottbusser Tor. **Open** from 9pm daily. **Map G4**
Predominantly a gay and lesbian venue, though Monday house and techno nights attract a mixed cross-section less defined by sexuality than the will to dance. *See chapter* **Gay & Lesbian**.

Wiener Blut

Wiener Straße 13, Kreuzberg, 10999 (618 9203). U1, U12 Görlitzer Bahnhof. **Open** from 6pm daily. **Map H5**
Thin, darkish bar with lazy booths and a well-abused football table, Wiener Blut sometimes features DJs who pack the place with wild beats and friends and the occasional video show. Otherwise it's just another red bar. Tables out front in the summer are a good alternative to the overcrowded terrace of Morena (*see chapter* **Cafés**) up the street.

Würgeengel

Dresdener Straße 122, Kreuzberg, 10999 (615 5560). U1, U8, U12 Kottbusser Tor. **Open** from 7pm daily. **Map G4**
Red walls and velvet upholstery convey an atmosphere aching for sin, while well-mixed cocktails and a fine wine list served by smartly dressed waitstaff make this a place for the more discerning drinker. The glass-latticed ceiling and a 1920s chandelier elegantly belie the fairly priced drinks and tapas on offer. Daily specials from the adjoining Gorgonzola Club (*see chapter* **Restaurants**) can also be ordered. Ideal in summer when a canopy of greenery curtains outdoor picnic tables.

Yaam

Cuvrystraße 50-51, Kreuzberg, 10997 (617 5959). U1 U12 Schlesisches Tor. **Open** *May-Sept* from noon Sat-Sun. **Admission** DM5. **Map H5**
A kind of combination urban playground and afternoon chill-out zone, patronised by clubbers who haven't gone home yet, or others for whom this is their first stop. There are stalls selling ethnic food, pick-up games of basketball, a soundsystem playing reggae and African stuff, occasionally a live band, and lots of people smoking reefers or sipping caipirinha in the sun or shade. Summertime only. *See also chapter* **Sport & Fitness**.

Zyankali Bar

Großbeerenstraße 64, Kreuzberg, 10965 (251 6333). U1, U7, U12 Möckernbrücke. **Open** from 8pm daily. **Map F5**
Once the most fun bar in Kreuzberg with its chemistry-set trappings and toxic-waste drink menu, the Zyankali is now veering dangerously close to theme-restaurant territory. Still worth checking out if you're in a loud and boisterous group or if it's Hallowe'en. Screens US indie classics on Sundays and features DJs on weekend nights.

Schöneberg

A smart, pleasantly gentrified borough where residents greet one another jovially in the streets and spend long afternoons reading the international papers over *Milchkaffee*. Civilised, tolerant and cosmopolitan, Schöneberg has several street festivals in the summer and loads of comfortable cafés and ethnic restaurants. Motzstraße and Fuggerstraße are the hub of gay life in Berlin, with numerous bars for cruising and shops catering to all manner of fetishists. The more conventional Winterfeldtplatz is a delightful place for summer carousing and the bars on nearby Goltzstraße fill in the evenings with trendy youth, architects and expats of varying ages and nationalities.

Many quirky little bars are nestled in the tree-lined streets around the Eisenacher Straße U-Bahn, offering understated-yet-local colour until the wee hours. Less ostentatious than Mitte's drinkers, and less adventurous than those in Friedrichshain, Schönebergers tend to be monogamous with their bars and cafés, choosing a favourite and then committing. For a bit on the side, the Metropol on Nollendorfplatz hosts regular concerts and the Kit Kat Club's stages infamous sex parties.

Caracas

Kurfürstenstraße 9, Tiergarten, 10785 (265 2171). U1, U12 Kurfürstenstraße. **Open** from 10pm daily. **Map E5**
A wild, wacky Latin American cellar bar decked in pink plastic flowers. A small alcove has tatty sofas to sink into when you've worked your way through the 20 kinds of rum or jigged around to salsa on the tiny dancefloor.

Green Door

Winterfeldtstraße 50, Schöneberg, 10781 (215 2515). U1, U2, U4, U12 Nollendorfplatz. **Open** 6pm-3am daily. **Admission** *women* DM15; *men* DM20; *couples* DM30. **Map D5**
It really does have a green door, and behind it there's a whole lotta cocktail shaking going on – the drinks menu is enormous. Nice long and curvy bar, perhaps a few too many yuppies, and a good location just off Winterfeldtplatz.

Kit Kat Club @ Metropol

Nollendorfplatz 5, Schöneberg, 10777 (2173 6841).
U1, U2, U4, U12 Nollendorfplatz. **Open** from 11pm
Fri; 11pm-8am Sat. **Map D5**
You want Berlin decadence? Here it is, turn-of-the-
century style – sex and stimulants and uplifting,
positive dance music. It's not in the least bit seedy
but no place for the narrow-minded, with half the
crowd in fetish gear, the other half in no gear at all,
and every kind of sexual activity taking place in full
view. In its way Kit Kat is the most relaxing club
night in Berlin. No one has anything to prove and
everyone knows why they're there – and will almost
certainly get it – but if you're not dressed up (or
down) enough, you probably won't get in. Be
warned: they're not overly fond of the English,
whom they regard as inhibited and prone to snig-
gering, and the door policy is rigorous.

Más y Más

Hohenstaufenstraße 69, Schöneberg, 10781 (2175
2927). U1, U2, U4, U12 Nollendorfplatz. **Open** 7pm-
3am Mon-Thur, Sun; from 7pm Fri-Sat. **Map D5**
This cool cocktail bar with occasional DJs, a Spanish
vibe, a shower cabinet in one room and a bed in the
other, is a newish addition to the Schöneberg scene
and feels like it might have been transplanted from
Prenzlauer Berg. Youngish crowd but it's yet to find
its feet and is struggling to compete with the heav-
ing **Mutter** (*below*) across the street.

Who's Hu? Happy hour at **Mister Hu**.

Mister Hu

Goltzstraße 39, Schöneberg, 10781 (217 2111). U7
Eisenacher Straße. **Open** 5pm-3am daily. **Map D5**
Dark and cosy bar decorated in greens and blues and
named after one of its owners, cigar-smoking
Chinese-Indonesian writer Husen Ciawi. Long cock-
tail list so at its best during happy hour.

Mutter

Hohenstaufenstraße 4, Schöneberg, 10781 (216
4990). U1, U2, U4, U12 Nollendorfplatz. **Open** 9am-
4am daily. **Map D5**
'Mother' tries to do everything at once: two bars; an
enormous selection of wines, beers and cocktails;
breakfasts from 9am-4pm; a sushi bar from 6pm,
plus a lot of other snacks on offer. It's a big place but
it can be hard to get a seat on weekend nights, when
trancey house plays in the front bar, more sedate
sounds in the café area at the back. It's roomy, the
decor is heavy on gold paint and the corridor to the
toilets is spectacular.

Pinguin Club

Wartburgstraße 54, Schöneberg, 10823 (781 3005).
U7 Eisenacherstraße. **Open** 9pm-4am daily. **Map D5**
Though a little past its heyday, this is still one of
Berlin's finest and friendliest institutions. It's decorated with original 1950s Americana and rock 'n' roll
memorabilia, plus assorted kitsch bits and pieces,
complete with sparkling mirror ball. Owners and
staff are all involved in music one way or another
and good sounds, varying from Dean Martin to
David Sylvian to dub, are a feature. Take your pick
from 156 spirits, and don't be surprised if the barman starts doing card tricks or everyone begins to
dance to disco or sing along to Nick Cave tunes.
Occasional weekend DJs play anything from old soul
to punky cover versions. Two-time winner of the
Time Out Berlin Guide Golden Shot Glass award for
best local bar.

Screwy Club

Frankenstraße 2, Schöneberg, 10781 (215 4441). U7
Eisenacher Straße. **Open** 9pm-2am Tue-Thur; 9pm-
4am Fri-Sat. **Map D5**
Small, friendly bar decorated with artwork by Chuck
Jones and Tex Avery. The barstools, for example,
are set on giant Bugs Bunny-style carrots.
Specialises in frozen cocktails.

Zoulou Bar

Hauptstraße 4, Schöneberg, 10728 (784 6894). U7
Kleistpark. **Open** 8pm-6am Mon-Thur, Sun; 10pm-
9am Fri, Sat. **Map E5**
Small, atmospheric bar with a funky vibe and occasional DJs. It can very crowded between 10pm and
2am; after that the crowd thins out and late is maybe
the best time for a visit. Usually full of staff from
nearby bars until the dawn light gets too bright.

Charlottenburg

There are pockets of life around Savignyplatz and
Karl-August-Platz, but Charlottenburg is essentially a place where nothing ever happens. The last

Screwy Club – *here are the carrots, now give it some stick.*

happening club checked out of this neighbourhood sometime in the late 1980s and the borough's ageing bars and stiff restaurants are no match for neighbouring Schöneberg, still less for newly redeveloped Mitte. Those establishments here that do business have to cater mostly to tourists, ageing businesspeople and a huge Russian population (*see page 68* **Charlottengrad**). There's much café life by day, but at night the best the Bezirk has to offer is **Abraxas**, where people make the best of the atmospheric void that is Charlottenburg by attempting to get laid.

Abraxas
Kantstraße 134, Charlottenburg, 10625 (312 9493). U7 Wilmersdorfer Straße. **Open** from 10pm Tue-Sun. **Admission** DM5-10. **Map B4**
A dusky, relaxed disco where you don't have to dress up to get in and where academics, social workers, bank clerks and midwives populate the floor. Flirtation rules. Dance to funk, soul, latino and jazz – like techno never happened.

Diener
Grolmanstraße 47, Charlottenburg, 10623 (881 5329). S3, S5, S7, S9 Savignyplatz. **Open** 6pm-2am Wed-Mon. **Map C4**
An old-style Berlin bar, named after a famous German boxer. There's no music and the walls are adorned with faded hunting murals and photos of famous Germans you won't recognise. You could almost be in 1920s Berlin. Almost.

Dralle's
Schlüterstraße 69, Charlottenburg, 10629 (313 5038). S3, S5, S7, S9 Savignyplatz. **Open** 11am-1am Sun-Thur; 11am-2pm Fri-Sat. **Map C4**

Hang-out for an oldish, formerly fashionable crowd. The decor is predominantly red, so avoid it if you have an aversion to the colour. Staff are efficient, drinks are pricey, snacks are also served and the place feels a bit like an American diner.

Rost
Knesebeckstraße 29, Charlottenburg, 10623 (881 9501). S3, S5, S7, S9 Savignyplatz. **Open** 9am-2am daily. **Map C4**
The name of this bar means 'rust', but the only thing remotely rusty here is the sign. The interior is designed simply with pale apricot walls and odd white lights extending from the ceiling. Cool, collected and catering to an older crowd, this is also a haunt of the theatre world.

Tiergarten

Bar am Lützowplatz
Lützowplatz 7, Tiergarten, 10785 (262 6807). U1, U2, U4, U12 Nollendorfplatz. **Open** 5pm-3am Sun-Thur; 5am-4am Fri-Sat. **Map D4**
Long bar with a drinks list to match where classy customers in Chanel suits and furs sip expensive, well-made cocktails and spend the evening comparing bank balances.

FouNaNa
S-Bahnbogen 475, Bachstraße, 10555 (391 2442). S3, S5, S7, S9 Tiergarten. **Open** varies. **Map D3**
Cavernous club in an S-Bahn arch that has become a meeting place for Berlin's African community and other lovers of zouk, highlife, rai, reggae, ragga, funk, R&B and hip hop – the full spectrum of African, Afro-Caribbean and African-American musical styles.

Kumpelnest 3000

Lützowstraße 23, Tiergarten, 10785 (261 6918).
U1, U12 Kurfürstenstraße. **Open** from 5pm daily.
Map E4
This used to be a brothel, the walls are carpeted and
some of the barmen are deaf. At its best at the end
of a long Saturday night: crowded, chaotic and with
people attempting to dance to disco classics.

Schleusenkrug

Müller-Breslau-Straße/Unterschleuse, Tiergarten,
10623 (313 9909). S3, S5, S7, S9 Tiergarten. **Open**
from 10.30am daily. **Map C4**
It has become a familiar story: a location that for
decades has catered to old couples is discovered by
young hipsters and becomes a cheesy-but-cool
lounge for undergroundish events. In this case, the
location is a bar and beer garden directly on the
canal in the Tiergarten, and the crowds descend on
it in droves for easy listening, mod and indie-pop
nights. During the day the place retains much of its
original flavour, hingeing on nautical themes and
large glasses of Pils.

Treptow

Insel

Alt-Treptow 6, Treptow, 12435 (534 8851). S6, S8,
S10 Planterwäld. **Open** from 10pm Fri-Sat.
Out of the way but a brilliant place – like a minia-
ture castle on a tiny Spree island, with several levels including a top-floor balcony overlooking east
Berlin. Once a communist youth club (the 'Island of
Youth'), these days it doubles as live venue and
colourful club – lots of neon and ultra-violet, Goa
and gabber, crusties and neo-hippies, techno and hip
hop, punk and metal. Great venue in summer.

Verein der Visionaire

Am Flutgraben 2, Treptow, 12435 (no phone). S6,
S8, S9, S10 Treptower Park/U1, U12 Schlesisches
Tor. **Open** varies.
On a narrow, wooded canal and open only when it's
warm enough to sit (or dance) outside, it's a lazy
lounge by day but at night, with its two small dancefloors, has the air of a Vietnamese peasant hut gone
disco. The furniture is tattered but the scenery makes
up for it and after a few drinks you won't even notice
the neighbouring former factory. The mini-Eiffel
Tower thing in the car park next door is the clue that
you're on the right canal, but getting past the doorman can sometimes be a tricky business.

Wilmersdorf

Berlin Bar

Uhlandstraße 145, Wilmersdorf, 10719 (883 7936).
U1 Hohenzollernplatz. **Open** 10pm-7am daily. **Map C5**
Small and narrow (if there's someone standing at the
bar, it's hard to squeeze by between them and the
wall) this venerable institution goes on serving when
all else around here has closed. You pay for the priv-
ilege, though. After about 4am it's full of people
who've finished working in other places.

Wessis at play in **Kumpelnest 3000**.

Galerie Bremer

Fasanenstraße 37, Charlottenberg, 10719 (881
4908). U1, U9, U12 Spichernstraße. **Open** from 9pm
Tue-Sun. **Map C5**
Hidden in the back room of a tiny gallery in this
quiet, exclusive street, this bar has a nice air of the
well-kept secret. Inside, it's all surprises: the room is
painted in deep, rich colours with a beautiful ship-
like bar designed by Hans Scharoun, architect of the
Philharmonie and Staatsbibliothek. When the per-
sonable assistant barman takes your coat and welcomes you, it's meant to make you feel at home, and
it's also the done thing to make a little conversation
with the majestically bearded owner – he'll remember next time you drop in. Then you can sit back and
feel privileged, and enjoy being nonplussed by the
odd member of parliament entering incognito.

Late eating

Most restaurants in Berlin will feed you up to midnight and many *Imbiße* stay open much later.
Below we list a few options for a late-night sit-down
dinner, but *see also chapter* **Restaurants**.

El Burriquito

Wielandstraße 6, Charlottenburg, 10625 (312 9929).
S3, S5, S7, S9 Savignyplatz. **Open** 7pm-5am daily.
No credit cards. Map C4
Lively Spanish bar/restaurant where you can stuff
yourself with tapas at a ridiculous hour in the morning, or perch at the bar and give yourself some serious hangover material.

Gambrinus

Linienstraße 133, Mitte, 10117 (282 6843). U8
Rosenthaler Platz. **Open** noon-4am Mon-Sat; 3pm-4am
Sun. **Average** DM15. **No credit cards. Map G3**
Traditional Berlin local restaurant serving varia-
tions on the meat, potato and cabbage theme.

Jimmy's Diner

Pariser Straße 41, Wilmersdorf, 10707 (882 3141).
U1, U12 Hohenzollernplatz. **Open** 11am-2am Mon-
Thur, Sun; 11am-4am Fri, Sat. **No credit cards.**
Map C5
Fake 1950s diner serving American beers and Tex-
Mex staples. Chili, burgers, ribs and fries make up
the bulk of the menu. Useless for vegetarians.

Presse Café
Corner Hardenbergstraße/Joachimstaler Straße,
Charlottenburg, 10623 (881 7256). S3, S5, S7,
S9/U2, U9 Zoologischer Garten. **Open** 9am-1am
daily. **No credit cards. Map C4**
Just opposite Bahnhof Zoo and with a decidedly
transient ambience.

Schwarzes Café
Kantstraße 148, Charlottenburg, 10623 (313 8038).
S3, S5, S7, S9 Savignyplatz. **Open** 24 hours Mon,
Wed-Sun. **No credit cards. Map C4**
Young and friendly if occasionally overstretched
service. Mixed clientèle. Good coffee and cheesecake
round the clock.

XII Apostoli
S-Bahnbogen 177-180, Georgenstraße, Mitte, 10117
(201 0222). S1, S2, S3, S5, S7, S9/U6 Friedrich-
straße. **Open** 24 hours daily. **No credit cards. Map**
F3
Popular upmarket pizzeria and croissanterie. If you
want a DM200 bottle of wine at six in the morning,
this is the place.
Branch: Bleibtreustraße 49 (Savigny Passage),
Charlottenburg, 10623 (312 1433).

Zwiebelfisch
Savignyplatz 7-8, Charlottenburg, 10623 (312 7363).
S3, S5, S7, S9 Savignyplatz. **Open** noon-6.30am
daily. **No credit cards. Map C4**
Greet the morning German-style with a plate of salami and a beer. Otherwise, just drink the superb coffee and wander home through Savignyplatz.

Imbiße & fast food

Bagels & Bialys
Rosenthaler Straße 46-48, Mitte, 10178 (283 6546).
U8 Weinmeisterstraße/S3, S5, S7, S9 Hackescher
Markt. **Open** 9am-4am daily. **Map F3**
Sandwiches, kebabs, bagels – a selection of snacks
from various cultures, all of it good and fresh.

City Imbiß
Oranienburger Straße/corner Linienstraße, Mitte,
10117 (no phone). U6 Oranienburger Tor. **Open**
10am-5am daily. **Map F3**
The usual range of German snacks – *Currywurst,*
Bouletten, Kartoffelsalat – available deeper into the
night than at most places around here.

Habibi
Goltzstraße 24, Schöneberg, 10781 (215 3332). U1,
U2, U4, U12 Nollendorfplatz. **Open** 11am-3am Mon-
Fri, Sun; 11am-5am Sat. **Map D5**
Freshly prepared Lebanese specialities served in this
favourite stop for ravenous night owls in the busy
Winterfeldtplatz neighbourhood. The branches
don't stay open quite so late.
Branches: Akazienstraße 9, Schöneberg, 10823 (787
4428); Körtestraße 35, Kreuzberg, 10967 (692 2401).

Traube
Danziger Straße 24, Prenzlauer Berg, 10405 (441
7447). U2 Eberswalder Straße. **Open** 9am-5am
daily. **Map G2**
Excellent Turkish Imbiß off Kollwitzplatz; salads
and veggie snacks as well as kebabs and chicken.

Galerie Bremer – *cocktails with the air of a well-kept secret.*

Cafés

In both traditional coffeehouses and designer cafés, Berliners still linger over Kaffee und Kuchen.

The pace of city life might be speeding up, but Berliners still find time to malinger over a coffee and savour a slab of cake. The café culture of the German capital is as lively, diverse and entrenched as that of any other central European city. These are the venues for Berlin breakfasts, light lunches with friends and colleagues, or spaces to spread out the daily papers – provided free for your perusal in most establishments – and laze around for an hour or two. Afternoon *Kaffee und Kuchen* – coffee and cakes – remains a widely observed ritual that cuts across all social classes, though the American way of coffee is beginning to mount a challenge. *See page 190* **Is *Kaffeekultur* in for a roasting?**

Note that in Berlin it's often a blurry line that separates the café from the bar. You can breakfast, lunch, snack, dine and then get horribly drunk all in the same place. And just as many bars open during the day, so many cafés linger deep into the night. Though most places listed are clearly based around coffee, cakes and other confections, those borderline cases that might at a pinch have been included in *chapter* **Nightlife** have ended up here because their daytime life is more important, because of the quality and selection of their snacks and light meals, or because they're better places for solitary sipping or sedentary socialising than for carousing or cocktail-quaffing. That said, in Berlin most cafés also alcohol, while many bars serve excellent coffee, and either kind of institution can offer mixing and mingling as well as whatever else is on sale.

Most cafés will not take credit cards. Assume this is the case unless otherwise stated.

Mitte

Aedes

Hof II, Hackesche Höfe, Rosenthaler Straße 40-41, Mitte, 10178 (282 2103). S3, S5, S7, S9 Hackescher Markt. **Open** 10am-2am daily. **Credit** AmEx, MC, V. **Map F3**
This small and stylish Hackesche Höfe café fills with insiders who know that the food here is better – and better-priced – than the expensive goodies on offer in the larger places in the first Hof. Aedes attracts a mixture of people from the nearby theatres, bars and offices, and thankfully fewer of the young western social climbers who otherwise haunt the Hackesche Höfe establishments.

Ici – *chez soi with wine and Camus.*

Barcomi's

Sophie-Gips-Höfe, Sophienstraße 21, Mitte, 10178 (2859 8363). U8 Weinmeisterstraße/S3, S5, S7, S9 Hackescher Markt. **Open** 9am-10pm Mon-Sat; 10am-10pm Sun. **Map F3**
Unlike the Kreuzberg Barcomi's, this new one draws a crowd less interested in macadamia nut-flavoured decaffeinated coffee than an atmosphere unusually serene and unpretentious by Mitte standards. Home-made baked goods and the wide variety of freshly roasted coffees are also a novelty. The inconspicuous entrances to the Höfe open from Sophienstraße and Gipsstraße. Cynthia Barcomi also runs the Café Bravo in the courtyard of Kunst-Werk – *see chapter* **Art Galleries**.
Branch: Bergmannstraße 21, Kreuzberg, 10961 (694 8158)

Café Beth

Tucholskystraße 40, Mitte, 10117 (281 3135). S1, S2 Oranienburger Straße. **Open** 10am-6pm Mon-Thur; 10am-3pm Fri. **Map F3**

Meeting place for the Jewish community in a bistro atmosphere. American and British Jews may puzzle over what gets delivered when they order familiar kosher favourites, since the knishes and Gefüllte Fisch Amerikaner Art bear scant resemblance to what they get at home, but this café wing of the Congregation Adass Jisroel guarantees kashruth and everything is tasty and well-made. Don't be put off by the gun-toting police in front of Berlin's Jewish-orientated businesses: they're friendly. Jazz accompanies Sunday brunches.

Gorki Park
Weinbergsweg 25, Mitte, 10119 (4487286). U8 Rosenthaler Platz. **Open** 10am-1am daily. **Map F2**
Tiny Russian-run café with surprisingly tasty and authentic snacks – blini, pierogi and the like. Guests range from students and loafers to the occasional guitar-toting Ukrainian and scenesters having a quiet coffee before heading down to pose at more centrally located bars. Interesting weekend brunch buffet includes a selection of warm dishes.

Hackbarths
Auguststraße 49a, Mitte, 10119 (282 7706). U8 Weinmeisterstraße. **Open** 9am-3am daily. *Breakfast* 9am-2pm. **Map F3**
Popular spot for a leisurely breakfast among ex-squatters, art-scenesters and other long-time Scheunenviertel residents. By night it's less a café than a busy local bar where it's possible to meet and mingle, thus bucking Mitte's general trend towards facelessness and over-design.

Ici
Auguststraße 61, Mitte, 10117 (281 4064). U6 Oranienburger Tor. **Open** 3pm-3am daily. **Map F3**
Featuring original painting and sculpture from local artists, a copy of Camus will help you feel at home among the self-consciously literary set that inhabits this quiet café. Good selection of wines by the glass.

Kapelle
Zionskirchplatz 22-24, Mitte, 10119 (4434 1300). U8 Rosenthaler Platz. **Open** 9am-3am daily. **Map F2**
A comfortable, high-ceilinged café/bar across from Zionskirch and named after Die Rote Kapelle, 'The Red Orchestra', a clandestine anti-fascist organisation. In the 1930s and 1940s the Kapelle's basement was a meeting place for the anti-Hitler resistance. A revolving menu features organic meat and vegetarian dishes, and proceeds are donated to local charities and social organisations.

Keyser Soze
Tucholskystraße 33, Mitte, 10117 (2859 9489). S1, S2 Oranienburger Straße. **Open** from 11am daily. **Map F3**
A stylistic extension of the more original **Hackbarths** up the street (*above*), albeit a bit larger and properly ventilated. Always packed around the Biennale, Kunstmesse and other large art openings. The friendly staff are veterans of Mitte's renovation, as are many of the regulars. Has the artiest male toilet design in the neighbourhood.

Opern Café
Unter den Linden 5, Mitte, 10117 (200 2269). U6 Französische Straße. **Open** 8.30am-midnight daily. **Map F3**
In the elaborately decorated palatial villa right next to the Staatsoper, this is a traditional coffee-stop for Berliners and music-loving visitors. Choose from a huge selection of beautifully displayed cakes. Excellent place to sit outside in summer and watch Unter den Linden go by.

Prenzlauer Berg

Alea Jacta
Lychener Straße 39, Prenzlauer Berg, 10437 (444 9018). U2 Eberswalder Straße. **Open** from 10am daily. **Map G2**
Only a few years old, this tiny café-bar has established itself as a local for the area's cross-section of long-term students, new-age tokers and people who make things out of wood and metal. There's a lot of talk, soft rattling of chess pieces and that rare phenomenon in Berlin: people leaning across to your table and making unsolicited conversation. Good place to relax at any time of day – although it does not do food.

Café Anita Wronski
Knaackstraße 26-28, Prenzlauer Berg, 10405 (442 8483). U2 Senefelderplatz. **Open** 10am-2am daily. **Map G2**
Friendly café on two levels with scrubbed floors, beige walls, hard-working staff and as many tables crammed into the space as the laws of physics allow. Excellent brunches at around DM12 and plenty of other cafés on this stretch if there's no room here.

Eckstein
Pappelallee 73, Prenzlauer Berg, 10437 (441 9960). U2 Eberswalder Straße. **Open** 9am-2am daily. **Map G1**
This beautiful café, with its broad corner front and deco-ish look, draws one of the most mixed crowds outside of the Hackesche Höfe. But unlike many cafés around the Wasserturm or Rosenthaler Straße, Eckstein maintains a following among the less-well-scrubbed residents of Prenzlauer Berg, adding a pleasingly old-school bohemian feel to a place otherwise clean enough to take your parents to.

Café Maurer
Templiner Straße 7, Prenzlauer Berg, 10119 (4404 6077). U2 Senefelderplatz. **Open** noon-midnight Mon; noon-1am Tue-Fri; 3pm-1am Sat; 10.30am-midnight Sun. **Map G2**
This spanking new café looks a little too posh and unlived-in (big marble tables, high ceilings), but makes up for it with its clever location in a leafy square behind the Pfefferberg, an outgoing staff of Anglophone Berliners, and a fantastically gooey selection of cakes and fine Genoese dishes (average DM15). A growing daytime melting-pot for recovering clubbers, people with kids and English-speaking locals and visitors.

Café November

Husemannstraße 15, Prenzlauer Berg, 10435 (442 8425) U2 Eberswalder Straße. **Open** 10am-2am daily. *Breakfast* 10am-4pm. **Map G2**
Friendly place that's especially nice during the day, when light floods into this bright, white café through show windows that also offer views of beautifully restored Husemannstraße.

Prater

Kastanienallee 7-9, Prenzlauer Berg,10435 (448 5688). U2 Eberswalder Straße. **Open** 6pm-2am Mon-Fri; 2pm-2am Sat-Sun. **Map G2**
Almost any evening this huge and immaculately restored swing-era bar, across the courtyard from the theatre of the same name, attracts a smart, high-volume crowd – a good place to drag a large gathering and add to the conversational roar, although the Pils-swilling lustiness can make you feel you've been teleported to Munich. In summer the shady beer garden edged by the sweeping concrete forms of an old GDR sports facility makes for more of an all-day buzz.

Cafe Torpedokäfer

Dunckerstraße 69, Prenzlauer Berg, 10437 (444 5763). U2 Eberswalder Straße. **Open** from 11am daily. **Map G1**
Cafés like this are rare in Prenzlauer Berg these days; not themed, anonymous but minimally stylish – and run by a relaxed collective. Many regulars have roots in the legendary Dunckerstraße squat, making it a welcome decompression cham-

ber after too much exposure to Prenzlauer Berg's growing gentrification. Drop in for a buffet breakfast on Sundays (from DM6) or after 10pm any night and contribute to the buzz of a café where a still-active political/literary journal has editorial meetings and readings.

Friedrichshain

Abgedreht

Karl-Marx-Allee 140, Friedrichshain, 10243 (294 6808). U5 Frankfurter Tor. **Open** from 10am daily.
Comes equipped with a mini-screening room, and decorated with classic examples of German film memorabilia, bits of old hardware and occasional pieces of celluloid. All this attracts a young crowd, and also features waiters in sweat pants and white-boy dreadlocks, old sofas and sewing machine tables. With Beck's for DM3.50 a bottle, the whole combination makes this a legitimate heir to the semi-legal joints that made Mitte cook in the early 1990s.

Conmux

Simon-Dach-Straße 35, Friedrichshain, 10245 (291 3863). U5 Samariterstraße. **Open** from 10am daily.
For those who love outdoor tables: here, even in winter there are seats outside, and the waiters will light one of the gas ovens to warm you up. Inside there are sewing-machine tables and pieces of scrap-metal art. The menu offers a huge variety of well-priced light meals. Service is at best monosyllabic, at worst downright indifferent.

Is *Kaffeekultur* in for a roasting?

Is it creeping Americanisation? A welcome addition to Berlin's gastronomic landscape? A major lifestyle change in the offing? Only one thing is certain: the coffee roasters have come to Berlin. To those who have watched the Starbucks-led change in the US and UK, the only question may be: 'What took them so long?' But others may wonder: 'What will become of our beloved *Kaffee und Kuchen?'*

From the moment the black stuff arrived here from Vienna, the mid-afternoon ritual of coffee and cake has been an integral part of the Berlin day. You take a break, slip out to a café and order coffee – usually a *Milchkaffee*, served in a sort of soup bowl – and a modest slice of pastry with an immodest calorie count. Everyone does it: construction workers stand around tables at a bakery; little old ladies meet somewhere with starched tablecloths; students at a bohemian joint with postered walls and a punky soundtrack.

What no one does, however, is enquire as to the variety of coffee being served. Or order it as takeaway. Or – and here's where connoisseurs

are ill-served – buy it as freshly roasted whole beans. And, apart from at bakeries, people sit, relax, socialise. It's never a gulp for the jolt and a quick trot back to the office. This may be about to change.

It started in Berlin in 1994, when Cynthia Barcomi opened her Bergmannstraße café with its small roaster. **Barcomi's**, which now sells coffee at both its original location and the one in the Sophie-Gips Höfe, set the pattern: several coffees both in the cup and in bean form, American-style pastries and a variety of preparations.

Barcomi, however, was more interested in catering and baking than establishing a coffee empire. That was left to **Cafe Einstein**, which began roasting its own beans at its Kurfürstenstraße location a couple of years ago, and which now has four locations in town, two of which are simple coffee bars à la Starbucks. At the Hackescher Markt location, the café has also attracted competition from a small roastery called **Coffee Mamas**, and surely more competition is on the way elsewhere in town.

Café 100Wasser

*Simon-Dach-Straße 39, Friedrichshain, 10245 (2900
1356). U5 Samariterstraße.* **Open** 10am-late.
The all-you-can-eat brunch buffet (Sundays,
DM14.50, coffee included) has a cult following among
students and other late-risers. Take your time and
don't panic as the buffet gets plundered. Just when
the food seems to be finished, out comes loads of new
stuff. Pleasant during the week, too, but when crowded it can be hard to flag down a waiter.

Intimes

*Boxhagener Straße 107, Friedrichshain, 10245 (2966
6457). U5 Samariterstraße.* **Open** from 10am daily.
Next door to the cinema of the same name, decorated with painted tiles and offering a good variety of
Turkish and vegetarian food as well as breakfast at
very reasonable prices. Pleasures can be as simple
as fried potatoes with garlic sausage; best deal is the
Wednesday special. Friendly service.

Kreuzberg

Café Adler

*Friedrichstraße 206, Kreuzberg, 10969 (251 8965).
U6 Kochstraße.* **Open** 8.30am-midnight Mon-Sat;
10am-7pm Sun. **Map F4**
Next to what used be Checkpoint Charlie, you could
once watch history in the making from this elegant
corner café. Today it's a bustling, businesslike corner and Adler is a well-lit oasis of calm, coffee and
decent light meals.

Café Torpedokäfer – *decompression.*

Naturally each of these operations has its
strengths and weaknesses. Barcomi's coffee is
excellent, but easily the most expensive. Her
baked goods, too, are pricey but (except for the
cakey bagels) also excellent and she offers a wider
menu of other foods. Einstein has reasonable
prices and a decor which recalls California chains
like Peet's. The baked goods selection is small but
good, various coffee-machines and books on coffee are available, but the workers clearly do not
partake of the product themselves, since service
is often slow and spaced out. Coffee Mamas has
good pastry and bagels by Solomon's, but the coffee tends to be over-roasted, making the resultant
brew rather bitter.

The cheapest place in town for coffee vari-
etals, however, is Café Malongo, a concession
run by the venerable Parisian firm in **Galeries
Lafayette**'s food floor (*see chapter* **Shopping
& Services**): it has the widest selection (including authentic Jamaican Blue Mountain) and
although it's not roasted on the premises, it is
impeccably fresh nonetheless.

Does this, then, spell the end of the Kaffee und
Kuchen ritual? Maybe not. Cynthia Barcomi
seems to have found a compromise in her cafés,
and reaps the benefit with packed houses.
Einstein and Coffee Mamas, however, are much
more in the American style, right down to high-
res, Starbucks-inspired graphics. The trend is
too new to predict which way the wind will blow.
Still, let it be noted that none of the above places
serves iced decaf frappuccinos. Yet.

Einstein Kaffee Bars & Shops

*Friedrichstraße 185-190, Mitte, 10117 (8096
2978). U6 Französische Straße.* **Open** 7.30am-8pm
Mon-Sat, 10am-6pm Sun. **Credit** AmEx, DC, V.
Map F3
Branch: An der Spandauer Brücke 8, Mitte, 10178
(2809 6223).
Website: www.cafeeinstein.com

Coffee Mamas

*S-Bahn Bogen 4, Hackescher Markt, Mitte, 10178
(2472 2225). S3, S5, S7, S9 Hackescher Markt.*
Open 7am-8pm daily. **No credit cards. Map F3**

Café Einstein – *hectic waiters, faux Viennese style, and famous Apfelstrudel.*

Café Bar Morena
Wiener Straße 60, Kreuzberg, 10999 (611 4716).
U1, U12 Görlitzer Bahnhof. **Open** 9am-5am daily.
Map H5
Famous breakfasts are served to people who wake
up at all hours. Make sure that you avoid the
'English Breakfast', though – it features the foulest
baked beans ever known to culinary science. In the
evening the Café Bar Morena bustles, and the service can be rather slow. The music isn't overpower-
ing and the half-tiled walls and parquet flooring give
it an art deco feel.

Freßco
Zossener Straße 24, Kreuzberg, 10961 (6940 1613).
U7 Gneisenaustraße. **Open** 10am-1am Mon-Fri;
10am-5pm Sat. **Map F5**
Bright and clean new addition to the cafés of the
Bergmannstraße neighbourhood. Good coffee and
fresh, tasty food – snacks, light meals, salads, sandwiches and pastries – chosen not from a menu, but
from the display case below the bar. Lots for vegetarians. Relaxing and roomy.
Branch: Stresemannstraße 34, Kreuzberg, 10963
(2529 9309)

Milagro
Bergmannstraße 12, Kreuzberg, 10961 (692 2303).
U7 Gneisenaustraße. **Open** 9am-1am Mon-Thur;
9am-2am Fri-Sat; 9am-1am Sun. **Map F5**
Light and friendly café, famous for its breakfasts,
which are served until 4pm. There are also cheap
but classy, tasty dishes being served until midnight.
Disorientating stairs lead to hospital-like toilets. On
a winter's afternoon, the front room can be too dim
to read your daily paper.

Café Übersee
Paul-Lincke-Ufer 44, Kreuzberg, 10555 (618 8765).
U1, U8, U12 Kottbusser Tor. **Open** 10am-2am
daily. *Breakfast* 10am-4pm daily. **Map H5**

Vines cover the outside, where summer tables offer
a popular spot for breakfast overlooking the
Landwehr canal. Nothing special inside and if it's
full, there are a couple of other places on this stretch.

Schöneberg
Café Berio
Maaßenstraße 7, Schöneberg, 10777 (216 1946).
U1, U2, U12 Nollendorfplatz. **Open** 8am-1am
daily. **Map D5**
The locals' choice for breakfast, it also has plenty of
home-made cakes and excellent ice cream. Café Berio
has been an institution since the 1930s and the tables
outside are a prime people-watching spot in summer.

Bilderbuch
Akazienstraße 28, Schöneberg, 10823 (7870 6057).
U7 Eisenacher Straße. **Open** 9am-1am Mon-Fri; 9am-
2am Sat; 10am-1am Sun. **Map D5**
Cavernous book-lined labyrinth whose inner dimensions are a surprise after the modest storefront
entrance. Vast spaces between the tables mean considerable room for discretion, though some parts of
the café are so far from the kitchen it's a surprise the
food isn't cold by the time it reaches your table.
Usefully located on one of Schöneberg's more interesting shopping streets.

Savarin
Kulmer Straße 17, Schöneberg, 10783 (216 3864).
S1, S2/U7 Yorckstraße. **Open** 10am-midnight daily.
Map E5
Gorgeously cosy little café with a sophisticated edge,
a staff who are glamorous in a worldly kind of way,
and famously excellent cakes and pies. On Sundays
it's not just that you can't find a seat – you can't even
get in the door for all the people queueing to take
away cheesecake slices and apple tarts.

Tim's Canadian Deli

Maaßenstraße 14, Schöneberg, 10777 (2175 6960).
U1, U2, U4, U12 Nollendorfplatz. **Open** 8am-1am
Mon-Fri; 9am-2am Sat; 9am-1am Sun. **Credit** AmEx,
MC, V. **Map D5**
Against the odds, this place seems to have con-
quered the Winterfeldtplatz area, though there's not
a café round here that's not full on a market day.
Lots of bagels and muffins, egg breakfasts until
4pm, various light meal options, but precious few
actual Canadians in evidence.

Charlottenburg

Café Aedes

*S-Bahn Bogen, Savignyplatz, Charlottenburg, 10629
(3150 9535). S3, S5, S7, S9 Savignyplatz.* **Open**
8am-midnight Mon-Fri; 9am-midnight Sat-Sun.
Breakfast 9am-3pm daily. **Map C4**
A small, trendy café tucked under the S-Bahn line at
Savignyplatz. A steady flow of fashionable yuppie
types pop in and out for a cappuccino, a late breakfast, or to look at the other fashionable yuppie types.

Café Hardenberg

*Hardenbergstraße 10, Charlottenburg, 10623 (312
2644). U2 Ernst-Reuter-Platz.* **Open** 9am-1am daily.
Map C4
Observe students in their natural habitat, day or
night, at the spacious and relaxing Hardenberg, next
to the Goethe-Institut and opposite the Technical
University. Most nurse a drink for hours, listening
to classical music or chatting. Others come for the
cheap eats. Furnishings include museum posters,
plants and ceiling fans.

Café Kranzler

*Kurfürstendamm 18, Charlottenburg, 10719 (882
6911). U9, U15 Kurfürstendamm.* **Open** 8am-
midnight daily. **Map C4**
Once dominating the Ku'damm Eck, but now somewhat cowed by the new Helmut Jahn structure rising right behind it, the three-storey Kranzler is one
of the city's oldest and most famous coffeehouses.
The terrace overlooking the Ku'damm is still a prime
spot in summer, but this institution is rather on the
wane and latterly little more than a tourist trap.
There has been talk of moving the operation east.

Gasthaus Lenz

*Stuttgarter Platz 20, Charlottenburg, 10627 (324
1619). S3, S5, S7, S9 Charlottenburg.* **Open** 10am-
2am daily. *Breakfast* 10am-11.30am daily. **Map B4**
An older crowd is drawn to this unpretentious, spacious café nestled in the cluster of bars on
Stuttgarter Platz. Cigarette-smoking intellectuals
pack the place day and night. If they can find a seat,
Guardian-reading 30-somethings will feel at home
here. No music.

Leysieffer

*Kurfürstendamm 218, Wilmersdorf, 10719 (8825
7480). U15 Uhlandstraße.* **Open** 9am-7pm Mon-
Wed, Fri-Sat; 9am-8.30pm Thur; 10am-8pm Sun.
Map C4
Indulge yourself in style at this recently refurbished
café housed in what used to be the Chinese Embassy.
Exquisite tortes and fruitcakes are served upstairs
in the high-ceilinged café which resembles an art
gallery. Mounds of truffles and bonbons, beautifully presented, are sold downstairs in the shop.

Café Savigny

*Grolmanstraße 53-54, Charlottenburg, 10623 (312
8195). S3, S5, S7, S9 Savignyplatz.* **Open** 10am-1am
daily. **Map C4**
It's hard to find a table at this small and airy café.
Sparsely decorated, painted white with round
arched doorways, the Savigny has a Mediterranean
feel. Good breakfasts, filled baguettes and cakes.
Tables outside in summer, nice bar within.

Schwarzes Café

*Kantstraße 148, Charlottenburg, 10623 (313 8038).
S3, S5, S7, S9 Savignyplatz.* **Open** 24 hours Mon,
Wed-Sun. **Map C4**
Centrally located, and open around the clock for
breakfasts and meals. It used to be all black and
somewhat anarchistically inclined (hence the name)
but these days the decor has been brightened up and
the political crowd moved out of this neighbourhood
ages ago. Service can get overstretched when it's
crowded, such as early on a weekend morning, when
clubbers stop by for breakfast on their way home.
See also chapter **Nightlife**.

Wintergarten im Literaturhaus

*Fasanenstraße 23, Charlottenburg, 10719 (882
5414). U15 Uhlandstraße.* **Open** 9.30am-1am daily.
Map C4
This is the café of the Literaturhaus, which has lectures, readings, exhibitions and an excellent bookshop in the basement (*see chapter* **Shopping &
Services**). The greenhouse-like sunny winter garden or salon rooms of the café are great for ducking
into a book or scribbling out postcards. Breakfast,
snacks and desserts are available.

Tiergarten

Café am Neuen See

*Lichtensteinallee 1, Tiergarten, 10787 (254 4930).
Bus x9, 100, 187, 341.* **Open** *Mar-Oct* 10am-11pm
daily; *Nov-Feb* 10am-8pm daily. **Credit** AmEx, V.
Map D4
Stretch out at one of the outside tables by a leafy
Tiergarten lake and it feels like you've slipped right
outside of the city. Coffee, cakes, drinks, light meals
and rowing-boats for hire nearby.

Café Einstein

*Kurfürstenstraße 58, Tiergarten, 10785 (261 5096).
U1, U2, U4, U12 Nollendorfplatz.* **Open** 10am-2am
daily. *Breakfast* all day. **Map D4**
A Viennese-style coffee house with hectic waiters in
bow-ties and waistcoats, international papers and
magazines, and a renowned Apfelstrudel. In summer you can sit in the garden at the back and enjoy
a leisurely breakfast. *See also chapter* **Restaurants**.
Branch: Unter den Linden 42, Mitte, 10117 (204 3632).

Love Parade

Music, dancing and shagging in the streets – each July Berlin becomes venue for the world's most over-the-top party.

Back on 1 July 1989, when around 350 people set off down the Ku'damm behind a couple of floats playing techno and house, no one could have predicted that the Love Parade would grow into the biggest and most important cultural event in Berlin. It was billed at the beginning by organiser Dr Motte as a demonstration, not against anything, but *for* love. Later the slogan was *Für Friede, Freude, Eierkuchen – For Peace, Joy and Pancakes.* A suitably Dada sentiment for an event that was always wacky and anarchic in the nicest possible way.

And the next year twice as many people turned up. And the next year twice as many as that. Until, after a decade of geometric growth, close to two million people turned out to party in July 1999. The Love Parade is these days akin to several Woodstocks dumped down right in the middle of a

major European capital. Apart from the Parade itself, which sprawls through the city from its epicentre at the Siegessäule, there are scores of raves in spaces scattered right from Spandau to Köpenick. The flyers alone would fuel a recycling plant. Every last hotel is crammed with party animals, and even non-raving Berliners watch it all on TV at home. It generates all kinds of excitement, from the euphoria of the participants, through much editorialising in the local press, to the outrage of conservationists and assorted boring old farts.

What miffs the conservationists is everyone trashing the Tiergarten, and this has become the main argument about the event. Formerly the beef was the clean-up bill. Over a million people partying their hardest for the whole weekend tend to leave a lot of litter. As it's classed as a political

demonstration, the city used to have to pay to tidy up afterwards. Now much of the clean-up is done courtesy of Alba, a private refuse collection concern which is effectively one of the main sponsors of the event, and the main issue is people pissing on Tiergarten trees and frightening all the rabbits.

On the other hand, over a million people partying their hardest for a whole weekend also tend to spend an awful lot of money. And this is what wins the day. Every year there are rumours that this will be the last Love Parade – it's almost a part of the event's mystique. And every year, after debates and much bargaining with the city government, the event finally goes ahead again. Berlin simply can't afford to turn away over one million tourists of any kind, and the Love Parade has become an internationally famous event that Paris, Berlin's ancient rival, would just love to get its hands on.

SEX ON THE STREETS

But what's it actually like being at the Love Parade? Well, it's hot, unbearably crowded, exhausting and very, very loud. It's also so mad and massive and exhilarating that your heart beats faster, even without any artificial stimulants, and there are certainly also plenty of those. If you're well-connected you might be lucky enough to get on one of the 50 or so

floats organised by clubs, labels and media outlets from Berlin and all over Europe. Otherwise you'll be adrift in an ocean of revellers, hopelessly lost in the party zone, and unable to get back to wherever you're staying even if you were still together enough to find the way. At night, you'll queue for ages outside every venue, queue to pay through the nose for a plastic cup of warm beer, queue to go for a piss, queue to get back on the dancefloor. But nothing can beat being in a crowd like this fired by top DJs giving their all to try and seal some legendary status at this dance music event of events. The Love Parade is a paradoxical thing: totally irritating and absolutely brilliant all at the same time.

It's also utterly over the top, with public sex now almost as much a feature as wild, abandoned dancing. In 1999 no fewer than three hardcore porn films were shot right in the middle of the parade, two of them on floats. Passengers on the float organised by the Kit Kat Club (*see chapter* **Nightlife**) basically shagged their way through the entire afternoon, their truck accompanied by hordes of horny bystanders craning to get a better look.

The music has always centred on techno, and still does, but these days you can hear almost anything it's possible to dance to, from African drumming to drum 'n' bass, from trance to wet & hard. It's easy to find out what's going on and where. At times it'll seem like everyone in Berlin wants to hand you a flyer advertising some huge outdoor

rave or a tiny trip hop club night. There's even a parallel parade, the Fuck Parade (*see chapter* **By Season**), which sees itself as a more underground alternative to the now arguably over-commercialised main event, and meanders on a different route through the city.

In 1999 the main Parade started at both the Brandenburg Gate and Ernst-Reuter-Platz, from where floats and floods of partying pedestrians slowly converged at the Siegessäule for the best light show since Nuremburg. At the time of writing, this looks likely to be the deal for 2000, though there are calls to shift it to the Avus, the dual-carriageway that runs south-west from the Funkturm – big and wide and safely out of town.

TOP PARADE TIPS

Whatever the route, there are some things you need to know. Take lots of water. People are going to spray you from high-velocity water pistols all afternoon but you're still going to need to drink lots of liquid. Beer is a bad idea, not least because it can be hard to find anywhere to piss. Take sun block, too. Many people strip off at least their shirts (some their entire kit) and end up with serious radiation burns. Remember that you won't be able to sit down and recuperate whenever you feel like it, and think about how you'll pace yourself over the whole weekend. Sleep will become a precious commodity. Glucose tablets are a good idea, because there are also few chances to eat. Veterans take a sandwich or some fruit.

The BVG issues a special Love Parade armband. In 1999 this cost DM10 and allowed the wearer unlimited travel on public transport for the weekend. This really is the best way to get about. You won't be able to park a car anywhere near the Parade, and traffic is disrupted from Saturday morning until Monday by scattered patches of dancing in the street. Police presence is low-key and friendly. Many cops even join in the dancing, cheered on by the surrounding crowds.

Above all, leap at the opportunity to get on any kind of guest list. Invitations to exclusive and relatively uncrowded events are like gold dust. In 1999, VIP passes for the Café am Neuen See in the Tiergarten (*see chapter* **Cafés**) were changing hands for up to DM2,000.

Ah yes, money. Sponsorship flows freely and there's no doubt that many people really rake it in, not least the city authorities, who apart from anything else licence the drink concessions along the route. There's a real danger that commercialisation could take over completely and lead to some sort of Pepsi Parade. But even then there'd still be all the autonomous events around the edges. And millions of participants in a state of mad summer abandon. And just about every DJ in the developed world. And the experience of Berlin transformed briefly into the backdrop for one colossal, city-wide party. The Love Parade is, quite simply, unique.

Love Parade

Date second Sat in July. **Admission** free for Parade; varies for evening raves. **Information** Planetcom (284 620).
Website: www.loveparade.de

Arts & Entertainment

Cabaret

Varieté is the spice of life.

First, the bad news. If you're longing to see a real Berlin cabaret of the 1920s – sorry. Life is another kind of cabaret now, old chum. But though the original clubs are long vanished, the feeling can sometimes be recaptured – it all depends on who's playing and where.

The good news is that modern Berlin cabaret has come into its own, without nostalgia to hold it back. In places like **Chamäleon Varieté** and **Kalkscheune** you can see anything from Burlesque talkshows to poetic jesters to drag queen theatre. Several venues have invested big money into recreating the look of an old Berlin cabaret but it's mostly just wishful thinking. The shows in these places are strictly tourist fluff. But **Wintergarten** does have gorgeous décor and can be lots of fun, especially if someone else is picking up the tab – table service in these places does not come cheap. This type of show is called 'varieté', meaning you can expect clowns, acrobats, magicians, dancing girls and maybe a snazzy band.

Other places might call the show a 'revue', which could include some of the above elements but mainly consists of song and dance and/or comedy sketches. This is what most of us would call cabaret. The German form of the word is *Kabarett* but shows billed as such have little in common with varieté – Kabarett is political satire sprinkled with original songs. This has always had a strong following in Berlin. Kartoon, (between premises as we go to press – call 204 4756 for information), is one of the premier contemporary exponents of the genre, but if you don't speak perfect German or have a good understanding of local politics, their shows won't make much sense.

In the **Roter** and **Grüner Salons**, on the other hand, there is something for everybody. These two separate clubs inside the Volksbühne (*see chapter* **Theatre**) host such a variety of acts that the shows can't be shoehorned into one particular category. It is, in the end, the performers that make the evening. A few to watch out for are: Teufelsberg Productions (clever drag cabaret); Stepinskis (tap-dancing female comediennes); the Lonely Husbands (slick but cosy male trio with fun musical numbers) and New Comedian Harmonists (funny male acappella). Interesting Anglophone entertainers include: Rick Maverick (stand-up comedy and poetry); Gayle Tufts (stand-up comedy with pop); Bridge Markland (gender-bending performance); and Priscilla Be (sardonic spoken-word).

Liza Minelli acts out the Weimar myth, but life is another kind of cabaret now, old chum.

Traditional

Chez Nous
Marburger Straße 14, Tiergarten, 10789 (213 1810). S3, S5, S7, S9/U2, U9 Zoologischer Garten. **Open** *box office* 10am-1pm, 1.30-6.30pm, daily. **Showtimes** 8.30pm and 11pm daily. **Admission** DM44-DM60. **No credit cards. Map D4**
Revue with classic drag queen numbers. Lots of feathers, falsies and celebrity lookalike lip-synching.

Friedrichstadtpalast
Friedrichstraße 107, Mitte, 10117 (2326 2474). S1, S2, S3, S5, S7, S9/U6 Friedrichstraße. **Open** 6pm-1am daily; *box office* 10am-6pm Mon, Sun; 10am-7pm Tue-Sat. **Admission** DM19-99. **No credit cards. Map F3**
Big venue, big shows – Las Vegas-like musical variety and revues, usually packed with German tourists.

Kleine Nachtrevue
Kurfürstenstraße 116, Schöneberg, 10787 (218 8950). U1, U2, U12, U15 Wittenbergplatz. **Open** 9pm-4am Mon-Sat. **Admission** *minimum charge* DM30. **Credit** AmEx, DC, V. **Map D4**
Opened by Sylvia Schmidt, a talented chanteuse who also appears in the show, the club is intimate sexy and as close to old Berlin as one can get. Forty-minute shows on and off during the evening, two longer shows on Saturdays at 10.30pm and 12.30am.

La Vie en Rose
Flughafen Tempelhof, Tempelhof, 12101 (6951 3000). U6 Platz der Luftbrücke. **Open** *box office* 11am-6pm Mon-Fri; *bar* from 7pm. **Showtimes** 9pm Wed-Sun. **Admission** DM30-45. **Credit** AmEx, DC, V. **Map F6**
Revue theatre and restaurant/piano bar recently relocated to premises left of Tempelhof Airport's main entrance. Dancing girls, glitter, soft porn, pricey drinks, German tourists and maximum cheese.

Wintergarten Varieté

Potsdamer Straße 96, Tiergarten, 10785 (250 0880/hotline 2500 8888). U1 Kurfürstenstraße. **Open** box office 10am-showtime daily. **Showtimes** 8pm Mon-Tue, Thur-Fri; 4pm, 8pm Wed; 6pm, 10pm Sat; 6pm Sun. **Admission** DM35-99. **Credit** AmEx, MC, V. **Map E4**
A classy place, run by astute impresario Andre Heller. The shows are slick, professional and very mixed – excellent acrobats, magicians and clowns, but often quite terrible dancing girls.

Modern

Bar Jeder Vernunft

Spiegelzelt, Schaperstraße 24, Wilmersdorf, 10719 (883 1582). U1, U9 Spichernstraße. **Open** box office noon-7pm daily. **Showtime** 8.30pm daily. **Admission** DM35-55. **Credit** MC, V. **Map C5**
This renovated circus tent is in a city park-like setting. The inside is lined with mirrors and on stage you can see some of Berlin's most celebrated entertainers. Friday and Saturday late-night shows are generally free and well-attended.

Chamäleon Varieté

Hackesche Höfe, Rosenthaler Straße 40-41, Mitte, 10178 (282 7118). S3, S5, S7, S9 Hackescher Markt. **Open** box office noon-9pm Mon-Thur; noon-midnight Fri, Sat; 4-9pm Sun. **Showtimes** 8.30pm Tue-Sat; 7pm Sun. **Admission** DM35-43. **No credit cards. Map F3**
A beautiful old theatre with classy and comfortable table seating, a modern attitude and a lot of flair. Earlier adventurousness seems, however, to be giving way to an attempt to become Wintergarten-Ost.

Kalkscheune

Johannisstraße 2, Mitte, 10117 (2839 0065). U6 Oranienburger Straße/S1, S2 Oranienburger Tor. **Open** box office noon-6pm daily. **Showtimes** vary. **Admission** DM7-30. **No credit cards. Map F3**
On the ball and close to the feeling of an old cabaret, a listed building from the 1840s, which also contains a lounge and party room. Challenging shows range from the warped to the wonderful.

Alternative

Apart from the spaces listed below, **Maria am Ostbahnhof** is also a venue for occasional events. *See chapter* **Music: Rock, Folk & Jazz.**

Cafe Theater Schalotte

Behaimstraße 22, Charlottenburg, 10585 (341 1485). U7 Richard-Wagner-Platz. **Open** varies. **Admission** DM25. **No credit cards. Map B3**
A friendly and comfortable café with a nice-sized theatre where a well-chosen assortment of acts can be seen. The European Acappella Festival every November is worth catching.

Open Space Art Laboratory

Adalbertstraße 32, Kreuzberg, 10999 (2759 0712). U1, U8 Kottbusser Tor. **Open** gallery 4-8pm Tue-Fri; 2-6pm Sat, Sun; performance varies. **Admission** varies. **No credit cards. Map G4**
Small, friendly and unpretentious space – just a few tables and a tiny bar – indulging a variety of exhibitions, performances, readings, concerts, films and cabaret events. Thursday evenings there are performances – somewhere between live art and cabaret – plus their 'Sexy Essen Volks-cuisine', a good and filling veggie plateful for DM5.

Roter Salon/Grüner Salon

Volksbühne, Rosa-Luxemburg-Platz, Mitte, 10178 (2406 5807/3087 4806). U2 Rosa-Luxemburg-Platz. **Open** varies. **Admission** DM10-20. **No credit cards. Map G3**
Sometimes the atmosphere in these two separate performance spaces can really take you back to the secret cabarets of the 1920s – you can get the feeling that you're doing something deliciously illegal. But these small clubs are actually legitimate and open-minded. Expect anything from drag talk shows to tango parties.

Scheinbar

Monumentenstraße 9, Schöneberg, 10829 (784 5539). U7 Kleistpark. **Open** from 8.30pm Wed-Sat. **Admission** DM12. **No credit cards. Map E5**
A hip and intimate storefront club exploding with fresh talent. One of the most experimental and fun-loving cabarets in town, with an excellent house troupe and a selection of guest performers. Wednesday night's open stage is often pretty wild.

Scheinbar – *an excellent house troupe.*

Children

Berliners love children – the idea of 'em, anyway.

Like all Germans, Berliners love the idea of childhood, but when it comes to kids in places where adults are supposed to hold sway – like the dinner table (or museums or churches) – well, sometimes they can be less than generous.

German educators and philosophers in the 19th century were among the first to recognise that children were more then mere inferior, pint-sized versions of adults. So the notion that kids (short for the German *Kinder*, by the way) deserve a special place in society is thoroughly incorporated in the modern German psyche.

So well-anchored, some would argue, that on occasion things have run out of control, with despots or even democratically elected politicians insisting like a stern parent on blind obedience, predictably resulting in a population which sooner or later either buckled under, or started raising hell and screaming uncontrollably. The behavioural borders between restrained adulthood and whining, pouting childhood here are so fluid that even today there is no idiom in the German language for the phrase, 'Grow up!'.

Instead, there are lots of places where kids can go about the business of being children in peace. In summer empty lots come alive with circuses and fun-fairs, called *Volksfeste*. The urban fabric is laced with small parks and squares with playgrounds. Museums and other attractions have reduced or free entrance for children, and public transport is free for kids under six. Buses can be entered easily with buggies from rear doors, and though many U-Bahn stations still don't have lifts, they are rarely more than a flight of stairs deep. Where escalators are available, they are technically off-limits to prams, but no one cares.

Berlin's Zoo and Aquarium are the traditional attractions for young tourists, and have been for generations. On a sunny summer day, nothing downtown competes. At press time Sony was preparing to open a spectacular urban entertainment centre under its new headquarters on Potsdamer Platz that points as far into the future as the Zoo does into the city's past.

Shopping for children

Necessities are available in any shopping district, with the Drospa and Kaisers Drugstore chains offering a good selection of baby food and supplies. Souvenirs for kids? Try fan articles for the

Berlin – swinging playground paradise.

local football team Hertha or stuffed-toy brands Steif and Sigikind, both available at department stores. *See chapter* **Shopping & Services**.

Bärenstark

Georgenstraße 201, Mitte, 10117 (208 2590). S1, S2, S3, S5, S7, S9/U6 Friedrichstraße. **Open** 11am-6pm Wed-Mon. **Credit** AmEx, MC, V. **Map F3**
New and antique teddy bears in what's almost a museum of plush kiddie companions.

Hennes & Mauritz (H&M)

Kurfürstendamm 234, Charlottenburg, 10719 (882 3844). U15 Uhlandstraße. **Open** 10am-8pm Mon-Fri; 9am-4pm Sat. **Credit** AmEx, DC, JCB, V. **Map C4**
Specialises in trendy baby, kids' and young adults' fashions and accessories. This branch is for babies and toddlers but a full range is at other H&M outlets all over town.
Branches: Karl-Marx-Straße 110; Arkaden am Potsdamer Platz.

Bärenstark – *top teddies.*

KaDeWe
*Wittenbergplatz, Charlottenburg, 10789 (212 10). U1,
U2, U15 Wittenbergplatz.* **Open** 9.30am-8pm Mon-Fri;
9am-4pm Sat. **Credit** AmEx, DC V. **Map D4**
Extensive but expensive children's wear department, a wonderful toy section, a food emporium on
the sixth floor, a no-smoking cafeteria in the rooftop
atrium, and nappy-changing tables in the toilets.

Spiele Max
*Wilmersdorfer Straße 54a, Charlottenburg, 10627
(390 8180). U7 Wilmersdorfer Straße.* **Open**
9.30am-8pm Mon-Fri; 9am-4pm Sat. **No credit
cards. Map C3**
The biggest local toy retailer, carrying a full selection of German and international brands plus seasonal stuff for fun outdoors.
Branch: Ring Center, Frankfurter Allee 111, 10247
(442 6410).

Von Winde Verweht
*Eisenacher Straße 81, Schöneberg, 10823 (7870
3636). U7 Eisenacher Straße.* **Open** 10am-6.30 pm
Mon-Fri; 10am-2pm Sat. **No credit cards. Map D5**
If it flies or floats and you can have fun with it, this
kite store will sell it to you. Named after *Gone With
the Wind.*

Baby-sitters

You may be able to arrange a baby-sitter through
your hotel. Otherwise, the following agencies can
provide English-speaking sitters.

Heinzelmännchen (Freie Universität)
(831 6071). **Open** 7.30am-5pm Mon-Fri.
A range of fees from DM18 depending on time and
availability.

Mickys Babysitterservice
(0330 569 3743/fax 0330 569 3745). **Open** 9am-
8pm Mon-Sat.
Experienced baby-sitters available for DM11 an
hour, plus a DM15 job fee and DM15 if it's a last-
minute booking.

TUSMA (Technische Universität)
(315 9340). **Open** 7am-6pm daily.
A range of fees from DM15 depending on time and
availability.

Attractions
Museums
Berlin has no large-scale, hands-on science museum, and few of the kid-friendly computer gimmicks standard by now in many museums around
the world. Germans are sceptical about the inter-
face of childhood and technology in general, and
specifically of the educational value of anything
transmitted via a video screen or keyboard.

But in addition to the museums listed below, it's
worth keeping in mind the following: the
Pergamon Museum's Greek altar and Babylonian
Ishtar Gate awe children as well as adults, and a
quick scoot around the museum's highlights is free
on Sunday; the **Egyptian Museum's** bust of
Cleopatra and sarcophagi appeal to even pre-school-
ers; the **Museum für Naturkunde** (Natural
History Museum) has the world's largest dinosaur
skeleton; the **Museum für Völkerkunde**
(Ethnological Museum) is more educational than
entertaining, but does have a large wooden clubhouse children can run around in, plus a boardable
replica of a catamaran from Tonga – there's also a
small Junior Museum in the basement with exhibits
designed for young people. One of Berlin's most kid-
friendly exhibits is at the **Museum für Verkehr
und Technik**, with trains to climb in and out of
plus computers and gadgets to play with. The
Spectrum annexe houses 200 interactive devices and
experiments, but most of them are primitive and
pretty boring. The cars used to smuggle people
through the Wall at the **Checkpoint Charlie
Museum** appeal to kids over the age of eight. For
listings *see chapter* **Museums**.

Museum Kindheit und Jugend des Stadtmuseums Berlin
Berlin Museum of Youth and Childhood
*Wallstraße 32, Mitte, 10179 (275 0383). U2
Märkisches Museum.* **Open** 9am-5pm Tue-Fri.
Admission DM3; DM1.50 children. **Map G4**
If you ever wanted to show your kids how lucky
they are to be going to school today and not 50 years
ago, this is the place to do it. Apart from old toys, it
shows artefacts from classrooms during the Weimar
Republic, the Nazi era and under Communism.

Museum Kindheit und Jugend.

Puppentheater-Museum Berlin

Berlin Puppet Theatre Museum
Karl-Marx-Straße 135, Neukölln, 12043 (687 8132).
U7 Karl-Marx-Straße. **Open** 9am-4pm Mon-Fri;
11am-5pm Sat-Sun. **Admission** DM5; DM4 children.
Map H6
Hand-made and antique puppets and marionettes
from around the world. Also occasional performances – a revelation for kids young enough not
quite to have sussed who's pulling the strings. A bit
out of the way but worthwhile.

Museum villages & farms

Domäne Dahlem

*Königin-Luise-Straße 49, Zehlendorf, 14195 (832
5000). U1 Dahlem-Dorf.* **Open** 10am-6pm Wed-Mon.
Admission DM3; children free.
On this working farm, children can see how life was
lived in the 17th century. Craftspeople including
blacksmiths, carpenters, bakers and potters preserve
and teach their skills. It is best to visit during one of
several festivals held during the year, when children
can ride ponies, tractors and hay-wagons. Also open
during the week, just to commune with the animals.

Jugendfarm Lübars

*Quickborner Strasse, Reinickendorf, 13469 (415
7027). S1 Wittenau, then bus 221.* **Open** 9am-7pm
Tue-Fri, Sun. **Admission** free.
Lübars was once at the edge of West Berlin, just
inside the Wall. The working farms in the charming
old village provided a haven from the bustle of the
city, and although west Berliners are no longer
hemmed in, Alt Lübars is still worth a visit. In the
nearby children's farm you can see farm animals,
watch craftspeople at work, and eat at the restaurant in the *Hof.* Adjacent is a great playground and
a hill of World War II rubble to climb.

Museumdorf Düppel

*Clauertstraße 11, Zehlendorf, 14163 (802 6671). U1
Oskar-Helene-Heim, then bus 115.* **Open** mid-Apr to
mid-Oct 3-7pm Thur; 10am-5pm Sun & hols.
Admission DM3; DM1.50 children.
A 14th-century village, reconstructed around arche-
ological excavations and surrounded by the Düppel
Forest. Workers demonstrate handicrafts, medieval
technology and farming techniques. Ox-cart rides
for kids. Small snack bar. A very quiet outing.

Zoos

Berlin Zoologischer Garten (Zoo) and Aquarium

*Hardenbergplatz 8, Tiergarten, 10787 (254 010).
S3, S5, S7, S9/U2, U9 Zoologischer Garten.* **Open**
9am-5pm daily. **Admission** *zoo* DM14; DM7
children; *aquarium* DM14; DM7 children; *combined
admission* DM22.50; DM11.50 children. **Map D4**
More species (1,500) than any other zoo in the world,
with an excellent playground. Highlights include a
petting zoo and giant pandas. The aquarium is also
extraordinary, and worth a separate visit to see trop-
ical fish, lizards, alligators and an insect zoo.

Tierpark Friedrichsfelde

*Am Tierpark 125, Friedrichsfelde, 10307 (515 310).
U5 Tierpark.* **Open** 9am-5pm daily. **Admission**
DM14; DM7 children.
The zoo in east Berlin is larger but has fewer animals than its western counterpart. It's good for long
walks and views of grassland animals (giraffe, deer)
in wide open spaces. Facilities for children include
a petting zoo, a playground and snack stands.

Entertainment

Music Box

*Sony Center, Kemperplatz 1, Tiergarten, 10785
(5513 7137). S1, S2/U2 Potsdamer Platz.* **Open**
10am-10pm daily. **Admission** DM20; DM12
children. **Map E4**
Opened in early 2000 in the basement of the Sony
Center, this interactive 'edutainment' exhibit features a series of attractions based around the theme
of music – including a *Yellow Submarine* 'adventure'
and the chance to conduct a virtual Berlin
Philharmonic. Children are guided by Egon the
Spider. At press time we'd only seen a press release
– impossible to tell if it would be wonderful or
cringeworthy. *See also chapter* **Museums**.

Children's films

Most films in Berlin are in German but check listings in *tip* or *Zitty* for the notation OF
(*Originalfassung* – 'original version') or OmU ('sub-
titled'). The **Berlin Film Festival** in February
(*see chapter* **Film**) features movies for children,
many in English. There's also usually something
educational at the **Haus der Kulturen der Welt**
(*see chapters* **Sightseeing** *and* **Music: Rock,
Folk & Jazz**).

Theatre & circus

For current theatre listings, check *tip* and *Zitty*
magazines. Visiting circuses hang their posters
everywhere around town. There's also a permanent circus show at the **UFA-Fabrik** (Victoria
Straße 13, Tempelhof, 752 8085). Because of the
language problem, theatre is not ideal, but Berlin
has several puppet theatres.

Hackesches Hof Theater

*Rosenthaler Straße 40-41, Mitte, 10178 (283 2587).
S3, S5, S7, S9 Hackescher Markt.* **Admission**
DM16; DM10 children. **Map F2**
Features a Sunday brunch programme from 10am
comprising a buffet followed by clowns and puppets.

Die Schaubude

*Greifswalder Straße 81-84, Prenzlauer Berg, 10405
(423 4314). S4, S8, S10 Greifswalder Straße.*
Performances 10am Mon-Fri; 10am, 2pm Wed;
3pm Sat; 11am Sun. **Admission** DM7-10.
High-quality puppet theatre for kids and adults,
used by a variety of local troupes plus visiting
artists from abroad.

Parks & playgrounds

The vast Grunewald is great for long walks, as is the more central Tiergarten. Paddle and rowing boats can be hired near the Café am Neuen See (Thomas-Dehler-Straße) in the Tiergarten, and just south of the S1 Schlachtensee station in the Grunewald. You can rent bicycles at the Grunewald S-Bahn station. Treptower Park, on the Spree river, has flowers, trees and standard German food. For a playground paradise, the Volkspark east of Bundesallee in Wilmersdorf (U7, U9 Berliner Straße) has myriad slides and playground paraphernalia, as well as a horizontal ski-lift ride and a duckpond. Viktoria Park in Kreuzberg (U6, U7 Mehringdamm) has a hill for climbing or tobogganing, Berlin's only waterfall, a small children's zoo and a good playground.

There are also some excellent playgrounds near tourist attractions: across the Spandauer Damm from the Schloß Charlottenburg at Klausenerplatz; Schustehruspark on Schustehrusstraße two blocks south of the Egyptian Museum; behind Museum Island just across the footbridge in Monbijou Park; and in the Tiergarten off John-Foster-Dulles-Allee on the way to the Reichstag.

Further afield, **Peacock Island** (Pfaueninsel) is a nice place to spend a quiet afternoon. Peacocks roam this island nature preserve near Wannsee, reachable by a short ferry ride. There's also an unusual castle built by Friedrich Wilhelm II with a small museum inside.

In summer there are plenty of places to go swimming or paddling – there are both outdoor public pools and lakes on the city outskirts. The Strandbad-Wannsee is the most accessible of the latter, a ten-minute walk from S-Bahn Nikolassee. Boat tours depart from nearby Wannsee Harbour and from other points around town. *See also chapters* Sightseeing *and* Getting Around.

FEZ Köpenick
Eichgestell, Köpenick, 12459 (5307 1504). S3 Wuhlheide. **Open** 10am-9pm Tue-Fri; 1-6pm Sat; 10am-6pm Sun; *school holidays* 10am-5pm Mon-Fri. **Admission** free.
Deep in the woods and refreshingly low-key, FEZ goes back to the days when the wife of GDR supremo Erich Honecker was East Germany's Minister for Education and Youth, and still retains some of that Socialist, kids-are-our-future idealism. Children can see immediately what's going on here – trampolines, forts, tricycles, wading ponds – and have a roaring good time without a burger or Disney character in sight. Nominal charge for each attraction.

Koppenplatz
Mitte, U8 Rosenthaler Platz.
Slap in Scheunenviertel, around the corner from a whole bunch of galleries and shops, a regular local playground – swings, roundabouts and alike – in a prime piece of real estate.

Charlottchen – *rump steak, rumpus room.*

Restaurants

Rule of thumb: the more interesting a restaurant looks to you, the discriminating adult, the less likely they will be overjoyed when you breeze through the door with your toddler on your arm. Solution: disarm them in advance by asking if they tolerate children. Of course no member of staff will dare to own up to it and say 'no', at which point you've been let off the hook. They might even offer to reduce prices on children's portions, but again, you generally be best to ask. In the summer much of the stress in dining out with children can be avoided in the leafy refuge of outdoor beer gardens or the al fresco dining scene in laid-back areas such as Winterfeldtplatz in Schöneberg or Wiener Straße in Kreuzberg. *See also chapter* Restaurants.

Chalet Suisse
Im Jagen, Zehlendorf, 14195 (832 6362). U1 Dahlem-Dorf/bus 108. **Open** 11.30am-midnight daily. **Average** DM30. **Credit** AmEx, DC, MC, V.
At the edge of the Grunewald on a forest path. The food here is pricey for the quality, but the fairy-tale setting of this 'Swiss Chalet' and its gingerbread-house appearance always makes it a big hit with kids. Adjacent playground.

Charlottchen
Droysenstraße 1, Charlottenburg, 10629 (324 4717). S3, S5, S7, S9 Charlottenburg. **Open** 3pm-midnight Mon-Fri; 10am-midnight Sat-Sun. **Average** DM30. **Credit** AmEx, DC, MC, V. **Map B5**
Adults eat in peace in the dining room while the kids tear it up in the rumpus room next door. A unique concept in Berlin. Theatre performances for the kids on Sundays at 11.30am.

Eis Henning
Kurfürstendamm 129b, Wilmersdorf, 10711 (892 8400). S4 Halensee. **Open** 8am-9pm Mon-Thur, Sun; 9am-10pm Fri-Sat. **Map B5**
The place for ice cream in Berlin, with a rather modest but excellent selection of hand-made ice cream dishes. There's other snacks on offer too, and even the facility of a play area.

Loretta am Wannsee
Kronprinzessinnenweg 260, Zehlendorf, 14129 (803 5156). S1, S7 Wannsee. **Open** 9am-midnight daily.
In the summer this is a beer garden with grilled meats, corn on the cob and cold salads, but the main attraction for kids are the swings and other playground gear.

Dance

Post-Wall Berlin boasts a thriving, quality dance scene – the only problem is paying for it.

Berlin's dance scene has made leaps and bounds since Reunification. If the standard in both halves of the city rarely passed the provincial mark before 1989, today it is nothing short of progressive. And while dance has become an increasingly important performing art within Berlin, Berlin dance has also asserted itself on the international stage.

There are reasons for this apart from the hard work of pre- and post-Wall choreographers and dancers determined to put Berlin on the map. For a start, they have been joined by an influx of artists – mainly from Britain and Holland – looking for the legendary creative energy which inspired New German Dance in the 1930s, when Berlin was home to such pioneers as Anita Berber, Rudolph von Laban and Mary Wigman. Most of them found that dynamic energy and many of them stayed – but not just out of historical romanticism. One of big attractions is the cross-fertilisation that takes place here. The fine arts scene is very open to co-operation, as is the music scene, and exciting productions have sprung from the artistic exchange between choreographers and interpreters of everything from jazz to the sounds of club culture.

The increasing number of dancers in the independent scene upped the competitive edge. That in turn gave rise to more professional training opportunities. There are now a handful of schools, though the city still lacks a state-funded institution such as the Volkwang School in Essen where Pina Bausch came to fame. Nevertheless, standards have improved tremendously. Half the productions showcased at the bi-annual Tanzplattform held in German cities in rotation now come from Berlin. Summer's Tanz im August (information from Tanzwerkstatt on 2474 9758 or Hebbel-Theater on 2590 0427) has evolved into Germany's leading annual festival, attracting experts from all over the world who seek out acts to show at home or to work together with their own troupes. Berlin's unique aesthetic and innovative atmosphere means these festivals can't be missed by anyone wishing to keep tabs on international developments.

FUSION AND DOWNSIZING

Developments too on the ballet front. The city is in the process of fusing the companies attached to Berlin's three opera houses into one 'Berlin Ballet'. To be in place by 2001, it's an effort to save money while addressing age-old complaints that dance is

Tanzcompagnie Rubato – leading Berlin.

the poor relation at these theatres. The company will consist of one large classical ensemble and two smaller contemporary groups, each maintaining the emphasis they have had at their respective opera houses. Plans foresee a director heading each ensemble.

Downsizing has been part of the cost-cutting measures, and the **Deutsche Oper** (tickets DM17-115) has had to let 18 dancers go. The house has had a swift turnover of ballet directors; Frenchwoman Sylviane Bayard is the fifth in ten years. She's returning company's focus to classical dramatic ballet, and inviting acclaimed choreographers like Angelin Preljocaj to stage their productions. The corps de ballet at the **Komische Oper** (tickets DM16-99) is also under new direction. Richard Wherlock has taken over from the experimental Dutch duo Marc Jonkers and Jan Linkens. He intends to continue the tradition of Tom Schilling, who for almost 30 years until his

Theater am Halleschen Ufer – indie home.

retirement in 1993 firmly established the company's roots in 'dance theatre'. The **Deutsche Staatsoper** (tickets DM10–150, premières up to DM200) is committed to the romantic classics and its corps will make up the largest ensemble in the Berlin Ballet. Its *Swan Lake* has met with huge success, touring the world and broadcast live in Spain and France. Daniel Barenboim himself sometimes conducts the scores to ballet evenings. For venue listings *see chapter* **Music: Classical & Opera**.

INDIES AND FESTIVALS

The 600-seat **Hebbel-Theater** in Kreuzberg is noted for international avant-garde dance, and director Nele Hertling books big-name companies such as Nederlands Dans Theater, Wim Wandeykebus and Lucinda Childs. February's Tanz im Winter is three weeks of performance highlighting current trends in modern dance. The Hebbel is also one of the main venues for Tanz im August. Berlin's dance scene got a big boost when Sascha Walz was appointed co-director of the prestigious **Schaubühne am Lehniner Platz** in 1999. Long a leading light of the independent scene, Walz is probably Germany's leading proponent of postmodern dance. The move has enabled her to double her company to 12 members and play her elaborate productions to larger audiences. For venue listings *see chapter* **Theatre**.

Known to have one of Europe's best stages for modern work, the **Theater am Halleschen Ufer** is the home of Berlin's independent dance scene. Its support of the city's choreographers has been instrumental in their success. Regular features include premières by Berlin's leading companies, including Anna Huber, Jo Fabian and Tanzcompagnie Rubato. The Tanzzeit festivals in June and November, and the Solo Duo festival in March, highlight new Berlin and global trends. The theatre co-produces with the Place in London. Meanwhile, Johann Kresnik's starkly expressive political dance theatre has kicked up a storm since his arrival at **Volksbühne** in 1994. For venue listings *see chapter* **Theatre**.

The Tanzwerkstatt organisation is based at the **Podewil** cultural centre. It scouts out fresh, promising talent at international festivals and

books young choreographers for Berlin events and Podewil's own stage. Workshops often run parallel to performances. Podewil's artist-in-residence programme has propelled young French choreographer Xavier Le Roy to international stardom. *See chapter* **Music: Rock, Folk & Jazz**.

Information

Check *tip* or *Zitty* for listings, or consult:

Tanz in Berlin

Monthly calendar of performances and dance-related events, free at theatres, cafes and hotels.

Classes & gear

Dock 11

Kastanienallee 79, Prenzlauer Berg, 10435 (448 1222). U2 Eberswalder Straße/U8 Rosenthaler Platz. **Open** 9.30am-10.30pm daily. **No credit cards. Map G2**
Two dancers who used this space to rehearse their company have turned it into the most successful school in the east. Daily professional training in modern, courses also for beginners with some experience and amateurs. Daily classes in yoga, Feldenkrais and Pilates.
Website: www.dock11-berlin.de

Pro Danse

Münzstraße 16, Mitte, 10178 (2472 2096). U8 Weinmeisterstraße. **Open** 10am-6.30pm Mon-Fri; 10am-2pm Sat. **No credit cards. Map G3**
Geared to professionals, this place is stocked with leotards, leg warmers, and tutus, jazz, tap and pointe shoes by all major brand names. The Australian owner is happy to answer any questions concerning dance in Berlin. Entrance in Max-Beer-Straße.

TanzFabrik Berlin

Möckernstraße 68, Kreuzberg, 10965 (786 5861). S1, S2/U7 Yorckstraße. **Open** 10am-noon, 5-8pm Mon-Thu; 10am-noon Fri. **No credit cards. Map E5**
Berlin's largest contemporary dance school, with about 50 classes a week and 600 students. A wide variety of techniques is on offer, including Limon, jazz, ballet, contact improvisation, new-dance, t'ai-chi, African and Afro-Brasileiro, street dance and samba. Daily training for professional dancers in modern, ballet and release. TanzFabrik also offers programmes for improvisation and performances on the tiny stage of its 100-seat theatre.
Website: www.tanzFabrik-berlin.de

Tanz Tangente

Kuhligkshofstraße 4, Steglitz, 12165 (792 9124). S1/U9 Rathaus Steglitz. **Open** 10am-noon, 4.30-6.30pm Tue; 4-6pm Wed; 4.30-6.30pm Thur; 10am-noon Fri. **No credit cards.**
Former Wigman student Leanore Ickstadt set up this school 20 years after she first arrived in Berlin in 1961 on a Fulbright Scholarship. Today Ickstadt only teaches children, but adult classes are held in modern, jazz, awareness through movement, tap and Feldenkrais.

Film

From vast new multiplexes to the world's most eclectic film festival, Deutschland's Kino capital caters for cineastes of every stripe.

Recent years have seen significant changes in Berlin's cinema landscape. Despite the closing of many small houses, the arrival of new multiplexes has increased the city's screens to more than 250 and counting. One result is that English-language programming, once the speciality of the small and daring, is becoming more the domain of the large, and largely conservative. Perhaps the most dramatic expression of this was the move, in 2000, of the Berlin Film Festival, one of the world's most important international film festivals, to that mighty new shopping mall called Potsdamer Platz.

But hey, even Paris is no longer the movie lover's paradise it once was, and if alternatives to the mainstream are shrinking, the number of screens available to the Anglophone contingent has markedly increased. Plus the larger venues now take reservations over the phone. And rabid cineastes should rest assured that all is not lost. Variety does survive and Berlin's cinemas offer many possibilities, from the most established (**Odeon**) to the most eclectic (**Arsenal**), from the wildest (**Eiszeit**) to the most Hollywood (**CineStar**) – with almost every level in between.

To find out what's going on check the listings in *tip*, *Zitty* or the freebie *[030]*, which can be picked up in bars and other venues. Most non-German movies are dubbed, so look for the notation OV or OF (original version or *Originalfassung*), OmU (original with subtitles) or OmE (original with English subtitles in the case of foreign films). The cinemas we list here are those most likely to show films in English, but keep your eyes open for sightings in other venues.

Berlin Film Festival

Before the days of the Love Parade, Berlin's biggest annual event was the Berlinale, the world's second-largest film festival (*see chapter* **By Season**). While the Berlin Festival may not equal the glamour of Cannes or Venice, it has both beaten hands down when it comes to its audience. What seems like the entire city turns out for 12 days every February to see what is arguably the widest and most eclectic mix of any film festival in the world. And if Cannes has been notorious for the hoopla created by bare-breasted starlets, Berlin has had its own rich history of uproar. If it wasn't the official denunciation of a pro-Vietnamese film

from West Germany in the early 1970s, it was public outcry against the programming of pro-Hollywood *Steel Magnolias* in the early 1990s. Jury president Gina Lollobrigida publicly slagged her colleagues over the awarding of the Golden Bear to a leftist film in 1986, while another president, George Stevens, led a mass resignation of the jury in protest over the entire programme in 1970. While the festival came under fire in the 1960s for recognising East Germany, the whole Eastern Bloc contingent walked out in a fury over the presentation of *The Deer Hunter* in 1976.

Traditionally a focal point of the Cold War, the festival had a distinctly political edge and was one of the few constructive ways for East and West to come together. The years surrounding the fall of the Wall were particularly exciting but recently the glow has been fading as the festival searches for a new identity. Jumping on the bandwagon of 'New Berlin', it has moved to new quarters on Potsdamer Platz, with screening facilities in the **CinemaxX** and CineStar multiplexes. The main competition screenings, previously hosted by the landmark **Zoo Palast**, will now be in the newly constructed Berlinale Palast (opposite the CinemaxX), otherwise dedicated to Broadway-esque musical productions. Only the Zoo Palast, **Delphi** and **Kino International** survive from the old régime, and now that they are only hosting repeat showings, should be easier to get into than before. At press time no other tips can be offered on how best to get around, and readers of this edition are advised to seek out specific information on site or via the Internet (*see below*).

What does remain constant, however, is the chance to see literally hundreds of films which are presented in seven sections, the most important of which are listed below.

The International Competition

The most visible part of the festival in terms of glamour and publicity, and also the most conservative in selection. Concentrating on big-budget major productions, with a heavy (and heavily criticised) accent on Hollywood, those films with the most popular appeal usually make it to general release afterwards. The International Competition provides the glitz and guest stars, both from the films and in the international jury, at its nightly gala presentations. Films compete for Gold and Silver Bears, often with a furore over the announcement of the winners. Since evening shows are the most expensive and most likely to sell out, either go for the afternoon shows or the repeats. All Berlinale Palast shows have simultaneous translation over headphones.

The International Forum of Young Cinema

The Forum was created as a direct opposition to the Competition (out of the above-mentioned revolt in 1970) and serves its position well, providing a vital selection of the challenging and eclectic that you may not have a chance to see anywhere else. Although it has the more rigorous selection, the Forum attracts a strong and loyal audience and it is here and in the **Panorama** (*see below*) where the real discoveries are to be found. Anything can happen here, from the latest American indie film, to African cinema, to midnight showings of Hong Kong action films. The likes of Bruce Willis can look pretty small waving from the stage of the Berlinale Palast but at the Forum, dialogues between audience and film maker are de rigueur. Shows at **CinemaxX, Arsenal, CineStar** and **Delphi** have simultaneous translation.

Panorama

Originally intended to showcase films that, for whatever reason, fell outside the strict guidelines of the Competition, the Panorama has spread its wings to give the Forum a run for its money in terms of innovative programming. Panorama is, however, less consciously serious than the Forum, and may be a good place to start for less hardcore cineastes, spotlighting world independent cinema with an accent on gay and lesbian films. Panorama films show in **CinemaxX** and **Zoo Palast** with repeats at **CinemaxX, CineStar** and **International**. No translations but most films have English subtitles.

Retrospective

The Retro section is one of the festival's surest bets for sheer movie-going pleasure and while it concentrates on the established mainstream, it's always an opportunity to catch films that you might never otherwise see on the big screen. Themes have included Colour, the Cold War, Robots, Nazi-era musicals and the work of directors such as Erich von Stroheim or William Wyler. There is also a homage to the work of still-living film personalities such as Jack Lemmon or Cathérine Deneuve, complete with personal appearances and gala screenings. Films show in the **CinemaxX**. Hollywood-oriented, but foreign-language films rarely have any translation.

Tickets

Tickets can be bought up to three days in advance at either the main ticket office in the **Arkaden am Potsdamer Platz**, the **Europa Center** or at **Kino International**. On the day of performance they can be bought at the theatre box office and last-minute tickets are often available. Queues for advance tickets can be insanely long so come early and buy as much as you can at once. Films are described in a Competition and Panorama catalogue which you can pick up for a nominal price

CinemaxX – *maximum screens. Page 210.*

at the Arkaden; the Forum has its own catalogue, available free at every Forum theatre. Films are usually shown three times. There is also a free daily *Berlinale Journal* available at all theatres with info and updates. It pays to plan ahead but keep your ears open for word-of-mouth.

Ticket prices have been ranging from DM10-25 depending on the show (hint: Berlinale Palast is cheaper during the day). A full festival pass (*Dauerkarte*) is available at the Arkaden am Potsdamer Platz from December until three days before the festival. The last reported price was DM250 (bring two passport photos). It's good for all sections but not all theatres or times, so familiarise yourself with the limitations to avoid disappointment. Check the festival website at *www.Berlinale.de* for current information and programming details. Day tickets for the festival are available at each of the following offices:

Arkaden am Potsdamer Platz

Potsdamer Straße 5, Mitte, 10785 (259 2000). S1, S2/U2 Potsdamer Platz. **Open** from 3 days before festival, 10am-8pm. **Map E4**

Europa Center

Breitscheidplatz 5, Tiergarten, 10787 (348 0088). S3, S5, S7, S9/U2, U9 Zoologischer Garten. **Open** from 3 days before festival, 11.30am-6.30pm. **Map D4**

Kino International

Karl-Marx-Allee 33 (corner of Schillingstraße), Mitte, 10178 (242 5826). U5 Schillingstraße. **Open** from 3 days before festival, noon-7pm. **Map G3**

Other film festivals

Berlin Beta Festival

Nominally a conference on New Media, but with a film programme attached which features a variety from America, Europe and Asia ranging from off-Hollywood to Swedish gang films and Malaysian road movies, all wild and strange. Programmed by **Eiszeit**, it takes place there and at **Central** and

Film Theatre Friedrichshain. Non-German films are in English or have English subtitles.
Website: www.berlinbeta.de

Fantasy Film Festival

Established summer event which shows the latest in fantasy, horror and sci-fi from America, Hong Kong, Japan and Europe as well as classic oldies. Films are often premières (at least in Europe), with occasional previews, programmed retrospectives and assorted rarities. Aside from the odd German film, all shows are screened in English or with English subtitles. Venues and dates are flexible but the last couple of years it's been in mid-August.
Website: www.fantasyfilmfest.com

Lesbian Film Festival

Every October the Lesbian Film Festival has a surprisingly wide international selection of films and performances. It seems to have found a home at the **Arsenal,** so as of 2000 it will be flying in the face of Potsdamer Platz's new mall culture. Most events are women-only, though some films could show up later at Arsenal or **Xenon.**
Website: www.woman-online.de/lesbenfilmfestival

On location

The images of cities such as London or New York are well known to travellers from their portrayal in the movies. Berlin is somehow harder to picture, its cinematic image difficult to reconcile with its tangible counterpart, an image owing as much to movie fantasy as to a reality that no longer exists.

Early German film-makers wanted as much control of their scenes as possible, so films such as *The Last Laugh* and Fritz Lang's *M* featured a Berlin built in the studio. If *Grand Hotel* and *Cabaret* are Weimar via Hollywood, one of the best snapshots of the period comes from *Berlin Sinfonie einer Großstadt* ('*Symphony of a City*'). This silent documentary presents a portrait of everyday life in the teeming metropolis, climaxing with the obligatory crawl through Berlin nightlife. A popular revival today, it's astounding how almost no view in the film is at all recognisable.

The aftermath of World War II made Berlin a big film location. With shattered remains referred to by one film critic as 'the most beautiful ruins in the modern world' it provided the background for such films as *The Young Lions*, picturing the decimated Lehrter Bahnhof; *A Time To Love And A Time To Die*, which plays amid the burnt-out façades of Charlottenburg; and Billy Wilder's *A Foreign Affair*, featuring a very unruined Marlene Dietrich. One of the most lasting impressions is in *The Big Lift*, a graphic portrayal of a city struggling to bring its streets back to life. The most memorable view is from

The Spy Who Came In From The Cold – *starring Dublin as divided Berlin.*

Cinemas

Arsenal

Potsdamer Straße 2, Tiergarten, 10785 (219 0010). S1, S2/U2 Potsdamer Platz. **Tickets** DM11. Two screens. **Map E4**

The Berlin Cinemathèque in everything but name. Its brazenly eclectic programming ranges from classic Hollywood to contemporary Middle Eastern cinema, from Russian art films to Italian horror, from Third World documentaries to the ever-popular silent films with live accompaniment. It shows many English-language films and sometimes foreign ones have English subtitles. Occasionally film-makers show up to present their work. Its recent move into these two state-of-the-art screening rooms in the Sony Center places it in the belly of the great Hollywood beast, which is probably right where we need it. Like its bigger neighbours, a major venue for the Berlin Film Festival.

Babylon A&B

Dresdener Straße 126, Kreuzberg, 10999 (614 6316). U1, U8 Kottbusser Tor. **Tickets** DM11-12; DM9 Tue-Wed; DM7 Mon. Two screens. **Map G4**

Angels over Berlin – the signature image of Wings Of Desire.

above, as Airlift planes fly in to Flughafen Templehof – a view of rooftops which feels remarkably the same today.

Cold-War Berlin was the setting for such films as *The Man Between* with James Mason; Billy Wilder's *One, Two, Three* and *The Spy Who Came In From The Cold* with Richard Burton. But the very political tensions which inspired the drama often made filming impossible, moving James Mason's Alexanderplatz scenes to Nollendorfplatz in the American Sector and forcing Wilder to recreate the Brandenburg Gate in a Munich studio. And the Berlin where Burton came in from the cold was actually filmed in Dublin.

The ultimate Cold War film, and perhaps the ultimate Berlin film, is Wim Wenders' *Wings Of Desire* which, particularly in hindsight, is emblematic of the tension in Berlin between the eternal and the ephemeral. Its signature image of the golden-winged Siegessäule will always be there, though these days the angels atop are looking down on the surging crowds of The Love Parade. The brooding, spaced-out, underground scene of West Berlin, pictured at the now defunct Schöneberg club, Ecstasy, is no more, though the looming Stadtsbibliothek is still there and every bit as spacey as it appears in the film. The no-man's land where the angels walked has been replaced by Potsdamer Platz reinvented as giant mall, and the ever-present Wall is now only recalled by the lone concrete strip of graffiti art on Mühlenstraße called The East Side Gallery. Finally, that fabulously ruined ballroom where Nick Cave and the Bad Seeds serenaded the fallen angels still survives – the former Hotel Esplanade Kaisersaal Café has been literally picked up and moved 50 metres to make way for, and be swallowed up by, the sprawling Sony Center – the beautiful decay erased and refurbished. A fitting allegory for the city itself.

A varied and almost totally English-language programme featuring off-Hollywood, indie crossover
and UK films. Not to be confused with **Filmkunsthaus Babylon** in Mitte (*see below*).

Camera in Tacheles

*Oranienburgerstraße 54-56, Mitte, 10117 (283
1498). U6 Oranienburger Tor/S1, S2
Oranienburger Straße.* **Tickets** DM11. One screen.
Map F3
Part of the multi-purpose Tacheles' many venues
(*see also chapter* **Theatre**), its film programming
offers an indefinable mix of independent and off-
Hollywood films plus interesting foreign movies in
a very long and narrow cinema. Films appear in
original English as often as not and foreign films
occasionally appear with English subtitles.

Central

*Rosenthaler Straße 39, Mitte, 10178 (2859 9973).
U8 Weinmeisterstraße.* **Tickets** DM11; DM8.50 Tue-
Wed; DM7 Mon. Two screens. **Map F3**
Newly built cinema in the Hackesche Höfe which
only occasionally offers programming in original
English except for special midnight shows (ranging
from Pam Grier retros to Pamela Anderson sex
tapes) and participation in Berlin Beta. Occasionally
a venue for the more kooky aspects of the Berlin
Film Festival Retrospective.

CinemaxX

*Potsdamer Straße 5, Tiergarten, 10785 (4431
6316/2592 2111). S1, S2/U2 Potsdamer Platz.*
Tickets DM13; DM9 Mon. 19 screens. **Map E4**
Biggest multiplex in town with at least two screens
regularly showing films in English. Strictly
Hollywood mainstream in mass-market mall surroundings. A main venue for the Berlin Film Festival.

CineStar

*Potsdamer Straße 4, Tiergarten, 10785 (2606
6260). S1, S2/U2 Potsdamer Platz.* **Tickets** DM6-
15; DM9.50 Mon. **Map E4**
Yet another new multiplex in town, this one in the
Sony Center, just opening as we were going to press.
Apparently most, if not all, of the screens will be able
to offer the possibility to show films in both English
and German simultaneously with the aid of headphones. Programming (surprise! surprise!) will be
strictly Hollywood mainstream, though considering
the increased competition, we may hope for some
unexpected developments. A main venue for the
Berlin Film Festival 2000.

Eiszeit

*Zeughofstraße 20, Kreuzberg, 10997 (611 6016). U1
Görlitzer Bahnhof.* **Tickets** DM11; DM8.50 Tue-
Wed; DM7 Mon. Two screens. **Map H4**
By far the most energetic cinema in town, established
by complete cinema aficionados in order to inflict
their unique tastes upon the world. However, the
recent renovations which have brought plush seats
and Dolby Surround have also ushered in a more conservative selection of films to pay the bills. But this
also means that audiences can now sit in comfort
when they choose to unleash their own special blend

Filmkunsthaus Babylon – *landmark theatre.*

of German underground, Japanimation, slash or
gangsta films, US indies and assorted weirdness.
Often stuff in English or with English subtitles. A
venue for Berlin Beta.

Filmkunsthaus Babylon

*Rosa-Luxemburg-Straße 30, Mitte, 10178 (242
5076). U2 Rosa-Luxemburg-Platz.* **Tickets** DM10.
One screen. **Map G3**
Not to be confused with the **Babylon** in Kreuzberg
(*see page 209*), this former East German première
theatre is a landmark building by Hans Poelzig,
who also designed the classic German silent *The
Golem*. Due to seemingly never-ending renovations,
shows take place in the lobby turned screening-
room. Heavy on retrospectives and thematic programming, a good venue for those interested in
Eastern Bloc films. Occasional Hollywood in
English, foreign films with English subtitles, independent series and gay programming.

Moviemento

*Kottbusser Damm 22, Kreuzberg, 10967 (692
4785). U8 Schönleinstraße.* **Tickets** DM11;
DM8.50 Tue-Wed; DM13 double features; DM15 all-
nighters; DM5 children 3pm Sat-Sun. Three
screens. **Map G5**
Loose and youthful upstairs cinema on the edge of
Kreuzberg showing indie crossover, occasional off-
Hollywood and new young German films with
periodic themed retro – often in English.

Odeon

Hauptstraße 116, Schöneberg, 10827 (7870 4019).
S9/U4 Innsbrucker Platz. **Tickets** DM13; DM9 Tue-Wed; DM7 Mon. One screen. **Map D6**
In deepest Schöneberg, Berlin's favourite English-language cinema. Though the largest, it's sometimes prone to sellouts, so it pays to get there a bit early. Shows a reasonably intelligent selection of big mainstream hits from Hollywood and the UK.

Olympia

Kantstraße 162, Charlottenburg,10623 (881 1978).
S3, S5, S7, S9/U2, U9 Zoologischer Garten. **Tickets** DM9-12; DM7 Mon. One screen. **Map C4**
Now exclusively English-language, this cinema often picks up films from Odeon or Babylon after their run. Threatened with closure for the last year or so, it continues in defiance of rumour.

UFA Arthouse Die Kurbel

Giesebrechtstraße 4, Charlottenburg, 10629 (883 5325). U7 Adenauerplatz. **Tickets** DM12-13; DM9 Tue-Wed. Three screens. **Map B4**
All the comforts of one of Berlin's first multiplexes with three screens showing Hollywood fare in original language. Sneak previews Monday at 11pm.

Xenon

Kolonnenstraße 5, Schöneberg, 10827 (782 8850). U7 Kleistpark. **Tickets** DM10; DM 8.50 Tue-Wed; DM5 children. One screen. **Map E6**
A small cosy cinema in large part dedicated to gay and lesbian programming (with very loosely defined boundaries). A lot of this is indie stuff from the US and Britain so a good deal of their programming is in English. Brought to you by the people at Eiszeit.

Zeughaus

Unter den Linden 2, Mitte, 10117. S1, S2, S3, S5, S7, S9/U6 Friedrichstraße. **Map F3**
At press time the Zeughaus is closed for renovations but is scheduled to reopen by 2001. Part of the **Deutsches Historisches Museum** (*see chapter* **Museums**), it might seem the last place in Berlin to look for English-speaking films, but it often hosts travelling retrospective shows such as Robert Wise, Powell & Pressburger, Douglas Sirk and Hollywood exiles, and also programmes series on thrillers, Westerns and British post-war films. The management always makes an effort to try to get the original versions and occasionally the foreign films have English subtitles.

Zoo Palast

Hardenbergstraße 29a, Charlottenburg, 10623 (2541 4777). S3, S5, S7, S9/U2, U9 Zoologischer Garten. **Tickets** DM12-14; DM9.50-10.50 Tue, Wed. Nine screens. **Map C4**
Berlin's flagship theatre since the 1950s and an architectural landmark. Before the Sony theatres were a gleam in the contractor's eye, two of the Zoo Palast's screens were able to play the original soundtrack to Hollywood hits over headphones (exchanged for some form of ID). Drop by to find out for which films this is available.

Video rentals

Note: all video rental outlets require ID and proof of residency to open an account (another good reason to make friends with the locals).

America-Gedenkbibliothek

Blücherplatz, Kreuzberg, 10961 (902 260). U1, U6 Hallesches Tor. **Annual membership** DM20; students free. **Open** 4-7pm Mon; 11am-7pm Tue-Sat. **Map F5**
Library offering a wide variety of interesting choices that range from film classics, musicals and comedies to Asian films and 1950s sci-fi, the majority of it in English or with English subtitles. Videos, like books, are free and can be kept out for two weeks (limit of four per customer). Best deal in town!

British Council Library

Hardenbergstraße 20, Tiergarten, 10623 (3110 9910). S3, S5, S7, S9/U2, U9 Zoologischer Garten. **Annual membership** DM60; students DM30. **Open** 2-6pm Mon, Wed-Fri; 2-7pm Tue. **Map C4**
Has a varied and ever-expanding collection of British contemporary and classic films as well as TV programmes. Prices range from DM2.50-7 and tapes can be kept out for a week.

Incredibly Strange Video

Eisenacher Straße 115, Schöneberg, 10823 (215 1770). U1, U2, U4 Nollendorfplatz. **Open** 2-10pm daily (with 24-hour return drop). **Map D5**
Selection ranges from crime, comedy, indie crossover and foreign films with English subtitles to the horror and sci-fi that was its original focus. At DM8 per night (DM6 for each additional tape) you don't come for the price, but the choice is worth it. Hefty deposit required in place of proof of residency. *Website: www.incredibly.de*

Negativeland

Dunckerstraße 9, Prenzlauer Berg, 10437 (4477 4477). U2 Eberswalder Straße. **Open** noon-midnight Mon-Sat. **Map G2**
The only English-language videos in Prenzlauer Berg and a nice meaty selection if your taste runs to Japanimation, biker films and lesbian vampires, though there's also a decent mainstream assortment. No English section per se – it's all mixed in with the German stuff so pay attention to what you're picking up. An in-store computer database makes searching less random or you can check out the catalogue online beforehand. Rentals are DM6 per day. *Website: www.snafu.de/negativeland*

Videodrome

Mittenwalder Straße 11, Kreuzberg, 10961 (692 8804). U7 Gneisenaustraße. **Open** noon-9pm Mon-Sat. **Map F5**
Nobody has everything, but Videodrome comes close. While its huge selection overlaps with Incredibly Strange, it excels in Japanimation, Splatter, Hong Kong films, and TV shows (including *Twilight Zone, Avengers* and the complete *Star Trek*), while also serving more conservative tastes. Rentals are DM7.50 per night. *Website: www.videodrome.dek*

Gay & Lesbian

With bars and clubs for every persuasion and more orgies than you can shake a riot stick at, Europe's gay mecca goes for it – big style.

Lab.oratory – *catering to every perverse taste. See page 217.*

In the 1920s Berlin became the the the first city in the world to have what we might recognise as a large-scale gay and lesbian community. The club Eldorado in Motzstraße, still an important gay street today, attracted Marlene Dietrich, Ernst Röhm and Christopher Isherwood, who lived at nearby Nollendorfstraße 17. Under the Nazi régime, gays were persecuted and forced to wear the Pink Triangle in concentration camps. They are commemorated on a plaque outside U-Bahnhof Nollendorfplatz.

Since the late 1960s, Berlin has resumed its role as one of the world's homosexual Meccas. The Berlin gay and lesbian scenes are big and bold, mostly concentrated in Schöneberg, Kreuzberg and Prenzlauer Berg. There are still some eye-catching differences between east and west but contrasts are disappearing as *Wessis* move east and vice versa, or outdated eastern institutions are renovated and replaced, leading to increasingly homogenous venue styles and clientèle.

Summer is the most exciting time, when all contingents of the sometimes fractious gay and lesbian scenes come together and much drinking and fun take place outside bars on the street. The **Schwullesbisches Straßenfest** on Motzstraße in mid-June is followed by **Christopher Street Day Parade** (*see chapter* **By Season**), a flamboyant annual event where up to 250,000 gays and lesbians unite to commemorate the Stonewall riots.

The scene includes much more than the venues listed here, especially cultural and subcultural events such as plays, trashy drag performances or the awarding of the Gay Teddy to the best gay-lesbian film during the annual FilmFest. MonGay at **Kino International** (*see chapter* **Film**) shows gay-lesbian films on Mondays and the stage company Teufelsberg produces hilariously vulgar comedy shows. Gay art and history is documented at the **Schwules Museum** (*see chapter* **Museums**) which also has an archive. If you wish, you can live an exclusively gay or lesbian life in

Berlin, working at a gay firm, working out at a gay gym, buying clothes at a gay shop, eating in a gay or lesbian restaurant... And when it's time to go, a gay undertaker can organise you a pink coffin lined with plush.

Advice & information

Berliner AIDS-Hilfe
Meinekestraße 12, Wilmersdorf, 10719 (885 6400). U15 Uhlandstraße. **Open** 10am-6pm Mon-Thur; 10am-3pm Fri. **Map C4**
Care, advice, information and counselling on every aspect of HIV and AIDS – legal, social, medical or psychological.

Lesbenberatung
Lesbian Advice Centre
Kulmer Straße 20a, Schöneberg, 10783 (215 2000/ lesbenberatung@w4w.net). S1, S2/U7 Yorckstraße. **Open** 4-7pm Tue, Thur; 2-5pm Fri. **Map E5**
Counselling in all areas of lesbian life as well as self-help groups, courses and cultural events.
Website: www.w4w.net/lesbenberatung

Mann-O-Meter
Motzstraße 5, Schöneberg, 10777 (216 8008/ info@mann-o-meter.de). U1, U2, U4 Nollendorfplatz. **Open** 5-10pm Mon-Fri; 4-9pm Sat-Sun. **Map D5**
Efficient and helpful drop-in centre and helpline with an exhaustive computer database. Regularly updated wall displays and stacks of listings magazines and newspapers detail weekly events. Cheap stocks of safer sex materials are also available. English spoken.
Website: www.mann-o-meter.de

Mitfahr 2000
Yorckstraße 52, Kreuzberg, 19420 (216 4020/ infoservice@mitfahrzentralen.de). S1, S2/U7 Yorckstraße. **Open** 8am-8pm daily. **Map E5**
Mitfahrzentralen are clearing houses for those offering or seeking lifts. This one caters to a gay and lesbian clientèle. Those requesting a ride pay a small fee to the agency and a set (very reasonable) fee to the driver depending on destination. A safe and reliable way to travel between German cities.
Website: www.mitfahrzentralen.de

Movin' Queer
Liegnitzer Straße 5, Kreuzberg, 10999 (618 6955/movinqueer@aol.com). U1 Görlitzer Bahnhof. **Open** by appointment. **Map H5**
Lesbian-run agency offering travel services including reservations at gay-friendly hotels, tours of the city and information about bars, nightclubs, restaurants and events.

Schwulenberatung
Gay Advice Centre
Mommsenstraße 45, Charlottenburg, 10629 (194 46). U7 Adenauerplatz. **Open** 9am-8pm Mon-Fri. **Map C4**
Information and counselling about HIV and AIDS. Crisis intervention, consultation and advice on psychotherapy – anonymously, if you wish.

Publications
Sergej and *Siegessäule* are monthly listings freebies which can be picked up at most venues. Apart from a what's-on calendar, *Siegessäule* also lists all gay and lesbian venues and pinpoints them on a city map. Also look out for *Gay Info*, *Box* and various other free magazines. For lesbians, *Blattgold* gives information on the women's scene.
 A free *Berlin Fun Map*, pinpointing all places of interest, can be picked up at venues, as well as the free *Siegessäule Kompass*, a classified directory of everything gay or lesbian.

Mixed venues

In West Berlin gays and lesbians have been treading separate paths for decades, but the situation was different in the east. Making common cause under the communists, homosexuals of both sexes shared bars, clubs and other spaces, a tradition maintained despite the powerful emergence of male-only cruise bars in Prenzlauer Berg.
 That said, the western half of the city is changing too. The late 1990s saw a proliferation of mixed gay and lesbian venues, and lesbians also made their voices felt in formerly gay-only organisations and political institutions. The formerly gay-only *Siegessäule* has become a gay and lesbian magazine, dealing with topics for both equally.
 This spirit of growing together also makes itself felt in an ever-greater mix in cafés, bars and clubs such as **Schall und Rauch** in the east or **SO36** and the unique dyke/queer bar that is **Roses** in the west. **Café Sundström** and **Anderes Ufer** are cafés where gays and lesbians mingle.
 Here we list a selection of genuinely mixed cafés, bars and clubs.

Mixed cafés & bars

Anderes Ufer
Hauptstraße 157, Schöneberg, 10827 (7870 3800). U7 Kleistpark. **Open** 11am-1am daily. **Map E5**
Established over 20 years ago, this is the city's oldest gay café. Lesbians often make up around 30% of the clientèle. Exhibitions of gay art and photography.

Café Amsterdam
Gleimstraße 24, Prenzlauer Berg, 10437 (448 0792). S4, S8, S10/U2 Schönhauser Allee. **Open** 4pm-6am daily. **Map G1**
Good bar to get wrecked in, with house and techno DJs on Fridays. Snacks and salads. Mixed crowd.

Café Sundström
Mehringdamm 61, Kreuzberg, 10961 (692 4414). U6, U7 Mehringdamm. **Open** 10am-late daily. **Map F5**
Daytimes this place serves as a café where rather uptight pseudo-intellectuals come to discuss poetry over coffee. In the evenings it's a Kreuzberg bar full

of gays too lazy to go to Schöneberg. At weekends the Café Sundström becomes the entrance to **SchwuZ** disco (*see below*) and the place is hectic and fun. It's best in spring and summer, when the big terrace opens until late and gays from all over Kreuzberg flock to loiter on the pavement.

Roses

Oranienstraße 187, Kreuzberg, 10999 (615 6570). U1, U8 Kottbusser Tor. **Open** 10pm-5am daily. **Map G4**

Whatever state you're in, you'll fit just fine in this boisterous den of glitter and kitsch, more or less next to SO36. It draws customers from right across the sexual spectrum – just about everybody who is gay or lesbian meets and mingles here.

Schall & Rauch

Gleimstraße 23, Prenzlauer Berg,10437 (448 0770). S4, S8, S10/U2 Schönhauser Allee. **Open** 10am-3am daily. **Map G1**

Relaxed and friendly atmosphere, good selection of food, central location – an ideal place to spend the afternoon or kick off an evening in Prenzlauer Berg.

Mixed clubs & one-nighters

Ackerkeller

Ackerstraße 12 hinterhof, Mitte, 10115 (280 7216). S1, S2 Nordbahnhof. **Open** 9pm-3am Tue; 10pm-late Fri, every second Sat. **Admission** DM3.50. **Map F2**

Grungy hole for gay punks and indie queens. Cheap drinks, hard music and rough decor. Sounds different? It is! Sounds exhilarating? Sorry. But one of the few venues where the more 'alternative' side of Berlin reveals itself to the gay visitor.

Die Busche

Mühlenstraße 11-12, Friedrichshain, 10243 (296 0800). S3, S5, S6, S7, S9/U1 Warschauer Straße. **Open** 9.30pm-5am Wed, Sun; 9.30pm-6am Fri; 10pm-6am Sat. **Admission** DM6-9. **Map H4**

Loud, tacky, resolutely mixed and always full, this is one of east Berlin's oldest discos for stylish lesbians and gays. In its current location since the early 1990s. A must for kitsch addicts and Abba fans.

SO 36

Oranienstraße 190, Kreuzberg, 10999 (6140 1306). U1, U8 Kottbusser Tor. **Open** 10pm-late Mon, Wed. **Admission** DM10 Mon; DM7 Wed. **Map G4**

A key venue for both gays and lesbians. Wednesday at SO is a fixed date for every gay man, and a lot of lesbians too – it's a fun-packed, very mixed, sociable evening and the dancefloor heaves. Monday ('Electric Ballroom') is not completely gay, but the hard techno sound draws a largely male following. Once a month is Gay Oriental Night, with belly-dancing transvestites and Turkish hits. Monthly Jane Bond parties bring together every imaginable manifestation of womanhood to dance to house and techno, funk and soul. Sunday is Café Fatal, where gays and lesbians get into ballroom dancing. Check local press for their sporadic one-nighters.

Gay

You don't need to look for the gay scene in Berlin. It'll find you in about ten minutes. Some areas, however, are gayer than others, especially Schöneberg's Motzstraße and Fuggerstraße, and Schönhauser Allee in Prenzlauer Berg. Bars, clubs, shops and saunas are so many and various it's impossible to take them all in on one visit.

The age of consent is 16 – same as for everyone else. Gays making contact in public is rarely of interest to passers-by. Nevertheless, bigots do exist and so does anti-gay violence. In the west it tends to be by gangs of Turkish teenagers, in the east by right-wing skinhead Germans. The most risky areas are Kreuzberg and Lichtenberg, but you're unlikely to enter the latter except for its train station. But compared to other cities, Berlin is an easy-going, innocuous place without much violence.

The scene is always shifting, so the places listed here may have changed by the time you read this. **Mann-O-Meter** (*see above*), *Siegessäule* and *Sergej* are the best sources of current information.

Accommodation

Most hotels know gays are important to the tourist industry and are courteous and efficient. Here are some options catering specifically for gay men.

Art Connection Cityhotel Berlin

Fuggerstraße 33, Schöneberg, 10777 (217 7028/fax 217 7030). U1, U2, U15 Wittenbergplatz. **Rates** single DM110; double DM140. **Credit** AmEx, MC, V. **Map D5**

Comfortable and spacious rooms (most en-suite), sumptuous breakfast included, prime location and next to Connection Disco.

Website: www.arthotel-connection.de

Enjoy Bed & Breakfast

c/o Mann-O-Meter, Motzstraße 5, Schöneberg, 10777 (215 1666/fax 2175 2219/info@ebab.com). U1, U2, U4 Nollendorfplatz. **Reservations** 5.30-9pm daily. **Rates** single DM80; double DM140. **No credit cards.** **Map D5**

Connection – *hot, esoteric. See page 216.*

Excellent accommodation service for gays and lesbians. Enjoy B&B can fix you up with a bed with gays or lesbians in their private apartment from as little as DM35.
Website: www.ebab.de

Schall und Rauch
Gleimstraße 23, Prenzlauer Berg, 10437 (448 0770). S4, S8, S10/U2 Schönhauser Allee. **Rates** *single* DM65; *double* DM120. **No credit cards. Map G1**
Clean, modern rooms next door to the café of the same name (*above*). All rooms are en-suite, complete with TV and telephone; rate includes breakfast.

Tom's House
Eisenacher Straße 10, Schöneberg, 10777 (218 5544). U1, U2, U4 Nollendorfplatz. **Rates** *single* DM130; *double* DM170. **No credit cards. Map D5**
An eccentric and unpredictable establishment deep in the heart of gay Schöneberg, with seven double rooms, a single one and first-rate buffet brunches from 10am-1pm.

Bars & cafés

Charlottenburg

Arc
Fasanenstraße 81, Charlottenburg, 10625 (313 2625). S3, S5, S7, S9/U2, U9 Zoologischer Garten. **Open** 11am-late Mon-Fri; 10am-1am Sat-Sun. **Map C4**
Underneath the S-Bahn arches, the Arc has rustic chic, exposed brickwork, wood interior, and both light snacks and an à la carte menu. From 8pm you can drop into the Banana Bar next door (staffed by the same team) and sample their professionally shaken cocktails.

Kleine Philharmonie
Schaperstraße 4, Wilmersdorf, 10719 (883 1102). U1, U9 Spichernstraße. **Open** 5pm-3am Mon-Fri, Sun; 8pm-3am Sat. **Map C5**
This eccentric umbrella-ceilinged parlour serves as a cosy living-room for the older local population.

Kreuzberg

Café Anal
Muskauer Straße 15, 10997 (6107 3030). U1 Görlitzer Bahnhof. **Open** 7pm-late Mon-Thur; 9pm-late Fri-Sat; 4pm-late Sun. **Map H4**
Tuntenbarock ('faggot-baroque') décor – lawdy it's gaudy – and indolent drinkers, laced with a tasteful fringing of political correctness. Punks, skinheads, students and drop-outs. Monday nights is women only.

Bierhimmel
Oranienstraße 183, Kreuzberg, 10999 (615 3122). U1, U8 Kottbusser Tor. **Open** 2pm-3am daily. **Map G4**
When Roses is too full you can always move to this nearby bar, where gays and heteros mix in a cooler atmosphere. Kitsch cocktail bar at the back, open at weekends. Popular with local drag queens.

Ficken 3000
Urbanstraße 70, Kreuzberg, 10967 (6950 7335). U7, U8 Hermannplatz. **Open** 10pm-late daily. **Map G5**
Big basement darkroom and a mix ranging from blue- and white-collar workers to students and night owls. Two drinks for the price of one on Tuesdays.

Prenzlauer Berg

Darkroom
Rodenbergstraße 23, Prenzlauer Berg, 10439 (444 9321). S4, S8, S10/U2 Schönhauser Allee. **Open** 10pm-6am daily. **Map G1**
Yes, there is a darkroom. And with the help of camouflage netting and urinals (in the actual darkroom) it often succeeds in pulling a slightly 'harder' clientèle, though on less busy nights things can feel a bit desperate. The fortnightly Naked Sex Party is a great success; after disposing of your clothes in a dustbin liner, feel free to roam about like a piece of trash.

Greifbar
Wichertstraße 10, Prenzlauer Berg, 10439 (444 0828). S4, S8, S10/U2 Schönhauser Allee. **Open** 10pm-6am daily. **Map G1**
Cruisy bar with a younger Prenzl'berg crowd looking for adventure and pleasure, either by picking someone up or by roaming about in the large darkrooms. Also good atmosphere for just drinking.

Pick Ab!
Greifenhagener Straße 16, Prenzlauer Berg, 10437 (445 8523). S4, S8, S10/U2 Schönhauser Allee. **Open** 10pm-late daily. **Map G1**
Late-night cruise bar for eastern action-seekers and insomniacs. Like most such bars it tends to fill up best during winter, when cruising heated backrooms is more comfortable than roaming freezing parks.

Stiller Don
Erich-Weinert-Straße 67, Prenzlauer Berg, 10439 (445 5957). S4, S8, S10/U2 Schönhauser Allee. **Open** 7pm-4am daily. **Map G1**
Formerly home to the local avant-garde but now attracting a mixed crowd from all over Berlin. The set-up is like a cosy café, but it gets high-spirited on weekends and Mondays.

Zum Burgfrieden
Wichertstraße 69, Prenzlauer Berg, 10439 (0177 5151299). S4, S8, S10/U2 Schönhauser Allee. **Open** 7pm-4am daily. **Map G1**
The former flagship of the eastern scene has hardly changed since Reunification. Many west Berliners who used to drop by when in the area have been lost to the new breed of cruise bars. In response the owners have tried to spruce up the joint with camouflage netting in the rear bar. This hasn't worked – only the old locals remain. Still, a taste of the east as was.

Schöneberg

Andreas Kneipe
Ansbacher Straße 29, Schöneberg, 10777 (218 3257). U1, U2, U12, U15 Wittenbergplatz. **Open** 11am-4am daily. **Map D5**

SchwuZ – a mixed crowd, but politically correct.

One of the oldest and most traditional bars in Berlin with a very mixed crowd. If you want real Berlin atmosphere, this is the place.

Connection Café
Martin-Luther-Straße 19, Schöneberg, 10777 (217 6809). U1, U2, U4, U12 Nollendorfplatz. **Open** 2pm-midnight daily. **Map D5**
The pot plants, mirrors and glitzy bar are a little tacky, but an established and popular meeting place.

Hafen
Motzstraße 19, Schöneberg, 10777 (211 4118). U1, U2, U4, U12 Nollendorfplatz. **Open** *summer* 8pm-4am daily; *winter* 9pm-4am daily. **Map D5**
A red plush and vaguely psychedelic bar in the centre of Schöneberg's gay triangle. Popular with the fashion- and body-conscious, especially at weekends, when it provides a safe haven from nearby heavy cruising dens. Usually very crowded.

Café PositHIV
Alvenslebenstraße 26, Schöneberg, 10829 (216 8654). U2 Bülowstraße. **Open** 3-11pm Mon-Fri, Sun; 6pm-late Sat. **Map E5**
Managed by voluntary staff for people affected by HIV and AIDS. Communal cooking and eating Thursday lunchtimes and Saturday evenings.

Prinzknecht
Fuggerstraße 33, Schöneberg, 10777 (2362 7444). U1, U2, U12, U15 Wittenbergplatz. **Open** 3pm-3am daily. **Map D5**

With a large but underused darkroom out back, this huge, open bar draws in all types of gays. Somewhat provincial, but nice for a chat and a beer. Free coffee and cake for bikers on Sunday afternoons.

Tom's Bar
Motzstraße 19, Schöneberg, 10777 (213 4570). U1, U2, U4, U12 Nollendorfplatz. **Open** 10pm-6am daily. **Map D5**
Once described by *Der Spiegel* as climax, or crash-landing, of the night. The front bar is fairly chatty, but the closer you get to the steps down to the darkroom, the more intense things become. Men only.

Clubs & one-nighters

With only a few real discos (**Die Busche, SchwuZ, Connection**), Saturday one-nighters have been the rage. Some quickly come and go; others run and run. Check *Siegessäule* or flyers.

Cocker Party
Changing its venue at press time, but you can't miss the muscle boy ads in *Siegessäule*. Huge monthly party with up to a thousand young gays dancing to pop and house. Check press for info.

Connection
Fuggerstraße 33, Schöneberg, 10777 (218 1432). U1, U2, U12, U15 Wittenbergplatz. **Open** 10pm-7am Fri-Sat. **Admission** DM12 (includes drink ticket). **Map D5**

Especially popular on men-only Saturdays when no one-nighters are on offer. A hot mixture of esoteric and Top 40 sounds ensure a packed dancefloor. Bored with dancing? Cruise through into the vast dungeons of **Connection Garage** (*below*).

House Boys

Kalkscheune, Johannisstraße 2, Mitte,10117 (2839 0065). U6 Oranienburger Tor. **Open** varies. **Map F3**
Excellent music and decoration makes this a must for every house-loving gay. Don your tightest t-shirt or ruffle your hair before coming. No fixed dates.

SchwuZ

Mehringdamm 61, Kreuzberg, 10961 (693 7025). U6, U7 Mehringdamm. **Open** 11pm-late Fri-Sat. **Admission** DM5-10. **Map F5**
Saturday is the main disco night at the Schwulen Zentrum ('Gay Centre'), Berlin's longest-running dance institution. Mixed crowd, but basically a politically correct scene covering all ages and styles. There are two dancefloors and much mingling between the three bars and **Café Sundström** (*above*) at the front. Friday hosts various one-nighters including the excellent Club 69 on the first Friday of the month, and the mixed **subterra** (*below*) on every second Friday. Parties also include a rock music night, trashy shows in the small theatre and the **Safer-Sex-Party** (*page 218*).

Leather, sex & fetish venues

Some very good leather-wear designers work and sell their wares in Berlin, but rubber and uniforms are also wildly popular with the younger hardcore crowd and skinhead-type gays. There are plenty of fascinating places to show off your preferred garb, including the eternally crowded Leather Meeting over the Easter holidays (information from MSC – *see below* **Knast**), the annual Gay Skinhead Meeting or fetish events such as those at SNAX-Club.

Over the last decade, since the first **Safer-Sex-Party** at **SchwuZ**, Berlin has developed into the gay sex party capital of the world. Nowhere else will you find such a number of different orgies, serving every need and desire on an almost daily basis. *Sergej* reported a staggering 95 sex parties in August 1999, including 26 naked and 21 SM/fetish ones. Orgies are well attended, especially in winter when weather forbids outdoor cruising.

Club Culture Houze

Görlitzer Straße 71, Kreuzberg, 10997 (6170 9669). U1 Görlitzer Bahnhof. **Open** 7pm-late Mon, Wed, Sun; 8pm-late Tue, Thur-Fri; 10pm-late Sat. **Admission** DM10. **Map H5**
Diverse sex parties (some of them mixed), ranging from 'naked' to 'dildo and fist night'. Gay nights feature on Monday and Friday morning (beginning at 5am) and Saturdays. Mostly body-conscious night owls visit the kitsch but inviting rooms, where mattresses make them feel like lying down. But actually they do it everywhere.

Erotik-Party AHA

Mehringdamm 61, Kreuzberg, 10961 (692 3600). U6, U7 Mehringdamm. **Open** 9pm-5am every second Friday. **Admission** DM12. **Map F5**
Every second Friday, this sex party is popular with guys under the age of 30 (or who look like it – no hairy chests here). What you wear is your business, but most put on some sexy shorts, which they then take off in the sex area, where mattresses invite you to have fun – if you can find an empty one.

Kit Kat Club in the Metropol

Metropol, Nollendorfplatz, Schöneberg, 10777 (2173 6841). U1, U2, U4, U12 Nollendorfplatz. **Open** varies. **Map D5**
Essentially a mixed/straight sex club but there are gay-only sex parties on Thurdays (Soirée Nudisme, entry 8-10pm) and Sundays (Naked Sex Party, open 9pm-midnight). The latter then mingles with MENtropolis (Sun from 11pm) a men-only gay T-dance where you must take off at least your shirt.

Knast

Fuggerstraße 34, Schöneberg, 10777 (218 1026). U1, U2, U12, U15 Wittenbergplatz. **Open** 9pm-5am daily. **Map D5**
The name means 'jail', and there are chains, helmets, and riot sticks galore: so much diversion that the porn videos go almost unnoticed. A small backroom exists although little happens there. The weekend is busiest and cruisiest, although the younger leather men prefer **Scheune** or **New Action** (*see below*). MSC (Motorsports and Contacts) Berlin meet here.

Lab.oratory

Mühlenstraße 26-30 (entrance Rummelsburger Platz), Friedrichshain, 10243 (290 0579). S3, S5, S6, S7, S9/U1 Warschauer Straße. **Open** varies. **Admission** DM8-10. **Map H4**
Gay hardcore discotheque for more perverse tastes. More darkroom than dancefloor. There is a 'normal' disco or Naked Sex Party on Fridays and special parties on Saturdays, including mud, scat, oil and grease, fist, watersports, rubber and sewer outfits. Watch out for flyers or check the press. Men only. *Website: www.lab-oratory.de*

New Action

Kleiststraße 35, Schöneberg, 10787 (211 8256). U1, U2, U4, U12 Nollendorfplatz. **Open** 8pm-7am daily. **Map D5**
Atmospheric and custom-designed hardcore bar with small darkroom. In early morning, when the atmosphere is at its most bizarre, it can become quite an *omnium gatherum* of eccentric weirdos, who either don't yet want to go to bed or else just got up. Leather, rubber, uniform, jeans – but also the odd woollen pullover creates a casual atmosphere.

Quälgeist

2nd backyard, Merseburger Straße 3, Schöneberg, 10823 (788 5799). U7 Eisenacher Straße. **Open** 10pm-late Fri-Sat. **Admission** DM15-30. **Map D5**
The first institution established solely to organise SM parties. And this they do every Friday and Saturday in this three-storey building dedicated to

the cause of hard sex. Tiled rooms in the basement, more than 20 slings upstairs. Parties include SM for beginners, bondage, slave-market and fist nights. Pick up their flyers at any leather bar or **Mann-O-Meter** (*page 213*). Usually a dress code.

Safer-Sex-Party @ SchwuZ

Mehringdamm 61, Kreuzberg, 10961 (693 7025). U6, U7 Mehringdamm. **Open** varies. **Admission** DM15. **Map F5**
The classic. A luxuriant orgy of food, draperies, cushions, kitsch and mattresses, inspired by fantasies of ancient Rome. It takes place on 24 December, at Easter and on the eve of other holidays, drawing an unconventional and youngish crowd and leaving behind hundreds of used condoms. Check out posters, flyers or the gay press.
Website: www.snafu.de/~megadyke.rainbow

Scheune

Motzstraße 25, Schöneberg, 10777 (213 8580). U1, U2, U4, U12 Nollendorfplatz. **Open** 9pm-7am Mon-Thur; non-stop 9pm Fri-7am Mon. **Map D5**
Small and popular leather hardcore bar. Action in the cellar is late and heavy. 'Naked Sex Party' Sunday afternoon and rubber night every second Friday.

SNAX-Club

Mühlenstraße 26-30 (entrance Rummelsburger Platz), Friedrichshain, 10243 (290 0597). S3, S5, S6, S7, S9/U1 Warschauer Straße. **Open** varies. **Admission** DM18. **Map H4**
The pervy party in Europe – the biggest hardcore event of its kind. Trance-techno and sex in a huge

former factory with darkrooms catering for every perverse need. The crowd of up to 1,000, all dressed in their best leather, rubber or uniform attire, look masculine and dangerous but mostly don't take themselves too seriously. First-comers can be distinguished by their blue jeans and amazed expressions. Held irregularly. Watch out for flyers or posters or check the gay press. Men only.
Website: www.snax-club.de

Stahlrohr

Greifenhagener Straße 54, Prenzlauer Berg, 10437 (4473 2747). S4, S8, S10/U2 Schönhauser Allee. **Open** 10am-6am daily. **Map G1**
Small pub in the front and a huge darkroom in the back. Sex parties for every taste, including one on Sunday afternoon called Coffee-Cake-Sex. Check the gay press for details.

Saunas

Saunas are popular and you may have to queue, especially on cheaper days. In-house bills can be run up on your locker or cabin number and settled on leaving. Penalties for lost keys.

Apollo City Sauna

Kurfürstenstraße 101, Tiergarten, 10787 (213 2424). U1, U2, U12, U15 Wittenbergplatz. **Open** 1pm-7am daily. **Admission** DM24 a day (DM21 Mon). Short-term cabin reservation. **Map D5**
A sprawling labyrinth of sin – with 130 lockers and 60 cabins. Dry and steam saunas, porn video den, TV

Prinz Eisenherz Buchladen *– one of the finest gay bookshops in Europe.*

lounge, weights room, sun beds and a well-stocked bar. If you don't end up in one of the cabins, there's plenty of action in the dark, cruisy steam bath.

Gate Sauna
Wilhelmstraße 81, Mitte, 10117 (229 9430). U2 Mohrenstraße/S1, S2 Unter den Linden. **Open** 11am-7am Mon-Thur; non-stop 11am-7am Fri-Mon. **Admission** DM22; Wed DM10 concs. **Map F4**
Newest but smallest addition to the sauna scene appeals to all ages and houses all the usual facilities. The sling in the basement is a prop most welcomed by the 'Heavy Teddies' who meet here every second Sunday afternoon of the month.

Steam Sauna
Kurfürstenstraße 113, Tiergarten, 10787 (218 4060). U1, U2, U12, U15 Wittenbergplatz. **Open** 11am-7am Mon-Thur; non-stop 11am-7am Mon. **Admission** DM21-25. **Map D4**
After Apollo, west Berlin's other classic sauna with 180 lockers and 38 cabins. It hasn't been redecorated for years, but the sex is plentiful. Clientèle of all ages plus sauna and steam rooms, whirlpool, bar and TV room showing porn.

Treibhaus Sauna
Schönhauser Allee 132, Prenzlauer Berg, 10437 (448 4503/449 3494). U2 Eberswalder Straße. **Open** 3pm-7am Mon-Thur; non-stop 3pm Fri-6am Mon. **Admission** DM19; cabin DM31. **Map G2**
Tucked in the first courtyard (buzz for entry), this has become a big favourite, especially with students. Facilities include dry sauna, steam room, whirlpool, cycle jet and solarium. Cabins equipped with TV and VCR on a first-come, first-served basis.

Cruising & sunshine

Cruising is a popular and legal pursuit in Berlin. Most action takes place in the parks. Don't panic or jump into a bush when encountering the police – they are actually there to protect you from local gay bashers and they never hassle cruisers. Some public toilets have a dangerous reputation: avoid the ones at Hermannplatz and in Preußenpark. Summer seems to bring out all of Berlin's finery. There is no taboo attached to nudity in large parks or large groups.

Grunewald
S7 Grunewald.
The woods behind the carpark at Pappelplatz. This popular daytime spot is also well frequented by night, when bikers and harder guys mingle among the trees.

Tiergarten
S3, S5, S7, S9 Tiergarten. **Map D4**
The Löwenbrücke (where the Großer Weg crosses the Neuer See) is the cruising focal point – but the whole corner south-west of the Siegessäule becomes a bit of a gay theme park in summer, including daytime, when hundreds of gays sun themselves on the 'Tuntenwiese' ('faggot meadow').

Volkspark Friedrichshain – *horny lads.*

Volkspark Friedrichshain
S3, S5, S7, S9/U2, U5, U8 Alexanderplatz/bus 100, 157, 257. **Map H3**
After sundown, the area around and behind the Märchenbrunnen monument fills with horny lads. Very active at night. Some activity by day, but it involves searching the nearby slopes for it.

Shopping
Books & art
Bruno's
Nürnberger Straße 53, Wilmersdorf, 10789 (2147 3293). U1 Augsburger Straße/U1, U2, U12, U15 Wittenbergplatz. **Open** 10am-10pm Mon-Sat. **Credit** AmEx, MC, V. **Map D4**
Large and rather plush shop with an extensive selection of reading and viewing material, plus cards, calendars and other paraphernalia.

Galerie Janssen
Pariser Straße 45, Wilmersdorf, 10719 (881 1590). U1, U9 Spichernstraße. **Credit** AmEx, MC, V. **Map C4**
Mainly a gallery, with some books. Regular art exhibitions, plus art pieces, posters and cards for sale.

Prinz Eisenherz Buchladen
Bleibtreustraße 52, Charlottenburg, 10623 (313 9936). S3, S5, S7, S9 Savignyplatz. **Open** 10am-6pm Mon-Fri; 10am-4pm Sat. **Credit** MC, V. **Map C4**
One of the finest gay bookshops in Europe, including, among its large English-language stock, many

titles unavailable in Britain. There's a good art and photography section, plus magazines, postcards and news of book readings and other events.

Toys & fetish outfits

Bad Boy'z
Schliemannstraße 38, Prenzlauer Berg, 10437 (440 8165). U2 Eberswalder Straße. **Open** 1pm-1am Mon-Sat; 3pm-1am Sun. **Admission** DM12; DM7 Mon, Sat. **Credit** AmEx, MC, V. **Map G2**
Darkroom and lockable cabins with beds, in which a choice of homo-erotica can be viewed alone or with anyone found lurking around the corridors.

Black Style
Seelower Straße 5, Prenzlauer Berg, 10439 (4468 8595). S4, S8, S10/U2 Schönhauser Allee. **Open** 1-6.30pm Mon-Wed, Fri; 1-8pm Thur; 10am-2pm Sat. **Credit** AmEx, MC, V. **Map G1**
From black fashion to butt plugs – if it can be made out of rubber or latex they've got it. High quality, reasonable prices and big variety. Mail order.
Website: www.blackstyle.de

Connection Garage
Fuggerstraße 33, Schöneberg, 10777 (218 1432). U1, U2, U12, U15 Wittenbergplatz. **Open** 10am-1am Mon-Sat; 2pm-1am Sun. **Credit** MC, V. **Map D5**
Rubber and leather novelties, T-shirts, magazines. The cruising area comes alive at weekends when it amalgamates with **Connection Disco** (*above*) into one large action-packed venue.

Good Vibration Toys
Nollendorfstraße 25, Schöneberg, 10777 (2175 2838/goodvibration@t-online.de). U1, U2, U4 Nollendorfplatz. **Open** noon-8pm Mon-Fri; 11am-4pm Sat. **No credit cards. Map D5**
Dildos and vibrators in every size and colour, plus condoms and a staggering selection of lubes. Next door at Mr B there's rubber- and leatherwear and a range of devices and appliances.

Leathers
Schliemannstraße 38, Prenzlauer Berg, 10437 (442 7786). U2 Eberswalder Straße. **Open** noon-7.30pm Tue-Fri; noon-4pm Sat. **Credit** AmEx, MC, V. **Map G2**
Attached to a workshop, producing leather and SM articles of the highest quality. No smut here – just well-presented products and helpful staff.

Playground
Courbièrestraße 9, Schöneberg, 10787 (218 2164). U1, U2, U4, U12 Nollendorfplatz. **Open** midnight-noon Mon-Sat. **Credit** AmEx, DC, MC, V. **Map D5**
All-round gay shop selling a fair selection of leather, rubber, toys, videos and magazines. Also an in-house piercing service and cruisy video cabins.

The Jaxx
Motzstraße 19, Schöneberg, 10777 (213 8103). U1, U2, U4, U12 Nollendorfplatz. **Open** noon-3am Mon-Sat; 1pm-3am Sun. **Admission** DM15; DM11 Tue. **Map D5**
A good selection of toys and videos, plus video cabins and cruising area. Popular with younger guys.

Lesbian

Few cities can compete with Berlin's impressive network of lesbian bars, clubs and institutions. Recent years have seen a shift in emphasis as (mostly unprofitable) women-only cafés make way for a revitalised scene populated by largely apolitical, fashion-conscious twenty-somethings. But Berlin caters for lesbians of all shapes and sizes. There are a few regular haunts but lesbian nightlife is mostly made up of one-nighters.

Yet, for all its vibrancy, Berlin's lesbian community can be difficult to penetrate (as it were). Like many Berliners, dykes can initially seem a little standoffish, although that seems to be changing and young lesbians can be seen having fun on Saturdays in the **SchwuZ**. In east Berlin lesbians tend to be more open and friendly, but that can still be said of most easterners.

Cafés, bars & restaurants

Begine
Potsdamer Straße 139, Schöneberg, 10783 (215 4325). U2 Bülowstraße. **Open** 5pm-1am Mon-Sat. **Map E5**
Women-only café frequented by lesbians.

Café am Senefelder Platz
Schönhauser Allee 173, Prenzlauer Berg, 10437 (449 6605). U2 Senefelderplatz. **Open** 8pm-3am daily. **Map G2**
Run by lesbians and attracting a mixed crowd.

Café Seidenfaden
Dircksenstraße 47, Mitte, 10178 (283 2783). S3, S5, S7, S9 Hackescher Markt. **Open** 11am-9pm Mon-Fri; 1-7pm Sun. **Map G3**
Run by women from a rehabilitation and therapy group of former addicts. Packed at lunchtime and quiet in the evenings. There are cultural events, readings, exhibitions and no drugs or alcohol at all.

Pour Elle
Kalckreuthstraße 10, Schöneberg, 10777 (218 7533). U4 Viktoria-Luise-Platz. **Open** 9pm-late daily; men admitted Mon, Wed. **Map D5**
Berlin's oldest lesbian bar/club. Kitsch gold décor and older and classic role-model lesbians. Camp and fun.

Schoko Café
Mariannenstraße 6, Kreuzberg, 10997 (615 1561). U1, U8 Kottbusser Tor. **Open** 5pm-late daily. **Map G5**
Part of the **Schoko-Fabrik** women's centre, this beautiful café is mostly frequented by lesbians (and other women). Cakes, soups, hot snacks and occasional dance parties. *See chapter* **Women**.

Clubs & one-nighters

Die 2 am Wasserturm
Spandauer Damm 168, Charlottenburg, 14059 (252 60). Bus 145. **Open** from 7pm daily; *disco* from 9pm Wed, Sat-Sun.

Energy-charged **MS TitaniCa** *– going down.*

A romantic garden promises wonderful summer nights. Inside they play oldies like 'La Vie En Rose' and 'Sex Machine'. Easy-going atmosphere. A true phenomenon, unchanged since the 1980s.

Diven Attacks
Kalkscheune, Johannisstraße 2, Mitte, 10117 (2839 0065). U6 Oranienburger Tor. **Open** call for details. **Map F3**
See-and-be-seen party for would-be divas. Live acts and go-go dancers enliven the atmosphere. Men may enter if accompanied by a woman friend.

Frauenparty im EWA e.V. Frauenzentrum
Prenzlauer Allee 6, Prenzlauer Berg, 10405 (442 5542). U2 Rosa-Luxemburg-Platz. **Open** 10pm-3am Sat. **Admission** DM3. **Map G3**
Dance party for women every Saturday. Check the press for other events at this venue.

Jane-Bond-Party @ SO36
Oranienstraße 190, Kreuzberg, 10999 (6140 1306). U1, U8 Kottbusser Tor. **Open** 10pm-late Mon, Wed. **Admission** DM8 Mon; DM7 Wed. **Map G4**
Every third Friday of the month, young and youngish progressive lesbians gather to dance and party in a slightly trashy and comic atmosphere. Women only; drags welcome. Go-go dancers. Wild.

Mega-Lesben-Party
Tränenpalast, Reichstagsufer 17, Mitte, 10117 (238 6211). S1, S2, S3, S5, S7, S9/U6 Friedrichstraße. **Information** *MegaDyke Productions (7870 3094/megadyke.rainbow@berlin.snafu.de).* **Admission** DM20. **Map F3**
One-nighter cropping up around once every six months, and a well-attended rallying point for the diverse factions of the extensive lesbian scene in Berlin. An upbeat housey soundtrack is interspersed with occasional performances by the likes of Mancunian contortionist Rose Zone and other unusual artists.
Website: www.snafu.de/~megadyke.rainbow

MS TitaniCa
Theaterschiff am Urban, Planufer 0, Kreuzberg, 10961, U1 Prinzenstraße. **Information** *MegaDyke productions (7870 3094/ megadyke.rainbow@berlin.snafu.de).* **Date** *Apr-Nov* first Fri of the month. **Admission** DM15. **Map G5**
Energy-charged women-only party aboard a boat moored in Kreuzberg's Urbanhafen. The sweltering lower deck churns out serious house beats. Upstairs gyrates to 1970s disco hits, 1980s classics and, inevitably, Abba.
Website: www.snafu.de/~megadyke.rainbow

Schatulle
Fasanenstraße 40, Wilmersdorf, 10719 (8827 7912). U1, U9 Spichernstraße. **Open** 9pm-6am daily. **Admission** free. **Map C5**
Disco with a 1980s atmosphere for women who want to dance but don't like techno. Men admitted.

subterra @ SchwuZ
SchwuZ, Mehringdamm 61, Kreuzberg, 10961 (693 7025). U6, U7 Mehringdamm. **Open** 10pm-5am every second Friday. **Information** *MegaDyke productions (7870 3094/megadyke.rainbow@ berlin.snafu.de).* **Admission** DM15. **Map F5**
Mixed party with slightly more lesbians than gays, downstairs in SchwuZ. Two dancefloors and a massage corner in the candlelight lounge, where a professional masseuse will knead anyone's flesh.
Website: www.snafu.de/~megadyke.rainbow

Shops & services
See chapter **Women** for Compania, an escort agency for lesbians or straight women.

Kadett Lederdesign
Pücklerstraße 31, Kreuzberg, 10997 (612 4457). U1 Görlitzer Bahnhof. **Open** 11am-7pm Mon-Fri; 10am-4pm Sat. **Map H5**
Leatherwear and accessories. Tell the proprietor your most intimate wishes – she will fashion them for you, be they snugly fitting chaps, gloves made from chains or leather dildo holders.
Website: www.kadettfetisch.de

Playstixx
Waldemarstraße 24 , Kreuzberg, 10999 (615 2410). U1, U8 Kottbusser Tor. **Open** 2-6pm Thur. **Map G4**
The dildos on offer at this workshop run by sculptress Stefanie Dörr come in the form of bananas, whales, fists or dolphins rather than simple phalluses. Most are made of non-allergenic, highly durable silicon. Usually customers are allowed to try them on before buying.

Sexclusivitäten
c/o Laura Merrit, Fürbringerstraße 2, Kreuzberg, 10961 (693 6666).
This ring of lesbian call-girls will visit you in your hotel, or wherever else you fancy. Also lessons in safer sex and SM plus porn videos, dildos, vibrators and other sex toys demonstrated at their legendary 'Fuckerware Parties'. By appointment only.

Media

Traditional media are fighting a losers-only battle, but advertising and PR agencies are spreading fast.

Berlin is rushing to regain some of its lost media savvy from the 1920s. But newspaper readership per household is these days lower than in any other major urban market in Germany, the radio scene suffers from overcapacity and local television is swooping downmarket to gain ratings among the city's largely proletarian viewers. Still, 'media' remains a buzzword in the new German capital.

While media sectors depending on the hard-hit local economy for income are ailing, those with clients or audiences beyond the city borders are growing fast. National and international news-gathering organisations have beefed up or installed new Berlin bureaux. The advertising agency scene is blossoming as Berlin becomes the preferred location for creative directors. And buoyed by budgets from newly arrived trade organisations and lobbying groups, public relations agencies are sprouting everywhere.

Radio is the most popular medium, with 26 stations competing for listeners via antenna alone. No other German city has this variety. However, the four largest stations have a stranglehold on 60 per cent of the region's radio advertising market, forcing newcomers to live on the edge. Most of Berlin is cabled, and TV viewers get more than 30 international, national and local channels of wildly varying quality. On the local scene, privately owned TVBerlin has declared war on the SFB affiliate of straight-laced national broadcaster ARD, extending its populist programming philosophy to include analysis and business information. SFB has yet to react, but when it does, it certainly won't be with a foray further upmarket.

Berlin's media mania has roots in the summer of 1990, when the government voted to relocate. Demographers predicted that Berlin's population would swell by 1.5 million to five million by the year 2000. In the boardrooms of Germany's publishing empires, those factors triggered huge investments in Berlin that have resulted in better newspapers, but have not paid off. The population has actually shrunk, and total daily newspaper sales have dropped by nearly a quarter of a million copies since 1994 – the biggest single reason being hordes of east Berlin readers deserting their *Berliner Zeitung* as new owner Gruner + Jahr pushed to expand readership in western districts. By contrast, established daily broadsheets in the west, such as *Der Tagesspiegel* from Holzbrinck

and *Berliner Morgenpost* from Springer, have gained some sales in the east without driving away too many of their core western readers.

All the local quality dailies hoped to find new readers among the tens of thousands of federal workers moving up from Bonn. But they were out-manoeuvred when national titles favoured by Bonners, such as *Die Welt, Frankfurter Allgemeine Zeitung* and the *Süddeutsche Zeitung,* responded with expanded coverage in Berlin editions, making a local read nearly superfluous. With tabloids like Springer's *BZ* or Gruner + Jahr's *Berliner Kurier* also stridently in the fray for daily buyers, few publishing executives now believe sustainable circulation gains are possible – for any title.

Foreign press

International publications are readily available at main stations, the Europa-Center and various International Presse newsagents. Book retailers **Dussman** and **Hugendubel** also carry a range of international titles, while **The British Bookshop** has a selection of London papers and magazines. (*See chapter* **Shopping & Services**.) Berlin currently has no English-language magazine or newspaper for expatriates.

Newspapers
National

Tabloid *BILD*, broadsheet *Die Welt*, and left-leaning *die tageszeitung* are Germany's only true national dailies, though for different reasons none of them reflect a national consensus on anything. *Frankfurter Allgemeine Zeitung* comes close to the task with exhaustive coverage, as does the *Süddeutsche Zeitung*, from Munich, with flair.

BILD

Flagship tabloid of the Axel Springer group. Though its credibility varies from story to story, *BILD* leverages the journalistic resources of the Springer empire and its four-million circulation to land regular scoops, so even the German intelligentsia pays attention to its daily riot of polemic.

Die Welt

Die Welt moved its main editorial office to Berlin well in advance of the government's arrival, appointed a new editor-in-chief, went through a redesign, and is now being held up by its owners, the Springer Group, as a success story. Once a lacklustre mouthpiece of conservative, provincial thinking, *Die Welt* has widened its political horizons, but at a circulation of around 17,000 for its Berlin edition, it's a non-starter in the capital. At the end of 1999, they added a page in English to the back of their Berlin section.

die tageszeitung

Set up in Berlin's rebellious Kreuzberg district in the 1970s, the '*taz*' was an attempt to balance the provincial world view offered by West German newspapers and give coverage to alternative political and social issues. Today, with many of its charter readers now making mainstream policies in the Bundestag, the *taz* is floundering. Still, the Berlin edition does a good job keeping watch on crooks in local government, and its regular appeals for funds are hilarious.

Frankfurter Allgemeine Zeitung

Germany's *de facto* newspaper of record. Stolid, exhaustive coverage of daily events, plus lots of background and analysis, particularly on the business pages. Designers are itching to give it a facelift, but the *FAZ* is too busy being serious to bother. Its Berlin section focuses on culture and arts, and in terms of listings is as good as the local papers.

Süddeutsche Zeitung

Based in Munich, the *Süddeutsche* blends first-rate journalism with enlightened commentary and, not unusual in Germany, uninspired visuals. Also with a Berlin edition, but only one page of local coverage, confining readership here to news junkies.

Handelsblatt

The closest Germany has to the *Financial Times* in terms of business slant and readability, but not for long. Holzbrinck's *Handelsblatt* is bracing for competition from a German-language version of the *FT*, which insiders give only a long shot at success.

Local

Berliner Zeitung

A black hole of investment since Gruner + Jahr bought it from Robert Maxwell in the early 1990s, this east Berlin newspaper sopped up the best journalistic talent and was redesigned in a bid to become the voice of Berlin. Gains through huge marketing in western strongholds only partly offset losses from its haemorrhaging core readership in the east. Running out of gimmicks just as the competition was preparing their own, the paper now lacks the spit and vigour of a few years ago, but remains a lively though unauthoritative read.

Der Tagesspiegel

Solid but predictable, this is the staple of Wilmersdorf solicitors and Dahlem academics. Once thought vulnerable to the *Berliner Zeitung*'s advance, its circulation has emerged as Berlin's most stable, and a new, younger editor-in-chief is slowly managing to bring a fresher viewpoint. Losing money hand over fist, *Der Tagesspiegel* is a matter of prestige for owner Holzbrinck.

Berliner Morgenpost

Fat, fresh and self-conscious, this broadsheet is the favourite of the petty bourgeois and a profitable concern for the Springer empire. Good local coverage, and gradually gaining readers in the east through the introduction of neighbourhood editions, but no depth on the national and international pages.

BZ

A classic tabloid, featuring the headline-writing talents of loose cannon editor-in-chief Franz Josef Wagner. The daily riot of polemic and pictures hasn't let up since it was demonised by the left in the 1970s – but its circulation has. Although still Berlin's largest seller with 270,000 copies daily, *BZ* sales are down by 70,000 copies since 1991.

15 Uhr Aktuell

Wimpy afternoon freesheet distributed by folks in daft white Parkas after 3pm in U-Bahn stations. Although the news is abbreviated, people theoretically take it because it is more current than the morning papers. In practice, readership is heavy among people who don't buy other papers, such as teenagers.

Weekly

Die Zeit

Every major post-war intellectual debate in Germany has been carried out in the pages of *Die Zeit*, the newspaper which proved to a suspicious world that a liberal tradition was alive and well in a country best known for excesses of intolerance. Now with a more friendly design, the wandering style of its élite authors still makes for a difficult read.

Jungle World

Defiantly left, graphically switched-on and commercially undaunted, the editors of this fairly new Berlin-based weekly can be relied on to mock anything approaching the comfortable views of the mainstream press. Born of an ideological dispute with the publishers of *Junge Welt*, a former East Berlin youth title, *Jungle World* lacks sales but packs a punch.

Magazines

Der Spiegel

Few journalistic institutions in Germany possess the resources and clout to pursue a major story like *Der Spiegel*, one of the best and most aggressive news weeklies in Europe. After years of firing barbs at the ruling Christian Democrats, *Der Spiegel* was caught off-guard when the Social Democrats were elected in 1999, but remains a must-read for anyone interested in Germany's power structure.

Focus

Once its spare, to-the-point articles, four-colour graphics, and service features were a welcome innovation in Germany. But the gloss has faded, and *Focus* has established itself as a non-thinking man's *Der Spiegel*, whose answer to the upstart was simply to print more colour pages and become warm and fuzzy by adding bylines.

Trevor Wilson – Radio Fritz's resident loon.

Stern

The heyday of news pictorials may have long gone, but *Stern* still manages to shift around a million copies a week of big colour spreads detailing the horrors of war, the beauties of nature and the curves of the female body. Nevertheless its reputation has never really recovered from the Hitler diaries fiasco in the early 1980s.

Listings magazines

Berlin is awash with listings freebies, notably *[030]* (music, nightlife, film), *Flyer* (a pocket-sized club guide), *Siegessäule* and *Sergej* (both gay). These can be picked up in bars and restaurants. The two paid-for fortnightlies, *Zitty* and *tip*, come out on alternate weeks and, at least for cinema information, it pays to get the current title.

Zitty

Having lost some counter-cultural edge since its foundation in 1977, *Zitty* remains a vital force on the Berlin media scene, providing a fortnightly blend of close-to-the-bone civic journalism, alternative cultural coverage, and a comprehensive listings interspersed with wry, often arcane German comics. The *Harte Welle* ('hardcore') department of its Lonely Hearts classifieds is legendary.

tip

A glossier version of *Zitty* in every respect, *tip* gets better marks for its overall presentation and readability, largely due to coated paper stock, four-colour pages throughout and a space-saving TV programme insert. This makes it more appealing to display advertisers – a double-edged sword depending on why you buy a listings magazine in the first place.

Television

At its best, German TV produces solid investigative programmes and clever drama series. At its worst there are cheesy 'erotic' shows and vapid folk-music programmes featuring rhythmically clapping studio audiences. Late-night TV is chock-a-block with imported action series and European soft porn, interspersed with nipple-pinching and finger-sucking adverts for telephone sex numbers.

A basic channel shakedown looks like this: two national public networks, ARD and ZDF, a handful of no-holds-barred commercial channels, and a load of special-interest channels.

ARD's daily *Tagesschau* at 8pm is the most authoritative news broadcast nationally. N-tv is Germany's all-news cable channel, owned partly by CNN but lacking the satellite broadcaster's ability to cover a breaking story. TVBerlin is the city's experiment with local commercial television and though more ambitious under new management, it's still catching up with ARD's local affilate SFB, which covers local news with more insight.

RTL, Pro 7 and SAT-1 are cable services offering a predictable mix of Hollywood re-runs and imported series, and increasingly producing their own produced fare, such as sensational magazine programmes. Special interest channels run from Kinderkanal for kids to Eurosport, MTV Europe and its German-language competitor Viva, to Arte, an enlightened French-German cultural channel with high-quality films and documentaries.

Channels broadcasting regularly in English include CNN, NBC, MTV Europe and BBC World. British or American films on ARD or ZDF are sometimes broadcast with a simultaneous soundtrack in English for stereo-equipped TV sets.

Radio

Some 33 stations compete for audiences in Berlin, seven from outside town, so even tiny shifts in market share have disastrous consequences for broadcasters. The race for ratings supremacy in the greater metropolitan area is thwarted by a clear split between the urban audience in both east and west and a rural one in the hinterland. The main four stations in the region have their audiences based in either Berlin (Berliner Rundfunk, 91.4; r.s.2, 94.3) or Brandenburg (BB Radio, 107.5; Antenne Brandenburg, 99.7). No station can pull in everyone.

Commercial stations 104,6 RTL (104.6) and Hundert,6 (100.6) offer standard chart pop spiced with news. Energy (103.4) and Fritz (102.6), featuring English DJ Trevor Wilson as resident loon, are a bit more adventurous but still far from cutting edge. Star FM's (87.9) rock format and Voice of America news broadcasts look back to the days when the frequency was occupied by the US Armed Forces Network in Berlin. Jazz is round the clock on Jazz Radio (101.9). Information-based stations such as Info Radio (92.05) and Berlin Aktuell (93.6) are increasing in popularity. The BBC World Service (90.2) is available 24 hours a day.

Internet

For websites *see chapter* **Further Media**; for Internet cafés *see chapter* **Essential Information**.

Music: Classical & Opera

At its biggest crossroads since the war, Berlin's classical scene looks to a sassy Scouser to soothe its internal strife.

Deutsche Staatsoper – *longer, grander and redolent of past glory. See page 228.*

Berlin can outdo any other city in the world when it comes the sheer number of opera houses (three, not counting several independent companies), orchestras (seven, with a number of private ones too) and venues (two major concert halls, plus a myriad smaller venues and churches). And yet the classical music scene is in a stage of transfiguration – some of it good, some of it bad – the like of which the city hasn't seen since the end of World War II. Read on.

'All change, please!' could be the motto of the current Berlin classical music scene, with most of the major musical figures due to step down by the year 2002 – including the musical directors of the Berlin Philharmonic Orchestra, the Deutsches Sinfonie-Orchester and the intendants of the Deutsche Oper and the Philharmonie. Virtually all of these changes should instill vigour, freshness and vitality in the musical landscape of Berlin. Now for the bad news.

STRIKE UP THE BAND

In the late 1990s a dispute that encapsulates the western half of the city's funding problems brought the **Deutsche Oper** to the brink of the abyss. The story starts in 1984 when the Deutsche Oper's orchestra was granted by the Senat a *Medienpauschale* (a quarterly hefty extra payment above the given salary) – exactly the sort of political please-just-stay-here-in-West-Berlin gesture that made the Western sector back then such a paradise for artists of all sorts. The Medienpauschale continued to be paid after 1989, although it no longer had any political purpose. In 1998, when the budget deficit problems of the Deutsche Oper reached crisis point, the orchestra agreed to play for one year with their Medienpauschale reduced by 50 per cent. The Senat promised to restore it in full after one year, but then-Kultursenator Peter Radunski, facing massive funding problems across the artistic spectrum, said no. In the late September of 1999 the Senat cancelled the orchestra's Medienpauschale and the fight was on. On 1 October 1999 15 members of the Deutsche Oper orchestra walked out (by phoning in sick) on the very afternoon of the premiere of that opera house's new production of Schönberg's *Moses und Aron*. Musicians had to be flown in from all over Europe to play this fiendishly difficult score unrehearsed – and were treated like traitors by the rest of the orchestra. Within a few days of the incident the entire DO orchestra was out on strike. The acrimony was as incredible as it was intense; the rest of the DO rounded on the treacherous orchestra, the orchestra rounded on the Senat and the public rounded on the DO's much-beleagured intendant, Götz Friedrich. For weeks not a single performance was given. It was the greatest musical crisis in Berlin since the war.

Compounding the problems of the Deutsche Oper, musical director Christian Thielemann announced in late 1999 that he wished to give up his position at the end of the 2001 season, claiming irreconcilable differences with incoming intendant, Udo Zimmermann. No wonder. Thielemann is an arch-classicist, whilst Zimmermann is a tried-and-tested avant-gardist. It appears, as of going to press, that the Deutsche Oper is setting itself up for a comprehensive and definitive cull from Berlin's classical music scene. Watch this space.

RING IN THE NEW

In 2002 **Berlin Philharmonic** will bid goodbye to their incumbent musical director, Claudio Abbado to welcome Britain's Sir Simon Rattle (*see below* **Rattle and hun**). This orchestra is always a must-see, even if its repertoire often seems frustratingly old-fashioned, although Rattle has pledged to change this. Tickets for the Berlin Phil are easier to come by than in the days when Herbert von Karajan led the orchestra, and the management has simplified booking procedures and finally introduced a credit-card facility.

The **Deutsches Symphonie-Orchester** (formerly the Berlin Radio Symphony Orchestra) also says adieu – in 2001 – to their musical director Vladimir Ashkenazy. He's being replaced by the dynamic Kent Nagano, who caused a stir in late 1999 by threatening to cancel his contract unless

Rattle and hun

When Herbert von Karajan died on 16 July 1989 it may have been a shock to many outside observers of the musical world, but to most members of the the the Berlin Philharmonic, it came as something of a relief. Karajan had led the orchestra for 34 despotic years, and while he consolidated the band's reputation as arguably the world's finest during his tenure, his methods were always tyrannical. As Norman Lebrecht puts it in his masterful polemic, *The Maestro Myth*, 'The price of working with Karajan was to accept his absolute autocracy'. A change at the orchestra's helm was long overdue.

Then in October 1989 55-year-old Claudio Abbado was declared the new musical director, just pipping the favourites, irascible Lorin Maazel, hauty Riccardo Muti and 'Big Jim' Levine. Tellingly, this orchestra itself elects its own musical director.

Abbado's non-authoritarian style proved a relief to the orchestra in the first few post-Karajan years, but by the late 1990s his star seemed to be waning. The orchestra experienced non-sell-out concerts for the first time in decades and it became clear that the relationship between the retiring Italian and his players was less than ideal. Towards the end of 1998 he announced that he would not renew his contract, which was due to expire in 2002.

Daniel Barenboim campaigned vigorously to replace Abbado but he's not all that popular with the band. His dream of a hat-trick (he already helms the Staatsoper and the Chicago Symphony Orchestra) came unstuck.

Enter Sir Simon Rattle, the greatest international musical phenomenon to come out of Liverpool since the Beatles. Born in 1955, he began studying conducting at the Royal Academy of Music at the age of 16 and by 25 was principal conductor (later musical director) of the City of Birmingham Symphony Orchestra, a then-mediocre provincial band which Rattle whipped up within a few years to world-class stature. He's since conducted every orchestra on the planet that counts, and – testimony to his pluralist, democratic and philanthropic musical philosophy – quite a few that don't; he simply wanted to help them.

When he first conducted the Berlin Phil in November 1987 things didn't go so smoothly for the young, shock-headed Scouser. A tale has it that the orchestra got bolshie and garrulous during rehearsal and Rattle replied: 'Ladies and Gentlemen, I've always known about the legendary sound this orchestra makes, but this is not the kind of sound I had in mind.' Over the years Rattle's distinctive blend of humility, wit and unquestionable musical authority won over

the Senat increased the orchestra's budget by DM6 million; at presstime, it looks like he'll get it. Although it may have nothing of the Berlin Philharmonic's cachet, the DSO gives it a run for its money and has developed into an orchestra which goes from strength to strength.

Berlin's dark-horse orchestra (and, at 77, its second oldest) is the venerable **Rundfunk Sinfonieorchester Berlin**. Playing at both the Philharmonie and the Konzerthaus, this band is currently under the fine musical directorship of Rafael Frühbeck de Burgos (to say nothing of its exceptional regular guest conductor, Michael Jurowski). Programmes by the RSO display taste combined with adventure and are always worth looking out for. And don't discount the Berliner Sinfonie-Orchester, which is based at the Konzerthaus and which can play superbly.

GOT ANY SPARES?

Unless you're in town in mid-summer when the opera houses and concert halls are generally dark, the choice of classical music events can be staggering. *Zitty* and *tip*, the German-language fort-nightly Berlin magazines, can be relied upon for classical listings, as can a few token listings on the new Anglophone daily back page of *Die Welt*.

The **Deutsche Staatsoper**, **Komische Oper** and **Konzerthaus** are within an easy stroll of one another, near Unter den Linden. While the Staatsoper and Konzerthaus only occasionally attract the megastars of the classical music circuit (the odd sell-out appearance by Domingo or Bartolli), and the Komische never does, they all offer a generally excellent standard of performance. Furthermore, concerts in the Konzerthaus and operas at the Komische can be considerably less expensive those than at the Berlin Phil, the Deutsche Oper or the Staatsoper. But concert-going in the east is not the bargain it once was. As Berlin teeters on the edge of bankruptcy (DM60 billion in debt and rising) and government arts subsidies are slashed, prices have risen accordingly as east Berlin's opera companies and ensembles scramble to stay afloat. You won't exactly break the bank in the east – except, perhaps, at the Staatsoper – but the days of DM5 opera and concert tickets have long since vanished.

the orchestra – despite his lack of German. On 23 June 1999 the Berlin Philharmonic elected him as Abbado's successor, effective from the start of the 2002-03 season. Changes to come? It's no secret that many Berlin Phil members are tired of the orchestra's overwhelmingly 19th-century repertoire and want to play more contemporary music. Sir Simon has pledged his commitment to doing just that. He should also bring to the orchestra a sharper-edged, less frilly sound than Abbado. And, in his short letter of thanks to the band following his election, he promised to make some personal changes: 'I look forward to many years of communication with you. However, in the near future, that will be in German. This long-delayed process starts now!'.

Naturally, the majority of classical music fans will be after tickets for the Berlin Philharmonic Orchestra at the Philharmonie. These can be hard come by, especially when the bigger names take to the podium, but nil desperandum. Make yourself a sign saying '*Suche eine Karte*' ('seeking a ticket') and stand outside the hall. Or try this sentence on people entering: '*Haben Sie vielleicht eine Karte übrig?*' ('Anyone got a spare ticket?'). With any luck, someone whose companion needed to work late will be able to help you out, or you might spot somebody holding a sign reading '*Karte(n) zu verkaufen*' ('ticket(s) for sale'). Be warned there may be ticket sharks.

The major Berlin music festival is the Berliner Festwochen (*see chapter* **By Season**). Started in 1950, this brings to Berlin the crème-de-la-crème of the world's soloists and orchestras, spanning the month of September. Each festival has a particular theme and details of where to get programmes are listed below.

Sadly, Berlin is still light years behind London for the amount of contemporary music on offer, but the contemporary music festival, the Biennale (every other March, *see chapter* **By Season**), as well as the presence of Berlin's première group for modern music, the Ensemble Modern, assures that those who want more challenging fare than Bach, Beethoven and Brahms are fairly well looked after. That said, the Biennale is often maddeningly biased towards serial and post-serial composers. Postmodernists scarcely get a look-in. At the other end of the historical scale, there's both July's Bach-Tage ('Bach Days'), a feast of Baroque music usually played on period instruments at various venues, and November's Wochen der alten Musik ('Early Music Weeks'), latterly including period instrument performances of operas at the Staatsoper. Additionally, 'alternative' opera performances at the small but creditable **Neuköllner Oper** or by the excellent **Berliner Kammeroper** should not be dismissed.

Ticket agencies

Tickets are sold at concert hall box offices or through ticket agencies, called *Theaterkassen*. At box offices, seats are generally sold up to one hour before the performance. You can also make a reservation by phone, except, as noted above, for concerts of the Berlin Phil. Theaterkassen provide the easiest means of buying a ticket, but you must be prepared to pay for the convenience as commissions can run as high as 17 per cent. Below are details of some of the major Theaterkassen in central Berlin. For details of the 50 or so other agencies around the city, look in the *Gelbe Seiten* ('*Yellow Pages*') under Theaterkassen. Beware that many places may not accept credit cards.

concert- & theaterkasse city

Knesebeckstraße 10, Charlottenburg, 10623 (0800 719 2710). S3, S5, S7, S9 Savignyplatz. **Open** 10am-6pm Mon-Fri; 10am-1pm Sat. **Credit** AmEx, DC, MC, V. **Map C4**

Hekticket

Kino Zoopalast at Bahnhof Zoo (230 9930). S3, S5, S7, S9/U2, U9 Zoologischer Garten. **Open** 9am-8pm Mon-Fri; 10am-8pm Sat; 4-8pm Sun. **No credit cards. Map C4**
Hekticket offers discounts of up to 50% on theatre and concert tickets, so it should be your first choice if using a ticket agency. For a DM2 commission, its staff will sell you tickets for the same evening's performance. Tickets for Sunday matinées are available on Saturday. At the time of going to press, Hekticket's Karl-Liebknecht-Straße branch was not able to accept telephone bookings.
Branch: Karl-Liebknecht-Straße 12, Mitte, 10178 (2431 2431).

Kant-Kasse

Krumme Straße 55, Charlottenburg, 10627 (313 4554; booking 834 4073). U7 Wilmersdorfer Straße. **Open** 10am-6.30pm Mon-Fri; 10am-2pm Sat. **Credit** AmEx, DC, MC, V. **Map B4**
Their telephone credit booking system is based at Birkbuschstraße 14, Steglitz, 1216.
Website: www.telecard.de

Major venues

Deutsche Oper

Bismarckstraße 35, Charlottenburg, 10585 (341 0249). U2 Deutsche Oper. **Open** 11am-7pm Mon-Fri; 10am-2pm Sat. **Tickets** DM17-200. **Credit** AmEx, DC, V. **Map B4**
As discussed above, Berlin's bolshiest orchestra. During a 1998 tour of Israel a musician was sacked for telling a local waiter, 'Adolf Hitler will pay my bill!'. By late 1999 the DO was at critical meltdown, walking out over a pay dispute and refusing to enter into negotiations. Even more drastic changes are coming up, when Götz Friedrich finally gives up his post of intendant in 2002 after two decades – generally thought to be one too many. He is due to be replaced by the intendant of the Leipzig Opera, Udo Zimmermann. If Zimmermann brings to the DO his Leipzig policy of regular contemporary operas, then this house will be in very good hands indeed artistically – even though the box office could suffer.
The DO was designed by Fritz Bornemann and built in 1961. The theatre interior is pleasant enough, although its exterior, an enormous tranche of granite, has led to Berliners nicknaming it 'Sing-Sing'.
Website: www.deutsche-oper.berlin.de

Deutsche Staatsoper

Unter den Linden 5-7, Mitte, 10117 (2035 4555). U6 Französische Straße. **Open** 10am-8pm Mon-Sat; 2-8pm Sun. **Tickets** DM13-120. **Credit** AmEx, MC, V. **Map F3**
The Deutsche Staatsoper has a longer and grander history than the Deutsche Oper. It was founded as

Komische Oper – *stimulation guaranteed.*

Prussia's Royal Court Opera for Frederick the Great in 1742, and designed along the lines of a Greek temple. Although the present building dates from 1955, the façade faithfully copies that of Knobelsdorff's original, twice destroyed in World War II. The elegant interior gives an immediate sense of the house's past glory, with huge chandeliers and elaborate wall paintings. Musical director Daniel Barenboim now divides his time between this house and the Chicago Symphony Orchestra – but he lost out to Sir Simon Rattle on his attempted hat-trick of becoming the new musical director of the Berlin Philharmonic. If you're very lucky (and if you can get a ticket), you may discover the likes of Domingo singing Wagner or Bartolli singing Mozart here. Beware of Harry Kupfer's jaw-droppingly awful Wagner productions, but if you have the chance to see the outstanding Peter Greenaway/Saskia Boddeke production of Milhaud's *Christophe Colomb*, then leap at it. Chamber music is performed in the small, ornate Apollo Saal, housed within the main building.

And beware of those Staatsoper DM10 opera tickets – they may seem a bargain until you realise you can't see half of the stage.
Website: www.staatsoper/berlin.org

Komische Oper

Behrenstraße 55-57, Mitte, 10117 (4799 7400). U6 Französische Straße/S1, S2 Unter den Linden. **Open** 11am-7pm Mon-Sat; 1-3pm Sun. **Tickets** DM16-99. **Credit** AmEx, DC, MC, V. **Map F3**
The Komische Oper is dominated by its artistic director, Harry Kupfer. One of the few *Ossis* whose career has not just continued but sailed since reunification, Kupfer runs a tight ship here. At present he is ably assisted by his dynamic young Russian-American musical director, Yakov Kreizberg, due to leave at the end of the 2001 season. Nevertheless Kupfer is one of the star directors in the German opera scene and is nothing if not bold; his radical but almost always incisive interpretations – especially, appropriately, of comic operas – virtually guarantee a stimulating evening's worth of opera. The singing (all operas are sung in German, which seems a pointless indulgence in this age of surtitles) may not always be exactly breathtaking, but prices are accordingly fair. Furthermore, all unsold tickets for that evening's performance are available from the box office for half-price after 11am. You can see an opera for the price of a cinema seat, a commendably wise financial policy courtesy of the house's appropriately named intendant, Albert Kost.
Website: www.komischeoper.line.de

Konzerthaus

Gendarmenmarkt 2, Mitte, 10106 (2030 92101). U6 Französische Straße. **Open** noon-7pm Mon-Sat; noon-4pm Sun & hols. **Tickets** DM10-110; some half-price concs. **Credit** AmEx, MC, V. **Map F4**
Formerly the Schauspielhaus am Gendarmenmarkt, this 1821 architectural gem by Friedrich Schinkel was all but destroyed in the war. Lovingly restored, it was reopened in 1984 under the rather confusing name 'Schauspielhaus', implying a theatre for plays (which it originally was), not concerts. There are no longer plays to be seen here, but there are two main spaces for concerts, the Großer Konzertsaal for orchestras, the Kleiner Saal for chamber music. Organ recitals in the large concert hall are a wonderful treat, played on a massive organ at the back of the stage. The Berliner Sinfonie-Orchestra is based here – and continuing the litany of new leaders, Michael Schönwandt is to be replaced as chief conductor by Eliahu Inbal in 2001. This house displays some of the most imaginative programming in Berlin; a healthy mixture of the old, the new and the rediscovered makes the Konzerthaus a wonderful venue for concert-goers. The Deutsches Sinfonie-Orchester, one of the finest in the land, also often plays here and is worthwhile particularly for its performances of contemporary music. There are also occasional informal concerts in the cosy little Musik Club in the depths of the building.

Finally, the Konzerthaus offers a 'ClassicCard'. For DM40 anybody under 27 can obtain one, which entitles the holder to any seats available at the *Abendkasse* (evening performance box office) for a mere DM10 – and they guarantee to hand over the best ones they've got.
Website: www.konzerthaus.de

Philharmonie

Herbert-von-Karajan Straße 1, Tiergarten, 10785 (2548 8126). U1 Kurfürstenstraße. **Open** 3-6pm Mon-Fri; 11am-2pm Sat-Sun. **Tickets** DM24-110; some last-minute concs. **Credit** AmEx, MC, V. **Map E4**
Berlin's most famous concert hall, home to the world-renowned Berlin Philharmonic Orchestra, is also its most architecturally daring; a marvellous, puckish piece of organic modernism. The hall, with a golden, reconstructionist vaulting roof, was designed by Hans Scharoun in 1963. The sad news is that it's now dwarfed by new monstrosities at Potsdamer Platz. Its reputation for superb acoustics is accurate but it depends very much on where you sit. Behind the orchestra the acoustics are appalling, but in front (where it is accordingly much more expensive) the sound is heavenly. The structure also incorporates a smaller hall, the Kammermusiksaal, about which the same accoustical notes apply. The Berlin Philharmonic Orchestra was founded in 1882 and has been led by some of the world's greatest conductors. Its greatest fame came under the baton of the late Herbert von Karajan and it will soon be under the leadership of Sir Simon Rattle (*see page 226-227* **Rattle and hun**). Elmar Weingarten has announced his intention to retire as intendant in 2001; he was frustrated at having too little real administrative power. Word on the street at press time is that if Rattle

asks him to stay, he will withdraw his resignation. On the negative side, The Berlin Phil continues to play the most boring, overplayed repertoire imaginable – safe and almost exclusively 19th-century – but that doesn't stop people flocking from all over the world to hear it, and it is still a magical orchestra. The Berlin Phil gives about a hundred performances in Berlin during its August-to-June season, with another 20 to 30 concerts around the world. See above about how to best get tickets. Tickets for visiting orchestras that play at the Philharmonie are usually easier to come by.

Website: www.berlin-philharmonic.com

Other venues

Many churches offer regular organ recitals. It's also worth enquiring if concerts are to be staged in any of the castles or museums in the area, especially in summer or at holiday time. Telephones are often erratically staffed, so check *Zitty* or *tip*.

Akademie der Künste

Hanseatenweg 10, Tiergarten, 10557 (390 760). U9 Hansaplatz. **Open** *enquiries* 1-7pm Mon; 10am-7pm Tue-Sun and one hour before performance. **Tickets** DM10-25. **No credit cards. Map D3**
The Academy of the Arts offers everything from art exhibitions to literary readings, from films to music, specialising in performances of 20th-century compositions. Concerts are either in the large (507-seater) or the small (195-seater) halls. Acoustics in both rooms of this 1960 building are reasonable.

Ballhaus Naunynstraße

Naunynstraße 27, Kreuzberg, 10997 (2588 6644). U8 Moritzplatz. **Open** *box office* 10am-6pm Mon-Fri. Reserve tickets by telephone. **Tickets** DM10-25. **No credit cards. Map G4**
Don't expect to hear anything ordinary at this Kreuzberg cultural centre. A varied assortment of western and oriental music is on the menu, with drinks and snacks in the café out front. The long, rectangular hall, which seats 150, plays guest to the excellent Berlin Chamber Opera, among others.

Berliner Dom

Lustgarten 1, Mitte, 10117 (2026 9136). S3, S5, S7, S9 Hackescher Markt. **Open** 10am-5.30pm Mon-Fri. **Tickets** DM10-30. **No credit cards. Map F3**
Berlin's cathedral, having just been fully restored from its war-damaged state, went up in flames a few years ago. It's been re-restored and now houses some recommendable concerts, usually of the organ or choral variety.

Hochschule der Künste

Hardenbergstraße 33, Tiergarten, 10623 (3185 2374). U2 Ernst-Reuter-Platz. **Open** *box office* 3-6.30pm Tue-Fri; 11am-2pm Sat. **Tickets** free for student concerts; DM20-50 for guest performers. **No credit cards. Map C4**
Berlin's wannabe musical luminaries study in the adjacent building. A grotesquely ugly but thoroughly functional hall plays host to both student soloists

and orchestras, as well as lesser-known, underfunded professional groups. There's a great deal of variety here, and the fact that it doesn't attract the best-known artists is certainly no reason to avoid it.

Kulturbrauerei (Kesselhaus)

Knaackstraße 97, Prenzlauer Berg, 10435 (441 9269). U2 Eberswalder Straße. **Open** *enquiries* 10am-6pm Mon-Sat. **Tickets** DM5-50. **No credit cards. Map G2**
Situated, as its name implies, in the boiler house of a converted brewery, which also houses art galleries, and a rather overpriced courtyard bar, this small theatre is rapidly establishing a reputation for itself among Berlin trendies who come to see occasional opera or music-theatre pieces performed here.

Meistersaal

Köthener Straße 38, Kreuzberg, 10963 (264 9530). S1, S2/U2 Potsdamer Platz. **Open** *enquiries* 11am-8pm Mon-Fri. **Tickets** DM10-35. **Credit** AmEx, MC, V. **Map E4**
The 'Maestro Hall' plays host to solo instrumentalists and chamber groups who can't afford to book the Kammermusiksaal of the Philharmonie. But don't let that fool you. Music-making of the highest rank occurs here in this warm and welcoming little salon with superb acoustics. The restaurant down the hallway could use some new enthusiasm.

Neuköllner Oper

Karl-Marx-Straße 131-133, Neukölln, 12043 (6889 0777). U7 Karl-Marx-Straße. **Open** *enquiries* 3-7pm Tue-Fri. **Tickets** DM14-39. **Credit** AmEx, DC, MC, V. **Map H6**
There's no grand opera here, but a constantly changing programme of chamber operas and music-theatre works much-loved by the Neuköllners who come here to see lighter, bubblier (and much less expensive) works than in Berlin's big three opera houses. An informal alternative to the champagne-and-chandeliers atmosphere of the Deutsche, Komische or Staatsoper. Current artistic director Peter Lund is one of Berlin's most promising young theatre directors. Pity about the appalling acoustics.

Staatsbibliothek-Otto-Braun Saal

Potsdamer Straße 33, Tiergarten, 10785 (26 60). S1, S2/U2 Potsdamer Platz. **Open** *enquiries* 8am-7.30pm Mon-Fri. **Tickets** vary according to event. **No credit cards. Map E4**
The Staatsbibliothek is everything to anyone looking for a bit of culture: exhibitions, historical archives and music are all on the programme. Smaller ensembles provide the lion's share of the music in this chamber of the state library.

St. Matthäus Kirche am Kulturforum

Matthäikirchplatz, Tiergarten, 10785 (261 3676). U1 Kurfürstenstraße. **Open** noon-6pm Wed-Sun. **Tickets** vary according to event. **No credit cards. Map E4**
Because it's next to the Philharmonie, locals have nicknamed this the 'Polka Church'. Check listings to see who's playing what, as it could be anything from a free organ recital to a heavenly chorus of Russian Orthodox Monks. Exquisite acoustics.

Music: Rock, Folk & Jazz

Despite a wave of rock 'Ostalgia', Berlin music retains its distinctive edge.

Berlin's music scene has always reflected the tension permeating city life. Cold War division infused the music with a sense of alienation, intrigue and even impending apocalypse. Post-1989, a spirit of improvisation and experimentation midwived techno culture and fashioned new club and performance spaces out of abandoned industrial and commercial buildings or the cellars of houses still riddled with World War II bullet holes – creative reactions to the dizzying and often disorienting changes of the last decade.

The post-war West German music industry shunned Berlin – even today, only V2 and soon Sony have head offices in Berlin. Left to their own devices, musicians helped themselves, with indie labels and alternative distribution. To compensate for the city's insular location, the West Berlin government offered generous subsidies for rock music, while the GDR entirely bankrolled music output. While this somewhat shielded Berlin bands from commercial pressure, the music was in danger of degenerating into state-sponsored mediocrity, or in the East, an instrument of state control.

UNDER THE INFLUENCE

The Allied media in divided Berlin played a significant role in spreading the music and myth of Anglo-American rock on both sides of the wall. The earliest example of this influence was Berlin Beat music with the success of groups like The Lords and, in East Berlin, Die Sputniks and the Franke Echo Quintett. West Berlin Beat tended to sound very British: upbeat, poppy and usually in English. What Easterners termed Beat leaned more towards American surf music, since instrumentals were less controversial than songs.

Purveyors of pop music in the West grew increasingly uncomfortable with the artificial heritage of Anglo-American rock. While the romance of foreign sounds never dwindled, Berlin's vanguard parted ways with the fare offered by military radio, and in the early 1970s moved off into experimental avenues led by bands like Ashra Tempel and Tangerine Dream or the radical politics of squatter patron saints Ton Stein Scherben.

*Pet Shop Boys do **Arena**. See page 232.*

The early 1980s witnessed a fresh burst of new music from Berlin, though the bulk of it, with its German lyrics, remains unknown in the Anglophone world. Industrial pioneers Einstürzende Neubauten stepped from the underground on to an international stage. Frenetic new wave bands, part of the Neue Deutsche Welle trend, emerged with a blaze of enthusiasm, and a series of Berlin acts stumbled upon sounds that gained wider international attention: Düsseldorf immigrants and techno forerunners DAF; power popper Nena; punk ironists Die Ärzte, and the radical girl group Malaria.

A NEW CAREER IN A NEW TOWN

Under Allied rule, residents of West Berlin were exempt from the draft. This attracted many young West Germans who helped to forge the alternative and avant-garde scenes in the city. But Berlin has also captured the imaginations of artists and musicians from abroad.

In the 1920s, the likes of Arnold Schönberg, Kurt Weill, Bertolt Brecht, George Grosz and Max Ernst founded Berlin's reputation for artistic experimentation. It was this cutting-edge legacy, along with the thrill and peril of life in the Walled City, that lured David Bowie and Iggy Pop to Berlin in 1976. In the early 1980s Nick Cave was a fixture at the legendary Risiko bar in Schöneberg, recruiting bartender and Neubauten member Blixa Bargeld to the Bad Seeds. Martin Gore moved in with his Berlin girlfriend around the same time and Depeche Mode added a Neubauten-influenced industrial flavour to their pristine synthpop.

In the late 1980s, the electronic avant-garde came upon techno – a form of music so primeval that it battered its way into the mainstream with a social and commercial strength previously unimaginable in experimental circles. The club culture that sprang up after Reunification evolved an infrastructure missing during the Cold War: new studios; graphic artists; promoters; management and video production companies. The way the experimental edge of Berlin music energised the mainstream had far-reaching implications – even U2 managed to reinvent themselves in Berlin with their *Achtung, Baby* album in the early 1990s.

While DJs such as Westbam and Paul van Dyk continue to enjoy large-scale success, a new experimentalism has asserted itself in techno's wake. The Kitty-yo label's eclectic stable, for example, offers original sounds reflecting the juxtaposition of demolition and construction at Berlin's heart. Laub mix breakbeats, reverbed guitar strumming, pastoral noise and restrained female vocals. Surrogat harness digital precision to the heft of layered guitars. And 'Original Prankster' Gonzalez

delivers absurdist raps over impressionist piano samples or industrial axe-grinding. Alec Empire, with band Atari Teenage Riot and his Digital Hardcore imprint, produces high-tech, high-adrenalin punk with topical and didactic lyrics.

Others largely ignore the jurassic beats of the 1990s. Flittchen ('tart') is a label run by former Lassie Singer Christiane Rösinger devoted to the feminine principle in rock. Flittchen signing Vermooste Vløten, delivering exquisite guitar/synth miniatures with Nicoesque vocal inflections, looks poised for international success. Second-generation Turkish immigrants harness hip-hop beats for their own agenda, rapping over samples of Turkish folk and pop music. Notable acts in this genre are Islamic Force and Aziza A, a Turkish Queen Latifah humorously dissing Muslim machismo.

Other acts worth catching: Howard Katz's mellifluous motormouth is accompanied by industrial wasteland electronic soundscapes or Carl Stalling samples; To Rococo Rot evoke Krautrock, cool jazz and minimalism; Stereo Total update the French chanson tradition with an array of second-hand machines and instruments; and Komëit offer dreamy lo-fi guitar and glockenspiel atmospherics.

For a comprehensive Berlin discography, *see* chapter **Further Media.**

Zitty and *tip* have comprehensive gig listings. Radio Eins (95.8FM) and Radio Fritz (102.6FM) are also good sources of news about upcoming events.

Rock venues

Arena/Arena Glashaus

Eichenstraße 4, Treptow, 12435 (533 7333). Bus 265, N65. **Open** according to event.
Former bus garage now hosting big concerts and other events needing space but not too worried about refinement. Prodigy, Chemical Brothers and Pet Shop Boys have all played here. No seating. The Arena Glashaus next door by the river hosts a variety of club events, including an American Breakfast served to house grooves on the first Sunday of the month. *Website: www.arena-berlin.de*

Bastard@Prater

Kastanienallee 7-9, Prenzlauer Berg, 10435 (0177 641 1424). U2 Eberswalder Straße/bus N52. **Open** varies. **Map G2**
Concert and club space with living-room charm – if your living-room is four metres high and covered with pictures torn from magazines. Local avant-rock acts perform several times a week in addition to club nights and multimedia happenings. Comfy sofas.

ColumbiaFritz

Columbiadamm 9-11, Tempelhof, 10965 (6981 2828). U6 Platz der Luftbrücke. **Open** according to event. **Map F6**
Former US Forces cinema now hosting alternative rock acts ranging from Ani DiFranco to Ocean Colour Scene. Namesake youth radio station Fritz regularly hosts drum 'n' bass, hip-hop and ragga events.

Local band Laub woo **Maria am Ostbahnhof.**

*Iggy plays the stooge at **ColumbiaFritz.***

Columbiahalle

Columbiadamm 13-21, Tempelhof, 10965 (698 0980). U6 Platz der Luftbrücke. **Open** according to event. **Map F6**

After Arena, the next biggest indoor concert venue for mainstream rock and pop. Blondie, Skunk Anansie, Nine Inch Nails and Iggy Pop have all played here recently. Next door to ColumbiaFritz.

Insel

Alt-Treptow 6, Treptow, 12435 (5360 8020). S6, S8, S9, S10 Plänterwald. **Open** according to event.

A three-storey tollhouse on a tiny, wooded island in the Spree converted to a multi-purpose space for concerts by international bands, popular Berlin acts and a variety of club nights. Insel also is the unofficial headquarters of the east Berlin hip-hop scene, hosting regular jams with DJ and MC battles.

Website: www.blinx.de/insel

Knaack Club

Greifswalder Straße 224, Prenzlauer Berg, 10405 (442 7061). Tram 2, 3, 4/bus N54. **Open** from 8pm Wed; from 9pm Fri-Sat. **Map H2**

An adventurous booking policy covers the full spectrum of alternative rock. Both dance floors and performance spaces lurk within this shabby multi-level complex, meaning sometimes as many as three different events on any given night – a concert ticket also gets you into the club events, but not vice versa.

Website: www.knaack-berlin.de

Maria am Ostbahnhof

Straße der Pariser Kommune 8-10, Friedrichshain, 10243 (2900 6198). S3, S5, S7, S9 Ostbahnhof. **Open** according to event. **Map H4**

A former main post-office building at the beginning of the Friedrichshain's new clubbing mile, Maria hosts local and international post-rock acts and musicians with multimedial aspirations – performances are often accompanied by video projections. If you can't fit into the cramped performance space, the sound carries well into the generous lounge.

SO 36

Oranienstraße 190, Kreuzberg, 10999 (6140 1306/6140 1307). U1, U12 Görlitzer Bahnhof/bus N29. **Open** according to event. **Map G5**

Epicentre of the early 1980s West Berlin scene, the 'Epicenter' hip-hop and crossover club night on Thursdays is just one facet of this eclectic venue. Expect gay and lesbian parties, Turkish hip-hop, oriental pop, house, dancehall and concerts ranging from riot girls L7 to Jimmy Somerville. No seating.

Velodrom

Paul-Heyse-Straße 29, Prenzlauer Berg, 10407 (4430 4430). S4, S8, S10 Landsberger Allee. **Open** according to event.

Spacious sports facility also hosts mainstream rock shows. *See chapter* **Sport & Fitness**.

Volksbühne/Roter Salon

Linienstraße 227, Mitte, 10178 (2406 5661). U2 Rosa-Luxemburg-Platz. **Open** box office noon-6pm daily. **Map F2**

One of Berlin's most popular and controversial theatres, the Volksbühne also turns over its stage to acts such as Stereolab or Billy Bragg. The smaller Roter Salon, which has its own side entrance, stucco moulding and glass chandeliers, is a venue for club nights and more marginal concerts.

Waldbühne

Waldbühne, Glockenturmstraße/Passenheimer Straße, Charlottenburg, 14053 (810 750). U2 Olympia-Stadion (Ost)/S5 Pichelsberg. **Open** varies.

Probably Berlin's nicest outdoor venue – a 22,000 amphitheatre in the woods near Olympiastadion that in summer hosts the likes of Phil Collins, Paul Simon or Depeche Mode.

Wild at Heart

Wiener Straße 20, Kreuzberg, 10999 (611 7010). U1, U12/bus N29 Görlitzer Bahnhof. **Open** from 8pm daily. **Map G5**

Restored after fire damage to its kitschy glory, a place to catch rousing live acts encompassing rock, punk, trash and various permutations thereof.

Folk & world music

With the return of the WOMEX world music trade fair to town in 1999, after years of exile in Brussels, Marseilles and Stockholm, Berlin hopes to rival Paris as a European worldbeat centre. Midway between eastern and western Europe, Berlin does offer opportunities to hear all sorts of eastern exotica, from Cossack choruses to Gypsy fiddlers. The resurgence of Jewish culture has brought a Klezmer boom, with local acts such as Joel Rubin and Karsten Troyke and international artists such as Hasidic New Wave, The Klezmatics and a deconstructionist/postmodern variant by John Zorn's Masada offering their traditional and modern interpretations of this east European-born and New York-bred Jewish folk music.

Several local bands, including Mutabor and Inchtabokatables, offer edgy takes on folk music, borrowing strings from eastern Europe or, in the case of Mutabor, influences from long stays in North Africa. Trio Bravo's Old World melancholy is also worth catching and *The Buena Vista Social Club*'s success has boosted the local Latin scene.

For info on world music events stop by the **Canzone** record shop (*see chapter* **Shopping**), tune to SFB4 MultiKulti radio on 106.8FM, or scan music listings in *tip* and *Zitty*. Touring acts rarely use set venues.

Hackesches Hof Theater

Rosenthaler Straße 40-41, Mitte, 10178 (283 2587). U8 Weinmeisterstraße/S3, S5, S7, S9 Hackescher Markt. **Open** *box office* from 8.15pm daily. **Map F3**

Intimate seated space offers daily concerts of Klezmer, Yiddish and east European folk music.

Ostalgia ain't what it used to be

Thousands of fans cheer in the sold-out Waldbühne as their idols tear into another goldien oldie. Stones? Bon Jovi? No, it's the Puhdys (*pictured*), the GDR's top-selling band, sliding into the chorus of their anthem, 'Alt wie ein Baum' ('Old as a Tree'). East German musicians from the 1970s and 1980s are enjoying a renaissance, not only with those who grew up with them, but also with curious neophytes in both east and west.

Just a few years ago they couldn't even get arrested. The fall of the Wall led to GDR audiences spurning home-grown heroes for Western artists, while Western audiences had never been interested in the first place. Acts such as the Puhdys had in any case been viewed with suspicion as stooges of a régime which nurtured the uncritical and stifled nonconformity. Measures such as a mandatory 60 per cent songs from socialist countries to be played at concerts or discos and the necessity of submitting a band's repertoire for state approval aimed to enforce an indigenous socialist rock culture and lure youths away from the decadent western media.

But by taking advantage of the loopholes in the system, a vital independent scene grew in the early part of the 1980s. Distributing their music on home-recorded tapes and often playing concerts under the auspices of the oppositional Protestant church, punk bands soon found themselves targeted by the Stasi, with many punks jailed or drafted. But after 1989 even mildly credible acts such as Feeling B or Freygang lost their audiences, despite their critical stance towards total annexation by the Federal Republic and pleas for a kinder, gentler GDR identity. Being 'Born in the GDR' just didn't cut it any more, neither for state-sponsored old farts nor incendiary dissidents.

But half a decade later, as disenchantment and identity crisis set in, east Germans began turning back to their former heroes for solace. Old stalwarts such as Puhdys, Karat, City and Silly enjoyed an unexpected revival.

The former GDR state record label Amiga, now owned by BMG, these days curates the east's musical legacy, along with smaller labels such as Buschfunk or Nasty Vinyl. The Test the West club night at the Kulturbrauerei plays music according to the old 60-40 regulation on Fridays to a sizeable, mixed east-west crowd. The strangest outgrowth of Ostalgia is IFA Wartburg, a Swedish combo singing polka, ska or lounge music paeans to the GDR youth organization FDJ or the 'Anti-Fascist Protection Rampart' in an idiosyncratic German gleaned from a rhyming dictionary. Ironic distance and yearning for the past coexist more or less peacefully within the realm of Ostalgia.

But many of the former GDR acts disdain Ostalgia and want their musical development since 1989 to be recognised. Dirk Zöllner is former frontman of Chicorée and Die Zöllner, a tight funk-rock combo and one of the few bands from the east to enjoy success immediately after 1989; Zöllner doesn't deny his roots but sees himself less an Ostalgia merchant than a representative of a new eastern identity.

Some former GDR indie groups went on to become major national and international players. Feeling B mutated into the industrial band Rammstein; the core of art punks Ornament und Verbrechen has regrouped as post-rock groups To Rococo Rot and Tarwater. The rediscovery of GDR rock not only satisfies (n)ostalgic impulses, but is also key to understanding today's music scene.

Da Capo

Kastanienallee 96, Prenzlauer Berg, 10435 (448 1771). U2 Eberswalder Straße. **Open** 11am-7pm Mon-Fri; 11am-4pm Sat. **No credit cards**. **Map G2**

Good selection of vinyl and comprehensive section devoted to releases on the old GDR Amiga label, including rare 1950s 10-inch records.

Haus der Kulturen der Welt

John-Foster-Dulles Allee 10, Tiergarten, 10557 (3978 7175). S3, S5, S7, S9 Bellevue/bus 100. **Open** *box office & information* 10am-9pm Tue-Sun. **Map E3**

Probably Berlin's most important world music venue. The Café Global, which overlooks the river Spree, occasionally also features live bands.

Pfefferberg

Schönhauser Allee 178, Mitte, 10119 (4438 3115). U2 Senefelderplatz/bus N52. **Open** varies. **Map G2**

Entrance below a colonnaded terrace leads up to a complex including a large beer garden and a roomy performance space for reggae and world music.

Werkstatt der Kulturen

Wissmannstraße 31-42, Neukölln, 12049 (622 2024). U7, U8 Hermannplatz. **Open** varies. **Map G6**

Small, community centre-style venue for more traditional, grassroots world music as well as ethno-jazz performances and club nights.

Jazz

Berlin's jazz scene is large and encompasses everything from pub jam sessions to major international festivals. The city also boasts Germany's only 24-hour jazz radio station. The major event in the jazz calendar, the JazzFest (*see chapter* **By Season**), has lost prestige due to inscrutable booking policies, largely ignoring both innovative forces and big names in favour of mediocrity. However, smaller events still offer cutting-edge music. The Berlin FMP (Free Music Production) label's concerts often feature some of the world's best improvisers, especially if they involve FMP founder Peter Brötzmann, an extremely physical baritone sax player. They're sometimes free when the sessions are being recorded. Another notable local act is jazz poet Anthony Baggette, who works with various jazz-funk formations, usually featuring trombonist Tony Hurdle and bebop-influenced saxman Fuasi Khaliq.

Be warned: Germans take jazz seriously. Even in small places, the appreciation is usually intense and often eerily intellectual. There's no chance of jazz regaining its original status as dance music and woe betide you if you talk while the band are playing.

For current concert information, check Jazz Radio 101.9, listings magazines, and flyers in shops such as **Gelbe Musik** (*see chapter* **Shopping & Services**).

A-Trane

Pestalozzistraße 105, Charlottenburg, 10623 (313 2550). S3, S5, S6, S9 Savignyplatz. **Open** *box office* from 8pm; *performances* from 10pm, daily. **Map C4**

A swanky attempt at a New York-style jazz bar where events are occasionally interesting enough to be heard over the yuppie trimmings. *Website: www.a-trane.de*

Be there or **B-Flat**.

B-Flat

Rosenthaler Straße 13, Mitte, 10119 (280 6349). U8 Rosenthaler Platz/bus N8, N52. **Open** from 9pm daily. **Map F3**

Cavernous bar fills up on weekend nights for mostly local, mostly mainstream jazz acts and DJ sets.

Badenscher Hof

Badensche Straße 29, Wilmersdorf, 10715 (861 0080). U7, U9 Berliner Straße. **Open** 3pm-1am daily. **Map D6**

Small, friendly club offers semi-avant jazz with a mostly African-American cast. Summer garden.

Bebop Bar

Willibald-Alexis-Straße 40, Kreuzberg, 10961 (6950 8526). U7 Gneisenaustraße. **Open** 6pm-4am daily. **Map F5**

Tiny bar with warm, subdued light and wood furnishing. In the back, live mainstream jazz, blues and folk are performed nearly every night of the week.

Jazz Café - Black Bar

Gneisenaustraße 18, Kreuzberg, 10961 (694 6603). U7 Gneisenaustraße. **Open** 5pm-late Mon-Fri; noon-late Sat-Sun. **Map F5**

Marital strife led former Junction Bar co-owner and jazz poet Corbett Santana to do his own thing – right next door. While the booking policies seem similar, the main difference is that the Junction Bar is in the cellar, while this place is overground – in a purely spatial sense, that is.

Junction Bar

Gneisenaustraße 18, Kreuzberg, 10961 (694 6602).
U7 Gneisenaustraße. **Open** 8pm-5am daily. **Map F5**
Jazz in all varieties – swing, Latin, contemporary, jazz
poetry – but not all on the same night. Occasionally
some blues and rock, too. After-show DJs spin soul,
funk and R&B. Mainly good music but the weirdo
quotient is so high some locals refer to it as the
Dysfunction Bar.

Miles the Club

Greifswalder Straße 212-3, Prenzlauer Berg, 10405
(4400 8140). **Tram** 2, 3, 4/bus N54. **Open** 9pm-late
Tue-Sun. **Map H2**
Slick but likeable club showcasing mainstream
jazz, blues, world music and occasionally rock.
Much the same fare as the **Quasimodo** (*see below*)
without the big names, a rare Gil Scott-Heron
appearance notwithstanding.

Parkhaus

Puschkinallee 5, Treptow, 12435 (533 7952). **S4, S6,**
S8, S9, S10 Treptower Park/bus 265. **Open** *box*
office from 7.30pm; *concerts* from 10pm, Wed-Sat.
A club that, with financial support from the Senate,
puts on a jazz programme every Friday and
Saturday night in the cellar of an old villa. The oldest jazz venue in Berlin.

Passionskirche

Marheinekeplatz 1-2, Kreuzberg, 10961 (6940
1241). **U7 Gneisenaustraße. Open** according to
event. **Map F5**
Lovely church with great acoustics hosts quieter
musical events in all genres. Also readings and spoken word performances.

Podewil

Klosterstraße 68-70, Mitte, 10179 (247 496). **U2**
Klosterstraße. **Open** *box office* 2-6pm Tue-Fri. **Map**
G3
Former HQ of the Communist youth organisation,
the FDJ, and music-vetting centre of the GDR. Jazz,
usually of the avant or free variety, is just one option
in its imaginative and eclectic programmes.
Website: www.podewil.de

Quasimodo

Kantstraße 12a, Charlottenburg, 10623 (312 8086).
S3, S5, S7, S9/U2, U9 Zoologischer Garten. **Open** *box*
office from 5pm; *concerts* from 10pm, daily. **Map C4**
Small, cramped and a stopping-off point for many
American bands touring Europe. Quasimodo's
booking policy has been expanded to include 1970s
rock, blues, roots and R&B. Notoriously the smoki-
est venue on Europe's jazz circuit, a fact which performers often bemoan.
Website: www.quasimodo.de

Tränenpalast

Reichstagsufer 17, Mitte, 10117 (2061 0011). **S1,**
S2, S3, S5, S7, S9/U6 Friedrichstraße. **Open** *box*
office from 7pm daily. **Map F3**
This former checkpoint is now a cosy mid-sized
venue not only for jazz notables such as Pharoah
Sanders, but also jam sessions, cabaret, laidback
rock acts and stand-up comedians.

Festivals

Fête de la Musique
Date June 21. **Admission** free.
For summer solstice, the city is transformed into
one grooving, vibing stage. Bands from over 100
countries offer everything from hip hop to folk,
rock, classical, worldbeat, blues and avant jazz. In
past years, acts such as Khaled, Fun Lovin'
Criminals, Stella Chiweshe and the New York Ska-
Jazz Ensemble have performed. *See chapter* **By**
Season.

Heimatklänge
Tempodrom, Straße der Pariser Kommune 8-10,
Friedrichshain, 10243 (6128 4235). **S3, S5, S7, S9**
Ostbahnhof. **Dates** July/Aug. **Admission** nominal.
Map H4
Berlin's biggest world music event. The
Tempodrom tent venue, at press time still located
next to Maria am Ostbahnhof, hosts acts from all
four corners of the globe, each of which gets five
days of shows. The event, and the Tempodrom
itself, are scheduled to move to Anhalter Bahnhof
before 2001. *See chapter* **By Season**.

Jazz Across The Border
Haus der Kulturen der Welt, John-Foster-Dulles
Allee 10, Tiergarten, 10557 (3978 7175). **S3, S5,**
S7, S9 Bellevue/bus 100. **Tickets** from May.
Map E3
Some 15 groups play five weekends of concerts over
June and July at the Haus der Kulturen der Welt.

Jazzfest Berlin
Haus der Kulturen der Welt, John-Foster-Dulles Allee
10, Tiergarten, 10557 (3978 7175). **S3, S5, S7, S9**
Bellevue/bus 100. **Date** Nov. **Admission** varies.
Map E3
A four-day event that aims to present a cross-section of European jazz along with some American
groups. Usually around 25 bands play, although the
days of attracting really big names have long gone.
The Total Music Meeting, a free jazz and improvised
music event, runs alongside the JazzFest, with concerts mostly taking place at **Podewil** (*see above*).
See chapter **By Season**.

Karneval der Kulturen
Information *(622 4232).* **Date** Whit weekend in
June.
A world music version of the Love Parade. Floats
wind through Kreuzberg on Saturday afternoon
while an assortment of open-air and traditional
venues around town offer everything from drumming to drum 'n' bass. *See chapter* **By Season**.
Website: www.karneval-berlin.de

Wie es ihr gefällt
Kulturbrauerei. For details *see chapter* **Women**.
Date November. **Map G2**
A forum for female musicians, 'As She Likes It' has
presented avant-garde doyenne Pauline Oliveros,
video artist Pippilotti Rist's combo Les Reines
Prochaines, violinist Iva Bittova and Finnish riot
grrls Thee Ultra Bimboos, among others.

Sport & Fitness

Berlin bristles with cycle lanes, skating rinks, lakes for sailing or windsurfing – and at last a decent local football team.

Olympiastadion – Nazi aesthetics, plastic seating, biting winds, biggest venue in town.

Berlin shows more muscle and confidence in its role as capital city these days, and its sports teams have been reflecting this. Spectator sports have gained a sheen of respectability and are no longer considered unhip, allowing artists, intellectuals and alternative types to come out of the closet as football fans, boxing enthusiasts or racing aficionados. Independent cinemas and trendy cafés have joined neighbourhood corner bars in broadcasting major sports events – and subscription satellite channel Premiere for regular live Bundesliga games – for knowledgeable punters. Remember Germany has two cable TV channels devoted entirely to sport. And Berliners lap it up.

This local sports mania could be attributed to the increasing significance in the wider arena of Berlin teams such as Hertha BSC, hotshot basketballers Alba or the successful ice hockey pair of the Eisbären and the Capitals. Internationally, the city is also an important stage for top-level sports events such as the Golden Four athletics meeting, the German Open tennis tournament and German national football team matches.

Participating in sport is also as popular as ever. Most sports are organised in national federations or *Verbände*. The local *Verband* offices provide information about clubs, facilities and events, encouraging the masses to be physically active (and pay membership dues). The city of Berlin also offers many facilities, from swimming pools to football fields. Students should check out the variety of university sports, with activities available at every proficiency level – and mostly at low prices. To find out where to buy sportswear and equipment *see chapter* **Shopping & Services**.

Major stadiums

Olympiastadion

Olympischer Platz 3, Charlottenburg, 14053 (300 633). U2 Olympia-Stadion (Ost)/S5 Olympiastadion. Impressive when built for the 1936 Olympics, this 80,000-capacity stadium is falling to bits. Albert Speer was part of the design team who conceived the Marathon Gate, clock tower and bell, all echoing the fascist aesthetic of the Nazi régime. Now, as lynchpin of Germany's bid to host the 2006 World Cup, the stadium will undergo a DM600-million transformation between 2000-2003, temporarily reducing capacity to 55,000. It's still the biggest venue in town and hosts Hertha games, the German Cup Final (*see chapter* **By Season**), athletics and concerts, but for now it's still uncomfortable and bitterly cold in winter. *See also chapter* **Sightseeing**.

Velodrom
Paul-Heyse-Straße 29, Prenzlauer Berg, 10407 (4430 4430). S4, S8, S10 Landsberger Allee.
Opened in early 1997, this is the only project linked to Berlin's abortive bid for the 2000 Olympics to have been completed. As well as cycling, the Velodrom hosts windsurfing exhibitions, handball tournaments and rock concerts.

Spectator sports

American football
Since 1999 Berlin has its own team in the newly created American Football league in Europe: Berlin Thunder, who play in the Friedrich-Jahn-Sportpark in Prenzlauer Berg. Due to the farm-team character of the European league, which acts as a testing-ground for the American NFL, the season is played throughout the summer.

Berlin Thunder
Friedrich-Jahn-Sportpark, Cantianstraße 24, Prenzlauer Berg, 10437 (tickets 3110 2222). U2 Eberswalder Straße. **Admission** DM5-60 **Map G1** *Website: www.berlin-thunder.de*

Athletics

ISTAF Athletics Meeting
Olympischer Platz 3, Charlottenburg, 14053 (243 1990). U2 Olympia-Stadion (Ost)/S5 Olympiastadion. **Date** late Aug. **Admission** DM25-80. **Tickets** *Kant-Kasse (313 4554).*
Instigated a year after the 1936 Olympics, this international one-day tournament is now the final event in athletics' Golden Four, featuring 250 athletes from 50 nations. Track stars hang out at TGI Friday's restaurant in the Radisson Hotel afterwards.

Basketball
Berlin team Alba dominate the German league. Crucial to their success is Alba's uniquely professional management, the club's 10,000-seat arena and most of all their coach, Sarajevo-born Svetislav Pesec, the only trainer ever to lead the German national team to a European championship. Alba's venue, the Max-Schmeling-Halle, is Germany's largest basketball arena. Regular sell-out crowds give the team enough financial support to invest in top foreign players to complement their home-grown talent. The season runs from September to May and tickets for domestic matches are cheaper than those for European ones.

Alba Berlin e.V. Basketball team
Max-Schmeling-Halle, Falkplatz, Prenzlauer Berg, 10437 (5343 8000). U2 Eberswalder Straße. **Admission** DM10-100. **Map G1**

Football
Not long ago, talking football in Berlin with local fans was a loaded topic – it was notoriously the largest city in Europe without a top-ranking club. But now Hertha BSC have been revived and even gave a good account of themselves in the 1999-2000 Champions League. Meanwhile, Chalottenburg's Tennis Borussia are challenging for Bundesliga status. It's a different story in the east, where FC Union and FCB Dynamo have been floundering since the end of communism. The teams in the amateur leagues – Croatia Berlin, Turkyimspor – reflect Berlin's ethnic mix.

Hertha BSC
Olympischer Platz 3, Charlottenburg, 14053 (300 633). U2 Olympia-Stadion (Ost)/S5 Olympiastadion. **Tickets** DM12-75.
After years in the doldrums, Hertha are back. Decimated by a bribery scandal in 1971, Hertha hit the skids until revived by media money in the mid-1990s. Back in the top division and in Europe, Hertha could be a real force for the future. (*see page* 239 **Berlin 0 Bavaria 1 (half-time)**). Their hardcore fans, however, are a different kind of force, numbering many racist skinheads among their ranks. The boys of Block O hardly do their city justice, and watch out for them in the two otherwise decent bars by the S-Bahn station.

Tennis Borussia
Mommsenstadion, Waldschulallee 34-42, Charlottenburg, 14055 (306 9610). S5 Eichkamp. **Tickets** DM10-40.
Perennially striving for the top division, Berliner Tennis- und Ping-Pong Gesellschaft Borussia, to give them their full name, are these days backed by an insurance company but still resemble a motley crew of half-hearted mercenaries with few ties to their few spectators, though the latter include many anti-racists who refuse to support Hertha because of their right-wing following.

1. FC Union
Stadion Alte Försterei, An der Wuhlheide 263, Köpenick, 12459 (6580 0329). S3 Köpenick. **Tickets** DM10-22.
This traditional east Berlin working-class club with an enduring fan base was recently bought by Kinowelt, a large film company. Sadly 'Iron Union' have failed to achieve top billing on the pitch, but can boast the best stadium bar in all Berlin, the Abseitsfalle ('Offside Trap'), by the main entrance.

Berliner Fußball Club Dynamo
Sportforum, Steffenstraße, Hohenschönhausen, 13053 (975 1178). S8, S10 Frankfurter Allee then tram 23/S8, S10 Landsberger Allee then tram 5, 15. **Tickets** DM6-25.

Berlin 0 Bavaria 1 (half-time)

Hertha vs. Chelsea, Champions League.

Mention the word 'Bayern' to the average German football fan and their eyes hit for the ceiling. For 30 years Germany's most successful club have ruled the domestic game. From their powerbase in Bavaria ('Bayern'), the Munich club have not only won more titles than any other club, but also sell a million replica shirts every year.

Few clubs have had the resources to challenge this hegemony – until media giant UFA became interested in Berlin's ailing flagship football club Hertha. The former film studio turned audio-visual arm of the vast Bertelsmann media empire, UFA saw parallels between the sorry state of the game in Germany's capital, and how it looked in Paris in the 1980s. That was before Canal Plus took over Paris Saint-Germain, helped them gain an image and a fan base – followed by domestic and international success.

When UFA decided to back Hertha in 1994, the club were in the Zweite Bundesliga (second division), playing in front of four-figure crowds. In three years the club were back in the top flight, pulling a regular 30,000-plus to the crumbling Olympic Stadium. The brain behind this revival – especially in terms of marketing, media coverage and image branding – was manager Robert Schwan, responsible for launching Bayern in the mid-1960s.

And, having got Hertha to the top, the manager Schwan has left in charge to keep them there is former international Dieter Hoeneß – brother of Uli, his managerial counterpart at Bayern Munich. A World Cup winner with West Germany in 1974, Uli is part of the so-called 'FC Hollywood' set-up – the clique of ex-Bayern stars (including Franz Beckenbauer, Karl-Heinz Rummenigge and Sepp Maier) who practically run the Munich club from top to bottom. And much as the younger Uli was more successful in his playing days than Dieter, so Uli's dream of having Bayern superstores in every major German city is far closer to being realised than anything Dieter might be planning with Hertha's so far exceedingly modest merchandising operation.

Moreover, this club rivalry has roots in politics and the media. Bertelsmann's powerbase is in the SPD stronghold of Rhine-Westphalia, whereas Bayern are backed by Bertelsmann's great rival, Leo Kirch, very much part of conservative Bavaria. For most of the 1990s, Bertelsmann had been looking for a high-profile city to challenge Kirch's Munich – now he has found it in Berlin.

For the time being, Bayern are well ahead of the game. In the last two decades, they've won the Bundesliga title ten times and very few clubs in Europe – Manchester United is the obvious exception, and indeed Bayern's role model – can match the Müncheners' marketing strength.

But for a club which has spent most of these same two decades in the doldrums, Hertha's revival is remarkable, reflected by a creditable performance in the 1999-2000 Champions League. Whether the club can also come to reflect Berlin's status as Germany's leading city remains to be seen.

BFC Dynamo are the infamous Dynamo Berlin in post-communist guise. As the figurehead club of the Stasi, they won the GDR title ten years running, becoming known as the *Schiebemeister*, the 'Cheating Champions'. Now they struggle on as BFC Dynamo, followed by some of the most evil skinheads ever to grace a crumbling football terrace.

Horse Racing

Galopprennbahn-Hoppegarten

Goetheallee 1, Dahlwitz-Hoppegarten, 15366 (033 423 8930). S5 Hoppegarten. **Admission** DM7-20. Races take place between April and October. The betting is run on similar lines to the English Tote.

Trabrennbetrieb-Karlshorst
*Treskowallee 129, Karlshorst, 10318 (500 170). S3
Karlshorst.* **Admission** free.
This and Mariendorf (*below*) host trotting events,
aka harness racing. This entails riders pelting
around in modern-day chariots, a kind of *Ben Hur*
for beginners. Meetings are held year-round on
Saturdays at 2.30pm, and Tuesdays from 6.30pm.

Trabrenn Verein-Mariendorf
*Mariendorfer Damm 222, Mariendorf, 12107 (222
298). U6 Alt-Mariendorf, bus x76, 176, 179
Trabrennbahn.* **Admission** DM5; Wed free.
Race meetings are on Sundays at 1.30pm and on
Wednesdays at 6pm.

Ice hockey

Since German ice hockey clubs set up a completely private national league and broke from the governing Verband in 1994, the sport has become big
business in Germany. In Berlin two perennial powers, the eastern Eisbären (a Dynamo descendent)
and the western Capitals (formerly the Prussian
Devils), have prospered under the new system.
Matches between these arch-rivals often induce
more fierce competition in the rafters than on the
rink. The Eisbären, under their trainer, former ice-
hockey star Lorenz Funk, had the edge for many
years, but the 'Caps' have recently awoken from
their hibernation, scoring several significant wins.
The season runs from September to April.

Berlin Capitals
*Eissporthalle, Jafféstraße, Charlottenburg, 14055
(885 6000). S5 Eichkamp.* **Admission** DM18-70.
Map A4

EHC Eisbären Berlin
*Sportforum, Steffenstraße, Hohenschönhausen,
13053 (971 8400). S8, S10 Frankfurter Allee then
tram 23/S8, S10 Landsberger Allee then tram 5, 15.*
Tickets DM25-65.

Motor sports

The closing of the AVUS for racing in 1999 due to
environmental concerns ended some 75 years of
racing history. The track, which played host to
Formula series races (not Formula 1), motorcycles
and touring cars, is actually a short stretch of
Autobahn heading from the Funkturm towards
Wannsee – and is still used by wannabe racecar
drivers hoping to relive the thrill of bygone days.

But the Berlin region won't be without an international racetrack for long. The Lausitzring
130km south-east of Berlin, opening in summer
2000, will become Europe's largest motor sports
facility. The 120,000-seater has several tracks
including the first European oval with elevated
curves, making it attractive for Nascar and Indie
Car series. Lausitzring is accessible via highway
A13 (exit Klettwitz) or by train to Senftenberg. For
information about races call 03573 3203.

Steffi – to be honoured at **LTTC Rot-Weiss**.

Tennis

The German Tennis Open, held each May, is the
world's fifth largest international women's tennis
championship and draws the world's top female
players. *See chapter* **By Season.**

LTTC Rot-Weiss
*Gottfried-von-Cramm-Weg 47-55, Grunewald, 14193
(8957 5510/ticket information 8957 5520). S7
Grunewald.* **Open** 8am-5pm Mon-Thur; 8am-noon Fri.
The German Open uses this club's clay courts. A
name change in honour of Steffi Graf was being considered by the club's membership body.

Activities

Verbände ('federations') are the national umbrella
organisations that help with co-ordination, facilities, financing and other logistical aspects of sport
of all kind. The Berlin offices can be invaluable
when trying to get involved in a sport here.

Landessportbund Berlin (LSB)
Berlin Regional Sports Federation
*Jesse-Owens-Allee 2, Charlottenburg, 10453 (300
020). U2 Olympia-Stadion (Ost)/S5 Olympiastadion.*
Open 9am-3pm Mon-Thur; 9am-2pm Fri.
The central office for Berlin co-ordinates other sport-
specific offices and provides general information.
The Landesausschuß Frauensport, the Regional
Committee for Women's Sport, shares the same
address. *See also page 245* **Women's Sport**.

Berlin Marathon – *sightseeing by track shoe.*

Athletics

Berlin's New Year Fun Run begins every 1 January at the Soviet Memorial on Straße des 17. Juni near the Brandenburg Gate. Information on 302 5370.

Berliner Leichtathletik-Verband

Berlin Athletics Federation
Glockenturmstraße 1, Charlottenburg, 14053 (305 7250). S5 Pichelsberg. **Open** 9am-5pm Tue; noon-7pm Thur; 10am-2pm Fri.
Contact this office for information about tracks, clubs and events in the city.

Berlin Marathon

Waldschulallee 34, Charlottenburg, 14055 (302 5370). **Date** September. **Map A5**
Upwards of 25,000 people participate in this annual event, making it the world's third largest marathon. The course winds past many historic sights. Taking part costs DM70-120, depending on when you register, and if it has been posted from abroad. There's also the Berlin Half-Marathon on the first Sunday in April. Information is available from the above address. *See also chapter* **By Season**.

Badminton

Of late, badminton has come into its own and is no longer considered a poor relation of tennis. Aside from Berlin's many parks, indoor courts are popular, and many have been freshly renovated.

Turngemeinde in Berlin 1848 e.V.

Columbiadamm 111, Kreuzberg (691 9315). U7 Südstern. **Open** 9am to 11pm daily. **Rental** *per hour* DM10-28. **Map G6**
Inexpensive courts near Tempelhof Airport.

Basketball

Though a relatively recent arrival, basketball has a strong following, with public courts springing up all over town. Contact the Verband for locations and club information. Temporary streetball installations pop up during the summer, notably on Sundays at the Yaam Club (*see chapter* **Nightlife**).

Berliner Basketball-Verband

Berlin Basketball Federation
Postfach 33 0 445, 14174 (893 6480). **Open** 10am-3pm Mon-Thur; 10am-2pm Fri.
Sign up for a club or get information about various streetball competitions or the Supercup.

Billiards

Tables can be found in many corner bars and pool halls. Most places have eight- and nine-ball pool, with a few billiard and snooker tables.

Billardparadies

Immanuelkirchstraße 14, Prenzlauer Berg, 10405 (442 8270). Tram 1. **Open** 24 hours daily. **Map G2**
Utilitarian establishment with 32 pool, three snooker and three billiard tables.

Köh

Sophienstraße 6, Mitte, 10119 (282 8420). U8 Weinmeisterstraße/S3, S5, S7, S9 Hackescher Markt. **Open** 4pm-3am daily. **Map F3**
Small and cosy, with leather couches and a better bar than normal halls.

Bowling

City Bowling Hasenheide

Hasenheide 108-114, Kreuzberg, 10967 (622 2038). U7, U8 Hermannplatz. **Open** 10am-midnight daily. **Prices** *per person per game* DM3-6. **No credit cards.**
Berlin's biggest bowling centre has 36 lanes. This neighbourhood place also has a bar and food.

Bowling Center Sport and Gastronomie

Rathausstraße 5, Mitte, 10178 (242 6657). S3, S5, S7, S9/U2, U5, U8 Alexanderplatz. **Open** 11am-midnight Mon-Fri; 10am-midnight Sat-Sun. **Prices** *per hour* DM24-36. **No credit cards. Map G3**
Not only 18 lanes, but billiards, darts, pinball machines and a restaurant. Near Alexanderplatz in the Rathauspassagen across from the Rotes Rathaus – look out for the big neon sign and head down the steps – this is a survivor from the communist era.

Chess

In summer, chess players of all nationalities and ages square off in Kreuzberg's Hasenheide (**map G6**) at open-air tables behind the animal enclosure.

Berliner Schachverband

Berlin Chess Federation
Blumenweg 17, Mariendorf, 12105 (705 6606). S2 Attilastraße. **Open** 10am-2pm Mon-Tue, Thur-Fri; 2pm-6pm Wed.
Information on joining clubs.

Cafe Belmont

Kurfürstenstraße 107, Schöneberg, 10787 (218 6365). U1, U2, U15 Wittenbergplatz. **Open** 24 hours daily. **Map D4**
The best place to get into the Berlin chess scene. Most of the hours this place is open you'll find a cosmopolitan crowd playing and talking chess.

Cycling

Getting around by bike is easy in flat Berlin, especially on the designated bike lanes that line most major roads. Sport cycling is popular, as is touring in the countryside via the S-Bahn into Brandenburg. Taking your bike on the U-Bahn is also allowed except during rush hour (defined as 6-9am and 2-5pm). *See chapter* **Getting Around**.

Allgemeiner Deutscher Fahrrad-Club

German General Cycling Club
Brunnenstraße 28, Mitte, 10119 (448 4724). U8 Bernauer Straße. **Open** noon-8pm Mon-Fri; 10am-6pm Sat. **Map F2**
The ADFC has an information and meeting point for cyclists and a self-help repair station.

Berliner Radsport-Verband

Priesterweg 3, Schöneberg, 10829 (784 5753). S2 Priesterweg. **Open** 10am-5pm Mon-Fri.
Information on clubs, races, and events. The International 4 Etappen Fahrt (a four-stage, 600-km race) takes place every year at the end of May.

Fitness Studios

Long-term residents may also want to check out aerobics and other fitness opportunities offered by Berlin's local adult education programmes (*Volkshochschulen,* details in the *Gelbe Seiten, Yellow Pages*). Their prices may be more reasonable than these private institutions listed below:

Gold's Gym

Immanuelkirchstraße 3-4, Prenzlauer Berg, 10405 (442 8294). U2 Senefelderplatz. **Open** 7am-11pm Mon, Wed, Fri; 10am-11pm Tue, Thur; 10am-6pm Sat-Sun. **Admission** *monthly minimum* DM89. **No credit cards.** **Map G2**
Moderately priced fitness studio offering two weeks' free use for Gold members.

Jopp Frauen-Fitness-Berlin

Tauentzienstraße 13, Charlottenburg, 10789 (210 111). S3, S5, S7, S9/U2, U9 Zoologischer Garten/U9, U15 Kurfürstendamm. **Open** 7am-11pm Mon-Fri; 10am-8pm Sat-Sun. **Admission** *monthly* DM75-139. **No credit cards.** **Map D4**
Women-only fitness centre with five locations in the city, endorsed by swimming champ Franziska van Almsick. The Mitte branch has the same opening hours and price structure.
Branch: Karl-Liebknecht-Straße 13, Mitte, 10178 (2434 9355).

Jump!

Togostraße 76, Wedding, 13351 (451 4712). U6 Seestraße. **Open** 10am-10pm Mon-Fri; 11am-6pm Sat; 11am-5pm Sun. **Admission** *day pass* DM25; *monthly pass* DM109. **No credit cards.** **Map D1**
Smallish sport studio run by a friendly, helpful team. Mixed but popular with gays. Universal weights and regular aerobic step classes.

Oasis

Stresemannstraße 74, Kreuzberg, 10963 (262 6661). S1, S2 Anhalter Bahnhof. **Open** 9am-11pm Mon-Fri; 10am-10pm Sat; 10am-6pm Sun. **Admission** *monthly fee* DM79-110. **No credit cards.** **Map F4**
Well-equipped, for both men and women, and with a great swimming pool.

Football

Football is Berlin's most popular sport. Pick-up games can be found in most parks at the weekend.

Berliner Fußball-Verband

Berlin Football Federation
Humboldtstraße 8a, Grunewald, 14193 (896 9940). S3, S5, S7, S9 Westkreuz. **Open** 8am-4.30pm Mon-Thur; 8am-7pm Fri. **Map A5**
Office for information about football in Berlin.

Golf

Believe it or not, golf is extremely popular as an alternative sport in Berlin, especially among young people. Although most courses are outside the city limits in Brandenburg and require membership, you can still practise your swing and enjoy some putting at the following facilities:

Öffentliches Golf-Zentrum Berlin-Mitte

Chausseestraße 94, Mitte, 10115 (285 7001). U6 Zinnowitzer Straße. **Open** 8am-dusk daily. **Admission** free. **Club rental** DM1. **Map E2**
A 100,000-sq m facility with 60-tee driving range, chip and pitch, and a putting green, partly roofed, open all year and free to the public. A relaxed place where polo shirts are not required. There are also 12 beach volleyball courts and BMX courses.

Öffentlichen Golf-Übungsanlage Berlin-Adlershof

Rudower Chaussee 4, Adlershof, 12489 (6701 2421). S4, S6, S8, S9 Adlershof. **Open** 10am-dusk daily. **Admission** DM15-20; DM10 concs. **Club rental** DM1.
'Public golf for all' and excellent facilities for the newcomer with four par-3 holes and a driving range.

Golfclub Schloß Wilkendorf e.V.

Am Weiher 1, OT Wilkendorf, Gielsdorf, 15345 (03341 330 960). S5 Strausberg Nord. **Open** 9am-5pm daily. **Admission** *Mon-Fri* DM50; *Sat-Sun* DM80. **Club rental** DM25; *half-set* DM15.
A short cab ride or fair walk away from the S5-line terminus, this is the only 18-hole course in the area open to non-members (at weekends only with a *Platzreife*, 'German Golf Certificate'). Also a six-hole course open to all daily for DM20-30.

Ice sports

Below are the best ice-skating rinks in the city. Also many of Berlin's lakes and canals freeze over in the winter – the federation has nothing to do with these, so just look for other skaters and hope their judgement is good. The Christmas market on Alexanderplatz has a small outdoor rink and there's another rink at scenic Gendarmenmarkt.

Berliner Eissport-Verband

Berlin Ice Sport Federation
Fritz-Wildung-Straße 9, Wilmersdorf, 14199 (823 4020). S4 Hohenzollerndamm. **Open** 8am-4pm Mon-Fri; 8am-2pm Fri. **Map B6**
Offers information on halls, clubs, and events.

Eisstadion Berlin Wilmersdorf

Fritz-Wildung-Straße 9, Wilmersdorf, 14199 (824 1012). S4 Hohenzollerndamm. **Open** *Oct-mid-Mar* 9am-6.30pm, 7.30-10pm, Mon, Wed, Fri; 9am-5.30pm, 7.30-10pm, Tue, Thur; 9am-10pm Sat; 10am-6pm Sun. **Admission** *two hours* DM6; DM3 concs. **Map B6**
With an outer ring for speed skating and an inner field for figure skaters and those with weak ankles who need to clutch the wall.

Get your skates on at **Eisstadion Berlin Wilmersdorf.**

Eisstadion Wedding

*Müllerstraße 185, Wedding, 13353 (4575 5555). U6
Wedding.* **Open** 9am-noon, 3-5.30pm, 7.30-9.30pm
Mon-Sat; 9am-noon, 2-5pm Sun; *adults only* noon-2pm
Mon-Sat. **Admission** 6DM; 3DM concs. **Map E1**
Cheapest public rink in town – admission gets you
up to three hours of skating pleasure.

Kayak & canoe

Much of Berlin is reclaimed land, to which the
many canals and embanked waterways in the city
can attest. There is also plenty of water in the surrounding countryside, notably the Spreewald to
the south (*see chapter* **Day Trips**), and to the
north and east. However you must be prepared to
paddle, as the flat Brandenburg plain means no
white water or strong currents.

Landes-Kanu-Verband Berlin

Berlin Regional Canoe Federation
*Eisenhammerweg 22a, Reinickendorf, 13507 (439
8070). U6 Alt-Tegel.* **Open** 8am-noon Tue-Wed, Fri;
1-7pm Thur.

Kanu Connection

*Köpenicker Straße 9, Kreuzberg, 10997 (612 2686).
U1 Schlesisches Tor.* **Open** *Mar-Nov* 10am-6pm
Mon-Fri. **Rental** *daily per boat* DM40-55; *weekends*
DM90-120. **Map H4**
Paddle through Kreuzberg's canals or take off into
the waterways winding through the forests east of
Berlin. Canoe and kayak rentals from four different
landings. Guides available.

Der Bootsladen

*Brandensteinweg 8, Spandau, 13595 (362 5685).
Bus 149.* **Open** *Mar-Oct* noon-7pm Tue-Fri; 9am-
7pm Sat-Sun. **Rental** *per hour* DM10-12.
Good starting point for tours of the western canal
system. Rental price depends on boat size, but you
can get good deals on more long-term rentals.

Sailing

The Wannsee provides an extensive area for sailing and water connections to Babelsberg and
Potsdam or north to Tegel and Spandau. To the
east, Müggelsee is also a swelling of the Spree.
North of Berlin in Brandenburg and Mecklenburg
are many lakes with further boating possibilities.

Berliner Segler-Verband

Berlin Sailing Federation
*Bismarckallee 2, Charlottenburg, 14193 (893
8420/fax 8938 4219). Bus 119.* **Open** 10am-5pm
Mon-Fri. **Map A5**
Information on certification, regulation and events.
If you want to sail or surf on the lakes, you'll need
an *Amtlicher Sportbootführerschein-Binnen* – sailing certificate, for which the federation sets an exam.
With enough practical experience, register for the
six-day theoretical course, which teaches the rules
and regulations of Berlin's waterways.

Am Großen Fenster

*Großes Fenster 1, Zehlendorf, 14129 (803 7137). S1,
S7 Nikolassee.* **Open** *Apr-Oct* 10am-7.30pm daily.
Boats for hire throughout the summer.

Sauna

Many of Berlin's public baths have saunas and women can use the Hamman Turkish Bath at the **Schoko-Fabrik** (*see chapter* **Women**).

Thermen

Europa-Center, Nurnberger Straße 7, Charlottenburg, 10777 (261 6031). U1, U2, U15 Wittenbergplatz. **Open** 10am-midnight Mon-Sat; 10am-9pm Sun. **Admission** *three hours* DM30; *one day* DM35. **Map D4**

Big, central, mixed facility offering Finnish saunas, steam baths, hot and cool pools, and a garden open until October. There is a pool where you can swim outside on to the roof, even in the depths of winter. Thermen also boasts a café, pool-side loungers where you can doze or read, table tennis, billiards and massage facilities.

Squash

An hour on a squash court will cost you about DM25. You can hire a racquet from the bigger sports centres.

Tennis and Squash City

Brandenburgische Straße 53, Wilmersdorf, 10707 (873 9097). U7 Konstanzer Straße. **Open** 7am-midnight daily. **Admission** *tennis* DM33-63; *squash* DM11-33; *badminton* DM11-30. **Map C5**

Apart from seven tennis courts, 11 squash courts and four badminton courts, this centre also offers a sauna, a solarium and a restaurant. Training available for all games, aerobics and classical dance.

Swimming (indoor)

Almost every district has at least one indoor pool. check the phone book for your nearest. Pools will be either *normale Bäder* (the water temperature at or below 26°c) or *Warmbäder* (above 27°c). Fewer crowds early in the morning or later in the evening.

Berliner Schwimm-Verband

Berlin Swimming Federation
Landsberger Allee 203, Hellersdorf, 13055 (971 0150). S4, S8, S10 Landsberger Allee. **Open** 8am-4.30pm Mon, Wed, Fri; 8am-7pm Tue; 8am-3pm Fri.

SEZ (Sport- und Erholungszentrum)

Landsberger Allee 77, Friedrichshain, 10249 (421 820). S4, S8, S10 Landsberger Allee. **Open** 11am-10pm Mon; 9am-10pm Tue-Sun. **Admission** DM10; DM5 concs.

Huge sports centre with many different facilities apart from swimming, including saunas, a solarium, a polarium, and even bowling.

Stadtbad Charlottenburg

Krumme Straße 6a-8, Charlottenburg, 10585 (3438 3860). U2 Deutsche Oper. **Open** 6-10am, 3-11pm, Tue; 10am-7.30pm Wed; 6am-3pm Thur; 6am-2pm, 4-6pm, Fri; 6am-11pm Sat; 4-11pm Sun. *women only* 6am-3pm, 5-8pm, Mon; *nudists* 6-11pm Tue; *nudists only* 7.30-11pm Wed; 6-11pm Thur; 6-11pm Fri. **Admission** DM6; DM4 concs. **Map B3**

The Stadtbad Charlottenburg is especially popular with nudists, so be aware of the times listed to either to whip your kit off or scuttle for cover.

Stadtbad Kreuzberg

Wiener Straße 59, Kreuzberg, 10999 (612 7057). U1 Görlitzer Bahnhof. **Open** 6am-11pm Mon-Sat; *women only* 2-5pm Mon. **Admission** DM6; DM4 concs. **Map H5**

Also known as the Spreewaldbad. Nice, but very crowded swimming facility with a wave pool, a lap pool and a whirlpool with slide. Good for kids.

Swimming (open-air)

These open-air pools and bathing beaches listed generally have been open from mid-May to September. However at press time the underfunded local swimming federation had scheduled a general meeting to consider which of its pools might have to be closed down. Because of the uncertainty of the situation at the start of the summer season 2000, it would be wise to phone your local pool before setting out. As such, it has not been possible to provide times and prices for each venue. There are also plenty of other places for swimming on the western lakes; Schlachtensee and Krumme Lanke are clean, set in attractive woodland and easily accessible by U- or S-Bahn.

Freibad Humboldthain

Wiesenstraße 1, Wedding, 13357 (464 4986). S1, S2 Humboldthain. **Map F1**
Complete with water slides.

Olympia Schwimmstadion

Olympischer Platz 3, Charlottenburg, 14053 (300 633). U2 Olympia-Stadion (Ost)/S5 Olympiastadion.
Regarded by many as the best pool in Berlin.

Seebad Friedrichshagen

Müggelseedamm 216, Friedrichshagen, 12587 (645 5756). S3 Friedrichshagen.
Pleasant bathing beach on the northern shore of the Müggelsee.

Sommerbad Kreuzberg

Gitschiner Straße 18-31, Kreuzberg, 10969 (616 1080). U1 Prinzenstraße. **Map F5**
Known as Prinzenbad, a popular outdoor complex for swimming and sunbathing. Nudist area.

Strandbad Müggelsee

Fürstenwalder Damm 838, Rahnsdorf, 12589 (648 7777). S3 Rahnsdorf.
North shore bathing beach, complete with nudist colony, on the bank of east Berlin's biggest lake.

Strandbad Wannsee

Wannseebadweg, Nikolassee, 14129 (803 5612). S1, S7 Nikolassee.
Europe's largest inland beach, with sand, sun beds, water slides, snack stalls and lots of Germans who like to get there early – just like being in Corfu, really. Nudist section.

Table tennis

If you've got bats and balls, stone tables with metal nets can be found in most public parks.

Berliner Tisch-Tennis Verband

Berlin Table-Tennis Federation
Bismarckallee 2, Charlottenburg, 14193 (892 9176).
S3, S5, S7, S9 Westkreuz. **Open** 10am-noon Wed, Fri; 3-6pm Thur. **Map A5**
Information about table-tennis clubs and events.

Lux Tischtennis Zentrum

Lobeckstraße 36, Kreuzberg, 10969 (614 9015). U8 Moritzplatz. **Open** 10am-6pm Mon-Fri; 9.30am-1.30pm Sat. **Map G4**
Satisfy your table-tennis needs at this centre, which can provide advice on which ping-pong club to join.

Tennis

Tennis is an expensive habit in Berlin. The cheapest time to hire a court is in the mornings, and even then it can cost DM30-60 for an hour for an indoor court of reasonable quality. Many badminton and squash establishments double up as tennis ones – *see also page 244* **Tennis and Squash City.**

Tennis-Verband Berlin-Brandenburg

Berlin-Brandenburg Tennis Federation
Auerbacher Straße 19, Charlottenburg, 14193 (825 5311). S7 Grunewald. **Open** 10am-2pm Mon-Fri.
Information about joining leagues and clubs.

tsf

Richard-Tauber-Damm 36, Marienfelde, 12277 (742 1091). U6 Alt-Mariendorf. **Open** 7am-11pm daily.
The Marienfelde facility has nine indoor courts, the Spandau branch has five. Winter prices are highest, ranging from DM32-50 per hour, depending on day and time. There is no membership fee. **Branch:** Galenstraße 33-45, Spandau, 13597 (333 4083).

TCW tennis center Weissensee

Roelckestraße 106, Weisensee, 13088 (927 4594). S4, S8, S10 Greifswalder Straße. **Open** 7am-midnight daily. **Map H1**
New hall with eight tennis courts and 12 badminton courts, all indoors. The surface is meant to approximate clay. Prices in winter are DM28-47 per hour, and include use of the sauna.

Windsurfing

With almost eight per cent of the city's area composed of lakes, ponds and inlets, not to mention the brisk breezes blowing over them, Berlin is a popular city for windsurfers.

Windchiefs

Horstweg 33-35, Charlottenburg, 14059 (3260 1777). U2 Sophie-Charlotte-Platz. **Open** 10am-6.30pm Mon-Wed; 10am-8pm Thur-Fri; 10am-4pm Sat. **Map B4**
A shop offering sales, service and rentals for windsurfing, in-line skating and snowboarding.

Women's sports

See also chapter **Women.**

Landesausschuß Frauensport

Regional Committee for Women's Sport
Jesse-Owens-Allee 2, Charlottenburg, 14053 (300 020). U2 Olympia-Stadion (Ost)/S5 Olympiastadion. **Open** 9am-3pm Mon-Thur; 9am-2pm Fri.
Promotes and provides info about women's sports.

In-line skating, BMX & skateboarding

Berlin's streets seem to have become one long in-line skating course. City landmarks such as Breitscheidplatz around Gedächniskirche and the terrace outside the Neue National Galerie serve as practice ramps for BMX cyclists and skateboarders. The following addresses offer facilities for all three activities unless otherwise indicated:

Böcklerpark

Prinzenstraße, Kreuzberg, 10969. U1 Prinzenstraße. **Map G5**
Jump ramps and course for cyclists and half-pipe for in-line skating and skateboarding.

Blade-Nite

Straße des 17. Juni and Unter den Linden. **Date** *May-Sept* 9-10.30pm every other Wed.
Two of Berlin's main thoroughfares are closed to traffic every fortnight while in-line skaters whizz from Ernst-Reuter-Platz past Siegessäule and through the Brandenburg Gate. This is officially listed as a demonstration by skaters rather optimistically seeking equal rights in street traffic.

Erlebniswerkstatt des Projektes Erlebnisräume

Sterndamm 82, Schöneweide, 12487 (631 0911). S4, S6, S8, S9, S10 Schöneweide.
Berlin's only trial track with jump ramps. The venue is also the right place to make contact with other cyclists as well as for latest info about hot spots.

Liberty Park

Senftenberger Straße/corner of Kastanienallee, Hellersdorf, 12629. U5 Hellersdorf.
Largest BMX and skater complex course in Berlin, with half-pipe and mini-ramps.

Search and Destroy

Oranienstraße 198, Kreuzberg, 10999 (6128 9064). U1, U8 Kottbusser Tor/U1 Görlitzer Bahnhof. **Open** noon-7pm Mon-Wed; noon-8pm Thur-Fri; 11am-4pm Sat. **Map G4**
Small skateboard scene shop with helpful staff.

Volkspark Wilmersdorf

Hans-Rosenthal-Platz (near playground), Wilmersdorf, 10820. U4 Rathaus Schöneberg/S4, U4, Innsbrucker Platz.
Three asphalt pools for BMX, in-line skating and skateboarding.

Theatre

Full of direction but lacking in directors, Berlin theatre is still haunted by its golden past.

Berlin is still a major international centre of the dramatic arts, even if the current theatre scene is nothing like as scintillating as during Berlin's two golden ages of theatre. During the Weimar period Berlin led the way in expressionism and made tremendous contributions to other theatrical styles, before Bertolt Brecht's **Berliner Ensemble** became arguably the greatest theatre company of the immediate post-war era.

From the late 1940s until 1989, theatre scene is nies, like other arts institutions on both sides of the Wall, were massively subsidised by their respective governments. But since Reunification, the political need to keep so many theatres afloat has vanished, leading to today's situation where many theatres have been closed down (most recently the Metropol Theater, axed in 1999) and companies wound up (the Berliner Ensemble, RIP 1999).

Great performances can still be seen at theatres such as the **Schaubühne**, **Maxim-Gorki-Theater**, **Deutsches Theater**, **Volksbühne** and, of course, the Berliner Ensemble – albeit increasingly rarely. It's difficult to explain exactly why, except perhaps to say that – with the possible exception of the Volksbühne's controversial Frank Castorf – in the late 1990s there was no single great director working in Berlin full-time. There *was* great direction, but more often than not it was for a one-off production – the days of the great intendant/director seemed to have gone in Berlin. But all that may be about to change.

THEATRE AGAINST DREAMS

Starting in 2000, all eyes are on one man: Claus Peymann. Peymann took over as intendant of the Berliner Ensemble in 1999. The company had proved virtually ungovernable since the death of Heiner Müller in 1996, seeming to be seriously adrift despite the occasional bravura production by visiting directors, such as Klaus Emmerich's *Die Massnahme* or Robert Wilson's *Dantons Tod*. For years German-born Peymann had been a colossus in the Austrian theatre scene, where he developed a reputation as an eternal rebel.

No shrinking violet, Peymann's brand of leftist politics will shake things up in a theatrical landscape largely either depoliticised or obsessed with dealing with the Nazi past. He has lambasted the new left as led by a 'generation of political chatshow hosts' and added: 'Everything you see on tele-

Schaubühne – *not yet demised. Page 247.*

vision is opportunism and fawning. All believability is gone. So much the greater, then, is the responsibility of Art...Theatre should be vigilant, a kind of sentry, so that the dreams of the powerful don't reach to the skies'. If anybody can revive the Berliner Ensemble, and in so doing up the stakes for other houses, then it's Peymann.

FRINGE FIGHTS ON

Fringe theatre, known in German as *Off-Theater*, has been fighting a tough battle for years. These groups rarely received more than token financial support from the Senat in the 1990s and now most of this has dried up, resulting in a much-reduced, if still valiant, fringe scene.

English-language theatre is of a high standard in Berlin. Several local groups comprised of excellent mother-tongued thespians as well as top-notch visiting ones from Anglophone countries (particularly Ireland and Britain) perform at several theatres in town – especially at the exclusively Anglophone **Friends of Italian Opera**.

Unless otherwise indicated, box offices open one hour before a performance and sell tickets for that performance only. Prices vary from the DM15-30 for Off-Theater productions up to DM75 or more for the best seats at a commercial show. An international student ID card should get you a discount at a smaller theatre on the night, but don't expect the same generosity from larger commercial or civic theatres. Audioloops (in German only) and wheelchair access (ring ahead to book for this) are indicated where available. Where no credit cards are listed, assume they are not accepted.

Ticket agencies

See chapter **Music: Classical & Opera**.

Civic theatres

Berliner Ensemble

Bertolt-Brecht-Platz 1, Mitte, 10117 (box office 282 3160/2840 8155). S1, S2, S3, S5, S7, S9/U6 Friedrichstraße. **Open** 8am-6pm Mon-Sat; 11am-6pm Sun. **Credit** AmEx, MC, V. **Map F3**
The House that Brecht built (and where *Threepenny Opera* was first seen in 1928). Technically speaking, the Berliner Ensemble as such doesn't exist anymore – the actual ensemble was disbanded in 1999 – and the theatre's proper name is Theater am Schiffbauerdamm. Following technical refurbishment it reopened in January 2000 under new intendant, Claus Peymann (*see introduction*). If you want to see the classic productions from Brecht's heyday, you've come way too late.
Wheelchair access and audioloop.
Website: www.berliner-ensemble.de/

Deutsches Theater/Kammerspiele des Deutschen Theaters

Schumannstaße 13a, Mitte, 10117 (box office 2844 1225; info 2844 1222). S1, S2, S3, S5, S7, S9/U6 Friedrichstraße. **Open** 11am-6.30pm Mon-Sat; 3-6.30pm Sun. **Map E3**
Two lovely adjacent houses on an equally attractive little courtyard in the quiet backstreets of Mitte provide the venue for hearty bourgeois theatrical fare of German and international classics. This is one of the most reliable companies in Berlin when it comes to good theatre. At press time they had in rep a creditable *Threepenny Opera* featuring Brecht's granddaughter, Johanna Schall.
Wheelchair access.
Website: www.deutsches-theater.berlin.net/

Hebbel-Theater

Stresemannstraße 29, Kreuzberg, 10963 (2590 0427). U1, U6 Hallesches Tor. **Open** 4-7pm daily. **Map F5**
Berlin's thinking person's theatre. Performances by the very best local and international rep companies and a varied, challenging programme make the Hebbel a haven of thought-provoking theatrical

quality. Chamber opera and occasional performances in English (and other tongues) further enhance this theatre's popularity amongst the Berlin intelligentsia, to say nothing of their annual feast of dance, Tanz im August. *See chapter* **Dance**.
Limited wheelchair access.
Website: www.hebbel-theater.de/

Maxim-Gorki-Theater and Studiobühne

Am Festungsgraben 2, Mitte, 10117 (box office 2022 1115; info 2022 1129). S1, S2, S3, S5, S7, S9/U6 Friedrichstraße. **Open** 1-6.30pm Mon-Sat. **Map F3**
Performs a catholic mix of classical and modern-classical works and contemporary drama. The company takes up temporary residence at the Schiller-Theater (Bismarckstraße 110, Charlottenburg, 10623) until summer 2000 while their home is renovated so check press listings during this period. Intendant Bernd Wilms is to be replaced in 2001 by Volker Hesse, ex-Neumarkt-Theater, Zürich. A worthy company.
Audioloop.

Renaissance Theater

Knesebeckstraße 100, Charlottenburg, 10623 (312 4202). U2 Ernst-Reuter-Platz. **Open** 10.30am-7pm Mon-Sat; 2-7pm Sun. **Credit** AmEx, DC, V. **Map C4**
A reputable house which invariable plays a rôle in Berlin's annual Festwochen (*see chapter* **By Season**). At this theatre some of Germany's most respected stage actors tread the boards in a repertoire that emphasises modern drama.

Schaubühne am Lehniner Platz

Kurfürstendamm 153, Charlottenburg, 10709 (890 023). S3, S5, S7, S9 Charlottenburg/ U7 Adenauerplatz. **Open** 11am-6.30pm Mon-Sat; 3-6.30pm Sun. **Credit** AmEx, MC, V. **Map B5**
Rumours of this theatre's demise have so far proven incorrect. Like the Renaissance (*above*), this is where some of Germany's greatest thespians perform. Mainly classical repertoire, but modern works occasionally taken out for an airing. An estimable house.
Limited wheelchair access & audioloop.
Website: www.schaubuehne.de/

Schloßpark Theater

Schloßstraße 48, Schöneberg, 12165 (793 5001/793 5002). S1/U9 Rathaus Steglitz. **Open** 1-7pm Mon-Sat; 5-7pm Sun. **Credit** AmEx, DC, MC, V.
A fairly standard but well-performed mix of classics with major modern dramas and comedies attracts a diverse audience.
Wheelchair access & audioloop.
Website: www.schlosspark.de

Volksbühne

Rosa-Luxemburg-Platz, Mitte, 10178 (2406 5661). U2 Rosa-Luxemburg-Platz. **Open** noon-6pm daily. **Map G2**
'The People's Stage' – and if your idea of theatre is not wildly avant-garde and extravagantly experimental, you'll probably feel that the people can bloody well keep it. Frank Castorf resides over this theatre in which provocation and re-interpretation rule the day. Hugely popular.
Limited wheelchair access.

Commercial theatres

Theater am Kurfürstendamm

Kurfürstendamm 206-9, Charlottenburg, 10719
(4799 7440). U15 Uhlandstraße. **Open** 10am-8pm
Mon-Sat; 3-8pm Sun. **Credit** AmEx, MC, V. **Map C4**
Here coachloads of provincial German tourists
decamp to see their favourite television stars cavort-
ing in light farce and Boulevard comedy.
Wheelchair access & audioloop.
Website: www.inter-tickets.com

Theater der Freien Volksbühne

Schaperstraße 24, Wilmersdorf, 10719 (8842
08510). U1, U9 Spichernstraße. **Open** 11am-7pm
Mon-Sat; 2-7pm Sun. **Credit** AmEx, MC, V. **Map C5**
Now under the aegis of the Theater des Westens,
what once used to be a bastion of high art (straight
drama, experimental theatre) seems to have gone the
way of too, too many Berlin theatres: musicals.
Website: www-theater-des-westens.de/

Theater des Westens

Kantstraße 12, Tiergarten, 10623 (8842 08510).
S3, S5, S7, S9/U2, U9 Zoologischer Garten. **Open**
11am-7pm Mon-Sat; 11am-2pm Sun. **Credit** AmEx,
MC, V. **Map C4**
Formerly the Städtische Oper Berlin, now it's a
house for musicals – and probably the best in Berlin.
In 1999 Elmar Ottenthal became the new intendant
and promises to inject new life into the TdW.
Wheelchair access.
Website: www.theater-des-westens.de/

Off-Theater

Berlin once boasted a hundred or so fringe companies, but only about two dozen exist today. Many
simply have been closed down; while others spring
up on a wing and a prayer, only to shut a few
months later. They're often rough-and-ready
spaces, but can provide real theatrical revelations.
The quality varies, but fringe prices are much
lower, audiences less stuffy and no matter what
you watch, chances are it will be at worst interesting and at best stunning.
  Most theatres will have an answering machine
with details of what's on. Box offices usually open
only up to an hour before each evening's performance – hence the absence of opening times here.

Theater am Halleschen Ufer

Hallesches Ufer 32, Kreuzberg, 10963 (251 0655).
U1, U6 Hallesches Tor/U1, U7 Möckernbrücke.
Credit MC, V. **Map F5**
Where Peter Stein made his name, hosting a variety
of theatre groups and solo artists, some in English.

Friends of Italian Opera

Fidicinstraße 40, Kreuzberg, 10965 (box office 691
1211; information 693 5692). U6 Platz der
Luftbrücke. **Map F5**
First-rate productions by the best local and visiting
English-language groups and performers (the com-
pany Out to Lunch in particular) make this 60-seat

courtyard theatre Berlin's premier address for the
Anglophone fringe. Booking advisable.
Website: www.thefriends.de

STÜKKE

Palisadenstraße 48, Friedrichshain, 10243 (7158
1143/st uekke@t-online.de). U5 Weberwiese. **Map H3**
At press time, it had been announced that STÜKKE
had been temporarily rescued from folding by EU
funding and the offer of a new space in the
Kulturhaus Palisadenstraße. The directors have
pledged to continue their laudable policy of staging
solely contemporary theatre works from across the
globe. Thoroughly recommended.

Tacheles

Oranienburger Straße 53-56, Mitte, 10969 (282
6185). U6 Oranienburger Tor. **Map F3**
Reviled by some as a glorified neo-hippy squat, cher-
ished by others as a vibrant and essential alternative
arts centre, this space often plays host to English-
language performances (such as those involving
English solo performer/writer Jon Flynn). Saved from
demolition in 1998 when the concern which owns this
delightful wreck of a building extended the lease to
this community of artists. *See also chapter* **Film**.
Website: www.tacheles.de/

Vagantenbühne

Kantstraße 12a, Charlottenburg, 10623 (312 4529).
S3, S5, S7, S9/U2, U9 Zoologischer Garten. **Map C4**
Next door to the glitzy Theater des Westens, this is
one of the few fringe theatres still to receive government subsidies, although they've rather abandoned their experimental roots – cynics might add
that they *had* to in order to continue receiving state
support. High performance standards.
Website: www.vaganten.de

Theater Zerbrochene Fenster

Fidicinstraße 3 (entrance Schwiebusser Straße 16),
Kreuzberg, 10965 (694 2400). U6 Platz der
Luftbrücke. **Map F6**
Another space where Anglophone productions
sometimes can be seen, the 'Broken Window
Theatre' is in a converted factory building – hence
the odd shape of the theatre area itself.

Festivals

Berliner Festspiele

Budapester Straße 50, Charlottenburg, 10787 (254
890). S3, S5, S7, S9/U2, U9 Zoologischer Garten.
Map D4
The office which oversees most of Berlin's major festivals is a reliable place to find information about
events it is sponsoring, in particular the Berliner
Festwochen each September, featuring some of the
world's greatest theatre companies.

Theater Treffen Berlin

A kind of pan-German theatrical trade congress, the
'Berlin Theatre Meeting' takes place every May, featuring performances and theatrical talks, lectures
and exhibitions. For information contact Berliner
Festspiele as above.

Trips Out of Town

Getting Started

How to get somewhere from the middle of nowhere.

S-Bahn to Potsdam – your carriage awaits.

Berlin is a city in the middle of nowhere. For miles around, fields, lakes and dense woods are scarcely interrupted by small towns and villages.

The hard details about what is to be seen, when and for how much, are available from central tourist offices, usually at or near main railway stations. Most of them keep up-to-date supplies of inexpensive or free tourist maps and leaflets, and are indefatigable promoters of themselves and other points of interest within reach.

Berlin Tourismus Marketing

Europa-Center, Budapester Straße, Charlottenburg, 10787 (01805 754 040). S3, S5, S7, S9/U2, U9 Zoologischer Garten. **Open** 8.30am-8.30pm Mon-Sat; 10am-6.30pm Sun. **Map D4**
Good website but phoning within Berlin costs an outrageous DM2.42 per minute.
Branches: Tegel Airport; Brandenburg Gate.
Website: www.btm.de

By bus

There are no buses to Leipzig, Dresden or Weimar.

Omnibusbahnhof am Funkturm

Masurenallee 4-6, Charlottenburg, 14057 (301 8028). U2 Kaiserdamm/S4 Witzleben. **Open** information 9am-6pm Mon-Sat.

To the **Baltic coast**: coach from Omnibusbahnhof to Usedom on the eastern German Baltic coast (Sat, Mar-Oct only); journey time about 4 hours.
To **Hamburg**: there are four departures daily from the Omnibusbahnhof; journey time about 3 hours.
To **Prague**: from Omnibusbahnhof on Mon, Wed, Fri at 11.55pm; journey time 6 hours 20 minutes; returns on Mon, Tue, Thur, Fri and Sat at 8pm.

By train

The S-Bahn system is integrated with the German rail network, reaching about 40km (25 miles) beyond the city boundary.

The welding together of the eastern and western rail systems into the Deutsche Bahn often creates changes in services. Information about timetable alterations is displayed on affected platforms. At popular times of the year longer-distance trains can be fully booked well in advance. You should also book a seat at weekends.

Trains are ruinously expensive in Germany, but trips into eastern Europe are still much cheaper even though most international services have been modernised.

Deutsche Bahn Information

Bahnhof Zoo, Hardenbergplatz, Charlottenburg, 10623 (0180 599 663). S3, S5, S7, S9/U2, U9 Zoologischer Garten. **Open** 24 hours daily. **Map C4**

To **Babelsberg**: from Potsdam take the S7 from Potsdam Stadt to Griebnitzsee. *Journey time* about 10 minutes. *Cost* DM2.50 from Potsdam Stadt.
To the **Baltic coast**: for Rügen from Bahnhof Lichtenberg every 2 hours from 5.37am to 7.26pm. *Journey time* 3 hours 30 minutes; last return 12.06am. *Cost* DM67 single; DM152 return.
To **Dresden**: from Bahnhof Zoo every 2 hours from 6.25am to 9.15pm. *Journey time* 2 hours; last return at 9.15pm. *Cost* DM59 single; DM118 return.
To **Frankfurt/Oder**: from Ostbahnhof hourly from 5.01am to 1.01am. *Journey time* 1 hour; last return 11.34pm. *Cost* DM15.10 single; DM30.20 return.
To **Hamburg**: from Bahnhof Zoo every 2 hours from 6.34am-9.06pm. *Journey time* 2 hours 30 minutes; last return 11pm. *Cost* DM88 single; DM176 return.
To **Leipzig**: from Bahnhof Zoo every 2 hours from 5.25am to 10.21pm. *Journey time* 2 hours 14 minutes; last return 1.15am. *Cost* DM58 single; DM116 return.
To **Potsdam**: S7 to Potsdam Stadt 3 times an hour from central Berlin. *Journey time* about 45 minutes from Bahnhof Zoo. *Cost* DM4.20.
To **Prague**: from Bahnhof Lichtenberg every 2 hours from 6.25am to 6.22pm and also at 7.45pm. *Journey time* 5 hours; last return 3.58am. *Cost* DM99.60 single; DM199.20 return.
To **Rostock**: from Bahnhof Lichtenberg every 2 hours from 6.56am to 6.08pm. *Journey time* 2 hours 50 minutes; last return 7.27pm. *Cost* DM65 single; DM130 return.
To **Sachsenhausen**: S1 Oranienburg, journey time about 45 minutes from Friedrichstraße, then a 15-minute walk: east along Straße des Friedens, left into

Straße der Einheit, and finally along Straße der Nationen to the camp entrance. *Cost* DM4.20.
To **Weimar**: from Bahnhof Zoo every 2 hours from 5.39am to 7.16pm. *Journey time* 3 hours; last return 2.30am. *Cost* DM75 single; DM150 return.

By car

If you own, borrow or hire a car, make sure you are well briefed before setting out. Speed limits are ruthlessly enforced; in built-up areas it's usually 30kmph; 50kmph is customary on main arterial roads; the *Schnellstrecke* – dual carriageway – functions in all but name as a motorway, with a limit of 100 or 120kmph; and on the Autobahn itself there is, as yet, no speed limit.

The motorway system has regular service and filling stations, all listed in free maps issued by the **ADAC** (German Automobile Association) and available at any of its outlets. Information on cars is available from the association:

ADAC Berlin-Brandenburg
ADAC Haus, Bundesallee 29-30, 10717 (information 868 60/breakdown & accident assistance 01802 222 222). S4/U9 Bundesplatz. **Map C6**

To the **Baltic Coast**: about 220km north of Berlin. Drive north to the Berliner Ring and then follow the A24 to Rostock (about 2 hours); continue on the B103 to Stralsund and Rügen. The motorway to Rostock also affords easy access to many lakes and forests en route. There are regular car-ferry links between Rügen and the mainland, as well as the Danish island of Bornholm. *Journey time* between 3 and 4 hours.
To **Dresden**: 200km south of Berlin. Take the AVUS to the Berliner Ring and then the A13. *Journey time* about 3 hours.
To **Hamburg**: 284km north-west of Berlin. Drive north from Jakob-Kaiser-Platz along Kurt-Schumacher-Damm to the A24. *Journey time* 3 hours 30 minutes.
To **Leipzig**: 192km south of Berlin. Take the AVUS to the Berliner Ring, then take the A9. *Journey time* about 3 hours, but be prepared for traffic jams during trade-fair times.
To the **Polish border**: take Frankfurter Allee to Münchenberg, and from there either take the A12 to Frankfurt-Oder or to Seelow. *Journey time* 1 hour.
To **Potsdam & Babelsberg**: take the AVUS as far as the Drewitz turn-off, then turn right into Großbeerenstraße and follow it until Babelsberg and then Potsdam.
To **Spreewald**: 100km south-east of Berlin, the Spree bisects the area in Unterspreewald and Oberspreewald. For Unterspreewald, Schepzig or Lübben are the starting points; for Oberspreewald go 15km further on to Lübbenau. *Journey time* around 90 minutes.
To **Weimar**: as for Leipzig (*above*), but continue on the E4055. Weimar lies 50km to the south-west of Leipzig across the state border in Thüringen (Thuringia). If you travel here by car, you can also explore the stunning Saale valley on the way. *Journey time* less than 4 hours.

Shared lifts

Germany has a well-established national lift-sharing network. Each city or town has at least one office, advertised in the phone book or *Yellow Pages* (*Gelbe Seiten*) under *Mitfahrzentrale*. Passengers can call the office, or visit in person, to find out if there are any drivers seeking companions. Usually a small fee is charged by the agent (about DM20). Theoretically, each agent recommends a fixed price per kilometre, but in practice the deal travellers strike up with each other is more important.

Lifts can sometimes be arranged just hours in advance of travelling, but if possible you do it two or three days earlier. Very long rides (say, Berlin to London) can be found but are not as common as short ones; you should prepare at least a week in advance and be flexible.

City-Netz
Joachimsthaler Straße 17, Charlottenburg, 10719 (194 44). U9, U15 Kurfürstendamm. **Open** 9am-8pm Mon-Fri; 9am-7pm Sat-Sun. **Map C5**
City-Netz has branches in every major German city.

Mitfahrzentrale am Alex
Alexanderplatz U-Bahn, Mitte, 10178 (241 5820). S3, S5, S7, S9/U2,U5,U8 Alexanderplatz. **Open** 10am-6pm Mon-Wed, Fri; 10am-8pm Thur; 11am-4pm Sat-Sun. **Map G3**

Hitching

Hitch-hiking is still common in Germany. Asking around at lorry parks and filling stations on the main routes out of the city can be a good way to cut your travel expenses.

If heading to Hamburg take bus 224 direction Henningsdorf and get off at Heiligensee. The bus stop is 150m from the car and lorry park known as Trämperparkplatz.

If heading in the direction of Hanover, Leipzig or Nuremberg take the S1 or S7 to Wannsee; exit towards Potsdamer Chaussee, then walk 300m to the slip road leading to the lorry park and petrol station at Raststätte Dreilinden. This is a busy spot, so arrive early and carry a clear sign indicating your desired destination. Standing on the hard shoulder is illegal and you may be moved on by the police.

Bicycles

Especially in fine weather, it is common for Berliners to pack their bikes on to the train and head off into the countryside. On the U-Bahn, there is a limit of two cycles at the end of carriages which have a bicycle sign on them. Bikes may not be taken on the U-Bahn during rush hour (defined as 6-9am and 2-5pm). More may be taken on to S-Bahn carriages, and at any time of day. In each case an extra ticket must be bought for each bike.

Day Trips

Beyond Berlin, day trippers will find forests, lakes, concentration camps and Germany's answers to both Versailles and Hollywood.

The area immediately around Berlin is full of lakes and forest, offering interesting bike rides and plenty of places to swim in summer. Potsdam is to Berlin what Versailles is to Paris, with a collection of palaces and other interesting things to see – almost more, in fact, than is manageable in one day. Neighbouring Babelsberg has the old UFA film studios, Germany's answer to Hollywood. The Spreewald, a forest filigreed with small streams,

is good for an afternoon's boat ride. More sombrely, KZ Sachsenhausen offers a reminder of one of history's more chilling passages.

With the exception of the Spreewald, which is only accessible by car, all of the destinations in this chapter can be reached on the S-Bahn. *See chapter* **Getting Started**.

Potsdam

Potsdam is capital of the state of Brandenburg and Berlin's closest and most beautiful neighbour. Its own millennial celebrations of 1993 coincided with a large new influx of tourists – before 1990 Potsdam had been a notoriously tricky destination for Westerners to obtain a visa – as well as shops, restaurants and cafés to cater for them. Since then, the number of visitors has been rising substantially every year, helped by the range and ease of transportation from Berlin – plus a regular ferry service from Wannsee – and summer weekends in this now chic exurb can become very crowded indeed. The main permanent attraction, then as

Sanssouci – *statues without cares at Potsdam's premier palace. See page 254.*

now, is the grandiose collection of palaces and out-buildings in Park Sanssouci. This in itself can take a whole day to see. Another afternoon can be pleasantly filled around Potsdam's baroque town centre, the Altstadt, as well as in Babelsberg.

Large parts of Potsdam town centre were destroyed in a single bombing raid on 14 April 1945, which claimed 4,000 lives. The vagaries of post-war reconstruction produced a ghastly 'restoration' of Schinkel's **St-Nikolaikirche**, whose dome can be seen for miles, as well as acres of featureless 1960s and 1970s flatblocks which crowd out Platz der Einheit ('Unity Square') and the surrounding streets.

Nevertheless, the unusual, mid-18th century, Palladian-style **Altes Rathaus** ('Town Hall') is worth admiring, particularly for its round tower, which until 1875 was used as a prison. It is now an arts centre (the **Kulturhaus Potsdam**). The Hans-Otto-Theater, resembling a nuclear plant, was finished (with post-Wall diminishing funds) in time to host open-air Millennium festivities. The park at the Alter Markt here covers the ruins of the first Stadtschloß, and a square of stones marks its oldest tower, dating from 1200.

Yorck- and Wilhelm-Raab-Straße retain their Baroque architecture: the Kabinetthaus, a small palace at Am neuen Markt 1, was the birthplace of Friedrich Wilhelm II (the only Hohenzollern both to have been born and to have died in the royal residence of Potsdam). The baroque centre, originally intended as a quarter to house people servicing the court, is bounded by Schopenhauerstraße, Hebbelstraße, Charlottenstraße and Hegel Allee. The dwellings were built between 1732 and 1742, at the behest of Friedrich Wilhelm I; the best of them can be seen running west along the pedestrianised Brandenburger Straße. Potsdam's Brandenburg Gate (by Gontard 1733), at the Sanssouci end of Brandenburger Straße, is a delightfully happy contrast to Berlin's sombre structure of the same name.

The Holländisches Viertel ('Dutch Quarter'), is between Gutenbergstraße, Friedrich-Ebert-Straße, Hebbelstraße and Kurfürstenstraße, and takes its name from the Dutch immigrant workers that Friedrich Wilhelm I, the inveterate builder, invited to the town. He ordered 134 gable-fronted red-brick houses to be built, most of which fell into neglect after the last war, but the survivors, particularly along Mittelstraße at the junction with Benkerstraße, have been scrubbed into shape. With the squatters long gone, private money has transformed the area to its current status as the place to dine and shop.

The best museum in town is the **Filmmuseum**, with an excellent documentation of the history of German cinema from 1895 to 1980. Indeed, it's one of the finest of its kind anywhere, underpinned by classic material from the UFA studios in nearby Babelsberg. Contained in the elegant former

Marstall ('royal stables'), which were given their current appearance by Knobelsdorff during the 18th century, it has rooms full of famous props, costumes, set-designs and projection screens. There's also a café and a large, comfortable cinema with an art-house programme, including talks and special events, that rivals anything on offer in Berlin. Behind it, bounded by Dortusstraße and Yorckstraße, lies another magnificent baroque neighbourhood awaiting restoration.

But without question the main draw for visitors lies in **Sanssouci** ('Without Cares'), given a French name because this was the language of the 18th-century Prussian court. It was a Francophile, Friedrich Wilhelm II, who originally began to build the extensive gardens here in 1740. They were intended to be in stark contrast to the style favoured by his detested father – German history is littered with examples of one generation doing the precise opposite of its predecessor. The first palace to be built, and the one which gives the park its name, forms a semi-circle at the top of a terrace on whose slopes symmetrical zig-zag paths are interspersed with vines and orange trees. It houses a collection of paintings, including a Caravaggio and several works by Dutch masters.

Gable vision – Potsdam's Dutch quarter.

Voltaire was brought to live in a suite here between 1750 and 1753, supposedly to oversee the library. But he devoted most of his time to his own writing, an act of defiance which eventually brought the relationship with his patron to an acrimonious end. Other abundant attractions include Friedrich Wilhelm II's huge Neue Palais, built 1763-69 to celebrate the end of the Seven Years War. So many statues were needed for the roof that they had to be mass-produced in a factory.

The last occupant, Kaiser Wilhelm II, took the Neue Palais' contents with him in 60 railway carriages when he fled into exile in Holland in 1918, where most of the items remained in boxes, unopened until they were returned to fill the restored palace in the 1980s. Also worth visiting in Sanssouci are: the gigantic Orangerie, in Italian Renaissance style; the Spielfestung ('toy fortress'), built for Wilhelm II's sons, complete with a toy cannon which can be fired; the Chinesisches Teehaus ('Chinese Teahouse'), with its collection of Chinese and Meißner porcelain; the Römischer Bäder, an imitation Roman villa by Schinkel and Persius; Schloß Charlottenhof, with its extraordinary blue-glazed entrance hall and Kupferstichzimmer ('copper-plate engraving room'), adorned with reproduction Renaissance paintings; and the Drachenhaus ('Dragonhouse'), a pagoda-style coffee shop where you can gorge on exquisite cakes.

While the park is open all the year round, much of the statuary – as is customary in this part of the world – is protected from the harsh winter by being encased in wooden boxes. For this reason, it's best to visit between April and October, a fact not lost on the vast crowds of tourists – aim to get there on a weekday.

Outside Sanssouci Park is Alexandrowka (between Puschkinallee and Am Schragen), a fake Russian village built in 1826 by Friedrich Wilhelm III to house Russian musicians and their families who came into Prussian hands as prisoners of war during the Napoleonic campaigns. The houses were arranged in the form of a St Andrew's cross and designed to look like log cabins. They still carry the names of the original tenants in inscriptions on their fronts, some in Cyrillic. The icon-filled Alexander-Newski-Kapelle, constructed three years later at the top of the densely wooded Kapellenberg hill, is named – strangely – after the celebrated Russian hero who defeated the medieval Teutonic Knights.

In the Neuer Garten, at the end of Johannes-Dieckmann-Allee, the **Marmorpalais** ('Marble Palace'), overlooking the beautiful Heiliger See, was where Friedrich Wilhelm II died. Nearby, **Schloß Cecilienhof**, the last royal addition to Potsdam's palaces, was begun in 1913 and completed four years later: its English-country-house style was unaffected by the war with Britain.

It was here that the Potsdam Conference (17 July to 2 August 1945) took place, and where Stalin, Truman and Attlee signed the Potsdamer Abkommen, the treaty which divided post-war Germany. The conference room, including the specially fashioned round table (so that none of the 'Big Three' would take precedence) was left untouched. The room was damaged in an arson attack in 1990, presumably by neo-Nazis. One wing of the building was converted into a hotel in 1960, and remains an expensive place to stay or dine, but cheaper alternatives abound.

Potsdam-Information

Friedrich-Ebert-Straße 5, Potsdam, 14467 (0331 275 580/fax 0331 275 5889/ information@potsdam.de). **Open** *Apr-Oct* 9am-8pm Mon-Fri; 9am-6pm Sat; 9am-4pm Sun; *Nov-Mar* 10am-6pm Mon-Fri; 10am-2pm Sat-Sun.
English spoken. Here you can find a WelcomeCard, a DM-32 book of vouchers which entitles you to three days' free travel on public transport in Berlin and Potsdam, as well as 50% reductions on entries to Potdam's tourist attractions. It is valid for one adult and up to three children. It is also available at VIP (the Potsdam public transport authority) ticket offices in the Platz der Einheit and Luisenplatz. The maps available are excellent, showing all the attractions and how best to move between them on the public transport system.
Website: www.potsdam.de

Potsdam-Ticket

Brandenburger Straße 18, Potsdam, 14467 (0331 275 580/fax 0331 275 899). **Open** 10am-7pm Mon-Fri; 10am-2pm Sat.
Mostly useful for tickets for cultural events.

Altes Rathaus: Kulturhaus Potsdam

Am Alten Markt, Potsdam, 14467 (0331 293 175). **Open** 10am-6pm Tue-Sun.

Filmmuseum

Marstall, Potsdam, 14467 (0331 271 810). **Open** 10am-6pm Tue-Sun. **Admission** DM4; DM2 concs.

Marmorpalais

Am Neuen Garten, Potsdam, 14414 (0331 969 4200). **Open** *Apr-Oct* 10am-5pm Tue-Sun; *Nov-Mar* 10am-4pm Sat-Sun. **Admission** DM4; DM3 concs.

St Nikolaikirche

Am Alten Markt, Potsdam, 14467 (0331 291 682). **Open** 2-5pm Mon-Fri; 10am-5pm Sat; 11.30am-5pm Sun. **Admission** free (tours by prior arrangement).

Sanssouci

(0331 969 4202). **Open** *for tours* (every 20 mins) 9am-5pm daily; *park* until dusk daily. **Admission** *Palace and exhibition buildings* DM8; DM4 concs; *Park* free. **Note**: Each of the various outbuildings has its own closing days each month, and some are only open 'during the season' of mid-May to mid-Oct. If you have a particular interest, call the number above for full information as to opening.

Gateway to Potsdam – the Nauener Tor.

Schloß Cecilienhof

Am Neuen Garten, Potsdam, 14414 (0331 969 4200/fax 0331 969 4107). **Open** *Apr-Oct* 9am-5pm Tue-Sun; *Nov-Mar* 9am-4pm Tue-Sun. **Admission** DM10; DM5 concs.

Babelsberg

If film palaces rather than royal palaces are your forte, then you should head over the Havel river to the finest one Europe ever saw: Babelsberg. Now officially part of Potsdam, Babelsberg was the centre of the pre-war German film industry, still the main reason why so many day trippers cross the Lange Brücke to land in Potsdam's otherwise prosaic east bank.

Indeed, the first thing they will see on the other side is the former state parliament building, Brauhausberg, known in communist times as the Kremlin, where the old authorities kept their archives. Beyond this, down Albert-Einstein-Straße, stands Telegrafenberg ('Telegraph Hill'). Here, in 1832, one of the mechanical telegraph stations linking Berlin to Koblenz was built. When electrification made it obsolete, an astronomical observatory was erected. Its expressionist tower by Erich Mendelsohn, the Einsteinturm, was added in 1920 with the hope of luring Albert Einstein here to test his Theory of Relativity.

But Einstein was not induced to stay, and neither are today's weekenders, who pour on to the buses running from Lange Brücke, stopping at **Filmpark-Babelsberg**, at the very gates of the Babelsberg Film Studios.

The first studio was opened here in 1912 by the Berlin production company Bioscop. But it was not until 1917, when the German General Staff decided that the war effort was suffering because of the inferior quality of their propaganda, that the Universum Film AG (UFA) was founded, with the financial support of the Deutsche Bank.

By the 1920s the studio had become the largest in the world outside Hollywood, making as many as a hundred films a year, including the Expressionist *The Cabinet of Dr Caligari*, the futurist *Metropolis* and the decadent *The Blue Angel* (the young Marlene Dietrich was so convinced she would not land the role of Lola that she came to her audition without a song to sing).

A mixture of success, the Depression and the rise of the Nazis saw most of the studios' talent leave for America, or the concentration camps.

During World War II, films such as the anti-Semitic *Jew Süß* and the colour, escapist fantasy *The Adventures of Baron Münchhausen* were made. Renamed Deutsche Film AG (DEFA) in the GDR, film-making resumed and included *Der Untertan (The Subject)*, possibly the best study of German totalitarianism ever made. It was banned immediately after its première in 1952 – a common fate.

The rediscovery, and sometimes reconstruction, of 'lost' DEFA films continues apace. Sections of the studio are open to the public but have been transformed into a tacky theme park where the product placement of international soft drink sponsors overshadow the exhibits on display. Avoid, unless you're turned on by inflatable Coca-Cola bottles. A walk by the pretty Griebnitzsee can be a far more appealing prospect – even in the rain.

Filmpark Babelsberg

August-Babel-Straße 26-53, entrance on Großbeerenstraße, Potsdam, 14482 (reservations 0331 721 2750/information 721 2755). Bus 698 from Lange Brücke, direction Am Gehöz. **Open** *22 Mar-1 Nov* 10am-6pm daily; last visitor 3.30pm. **Tickets** DM28; DM25 concs. Special group rates.

Potsdam-Information

Friedrich-Ebert-Straße 5, Potsdam, 14467 (0331 275 580/fax 0331 275 5889/information@potsdam.de). **Open** *Apr-Oct* 9am-8pm Mon-Fri; 9am-6pm Sat; 9am-4pm Sun; *Nov-Mar* 10am-6pm Mon-Fri; 10am-2pm Sat-Sun.

Spreewald

This filigree network of tiny rivers, streams and canals, dividing dense patches of deciduous forest interspersed with market garden farmland, is one of the most spectacular excursions out of Berlin. The area is extremely crowded in season, and particularly at weekends, giving the lie to its otherwise justified claim to be one of the most perfect areas of wilderness in Europe.

Located 100km to the south-east of Berlin, the Spree bisects the area into Unterspreewald and Oberspreewald. For the former, Schepzig or Lübben are the best starting points; for the latter go 15km further on the train to Lübbenau.

The character of both sections is very similar. The Oberspreewald is perhaps better, for its 500sq km of territory contains more than 300 natural and artificial channels, called Fliesse. You can travel around these on hand-propelled punts – rent your own or join a larger group – and also take out kayaks. Motorised boats are forbidden. Here and there in the forest are restaurants and small hotels.

Theodor Fontane described the Spreewald as resembling Venice more than 1,500 years ago. The local population belongs to the Sorbisch Slav minority, related to Czechs and Slovaks, with their own language much in evidence in street names, newspapers and so on. This can be an exotic attraction, unlike the folk festivals regularly laid on for tourists in the high season.

Spreewald Information

Ehm-Welk-Straße 15, Lubbenau, 03222 (03542 36 68). **Open** *Apr-Oct* 9am-4pm daily; *Nov-Mar* 9am-4pm Mon-Fri.

KZ Sachsenhausen

Many Nazi concentration camps (*Konzentrationslager*) have been preserved and opened to the public as memorials to what happened and how. Sachsenhausen is the one nearest to Berlin.

Immediately upon coming to power, Hitler set about rounding up and interning his opponents. From 1933 to 1935 an old brewery on this site was used to hold them. The present camp received its first prisoners in July 1936 (coinciding with the Berlin Olympic Games). It was designated with cynical euphemism as a *Schutzhaftlager* ('Protective Custody Camp'). The first *Schutzhäftlinger* were political opponents of the government: communists, social democrats, trade unionists. With time, the number and variety of prisoners widened to include anyone guilty of 'antisocial' behaviour, homosexuals and Jews.

About 6,000 Jews were forcibly brought here after Kristallnacht alone. It was here that some of the first experiments in organised mass murder were made: tens of thousands of prisoners of war from the Eastern Front were killed at the neighbouring Station Z, where the cells for *Prominenz* ('privileged detainees') housed Pastor Martin Niemöller, a decorated World War I U-Boat captain and one-time supporter of the Nazis.

The SS evacuated the camp in 1945 and began marching 33,000 inmates to the Baltic, where they were to be packed into boats and sunk in the sea. Some 6,000 died during the march before the survivors were rescued by the Allies. A further 3,000 prisoners were found in the camp's hospital when it was captured on 22 April 1945.

But the horror did not end here. After the German capitulation, the Russian secret police, the MVD, re-opened Sachsenhausen as 'Camp 7' for the detention of war criminals; in fact it was filled with anyone suspected of opposition. Following the fall of the GDR, mass graves were discovered, containing the remains of an estimated 10,000 prisoners.

On 23 April 1961, the partially restored camp was opened to the public as Nationale Mahn- und Gedenkstätte Sachsenhausen, a national monument and memorial. As far as the GDR was concerned, it was absolved of all complicity in the actions of the Hitler régime, whose rightful successors, it claimed, could be found across the border in West Germany. The inscription over the entrance, Arbeit Macht Frei ('Work Sets You Free'), could be found over the gates of all concentration camps.

The parade ground, where morning roll-call was taken, and from where inmates were required to witness executions on the gallows, stands before the two remaining barrack blocks. One is now a museum and the other a memorial hall and cinema, where a film about the history of the camp is shown hourly, on the hour. The scale and the grisliness of the horror remembered here can be very disturbing, but it is worth noting that there are people even today who would like to pretend that none of it ever happened – some of them burned a couple of the buildings here in 1996.

KZ Sachsenhausen

Straße der Nationen 22, Oranienburg, 16515 (03301 803 715). **Open** 8.30am-4pm Tue-Sun. **Admission** free.

Overnighters

History, culture and solitary beaches in east Germany's hinterland – but you'll need a car and a map to find it all.

It is possible to get to and from the following destinations within one day, but as day trips these would be arduous, especially for inveterate museum-goers. Better, we reckon, to make them an overnight stay. All of them are sited in the former GDR, where affordable hotel accommodation is at a general premium. However such is the regeneration of its two great cities, Leipzig and Dresden, that many mid-range and top-level hotels have sprung up, with the knock-on effect of a far wider range of shops, bars and restaurants than could previously have been imagined.

Nevertheless the economic, political, social and cultural base is of an entirely different character, not only from the west, but also from eastern Berlin, which enjoyed a comparatively favoured position in the former Eastern Bloc. Federal subsidies for rebuilding have been eagerly seized, and construction is rampant, meaning some landmarks, particularly once-neglected churches, may be closed or clad in scaffolding.

Even so, a longer excursion into the east German hinterland not only affords an unrepeatable experience as the continent of Europe continues to move into a new era, but a chance to see some of the country's other regions which played their own parts in Berlin's history.

Baltic Coast

The Baltic coast was the favoured holiday destination of the GDR citizen; post-Reunification it is still the most accessible seaside resort for all Berliners. The coast forms the northern boundary of the modern state of Mecklenburg-Vorpommern. Bismarck said of the area: 'When the end of the world comes, I shall go to Mecklenburg, because there everything happens a hundred years later.'

The large island of Rügen is gradually resuming its rivalry with Sylt in the North Sea – both islands claim to be the principal north German resort. In July and August it can get crowded (don't go without pre-booked accommodation), and Rügen's handful of restaurants and lack of late-night bars mean visitors are early to bed and early to rise. Go out of season and enjoy the solitude.

Rostock was one of the founder members of the medieval Hanseatic League, and, until wrecked by bombing in the last war, was an attractive port full of grandiose, gabled merchants' houses and sea-

men's cottages. The GDR did a good job of putting Rostock back together again and, though it is no longer the vital trading link it once was, it is a quietly attractive, if slightly melancholy town, especially off-season. Much of the past flavour can still be found around the waterfront, where cafés, restaurants and hotels have recently opened. But Rostock's reputation has not yet recovered from the ugly racial incident in 1992, when people and police alike stood and watched as neo-Nazis stormed and fired a hostel for asylum seekers.

Forty kilometres to the east of Rostock is Peenemünde, at the very tip of the island of Usedom, site of secret weapons development in the closing years of World War II. Here, a group of engineers and technicians produced the Vergeltungswaffen ('revenge weapons'), V1 and V2, and several rockets were fired from the island. Part of the complex has been preserved as a museum, and examples of the rockets are on display. After the war, both the Americans and Russians were quick to requisition the services of the scientists responsible for the rockets' creation. One of the boffins, Werner von Braun, became the leading expert of NASA's Apollo programme.

Fremdenverkehrsverband 'Insel Usedom'

Insel Usedom Tourist Information Office
Bäderstraße 4, Ueckeritz, 17459 (038375 76 93).
Open 9am-4pm Mon-Fri.

Rostock Information

Schnickmannstraße 13-14, Rostock, 18055 (0381 497 9914). **Open** *May-Sept* 10am-6pm Mon-Fri; 10am-2.30pm Sat-Sun; *Oct-Apr* 10am-5pm Mon-Fri; 10am-2.30pm Sat.

Tourismus Verbund Rügen

Markt 4, Bergen, 18528 (03838 807 70). **Open** 8am-4pm Mon-Fri.

Tourist Information Bad Doberan

Goethestraße 1, Bad Doberan, 18203 (038 203 2120). **Open** 8am-5pm Mon-Thur.

Dresden

Destroyed twice and rebuilt one-and-a-half times, the capital of Saxony boasts one of Germany's best art museums and many historic buildings.

Modern Dresden is built on the ruins of its past. A fire consumed Altendresden on the bank of the

Elbe in 1685, provoking a wave of rebuilding throughout the city. On the night of 13 February 1945, the biggest of Sir Arthur 'Bomber' Harris' raids caused huge fire storms killing up to 100,000 people, mostly refugees from the Eastern Front. After the war, Dresden was twinned with Coventry, and Benjamin Britten's *War Requiem* was given its first performance in the Hofkirche by musicians from both towns. Under the GDR reconstruction was erratic, but a maze of cranes and scaffolding sprang up in the 1990s – Dresden is making up for lost time.

Dresden's main attraction remains the buildings from the reign of Augustus the Strong (1670-1733). The Hofkirche (Am Theaterplatz 1), the Zwinger, a garden containing a complex of museums, and the Grünes Gewölbe, a collection of Augustus' jewels and knick-knacks in the **Albertinum**, all give a flavour of the city's Baroque exuberance. They can be reached via the Hauptbahnhof's Prager Straße exit and through the pedestrianised mall that competes with Alexanderplatz for the honour of ugliest GDR public space.

Building was continued by Augustus' successor, Augustus III, who then lost to Prussia in the Seven Years War (1756-63). Frederick the Great destroyed much of the city in this war, although not the Brühlsche Terrassen in the old part of the city. A victorious Napoleon ordered the demolition of the city's defences in 1809. In 1985 the **Semperoper** opera house, named after its architect Gottfried Semper (1838-41), was fully restored to its earlier elegance. The **Gemäldegalerie Alte Meister** in the Zwinger has a superb collection of Old Masters, particularly Italian Renaissance and Flemish, and there are also exhibitions of porcelain from nearby Meißen, and collections of armour, weapons, clocks and scientific equipment.

The industrialisation of Dresden heralded a new phase of construction that produced the Rathaus ('Town Hall', built 1905-10) at Dr.-Külz-Ring, the Hauptbahnhof (1892-95) at the end of Prager Straße, the Yenidze cigarette factory (1912) in Könneritzstraße, designed to look like a mosque, and the grandiose Landtagsgebäude (completed to plans by Paul Wallot, designer of Berlin's Reichstag, in 1907) at Heinrich-Zille-Straße 11. The finest example of inter-war architecture is Wilhelm Kreis' Deutsches Hygienemuseum (1929) at Lingner Platz 1, constructed to house the German Institute of Hygiene.

Relatively recent reconstruction of the Frauenkirche at Neumarkt, the Schloß, and most prominently the Altstadt, should see the city in its best light for its 1,000th anniversary in 2006.

In the GDR days, this part of the country, behind the Saxon hills, could not receive Western television or radio broadcasts and was called 'Tal der Ahnungslosen' ('Valley of the Clueless'). In the process of catching up, a vibrant alternative scene has developed in the Neustadt, particularly in the bars and cafés on and around Alaunstraße.

The Striezelmarkt (named after the savoury pretzel you will see everyone eating), is held on Altstädtermarkt every December. The Christmas market is one of the most colourful events of the year. Dresden is also home to the best *Stollen*, a German variety of yuletide cake.

Dresden's Zwinger complex – gardens, museums and lots of Old Masters.

Semperoper – *restored to earlier elegance.*

Dresden Tourist Information

Prager Straße, Dresden, 01069 (0351 491 920/fax 495 1276/info@dresden-tourist.de). **Open** 10am-6pm Mon-Fri; 10am-2pm Sat-Sun.
Neustädter Markt, Dresden, 01097 (0351 491 920/fax 0351 495 1276/info@dresden-tourist.de). **Open** 10am-6pm Mon-Fri; 10am-2pm Sat-Sun.
Efficient, English-speaking service with two main offices in town, both with the same contact details. The Dresden-Card also available in both, DM26, valid for 48 hours for one adult and child, allowing free travel on public transport, and free and reduced admission to the city's museums.
Website: www.dresden-tourist.de

Albertinum

Brühlsche Terrasse, Dresden, 01067 (0351 491 4622/fax 0351 491 4616). **Open** 10am-6pm Mon-Wed, Fri-Sun. **Admission** DM7; DM4 concs.
Houses two major collections of paintings and treasures, the Gemäldegalerie Neue Meister and the Grünes Gewölbe.

Altstädter Wache

Theaterplatz, Dresden, 01067 (0351 484 2323). **Open** box office for the Semperoper noon-5pm Mon-Fri; 10am-1pm Sat. **Tickets** DM5-DM65; DM8 concs.

Gemäldegalerie Alte Meister

in the Zwinger at the Theaterplatz, Dresden, 01067 (0351 491 4622). **Open** 10am-6pm Tue-Sun. **Admission** DM7; DM4 concs.
Website: www.staatl-kunstsammlungen-dresden.de

Semperoper

Theaterplatz, Dresden, 01067 (0351 484 2323). **Open** box office see Altstädter Wache.

Leipzig

One of Germany's most important trade centres and former second city of the GDR, Leipzig is both Bach's city and the place where the mass movement for political change began. Once one of Germany's biggest industrial strongholds, trade fairs (*Messen*) are its bread and butter these days. The recent influx of western businesspeople (and

their spouses) has resulted not only in the scrubbing clean of the city, but also in a proliferation of pricey shops and boutiques.

All forms of transport between Berlin and Leipzig are liable to be overcrowded or fully booked during important trade fairs – ask at a tourist information office for details. The advantage of taking a slower train is that it enables you to make stops en route (perhaps Wittenberg, former home of Martin Luther and a pretty, medieval town). Another sight which cannot be overlooked on a trip by train is the gigantic chemical works at Leuna. The factories were originally built in the early 1900s for the immense conglomerate IG Farben, which produced the poison gas used on the Western Front during World War I and the Zyklon B for Nazi gas chambers.

Visitors to Leipzig will arrive at its extensively restored main train station, one of the world's largest, with a three-level shopping mall and a comprehensive international press shop.

From the Hauptbahnhof, it is a short walk to the compact town centre, surrounded by the Ring, a wide road built on the site of the old city wall torn down in the last century. Most things worth seeing are within this ring. Leipzig was heavily bombed during the last war and restoration has been piecemeal, if not chaotic. But examples of grand, turn-of-the-century civic pomp survive, dotted among the communist blandness.

The Neues Rathaus ('New Town Hall'), at Martin-Luther-Ring 2, dates from the end of the last century, and competes well with the University skyscraper for ugliness. The Reichsgerichtsmuseum opposite, with its **Museum für Bildende Künste** ('Museum of Arts Picture Gallery') is worth a visit just to look at the building. Farther along the ring is the Runde Ecke, where the dreaded Stasi had their headquarters. It now houses a museum about their activities – the **Museum in der Runden Ecke**. Across the park and back south is the Thomaskirche, where Bach spent the last 27 years of his life as *Kapellmeister* ('Music Director'). He is buried in the choir, and fans won't want to miss the **Johann-Sebastian-Bach-Museum**, located in the Bosehaus behind the church, or the small monument in the park, which was erected by another Leipziger, Felix Mendelssohn, in Bach's honour.

Continue down Thomaskirchhof as it turns into Grimmaische Straße and you reach the Altes Rathaus ('Old Town Hall'), which dates from the Renaissance and has the longest building inscription in the world. It also houses the city's History Museum. The covered Galerie Mädler Passage on the other side of the street has been completely rebuilt, one of the older of the passages which have sprung up post-1990, attracting expensive shops and boutiques. In its basement is **Auerbachs Keller**, one of the most famous restaurants in

Leibniz and Leipzig University.

Germany. Goethe came here regularly to dine, and especially to drink, and used it as a location for a scene in his epic drama, *Faust*. Two bronze models at the entrance and paintings inside depict scenes from Goethe's drama. The restaurant, which is more than 300 years old, was extensively refurbished in 1911.

Reichstraße leads past the Alte Börse, sparkling with its gilding, to Sachsenplatz, the city's main outdoor market. But turn just before the market to see the Nikolaikirche, Leipzig's proud symbol of its new freedom. This medieval church, with its Baroque interior featuring columns that imitate palm trees, is the place where regular free-speech meetings started in 1982. These evolved into the Swords to Ploughshares peace movement, which led to the first anti-GDR demonstration on Monday, 4 September 1989 in the Nikolaikirchhof. (Today, there is the excellent Kulturcafé in the church's former school.)

By 6 November, the Monday Demonstrations had swelled into 600,000-strong rallies in Augustusplatz (formerly Karl-Marx-Platz) just down the street by the University. The crowd chanted, *'Deutschland einig Vaterland'* and *'Wir sind das Volk'*, and listened to speakers such as Kurt Masur, chief conductor of the **Leipziger Gewandhaus Orchester** (housed in the brown glass-fronted buildings on the south side), one of the finest orchestras in the world.

Augustusplatz was a project of GDR communist party leader Walter Ulbricht, himself a Leipziger, and the staggeringly ugly skyscraper is supposed to represent an open book. Be sure to catch the inscription memorialising the Universitätskirche, a medieval building destroyed to make way for this eyesore. On the north side of the square stands the **Opernhaus Leipzig** (opened in 1960), which also has an excellent reputation.

Wandering through the city centre, you can see many of the handsome, prosperous homes of Leipzig's industrialists that survived the ravages of recent history. Now most of the stores in the city centre built to cater for this élite have been restored. As a contrast, the offices of the Universität Leipzig, Augustusplatz, still have an impressive bronze bas-relief of Marx urging workers of the world to unite.

Leipzig Tourist Service
Richard-Wagner-Platz 1, Leipzig, 04109 (0341 710 4260). **Open** 9am-7pm Mon-Fri; 9am-4pm Sat; 9am-2pm Sun.
The best stop for all enquiries. English is spoken here, and the staff can provide an excellent information booklet in a dozen languages. You can also buy a Leipzig Card, allowing free transport in the city and discounts on tours and museums, DM9.90 for one day, DM21 for two adults and three children. *Website: www.leipzig.de*

Auerbachs Keller
Mädlerpassage, Grimmaische Straße 2-4, Leipzig 04109 (0341 216 100). **Open** 11.30am-midnight daily. **Average** DM35. **Credit** AmEx, DC, JCB, V.
Both the menu and the wine list are of excellent quality at Auerbachs. Specialities include Leipziger Allerlei, a dish of steamed mixed vegetables and mushrooms with crayfish.

Johann-Sebastian-Bach-Museum
Thomaskirchhof 16, Leipzig, 04109 (0341 78 66). **Open** 10am-5pm daily. **Tickets** DM2; DM1 concs. *Website: www.bach-leipzig.de*

Leipziger Gewandhaus Orchester
Augustusplatz 8, Leipzig, 04199 (0341 127 00/127 080). **Open** 1-6pm Mon; 10am-6pm Tue-Fri; 10am-2pm Sat. **Admission** varies. *Website: www.gewandhaus.de*

Museum für Bildende Künste
Grimmaische Straße 1-7, Leipzig, 04109 (0341 216 990). **Open** 10am-6pm Tue, Thur-Sun; 1-9.30pm Wed. **Tickets** DM5; DM2.50 concs.

Museum in der Runden Ecke
Dittrichring 24, 04109 Leipzig (0341 961 2443). **Open** 2-6pm Wed-Sun.

Opernhaus Leipzig
Augustusplatz 12, Leipzig, 04109 (0341 126 10). **Open** box office 10am-6pm Mon-Fri; 10am-1pm Sat. **Admission** varies.
Call for information about tours of the building. *Website: www.leipzig-online.de/oper/*

Polish border region

The Polish border region is a must for World War II buffs, since it is the place where the Russians broke through the German lines to start the final assault on Berlin. But it is also a place of peaceful countryside dotted with relatively untouched villages that are quite unlike anything in western Germany. For anything except a day trip to Frankfurt-an-der-Oder, a car and a detailed map are essential, since transport in this part of the country is severely underdeveloped and the places referred to below are way off the usual routes. Floods in 1997 wreaked havoc with many of the small towns here, and recovery has been slow.

Frankfurt-an-der-Oder is the main metropolis of the border region, a 13th-century market town that was almost completely destroyed during the war. GDR reconstruction leaves little to recommend the place – use it as a jumping-off point to Poland to the east. A bridge across the river leads to the Polish town of Słubice, where flea markets depressingly reminiscent of those on the US-Mexican border sell cheap cigarettes, meats, cheese, and horrid clothing and knick-knacks.

Seelow, just north of Frankfurt, is another 13th-century town that suffered horrible wartime devastation. The battle for the Eastern Front is commemorated at the **Gedankstätte Seelower Höhen**, a hill topped with a statue of a Russian soldier. Today the museum pays homage to both sides, and a slide presentation (available in English) with a light-up map and a rather tendentious narration will explain the struggle to break through and take Berlin. Going back south from Seelow, you'll find an even grimmer reminder in the recent German Military Cemetery in Lietzen, where so far 890 graves have been installed. Few of the inhabitants are over 20.

A drive through the villages near Seelow, in the area known as the Oderbruch, will turn up a Russian war memorial in every village square. Neu Hardenburg has a Schinkel church, built as part of the reconstruction of the village after a disastrous fire, and one of the first projects overseen by the teenage genius. The Schloß was the family home of Graf von Hardenburg, one of the plotters against Hitler, and it was here that he was captured by the SS and taken to Sachsenhausen. The Oderbruch was a special project of Frederick the Great after his release from prison in Kostryzn across the Polish border. Here he built a huge levee, on what is now the German side of the river, to control the flooding so that the area could be settled for agriculture. Wilhelmsaue has the area's only windmill, which is sometimes open as a museum. North of Seelow, Neutrebbin was a village personally founded by the king, and today it is a gem which hardly looks touched by the 20th century, let alone the GDR. The statue of Frederick in the town

square is brand new, a replica of one melted down by the GDR authorities in 1953. The one in the town square at nearby Letschin, however, is original, albeit restored, and the centre of a hilarious story involving the innkeeper at the nearby **Zum Alten Fritz** and several of his buddies, who hid the statue in a cow shed and one drunken night managed to drag it out as far as the busstop. The steeple in the town's centre is all that remains of another of Schinkel's first churches, the only one the architect did in red brick. Accommodation is available in several Gästtätte in villages nearby.

Frankfurt-an-der-Oder Verkehrsverein

Karl-Marx Straße 8a, Frankfurt-an-der-Oder, 15230 (0335 325 216). **Open** *winter* 10am-6pm Mon-Fri; 10am-1.30pm Sat; *summer* 10am-noon Sun.
If the staff's phone manner's anything to go by, don't expect an excess of help at this tourist office.

Gedenkstätte Seelower Höhen

Küstriner Straße 28a, Seelow, 15306 (03346 597). **Open** 9am-4.30pm Tue-Sun. **Admission** DM3; DM1.50 concs.

Zum Alten Fritz

Karl-Marx Straße 1, Letschin, 15324 (033475 223). **Open** 10am-6pm Tues; 10am-11pm Wed-Thu, Sun; 10am-noon Fri-Sat. **Average** DM12.
Mammoth portions of typical Oderbruch cuisine in a family-run inn typical of the area. Ask to see the Frederick the Great room, with souvenirs of the notorious battle to rehabilitate the statue.

Weimar

Lying 50km south-west of Leipzig and across the state border into Thüringen (Thuringia), Weimar is known as Kulturstadt Deutschlands ('Home of German Culture'), and was the European City of Culture in 1999. It is a small town stuffed to the gunnels with monuments to the country's literature, music and other arts.

Goethe and Schiller both lived and worked here, although the town's charm is such that you can have an enjoyable visit without having read them. Weimar was bombed heavily in the last war, but after decades of work, most of it has now been restored. Apart from writing, directing the State Theatre and working on assorted scientific theories, Goethe also held various posts in the government of Weimar. His house is now a museum, and the office where he did much of his writing has been preserved intact – complete with original desk, quills and paper at the ready.

Nearby is the more modest house (now also a museum) of Schiller, the first German to make a career out of writing plays. Both Schiller and Goethe had their plays performed at the **Deutches Nationaltheater**. The building was the assembly point of the 1919 conference which drew up Germany's first republican constitution, thereafter known as the Weimar Republic. Weimar was also the first German town to elect a Nazi-dominated council – an event which caused the Bauhaus, the famed school of design founded here, to move on to Dessau and Berlin. A small museum devoted to the Bauhaus now stands opposite the Nationaltheater.

Bach lived here and worked at the Stadtkirche St Peter und Paul on Herderplatz. The church is also known under the name Herder Kirche; it was built in 1498 in late Gothic style and renovated in early Baroque style. In the mid-19th century, when the great Austro-Hungarian composer Franz Liszt arrived, music became a focal point of town life. Today you can still see regular concerts of the highest quality at the Hochschule für Musik Franz Liszt, the music school of which Liszt was first director, in Platz der Demokratie. Check with the tourist office for concert details.

The castle and former home of the court of Thüringen is now a museum housing the **Kunstsammlung zu Weimar**, a collection of Weimar artists from the turn of the century and a superb collection of Lucas Cranach the Elder, who lived here in the year preceding his death. It stands beside a large, handsome park which also holds Goethe's summer home. The town square houses an open-air market selling local specialities like the justly celebrated Thüringer Rostbratwurst, and the **Ratskeller** has a good selection of inexpensive regional dishes. But for a choice of bars and cafés, explore the pedestrianised section of the town, especially near the Schillerhaus.

Tourist Information

Burgplatz 3, Weimar, 99421 (03643 240 021). **Open** *Apr-Oct* 9.30am-7.30pm Mon-Fri; 9.30am-5pm Sat; 9.30am-4pm Sun; *Nov-Mar* 10am-6pm Mon-Fri; 10am-2pm Sat-Sun.
Helpful, English-speaking service, which can also help with accommodation requests. WeimarCards, offering free and reduced entry to the city's museums, available here for DM20 daily.
Website: www.weimar.de

Die Kunstsammlung zu Weimar

Burgplatz 4, 99423 Weimar (03643 618 31). **Open** 10am-6pm Tue-Sun. **Tickets** DM6; DM3 concs.

Deutsches Nationaltheater

Theaterplatz, 93401 Weimar (03643 755 305; telephone ticket service 03643 755 334). **Open** *box office* 2-6pm Mon; 10am-6pm Tue-Sat; 10am-1pm Sun. **Tickets** DM9-DM40; half-price concs.

Goethe House and Museum

Am Frauenplan, 4 (03643 54 50). **Open** *Mar-mid-May, Sep-Oct* 9am-6pm Tue-Sun; *mid-May-Aug* 9am-7pm Tue-Sun; *Nov-Mar* 9am-4pm Tue-Sun. **Tickets** DM8; DM5 concs.

Ratskeller

Markt 10, 99420 Weimar (03643 641 42). **Open** 11.30am-midnight daily. **Average** DM30. **Credit** AmEx, V.

Schiller House and Museum

Schillerstraße, (03643 54 50). **Open** *Mar-mid-May, Sep-Oct* 9am-6pm Wed-Mon; *mid-May-Aug* 9am-7pm Wed-Mon; *Nov-Mar* 9am-4pm Mon-Wed, Sun. **Tickets** DM5; DM2.50 concs.

Weimar's Marktplatz – get your Thüringer Rostbratwurst here.

Hamburg

Rough trade and free trade in Germany's most independent city.

TV tower – symbol of this major media centre.

Hamburg is all about free trade. Well, that's not strictly true, most think of a different kind of trade when they think of Hamburg – the oldest trade in fact – but the wealth and reputation of this city state was built on its legacy of mercantile independence. Today it's also major media centre, it's Europe's second biggest port, it's Germany's richest city – and it's full of titty bars. It houses the most notorious stretch of sidewalk in Germany, the Reeperbahn, street of sleaze, but Hamburg has much more to offer than just titties and beer.

The Free and Hanseatic City of Hamburg holds an important place in German history. The Hanseatic League was founded here as a protected trade zone stretching along the North Sea and Baltic coasts. Hamburg has enjoyed eight centuries of free trade, and the city tends to think of itself as somewhat separate from the rest of Germany. Always a wealthy city, one in a hundred Hamburgers is a millionaire. There is also a long history of social democracy and the SPD has a virtual monopoly of power, even with its current liaison with the Green Party.

Hamburg is built on the lower reach of the Elbe, where the river is joined by the waters of the Binnen- and Aussenalster lakes. The city has more canals than Venice, most of them around the harbour area, one of the main tourist attractions.

Much of Hamburg was destroyed during the war, but restoration has been kind, leaving an attractive city in its wake. In winter, the city, set on the flat northern expanse stretching from the Dutch coast to the Asian steppes, can be bleak and bitterly cold. But in spring and summer, it is transformed by its abundant greenery. The city then has a relaxing feel, with canals, lakes and parks to laze around, recuperating from heavy club nights in St Pauli, Hamburg's nightlife hub.

There is a ferry service from Newcastle or Harwich, but if travelling from Berlin, the four-hour train journey will land you at Hamburg's main railway station, built in the 19th century to resemble a fortress. Inside there's an efficient tourist office and scores of fast-food joints, one offering the local delicacy of roast mushrooms. Immediately outside you'll find sleaze a go-go after dark, with gaggles of junkies and their dogs hanging out by the main entrance. Watch your pockets.

Nearby are a number of reasonably priced hotels, some of them brothels, plus the **Deutsches Schauspielhaus** ('German Playhouse') with its mainstream programme and occasional live, large-screen video relays shown in the square. Nearby is the top museum in town, the **Kunsthalle** ('Art Gallery') on Glockengießerwall, with its extensive collection of German medieval, 19th-century, Impressionist and Brücke movement artists.

Also walking distance from the station is the area of St Georg, packed with hotels. From here, down café-lined Lange Reihe, leafy Danziger Straße, and seedy Steindamm, you'll find your vision soon blurred by concrete and steel. Welcome to the home of the one-in-a-hundred Hamburgers, the city's commercial quarter. A few half-decent nightclubs shine out amid the faceless commerce, but you might be better off exploring the pedestrianised old town, where you'll find one of the oldest breweries in Germany, **Gröningers**, serving home-brewed dark and light beers.

To go further afield, city transport is integrated and efficient, with day cards, three-day cards and museum-friendly Hamburg Cards available.

The Hafengelände – Hamburg's heart.

But, let's face it, you're all going to be heading to the Reeperbahn (served by U- and S-Bahn stops U3 St Pauli or S1/S2 Reeperbahn), just west of the centre. Unrivalled for its permissiveness, the Reeperbahn is a long, neon strip of fun and vice, deliciously corrupt, there for the taking, ripe for the trawling. In fact, it runs practically to the harbour, which originally provided it with boatloads of pleasure-hungry seafaring clientèle. You'll still see them on the town, stumbling into each other in the Reeperbahn's raucous drinking bars, kebab joints and bordellos. Anthropologists would have a field day in the dreg-friendly Leihnitz at number 22, for example, but after a while it all becomes one big binge blur of bars, walk-up hotels and drug dealers. Broken glass, cigarette ends and used condoms scatter the sticky pavement every morning. The Star Club – where The Beatles first grew up – was at Große Freiheit 39, just off the Reeperbahn. Indeed, off Reeperbahn is often a better place to be, particularly the streets leading from Hans-Albertz-Platz, Hamburger Berg and Große Freiheit itself. Louche cabaret sounds fill the air. Seedier still is Herbertstraße. This is the side street of sleaze, bordered off by a metal barriers, eerily quiet as punters wander around gaping at the women of varying age and beauty tapping at them from illuminated bay windows.

Leaving lust aside, Hamburg has bars to suit all tastes, all serving local Astra beer and shots of Sauer, bitter lemon mixed with any spirit to hand. At the harbour end of the Reeperbahn lies Hafenstraße, once the scene of pitched territorial battles between riot police, squatters, punks,

pinkos, anarchists and diehard soapdodgers. As if in their honour, some oddly interesting, transient bars and clubs can sometimes be found in saggy-breasted stripjoints. Standing out from the bunch is the Golden Pudles Club, near Landungsbrücke U-Bahn stop, an old favoured nightspot for locals in the know. You'll also find Harry's Bazaar, a musty, decidedly bizarre junk shop where sailors come to offload their sharktooth necklaces, stuffed armadillos and other weird souvenirs picked up on their travels.

Rather quieter but no less interesting is the traditional workers' district of St Pauli, just north of the Reeperbahn, with its populist football club. Although the club are in decline, their spiky-haired fans sing on, spurred on by the tacky jukebox in the Clubheim bar more than by the sorry action on the pitch. Around the ground hides a dark network of narrow streets and tiny, cheap restaurants.

To the west of St Pauli stands Altona. Here the streets are lined with handsome villas and rows of smaller cottages, but the biggest attraction for the visitor is the range of international restaurants, particularly Portuguese, a legacy of Altona's traditional welcome mat to foreign residents. Also you can get great views of the Elbe from Altonaer Balkon Hill, the sandy shore down below a favoured bathing spot in good weather.

Other less promiscuous activities include regular tours of Hamburg's big harbour (Hafengelände) and visits to the market there early Sunday mornings, fishermen diligently landing their hauls while onlookers test out that first beer of the day at one of the dozens of open-air stalls.

The best time to visit the city is in the spring. On 7 May the city celebrates Überseetag (Overseas Day), which commemorates Frederick Barbarossa's decree giving Hamburg the right to trade freely on the lower Elbe in 1189. The anniversary itself is straddled by a variety of events all week, with an outdoor music festival taking up much of the available public space, given over to rock, folk, jazz and classical concerts.

Tourismus-Zentrale Hamburg
Steinstraße 7, Hamburg, 20095 (040 300 510).
Open 8.45am-5.15pm Mon-Fri.

Deutsches Schauspielhaus
Kirchenallee 39, Hamburg, 20099 (040 248 713).
Open box office 10am-6pm Mon-Sat; 10am-1pm Sun.
Tickets prices vary. **Credit** AmEx, DC, MC, V.

Gröningers Brewery
Gröninger Braukeller, Ost-West-Straße 47,
Hamburg, 20457 (040 331 381). **Open** 11am-
midnight Mon-Fri; 5pm-midnight Sat. **Credit** AmEx,
DC, MC, V. **Average** (meal) DM38.

Kunsthalle
*Glockengießerwall 1, Hamburg, 20095 (040 4285
42612).* **Open** 10am-6pm Tue-Sun. **Tickets** DM8;
DM4 concs.

Prague

Europe's most enchanting city is only a short hop from Berlin.

Less than five hours from Berlin by train – a beautiful journey on the stretch south of Dresden as the line winds through the mountains along the Elbe – Prague is both one of Europe's most stunning cities and a complete contrast to Berlin.

Unlike most European metropolises, Prague was never bombed. It still retains the look, feel and smell of genuine medieval stonework – the scent of old Europe. There's something ghostly, something dark, something inspirational about this ancient city, whose ancient buildings have survived the tragic events of the last millennium with barely a scratch. Prague is a city people come to visit for a few weeks and end up staying for years. But if you've only got a weekend, it's still more than worthwhile to surrender yourself to its mystery and confusion.

Built around a bend of the Vltava river, Prague first grew into a major town to support the Přemyslid dynasty in the early 9th century.

Above its left bank, Prague Castle and the looing towers of St Vitus' Cathedral dominate, with the roofs of Malá Strana, the traditional craftsmen's quarter, reaching down to the river. Charles Bridge links Malá Strana to the flat, twisting, medieval streets of Old Town on the right bank. This district's north-west corner makes up the eerily quiet former Jewish ghetto of Josefov. Franz Kafka mourned the loss of ghetto life a generation earlier when Josefov was cleared and rebuilt into Paris-style Art Nouveau boulevards. But the cleanup, fortunately, never really took. Acid rain, unregulated diesel smoke, and a millennium of cursory maintenance have slowly moulded façades into an architectural jigsaw that is unmatched anywhere. Romanesque, Gothic, Baroque, Neo-Classical, Art Nouveau, Cubist, Art Deco and Functionalist, all squeezed in side-by-side.

Bordering Prague 1 to the east is gritty Žižkov, Prague 3. To the south are Prague 2's Nové Město and leafy Vinohrady, where the lanes widen into trafficked thoroughfares lined with graceful apartment blocks, and less graceful shops and eateries. Bordering Prague 1 to the north are the rambling parks and overlooked cafés of Prague 7's Holešovice and Prague 6's Hradčanská districts.

Getting around town is cheap, thanks to a three-line metro system and a thorough network of trams. The yellow ticket-dispensing machines, however, are fiendishly complicated – it may be easier to buy a strip of Kč12 tickets from any news-

Perfectly preserved – St George's Basilica.

stand, and validate one for an hour's or 90 minutes' travel, depending on the time of day. Only take a taxi as a last resort or call one of the few honest ones like Profi (1088) or AAA (1080). Better yet, walk. Prague lends itself to sightseeing on foot.

The city's icon is Hradčany, the Castle District, site of the Castle of Kafka fame, once the Old Royal Palace, now the Presidential one, home to a thousand years of Czech history. Attractions here are in the third courtyard: the spires and stained glass of St Vitus' Cathedral and the perfectly preserved baroque façades of St George's Basilica.

Although steep, you'll find the climb a welcome relief from the crowds swarming the Old Town, or Staré Město, with its Old Town Square (Staroměstské náměstí), an astonishing jumble of Baroque and medieval structures. All visitors gravitate here, not least to see the 15th-century Astronomical Clock strike on the hour. Most, however, leave disappointed, badgered by gift-sellers, and in need of a nearby beer.

From Staré Město, one option is to walk down twisting, cobbled Karlova which leads to another of the city's icons, Charles Bridge (Karlův most), lined with pickpockets, backpackers and two rows

Glazed expression – St Vitus' Cathedral.

but caters to more commercial sounds. All the best DJs from the above places also pull shifts at the recently opened megaclub Karlovy lázně at the Old Town end of Charles Bridge. For something more off-the-wall, Železne Dveře (Jilská 18), is a louche lounge, offering flaming abinsthe, flaming blondes and flaming hangovers, run by the same imaginative management team responsible for De Lux, at the lower end of Wenceslas Square, a club/restaurant of taste. Both are open until 4am.

Whereas De Lux offers Vietnamese specials, the average local *hostinec* will serve bog-standard Bohemian fare, a steadfast supply of schnitzel, *guláš* and dumplings. For a decent bite of something local try U medvídků (Na Perštýně 7) or U Ševce Matouše (Loretánské náměstí 4). The riverside terrace at Kampa Park (Na Kampě 8b) serves up seafood to the landlocked. Others are fusing Bohemian traditional with continental, even Californian, as seen at Gargoyle's (Opatovická 5, 2491 6047) and the adjoining Red Room. The posh, crystal-chandeliered Bellevue (Smetanovo nábřeží 18, 2222 1438) marks the high end of the trend, while the cosy and cheap Globe Bookstore and Coffeehouse (Janovského 14, 667 1261) feeds the foreign masses.

Accommodation in Prague does not deliver particularly good value for money, but a reasonable compromise is the Hotel Sax (Jánský vršek 3, 538 422) or the nearby Penzion Dientzenhofer (Nosticova 2, 531 672) – book ahead. Another small, and notable charmer, above a 17th-century pub on Kampa Island, is Na Kampě 15 (5731 8996).

Two comfortable hostels are the former police jail Pension Unitas at Bartolomějská 9 (232 7700) in the Old Town, where Václav Havel was once held, and the Penzion Chaloupka, at Nad hradním vodojemem 83 (2051 1761), a bit further out in Prague 6 but conveniently on a night tram line. Otherwise it's dorm living and backpackers at Travelers Hostels (Dlouhá 33, 2482 6662).

For faded elegance, the Grand Hotel Evropa on Wenceslas Square (Václavské náměstí 25, 2422 8117/fax 2422 4544) is Art Nouveau in the right place at the wrong time. Or you can do like Dubček and room at the Grand Hotel Bohemia (Králodvorská 4, 2480 4111), an Old Town Art Nouveau treasure once reserved for communist high officials and now efficiently run by an Austrian firm.

of statues of medieval saints. The best time to come is at night when the Castle above is floodlit – until midnight, when a switch is thrown and everything disappears into the night.

Across Charles Bridge is Malá Strana, the 'Little Quarter', with the bar-blessed Malostranská náměstí as its centrepiece square. This former Bohemian quarter is ornate, crumbling and ever more upmarket.

Another option from the Old Town Square is to head through the Powder Gate to what is referred to as Nové Město, or 'New Town' – even though it was founded in the 14th century. The main attractions here are Wencelas Square (Václavské náměstí), more a boulevard than a square, site of the 1989 demonstrations that led to the overthrow of the communist régime, and, at the far end of it, a short walk from the main railway station, the National Museum.

Although these are Prague's main attractions, any walk down a cobbled street around the Old Town can turn up an unusual bar or three, serving, as if by some miracle, both the best and the cheapest beer in the world. Although many brands will be familiar – Pilsner Urquell, Budvar, Staropramen – other local favourites such as Gambrinus or Radegast may provide equal satisfaction. These can be chased with Becherovka, a local herb liqueur, or, for the really brave, absinthe.

Prague nightlife is not sophisticated – any dip into an off-Wenceslas Square disco will tell you that – but a few trusty standbys can be relied on to offer as good a time as you're going to get west of Moscow and east of Vienna. The veteran Roxy club (Dlouhá 33) has for five years been the city's leading venue for dance music; Radost FX (Bělehradská 120) has been around even longer,

Tourist Information

Prague Information Service
Na příkopě 20 (264 0221). **Open** 9am-7pm Mon-Fri;
9am-5pm Sat-Sun.
On the main drag between Wenceslas Square and náměstí Republiky, the former state agency has events info, an English-language monthly listings booklet and an accommodation booking facility.
Branch: Old Town Hall, Staroměstské náměstí (2448 2202).

Directory

Directory

Essential information

Directory

Climate

Berlin has a continental climate, hot in summer and cold in winter, especially when the wind blows in from the surrounding lowlands. At the end of October temperatures can fall below zero and in January and February Berlin often ices over. Spring begins in late March or April. The average range of temperatures are: January to February -3°C to 4°C; March to May 8°C to 19°C; June to July 21°C to 24°C; August to September 22°C to 19°C; October to December 13°C to 3°C.

Crime

Though crime is increasing, Berlin remains a reasonably safe city by western standards. Even for a woman, it's pretty safe to walk around alone at night in most central areas of the city. Avoid the eastern suburbs if you look gay or non-German. Pickpockets are not unknown around major tourist areas. Use some common sense and you're unlikely to get into any trouble.

Customs

EU nationals over 17 years of age can import limitless goods for personal use, if bought tax paid.

For non-EU citizens and for duty-free goods, the following limits apply:
• 200 cigarettes or 50 cigars or 250 grams of tobacco;
• 1 litre of spirits (over 22 per cent alcohol), or 2 litres of fortified wine (under 22 per cent

alcohol), or 2 litres of non-sparkling and sparkling wine;
• 50 grams of perfume;
• 500 grams coffee;
• 100 grams tea;
• Other goods to the value of DM350 for non-commercial use;
• The import of meat, meat products, fruit, plants, flowers and protected animals is restricted or forbidden.

Dentists

See **Health.**

Disabled travellers

Only some U- and S-Bahn stations have wheelchair facilities; the full map of the transport network (*see pages 312-313*) indicates which ones. The BVG is slowly improving things, adding facilities here and there, but it's still a long way from being a wheelchair-friendly system. You may prefer to take advantage of the Telebus, a bus service for people with disabilities.

Berlin Tourismus Marketing (*see below* **Tourist information**) can give details on which of the city's hotels have disabled access, but if you require more specific information, try the **Beschäftigungswerk des BBV** or the **Touristik Union International.**

Beschäftigungswerk des BBV

Berlin Centre for the Disabled
Bizetstraße 51-55, Weissensee, 10388 (927 0360). S4, S8, S10 Greifswalder Straße. **Open** 8am-4pm Mon-Fri.
The centre provides legal and social advice, together with a transport service and travel information.

Blisse 14 Sozial Therapeutisches Zentrum und Café

Blissestraße 14, Wilmersdorf, 10713 (821 1091/fax 821 5673). U7 Blissestraße. **Open** 10am-11pm Mon-Fri; 10am-5pm Sat-Sun; *office* 9am-1pm Mon-Fri. **Map C6**
Café-bar at this social therapy centre, designed especially for the disabled, is popular with a mixed clientèle.

Gästehaus der Fürst-Donnersmarck-Stiftung

Wildkanzelweg 28, Frohnau, 13465 (406 060). S1 Frohnau. Berlin's only hostel that's specially adapted for people with disabilities.

Telebus-Zentrale

Esplanade 17, Pankow, 13187 (410 200). U2 Vinetastraße. **Open** *office* 7am-5pm Mon-Fri.
The Telebus is available to tourists if they contact this organisation in advance. A pass has to be issued for each user, so give plenty of notice. *See also chapter* **Getting Around.**

Touristik Union International (TUI)

Kurfürstendamm 119, Charlottenburg, 10711 (896 070). S4 Halensee. **Open** 9am-6pm Mon-Fri. Call or write for appointment. **Map B5**
Provides information on accommodation and travel in Germany for disabled people.

Driving in Berlin

Though the city is increasingly congested, particularly in areas still undergoing heavy construction, driving in Berlin, with its wide, straight roads, presents few particular problems. Visitors from the UK and US should bear in mind that, in the absence of signals, drivers must yield to traffic from the right, except at crossings marked by a diamond-shaped yellow sign. In the east side, trams always have right of way. An *Einbahn-straße* is a one-way street.

Emergencies

The following emergency services are all open 24 hours daily.

Ambulance/Krankenwagen *(112)*.
Fire Service/Feuerwehr *(112)*.
Police/Polizei *(110)*.
ADAC Auto Assistance/ADAC-Stadtpannendienst *(868 60)*.
Emergency Dental Service/Zahnärztlicher Notdienst *(8900 4333)*.
Emergency Doctor's Service/Ärztlicher Notdienst *(011 41)*.
Emergency Pharmaceutical Services/Apotheken Notdienst *(011 41)*.
Emergency Veterinary Surgeon/Tierärztlicher Notdienst *(365 4056)*.
Emergency Poison Unit/Vergiftungs Notdienst *(192 40)*.

Parking

Parking is free in Berlin side streets, but spaces are increasingly hard to find. If you park illegally (pedestrian crossing, loading zone, bus lane and so on), you risk getting your car clamped or towed away. Meters are appearing in some areas.

There are long-term car parks at Schönefeld and Tegel airports (*see chapter* **Getting Around**). Otherwise there are numerous *Parkgaragen* and *Parkhäuser* (multi-storey and underground car parks) around the city, open 24 hours, that charge about DM3 an hour.

Schönefeld Airport Car Park

(6091 5582). **Cost** *1 day* DM18; *1 week* DM59; *2 weeks* DM77. **Credit** V.

Tegel Airport Car Park

(4101 3378). **Cost** *1 day* DM20-30; *per week* DM140-180. **No credit cards**.

Breakdowns

The following garages offer 24-hour assistance. Minimum call-out charge is about DM100, but they won't take credit cards.

Abschleppdienst West

Mansfelder Straße 58, Wilmersdorf, 10709 (883 6851).

Eichmanns Autodienst

Rothenbachstraße 55, Weissensee, 13085 (471 9401).

Drugs

Berlin is relatively liberal in its attitude to drugs. Despite illegalities, possession of hash or grass has been effectively decriminalised. Anyone caught with an amount under ten grams is liable to have the stuff confiscated, but can expect no further retribution. Joint-smoking is tolerated in some of Berlin's younger bars and cafés. It's usually easy to tell whether you're in one. If in doubt, just ask – they can only say no – but be both considerate and discreet. Anyone caught with small amounts of harder drugs will net a stiff fine, but is unlikely to be incarcerated.

Drogen Notdienst

Emergency Drug Service
Ansbacher Straße 11, Schöneberg, 10787 (192 37). U1, U2, U15 Wittenbergplatz. **Open** *advice* 8.30am-10pm Mon-Fri; 2-9.30pm Sat-Sun. **Map D4**
Open 24 hours daily for emergencies, overnight stays possibl e. No appointment necessary if you're coming for advice.

Education

There are more than 160,000 students in Berlin, spread between three universities and 17 subject-specific colleges (*Fachhochschulen*). Studies last at least four years but most students take longer.

Since Reunification the lot of students has worsened. Rents have risen, libraries and lecture halls are congested, while the official budget is eaten up by Reunification programmes.

Universities

Freie Universität Berlin

Central administration, Kaiserswertherstraße 16-18, Dahlem, 14195 (83 81). U1 Dahlem-Dorf.
What is today Germany's biggest university was founded by a group of students in 1948 after the Humboldt was taken over by East German authorities. It began with a few books, a Dahlem villa provided by the US military government and a constitution which gave students a vote on all decision-making bodies. It was to be free of government interference. But today, the huge anonymous university is far from being a community of professors, tutors and students. The AStA (Allgemeiner Studentenausschuß, 'General Student Committee') elected by the student parliament, now has no decision-making powers. The financial situation is also getting worse: more students, fewer books, professors, tutors and services. *Website: www.FU-Berlin.de*

Humboldt Universität zu Berlin (HUB)

Unter den Linden 6, Mitte, 10117 (209 30). S1, S2, S3, S5, S7, S9/U6 Friedrichstraße. **Map F3**
Berlin's first university was founded by the humanist Wilhelm von Humboldt in 1810. Hegel taught here in the 1820s, making Berlin the centre of German philosophy. His pupils included Karl Marx. Other departments have boasted Nobel Prize winning chemists van t'Hoff and Otto Hahn; physicists Max Planck, Albert Einstein and Werner Heisenberg; and physicians Rudolph Virchow and Robert Koch. During the Nazi period, books were burned, students and professors expelled and murdered. When the Soviets reopened the university in 1946, there were hopes of a fresh start but these were stifled at birth. After the 1989 revolution, students briefly fought, with partial success, against plans to close some faculties. Today jobs, not political activism, are the priority. *Website: www.HU-Berlin.de*

Technische Universität Berlin (TU)

Straße des 17. Juni 135, Tiergarten, 10623 (31 40). U2 Ernst-Reuter-Platz. **Map C4**
The Technical University, or TU, started life as a mining, building and

Directory

gardening academy in the 18th century. With its focus on engineering, machinery and business, the university was given financial priority by the Nazi government. It was reopened in 1946 with an expanded remit including the social sciences, philosophy, psychology, business studies, computers and analytical chemistry. With roughly 40,000 students, the TU is one of Germany's ten largest universities. It also has the highest number of foreign students (17 per cent). There are special supplementary classes and a Language and Cultural Exchange Programme for foreigners (Sprach- und Kulturbörse, SKB, *below*), where you can take intensive language courses, join conversational groups, attend seminars on international issues and apply for language exchange partnerships. The SKB services are open to students at any Berlin university. *Website: www.TU-Berlin.de*

Sprach-und Kulturbörse an der TU Berlin

Room 3012, Franklinstraße 28-29, Charlottenburg (3142 2730/fax 3142 1117). U2 Ernst-Reuter-Platz. **Open** 1-5pm Tue, Thur. **Map C4**

Information

Studentenwerk Berlin

Hardenbergstraße 34, Charlottenburg (311 2313). U2 Ernst-Reuter-Platz. **Open** 9am-3pm Mon-Fri. **Map C4**
The central organisation for student affairs runs hostels, restaurants and job agencies.

Learning German

Goethe-Institut

Friedrichstraße 209, Mitte, 10969 (259 063). U6 Kochstraße. **Open** 9am-6pm Mon; 9am-5pm Tue-Thur; 9am-2pm Fri. **Map F4**
The Goethe Institute is well-organised, solid and reliable. Facilities include a cultural extension programme (theatre, film and museum visits), accommodation for students, and a media centre with computers. A four-week intensive course costs DM1,690; eight-week courses cost DM3,170. Exams can be taken at the end of each course.

Tandem

Lychenerstraße 7, Prenzlauer Berg, 14037 (441 3003/fax 441 5305). U2 Eberswalder Straße. **Open** 11am-2pm, 4pm-7pm, Mon-Thur; 11am-2pm Fri. **Map G1**
For DM30 Tandem will put you in touch with two German speakers who want to learn English, and are prepared to teach you German.

Electricity in Germany runs on 220v. To use British appliances (which run on 240v), simply change the plug or use an adaptor (available at most UK electrical shops). American appliances run on 110v and require a converter.

Embassies & consulates

See also *Botschaften* in the *Gelbe Seiten (Yellow Pages)*.

Australian Embassy

Friedrichstraße 200, Mitte, 10117 (880 0880). U2, U6 Stadtmitte. **Open** 8.30am-1pm, 2-5pm, Mon-Thur; 8.30am-4.15pm Fri. **Map C4**

British Embassy

Unter den Linden 32, Mitte, 10117 (201 840). S1, S2 Unter den Linden. **Open** 9am-noon, 2pm-4pm, Mon-Fri. **Map F3**

Irish Consulate

Ernst-Reuter-Platz 10, Charlottenburg, 10587 (3480 0822). U2 Ernst-Reuter-Platz. **Open** 10am-1pm Mon-Fri. **Map C4**

US Embassy

Neustädtische Kirchstraße 4, Mitte, 10117 (238 5174). S1, S2 Unter den Linden. **Open** 24 hours daily. **Map F3**

US Consulate

Clayallee 170, Zehlendorf, 14195 (8305 1200). U1 Oscar-Helene-Heim. Visa enquiries 8.30-11.30am Mon-Fri; *consular enquiries* 8.30am-noon Mon-Fri.

Health

EU countries have reciprocal medical treatment arrangements with Germany. All EU citizens will need the form E111. British citizens can obtain this by filling in the application form in leaflet SA30, available in all Department of Social Security (DSS) offices or over any post office counter. You should get your E111 at least two weeks before you leave, but it does not cover all medical costs (for example, dental treatment) so you may wish to take out

private insurance before leaving for Germany.

Citizens from non-EU countries should take out private medical insurance before their visit. German medical treatment is expensive: the minimum charge for a visit to the doctor will be DM70.

The British Embassy (*see above* **Embassies & consulates**) publishes a list of English-speaking doctors, dentists and other medical professionals, as well as lawyers and interpreters.

Should you fall ill in Berlin, take a completed form E111 to the AOK (*below*) and staff will exchange it for a *Krankenschein* (medical certificate) which you can present to the doctor treating you, or to the hospital in an emergency.

If you require non-emergency hospital treatment, the doctor will issue you with a *Notwendigkeitsbescheinigung* ('Essential Certificate') which you must take to the AOK. They in turn will give you a *Kostenübernahmeschein* ('Cost Transferral Certificate') which entitles you to hospital treatment in a public ward.

All hospitals have an emergency ward open 24 hours daily. Otherwise, it is customary in Germany for patients to be admitted to hospital via a practising physician. For a complete list of hospitals in and around Berlin, consult the *Gelbe Seiten (Yellow Pages)* under *Krankenhäuser/Kliniken*.

AOK Auslandsschalter

Foreign Section AOK
Karl-Marx-Allee 3, Mitte, 10957 (2531 8187). S3, S5, S7, S9/U2, U5, U8, Alexanderplatz. **Open** 8am-2pm Mon, Wed; 8am-6pm Tue, Thur; 8am-noon Fri. **Map G3**

Complementary medicine

There is a long tradition of alternative medicine (*Heilpraxis*) in Germany and your medical insurance will usually cover treatment costs.

For a full list of practitioners, look up *Heilpraktiker* in the *Gelbe Seiten* (*Yellow Pages*). There you'll find a complete list of chiropractors, osteopaths, acupuncturists and homoeopaths. Homoeopathic medicines are harder to get hold of and much more expensive than in the UK, and it's generally harder to find an osteopath or chiropractor.

Contraception & abortion

Family-planning clinics are thin on the ground in Germany, and generally you have to go to a gynaecologist (*Frauenarzt*).

The abortion law was amended in 1995 to take into account the differing systems which existed in east and west. East Germany had abortion on demand; in the West abortion was only allowed in extenuating circumstances, such as when the health of the foetus or mother was at risk. In a complicated compromise, abortion is still technically illegal but is not punishable. Women wishing to terminate a pregnancy can do so only after receiving certification from a counsellor. Counselling is offered by state, lay and church bodies. Counsellors are not there to talk women out of having an abortion, though may seek to persuade women to think again. The following agency can advise you:

Pro Familia
Ansbacher Straße 11, Schöneberg, 10787 (213 9013). U1, U2, U15 Wittenbergplatz. **Open** 10am-1pm Mon, Wed; 4-6pm Tue; 1-3pm Thur. **Map D5**
Free advice about sex, contraception and abortion. Best to call for an appointment. Staff speak English.

Doctors & dentists

If you don't know of any doctors or are too ill to leave your bed, phone the Emergency Doctor's Service (Ärztlicher

Bereitschaftdienst, 310 031), which specialises in dispatching doctors for house calls. Charges vary according to treatment.

In Germany you choose your doctor according to his or her speciality. You don't have to get a referral from a GP. The British Embassy (*see above* **Embassies & consulates**) will provide you with a list of English-speaking doctors, but many doctors can speak some English. They will all be expensive, so either have your E111 at hand or your private insurance document. The following are English-speaking doctors and dentists:

Dentists

Dr Andreas Bothe
Kurfürstendamm 210, Charlottenburg, 10719 (882 6767). U15 Uhlandstraße. **Surgery hours** 8am-2pm Mon, Fri; noon-7pm Tue, Thur. **Map C4**

Mr Pankaj Mehta
Schlangenbader Straße 25, Wilmersdorf, 14197 (823 3010). U1 Rüdesheimer Platz. **Surgery hours** 9am-noon, 2-6pm, Mon, Tue, Thur; 8am-1pm Wed, Fri. **Map B6**

General Practitioners

Herr Dr U Beck
Bundesratufer 2, Tiergarten, 10555 (391 2808). U9 Turmstraße. **Surgery hours** 9.30am-noon, 4-6pm, Mon, Tue, Thur; 9am-noon Wed, Fri. **Map D5**

Frau Dr I Dorow
Rüsternallee 14-16, Charlottenburg, 14050 (302 4690). U2 Neu-Westend. **Surgery hours** 9-11.30am Mon-Fri; 5-7pm Mon, Thur; 4-6pm Tue. **Map A3**

Dr Christine Rommelspacher
Gotzkowskystraße 19, Tiergarten, 10555 (392 2075). U9 Turmstraße. **Surgery hours** 9am-noon, 3-6pm, Mon-Wed, Fri. **Map C3**

Gynaecologists

Dr Lutz Opitz
Tegeler Weg 4, Charlottenburg, 10589 (344 4001). U7 Mierendorffplatz. **Surgery hours** 8am-2pm Mon; 3-7pm Tue, Thur; 8am-noon Wed, Fri. **Map B3**

Pharmacies

Prescription and non-prescription drugs (including aspirin) are sold only at pharmacies (*Apotheken*). You can recognise these by a red 'A' outside the front door. A list of pharmacies offering Sunday and evening services should be displayed at every pharmacy. For information, phone:

Emergency Pharmaceutical Services
(192 92). **Open** 24 hours daily.

Sexually transmitted diseases

For most problems, see a general practitioner.

Berliner Aids-Hilfe (BAH)
Büro 15, Meinekestraße 12, Wilmersdorf, 10719 (885 6400; advice line 194 11). U9, U15 Kurfürstendamm. **Open** noon-6pm Mon-Thur; noon-3pm Fri. **Map C4**
The BAH runs a 24-hour advice line; information is given on all aspects of HIV and AIDS. Free consultations, and supplies of condoms and lubricant, are also provided. Staff speak English.

Deutsche Aids-Hilfe (DAH)
Dieffenbachstraße 33, Kreuzberg, 10967 (690 0870). U8 Schönleinstraße. **Open** 11am-5pm Mon; 10am-5pm Tue-Thur; 10am-2.30pm Fri. **Map G5**
This is the Germany-wide version of the BAH (*see above*) and can also provide information on other sexually transmitted diseases.

Helplines

Alkoholkranken-Beratung
Alcoholic Advice Centre
Gierkezeile 39, Charlottenburg, 10585 (348 0090). U7 Richard-Wagner-Platz. **Open** advice 3-6pm Mon; 2-4pm Tue, Fri; 10am-noon Thur; *telephones manned* 9am-noon, 1-6pm, Mon-Fri. **Map B3**
Advice and free information on self-help groups. Outside consultation hours, by appointment only.

KUB
Crisis & Advice Centre
Turmstraße 21, Tiergarten, 10559 (781 8585). U9 Turmstraße. **Open** 4pm-midnight daily. **Map D3**
Free and confidential advice for people in need of emotional counselling. This is the central office; they will probably refer you to a local branch.

Directory

Overcoming the inner pigdog

Ever since Mark Twain's 'That Awful German Language', Deutsch has had something of a bad press. While French is regarded as a lover's tongue, and Italian can sound operatic even when reciting a shopping list, German is either grudgingly complimented for its philosophical exactitude, or else regarded as suitable only for snarling *verboten*. Rampant German polysyllabicisms can indeed be frightening – but then so can English words like 'polysyllabicisms'. Everyday Deutsch is actually rich in bizarre idiom and precise put-downs – many without English equivalents – and Berliners deploy them with zest. Here we present five crucial colloquialisms. Even if you don't get around to using any, they will at least make listening in to bar conversations a more edifying touristic experience.

Feierabend

Literally 'party evening', but when a barkeeper announces this at four in the morning, don't take it as an invitation to dance on the tables. It's actually a more poetic version of the English 'knocking-off time' or the cringeworthy American 'Miller time'. Bond with your local greengrocer by wishing him a schön Feierabend ('beautiful party evening') at the end of a long working day, and then nip right out for a Feierabendsbier yourself.

Scheißladen

A handy term which, once mastered, can be used time and time again on any visit to Berlin. Literally 'shit shop', but the word Laden can also mean a bar, club, restaurant or any place where you part with your money and expect value in return. When the waiter forgets your order, the barman brings you the wrong drink, or you queue for 20 minutes only to find that some obvious item is out of stock and then get barked at by the shopkeeper, communicate your disdain for their establishment by spitting back Scheißladen!

Arsch

German swearing tends to the scatalogical. Literally 'arse', Arsch is German's most common amplifier. Weather can be arschkalt (very cold), an observation might be arschklar (blindingly obvious) goods are often arschteuer (extremely expensive) and someone who talks a lot of crap and gets on your nerves is an Arschgeige ('arse violin'). To be the recipient of an Arschkarte ('arse ticket') is to get the short end of the stick, if you're verarscht (or gearscht) you've been tricked or made a fool of, and when everything's going wrong all at once you say there's an Arschprogramm going on. Be warned: Arschloch ('arsehole') is a way more serious insult than it is in English. Avoid using it unless you want to end up am Arsch (fucked up).

Geil

The German equivalent of English 'wicked' or American 'awesome' literally means 'horny' as in 'gagging for it'. Berliners deliver the dipthong with great gusto: 'Guy-ull!'

Wurst

The centrality of the sausage in German culture is evidenced in a wealth of idiom. For 'I don't care' try Mir ist Alles Wurst! – 'It's all sausage to me!'. When things are coming to the crunch, you might say Es geht um die Wurst! – 'It goes around the sausage!' And when someone's sulking tell them: Sei keine beleidigte Leberwurst! – 'Don't be an insulted liver sausage.'

Schwein

The humble porker looms large in the zoology of Deutsch. Stuck at home alone and feeling sorry for yourself, say Kein Schwein ruft mich an! – 'No pig telephones me!' – but when you've had a stroke of luck declare Ich habe Schwein gehabt! – 'I have had pig!' (The opposite is to have Pech – 'pitch'.) To express incredulity, try Ich glaube mein Schwein pfeift! – 'I believe my pig whistles!' A Schweinepriester ('pig priest') is a dishonest person, Schweinarbeit is a hell of a job, a Schweinerei is a real mess, and if a stranger's getting over-familiar, ask them: Haben wir mal zusammen Schweine gehütet? – 'Have we sheltered pigs together?' And if anyone talks of overcoming their innere Schweinehund ('inner pigdog'), they're talking about their lack of will-power.

Emergency psychiatric help

Help & Advice Line

(080 0111 0111).
A crisis telephone line for the depressed and suicidal, where some staff speak English.

Psychiatrischer Notdienst

Horstweg 2, Charlottenburg, 14059 (322 2020). U2 Sophie-Charlotte-Platz. **Open** 4pm-midnight daily. **Map B4**
The staff here are able to put you in touch with your local psychiatric clinic.

Hitch-hiking

On major routes out of the city heading westwards, you should be able to get a ride, but eastern directions may prove troublesome.

Mitfahrzentrale match car drivers to prospective travellers for a small fee. This is a safe and cheap method of travel. The following are among the many companies offering this service. *See also chapter* **Gay & Lesbian**.

Mitfahrzentrale am Alex

Alexanderplatz U-Bahn, in the hall between lines 8 and 2, Mitte, 10178 (241 5820). S3, S5, S7, S9, S75/U2, U5, U8 Alexanderplatz. **Open** 10am-6pm Mon-Wed, Fri; 10am-8pm Thur; 8am-6pm Sat; 10am-6pm Sun. **Map G3**

Mitfahrzentrale am Zoo

Zoo Station U-Bahn, platform of line 2 (direction Vinetastraße), Zoologischer Garten, Hardenbergplatz, Charlottenburg, 10623 (194 40). S3, S5, S7, S9, S75/U2, U9 Zoologischer Garten. **Open** 9am-8pm Mon-Fri; 10am-6pm Sat, Sun. **Map C4**

Internet

For Internet access on a short visit, try one of the cybercafés listed below. If staying longer, Snafu are reputed to be Berlin's best internet service provider. Call them on 2543 1112 or check their website at *www.snafu.de*. *For websites see chapter* **Further Media**

Internet Café Alpha

Dunckerstraße 72, Prenzlauer Berg, 10437 (447 9067). U2 Eberswalder Straße. **Open** 2pm-midnight daily. **Map G1**
Using one of their 12 computers costs DM6 for 30 minutes. Staff offer wine, beer and assorted snacks such as omelettes and baked camembert. *Website: www.alpha.berlinonline.de*

Internet Café Haitaick

Brünnhildestraße 8, Schöneberg, 12159 (8596 1413/ office@haitaick.de). S4/U9 Bundesplatz. **Open** 11am-1am daily.
Half an hour on one of their 11 machines costs DM6. Expect beer, wine, salads, baguettes, assorted arcade games and a scanner. Also Internet classes. *Website: www.haitaick.de*

Website

Joachimstaler Straße 41, Charlottenburg, 10623 (8867 9630/cafe1@cybermind.de). U9, U15 Kurfürstendamm. **Open** 10am-2am daily.
As much a cyber-cocktail bar as a café, they have 30 computers (DM7 for 30 minutes) and virtual reality games. *Website: www.cybermind.de*

Webtimes

Chausseestraße 8, Mitte, 10115 (2804 9890). U6 Oranienburger Tor. **Open** 9am-midnight Mon-Fri; 10am-midnight Sat-Sun. **Map E2**
Dodgy coffee and no eats, but friendly and inexpensive at DM7-9 (depending on time of day) for an hour on one of the 13 iMacs. Classes in Internet usage and free e-mail accounts. *Website: www.webtimes.de*

Jaywalking

In Berlin, as elsewhere in Germany, jaywalking is a fineable offence. Even the generally unruly Berliners tend to obey the little red man on the traffic light; ignore it and you may well find yourself reproached by solid citizens or spot-fined DM20.

Language schools

See **Education**.

Legal help

If you get into legal difficulties, the British Embassy (*see above* **Embassies & Consulates**) can provide a list of English-speaking lawyers in Berlin. If you can't afford a lawyer, contact your local *Sozialamt* ('Social Services Office', listed in the telephone book).

Libraries

There are dozens of *Bibliotheken* or *Büchereien* ('public libraries') in Berlin. To borrow books, you will need your stamped *Anmeldungs-formular* ('Certificate of Registration', *see below* **Residency**) and your passport. There will also be a small joining fee.

Amerika-Gedenkbibliothek

Blücherplatz 1, Kreuzberg, 10961 (690 840). U1, U6 Hallesches Tor. **Open** 3-7pm Mon; 11am-7pm Tue-Sat. **Map F5**
This library has a small collection of English and American literature, but an excellent collection of videos. *See chapter* **Film**.

British Council

Hardenbergstraße 20, Charlottenburg, 10623 (3110 9910). S3, S5, S7, S9/U2, U9 Zoologischer Garten. **Open** 2-6pm Mon, Wed, Thur-Fri; 2-7pm Tue. **Membership** *per year* DM40; *students and teachers* DM30. **Map C4**

Staatsbibliothek

Potsdamer Straße 33, Tiergarten, 10772 (26 60). S1, S2/U2 Potsdamer Platz. **Open** 9am-9pm Mon-Fri; 9am-7pm Sat. **Map E4**
Books in English on every subject are available at this branch of the State Library – as featured in Wim Wenders' *Wings of Desire*.

Staatsbibliothek

Unter den Linden 8, Mitte, 10102 (26 60). S1, S2, S3, S5, S7, S9/U6 Friedrichstraße. **Open** 9am-9pm Mon-Fri; 9am-5pm Sat. **Map F3**
This branch has a smaller range of English books than the above, but is still worth a visit, not least for its café.

Lost or stolen property

If your belongings are stolen, you should go to the police station nearest to where the incident occurred (listed in the *Gelbe Seiten/Yellow Pages* under *Polizei*), report the theft and fill in report forms for insurance purposes. If you can't speak German, the police will call in one of their interpreters at no extra cost.

If you've lost a credit card, or had one stolen, phone one of the emergency numbers listed below. All lines are open 24 hours daily.

Mastercard/Visa
(0697 933 1910).

American Express
(0180 523 2377).

Diners' Club
(069 260 3050).

BVG Fundbüro
Potsdamer Straße 180-182, Schöneberg, 10783 (lost property 2562 3040/customer services 194 49). U7 Kleistpark. **Open** 9am-6pm Mon-Thur; 9am-2pm Fri. **Map E5**
Contact this office with any queries about lost property on Berlin's public transport system.

Zentrales Fundbüro
Central Lost Property Office
Platz der Luftbrücke 6, Tempelhof, 12101 (69 95). U6 Platz der Luftbrücke. **Open** 7.30am-2pm Mon; 8.30am-4pm Tue; noon-6.30pm Wed; 1-7pm Thur; 7.30am-noon Fri. **Map F6**

Maps

The city map of choice is the *Falk Plan Berlin* (DM10.90) – available in petrol stations, newsagents and bookshops around town. Falk's weird folding system make the maps difficult to open right out but is easy to use once you get used to it. This map scores over its competitors by providing house numbers and bus and tram routes as well as the U- and S-Bahn, places of public interest and most of the larger structures.

Directory

Money

The unit of German currency is the Deutschmark, abbreviated to DM. The DM is divided into 100 Pfennigs (pfg).

Berliners prefer to use cash for most transactions, although the larger hotels, shops and most restaurants will accept one or more of the major credit cards (American Express, Diners' Club, Mastercard, Visa) and many will take Eurocheques with guarantee cards, and travellers' cheques with ID. In general, the German banking and retail systems are less enthusiastic about credit than their UK or US equivalents, though this is slowly changing.

If you want to take out cash on your credit card, banks will give an advance against Visa and Mastercard cards. But you may not be able to withdraw less than the equivalent of US$100. There are cash machines all over town, linked to the major international systems.

American Express

Bayreuther Straße 37, Schöneberg, 10789 (214 9830). U1, U2, U15 Wittenbergplatz. **Open** 9am-6pm Mon-Fri; 10am-1pm Sat. **Map D5**
Holders of an American Express card can use the company's facilities here, including the cash-advance service.

Banks

Most banks are open 9am-noon Mon-Fri, and 1-3pm or 2-6pm on varied weekdays.

Wechselstuben ('bureaux de change') are open outside normal banking hours and generally give better rates than banks, where changing money involves much queuing.

Reisebank AG

Zoo Station, Hardenbergplatz, Charlottenburg, 10623 (881 7117). S3, S5, S7, S9/U2, U9 Zoologischer Garten. **Open** 7.30am-10pm daily. **Map C4**
The *Wechselstuben* of the Reisebank offer some of the best rates of exchange in the city. There are other branches at Ostbahnhof and Bahnhof Lichtenberg.

Opening times

Shops can stay open until 8.30pm on weekdays, and 4pm on Saturdays, though many close earlier. Most big stores open their doors at 8.30am, newsagents a little earlier, and smaller or independent shops tend to open around 10am or later.

Many Turkish shops are open on Saturday afternoons and on Sundays from 1pm to 5pm. Many bakers open to sell cakes on Sundays from 2pm to 4pm. Most filling stations that stay open 24 hours also sell basic groceries. *See also* chapters **Shopping & Services** *and* **Nightlife**.

Bar opening times vary considerably, but many are open during the day, and most stay open until at least 1am, if not through until morning.

Passports

By law you are required to carry some form of ID, which for UK or US citizens will mean a passport. If police catch you without one, they may go with you to wherever you've left it. But if the offence is trivial and you play the dumb foreigner, you'll probably get away with a telling-off.

Pharmacies

See **Health**.

Police

You are unlikely to come in contact with the German police, unless you commit a crime or are the victim of one. Most of the time they seem fairly distant figures, buzzing around town in their green and white vans, though they come out in droves for a riot. There are very few pedestrian patrols or traffic checks (and often they announce on local radio news in which areas to watch out for them).

Post offices

Main Post Office

Budapester Straße 42, Charlottenburg, 10787 (2693 8831). S3, S5, S7, S9/U2, U9 Zoologischer Garten. **Open** 8am-midnight Mon-Sat; 10am-midnight Sun. **Map C4**
If your mail is urgent, send it from here and it should get to the UK in three to four days, to America about seven or eight days. Letters for *poste restante* should also be sent to this post office, addressed: (Recipient's name), Postamt 120, 10612 Postlagernd. They can be collected from the counter marked *Postlagernde Sendungen*. Take your passport. Fax and telex facilities are also available here, and at many modern hotels and some copyshops. Most other post offices (simply *Post* in German) are open from 8am-6pm Mon-Fri; 8am-1pm Sat. For non-local mail, use the Andere Richtungen ('other destinations') slot in post-boxes. Letters of up to 20 grams (7oz) to anywhere in Germany and the EU need DM1.10 in postage. Postcards require DM1. For anywhere outside the EU, a 20-gram airmail letter costs DM3, a postcard DM2.

Public holidays

On public holidays (*Feiertagen*) you will find it very difficult to get things done, but most cafés, bars and restaurants stay open. Public holidays are: New Year's Day 1 January; Good Friday; May Day 1 May; Ascension Day; Whitsun; Day of German Unity 17 June; Reunification Day 3 October; Day of Prayer and National Repentance third Wednesday in November; Christmas Eve 24 December; Christmas Day 25 December; Boxing Day 26 December.

Public toilets

Berlin public toilets can be pretty scummy but the authorities have been trying to clean them up. Single-occupancy, coin-operated 'City Toilets' are becoming the norm. The toilets in main stations are looked after by an attendant and are relatively clean. Restaurants and cafés have to let you use their toilets

Essential vocabulary

Most west Berliners will have at least a smattering of English, though not all enjoy using it. In the east, Russian was the first language learned at school; although English is rapidly being acquired, it is useful and polite to have at least a few German words, especially if you intend to venture out of the city.

Pronunciation

z – pronounced ts
w – like English v
v – like English f
s – like English z, but softer
r – like a french r, throaty
a – as in father
e – as in day
i – as in seek
o – as in note
u – as in loot
ch – as in Scottish loch
ä – combination of a and e, sometimes like ai in paid and sometimes like e in set
ö – combination of o and e, as in French eu
ü – combination of u and e, like true
ai – like pie
au – like house
ie – like free
ei – like fine
eu – like coil

Useful phrases

hello – *guten Tag*
goodbye – *aufwiedersehen, tschüß*
good morning – *guten Morgen*
good day – *guten Tag*
good evening – *guten Abend*
good night – *gute Nacht*
yes – *ja;* (emphatic) *jawohl*
no – *nein, nee*
maybe – *vielleicht*
please – *bitte*
thank you – *danke schön*
excuse me – *entschuldigen Sie mir bitte*
sorry! – *Verzeihung!*
I'm sorry, I don't speak German – *Entschuldigung, ich kann kein Deutsch*
do you speak English? – *sprechen Sie Englisch?*
can you speak more slowly, please? – *können Sie bitte langsamer sprechen?*
my name is…– *ich heiße…*
do you have a light? – *haben Sie Feuer?*
open/closed – *geöffnet/geschlossen*
with/without – *mit/ohne*
cheap/expensive – *billig/teuer*
big/small – *groß/klein*
entrance/exit – *Eingang/Ausgang*
push/pull – *drücken/ziehen*
I would like… – *ich möchte…*
how much is… ? – *wieviel kostet… ?*
could I have a receipt? – *darf ich bitte eine Quittung haben?*
how do I get to… ? – *wie komme ich nach… ?*
how far is it to… ? – *wie weit ist es nach… ?*

where is… ? – *wo ist… ?*
airport – *der Flughafen*
railway station – *der Bahnhof*
bus station – *der busbahnhof*
metro – *die U-Bahn*
petrol – *das Benzin*
diesel – *das Dieselöl*
lead-free – *bleifrei*
can you call me a cab? – *können Sie bitte mir ein Taxi rufen?*
left – *links*
right – *rechts*
straight ahead – *gerade aus*
far – *weit*
near – *nah*
street – *die Straße*
square – *der Platz*
gate – *das Tor*
help! – *Hilfe!*
I feel ill – *ich bin krank*
doctor – *der Arzt*
pharmacy – *die Apotheke*
hospital – *das Krankenhaus*

Numbers

0 *null*; 1 *eins*; 2 *zwei*; 3 *drei*; 4 *vier*; 5 *fünf*; 6 *sechs*; 7 *sieben*; 8 *acht*; 9 *neun*; 10 *zehn*; 11 *elf*; 12 *zwölf*; 13 *dreizehn*; 14 *vierzehn*; 15 *fünfzehn*; 16 *sechszehn*; 17 *siebzehn*; 18 *achtzehn*; 19 *neunzehn*; 20 *zwanzig*; 21 *einundzwanzig*; 22 *zweiundzwanzig*; 30 *dreißig*; 31 *einunddreißig*; 32 *zweiunddreißig*; 40 *vierzig*; 50 *fünfzig*; 60 *sechszig*; 70 *siebzig*; 80 *achtzig*; 90 *neunzig*; 100 *hundert*; 101 *hunderteins*; 110 *hundertzehn*; 200 *zweihundert*; 201 *zweihunderteins*; 1,000 *tausend*; 2,000 *zweitausend*.

by law and legally they can't refuse you a glass of water – though of course they can get stroppy about it.

Repairs

There are surprisingly few 24-hour emergency repair services dealing with plumbing, electricity, heating, locks, cars and carpentry. They usually charge a minimum of DM40 for a call-out, plus around DM25 per hour's labour, plus parts.

Water, gas & heating

Ex-Rohr
(6719 8909).

Kempinger
(851 5111).

Meisterbetrieb
(703 5050).

Lock-opening & repairs

For a local locksmith, look in the *Gelbe Seiten* (*Yellow Pages*) under *Schlösser*. Schloßdienst (834 2292) provides emergency assistance 24 hours daily.

Gas & electricity

In Berlin gas is supplied by Berliner Gaswerke (GASAG) while electricity comes courtesy of the Bewag (Berliner Kraft-und Licht AG).

Berliner Gaswerke (GASAG) Service

Torgauer Straße 12-15, Schöneberg, 10829 (787 20/ emergency 787 272). S1, S4 Schöneberg. **Open** 24 hours daily. **Map D6**

Berliner Kraft-und Licht (Bewag) AG Service

Puschkinallee 52, Prenzlauer Berg, 12435 (26 70/emergency2671 2525/heating 2672 7106). **Open** 24 hours daily.

Residence permits

For stays of longer than three months, you'll need a residence permit. EU citizens and those of Andorra, Australia, Canada, Cyprus, Israel, Japan, Malta,

End of the *Eszett*

Learning German was never easy. The language is riddled with so many rules governing grammar and spelling that even native speakers can come unstuck when choosing where to put a comma, how to hyphenate a word, or just how many words can be stuck together to form one of those interminable compound nouns.

With such complexities in mind, language experts, politicians and civil servants got together in the mid-1980s to dream up ways of making German easier. Over ten years and much philological hair-splitting later, the result was the *Rechtschreibereform* or 'correct writing reform'.

The reform includes a cut in the number of rules governing grammar and spelling from 212 to 112 and in those governing commas from 58 to 9. Compound nouns are to be broken up and the *Eszett* (ß) will be phased out.

The reformers also proposed new spelling for words to reflect their etymological roots or common pronounciation. The verb *numerieren* ('to number'), for instance, will

acquire a second 'm' to show its provenance from the noun *Nummer*. The reformers also recommended Germanifying foreign words, so that in future people will eat *spagetti* or study *geografie*.

In 1996, the federal states passed the reforms, which are also to be adopted in Austria and the German-speaking parts of Switzerland, Luxembourg, and northern Italy. They set August 1998 as the launch-date for their official introduction. The decision of some states (including Berlin) to introduce the reforms early in schools in 1997 unleashed a wave of popular protest. Parents went to court to protest against what they saw as a state diktat to change the common property of language. Writers such as Günter Grass raged against the bureaucratisation of language. Pleas were made to the constitutional court, the highest body in the land, and the matter was raised in parliament.

But despite all these protests the reforms are going ahead. By the end of 2001, the ß will be an ex-*Eszett*.

New Zealand and the United States can obtain this from the Landeseinwohneramt Berlin (*see below*).

A residence permit is free and can normally be obtained on the day of application. Appointments are not required but queues start at around 6am and you can expect a wait of up to two hours. Once you have queued it only takes a few minutes for the interviewer to process your application and grant you a visa. You will need your passport, two photos and proof of an address in Germany (your *Anmeldungsbestätigung* – a form confirming you have registered at the Anmeldungsamt, or registration office). If you have a work contract, take that along too and you may be granted a longer stay than you would otherwise.

If unsure about your status, contact the German Embassy in your country of origin, or your own embassy or consulate

in Berlin. *See above* **Embassies & consulates**.

Landeseinwohneramt Berlin

Friedrichstraße 219, Mitte, 10958 (6995). U6 Kochstraße. **Open** 7.30am-2pm Mon-Tue, Thur; 1pm-7pm Wed; 7.30am-noon Fri. **Map F4**

Smoking

Many Berliners smoke, and though the habit is in decline, there is a lot less stigma attached than in the UK or US. Smoking is banned on public transport, in theatres and cinemas and in many public institutions, but is tolerated just about everywhere else.

Telephones
Phone boxes

At post offices you'll find both coin- and card-operated phones, but most pavement phone boxes are card-only. You can

sometimes find a coin-operated phone in a bar or café. Phonecards can be bought for DM12 or DM50 at post offices and newsstands. The minimum fee for a call from a phone-box within Berlin is 30 pfennigs. The DM50 card works out cheaper in the long run by 5 pfennigs per call. Look for phone-boxes marked international and with a ringing-bell symbol – you can be called back on them. At the Zoo Station post office (*see above* **Post offices**) you can send telexes, faxes and use the metered pay-phones.

International calls

To phone Berlin from abroad, dial the international code then 49 30. To phone out of Germany dial 00, then the appropriate country-code: Australia 61; Canada 1; Ireland 353; New Zealand 64; United Kingdom 44; United States 1.

For calls to the UK, Ireland, US and Canada, charges start at DM0.48 per minute. Calls to Australia cost DM2.16 per minute at all times. You can call 0130 1118 to check the price at any time.

Most international calls are a lot cheaper (DM0.13 per minute to the UK, for example, at any time of day or night) if you simply dial the prefix 01051 before the international code.

Operator services

Alarm calls/Weckruf
(011 41).
International directory enquiries
(118 34).
Operator assistance/German directory enquiries
(118 33).
Phone repairs/ Störungsannahme
(080 0330 4000).
Telegram/ Telegrammaufnahme
(01805 121 210).
Time/Zeitansage
(011 91).
Weather/ Wettervorhersage
(0190 116 400).

Time

Germany is on Central European Time – one hour ahead of Britain, except briefly at the end of March and the end of September.

Germany uses a 24-hour system. 8am is '8 Uhr' (usually written 8h), noon is '12 Uhr Mittags' or just '12 Uhr', 5pm is '17 Uhr' and midnight is '12 Uhr Mitternachts' or just 'Mitternacht'.

8.15 is '8 Uhr 15' or 'Viertel nach 8'; 8.30 is '8 Uhr 30' or 'halb 9'; and 8.45 is '8 Uhr 45' or 'Viertel vor 9'.

Tipping

The standard tip in restaurants is around ten per cent, but tipping is not obligatory. Check for the words *Bedienung Inclusiv* (service included) on your bill. In a taxi round up the bill to the nearest Mark.

Tourist information

Berlin Tourismus Marketing

Europa-Center, Budapester Straße, Charlottenburg, 10787 (01805 754 040). S3, S5, S7, S9/U2, U9 Zoologischer Garten. **Open** 8.30am-8.30pm Mon-Sat; 10am-6.30pm Sun. **Map D4**
Good website but phoning within Berlin costs an outrageous DM2.42 per minute.
Branches: Tegel Airport; Brandenburg Gate.
Website: www.btm.de

Universities

See **Education**.

Visas

A valid passport is all that an EU national needs for a stay of up to three months in Germany. Officially, within a week of arriving you are supposed to register your address at the Anmeldungsamt ('Local Registration Office'). To find the nearest one in your district phone the Landeseinwohneramt ('State Registration Office') on 6995.Take your passport and expect to queue.

However, your passport probably won't be stamped when you arrive in the country, so unless you need to register to enrol as a student or extend your stay beyond three months, don't worry about it. *See also* **Residence permits**.

Working in Berlin

Berlin offers a wealth of opportunity for people wanting to stay and work. However, the price of accommodation is soaring and the jobs market is beginning to shrink.

The small ads in the magazines *Zitty*, *tip* and *Zweite Hand* (*see chapter* **Media**) are good places to start the search for work, but jobs are filled quickly so move fast. Teaching English is a popular choice: there is always a demand for native English speakers.

If you're studying in Berlin, try the Studentische Arbeitsvermittlung ('Student Job Service'). You'll need your passport, student card and a *Lohnsteuerkarte* ('tax card'), available from your local Finanzamt ('tax office' – listed in the *Gelbe Seiten*). Your tax is reclaimable – get details from the tax office. Students looking for summer work can contact the Zentralstelle für Arbeitsvermittlung (*see below*).

The British/German Chamber of Commerce publishes a list of English companies who have associates in Germany. There's a copy in the commercial department of the British Embassy (*see above* **Embassies & consulates**).

The German equivalent of the Job Centre is the Arbeitsamt ('Employment Service'). There are very few private agencies. To find the address of your nearest office in Germany, look in the *Gelbe Seiten* under *Arbeitsämter*.

EU nationals have the right to live and work in Germany without a work permit. UK nationals working in Germany have the same rights as German nationals with regard to pay, working conditions, access to housing, vocational training, social security and trade union membership. Families and immediate dependants are entitled to join them and have similar rights. For information about registration in Germany and residence permits *see* **Visas**.

Studentische Arbeitsvermittlung (TUZMA)

Hardenbergstraße 9a, Charlottenburg, 10623 (315 9340). U2 Ernst-Reuter-Platz. **Open** 7am-6pm Mon-Fri; 8am-1pm Sat. **Map C4**

Zentralstelle für Arbeitsvermittlung (ZAV)

Kurfürstendamm 206, Charlottenburg, 10719 (885 9060). U12, U15 Uhlandstraße. **Open** 8.15am-4pm Mon-Wed; 8.30am-6pm Thur; 8.15am-2pm Fri. **Map C4**

Directory

Getting around

Berlin is served by a comprehensive and interlinked network of buses, trains, trams and ferries. Divided into three zones – though visitors will rarely stray beyond zones 1 and 2, making it effectively a flat-fare system – it's efficient and punctual but hardly cheap. Various ticket deals are detailed below.

The respective transport systems of former East and West Berlin have mostly been sewn back together, though it can still sometimes be complicated travelling between eastern and western destinations. Even within one half of the city, journeys can involve several changes of route or mode of transport. But services are usually regular and frequent, and timetables can be trusted.

Taxis are also efficient but pricey, and subject to the same delays that currently affect traffic all over Berlin. The city is excellent for cycling – flat and criss-crossed by dedicated bike paths.

Arriving in Berlin

From Tegel Airport

Airport Information (4101 2306). **Open** 6am-10pm daily. **Map B1**
Take buses 109 or X9 (the express version) to the Zoologischer Garten (known as Zoo Station or just Zoo) in the centre of the city. This costs DM3.90. From Zoo you can connect by bus, U-Bahn or S-Bahn to anywhere in the city. You will also find rail and tourist information offices at Zoo (*see below*).
Alternatively, you can take bus 109 to Jacob-Kaiser-Platz U-Bahn, or bus 128 to Kurt-Schumacher-Platz and transfer to the U-Bahn, for which your bus ticket is valid (*see below* **Tickets & travel passes**). A taxi to anywhere central will cost around DM30-40.

From Berlin Tempelhof Airport

Airport Information (695 10). Flight Information (6951 2288). **Open** 6am-10pm daily. **Map F6**
Berlin Tempelhof is just south of the city centre on the U6 line. Connections to the rest of Berlin are easy. The U-Bahn station (Platz der Luftbrücke) is a short walk from the terminal building, as are bus connections.

From Schönefeld Airport

Airport Information (609 10). **Open** 24 hours daily.
The airport of east Berlin is a long way to the south-east of the city. A taxi to Zoo station will cost you about DM60. The 171 bus takes you to the S-Bahn, which provides easy access to the east and west, with S9 going to Alexanderplatz, Friedrichstraße and Zoo (change at Ostkreuz for Bahnhof Lichtenberg), and the S45 taking a southern route to Westend. Alternatively you can also take the 171 bus on to Rudow U-Bahn station and connect with the rest of the underground via line 7.

From train stations

Deutsche Bahn Information, Zoologischer Garten (Bahnhof Zoo), Hardenbergplatz, Charlottenburg, 10623 (0180 599 6633). **Open** 5am-11pm daily. **Map C4**
Bahnhof Zoo is the point of arrival from most destinations to the west, including Hamburg, Hanover and Amsterdam. Bahnhof Lichtenberg, out in the wilds of east Berlin on lines U9, S5, S7 and S75, is the main station for destinations to the south and east, including Vienna, Warsaw, Prague, Budapest, Dresden and Leipzig.

From bus stations

Information (301 8028). **Open** 5.30am-9.30pm Mon-Sat.
Buses arrive in west Berlin at the Central Bus Station at Messedamm 8, Charlottenburg, 14057, opposite the radio tower (Funkturm) and the ICC (International Congress Centrum). From there, continue by U-Bahn line U2, direction Vinetastraße (station Kaiserdamm), to the centre. There is no bus station in the eastern half of the city.

Public transport

The Berlin transport authority, the **BVG**, operates the bus, **U-Bahn** (underground, some of which runs on the surface), **S-Bahn** (surface rail, some of which runs underground) and tram networks (only in the eastern half of the city). These, plus a few ferry services on the lakes, are all connected on the same three-zone tariff system.

A DM3.90 ticket allows travel for two hours on all forms of transport in two adjacent zones. A three-zone ticket costs DM4.20.

Berlin is also served by the **Regionalbahn** ('regional railway') which in former times connected East Berlin with Potsdam via the suburbs and small towns that had been left outside the Wall. It still circumnavigates the entire city. The Regionalbahn is run by Deutsche Bahn and ticket prices vary according to the journey.

Renovation work on the S-Bahn system is almost complete, though there are still temporary disruptions. The final piece of the puzzle will be the northern segment of the inner Ringbahn – from Jungfernheide to Schönhauser Allee – scheduled for completion in 2002.

U-Bahn

The first stretch of Berlin's U-Bahn was opened in 1902 and the network now consists of nine lines and 163 stations. The first trains run shortly after 4am; the last ones between midnight and 1am, except weekends on the U1/15 and U9 lines when trains run all night. The direction of travel is indicated by the name of the last stop on the line.

S-Bahn

Under constant renovation for over a decade, the S-Bahn system is no longer the rattly ride through the city's 'ripped backsides', as celebrated in Iggy Pop's *The Passenger*. It's especially useful in eastern Berlin, covers long distances much faster than the U-Bahn and is an efficient means of getting to Berlin's outlying areas.

Buses

Berlin has a dense network of bus lines (155), and a restricted number (45) run in the early hours (*see below* **Travelling at night**). The day lines run from 4.30am to about 1am the next morning. Enter at the front of the bus and exit in the middle. The driver sells only individual tickets, but all tickets from the orange or yellow machines on the U-Bahn are valid. Most bus stops have clear timetables and route maps.

Tram

There are 30 tram lines, all originating in the east, though some have now been extended a few kilometres into the western half of the city, mostly in Wedding.

Maps

The Liniennetz, a map of all BVG U-Bahn, S-Bahn, bus and tram routes for Berlin and Potsdam, costs DM4.50 from ticket offices and includes an enlarged map of the city centre. A simpler, schematic map of the U- and S-Bahn can be picked up free at the same ticket offices or from the grey-uniformed *Zugabfertiger* – 'customer assistance personnel' – who can be found bored and loitering in some of the larger U-Bahn and S-Bahn stations. *See pages 312-313.*

Tickets & travel passes

Apart from the *Zeitkarten* (longer-term tickets, *see below*) and the WelcomeCard (sic), tickets for Berlin's public transport system can be bought from the yellow or orange machines at U- or S-Bahn stations. These take coins and sometimes notes, give change and have a limited explanation of the ticket system in English. Once you've purchased your ticket, validate it in the small red or yellow box next to the machine, which stamps it with time and date. If you're caught without a valid ticket you will be fined DM60 on the spot by one of the gangs of blue-uniformed officials. Ticket inspections are fairly frequent, particularly at weekends and at the beginning of the month, when they hope to collar miscreants who haven't renewed their passes.

The BVG says the current ticket system is unlikely to change in the near future, and though prices will certainly rise at some point, in early 2000 they had no increases planned.

Single Ticket (Normaltarif)

Single tickets cost DM3.90 for travel within two zones or DM4.20 for all three zones (DM2.60 or DM3 for children between the ages of 6 and 14). Your ticket allows you to use the BVG network for two hours, with as many changes between bus, U-Bahn and S-Bahn and with as many breaks as you like – an excellent system for running around town doing errands.

Short-Distance Fare (Kurzstreckentarif)

The Kurzstreckentarif (ask for a Kurzstrecke) costs DM2.50 (DM2 concessions). It is valid for three U- or S-Bahn stops, or six bus stops. No transfers allowed.

Day Ticket (Tageskarte)

The Tageskarte allows travel anywhere in two zones (DM7.80; DM5.20 concs) or in all three zones (DM8.50; DM6.30 concessions) until 3am the day after validating.

Group Day Ticket (Gruppentageskarte)

Same as the Day Ticket for a group of up to five people. DM20 for two zones or DM22.50 for all three.

Longer-Term Tickets (Zeitkarten)

If in town for a few days with a family, the WelcomeCard is the way to go. For DM29 it allows 72 hours of travel throughout all three zones with up to three under-14s. If you're in Berlin for longer, it makes sense to buy a Sieben-Tage-Karte ('seven-day ticket'), for DM40 for two zones or DM48 for all three (no concessions available).

A stay of over two weeks makes an Umweltkarte ('environment ticket') economical. Get the basic card free from station ticket offices, and then purchase the validating stamp either there, or from a machine. This costs DM99 for two zones or DM120 for all three. This works for one calendar month across the network, and is transferable to other users.

Lost property & customer services

See chapter Essential Information.

Travelling at night

Berlin has a comprehensive Nachtliniennetz ('night bus network') that covers all parts of town via 60 bus and tram routes running every 30 minutes between 1-4am. Before and after these times the regular timetable for bus and tram routes applies. In addition, the U12 (Ruhleben to Warschauer Straße) and U9 (Osloer Straße to Rathaus Steglitz) lines run all night on Fridays and Saturdays, with trains every 15 minutes.

Night-line network maps and timetables are available from BVG information kiosks at stations. Ticket prices are the same as during the day. Buses and trams that run at night are distinguished by an 'N' in front of the number.

Note: The N16 to Potsdam runs only once an hour. S-Bahn lines 3 to 10 provide an hourly service. On lines N11 and N41 the bus will actually take you right to your front door if it's close to the official route.

The BVG also operates a Taxi-Ruf-System ('taxi calling service') on the U-Bahn for people with disabilities and for female passengers from 8pm every evening until the network closes for the night. Just ask the uniformed BVG employee in the platform booth to phone, giving your destination and method of payment, since you will have to pay the full taxi fare.

Boat trips

Besides the BVG there are several private companies operating on Berlin's waterways.

Reederei Heinz Riedel

Planufer 78, Kreuzberg, 10967 (691 3782). U8 Schönleinstraße. Open 8am-4pm Mon-Fri. *May-Sept* (also fair weather days in October) daily. Map F5

Excursions are available which start in the city and pass through industrial suburbs into rural Berlin. A tour through the city's rivers and canals costs DM21.

Stern und Kreisschiffahrt

Puschkinallee 16-17, Treptow, 12435 (536 3600). S6, S8, S9 S10 Treptower Park. Open 7.30am-4pm daily.

Various cruises along the Spree and around lakes in the Berlin area. Departure points and times vary. A round trip will cost about DM15.

Taxis

Berlin taxis are numerous, pricey, reasonably efficient and frustratingly lackadaisical. You can walk half an hour in the rain without seeing a single cab, and then find two dozen parked at a rank. Often they cruise in the outside lane and can't stop even if they see you.

The starting fee is DM4 and thereafter the fare is DM2.10 per km (about DM3.36 per mile) for the first six kilometres. At night this rises to DM2.30 per kilometre (about DM3.68 per mile). For short journeys ask for a Kurzstrecke. For DM5 this will allow you to travel for 2km or 5 minutes, whichever comes first. These are only available when you've hailed a cab and not from taxi ranks. Taxi stands are relatively numerous, especially in central areas, and can usually be found near stations and at major intersections.

You can phone for a cab 24 hours daily on 261 026. Cabs ordered by phone start at DM6 rather than the normal DM4.

Most taxi firms can transport the disabled, but require advance notice.

Most cabs are Mercedes. If you want an estate car (station wagon) ask for a 'combi'. There's also a company called Berlin Taxi which operates vans capable of transporting up to seven people. Call 813 2613.

Car hire

Car hire in Germany is not generally expensive and all major companies are represented in Berlin. Look under *Autovermietung* in the *Gelbe Seiten* (*Yellow Pages*) and be sure to shop around.

Bicycle hire

The western half of Berlin is wonderful for cycling – flat, well equipped with cycle paths and with lots of parks to scoot through and canals to cruise alongside. East Berlin is no less flat, but has far fewer cycle paths and a lot more cobblestones, tram lines and holes in the road.

On the U-Bahn, there is a limit of two cycles at the end of carriages which have a bicycle sign on them. Bikes may not be taken on the U-Bahn during rush hour (defined as 6-9am and 2-5pm). More may be taken on to S-Bahn carriages, and at any time of day. In each case an extra ticket must be bought for each bike. The **ADFC Fahrradstadtplan**, available in bike shops for DM13, is an excellent guide to the city's cycle routes. The companies below will rent bikes. Or look under *Fahrradverleih* in the *Gelbe Seiten* (*Yellow Pages*).

Bikes & Jeans

Reinhardtstraße 6, Mitte, 10117 (447 6666).U6 Oranienburger Tor. **Open** 10am-7pm Mon-Fri; 10am-1pm Sat. **Rates** *per day* DM15-20. **Map F3**

Fahrradverleih

Uhlandstraße 106a, Wilmersdorf, 10717 (861 5237). U7 Blissestraße. **Rates** *per day* DM10. **Map C5**

Disabled travellers

See chapter **Essential information.**

Business

Well, you can't have everything. Contrasting with Berlin's great nightlife, expansive cultural scene and rich history, is a business sector which pretty much puts it in last place in terms of gross domestic product of all Germany's federal states.

At first glance it doesn't look that way. Berlin is the largest urban market in Germany, and with all those glittering new office buildings at Potsdamer Platz, anyone could be forgiven for thinking the place is an absolute powerhouse of business activity.

But in fact, nearly 15 per cent of the population is unemployed, and lots of the new office space is vacant or rented by temporary tenants. Referring to

the city's mountain of public debt, one lawyer recently remarked that the only people making a profit out of Berlin these days were people lending money.

That's a bit of an overstatement, harking back to the halcyon days, when geopolitical considerations kept West Berlin businesses afloat with generous grants, subsidies and interest-free loans. The legacy is a business sector inexperienced in the ups and downs of economic cycles and ill-prepared for the challenges of a free market. A further complication is that the traditional Berlin workforce was comprised of public sector drones or skilled factory workers made light bulbs, razor

blades and cigarettes – not exactly the profile you need for the third-wave industries the city is anxious to attract.

In the early 1990s, optimism ran high as the city assumed it would regain its status as a gateway to eastern Europe, becoming the headquarters of international companies poised to exploit emerging markets to the east. In fact, most companies bypassed the expensive labour and social costs in Berlin, and went straight to low-wage cities like Prague or Budapest to do their exploiting. One result is that Berlin's population did not grow as predicted, leaving investors in building projects holding the bag.

The most salient characteristic of the business

Directory

sector today is that it is financed by money from out of town. A thriving trade fair business brings in millions through trade events such as the Internationale Funkaustellung (*see chapter* **By Season**). The exhibitors spend both for their stands and on hotels and restaurants. Same with the Love Parade (*see chapter* **Love Parade**) which draws hundreds of thousands and creates a mini-boom in the tourism and retail sectors.

Experts predict that the city's extended period of slow or no economic growth has come to an end, however, and that the negative aspects of doing business here are finally being outweighed by positive factors such as the arrival of the government from Bonn, a streamlined public sector and completion of large building projects. Other observers say the business climate will remain dismal until macro-economic reforms, including lower corporate taxes, are implemented nationwide by the federal government.

PRACTICALITIES

Ideas about efficiency in Germany, based on method, not speed, are changing. Formerly things were done properly, but took forever. With the advent of computerised work stations and digital telephone lines business is a bit faster, but, frankly, with less paper to rubber stamp, a new generation of office workers is less methodical. For safety, keep a record of all your business transactions.

Be prepared for lots of form-filling. If you are signing any contracts you will need to have them notarised by a state-approved notary. By law you are required to be able fully to comprehend the terms of the contract which, if you cannot understand German, means it will need to be professionally translated. One way of avoiding this expense is to give your right of signature to a

trusted German-speaking colleague or lawyer.

Despite their workaholic reputation, Germans work fewer hours than anyone else in Europe. Lunch-hours devour afternoons and few are at their desks after 3pm on Fridays.

Finally, foreigners are often surprised at the extent of graft and corruption that accompany even small transactions in Berlin: another reason to be sure you work through a reputable law firm when doing business here.

Stock exchange

Börsengebaüde

Stock Exchange
Fasanenstraße 85, Charlottenburg, 10623 (315 100). S3, S5, S7, S9/U2, U9 Zoologischer Garten. **Open** 8am-6pm Mon-Thur; 8am-5pm Fri. **Map C4**
Individuals and small groups are allowed in the visitors' gallery during operating hours.

Börsenverwaltung

Stock Exchange Administration
Fasanenstraße 3, Charlottenburg, 10623 (311 0910/fax 3110 9178/79). S3, S5, S7, S9/U2, U9 Zoologischer Garten. **Open** 9am-5pm Mon-Fri. **Map C4**
Groups wanting to be shown round the Börsengebaüde (*see below*) should arrange the tours at these offices.

Banks

Head offices for the major banks in Berlin:

Berliner Bank

Hardenbergstraße 32, Charlottenburg, 10623 (310 90/fax 3109 2548). S3, S5, S7, S9/U2, U9 Zoologischer Garten. **Open** 9am-2pm Mon, Wed, Fri; 9am-6pm Tue, Thur. **Map C4**

Berliner Commerzbank

Potsdamer Straße 125, Schöneberg, 10783 (2653 3953/fax 2653 2746). U1 Kurfürstenstraße. **Open** 9am-6.30pm Mon-Thur; 9am-4pm Fri. **Map E5**
Has an 'International Counter', which can deal with your needs in English.

Deutsche Bank

Otto-Suhr-Allee 6-16, Charlottenburg, 10585 (340 70/fax 3407 2788). U2 Ernst-Reuter-Platz. **Open** 9am-6pm Mon-Fri. **Map C4**

Dresdner Bank

Kantstraße 81, Charlottenburg, 10623 (31530/fax 312 4041). U15 Uhlandstraße. **Open** 8.30am-2pm Mon, Wed, Fri; 8.30am-6pm Tue, Thur. **Map C4**

IKB Deutsche Industriebank

Bismarckstraße 105, Charlottenburg, 10625 (310 090/fax 3100 9109). U2 Deutsche Oper/Ernst-Reuter-Platz. **Open** 7.45am-6pm Mon-Thur; 7.45am-5pm Fri. **Map C4**

Embassies & agencies

American Embassy Commercial Department

Neustädtische Kirchstraße 4-5, Mitte, 10117 (8305 2730/fax 2045 4466). S1, S2, S3, S5, S7, S9/U6 Friedrichstraße. **Open** 8.30am-5.30pm Mon-Fri. **Map E3**

American Chamber of Commerce

Budapester Straße 16, Tiergarten, 10787 (261 5586/fax 262 2600). S3, S5, S7, S9/U2, U9 Zoologischer Garten/U1, U2, U15 Wittenbergplatz. **Open** 9am-5pm Mon-Fri. **Map D4**

Berlin Chamber of Commerce

Hardenbergstraße 16-18, Charlottenburg, 10623 (315 100/fax 3151 0278). S3, S5, S7, S9/U2, U9 Zoologischer Garten. **Open** 9am-5pm Mon-Fri. **Map C4**

Berlin Economic Development Corporation

Wirtschaftsförderung Berlin GmbH
Hallerstraße 6, Charlottenburg, 10587 (399 800/fax 3998 0239). U2 Ernst-Reuter-Platz. **Open** 8.30am-5pm Mon-Fri. **Map C3**
Help for foreign investors settling in Berlin.

British Embassy Commercial Department

Unter den Linden 32-34, Mitte, 10117 (201 840/fax 2018 4157). S1, S2 Unter den Linden. **Open** 9am-noon, 2-4pm, Mon-Fri. **Map F3**
Basic assistance and advice for British businesses.

Partner für Berlin

Charlottenstraße 65, Mitte, 10117 (2024 0100/fax 2024 1067). U2, U6 Stadtmitte. **Open** 9am-5.30pm Mon-Fri. **Map F3**
City marketing agency, funded by big companies with large stakes in the city, specialising in courting international investors.

Senate for Economics and Industry

Senatsverwaltung für Wirtschaft und Betriebe
Martin-Luther-Straße 105, Schöneberg, 10820 (787 60/fax 7876 3541). U4 Rathaus Schöneberg. **Open** 9am-3pm Mon-Fri. **Map D6**
Responsible for overall economic planning in the city. Will provide advice and guidelines for investors.

Business services

Accountants & consultants

The major international accountants and consultants are all represented in Berlin.

Bossard Consultants
Bleibtreustraße 38, Charlottenburg, 10623 (886 0694/fax 883 6958). U15 Uhlandstraße. **Open** 8.30am-5pm Mon-Fri. **Map C4**

Deloitte and Touche
Lützowufer 33, Tiergarten, 10787 (254 6803). U1, U2, U15 Wittenbergplatz. **Open** 9am-7pm Mon-Fri. **Map D4**

McKinsey and Company
Kurfürstendamm 185, Tiergarten, 10707 (884 520). U7 Adenauerplatz. **Open** 8.30am-5.30pm Mon-Fri. **Map C4**

Price Waterhouse Consulting
Lise-Meitner-Straße 1, Charlottenburg, 10589 (439 020). U7 Mierendorffplatz. **Open** 8am-8pm Mon-Fri.

Conference facilities

Messe Berlin
Messedamm 22, Charlottenburg, 14055 (303 80/fax 3038 2325). U2 Theodor-Heuss-Platz. **Open** 10am-6pm. **Map A4**
The city's official trade fair and conference organisation can advise on setting up small seminars and congresses, or big trade fairs.

Regus Business Centre
Kurfürstendamm 11, Tiergarten, 10719 (884 410/fax 8844 1520). S3, S5, S7, S9/U2, U9 Zoologischer Garten. **Open** 8.30am-6pm Mon-Fri. **Map C4**
Offices for short-term rent, multilingual secretarial services and conference facilities in two central locations.
Branch: Lindencorso, Unter den Linden, Mitte, 10117 (0130 110 311).

Couriers

A package 1kg (2.2lb) or under within Berlin will cost you about DM15-30. These companies use both motorbike and cycle couriers.

Heikosprint
(2327 6660). **Open** 7am-7pm daily.

Messenger
(2355 000). **Open** 24 hours daily.

Moskitos
(616 7900). **Open** 7.30am-7.30pm Mon-Fri.

Prices vary considerably, but a package up to 5kg delivered within Germany will cost about DM85; to the UK about DM160; and to America about DM210. It might be worth going to the post office and using their express service.

DHL
Kaiserin-Augusta-Allee 16-24, Tiergarten, 10553 (2529 4927/fax 345 7762). U9 Turmstraße. **Open** 8am-6pm Mon-Fri. **No credit cards. Map C3**
Delivers to 180 countries worldwide. Overnight to most European centres and New York.

Federal Express
Mahlower Straße, Neukölln, 12049 (0130 7573). **Open** 8am-7pm Mon-Fri. **Credit** AmEx, MC, V. **Map H5**

UPS
(0130 826630).

Estate agents

The estate agents listed here are able to do business with you in English.

Healey and Baker
Mommsenstraße 68, Charlottenburg, 10629 (882 5724/fax 882 5670). U12, U15 Uhlandstraße. **Open** 9am-5.30pm Mon-Fri. **Map C4**

Jones Lang Wooton Investment Team Berlin
Charlottenstraße 57, Mitte, 10117 (203 9800/fax 2039 8040). S1, S2, S3, S5, S7, S9, S75/U6 Friedrichstraße. **Open** 10am-5pm Mon-Fri. **Map F3**

Saddelhoff Deutschland
Friedrichstraße 60, Mitte, 10117 (201 7050/fax 201 7011). U6 Französische Straße. **Open** 8.30am-6pm Mon-Fri. **Map C4**

Office equipment

DEHA Einrichtungen
Lietzenburger Straße 48-50, Charlottenburg, 10789 (881 4011). U1 Augsburger Straße. **Open** 10am-6.30pm Mon-Fri; 11am-2pm Sat. **No credit cards. Map D4**
Office furniture and stationery.

L&W Büroeinrichtungen
Groß-Berliner Damm 73c, Treptow, 12487 (639 9630). S4, S6, S8, S9, S10 Schöneweide. **Open** 10am-6pm Mon-Fri; 10am-2pm Sat. **Credit** V.
Furniture, office software and communications technology.

Office space

Regus Business Centre
Kurfürstendamm 11, Charlottenburg, 10719 (2092 4000). U9, U15 Kurfürstendamm. **Open** 8.30am-6pm Mon-Fri. **Map C4**
Market leader in rental of temporary office space.

Lawyers

The British Embassy (*see above* **Embassies & consulates**) can supply a list of English-speaking lawyers. Here are two that specialise in commercial law and speak English:

Guentsche and Partner
Hr. Johann Peter Sieveking, Hubertusbader Straße 14a, Wilmersdorf, 14193 (825 2085/fax 825 2080). S7 Grunewald. **Open** 9am-6.30pm Mon-Fri.

Peter Evers
Oliver Platz 16, Charlottenburg, 10707 (880 3300/fax 880 3330). U7 Adenauer Platz. **Open** 10am-6pm Mon-Fri. **Map C5**

Relocation services

The following can offer assistance in looking for homes and schools, and will help deal with residence and work permits.

Hardenberg Concept
Burgunder Straße 5, Zehlendorf, 14129 (8040 2646). S1, S7 Nikolassee. **Open** 9am-5pm Mon-Fri.

Staff hire agencies

Here are two temp agencies specialising in technical and sales personnel. A secretary will cost about DM35 an hour.

City Büro
Wexstraße 1 (on Innsbrucker Platz),
10825 (854 1094/fax 854 1097).
S4/U4 Innsbrucker Platz. **Open** 8am-
4.30pm Mon-Fri. **Map D6**
Agency for temps and secretarial
staff.

Personal Partner
Tauentzienstraße 18a, Schöneberg,
10789 (213 1051/fax 213 2527).
U1, U2, U15 Wittenbergplatz. **Open**
8am-5pm Mon-Fri. **Map D4**
This agency places multilingual secretarial staff.

Translators & interpreters

See also *Übersetzungen* in the
Gelbe Seiten (*Yellow Pages*) for
other translation services. A
thousand words will cost about
DM500 at professional rates.

Amerikanisch/Englisch Übersetzerteam
Kurfürstendamm 11, Tiergarten,
10711 (881 6746). U9, U15

Kurfürstendamm. **Open** 9am-5pm
Mon-Fri. **Map C4**
Specialists in English-language
business, technical and legal
documents.

K Hilau Übersetzungsdienst
Innsbrucker Straße 58, Schöneberg,
10825 (781 7584/fax 782 2680).
U4, U7 Bayerischer Platz. **Open**
10am-5pm Mon-Fri. **Map D6**
Interpreters specialising in the
translation of legal, technical and
business documents.

Women

Berlin is an easy city to be a
woman, one of the few major
cities where women can move
around safely at night on their
own. There is virtually no
hassle from men, not even
whistling or staring. It is just
not done. In the words of one
connoisseur, 'Most German
men only become macho after
they've been going out with
you for a few years – and even
then, they wouldn't dare do it in
public'.

Women play a prominent
role in public life in Berlin,
especially in politics. More than
one third of local
parliamentarians are women.
West Berlin feminists, the most
radical in the country in the
1960s and 1970s, fought hard
for today's freedoms. One of
their legacies is an intricate network of women's organisations
– from carpenters' associations
and hotels to didgeridoo classes
and brothels. A number of
subsidised cafés and projects
have been forced to close as the
local government tightens its
belt. However, many of the
surviving women's centres are
equipped with computers, and
one even has an editing suite
(*see below*). Initiative and talent
also continue to thrive at places
such **Weiberwirtschaft** (*see
below*), a pioneering business
centre which has created
thousands of jobs for both
women and men.

This well-endowed
infrastructure is a testament to

the self-confidence of women in
a city which, over the last two
centuries, has nurtured a distin-
guised array of female
politicans, thinkers and artists.

These include intellectuals
such as Henrietta Herz and
Rahel Varnhagen von Else,
who advanced the cause of
emancipation in the late 18th
century by setting up literary
and cultural salons. Another
key figure was the communist
Clara Zetkin – after the 1871
unification of Germany she
presented her ground-breaking
Theory of Emancipation before
going on to orchestrate the
campaign for women's
suffrage. The vote for women
was eventually won in 1919, the
year which saw the murder of
another great revolutionary,
Rosa Luxemburg. During the
interwar years women began to
make significant inroads into
the world of arts and
entertainment – before being
stripped of their rights by the
Nazis. Marlene Dietrich shot to
international fame as the
femme fatale in Josef von
Sternberg's *The Blue Angel*,
and Anita Berber, immortalised
in red by painter Otto Dix,
gained notoriety as the city's
first nude dancer. After the war
it was the *Trümmerfrauen*
('rubble women') who rebuilt
the city. And in the late 1960s,
it was the women of Berlin who
instigated a nationwide protest
against the country's restrictive
abortion legislation.

It is a sad fact that, at the
start of the new millennium,
Berlin women are suffering
disproportionately from the
city's economic woes. They
have borne the brunt of soaring
unemployment, particularly
those in the east who were fired
in droves after the collapse of
the GDR. Despite this trough,
they still manage to live up to
their reputation of being feisty,
resilient, innovative and in
charge.

Help & information

The monthly German-language
women's calendar and
magazine, *Blattgold* (DM8) – on
sale at health food shops and
women's cafés – provides a
good overview of women's
events, clubs and associations.

Frauenkrisentelefon
(615 4243/615 7596). **Open** 10am-
noon Mon, Thur; 10am-noon, 7-9pm,
Tue-Wed, Fri; 5-7pm Sat-Sun.
Offers advice and information on anything and everything.

Notruf
Rape Crisis Phone Line
(251 2828). **Open** 6-9pm Tue, Thur;
noon-2pm Sun.
Advice and help on rape and sexual
harassment, as well as help dealing
with the police and doctors.

Accommodation

artemisia
Brandenburgische Straße 18,
Wilmersdorf, 10707 (873
8905/frauenhotel-berlin@t-online.de).
U7 Konstanzer Straße. **Rates** *single*

Directory

DM109-149; *double* DM170-198.
Credit AmEx, DC, MC, V. **Map B5**
A shabby elevator brings you to the
fourth floor of this art nouveau
building near the Ku'damm, where
Germany's first women-only hotel
opened in 1989. The artemisia is
comfortable and bright. Each room is
dedicated to a famous woman from
Berlin's history. There are two conference rooms, and the hotel welcomes
groups and businesswomen. Further
extras: a roof terrace; a small bar and
a Queen's Suite.

Intermezzo
*An der Kolonnade 14, Mitte, 10117
(2248 9096). S1, S2/U2 Potsdamer
Platz.* **Rates** *single* DM75; *double*
DM65. **Credit** AmEx, MC, V. **Map
F4**
Centrally located hotel with well-
priced rooms and friendly service.

Art & museums

Goldrausch Künstleinnenprojekt
*Dircksenstraße 47, Mitte, 10178
(283 2776). S3, S5, S7, S9
Hackescher Markt.* **Map G3**
Organises year-long seminars for
women artists, as well as exhibitions
at venues across the city. Leave your
details on the answering machine.

Das Verborgene Museum
The Hidden Museum
*Schlüterstraße 70, Charlottenburg,
10625 (313 3656). S3, S5, S7, S9
Savignyplatz.* **Open** 3-7pm Thur, Fri;
noon-4pm Sun. **Map C4**
The amount of art by women that is
rotting unseen in Berlin's museum cellars is alarming. With temporary
exhibitions and lectures, the Hidden
Museum tries to rescue female artists
from historical oblivion.

Baths & massage

Hamam Turkish Bath
*Schoko-Fabrik, Naunynstraße 72,
Kreuzberg, 10997 (615 1464). U1,
U8 Kottbusser Tor.* **Open** *Sep-June*
3-10pm Mon; noon-10pm Tue-Sun.
Admission DM20. **Map G4**
Daylight filters through the glass
cupola of the main hall, where women
sit in small alcoves, bathing in the
warm water of the baths. Enjoy
Turkish tea and a reviving massage
afterwards. The bustle of Berlin
seems miles away. Friendly and laid-
back, the Hamam attracts a very
mixed clientèle, from mature Turkish
women to gay German teenagers.
Thursday is children's day – children
are not permitted on Tuesdays and
Fridays. *See also below* **Women's
Centres**.

Bookshops

See also **Marga Schoeller
Bücherstube** *in chapter*
Shopping & Services.

Adhara Büchertempel
*Pestalozzistraße 35, Charlottenburg,
10627 (312 2462). U7
Wilmersdorfer Straße.* **Open** 10am-
7pm Mon-Fri; 10am-6pm Sat. **Credit**
MC, V. **Map B4**
A good selection of feminist and
lesbian literature as well as books on
astrology and homeopathy. Also oils,
tarot cards, jewellery, incense, CDs.

Schwarze Risse
*Gneisenaustraße 2a, Kreuzberg,
10961 (692 8779). U6, U7
Mehringdamm.* **Open** 10am-6.30pm
Mon-Fri; 11am-2pm Sat. **No credit
cards. Map F5**
In the Mehringhof, a courtyard
housing over 30 left-wing projects
including a kindergarten, school, bar
and bike shop, this political bookshop
sells international women's and
lesbian literature.

Business

Weiberwirtschaft
*Anklamer Straße 38, Mitte, 10115
(440 2230/infos@weiberwirtschaft.de).
U8 Bernauer Straße.* **Open** varies.
Map F2
Unique in Europe, this impressive
complex of buildings houses more
than 60 women-owned businesses,
including media consultants, lighting
designers, travel agents, dentists and
psychotherapists. Once the site of a
decrepit East German cosmetics factory, the building was taken over and
modernised by a group of female
entrepreneurs in 1992. Their aims
were to create jobs for women
(although many of the firms now also
employ men) and to help women start
up their own businesses. There is also
a café and a restaurant for those just
wanting to look around.
Website: www.weiberwirtschaft.de

Cafés

All the venues listed are
women-only. *See also*
Women's Centres (*below*)
and *chapter* **Gay & Lesbian**.

Amanda
*Humboldt-Universität, Unter den
Linden 6, Mitte, 10117 (209 30). S1,
S2, S3, S5, S7, S9/U6
Friedrichstraße.* **Open** from 7.30pm
Thur. **Map F3**
Weekly women's café on the ground
floor of the East Wing of Humboldt

University with readings, concerts
and film shows.

Begine
*Potsdamer Straße 139, Schöneberg,
10783 (215 4325). U2 Bülowstraße.*
Open 5pm-1am Mon-Sat. **Map E5**
Café and cultural centre named after
the Beginen, women who shared a
common social and economic network
in the Middle Ages. A popular meet
for all kinds of women. Hot snacks,
soups and salads available. *See also
chapter* **Gay & Lesbian**.

Schoko-Café
*Mariannenstraße 6, Kreuzberg,
10997 (615 1561). U1, U8
Kottbusser Tor.* **Open** 5pm-late
daily. **Map G5**
Part of the women's centre Schoko-
Fabrik (*see below* **Women's
Centres**) this factory-style café is
mostly frequented by the women who
participate in the many courses and
activities, or who finish their
afternoon in the Turkish bath. Cakes,
soups and hot snacks are served.
Dancing parties are held once a
month, call for details. There are also
readings and occasional
performances. *See also chapter* **Gay
& Lesbian**.

Café Seidenfaden
*Dircksenstraße 47, Mitte, 10178
(283 2783). S3, S5, S7, S9
Hackescher Markt.* **Open** 11am-9pm
Mon-Fri; 1-7pm Sun. **Map G3**
Alcohol and drug-free café.

Health

Aids Beratungen für Migrantinnen
*Skalitzer Straße 138, Kreuzberg,
10999 (615 3232). U1, U8
Kottbusser Tor.* **Open** 9am-noon
Mon; 3-6pm Tue, Thur; 11am-3pm
Fri. **Map H5**
Helpline for female immigrants
offering advice on AIDS in over 20
languages, including English.

Berliner Aids-Hilfe
*Meinekestraße 12, Wilmersdorf,
10719 (885 6400). U9, U15
Kurfürstendamm.* **Open** noon-6pm
Mon-Thur; noon-3pm Fri. **Map C4**
The Berlin equivalent of the Terence
Higgins Trust has a special service
for women.

Feministisches Frauengesundheitzentrum (FFGZ)
*Bamberger Straße 51, Schöneberg,
10777 (213 9597). U4, U7
Bayerischer Platz.* **Open** 10am-1pm
Tue; 10am-1pm, 3-6pm, Thur. **Map
D5**
Courses and lectures on natural
contraception, pregnancy, cancer,

abortion, AIDS, migraines and sexuality. Self-help and preventative medicine are stressed. Information on gynaecologists, health institutions and organisations can also be obtained. The FFGZ's archive holds an international collection of books, magazines and articles on issues concerning women and health.

Music

Lärm und Lust

Frauenmusikzentrum, Schwedenstraße 14, Wedding, 13357 (491 5304). U8, U9 Osloer Straße. **Open** varies. **Map E1**
A women's music centre providing rehearsal rooms and courses.

'Wie es Ihr gefällt'

Kulturbrauerei, Knaackstraße 97, Prenzlauer Berg, 10435 (441 9269). U2 Eberswalder Straße. **Date** November. **Map G2**
"As She Likes It" features an eclectic mix of bands, from avant-garde and classical to drum 'n' bass and techno. Set up in 1990 to provide a platform for all-female bands, it attracts top-notch artists from the USA, Japan and the Czech Republic. The standard is extremely high and men make up at least half the audience. *See also chapter* **Music: Rock, Folk & Jazz.**

Politics

Die Frauen

Feministische Partei, c/o Liz Schmidt, Manteuffelstraße 58, Kreuzberg, 10999 (612 1350). U1 Görlitzer Bahnhof. **Map H4**
Die Frauen hold monthly discussion groups on political topics. See *Blattgold* for details.

Sightseeing tours

Compania

Anklamer Straße 38, Mitte, 10115 (4435 8704/ brigitta.schilk@berlin.de). U8 Bernauer Straße. **Open** 11am-6pm Mon-Fri. **Map F2**
Housed within Weiberwirtschaft (*see above* **Business**), Berlin's first escort service for women and lesbians organises Friday night city tours which stop off at women's bars, clubs and other places of historical, cultural and architectural interest. The agency also provides individual guides for DM150. *See also chapter* **Gay & Lesbian.**

Frauentouren

Sophienstraße 32, Mitte, 10178 (281 0308/ frauentouren@t-online.de). U8 Weinmeisterstraße. **Map F3**

These popular walking tours cover more than 700 years of women's history. Visiting buildings, streets, memorials and parks, they provide an insight into the lives of prominent and ordinary women, from the washerwomen of Köpenick to the founders of the literary salons of the late 18th century. Open to both men and women.
Website: www.home.t-online.de/home/frauentouren

Sport

Seitenwechsel

Kulmer Straße 20a, Schöneberg, 10783 (215 9000). S1, S2/U7 Yorckstraße. **Open** 5-7pm Tue; 4-6pm Thur. **Map E5**
A sports club for women offering courses in badminton, basketball, aerobics, self-defence, swimming, tennis, volleyball and other disciplines. Events take place at sports centres across the city. Phone for details.

Travel

Frauen Unterwegs

Potsdamer Straße 139, Schöneberg, 10783 (215 1022). U2 Bülowstraße. **Open** 10am-2pm, 5-7pm, Mon-Thur; 10am-2pm Fri. **Map E4**
If you want to take a trip out of Berlin, you can book a women-only cultural tour with this association. Staff will organise tours for small groups, which involve meeting local people and retracing the steps of important women, as well as city trips, sporting and walking vacations, language holidays and workshops.

Women's centres

EWA Frauenzentrum

Prenzlauer Allee 6, Prenzlauer Berg, 10405 (442 5542). U2 Senefelderplatz. **Open** 10am-6pm Mon-Fri; café and gallery 6-11pm Mon-Thur. **Map G2**
The Erster Weiblicher Aufbruch ('First Feminine Awakening') was the first women's centre to open in east Berlin after the Wall came down. Women at the centre offer legal advice and psychological counselling, but you can also just pop into the café. The centre runs dozens of courses, in everything from computing and belly dancing to yoga, jewellery-making and foreign languages. It also hosts concerts, readings and regular discussion groups. The media workshop on the fifth floor is equipped with PCs, a darkroom, an editing suite, a well-stocked library and archive.

Frieda Frauenzentrum

Proskauer Straße 7, Friedrichshain, 10247 (422 4276). U5 Frankfurter Tor. **Open** 3-9pm Mon; 9am-11pm Tue; 9am-11pm Thur; 9am-midnight Fri; 11am-midnight Sat; 3-6pm Sun.
Communication centre and café for the women of Friedrichshain. Monthly programme includes exhibitions and poetry-readings as well as political debates. Also weekly meetings of self-help and conversational groups, plus courses and advisory services.

Schoko-Fabrik

Mariannenstraße 6, Kreuzberg, 10997 (615 2999). U1 Görlitzer Bahnhof. **Open** office 10am-2pm Mon-Thur. **Map G5**
Old chocolate factory turned women's centre. On the first floor there's a joinery. Women practise self-defence on the second floor. Cultural events take place in the café (*see above* **Cafés**). There is also a Turkish bath Hamam (*see above* **Baths & massage**) as well as fitness classes, language courses, bicycle repair workshops and medical advice.
Website: www.schokofabrik.de

Women's studies

FFBIZ

Danckelmannstraße 15 and 47, Charlottenburg, 14059 (322 1035). U1 Sophie-Charlotte-Platz. **Open** archive and library 2-6pm Tue; 3-6pm Thur; 3-8pm Fri. **Map B4**
A women's research, education and information centre. The huge archive contains leaflets, press cuttings, posters, exam papers and other documents. You can also read, though not borrow, books in the library.

Zentraleinrichtung zur Foerderung von Frauenstudien und Frauenforschung

Freie Universität, Königin-Luise-Straße 34, Dahlem, 14195 (838 6256). U2 Dahlem-Dorf. **Open** information and library 9-25pm Tue; 10am-6pm Wed. 10am-noon Fri.
The Department of Promotion of women's studies and research at the Free University.

Zentrum Interdisziplinaere Frauenforschung (ZIF)

Humboldt-Universtät, Sophienstrasse 22a, Mitte, 10178 (3088 2301). U8 Weinmeisterstraße. **Open** information and documentation 9am-noon Mon-Fri.
Gender Studies Department of Humboldt Uni organises seminars and lectures and stores information relevant for women's research.
Website: www.hu-berlin.de

Further media

Books

We've chosen these books for quality and interest as much as for availability. Most are currently in print, but some will only be found in libraries or second-hand shops. The date given is that of the first publication in English.

Fiction

Deighton, Len: *Berlin Game, Mexico Set, London Match* (London 1983, 1984, 1985)
Epic espionage trilogy with labyrinthine plot set against an accurate picture of 1980s Berlin. The next six books in the series aren't bad either.
Deighton, Len: *Funeral In Berlin* (London 1964)
Best of Deighton's 1960s novels.
Döblin, Alfred: *Berlin-Alexanderplatz* (London 1975)
Devastating expressionist portrait of the inter-war underworld in working class quarters of Alexanderplatz.
Eckhart, Gabriele: *Hitchhiking* (Lincoln, Nebraska 1992)
Short stories viewing East Berlin through the eyes of street cleaners and a female construction worker.
Grass, Gunther: *Local Anaesthetic* (New York 1970)
The Berlin angst of a schoolboy who threatens to burn a dog outside a Ku'damm café to protest the Vietnam War is firmly satirised, albeit in Grass's irritating schoolmasterly way.
Harris, Robert: *Fatherland* (London 1992)
Alternative history and detective novel set in a 1964 Berlin as the Nazis might have built it.
Isherwood, Christopher: *Mr Norris Changes Trains, Goodbye To Berlin* (London 1935, 1939)
Isherwood's two Berlin novels, the basis of the movie *Cabaret*, offer finely drawn characters and a sharp picture of the decadent city as it tipped over into Nazism.
Johnson, Uwe: *Two Views* (New York 1966)
Love story across the East-West divide, strong on the mood of Berlin in the late 1950s and early 1960s.
Kerr, Philip: *Berlin Noir* (London 1994)
The Bernie Gunther triology now available in one volume, about a private detective in Nazi Berlin.
Le Carré, John: *The Spy Who Came In From The Cold* (London 1963)
The prime shot-going-over-the-Wall thriller.

Markstein, George: *Ultimate Issue* (London 1981)
Stark thriller of political expediency leading to uncomfortable conclusion about why the Wall went up.
McEwan, Ian: *The Innocent* (London 1990)
Tale of naive young Englishman recruited into Cold War machinations with tragi-comic results.
Müller, Heiner: *The Battle* (New York 1989)
Collection of plays and pieces strong on the grimness of the Stalinism and false temptations from the West.
Nabokov, Vladimir: *The Gift* (New York 1963)
Written and set in 1920s Berlin, where impoverished Russian émigré dreams of writing a book very like this one.
Schneider, Peter: *The Wall Jumper* (London 1984)
Somewhere between novel, prose poem and artful reportage, a meditation on the madhouse absurdities of the Wall.

Children

Kästner, Erich: *Emil And The Detectives* (London 1931)
Classic set mostly around Zoo Station and Nollendorfplatz.

Biography & Memoir

Baumann, Bommi: *How It All Began* (Vancouver, 1977)
Frank and often funny account of the Berlin origins of West German terrorism, by a former member of the June 2nd Movement.
Bielenberg, Christabel: *The Past Is Myself* (London 1968)
Fascinating autobiography of an English woman who married a German lawyer and lived through the war in Berlin.
F, Christiane: *H – Autobiography Of A Child Prostitute And Heroin Addict* (London 1980)
Stark account of life around the housing estates and heroin scene of 1970s West Berlin. Later filmed as *Christiane F*.
Friedrich, Ruth Andreas: *The Berlin Underground 1938-45* (New York 1947)
A few courageous souls formed anti-Nazi resistance groups. The journalist-author's diaries capture the day-to-day fear.
Millar, Peter: *Tomorrow Belongs To Me* (London 1992)
Memoir of a Prenzlauer Berg local pub by a former East Berlin Reuter's correspondent.
Rimmer, Dave: *Once Upon A Time In The East* (London 1992)
The collapse of communism seen stoned and from ground level – strange tales of games between East

and West Berlin and travels through assorted East European revolutions.
Schirer, William L: *Berlin Diaries* (New York 1941)
Foreign correspondent in Berlin from 1931-1941 bears appalled witness to Europe's plunge into Armageddon.

History

Friedrich, Otto: *Before The Deluge* (New York, 1972)
Vivid and entertaining portrait of Berlin in the 1920s, much of it based on interviews with those who survived what followed.
Garton Ash, Timothy: *We The People* (London 1990)
Instant history of the 1989 revolutions.
Gelb, Norman: *The Berlin Wall* (New York 1986)
Gripping narrative history of how the Wall went up.
Jelavich, Peter: *Berlin Cabaret* (Harvard 1993)
Definitive history of Berlin cabaret from 1901 to Nazi times.
McElvoy, Anne: *The Saddled Cow* (London 1992)
Lively history of East Germany by a former Berlin *Times* correspondent.
Read, Anthony and Fisher, David: *Berlin – The Biography Of A City* (London 1994)
Readable, lightweight history.
Richie, Alexandra: *Faust's Metropolis* (London, 1998)
The most detailed and exhaustive one-volume history of Berlin, but a little too heavy for holiday reading and with a rather too right-wing agenda.
Schirer, William L: *The Rise And Fall Of The Third Reich* (New York 1960)
Still the most readable history of Nazi Germany.
Tusa, Ann & John: *The Berlin Blockade* (London 1988)
Absorbing account of the 11 months when the Allied sector was fed from the air and Berlin, Germany and Europe proceeded to fall into two.

Architecture

Ladd, Brian: *The Ghosts of Berlin: Confronting German History in the Urban Landscape* (Chicago, 1997)
Erudite and insightful look into the relationship between architecture, urbanism and Berlin's violent politi cal history.
Berlin-Brandenburg – An Architectural Guide (Berlin 1993)
Berlin by building, with quirky text in both English and German.
Berlin: Open City (Berlin 1999)
Excellent guide to both new building and extant architectural curiosities, built around city walks excellently detailed in fine fold-out maps.

Miscellaneous

Bertsch, Georg C & Hedler, Ernst: *SED* (Cologne 1990)
Schöne Einheits Design: over 200 illustrations of crazy East German consumer product designs.

Friedrich, Thomas: *Berlin – A Photographic Portrait Of The Weimar Years 1918-1933* (London 1991)
Superb photographs of lost Berlin, its personalities and its daily life, with a foreword by Stephen Spender.

Discography

From Brecht to Bowie, from Marlene to Malaria!, from Tangerine Dream to techno – 50 essential Berlin releases.

AG Geige: *Raabe?* (Zensor)
One of the first post 1989 discs to emerge from the East Berlin underground came from a bizarre electronica outfit rooted in The Residents and Die Tödliche Doris.

Ash Ra Tempel: *Join Inn* (Temple/Spalax)
The 1972 hippy freakout incarnation of guitarist Manuel Göttsching, before he was reborn as techno's most baffling muse.

Meret Becker: *Noctambule* (Ego)
Actress/chanteuse Becker restages Weimar alongside Berliner Krankheit classics like Neubauten's 'Schwarz'.

The Birthday Party: *Mutiny/The Bad Seed EP* (4AD)
Nick Cave and cohorts escaped drab London for the fevered creativity of early 1980s Berlin to record their two most intense EPs, here compressed into one volatile CD.

David Bowie: *'Heroes'* (EMI)
In which Bowie romanticises the Wall and captures the atmosphere of (misspelt) 'Neuköln'.

David Bowie: Low (EMI)
Begun in France, completed at Hansa Studios, the album that heralded Bowie's new career in a new town.

Brecht/Weill: *Die Dreigroschenoper Berlin 1930* (Teldec)
Historic shellac transcriptions from 1930 featuring a young and shrill Lotte Lenya, who also contributes a brace of *Mahagonny* songs.

Peter Brötzmann: *No Nothing* (FMP)
Uncharacteristically introspective recording from the sax colossus of German improvisation for Berlin's vital Free Music Production label, which he co-founded 30 years ago.

Caspar Brötzmann/FM Einheit: *Merry Christmas* (Blast First/Rough Trade Deutschland)
Guitarist son Caspar is no less noisy than père Brötzmann, especially on this frenzy of feedback and distortion kicked up with ex-Neubauten man-mountain FM Einheit on, er, stones.

Ernst Busch: *Der Rote Orpheus/Der Barrikaden Tauber* (BARBArossa)
Two-CD survey of the great revolutionary tenor's 1930s recordings covers Brecht, Eisler and Weill, plus his morale boosters for the Spanish International Brigades.

Nick Cave: *From Her To Eternity* (Mute)
The Australian expat in best Berlinerisch debauched and desperate mode, with a title track later featured in *Wings of Desire*.

Crime & The City Solution: *Paradise Discotheque* (Mute)
Underrated Berlin-Australian émigré group's finest disc (1990) is an oblique commentary on the heady 'neo-black market burnt-out ruins' amorality of the immediate post-1989 era.

DAF: *Kebabträume* (Mute)
Exhilarating German punk satire of Berlin's cold war neuroses, culminating in the coda 'We are the Turks of tomorrow'.

Marlene Dietrich: *On Screen, Stage And Radio* (Legend)
From 'I Am The Sexy Lola' through 'Ruins Of Berlin', the sultry Schöneberg songstress embodies the mood of decadent Berlin.

Effective Force: *Illuminate The Planet* (MFS)
Berlin ambient techno, here represented by Johnny Klimek and Paul Browse, struggles optimistically towards the light.

Einstürzende Neubauten: *Eclipse Of The Sun EP* (Mute/Rough Trade Germany)
Recorded in the run-up to their year 2000 celebrations of two decades spent in a state of permanent collapse, *Eclipse* shades in a more reflective side to Neubauten's destructive character.

Alec Empire: *The Geist Of…* (Geist)
Wonderful triple CD compilation of ATR mainman Empire's less combative electronica explorations for Frankfurt brainiac label Force Inc/Mille Plateaux.

Thomas Fehlmann: *one to three. Overflow. Ninenine/nd* (R&S)
Berlin techno's backroom 'fixer' and occasional Orb member consolidates a decade's worth of ideas that electronica was in too much of a rush to finish properly at the time.

Manuel Göttsching: *E2-E4* (Racket)
The great lost waveform guitar album by the ex-Ash Ra Tempel leader beloved by Berlin technoheads.

Gudrun Gut & Various: *The Ocean Club* (Alternation)
Ex-Malaria! member Gudrun Gut's Ocean Club is a congenial cyberport for ambient song collaborations between singers, artists and programmers as disparate as Blixa Bargeld, Anita Lane, Katherine Franck, Thomas Fehlmann and Johnny Klimek.

Die Haut: *Head On* (What's So Funny About)
Avantish Berlin equivalent of The Ventures lay down Morricone-meets-Loony-Tunes backdrops for guest singers like Alan Vega, Lydia Lunch, Kim Gordon and Jeffrey Lee Pierce.

Anita Lane: *Dirty Pearl* (Mute)
The only album to date from Nick Cave's former muse anthologises her legendary unreleased Birthday Party collaboration 'The Fullness Of His Coming', alongside work with Blixa Bargeld, Mick Harvey, Alex Hacke and Die Haut.

Liaisons Dangereuses: *Liaisons Dangereuses* (Roadrunner)
Formed by Ex-DAF member Chrislo Haas, their solitary 1982 album of chipped beats and industrial atmospheres was a key influence on Detroit's techno pioneers.

Malaria!: *Compiled* (Moabit Musik)
What with their telltale songtitles – 'Passion', 'Jealousy', 'Power' and 'Death' – and suffocating swirls of synths and heavy-stepping beats, Malaria! was girl-pop, Berlin-style.

Maurizio: *M* (M)
Essential CD compilation of Basic Channel mainman Moritz Von Oswald's vinyl releases, which lights up Chicago house with streaming beats diverted from the Berlin-Detroit techno grid.

Monolake: *Hong Kong* (Chain Reaction)
Again from the Basic Channel family, Monolake's debut album is an improbable fusion of cool central European electronica and sub-tropical humidity, rippling with strangely distressed pulses.

Pole: *CD1* (Kiff SM)
Ex-Basic Channel engineer Stefan Betke is now at the cutting edge of the digidub school of blunted beats and vinyl glitches.

Iggy Pop: *The Idiot* (Virgin America)
With Bowie in the producer's chair, Iggy begins to absorb the influence of early German electronica and the city of bright, white clubbing.

Iggy Pop: *Lust For Life* (Virgin America)
Way back in West Berlin, Iggy the passenger cruises through the divided city's ripped-back sides and finds himself full of lust for life.

Lou Reed: *Berlin* (RCA)
Although he'd never even been to the city, Lou somehow still got it right in this melancholy *Meisterwerk*.

Spacebow: *Big Waves* (Noteworks)
Extraordinary set of reverberating metallic sound sculptures hewn from Berlin-based American expatriate artist Robert Rutman's steel cellos.

Stereo Total: *My Melody* (Bungalow)
Demented chansons with cheesy lounge backing – Mitte's kitsch aesthetic plus a Francophone spin.

Tangerine Dream: *Zeit* (Jive Electro)
Where cosmic consciousness and electronic minimalism first met by the Wall.

Terranova: *Close The Door* (K7)
Dark and intelligent trip hop from the WMF axis, featuring guest appearance by Tricky.

Die Tödliche Doris: *Die Unsichtbare 5te LP Materialisiert Als CD* (Die Tödliche Doris Schallplatten)
The 1980s Berlin dada trio's only CD is the product of the union of two separate vinyl albums played simultaneously.

Ton Steine Scherben: *Keine Macht Für Niemand* (David Volksmund)
Ernst Busch reincarnated as the early 1970s rock commune which provided Kreuzberg's anarchists with their most enduring anthems.

U2: *Achtung Baby!* (Island)
It took newly reunified Berlin to inspire the U2 album for people who don't like U2.

Paul van Dyk: *Seven Ways* (MFS)
Eisenhüttenstadt's prime export is trance's one-trick pony, but here shows it off at its best.

Various: *Als Die Partisanen Kamen* (Zensor)
Definitive roundup of great lost West Berlin underground 'hits' from the golden period (1979-83), including Mania D, Rainy Day Women, Neubauten and Borsig's 'Hiroshima'.

Various: *Assorted Stadtansichten* (MFS)
The MFS stable circa 1999 respond to the changing cityscape and honour the innovators of Berlin techno. Selection includes Corvin Dalek, Chris Zippel, Cal-Q-Lator and Cybersecrecy.

Various: *Das Beste aus der DDR Parts I-III* (Amiga)
Three-part retrospective of East German rock, divided into rock, pop and 'Kult', including such Ostalgia stalwarts as Puhdys, Silly and Karat plus Sandow's alternative anthem 'Born in the GDR' and an early Nina Hagen ditty.

Various: *Basic Channel* (Basic Channel)
BC's Mark Edwardus and Moritz Von Oswald mix down their nine vinyl releases into a seamless 66-minute mix that transmutes Berlin-Detroit-Chicago beats into Tarkovsky-like atmospheres.

Various: *Berlin 1992* (Tresor)
On the first of several Tresor compilations Berlin techno is captured in its early, apocalyptic phase. Includes Love Parade anthem 'Der Klang der Familie' by 3Phase (at that time, Dr Motte & Sven Röhrig).

Various: *Cabaret: Music From The Original Soundtrack* (MCA)
Life is a cabaret, old chum: the very definition of the Berlin myth.

Various: *Digital Hardcore Recordings... Riot Zone* (DHR)
Atari Teenage Riot's 1997 riotbeat label compilation also showcases the anarcho-comicbook radicalism of acolytes Shizuo, Christoph De Babalon and EC8OR.

Various: *Freischwimmer* (Kitty-Yo)
Sampler covering five years of work on Mitte's premier post-rock indie label. Acts include Laub, Tarwater, Raz O'Hara, Gonzalez.

Various: *Tranceformed From Beyond* (MFS)
The compilation that defined Berlin trance. The segued selection includes Cosmic Baby, Microglobe, Effective Force and others.

Vermooste Vlöten: *ngongo* (Flittchen)
Nico-like debut from most promising signing of women-orientated label run by former Lassie Singer Christiane Roesinger.

Westbam: *A Practising Maniac At Work* (Low Spirit)
Album that effectively summarises the best of Berlin's best-known DJ, veering from stomping techno to twisted disco.

Websites

A selection of the best Berlin-orientated websites.

General information
www.timeout.com/berlin/index/html
Naturally, we think this is pretty good, with numerous extracts from this book, in case you haven't read it all yet, plus the useful International Agenda, a weekly calendar of things to do and see, written by residents.
www.berlinfo.com
Technologically primitive and with a bad case of apologising for itself, it's produced by an idealistic group of locals and will, if plans work out, soon feature a huge searchable database of information for residents and visitors alike. Best thing so far is its list of professionals – doctors, tax accountants, lawyers – who speak English.
www.berlin-info.de/index_e.html
Pretty, comprehensive, but with a nasty habit of returning a page which says 'Sorry, this information is only available in German' when you click a link on its front page. Operated by **Berlin Tourismus und Marketing**, and orientated to upmarket tourism.
www.berlin.de
Berlin's official site, stuffy and conservative albeit with nice graphics. If nothing else, in its perverse way it's an interesting take on how the city wishes itself to be seen.

userpage.chemie. fu-berlin.de/adressen/ berlin/html
Very basic page run by students at the Freie Universität, with some history and some useful links to other basic information.

Accommodation & dining
berlin.hotelguide.net/
A commercial site which sends you to the most expensive hotels, but then they're the ones which have online reservation services.
www.net4berlin.com
A goofy site, very Kreuzberg-orientated, with some hotel and restaurant listings, and a few very odd essays by Germans in English.

'Fan' sites
www.mbihler.demon.co.uk/berlin.html
Run out of Britain by a young man who loves the city and spends a lot of time here. Again, not too useful as a planning tool but his friend Steffi has some fine shopping tips (in German) and his page on clubs outlines some essential dos and don'ts.
www.appropriatesoftware.com/BerlinWall/Welcome.html
Chris deWitt is another Brit who is clearly haunted by the Wall. Essays on the Wall and a fine gallery of his photos of the city. Plus a link to a page which will, he claims, sell you a genuine Wall chunk.

Links & service pages
www.links2go.com/channel/Berlin
Numerous Berlin links, some more useful than others, well-organised.
www.gates96.com/carn/Europe/Germany/Berlin
Astonishing link page which will send you to every media outlet, weather service, academic publication, you name it, in town. Most links are in German, but this is thorough. Extra bonus: live webcams all over the city.
www.stadtplandienst.de
Interactive map which will find any address in the city, zoomable so you can figure out how to get there.
www.platten.net
Ambitious project to link up all of Germany's record stores and help you find what you've been searching for. Bilingual, with a bulletin-board so you can post your want-list.

Miscellaneous
www.loveparade.de
Berlin's techno-fest has a fine page – with music, chat-room and bulletin-board to help find everything from accommodation to the best parties.
www.berlin-style.com/
A miscellaneous selection of stuff for sale, including fashion, records and that all-important solar-powered milk steamer for your cappuccino.

Index

Advertisers Index

Please refer to the relevant sections for
addresses/telephone numbers

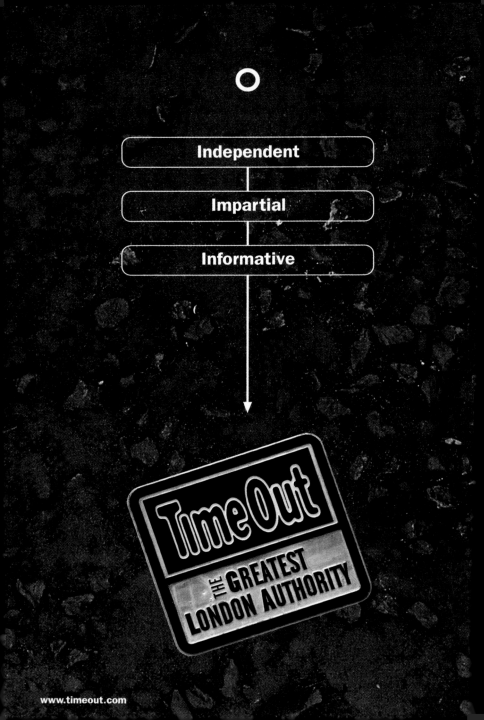

Maps

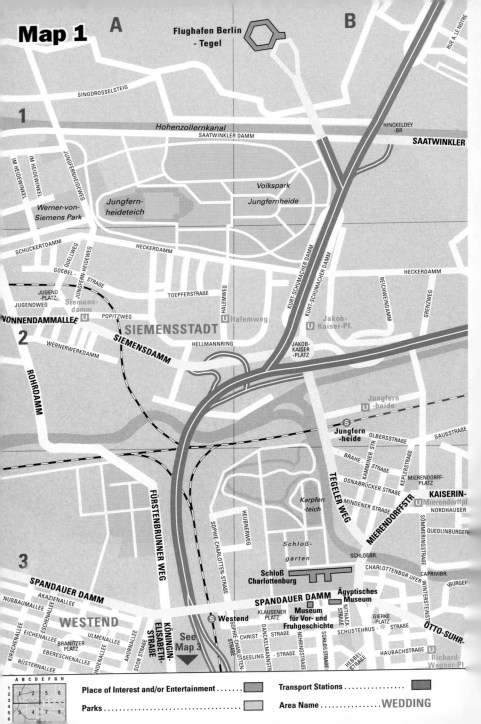

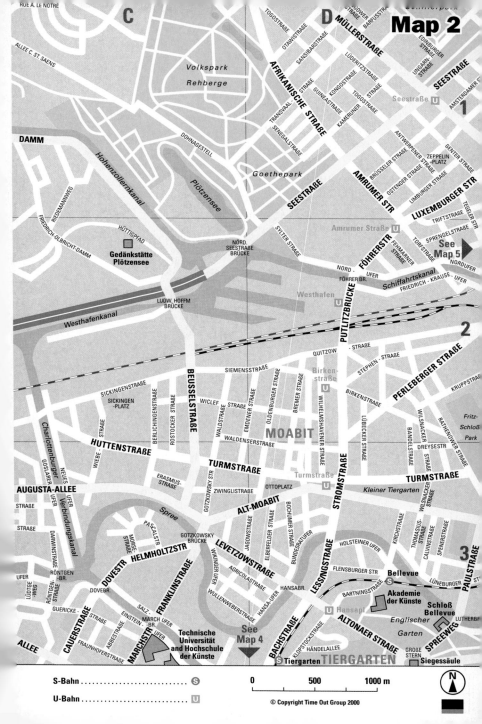

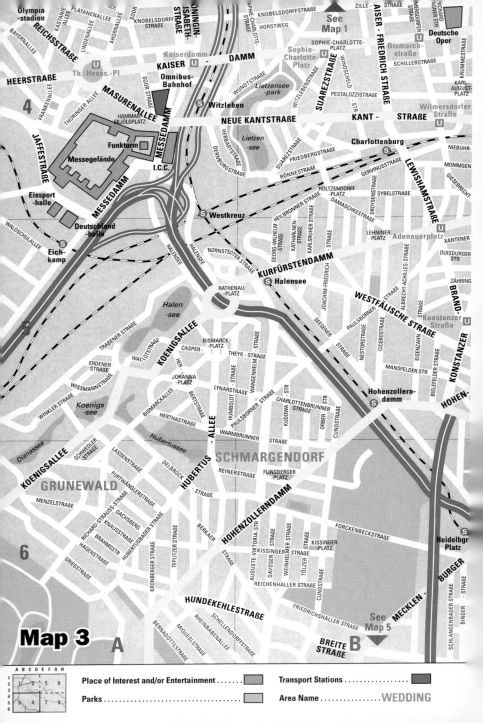

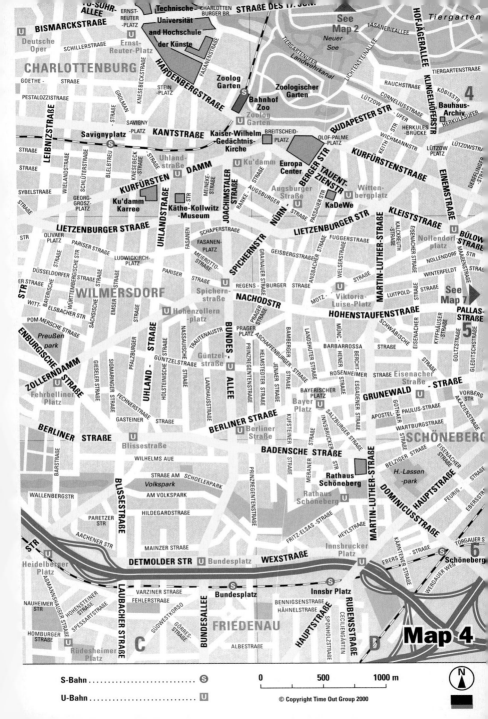

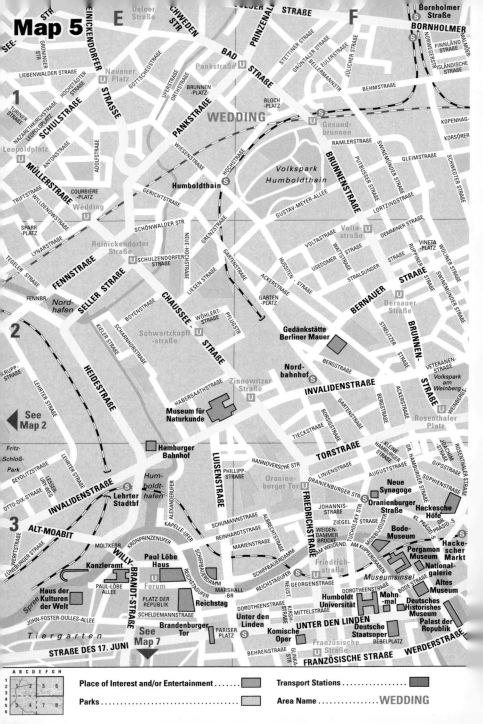

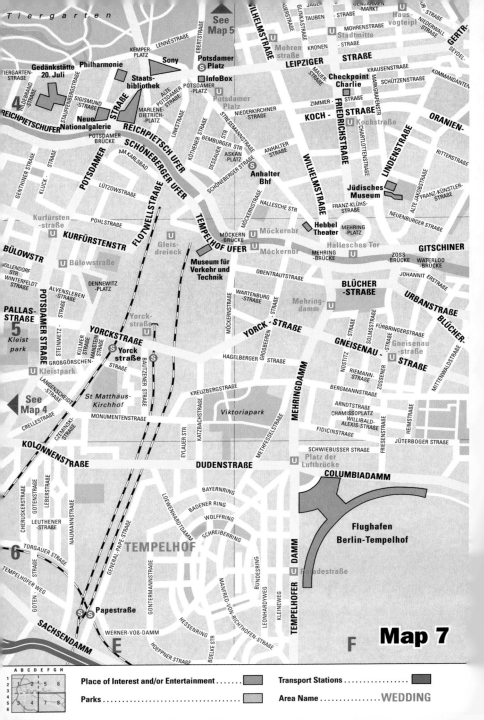

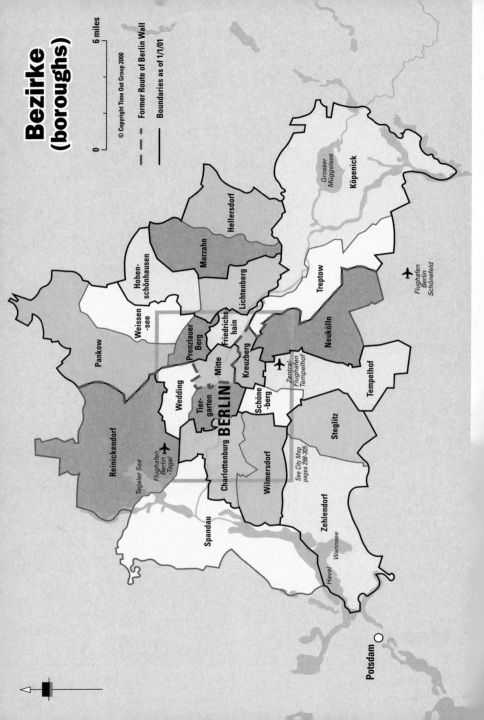

Bezirke (boroughs)

© Copyright Time Out Group 2000

— — — Former Route of Berlin Wall

———— Boundaries as of 1/1/01

0   6 miles

BERLIN

Reinickendorf

Spandau

Pankow

Weissen-see

Hohen-schönhausen

Hellersdorf

Marzahn

Lichtenberg

Prenzlauer Berg

Friedrichs-hain

Wedding

Tier-garten

Mitte

Kreuzberg

Treptow

Köpenick

Grosser Müggelsee

Neukölln

Charlottenburg

Schöne-berg

Zentral-Flughafen Tempelhof

Tempelhof

Wilmersdorf

Steglitz

Zehlendorf

Flughafen Berlin-Tegel

Tegeler See

Havel

Wannsee

See City Map pages 298-305

Flughafen Berlin Schönefeld

Potsdam

Street Index

Eichenallee - A3
Einemstraße - D4
Einsteinstraße - G2
Einsteinufer - C3
Eisenacher Straße - D5
Eisenbahnstraße - H4
Eisenzahnstraße - B5
Elberfelder Straße - D3
Elbestraße - H6
Ella-Kay-Straße - H2
Elßholzstraße - D5
Emdener Straße - C2/3/D2
Emser Straße - C5
Engeldamm - G4/H4
Erasmusstraße - C3
Erdener Straße - A5
Erich-Weinert-Straße - G1/H1
Erkstraße - H6
Ernst-Reuter-Platz - C4
Eschenallee - A3
Eschengraben - G1
Eulerstraße - F1
Eylauer Straße - E5/6

Falkplatz - F1/G1
Falkstraße - H6
Fasanenplatz - C5
Fasanenstraße - C4/5
Fasanerieallee - D4
Fechnerstraße - C5
Fehlerstraße - C6
Fehmarner Straße - D2
Fehrbelliner Straße - F2/G2
Fennbrücke - E2
Fennstraße - E2
Feurigstraße - D6/E6
Fichtestraße - G5
Fidicinstraße - F5
Finnländische Straße - F1
Fischerinsel - G4
Flensburger Straße - D3
Flinsberger Platz - B6
Flotwellstraße - E4/5
Flughafenstraße - G6/H6
Föhrer Brücke. - D2
Föhrerstraße - D2
Forckenbeckstraße - B6
Forster Straße - H5
Fraenkelufer - G5
Frankenallee - A4
Franklinstraße - C3
Franz-Klühs-Straße - F4
Franz-Künstler-Straße - F4
Französische Straße - F3
Fraunhoferstraße - C3
Fredersdorfer Straße - H3/4
Friedbergstraße - B4
Friedelstraße - H5
Friedenstraße - H3
Friedrich-Krause-Ufer - D2
Friedrich-Olbricht-Damm - C1/2
Friedrichshaller Straße - B6
Friedrichstraße - F3/4
Friesenstraße - F5/6
Fritz-Elsas-Straße - D6
Fröbelstraße - G2/H2
Fuggerstraße - D5
Fürbringerstraße - F5
Fürstenbergstraße - H2
Fürstenbrunner Weg - A3
Furtwänglerstraße - A6

Ganghoferstraße - H6
Gartenplatz - F2

Gartenstraße - E2/F 2
Gasteiner Straße - C5
Gaudystraße - G1
Gaußstraße - B2
Geisbergstraße - D5
Gendarmenmarkt - F4
General-Pape-Straße - E6
Genter Straße - D1
Genthiner Straße - E4
Georg-Grosz-Platz - C4
Georg-Wilhelm-Straße - B5
Georgenstraße - F3
Gerichtstraße - E1
Gertrauden Straße - F4/G4
Gervinusstraße - B4
Gierkeplatz - B3
Giesebrechtstraße - B4/C4
Gieseler Straße - C5
Gipsstraße - F3
Gitschinerstraße - F5/G5
Glasgower Straße - D1
Gleditschstraße - D5
Gleimstraße - F1/G1
Glinkastraße - F3/4
Gneisenaustraße - F5
Goebelstraße - A2
Goerdelerdamm Brücke. - C2
Goethestraße - B4/C4
Goethestraße - H1
Goltzstraße - D5
Gontermannstraße - E6
Görlitzer Straße - H5
Görlitzer Ufer - H5
Görresstraße - C6
Goslarer Ufer - C3
Gotenstraße - E6
Gothaer Straße - D5/6
Gottschedstraße - E1
Gotzkowskybrücke - C3
Gotzkowskystraße - C3
Große Hamburger Straße - F3
Große Präsident Straße - F3
Grabowstraße - H5
Graefestraße - G5
Grainauer Straße - D5
Greifenhagener Straße - G1
Greifswalder Straße - G2/3/H1/2
Grellstraße - H1
Grenzstraße - E1/2
Grenzweg - B2
Griegstraße - A6
Grolmanstraße - C4
Gröninger Straße - E1
Großbeerenstraße - F5
Große Stern - D3/4
Großgörschenstraße - E5
Grunerstraße - G3
Grunewaldstraße - D5
Grüntaler Straße - F1
Gubener Straße - H4
Gubitzstraße - H1
Gudvanger Straße - G1
Guerickestraße - C3
Guineastraße - D1
Güntzelstraße - C5
Gürtelstraße - H1
Gustav-Adolf-Straße - H1
Gustav-Meyer-Allee - F1

Hildeg-Jadamowitz-Straße - H3
Habersaathstraße - E2
Hagelbergerstraße - E5/F5
Hagenstraße - A6
Hähnelstraße - D6

Halemweg - A2
Halensee - A5
Hallesche Straße - F4
Hammarskjöldplatz - A4
Händelallee - D3
Hannoversche Straße - F3
Hanns-Eisler-Straße - H1
Hans-Otto-Straße - H2
Hansabrücke - D3
Hansaufer - D3
Hardenbergstraße - C4
Harzer Straße - H5/6
Hasenheide - G5
Haubachstraße - B3
Hauptstraße - D6
Hebbelstraße - B3/4
Heckerdamm - A2/B2/C2
Heerstraße - A4
Heidestraße - E2
Heilbronner Straße - B4
Heimstraße - F5
Heinrich-Roller-Straße - G2
Heinrich-Heine-Platz - G4
Heinrich-Heine-Straße - G4
Hellmannring - A2/B2
Helmholtzstraße - C3
Helmholzplatz - G1
Helmstedter Straße - D5
Helsingforser Straße - H4
Herbartstraße - A4
Herbertstraße - A5
Herkulesbrücke - D4
Herkulesufer - D4
Hermannstraße - G6/H6
Herrfurthplatz - G6
Herthastraße - A5
Hessenring - E6
Heubnerweg - B3
Heylstraße - D6
Hildebrandstraße - E4
Hildegardstraße - C6
Hinckeldeybrücke - B1
Hirtenstraße - G3
Hobrechtbrücke - H5
Hobrechtstraße - G5/H5
Hochstädter Straße - E1
Hochstraße - E1/F1
Hoeppner Straße - E6
Hofjägerallee - D4
Hohenstaufenstraße - D5
Hohensteiner Straße - C6
Hohenzollerndamm - A6/B6/C5
Holsteiner Ufer - D3
Holsteinische Straße - C5
Holtzendorffplatz - B4
Holzmarktstraße - G4/H4
Homburger Straße - B6/C6
Horstweg - B4
Hosemann Straße - H1
Hubertusallee - A5/6
Hubertusbader Straße - A6
Hufelandstraße - H2
Humannplatz - G1
Humboldtstraße - A5
Hundekehlestraße - A6/B6
Husemannstraße - G2
Hussitenstraße - F2
Huttenstraße - C2/3

Ibsenstraße - G1
Iburger Ufer - B3/C3
Im Heidewinkel - A1
Immanuelkirchstraße - G2
Innsbrucker Straße - D5/6

Mittelstraße - F3
Mittelweg - H6
Mittenwalder Straße - F5
Möckernbrücke - F5
Möckernstraße - E5/F4/5
Mohrenstraße - F4
Mollstraße - G3/H3
Moltkebrücke - E3
Moltkestraße - E3
Mommsenstraße - B4/C4
Monbijoustraße - F3
Monumentenstraße - E5
Morsestraße - C3
Morusstraße - H6
Motzstraße - D5
Mühlendamm - G3
Mühlenstraße - H4
Mühsamstraße - H3
Mulackstraße - G3
Müllerstraße - D1/E1
Münchener Straße - D5
Muskauer Straße - H4

Nachodstraße - C5/D5
Nassauische Straße - C5
Nauheimer Straße - B6/C6
Naumannstraße - E6
Naunynstraße - G4
Nazarethkirchstraße - E1
Nehringstraße - B3/4
Nestorstraße - B5
Neue-Hochstraße - E2
Neue Kantstraße - A4/B4
Neue-Roßstraße - G4
Neuenburger Straße - F4/5
Neues Ufer - C3
Neumannstraße - G1
Neustädische Kirchstraße - F3
Niebuhrstraße - B4/C4
Niederkirchnerstraße - F4
Niederwallstraße - F4
Nithackstraße - B3
Nollendorfstraße - D5
Nonnendammallee - A2
Nordhauser Straße - B3/C3
Nordufer - D2
Norwegerstraße - F1
Nostitzstraße - F5
Nürnberger Straße - D4
Nußbaumallee - A3

Obentrautstraße - F5
Oderberger Straße - G2
Oderstraße - G6
Ohlauer Straße - H5
Okerstraße - G6
Olbersstraße - B2
Oldenburger Straße - D2
Olivaer Platz - C5
Olof-Palme-Platz - D4
Onckenstraße - H5
Oppelner Straße - H5
Oranienburger Straße - F3
Oranienplatz - G4
Oranienstraße - F4/G4/5
Orber Straße - B5
Orthstraße - E1
Osloer Straße - E1/F1
Osnabrücker Straße - B3
Ostender Straße - D1
Ostseestraße - H1
Otawistraße - D1
Otto-Braun-Straße - G3
Otto-Dix-Straße - E3

Otto-Suhr-Allee - B3/C3
Ottoplatz - D3

Palisadenstraße - H3
Pallasstraße - D5/E5
Pankstraße - E1
Pannierstraße - H5
Pappelallee - G1
Paretzer Straße - C6
Pariser Platz - E3
Pariser Straße - C5
Pascalstraße - C3
Passauer Straße - D4
Pasteurstraße - H2
Paul-Lincke-Ufer - H5
Paul-Lobe-Allee - E3
Paul-Robeson-Straße - G1
Paulsborner Straße - B5
Paulstraße - D3
Perleberger Straße - D2
Pestalozzistraße - B4/C4
Pfalzburger Straße - C5
Pflügerstraße - H5
Pflugstraße - E2
Phillippstraße - E3/F3
Pistoriusstraße - H1
Planufer - G5
Platanenallee - A4
Platz Der Republik - E3
Pohlstraße - E4/5
Pommersche Straße - C5
Popitzweg - A2
Potsdamer Platz - E4
Potsdamer Straße - E4/5
Potsdamer Brücke - E4
Prager Platz - C5
Prager Straße - D5
Prenzlauer Allee - G2/3/H1
Prenzlauer Promenade - H1
Prinzenallee - F1
Prinzenstraße - G4/5
Prinzregentenstraße - C5/6
Pücklerstraße - H4
Pufendorfstraße - H3
Putbusser Straße - F1
Putlitzbrucke - D2

Quedlinburger Straße - B3/C3
Quellweg - A2
Quitzowstraße - D2

R.-Schwarz-Straße - H2
Ramlerstraße - F1
Rankestraße - C4/D4
Rathausstraße - G3
Rathenauplatz - A5
Rathenower Straße - D2/3
Ratiborstraße - H5
Rauchstraße - D4
Raumerstraße - G1/2
Regensburger Straße - C5/D5
Reichenberger Straße - G4/5/H5
Reichenhaller Straße - B6
Reichpietschufer - D4/E4
Reichsstraße - A4
Reichstagufer - E3/F3
Reichweindamm - B2
Reinerstraße - A6/B6
Reinhardtstraße - E3/F3
Reinickendorfer Strasse - E1
Reuterplatz - H5
Reuterstraße - H6
Rheinbabenallee - A6
Richard-Sorge-Straße - H3

Richard-Strauss-Straße - A6
Richard-Wagner-Straße - B3/4
Richardplatz - H6
Richardstraße - H6
Riedemannweg - C1/2
Riemannstraße - F5
Ritterstraße - F4/G4
Rochstraße - G3
Rodenbergstraße - G1
Roelckestraße - H1
Rohrdamm - A2
Rolandufer - G3
Rollbergstraße - H6
Rönnestraße - B4
Röntgenbrücke - C3
Röntgenstraße - C3
Rosa-Luxemburg-Platz - G3
Rosa-Luxemburg-Straße - G3
Rosenheimer Straße - D5
Rosenthaler Straße - F3
Rostocker Straße - C2
Rubensstraße - D6
Rue A. Le Notre - B1/C1
Rungestraße - G4
Ruppiner Straße - F2
Rüsternallee - A3/4
Rütlistraße - H5
Rykestraße - G2

Saarbrücker Straße - G2
Saatwinkler Damm - A1/B1/C1
Sachsendamm - D6/E6
Sächsische Straße - C5
Salzburger Straße - D5/6
Salzufer - C3
Sanderstraße - G5/H5
Sansibarstraße - D1
Savignyplatz - C4
Schaperstraße - C5/D5
Scharnhorstraße - E2
Scheldemannstraße - E3
Schellendorffstraße - A6/B6
Schiffbauerdamm - E3/F3
Schillerstraße - B4/C4
Schillingbrücke - H4
Schillingstraße - G3
Schivelbeiner Straße - G1
Schlangenbader Straße - B6
Schlesische Straße - H5
Schloßbrücke - B3
Schloßstraße - B3/4
Schlüterstraße - C4
Schmidstraße - G4
Schmollerplatz - H5
Schöneberger Straße - E4/F4
Schöneberger Ufer - E4
Schonensche Straße - G1
Schönhauser Allee - G1/2
Schönleinstraße - G5
Schönwalder Straße - E2
Schreiberring - E6/F6
Schuckertdamm - A2
Schulstraße - E1
Schulzendorfer Straße - E2
Schumannstraße - E3/F3
Schustehrusstraße - B3
Schützenstraße - F4
Schwäbische Straße - D5
Schwedenstraße - E1
Schwedlerstraße - A6
Schwedter Straße - F1/G2
Schwiebusser Straße - F6
Sebastianstraße - G4
Seelingstraße - B3

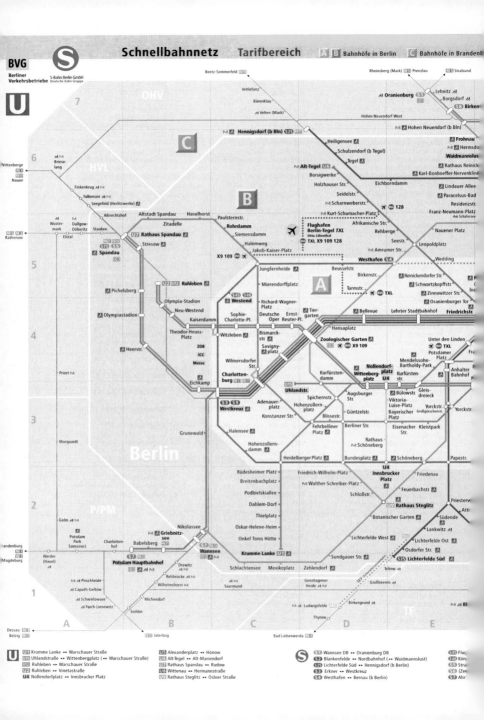

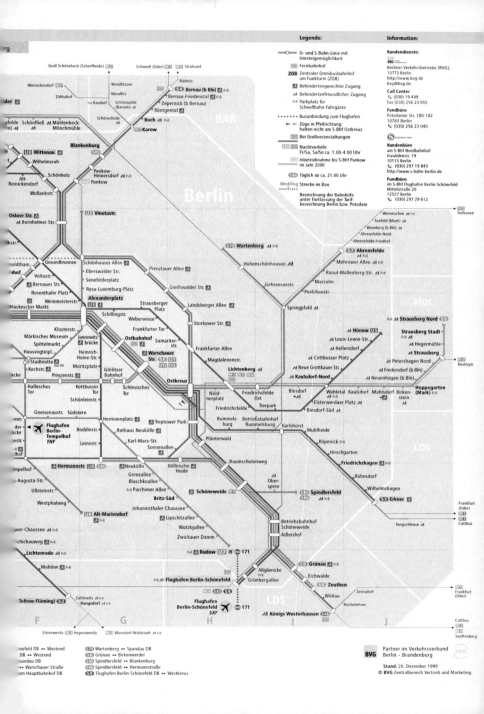

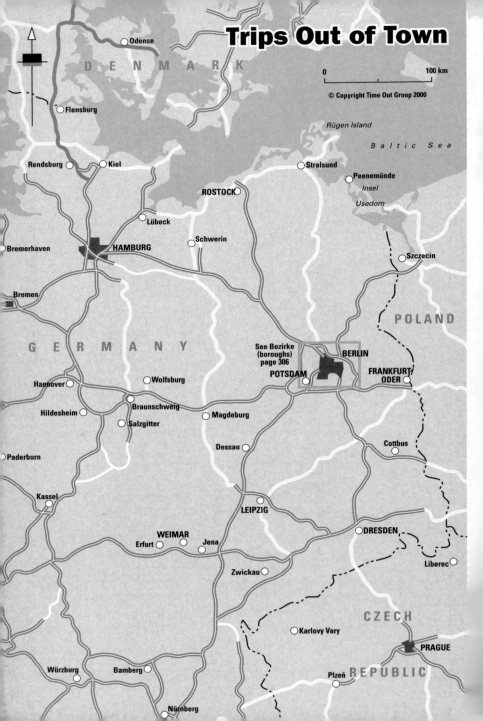

Trips Out of Town

© Copyright Time Out Group 2000

0   100 km

DENMARK

Odense

Flensburg

Rendsburg   Kiel

Lübeck

ROSTOCK

Schwerin

Stralsund

Peenemünde

Rügen Island

Baltic Sea

Insel Usedom

Bremerhaven   HAMBURG

Bremen

Szczecin

GERMANY

POLAND

Hannover   Wolfsburg

Braunschweig

Hildesheim   Salzgitter

Magdeburg

See Bezirke
(boroughs)
page 306

BERLIN

POTSDAM

FRANKFURT/
ODER

Paderborn

Dessau

Cottbus

Kassel

LEIPZIG

DRESDEN

Liberec

WEIMAR

Erfurt   Jena

Zwickau

Karlovy Vary

CZECH

PRAGUE

Würzburg   Bamberg

Plzeň

REPUBLIC

Nürnberg